BALL OF FIRE

By the same author
REPORT MY SIGNALS

(C.I.S. Historical Section)

THE GREAT SAND SEA

BALL OF FIRE

THE FIFTH INDIAN DIVISION IN THE
SECOND WORLD WAR

BY

ANTONY BRETT-JAMES

FOREWORD BY

VICE-ADMIRAL EARL MOUNTBATTEN OF BURMA

The Naval & Military Press Ltd

Published by

The Naval & Military Press Ltd
Unit 10 Ridgewood Industrial Park,
Uckfield, East Sussex,
TN22 5QE England

Tel: +44 (0) 1825 749494
Fax: +44 (0) 1825 765701

www.naval-military-press.com
www.military-genealogy.com

In reprinting in facsimile from the original, any imperfections are inevitably reproduced and the quality may fall short of modern type and cartographic standards.

CONTENTS

		Page
	FOREWORD BY VICE-ADMIRAL EARL MOUNTBATTEN OF BURMA, K.G., P.C., G.M.S.I., G.M.I.E., G.C.V.O., K.C.B., D.S.O.	xi
	PROLOGUE	1
I.	BLUFF IN THE SUDAN	13
II.	GALLABAT	22
III.	KASSALA TO BARENTU	38
IV.	KEREN	51
V.	THE FALL OF KEREN	72
VI.	THE ROAD TO ASMARA	81
VII.	MASSAWA BY THE SEA	93
VIII.	AMBA ALAGI	101
IX.	SURRENDER WITH HONOUR	123
X.	FROM PILLAR TO POST	137
XI.	GIARABUB AND GIALO	143
XII.	CYPRUS INTERLUDE	153
XIII.	ENTRY INTO THE DESERT	160
XIV.	ROMMEL'S OFFENSIVE	171
XV.	THE CAULDRON	181
XVI.	FIGHTING RETREAT	202
XVII.	RUWEISAT RIDGE	223
XVIII.	OUTSIDE BAGHDAD	240
XIX.	TRAINING FOR BURMA	249
XX.	ARAKAN	254
XXI.	THE NGAKYEDAUK BOX	273
XXII.	RAZABIL FORTRESS	294
XXIII.	KOHIMA	303
XXIV.	IMPHAL	322
XXV.	THE ROAD TO TIDDIM	355
XXVI.	VITAL CORNER AND KENNEDY PEAK	382
XXVII.	TRAGEDY AT JORHAT	391
XXVIII.	MEIKTILA	399
XXIX.	THE RACE FOR RANGOON	410
XXX.	MOPPING-UP IN BURMA	420
XXXI.	SINGAPORE REOCCUPIED	427
XXXII.	SOERABAJA	444
	EPILOGUE	466
	APPENDIX I	471
	APPENDIX II	472
	PERSONAL INDEX	475

ILLUSTRATIONS

THE GREAT SAND SEA	*Frontispiece*
	Facing page
MAJOR-GENERAL L. M. HEATH	34
MAJOR-GENERAL A. G. O. M. MAYNE	34
BRIGADIER W. J. SLIM	35
BRIGADIER J. C. O. MARRIOTT	35
BRIGADIER F. W. MESSERVY	35
BRIGADIER T. W. REES	35
BRITISH TROOPS ATTACKING	50
CAMERON RIDGE, BRIGS PEAK, SANCHIL	50
FORT DOLOGORODOC	51
MADRASSI LINEMEN WITH MULE	51
THE MULE TRACK AND SANCHIL	98
THE HIGHLAND LIGHT INFANTRY ENTER ASMARA	99
MAJOR GRAHAM, COLONEL RUSSELL, BRIGADIER REES, MAJOR-GENERAL HEATH AT ASMARA	99
NEAR AD TECLESAN	114
DISTANT VIEW OF AMBA ALAGI	114
TRIANGLE AND AMBA ALAGI	115
COLONEL RUSSELL, MAJOR-GENERAL MAYNE, THE DUKE OF AOSTA	115
SURRENDER WITH HONOUR	146
PASSING THE GUARD OF HONOUR	146
GIALO	147
WHEEL-MARKS IN THE SAND	162
A DESERT TRACK	162
A TENT IN THE DESERT	163
MR. CASEY WITH MAJOR-GENERAL BRIGGS ON RUWEISAT RIDGE	163
GENERAL ALEXANDER INSPECTS THE 3/2ND PUNJAB	242
MAJOR-GENERAL H. R. BRIGGS	243
THE KING OF IRAQ VISITS THE DIVISION	243
BRIGADIER D. W. REID	258
BRIGADIER B. C. FLETCHER	258
BRIGADIER C. H. BOUCHER	258

ILLUSTRATIONS

	Facing page
BRIGADIER W. H. LANGRAN	258
ARAKAN LANDSCAPE	259
THE MAYU RANGE	259
THE 25TH DRAGOONS NORTH OF RAZABIL	290
MEN OF 123 BRIGADE CLAMBER UP A JUNGLE PATH	290
BRIGADIER G. C. EVANS	291
BRIGADIER J. A. SALOMONS	291
CORPORAL ASKE BANDAGES A WOUNDED RAJPUT	291
THE WAR MEMORIAL AT KOHIMA	306
ACROSS THE IMPHAL PLAIN	307
A PUNJABI DEFENCE POST	307
DOGRA STRETCHER-BEARERS BELOW NUMSHIGUM	338
MILESTONE 109 ON THE KOHIMA–IMPHAL ROAD: MAJOR-GENERAL GROVER, BRIGADIER SALOMONS, LIEUT.-GENERAL STOPFORD, BRIGADIER SMITH	338
CROSSING THE FRONTIER	339
MUD ON THE TIDDIM ROAD	339
BRITISH GUNNERS	354
SAPPERS CROSS THE RIVER	354
SUPPLY DROPPING	355
FALLEN PARACHUTES ON THE 'CHOCOLATE STAIRCASE'	355
MOVING UP THE TIDDIM ROAD	386
TIDDIM	386
THE 3RD CARABINEERS ON KENNEDY PEAK	387
MADRASSI WIRELESS OPERATORS	387
MAJOR-GENERAL D. F. W. WARREN	402
MAJOR-GENERAL E. C. MANSERGH	402
LORD LOUIS MOUNTBATTEN INSPECTS 3/2ND PUNJAB GUARD OF HONOUR AT JORHAT	403
MAJOR-GENERAL MANSERGH IN CONFERENCE NEAR MEIKTILA	403
A YORK AND LANCASTER PATROL AT YAMETHIN	434
SAPPERS REPAIR THE ROAD TO PEGU	434
APPROACHING SINGAPORE	435
LANDING AT SINGAPORE	435
BRIGADIER DENHOLM-YOUNG AND A JAPANESE INTERPRETER	450
LORD LOUIS MOUNTBATTEN INSPECTS 1/17TH DOGRA GUARD OF HONOUR	450
BRITISH TROOPS AT SOERABAJA	451
THE 4/7TH RAJPUTS BESIDE A RAILWAY TRACK OUTSIDE SOERABAJA	451

MAPS

	Page
ABYSSINIA, SUDAN, ERITREA	21
KEREN	50
AMBA ALAGI	103
MIDDLE EAST	138
GAZALA LINE	172
EL ALAMEIN	222
INDIA AND BURMA	248
ARAKAN	255
KOHIMA	302
IMPHAL—NORTHERN FRONT	323
TIDDIM—KALEMYO	376
CENTRAL BURMA	401

FOREWORD

By Vice-Admiral Earl Mountbatten of Burma,
K.G., P.C., G.M.S.I., G.M.I.E., G.C.V.O., K.C.B., D.S.O.

I AM proud to pay my tribute in this foreword to the Fifth Indian Division. When the Division came under my command in South-East Asia towards the end of 1943, it had already had three years' hard fighting in Africa. In 1941 it had played a leading part in the defeat of the Italian Army in the Sudan, Eritrea, and Abyssinia; in the summer of 1942 it had been very heavily engaged with the Germans and Italians in the crucial battle of the Knightsbridge 'Cauldron,' and in the fighting withdrawal across North Africa to the defence of the Alamein line.

Thus when I first met the men of this Division, soon after the formation of the South-East Asia Command—indeed it was the first Division that I visited—its reputation was already high. At that time it was under the command of Major-General Briggs, and was facing 55 Japanese Division on the coastal flank of the Arakan front. By a coincidence, it was also the last division that I visited before I left South-East Asia in the early summer of 1946—when it was in Java, under the command of Major-General Mansergh.

Soon after my first visit, the Division was heavily engaged in the first land battle to be fought since the Command had been set up. I remember feeling how greatly the future trend of operations would depend on the outcome of this battle; and a large share of the credit must go to the Fifth Indian Division for the first decisive victory against the Japanese since they had invaded two years previously.

Immediately after this, three Japanese divisions attacked 4 Corps in the Imphal Plain: and the Fifth Indian Division was at once flown in, straight from its victorious battle in Arakan, to take part in the vital struggle which was developing on the Central front. 161 Brigade joined 33 Corps, which was beginning to arrive at Dimapur, and fought in the battle of Kohima; the remainder of the Division reinforced 4 Corps, whose land victory at Kohima and Imphal, in which the Division played an important part, proved to be the turning-point of the Burma Campaign.

The Division continued to fight and to advance throughout the rest of the war, except for one period of rest and reorganization; and took part in the final thrust by 4 Corps down to Rangoon. Its record was second to none and I was proud to have such a fine formation under my command.

Mountbatten of Burma

ACKNOWLEDGMENTS

WITHOUT the most generous and painstaking help given to me by more than eighty former members of the Division, its History could not have been written, for many of the experiences that they brought out from the depths of their memories and set down on paper had never before been recorded. Some wrote many pages about the particular campaigns in which they served; others lent their personal diaries, maps, private letters, newspaper cuttings, articles they once wrote for journals, photographs, regimental histories as yet unpublished, war-time copies of regimental journals and news-letters. Some have recorded their impressions of the senior commanders under whom they served; others have patiently answered the questions put to them on varied and often perplexing subjects. Some have given of their best in conversation over a drink or a meal, or by telephone; others have taken great trouble to read through the draft chapters submitted to them for criticism, and have suggested many amendments, recastings, and improvements, besides pointing out errors of fact, half-truths, and misinterpretations. For any such blemishes that remain, they are not to blame.

To all those who have given their aid I am deeply grateful. My particular thanks are due to the following: Lieutenant-General Sir Harold Briggs; Lieutenant-Colonel W. F. Dean; Brigadier B. C. Fletcher, D.S.O., M.C.; Captain B. C. Gomm; Lieutenant-Colonel A. P. Harrington, M.B.E.; Lieutenant-General Sir Lewis Heath; Captain P. M. Leslie-Smith; Lieutenant-General Sir Robert Mansergh; Major-General Sir John Marriott; General Sir Mosley Mayne; General Sir Frank Messervy; Major C. Morshead, M.C.; General Sir William Platt; Major-General D. W. Reid; Lieutenant-Colonel T. C. W. Roe, O.B.E.; Lieutenant-General D. Russell; Brigadier J. A. Salomons, D.S.O., O.B.E.; Colonel B. L. Sundius-Smith, D.S.O.; Mrs. D. F. W. Warren; Brigadier G. de V. Welchman, C.B.E., D.S.O.; and Major J. Wiberg. The names of all others who helped in the writing of this book are listed at the end.

I am indebted to the late Field-Marshal Earl Wavell and Messrs. Harrap for permission to quote a passage from his book, *Allenby*; to

ACKNOWLEDGMENTS

Mr. Winston S. Churchill and Messrs. Cassell for permission to quote from one of his war-time speeches and from his book, *Their Finest Hour*; also to Lord Camrose and the *Daily Telegraph* for the latter excerpt.

Thanks are due to the Imperial War Museum, the Combined Inter-Services Historical Section (India and Pakistan), Elliott & Fry Ltd., Lafayette Ltd., and J. Russell & Sons Ltd., for permission to reproduce copyright photographs. Also to Sir Charles Pawsey, K.C.I.E., C.S.I., M.C., who lent me his collection of photographs of Kohima.

I have received the greatest help from Lieutenant-Colonel J. E. B. Barton, of the Cabinet Office (Historical Section), who gave me access to the narrative of the campaign in the Sudan, Eritrea, and Abyssinia, which he compiled for the Official History of the Second World War; he also read through the early chapters, and made many valuable comments. I am further indebted to him for the use of several photographs which he took during a tour of the battlefields.

I am grateful to Brigadier H. B. Latham and the staff of the Cabinet Office (Historical Section) for enabling me to study the war diaries of the Division, documents that were largely dull but occasionally rewarding.

I owe much to Miss N. S. Peppard, who read large parts of the manuscript and saved me from a number of grammatical faults and clumsy phrases; and to Mr. R. P. Jago and Mr. David Bowen, who read the proofs.

To Miss Mary Scorer, of Winnipeg, I dictated parts of this book, and she typed and in many cases retyped the manuscript with great efficiency and understanding. She has my very warmest thanks.

All the maps were drawn by Captain J. A. Hepburn, who deserves special recognition.

Lastly I express my gratitude to my father, who helped me so nobly during the often tedious work of research upon the war diaries, and who, with my mother, read through the book in manuscript, transferred corrections and additions from one copy to the two spare copies, read the proofs with such care, and helped with the Index.

A. B.-J.

MILL HILL.

PROLOGUE

"Long dark months of trials and tribulations lie before us. Not only great dangers but many more misfortunes, many shortcomings, many mistakes, many disappointments will surely be our lot. Death and sorrow will be the companions of our journey; hardship our garment; constancy and valour our only shield. We must be united, we must be undaunted, we must be inflexible."

WINSTON S. CHURCHILL.
Speech to the House of Commons, October 8, 1940.

THIS is the story less of a military formation of tactical importance than of some thousands of British and Indian soldiers who fought against three strong and different enemies across the continents of Africa and Asia. They served both in battle and in training from the highlands of Eritrea and Abyssinia to the glaring sands of ridge and wadi in the Western Desert; from the jungle-clad mountains and valleys, with their waterways and rare villages, to the sunburnt plain of the Irrawaddy in Central Burma. They worked and played in Cyprus and Baghdad, in Singapore and beneath the shadow of the Pyramids.

The story covers six long and varied years in which these men took their part in the fight and performed the tasks and duties allotted to them. Great were the distances travelled, the mountains climbed, the wounds and discomforts endured, the dangers shared, and the comradeship enjoyed. By all these were the soldiers welded together into companions of history.

They did not constantly think of the cause for which they fought; their minds grasped more readily the simpler pattern of local circumstances. Momentarily they forgot that their small corner of the battlefront was not the centre of the world-wide struggle. Of distant events they learned from letter, newspaper, and from voices in the air. They lived in the present and reminisced of past achievements, for the road into the future wound among shadows of uncertainty. They believed in ultimate victory, but no man could tell how far ahead that lay. Passing frictions and swift prejudice might dull the harmony of their existence; discontent, apathy, and jealousy mingled with selfless effort and enthusiasm; prudence and wisdom did not go always beside daring or bravado. Yet tolerance and justice mingled with the ultimate demand for individual and corporate efficiency and endurance, under the steel laws of military conduct and discipline. No man might with impunity or pleasure falter by the wayside or fail his companions. Rather must he plod onwards in their good company, while those who led the way urged themselves to still greater exertions and sacrifice by virtue of the example that they had to set.

There were moments when doubt, anxiety, and despair had the upper hand. Impatience and exuberant triumph had their hours of influence. Sadness or exultation might hold momentary sway. But at the end of a long and perilous journey victory was attained. It is the course of this journey that we shall now follow. But first, what was the Division, and who were its members?

* * * * *

The Division had three brigades, and was commanded by a major-general. Each brigade had one British and two Indian infantry battalions. Under the senior officers of Divisional Headquarters came the supporting arms, the artillery regiments of field, mountain, anti-tank, or anti-aircraft guns; the Field Companies of Indian Sappers and Miners; the companies and sections of Divisional Signals; the Field Ambulances; the Workshop Companies and Transport Companies; the Supply sections; the Divisional Provost unit of Military Police; the Animal Transport Companies; and many other units and sections that were from time to time attached to the Division to give their aid during a particular campaign.

Sometimes these companies and sections were commanded directly from Divisional Headquarters; at other times they were placed under command of one or other of the three brigades, and formed what became known as a 'brigade group,' independent and composed of all arms. During certain operations armoured regiments joined the Division and supported the infantry. So, too, did armoured car units. Local porters, guides, interpreters appeared

PROLOGUE

on the scene from time to time. And medium guns, veterinary officers, salvage and laundry and bakery units, hospitals and nursing sisters, canteens and concert parties, war correspondents and photographers made their appearance in various battle areas.

It took all sorts of officers and men to make a division—professionals and war-time amateurs, some quiet, some dashing, some suave and charming, others abrupt and tactless. One man looked the regular soldier that he was, while another might resemble more closely a country squire or farmer.

Casualties from battle and disease caused vacancies, sometimes filled from outside the Division, but more often by a second-in-command, or deputy staff officer, or a battalion commander when the vacant post was that of brigadier.

There was a constant flow of men in and out. As the months passed, losses came from death in action, death from disease, wounds and illness, promotion and posting, repatriation and courses. Some were lost to the Division for the rest of the war, others returned after many months in hospital or at Staff College or on leave. And then there were losses when whole battalions and regiments were transferred from the Division, and during the summer of 1942 the flower of whole brigades was destroyed or captured in the Western Desert.

Though membership of the Division brought similar experiences to all, there were as many different viewpoints as jobs. Though in the Desert what happened to 'A' Company was much the same as what happened to 'B' Company, in the jungles of Burma what the leading scout saw differed from what the section or company commander saw. And so the picture obtained by any one individual was smaller. A sepoy out on patrol along a *chaung* in Arakan or prowling in No-Man's-Land in the Desert saw quite different things from the medical orderly who helped to give blood transfusions, and the orderly room clerk who spent his days before a typewriter, filling in reports and returns. Different, again, were the viewpoints of the mechanic lying on his back in oily dungarees under a lorry, seeking a fault or using a grease-gun; the mule-driver combing and brushing his mule and fitting the saddle so that it rubbed no sores; or a telephone switchboard operator, whose English was indifferent, plugging in when the little bulbs lit up, and linking one caller with another, all day and all night.

A farrier, a stretcher-bearer, an officer's orderly and driver, a dispatch rider whose life might depend upon how well he kept his motor-cycle in good repair, the driver of a lorry laden with rations or ammunition, a lance-bombardier man-handling a gun—all these played their part. But their role was not the same as that of a postal orderly who sorted the precious letters and airgraphs; or the sapper prodding and searching for mines hidden in sand or below the muddy surface of some mountain track; or again, the battalion chaplain taking a Communion Service beside a truck in the open desert, burying the dead on the edge of a paddy-field, or tending the wounded; a surgeon performing an amputation in some tent or dugout; a staff officer writing out an operation order, preparing documents for a court-martial, or marking up his map with the locations of our own and the enemy's troops; the field cashier paying out rupees, dinars, Egyptian pounds, and Cyprus piastres; or the Signals adjutant keeping a clear head to work out the wireless three-letter call-signs for every major unit in the Division.

And it was towards the defeat of three enemies and to the building and maintenance of the Division's high reputation and *izzat* that these manifold activities were directed. In the Division, and all that it stood for, did these diverse efforts find their unity. A common pride in achievement, spirit, and tradition was given an outward symbol in the shoulder flash of the red ball of fire. And at the head of the Division worked the Commander. His viewpoint was different again, and his shoulders were more weighted with responsibility, and his breast with ribbons.

There are times when the Divisional Commander has a sense of loneliness and isolation.

The new commander in his first contact with his subordinate commanders becomes aware that they are summing him up. Whether they accept him or whether they do not may be a slow process or a quick one. Equally, the commander is very quickly aware of whether or not he has gained their confidence and become accepted. Their genuine friendliness is also quickly discernible.

"It is an intangible affair, but one that to look back on has much humour in it. Memorable are the steady, sometimes very cool and appraising eyes gradually giving way to friendliness, kindliness and, much more important, understanding.

"It is quite remarkable how you find yourself suddenly com-

PROLOGUE

pletely alone. Some impending battle, or an obviously impending decision to be taken will bring this loneliness about. There seems to be a withdrawal of your subordinates into themselves. They will have nothing to do with these decisions. These are yours to make—in some cases, no doubt, they murmur 'Thank Heavens!'—and it is entirely up to you. The decision once made, all goes well again. The spiritual withdrawal of comradeship, if for a moment only, has briefly occurred, and you are back again with them and knit once more in one wonderful spirit and camaraderie of confidence. Remarkable it all is, and most difficult to explain, but intriguing and rather exhilarating."[1]

Everyone on his staff, except perhaps the C.R.A. (Commander, Royal Artillery), is younger, and somewhat diffident to be too much with him. And they are not always natural in his presence. It is important that the senior officers, at least, should be good companions. And the main thing about a staff, in General Briggs' words, is to find "a real happy and loyal team, and then to trust them to do the job. I found that they always did, and was never let down. Had I been, I should have had to dismiss the officer."

"If troops are to have good morale, they must have confidence in their weapons, in their commanders, and in their cause. Commanders, however, need one more confidence—in themselves."[2] "If one has the knowledge and can truthfully say to oneself, 'I have done everything possible to achieve success,' then self-confidence comes automatically. You must have it, or you will be vacillating, and inclined to change things with insufficient cause; a number of plausible people will always ask you to make changes to suit them."[3]

"People will frequently ask you to change something soon after the battle starts. I used to resist this with determination. The fellow who asked probably had a local view surrounded by the smoke and fog of war. A change might affect others, communication of such a change might be difficult, and a plan made carefully and deliberately in cold blood should not be lightly changed in the heat of battle. I usually told the man that he was doing fine, and that I would consider his suggestion after I had let

---

[1] Major-General Denys W. Reid, C.B., C.B.E., D.S.O., M.C.
[2] Brigadier B. C. Fletcher, D.S.O., M.C.
[3] Lieutenant-General Dudley Russell, C.B., C.B.E., D.S.O., M.C.

things go on a little longer as they were. I usually found that no change was necessary.

"As soon as I knew that my command was destined to play an important part in an operation, I always tried to get in on it at the highest level during the planning stage.

"Then came the personal planning stage. During his working hours the commander is usually turning over in his mind the best way to do it. I used to go for long walks in the beautiful Italian[1] country thinking things out. He will probably discuss the matter freely with the more important subordinates. I always used to think out as a Divisional Commander how I would carry out the Brigade tasks and as a Brigadier the Battalion tasks, and frequently made notes. This helped in discussion of the subordinates' outline plan. I always reached agreement personally with the more important subordinates before a vital conference.

"When I had given it all the thought I could and felt I had the best plan possible, I would sleep at night like a child, quite regardless of battle noises. Until then, however, I used to lie awake and think a bit, unless I was very tired. Having put the plan 'to bed,' the Staff got on with the operation order, and I had a chance to go around and see the chaps who were to do the job. I tried never to interfere with what subordinates were doing, but let it be understood that I was always available to sort something out."

An intermediate commander is often faced with the problem of acting as a buffer between those above and those below. Sometimes a commander might be ordered to carry out a task which he did not think worth while in relation to the casualties which would more or less have written the Brigade off. Shall he say so, refuse to do the job, and suggest a more reasonable alternative? Shall he ignore pressure from above, messages from Corps and Army Headquarters asking why the objective has not yet been captured, and displaying extreme impatience? Shall he, like Russell, in Italy, keep all these impatient messages in his pocket, because he knew that his brigadier was doing his best and realized just as well as did his divisional commander that the village *must* be taken from the Germans?

He should not display disappointment to his subordinate

---

[1] Russell later commanded the 8th Indian Division in Italy.

PROLOGUE

commanders, nor harass them with repeated order surging greater speed.

How far does peace-time training fit a man for command in war? No doubt the requisite knowledge can be acquired, but no one really knows how he is going to react to modern warfare until he has tried it. "Once he is sure that he can think clearly in spite of all that is going on around him in battle—losing key men; essential equipment being blown up; unforeseen delays; a temporary breakdown in communications; being surrounded; noise and near misses—then a commander can apply his peace-time training and will find it adequate, though he will continue to learn every day. But if he reacts unfavourably to the battle background, then no amount of peace-time training will put him right.

"He must be a good 'mixer' with officers, men, allies, regardless of caste, creed, colour, or status. This can be acquired in peace time to a certain extent, but is sometimes overlooked. And it is probably easier to acquire in war if the germ is somewhere in a man's make-up. A nice balance is required in this matter; not a familiar but a comrade commander, who is obviously the best man for the job, knows his profession, is fully qualified as captain of the team, but uses his position to help all those under his command. He must be approachable and sympathetic to those in trouble, and do something about it himself rather than 'pass the baby.' A cheerful word readily on the tongue, a smile, an amusing story in the sergeants' mess over a glass of beer with the R.S.M.; the correct attitude when visiting hospitals and field ambulances and talking to the wounded and dying; a letter to the deceased's relatives about how the chap went out doing his duty gallantly—all these things help."[1]

A commander's predominant thoughts might well be: Is there anything more that I could do to help before the start, without cramping my subordinates' initiative? Where are my headquarters to be, so that I can be right in the picture, with good communications, able to move my reserves or arrange for additional support as required?

"A good commander requires to be intelligent, but if he is sensitive this will be a strain added to the strains which he shares with his fellow commanders in battle.

---
[1] Lieutenant-General Dudley Russell.

"To command in battle when things are going wrong combines the horror of a nightmare with the added consciousness of reality; that is, if you stop to think about it. In point of fact, however, the heat of action, the urgency of remedies, prevent one from thinking, and the mind is absorbed in the problem of warning so-and-so, and of saving such and such a unit from what they have not realized may happen. Anxiety is greatest when nothing is happening, but when a great deal may happen."[1]

Having to launch troops against difficult objectives is a question of confidence and of putting confidence across. "Where half the failures in battle have occurred is in not appreciating or *knowing* what terrific tasks you *can* ask of troops. Another thing is to have experienced personally one or two what might be termed almost impossible assignments. If these have been successful it has been due mainly to the fact that the stark facts were clear, that the chance of success was simply and clearly indicated, and that the task would obviously not go through unless it was carried out with punch, drive and confidence.

"The feeling of gratitude, humbleness, and abasement that you get when your troops have achieved such a task is quite impossible to describe. Humbleness, and why you should have been permitted such devotion and selflessness leaves you wondering and—yes—worshipping."[2]

* * * * *

To the British officers and men who came to the Division without ever having set foot in India, the Indian other ranks—I.O.Rs. as they were called—provided the deepest source of interest and fresh experience. The bonds of respect and affection that were forged during the campaigning years were strong and vital. The loyalty and trust displayed by the Indian sepoy spurred on his British officers and senior N.C.Os. to their finest efforts. The Indians were friendly and proud, sensitive, and bright with smiles.

And what variety in the types of Indian soldiers who served with the Division! Mahrattas, Jats, Dogras, Madrassis, Sikhs, Garhwalis, Punjabi Mussulmen, Rajputs, Pathans, and many others.

---

[1] Brigadier B. C. Fletcher.
[2] Major-General Denys W. Reid.

PROLOGUE

They fought side by side in the same army, but how utterly different was the background they had left when they joined the armed forces of the King Emperor. How immense was the continent of India, hot, turbulent, swarming with its hundreds of millions, a Babel of different tongues, a home for varied religions and gods, beliefs and customs, tribes and castes. And yet most of these sepoys had seen but little of their vast country. Their horizon was so often bounded by a score of miles, a village in the hills of Jammu or beside one of the five rivers of the Punjab or along the coast of Malabar.

In their mind's eye flitted scenes from an Indian village, their village with its thatched mud huts half concealed among palm or banyan trees. There passed scenes of the village pond to which the women carried brass jars on their heads, washed their laundry, and gossiped while they filled these jars with water, the same water in which the cattle bathed or drank. And the women, moving barefooted, their arms and right shoulder bare, wearing gay saris of crimson, green, purple or pink, and jangling with brass anklets, glass bangles and cheap jewellery. Or the naked children running about the dusty tracks of the village, or men clad only in loincloth and turban guiding the plough drawn by a bullock.

These soldiers thought back to the evenings spent in the little room of their home, smoking the hubble-hubble hookah, talking of how they might save up money with which to pay a dowry for their daughter, or eating with their fingers the boiled rice, the crisp flat chapathis, the curried vegetables, or chewing the betel-leaf that made them spit out scarlet saliva. They would recall the mingled smell of sandal-wood and sunbaked mud walls, the smoke-blackened thatched roof, and the greasy aroma of *ghi*. To the ears came the hum of the spinning wheel, the beating of drums at one of the Hindu festivals, the sight of an open cooking fire that burnt cakes of dried cow dung as fuel.

Self-contained and restricted had been the existence they had led in their villages, both in north and south India. Contacts with the outside world had been rare. Threatened by famine and poverty, burdened by arrears of taxation or by the interest to be paid on old debts, they were constantly obliged to contract new debts with the powerful money-lender. Most of these soldiers were small farmers, who tended their plot of land with buffalo and ox, and struggled to eke out a living in the face of drought and flood, storms of hail and sand, and damage to crops from locusts and other pests.

Some of them believed in Mahomet and turned daily towards the east to pray and prostrate themselves on little mats. Others, believing in horoscopes and evil spirits, made sacrifices to their many gods: Brahma, creator of all things, and Vishnu, the preserver of life, and Siva, the destroyer of life. They worshipped the monkey god, Hanuman, and Ganesh, with his elephant's head, Lakshmi, the goddess of prosperity, and Krishna, the flute-player and god of joy. Others, though a minority, and mostly from Madras, were Christians.

Great was the variety in the names of these Indians: Sikhs like Rattan Singh, Sardara Singh, and Balwant Singh; Punjabi Mussulmen called Mohd Sharif, Rab Niwaz, or Fateh Mohd; Madrassis with names like Balakrishna Pillai, Muthuswamy, Krishna Nair; Mahrattas named Ganpat Chawan, Balu Powar, Shrirang Lawand, Vishnu Mane; Dogras called Tulsi Ram and Gian Chand; Garhwalis like Alam Sing Bisht, Bahadur Sing Rawat; and a thousand other names and combinations of such names.

The ranks of the Indian troops had different names: *lance-naik* (lance-corporal); *naik* (corporal); *havildar* (sergeant); and *havildar-major* (sergeant-major). Higher up the scale, though lower than the officers who received their commissions from the King, were the Viceroy's Commissioned Officers—known as V.C.Os.: *jemadar*, *subadar*, and *subadar-major*. And at the other end of the scale were the non-combatants or 'followers': the *mochi* who repaired your boots and shoes; the *dhobi* who did the laundry; the *dherzi* who made bush-jackets and pairs of shorts, who would sew on medal ribbons and stripes of rank; the *nai* (barber); the *bhisti* (water-carrier); the *babaji* (cook); and the sweeper, who cleaned up the camp and latrines.

In their homes they spoke Punjabi, Pushtu, Mahratti, Telugu, Tamil, Malayalam, but in the Army their common language became Urdu. And some of them learned more than a smattering of English. All officers who served in Indian units had to learn to speak Urdu with fluency; they studied with *munshis* or from books on their own, and they passed their examinations. But there was scarcely a single British officer or other rank in the British units,

PROLOGUE

or among the few N.C.Os. and men in Indian Signal and Sapper companies, who did not pick up a score of Urdu words and phrases that passed into his own current vocabulary. Consciously they used these words when talking with their Indian companions; and unconsciously they spoke the same words among themselves, so inextricably had the Urdu vocabulary become interwoven with their English language.

The English spoken by the Indians varied widely from one unit to another. In an Indian infantry battalion very few would speak any, apart from the Viceroy's Commissioned Officers and the clerks. But in the Signal sections formed of Madrassis, these operators and dispatch riders and linemen spoke a most fluent and picturesque version of the English language, learned in part from the Mission schools, in part from contact with British officers and men.

They slept in their little *tambu*, the adjutant and his *babus* worked in the *daftar*, they all drank *char* out of a *piyala*, and slept on a *charpai*, wrapped in their *bistra*. They would eat their *khana* in the *langar*. They eagerly read their *dak* when it came from the post office, and they wrote more letters in reply. They wore one or other form of *topi* on their heads, earned and spent their *paisa* in rupees and annas, or in piastres and fils. They said *kitne baje* when they wanted to know the time, their every vehicle became a *ghari*; when they were hot and thirsty and there was no tea to refresh them they would ask for *tanda pani*, their bread was referred to as *roti*, and when darkness fell they lit the *batti* in the tent. British soldiers riding beside an Indian driver might shout out *roco!* when they wanted to stop, *ahista* (pronounced *arsti*) *jao* or *jaldi jao* when the driver was to slow down or to hurry along the road. An order was a *hukm*, any swap became a *badali*, and in the long *larai* that was being waged, the various Italian, German and Japanese opponents were termed the *dushman*. The words of understanding or approval alternated between the ubiquitous 'O.K.' and the enchanting *Tikh hai*, while praise was given so easily by a shout of *shahbash!*

*   *   *   *   *

Some there were who stayed with the Division for years on end, others departed after a few weeks, or even days. There were those who shared in the first scenes of the Division's story, those who served through the central episodes, and others who came out to join in the final campaigns. A very few veterans, mostly Indians, travelled right through with the Division from India in 1940 to India in 1943, and then back again to India in 1946.

And as the war progressed, scattered with the Eighth Army, in the War Office, on staff posts and commands in Tunisia and in Italy, in Cairo and Delhi, in senior appointments from the Middle East to Normandy, worked former members of the Division who had gained their early war experience, their opportunity for distinguished leadership, with one of the units. Though these officers and men never followed the Division on its travels to Burma and beyond, they were proud to hear of its achievements, and would turn to a companion and say with pride that they had once served with the Fifth Indian Division.

CHAPTER I

BLUFF IN THE SUDAN

JUNE—OCTOBER 1940

EARLY in July, 1940, a month after Italy entered the war, the Italian forces in Eritrea were under the command of General Tessitore, and he was responsible to his superior officer, General di Corpo D'Armante Luigi Frusci, the Governor of Eritrea and Commander-in-Chief of the Italian Northern Army. These forces attacked Kassala. They crossed the frontier from Metemma and drove us from Gallabat. But then they went no farther. From Kassala they might have crossed a hundred and fifty miles of flat desert that was almost waterless in the dry weather, but where the tracks—no proper roads existed—were becoming impassable to motor traffic with the rains that fall from June to October. Had the Italians made this crossing they would have threatened Khartoum, a capital that was all but defenceless. They made no move towards Khartoum. Their communications would, they feared, be too long and too vulnerable.

Nor was any move made by the Italians against our strategic base at Port Sudan, held by a very small force. They might have advanced from Um Hagar to cut the railway forty miles south-west of Kassala, at the vital Butana Bridge that carries both road and railway across the River Atbara. They did no such thing. And Gallabat might have been the starting-point for an offensive over some ninety miles to the market town of Gedaref, though, with the winding dust track liable to become like a quagmire any day with the rains, such a drive would have been fraught with problems. In no instance did the Italians venture forth.

Their lack of initiative was astounding. For they possessed great superiority in numbers, weapons, aircraft, and war materials, disposing as they did of a quarter of a million troops, white and colonial, in their East African Empire. By contrast, the Kaid (Commander-in-Chief) in the Sudan, Major-General William

Platt, C.B., D.S.O., had at his command during that fateful summer of 1940 no more than three British battalions of infantry—the 2nd West Yorkshires, the 1st Essex, the 1st Worcestershires—and the Sudan Defence Force, with its highly mobile machine-gun companies and its Camel Corps. After the loss of British Somaliland in August, General Platt was reinforced by an Indian battalion, the 2/5th Mahrattas from Aden, and by one British artillery unit, the 4th Field Regiment.

For all this welcome addition to his strength, General Platt was still heavily outnumbered, and committed to the defence of a territory that was a thousand miles in width, cut in two from north to south by the Nile Valley, and of still greater extent from the bare, rocky desert in the north to the forests and mountains of the southern tracts. The Kaid's meagre forces, disposed in groups along his 1,200 miles of front, watched the Red Sea coast between Port Sudan and Suakin, guarded the all-important Butana Bridge, the Atbara and Gash rivers, the approaches to Gedaref and Khartoum, the enemy's activities in his newly won positions at Kassala and Gallabat.

And this was no ordinary task. It imposed a tremendous strain. But for all this, as the months of that memorable summer went by one by one, when Britain looked to her defence after the grim losses of Dunkirk, and the people of the island girded their loins to face the promised "blood, sweat, toil and tears," our troops in the Sudan broke the threat of an Italian invasion.

If the Kaid lacked the resources for an offensive, he did not hesitate to defend offensively, provided only that we did not incur losses that we could not afford. Information was required about the enemy. The initiative must be wrested from the supine Italians. An impression must be given of a strength greater than we actually possessed. To this end our small detachments hurried from point to point, raided and nibbled, showed themselves up and down the long frontier, harassed the opponent, stabbed him across the border, shelled Kassala in the first days of September, disguised our weakness by unprecedented activity—all to such good effect that the Italians came to fear a major British offensive.

For all their strength, they yielded to Platt's soldiers the moral ascendancy, the spirit of attack, the energy that should have been their own. The enemy contented himself with strengthening his frontier garrisons and outposts, and turning still more fatally to the defensive. And our strength was, as we intended, overestimated by the Italian commanders, who were soon bluffed into the conviction that any further advance they might make against Port Sudan, Atbara or Khartoum would encounter very considerable opposition. The Kaid's policy had succeeded. And in September came powerful reinforcements from India in the form of the Fifth Indian Division.

This Division had been formed from the Deccan District, composed at the beginning of the war of the 7th Poona Brigade, later to be commanded by Brigadier H. R. Briggs, the 9th Secunderabad Brigade, under Brigadier A. G. O. M. Mayne, D.S.O., and the 10th Jhansi Brigade, led by Brigadier W. J. Slim, M.C.

The first member of the new Divisional Headquarters to arrive in Secunderabad was the G.S.O.1, Colonel F. W. Messervy, who hurried there from command of the 13th Lancers. When he found that his posting was to Deccan District, he was indignant and wrote a letter of complaint to the Commander-in-Chief. He was told to be patient; his new appointment would not remain so dull and unexciting as he imagined. And within a few days the Fifth Indian Division emerged out of Deccan District, and Secunderabad took on a new spirit of anticipation. But the training was difficult through lack of the most recent equipment and the latest types of guns. When complaints were lodged on this score, the Division was informed that the Cabinet had decided that the Indian Army would not take part in first-class war at all. In consequence, all the new equipment was being sent to the British Army in France. It was later alleged that the Division was only sent to fight in the Sudan and Eritrea because the Italians were considered as second-class enemies. The Fifth Indian Division was one of the few formations to fight all three enemies during the war, and whatever might have been said against the Italians, the Germans and Japanese were never accused of being anything but first-class soldiers.

* * * * *

The first Divisional Commander was Major-General L. M. Heath, C.B., C.I.E., D.S.O., M.C. Before the First World War he raised the Indian contingent in Nyasaland. He fought with the Scinde Rifles in operations for the relief of Kut el Amara, was severely wounded in the left arm during the action of the Dujailah Redoubt in March, 1916, and spent eighteen months in hospital. Then, having deliberately surrendered a nomination to the Staff College—the passport of advancement to posts beyond that of battalion commander—Heath accepted command of the Seistan Levy Corps, in the south-west corner of Afghanistan.

The Levy Corps was disbanded in 1921. Heath served with his regiment, the 14th Punjab, in Palestine, returned to India to command the Indian Army School of Education, and in 1929 assumed command of the 1/11th Sikh Regiment. For three years he served on the North-West Frontier, then found himself an Instructor at the Senior Officers' School, with the rank of full Colonel. Another three years elapsed before Heath was promoted to command the Wana Brigade, once again on the Frontier, where he remained until 1939. Then he was raised to Major-General, only to find that there was little hope of a vacancy; so he went home, but was recalled soon afterwards on the outbreak of war. The Fourth Indian Division had just moved to the Middle East, and there was a vacant appointment in Deccan District.

It was to the personality, ability and energy of General Heath that the Division owed the solid foundation upon which were achieved its battles during the long years to be lived through between the Sudan and Java. Having thrust and dash, cheerfulness, and a calm mastery of the situation, he inspired his troops, who had complete confidence in his leadership. As a commander he looked and was the part. Badly scarred from previous battles, he could not but inspire trust in all who were near him during the many unpleasant days that lay ahead. His almost fatherly manner in the mess, his sense of humour and gay charm, and his ready accessibility to anyone who wished to talk things over, endeared him to the Division.

He always wanted to see his battles, and the observation points and tactical headquarters he chose were sometimes unduly advanced. He was present at the battle whenever the fighting was at its fiercest. General Heath was a keen flyer—he could pilot an aircraft himself, though his damaged arm prevented his being given a licence—and whenever possible he made an aerial reconnaissance of the ground before the battle was engaged. He made one such expedition in a Hardy, and leaned so far out that the pilot was afraid of losing him overboard.

When he had a decision to make he thought the matter out from every angle. Then, at a conference, he appeared to throw up his withered arm to a comfortable position, before issuing his orders briefly and without possible ambiguity. And he kept to his custom of sleeping for an hour every afternoon, because he said that he was then fit to direct operations late into the night. He refused to be hurried, never seemed depressed, and timed his attacks and manœuvres with skill.

It was under his wise and trustful leadership, and with the team of commanders and staff officers that was selected so admirably, that the spirit of the Division grew and flowered at the outset of a long and arduous journey.

His Christian names were Lewis Macclesfield, but he was called either "Mac" or by his nickname "Piggy," the origin of which the General has himself recorded. "This name was given to me when I was a very small boy at Wellington: I was then a rather rotund and well-covered lad rising twelve years of age. Going up the stairs after Chapel one evening a boy named Richardson slapped me on the bottom and said 'You fat little piggy.' That name was used in the dormitory first, and later became common throughout the school. It followed me to Sandhurst and stuck to me all through my service and even into retirement, over half a century later."

*   *   *   *   *

In common with all other major formations during the war, the Fifth Indian Division possessed a sign of its own, that was worn on the sleeves of shirts or battle-dress blouses, and painted on trucks and lorries, jeeps and staff cars. Its origin is less certain than that of General Heath's nickname, though the two are connected. The G.S.O.1 of the Division, Colonel Frank Messervy, submitted to units for their approval the suggestion that the design of the flash should be a boar's head; in this way it would be linked with the nickname of its first commander. But vehement objections to this idea were raised on the grounds that such an insignia would arouse resentment among the Muslim troops in the Division, whose religion forbade them to eat the flesh of the pig. This objection was recognized, and the boar's head cancelled. Messervy then tried the heads of other animals, but each one he devised had already been selected by some other formation. So a plain red circle was chosen. It was simple and distinctive; General Heath approved. The red circle, standing as it did on a black background, gradually came to symbolize a Ball of Fire.

* * * * *

When the Division and its two brigades arrived in the Sudan various changes were made. The 29th Brigade, composed of the three British battalions already in the country, was split up. The 1st Worcestershires remained, the 2nd West Yorkshires went to Mayne's Nine Brigade, while the 1st Essex joined Ten Brigade. Each of the three brigades now had one British and two Indian battalions. Brigadier J. C. O. Marriott, C.V.O., D.S.O., M.C., a Scots Guardsman commanding the newly constituted 29 Brigade, had the 3/2nd Punjab and 6/13th Frontier Force Rifles. Mayne's two Indian battalions were the 3/5th Mahratta Light Infantry and 3/12th Frontier Force Regiment; Brigadier Slim had the 4/10th Baluch and 3/18th Royal Garhwal Rifles.

By October the rains had almost ceased. The Division was distributed along the northern part of the immense frontier that the Kaid's scanty force had so skilfully dominated throughout the summer. While Marriott's battalions were split between Port Sudan and the Sennar Dam, and while Nine Brigade guarded a central area from Butana Bridge to Showak, Slim's Ten Brigade held Gedaref and Doka and watched the enemy at Gallabat and Metemma. Later, the Kassala area was taken care of by Gazelle Force.

The nucleus of this force was one of the two groups of Sudan Defence Force machine-gun companies, based on Butana Bridge. It was now strengthened by Skinner's Horse and a battery of field guns, the whole being placed under command of Colonel Frank Messervy, who handed over his work as G.S.O.1 of the Division to Colonel Dudley Russell of the 6/13th Frontier Force Rifles.

Messervy, a man brimming over with energy, ideas, and cheerfulness, tempered the thrust and impetus of a cavalry officer with the sound planning of a former instructor at the Staff College. His figure was tall, his head very bald, his face eager and alert of expression. To the cautious and ponderous he may, at times, have appeared to be rash and even foolhardy, but those who offered such criticisms failed to realize just how astute and quick-witted was Frank Messervy. Perhaps there were moments when he realized that the demands he was making on his men were excessive, but those who served with him responded to his every call for endeavour. To say that he had no fear might be false. But on one occasion, during a nasty bout of enemy shelling, he was heard to say cheerily to a fellow-commander who had himself earned a triple D.S.O. and was shouting to Messervy to take cover: "Oh, it's all right. They're not aiming at me!"

Some have said, and no doubt many others have thought, that Messervy was blessed with uncommon luck in battle. But this he attributed to his reliance upon the shielding arm of Providence (he is a staunch Roman Catholic) and to his inherent belief in the ancient motto that "Fortune favours the brave." His military life illustrates those beliefs.

'Gazelle' was, as General Heath later noted, a misnomer for that fleet-footed animal of the desert which is essentially a timid creature, whereas the 'Gazelle' as welded and wielded by Messervy had the cunning and ferocity of a man-eating leopard. Messervy was charged with the task of dominating the Gash Delta and deceiving the enemy. In both respects he succeeded admirably. By great mobility, daring, and an enterprise that often amounted to impudence, Gazelle Force led the Italians to believe that at least two divisions faced them—there were scarcely more than a thousand men. Messervy's columns harassed and ambushed enemy maintenance convoys, and raided behind Italian outposts—the Sudan Defence Force officers' mess supplied itself with fresh fruit and vegetables from Italian gardens in Kassala itself. Characteristic of their day-to-day achievements was the rounding up of a party that was repairing the telephone line from Kassala to Tessenei; when a small enemy force came out to search for the missing line party, it, too, was destroyed.

An interesting example of our deception policy during this period of preparation was the suggestion that the phrase "Fifth Indian Division" should be converted, in the course of purposely indiscreet talk, into "five Indian Divisions." Within ten days this new 'fact' was inserted in Italian Intelligence reports!

* * * * *

As the weeks passed the men of the Division grew familiar with the rocks and sand and dust of the Sudan; with the local villages and the *tukls* (mud huts with thatched roofs), the little tin railway stations. They learned to camouflage their vehicles at every halt and to dig slit trenches—the enemy held sway in the air. Slowly our troops gained experience in the difficulties of navigation through the bush. All this time the heat was fierce, and the few eggs and chickens purchased from Sudanese villagers could well have been cooked on the railway lines. Those officers who on reconnaissance travelled across country by railway scooter saw numbers of giraffe and ostrich moving against the monotonous landscape of hard sand, that rolled away to a horizon broken only by an occasional *jebel* (mountain) of solid rock.

The mirage whose outline faded and then vanished as you drew near, the heat shimmer from which tree-ringed lakes and the likeness of still water might be stared at, were a frequent and memorable feature of many a drive over the desert. Wells became important and recognizable by the swarms of flies as well as by the camels, cows, goats and donkeys that watered there in daylight. To pick out the one camel track to be followed among many such tracks was often perplexing, and a glance at the sun or a compass would be necessary to avoid taking the wrong route. Patches of long *tubbas* grass grew on the sand now that the rains were falling, and camel-thorn bushes studded the ground. Where these bushes flourished, particularly round Gedaref, men found it difficult to walk any distance without getting caught up in thorns like fish-hooks. The scratches festered into septic sores, and in certain units there was hardly a man without bandages on one or both arms and knees.

Farther south, towards Gedaref and Butana Bridge, and in the Gash Delta cotton-growing district, the sand gave place to loamy, black-cotton soil, badly cracked and bumpy in the sun's glare, and, in the rainy season, holding pools of water. Trucks could be hidden beneath the quaint evergreen *tebeldi* trees, shaped like umbrellas, and beneath numerous gum trees. And some of the troops would defy the risk of crocodiles and bathe in the clear waters of the Atbara, sharing the shallow reaches with families of hippopotami.

CHAPTER II

GALLABAT

NOVEMBER—DECEMBER 1940

DURING this initial period, when the Division concentrated its units, adapted itself to the new theatre of operations, learned something of the enemy's strength and methods, and laid the foundations of spirit, teamwork and tradition, the main offensive gesture was made by Slim's Ten Brigade. And it was a gesture with a twofold purpose. The activity and confidence of the Abyssinian patriots between Gallabat and Gondar were to be stimulated. Local guerilla pinpricks against the Italians would receive encouragement from the news of an attack against Gallabat by our land and air forces. But apart from the need of impressing the Abyssinians, General Heath was keen that as many troops in the Division as possible should gain experience of conditions of modern warfare.

Ten Brigade, supported by the 28th Field Regiment, R.A. (Lieutenant-Colonel G. de V. Welchman), bivouacked for several days in Gedaref, a dirty, smelly little town, and then set off towards the south-east. The journey of some ninety miles lay across country which was in turn open and heavily wooded—tall and thickish jungle covered by drying yellow elephant grass as high as a standing man.

Brigadier Slim, accompanied by certain members of his staff and by his Gunner commander, Welchman, made the first main reconnaissance on October 28. They were riding ponies loaned by the Sudan Defence Force, and had just reached one *khor* (watercourse) on their way to an excellent observation point named Signal Hill when an Italian plane came over at low altitude to have a look. Its progress was leisurely, its silver paint attractive. But the aircraft might have been menacing, so Slim's party all dismounted and took cover underneath their ponies. The Italian observer failed to see them, or perhaps mistook their ponies for giraffe, and nothing more happened to disturb the peace of the reconnaissance.

Many glimpsed Gallabat for the first time from the Baluch positions on Signal Hill. The forward edge of Gallabat fort was plainly to be seen in a clearing amid a wide panorama of jungle. Behind and to the left rose the jungle-clad slopes of Jebel Mariam Waha. On the lower slopes of this hill lay Metemma, less than two miles from Gallabat. Between these two places ran the steep Boundary *khor* that marked the frontier between the Sudan and Abyssinia. In the background, far distant, ran the line of the main Abyssinian mountains.

Those who had field glasses on Signal Hill or on other hillocks—more sparsely covered with forest trees than the rest of the country, and used by the supporting Gunners for observation posts—could pick out the native huts of Metemma, the white walls of the Italian barracks, and two long white storage sheds, the more readily against the darker surroundings. Half a mile to the south stretched the landing ground. Gallabat fort, too, stood out prominently in the landscape, surrounded by an outer thorn hedge, by belts of barbed wire, and by low defence emplacements. Here, too, were native *tukls* and a pair of tin huts. The country between the forward positions on the line of hillocks and Gallabat itself was undulating and wooded. But to the north-west and north-east were two open brown clearings, known by the troops as the Right and Left Golf Courses.

Small Italian working parties could be seen marching in and out of Gallabat, and this first glimpse of the enemy in the flesh was no small excitement to our troops.

The surface of the road to Gallabat was marked as suitable for all weathers, and composed of the heavy black cotton soil characteristic of these parts. But the road had become heavily corrugated; the bumps and ridges, being as much as three inches high, rendered travel by any means of motor transport most painful. Accordingly, the Sappers and Miners were constantly at work with their graders to level off the surface.

* * * * *

Slim chose November 6 for his first attack on Gallabat and Metemma. It was the first offensive action to be taken in Africa or on any other front by our land forces since the outbreak of war with Italy five months earlier.

Night fell on Guy Fawkes' Day with everyone in the Brigade wondering how much the Italians knew about our impending assault. During the previous three days units had taken up their battle positions, ammunition had been brought up for Welchman's guns. Whatever the Italians might be doing or thinking, our men had little sleep, and were keyed up for this, the Division's first attack.

A little before midnight the 3/18th Royal Garhwal Rifles (Lieutenant-Colonel S. E. Tayler) and the 1st Essex moved forward. The Brigade firm base was held by the 4/10th Baluch (Lieutenant-Colonel B. L. Sundius-Smith) on Signal Hill and on either side of the Gedaref road. The darkness was black as the proverbial pitch. Rain was falling. The slimy surface of the ground made progress slow and awkward. Later, when the cover of the hills was behind the infantry and, in front, the more level ground that led away towards Gallabat fort, visibility and movement were much reduced by the tall elephant grass. The battalions then waited for the dawn.

Slim's plan provided for our bombardment to open with the bombing of Gallabat and Metemma by the Royal Air Force. The planes were late. The minutes ticked past. The infantry and gunners waited, the excitement within them contrasted sharply with the peace of the morning landscape. It was later discovered that the night's fall of rain had been heavy elsewhere and had turned our advanced landing ground into a muddy expanse. And the bombers had been unable to take off from the treacherous black cotton soil until it had dried a little.

Then at last our expectant troops, and the Italians, heard the drone of our approaching aircraft. Over flew eight Wellesleys and Vincents, to bomb Metemma and Gallabat forts, and to attack the two enemy Colonial battalions in positions outside the wire at Metemma. Welchman's 28th Field Regiment, who had registered their targets during the air bombardments for reasons of secrecy, fired a series of concentrations at the crest of Gallabat hill and at the wireless station and command post in Metemma. Bombs crumped, aircraft engines throbbed overhead, shells whined towards their several targets. Gallabat became overhung by a pall of smoke.

Soon after first light the fighters on both sides came into action.

GALLABAT

Our ten Gladiators were opposed by about an equal number of Fiat C.R.42's. Within half an hour five of our machines had been destroyed at little or no cost to the Italians, and other Gladiators had been damaged. In this brief period we lost control of the air above our attacking troops.

The descent in flames of British aircraft and the gentle drifting of parachutes from which dangled the tiny silhouetted figures of our pilots was witnessed from Ten Brigade Headquarters with astonishment and dismay. It was known that the C.R. 42 was a faster aircraft, but the Gladiator was more manœuvrable, and in previous encounters over the Sudan aerodromes the more skilfully handled British machines had proved at least a match for the Italian fighters.

After the battle it was learned that the enemy machines, which were armed with cannons, had recently received a new type of incendiary bullet which proved much more effective than their old type of ammunition, and infinitely more so than our own.

Once our Gladiators had been destroyed, the Italian commander at Gallabat summoned bombers to come to his assistance, and from about seven o'clock onwards these flew backwards and forwards, quite unhindered, and in ever-increasing strength, over the battlefield.

But let us return to the action of the ground troops. While dog fights still persisted overhead and the smoke thinned away from Gallabat, Tayler's Garhwalis, with a squadron of the 6th Royal Tank Regiment, advanced across the last few hundred yards of rocky ground. They approached the fort. The fort fell to the Indian battalion. Soon the first of over two hundred Italian prisoners, mostly native Eritrean troops with a handful of white officers, began to trickle back. This success was gained against hard opposition from the Italian Colonial battalions and fierce hand-to-hand fighting that surged in and around the fort for three-quarters of an hour. The Garhwalis had reached their objective at half-past six.

If the air support had failed to come up to expectations, so too had the tanks. They were a mixed squadron that had been sent down the Nile from the Western Desert. The tank drivers had no experience of driving in such country. They had switched from open sand to rock, bush and hills. Mechanical breakdowns, broken tracks, rough boulders that could not be seen in the long grass, and mines caused severe losses. Of twelve cruiser and light tanks, three were out of action from mines, and six more from damaged track pins. Three that broke down inside Gallabat fort still continued to fire their guns in support of the Garhwalis. In assessing the efficiency of these tanks, it should be realized that the squadron, the only one that could be spared from Middle East, was long overdue for repair and refitting.

The bombardment of our artillery lifted from Gallabat to Metemma, and the infantry attack began. The Pathan company of the Baluch (Major Sherwood) had, by six o'clock, captured Jebel Um Zareba, a little hillock two miles north-west of the fort.

Soon after half-past seven, when the green success signal flared into the air, Brigadier Slim decided that the moment had come for himself, Welchman, and his Intelligence Officer, Captain Mark Ash, to drive up to Gallabat. Welchman had a Bren carrier standing by for this very purpose, so they set off up the road that had not been used since the outbreak of war with Italy. When obstructions and difficult stretches of going were met, the Brigadier and his two companions had to climb out and guide the driver through. At last the carrier reached the fort without mishap. Here a number of Italian officer prisoners were being checked over. One of these fresh captives, excessively polite despite his agitation, kept on saluting and introducing himself to Slim and Welchman as "Capitano Italiano, Capitano Italiano." Unfortunately, this introduction was accompanied by a frequent double knees-bend, for machine-gun bullets from an Italian counter-attack were swishing overhead all the time. The Brigade Commander thought it wiser to close the interview and hasten forward into the fort. But Slim's party were still not out of trouble, for no sooner had they walked on a short distance than they found themselves involved between a Garhwali company and a fresh enemy counter-attack. Excited riflemen were shouting at the Brigadier to get out of the way. It was as well that this attack was beaten off without delay.

In the centre of the fort sat the redoubtable "Snap" Tayler—commander of the Garhwalis—sitting, as Welchman described it, "placidly on a rock like Mr. Pickwick with a moustache, getting his wind, and a little pleased at having captured an Italian officer by himself." On every side lay dead men and mules. Already flies buzzed avidly upon the corpses. Very soon Italian bombers, with fighter protection above, delivered the first of a succession of attacks on Gallabat. Having shot down or crippled our fighters, the Italians were free to mobilize, from every airfield held in Eritrea and Abyssinia, all the bombers they could make available. Gallabat, lying conspicuously as it did, presented almost the ideal target. Four air raids had come by half-past three, each more intense than its predecessor.

Meanwhile, Slim and Welchman had looked across to Metemma. Its stone walls and barbed-wire defences, covered by guns, looked formidable. There was also the deep Boundary *khor* to be contended with. The Royal Garhwal Rifles had had a gruelling morning, the Baluch were in reserve, and the 1st Essex were in readiness to advance up to the fort, which they actually entered at eleven o'clock. Overhead the enemy had domination. Without tanks—which alone could break the wire—an attack against Metemma would be at once uncertain and costly. Reinforcements were no nearer than at three days' call.

For Brigadier Slim this was a testing experience. He had planned and executed a successful attack on Gallabat. The fort had been recaptured. And now within his grasp was the chance of commanding the first attack of the war on to Italian soil. But Slim realized the grave difficulties. Success was in the balance. With imperturbable confidence he took the decision to call off any further attack beyond the *khor*. Instead, Ten Brigade was to consolidate its positions round Gallabat.

But our casualties were mounting. Their evacuation was slow and difficult. By nine o'clock it was evident that if the Italian Air Force continued to hold supremacy, Gallabat would become untenable. Our tanks were still not repaired: an L.A.D. lorry had been bombed, three fitters wounded, and most of the spare parts and tools lost. For the infantry alone, with neither tank nor air support, to attack the double-apron wire that encircled Metemma was out of the question. Further, the battalions had suffered too severely from the bombings to make the difficult flank attack against the enemy outside the wire on the hill-slopes.

At half-past three that afternoon some elements of the 1st Essex withdrew in some disorder from their positions in and about

Gallabat fort. So hard and rocky was the ground that even the defence-minded Italians had failed to dig trenches. And when the Italian bombers delivered their most concentrated attack of the day, the troops were still not properly consolidated, and were unsheltered and defenceless against aerial attack. In the midst of this unnerving ordeal an ammunition lorry was set on fire by burning grass, and the noise was thought to be an enemy counter-attack from the rear. One platoon deliberately advanced with bayonets fixed towards the sound of popping bullets to deal with the situation. Other troops mistook this move for a general retirement, and some confusion ensued.

General Heath, who was forward with Russell, his G.S.O.1, informed Brigadier Slim that he was there if wanted. Slim came up and frankly described what was happening. General Heath said very quietly:

"I think we ought to write an appreciation."

The three officers then sat down and on the backs of message pads, without collaboration, wrote appreciations. They went through these, each commenting on the others, and a plan for the future was evolved. But, more important still, this simple action served, in a subtle way, to bring an atmosphere of unruffled control over the whole operation.

It was decided, reluctantly enough, to retire to positions within artillery range of Metemma, and to render that base untenable to the Italians.

* * * * *

Ten Brigade withdrew from Gallabat that evening. Sappers from 21 Field Company remained behind to destroy all usable buildings and stores in the fort. Our Gunners bombarded it and Metemma. This bombardment was spectacular: direct hits set off most of the Italian ammunition dumps, and these contained large stocks of fireworks and rockets.

Slim's policy was not to reoccupy Gallabat but to patrol vigorously and deny the fort to the enemy. On November 9 two companies of the Baluch attacked, and held the fort throughout the day, retiring in the evening. That night a strong enemy counter-attack was repulsed by our defensive fire. Next morning our infantry reoccupied the fort, without opposition. Ambushes were laid with great effect. Though we did not hold Gallabat, we prevented the heavily reinforced Italians from occupying the place again and we kept our grip on the flanking hills despite daily bombing.

What had been the results of this fighting? True it is that the enemy forces in the area had not been destroyed, though one Colonial battalion had been virtually annihilated, and two others mauled. But we had shown that we were prepared to take the offensive with artillery and tanks, that we were superior to the Italians in fighting capacity. And this did much to hearten the morale of the Abyssinian Patriots. Prior to the action at Gallabat the efforts of their leaders had been faint-hearted. Besides, the Italians assisted the change of heart by withdrawing a considerable number of troops from north-west Abyssinia to reinforce the garrison in Metemma. From this time dates not merely the real aid we received from the Patriots, but also the desertion of many Abyssinian soldiers serving in the enemy's Colonial battalions. This defection was a direct result of our local success at Gallabat, and as the campaign progressed these Abyssinians proved themselves most ready to give away details about enemy troop movements and dispositions. This source of information concerning the enemy order of battle gave our commanders a picture of what was happening on the other side seldom surpassed in any other theatre of war.

Ten Brigade had been introduced to the noise, strain and horror of modern war. To quote Brigadier Slim's notes on training issued after the battle: "The majority of the troops who assaulted Gallabat had hardly seen an aeroplane or tank, let alone co-operated with or been attacked by them; they had never seen or heard an artillery bombardment or had a shell pass over their heads. The noise alone of these, heard for the first time, is distressing and bewildering."

Brigadier W. J. Slim had joined the 6th Gurkha Rifles after serving in Gallipoli and Mesopotamia with the Royal Warwickshire Regiment. When, one day in 1940, he confided to a staff officer that he did not really want to serve on and that had no war come he would have been happy to retire and write books, he little knew the path that lay before him between command of Ten Brigade and that of the Fourteenth Army and, later, the post of Chief of the Imperial General Staff. Not only was he confident in himself, but the confidence that he showed in his troops aroused their confidence in him as their commander. It is not certain that his companions foresaw the brilliant future in these early days in the Sudan, but there is no doubt that Brigadier Slim was imperturbable in the worst of circumstances, and a high level tactician. To have won his first engagement of the campaign—at Gallabat—and then to have lost it would have rattled many another commander. But Slim stabilized the situation that had turned against his brigade through no fault of his own.

For all the thrust and stubbornness of his chin, which was not deceptive, he was most approachable, and a ready listener to the ideas of his officers. If he was prepared to shoulder blame with equanimity, he was also quick to pass on credit to his subordinates rather than accept it for himself.

The celebrated tale is told of Slim's first visit to the Highland Light Infantry, who joined Ten Brigade after Gallabat. At the end of the Brigadier's talk to the officers and N.C.Os. of the battalion, a Jock jumped to his feet and cried: "Don't you worry, sir! We'll follow you anywhere." Like a flash came the retort from Slim: "Don't you be so bloody sure about that. I'm going to follow you!"

*　　*　　*　　*　　*

For two and a half months our troops stayed there before a general advance was made. By vigorous patrolling they maintained complete ascendancy over the enemy on the ground, though the Italians in that area outnumbered us by three to one. Patrolling in the tall elephant grass was a nervy procedure, and small patrols might well come unexpectedly face to face with an Italian party. Then the men in front would shoot it out while their companions behind tried to outflank the opposite side. Already the vultures were feasting in Gallabat, or what remained of it after the fighting and bombardments. Care was essential when approaching the fort, because the sudden rising of a flock of these sinister birds could reveal our presence to a watchful foe. False alarms were many, and often caused by the baboons which abounded in the district.

The tinder-like elephant grass was also a problem to the Gunners. Several fires started in the gun-pits when fragments of burning cordite set the grass alight. Buckets of water had constantly to be kept at hand, and smoking was strictly forbidden. Because of the visits of hostile aircraft day after day, these gun-pits were elaborate with their camouflage nets draped on poles. The Gunners went to the length of cutting sods with the grass attached and of 'planting' these on top of the camouflage nets to simulate the normal jungle grass growing on every side. As these covers had to be taken down every time the guns were fired, and then replaced immediately afterwards, the trouble involved was great, but amply repaid. Never once were the Gunners spotted by Italian pilots.

The local superiority enjoyed by the enemy in the air was a salutary training in care and concealment to our men. Track discipline was rigorously enforced. Trucks of all kinds were parked under trees and liberally draped with foliage. The troops lived in huts constructed of boughs and named *tukls*. These had to be dug in, for protection against the 'egg-basket' type of Italian bomb, a series of anti-personnel grenades that were virtually shovelled out of the enemy bombers. Along the banks of the local *khors* the trees were particularly heavy and green. At this season the streams were mostly dry, with an occasional pool, and away from their proximity the bush was scorched by heat and drought, the leaves burnt off, and the landscape consequently more open than a few months earlier when the vegetation had been dense and tall.

Soon after the withdrawal from Gallabat, Colonel Welchman was presented with a hunting spear, which became one of his most treasured possessions. He converted it into a sort of *khud* stick, and found it an invaluable aid on the climb, which he did several times a day, up the steep paths of Signal Hill—his Observation Post. Though Welchman was soon practised enough to avoid poking the point of the spear through one of his own feet, he also noticed that those who accompanied him were careful to keep at a respectful distance. When there was no need for silent movement, the metal point made a friendly tinkling sound on the rocks, and often Welchman would hear, as he approached his O.P., the telephone operator on duty saying to the batteries of the 28th Field Regiment: "'Ere 'e comes. Get the smoke shell ready." The Colonel also recalls with satisfaction that when his spear went tinkling down the path once again, he would hear a message such as: "'E's on the way down now. An M.G. emplacement blowed up and ten —— *tukls* burning grand."

Colonel Sundius-Smith has recorded that Welchman often tarried at the Baluch officers' mess hut for lunch on his way to or from Signal Hill. On one occasion, when Sundius-Smith reminded him of something he was to have done but had forgotten, Welchman's comment was: "Oh, yes, I must tie a knot in my spear."

Welchman was soon given the title of "Abu harleyah," meaning "Father of all spears," by the Sudan Defence Force, and "Ballum sahib" by the sepoys. He instituted his own system of numbering purely personal messages, and this started with the quite illegal number of O.B.W.S. ("Old Blighter with Spear") 72, or whatever the reference was.

* * * * *

During the second week of December Ten Brigade was relieved in the Gallabat-Metemma district by Mayne's Nine Brigade. In came the 2nd West Yorkshires (Lieutenant-Colonel R. M. Rodwell), the 3/5th Mahratta Light Infantry (now commanded by Lieutenant-Colonel Denys Reid), and the 3/12th Frontier Force Regiment (Lieutenant-Colonel J. A. Blood).

Brigadier Mosley Mayne, affectionately known far and wide as "Mo," had passed his fiftieth year. After a year with the East Lancashire Regiment in India, he joined the 13th Duke of Connaught's Lancers, and spent the next five years on the North-West Frontier. All through the 1914-18 war he served as adjutant, and in 1917 was wounded in Mesopotamia. Thirty years later he was still in receipt of a disability pension for his leg that was damaged in that fighting. Within two years Mayne sustained a permanent injury to his back as the result of an air crash while making a battle reconnaissance in Kurdistan. Then, in 1924, when Chief Instructor at the Cavalry School in India, he had a serious polo accident, lay unconscious for several days, spent three and a half months in a dark room, and was forced to take eighteen months' sick leave. No sooner had he rejoined his regiment, now the 6th Lancers, than Mayne was again injured in a practice polo game. This cost him a further six months in bed, and he came home to England.

Both at the War Office and, in 1933, at the Imperial Defence College he forged many friendships with men who were destined to rise to fame in the Second World War. Three years later saw him back once more in India, this time as Director of Military Operations, during a period when it was clear that war was impending. He worked in close touch with Auchinleck on strategic planning, with particular reference to the employment of the "Army in India" on overseas service.

To the Fifth Indian Division Brigadier Mayne brought a cavalry outlook, tempered by a realization and experience of the wider issues of war, sharpened by the keen brain of a tried senior staff officer, who learned all he could about the handling of infantry in the field by inquisitive and searching questions to his battalion commanders.

Always he seemed delighted to see you; no officer or man was too junior to receive from him a few cheerful words and an engaging smile that lit up his lined face. He was keenly interested in their welfare and success, and when visiting a unit would invariably inquire whether there was anyone to whom he ought to speak: one who had lost his mother, an officer whose son had been killed in the Royal Air Force, an Indian Christian clerk who had recently married.

Beneath his charm of manner, with his monocle, cigarette holder, quivering salute, and jerky mannerisms, lay a quick mind, a human approach to his troops, a meticulous attention to detail, an understanding of both staff and common problems, an unusual aptitude for paper-work, and great determination.

* * * * *

The Brigade's task was to prevent the enemy entering Gallabat, to disorganize his defensive arrangements, and to demoralize his troops. Later, in conjunction with other arrangements for the advance into Eritrea, it was to simulate a full division and lead the Italians to believe that our harassing operations on the Kassala front were mere bluff, and that our main offensive was to be staged along the Gallabat–Metemma–Wahni–Gondar line. A programme of deception was drawn up. Dummy landing grounds, dumps, and medical posts were established on our lines of communication. Concentrations were fired by guns of various calibres. At dawn each day Welchman sent his guns forward to their outpost positions, in order to use to the best advantage the comparatively short range of the 4.5-inch howitzers. At dusk these guns were withdrawn.

And the fact that all this movement to and fro was possible without the enemy being aware of it indicates at once the skill with which it was effected, the thickness of the bush, and the dense interlacing of the branches above the dusty tracks.

These were busy weeks of raids and fighting patrols, and the dive-bombing of Italian positions from time to time by our Hardys. When the enemy's obsolete biplanes came trundling over at intervals, their slow speed and loud noise gave good warning of their approach, and our anti-aircraft defence, comprising twelve Bredas—part of a consignment of forty from an Italian vessel captured in the Red Sea—went into action.

Then, early in the new year, 1941, 28 Field Regiment was ordered back to Gedaref. In its place came the 25-pounders of 144 Field Regiment (Surrey and Sussex Yeomanry).

144 Field Regiment had the reputation among other units for being clannish and something of a 'private army.' The story is told that when all commanding officers were urged to ensure that the men made provision for their dependents, a certain battery commander in this regiment, noting that one of his men was making no allotment to his mother, requested him to do so. The man replied that, before leaving for active service, he had made over to his mother ten thousand pounds. If the battery commander thought this inadequate, he would consider raising it. This, a true story, is some indication of the texture of the Territorial Army units at that period.

And Major George Munn, himself a battery commander with the regiment, records the evident amazement of General Heath when he inspected his battery, and asked the officers what they did in civilian life. The replies were: stockbroker, barrister, printer, master of foxhounds, Lloyd's broker, racehorse trainer, and architect.

*　　*　　*　　*　　*

During our initial advance into Eritrea, Brigadier Mayne, who was neither able nor allowed to stage a full stage brigade attack, was constantly trying to discover if and when the enemy would withdraw from the Gallabat front, and a mobile column was made ready for the pursuit when it came. It is convenient here to forestall the narrative of earlier events on the main front of the

Major-General L. M. Heath

Major-General A. G. O. M. Mayne

(C.I.S. Historical Section)

BRIGADIER W. J. SLIM

(Walter Stoneman, F.R.P.)

BRIGADIER J. C. O. MARRIOTT

(Elliott & Fry)

BRIGADIER F. W. MESSERVY

BRIGADIER T. W. REES

Fifth Indian Division by recounting the sequence of events which occurred much later on the Gallabat front.

Early on the morning of February 1 routine patrols from the 2nd West Yorkshires, having instructions always to draw fire in order to establish the enemy's continued presence, found that there was no more fire to be drawn. The Italians had slipped away, after several days of increased activity with shelling, aggressive patrols, night demonstrations against our forward lines, and air attacks. And so the chase began.

The mobile column, under the command of Major Hugh Stewart, comprised twelve carriers from the West Yorkshires and 3/12th Frontier Force Regiment, one company of the West Yorkshires, an O.P. party from Munn's battery, with a troop of guns, and a detachment of Philbrick's 21 Field Company, led by Second-Lieutenant Bhagat.

The pursuit progressed well, but was frequently delayed by extensive minefields. Bhagat, the Sapper, led the column in a carrier, in which he stood next to the driver. He kept his eyes on the road, watching for any disturbance of the surface which might indicate a buried mine. All *wadi* beds—and they crossed many—were automatically suspect and examined minutely, since it was possible to bury mines under the uneven surface without leaving a trace. The outstanding performance of the detachment of Sappers during this advance was responsible for the award of the Victoria Cross to Second-Lieutenant Premindra Singh Bhagat. It was the first V.C. to be won by the Indian Army in the Second World War, the first to be earned by an Indian Commissioned Officer. From the citation we may quote this passage:—

"For a period of four days and over a distance of 55 miles this officer in the leading carrier led the column. He detected and supervised the clearing of fifteen minefields. Speed being essential, he worked at high pressure from dawn to dusk each day. On two occasions when his carrier was blown up with casualties to others, and on a third occasion when ambushed and under close enemy fire, he himself carried straight on with his task. He refused relief when worn out with strain and fatigue and with one eardrum punctured by an explosion, on the grounds that he was now better qualified to continue his task to the end.

"His coolness, persistence over a period of 96 hours, and gallantry not only in battle but throughout the long period when the safety of the column and the speed at which it could advance were dependent on his personal efforts, are deserving of the highest recognition."

And that recognition was forthcoming.

* * * * *

Soon after leaving Metemma the column caught up two stragglers —ragged Eritreans they were, with a mule that carried medical equipment. Camps were passed, previously occupied by the retreating enemy and now littered with refuse, food, dead mules and lumps of raw meat, and alive with flies. The Gandwa river, that was reached on February 3, proved a real obstacle, covered as it was by the fire of an Italian rearguard and by well-placed minefields. Neither carriers nor trucks could be manœuvred in the dense bush or across the river and its tributaries. To disperse the rearguard and clear the mines took two hours.

The next twenty miles to Wahni were rapidly covered, despite an ambush and two attacks on our advanced camp by native troops. Early on the 7th Wahni was occupied, the enemy having withdrawn during the night; we had shelled the place for two hours the previous afternoon. A number of prisoners and stragglers had been left for us to collect.

We are indebted to General Mayne for the story of an incident during this pursuit of General Martini's forces to Wahni and beyond. Mayne had established his tactical headquarters some miles short of Gandwa, and wanted signal communications with the mobile column very urgently. His Signals Officer, Captain T. H. Jessop, went forward with a small line party to lay the cable. And this, according to the General, was the only occasion on which he ever saw Jessop defeated, for the latter had guaranteed proper line communication with Wahni.

"Having set off into the bush as the sun was setting, he rang me up from Gandwa six hours later, received my thanks and congratulations, and then started back to my headquarters again. I was delighted, and after a comforting talk with my O.C. Mobile Column, I closed down for the night and went to sleep, telling the Signals to snatch some rest too.

"At dawn I went round to the Signal Office to find out how the Wahni column had fared during the night, and to give them the latest news from my end. I found Jessop there asleep, but with one ear open, for he jumped to his feet the moment after I arrived and seized the phone to put me through to Gandwa. Failure! Not a buzz! Jessop looked the picture of astonishment, and misery; I expect I, too, looked worried. Then came the explanation in the form, or rather in the person, of a beaming corporal of British infantry. He had been out on salvage duty—there was a mass of valuable Italian salvage to collect—and, with commendable enthusiasm but regrettable lack of judgment, had stayed out all night and had salvaged almost every scrap of line that poor Jessop had so laboriously and skilfully laid! Jessop was habitually a man of few words, but on this occasion he broke custom."

All idea of a further advance towards Gondar was for the time being abandoned by the Kaid, on January 26. He had kept this front open in case serious opposition round Kassala persuaded him to switch his main thrust towards Gondar. But Kassala had, as will be seen, been evacuated by the enemy. Our progress there was good, and General Platt could not supply both fronts. He rightly chose to reinforce success. Moreover, administrative difficulties were becoming insuperable. The pursuit, except for small motorized patrols, had almost come to a standstill, for Nine Brigade Group, having advanced sixty miles from Metemma over an outrageous road, still had to maintain itself all the way from Gedaref, yet another ninety miles to the north, on unit first-line transport alone.

Early in February Mayne was promoted Major-General, handed over Nine Brigade to Colonel Messervy of Gazelle Force, and went to G.H.Q., Middle East, to wait for an appointment in his new rank. Then, on February 10, Messervy withdrew his troops to Gedaref, leaving behind two companies of the 3/12th Frontier Force Regiment to keep watch at Wahni and by the Gandwa crossing. After hunting a side line very hard and not without success for a period of nearly three months, Nine Brigade prepared to rejoin the main Divisional pack on the Kassala front, where the limelight was shining.

CHAPTER III

FROM KASSALA TO BARENTU

JANUARY—FEBRUARY 1941

AT the beginning of December 1940 the Commander-in-Chief in the Middle East, General Sir Archibald Wavell, had laid down as his general policy that the troops under Platt's command were to prepare for the recapture of Kassala in the New Year, provided that the necessary reinforcements could be made available from Egypt. Pressure was to be maintained in the Metemma area. The fomentation of the Patriots in Abyssinia offered an excellent prospect of rendering intolerable the enemy's position and of aiding our eventual recapture of the country. With the victory of Sidi Barrani in North Africa behind him, Wavell was enabled to release the Fourth Indian Division, led by Major-General Sir Noel de la P. Beresford-Peirse. But although Eleven Brigade (Brigadier R. A. Savory) arrived in the Sudan before the end of the year, the Division as a whole could not be concentrated and ready for action for a further six weeks.

The piecemeal arrival of the new division during this period should not be forgotten, for troops were brought forward ahead of programme according to the means of transport available, and they went into battle and pursuit of the enemy as soon as they reached their destination. When Briggs' Seven Brigade relieved 29 Brigade on the Lines of Communication between Port Sudan and Atbara, there were left free for the offensive against Kassala only Gazelle Force, Eleven Brigade of the Fourth Indian Division, and Heath's Ten and 29 Brigades, with Nos. 3 and 5 M.M.G. Companies of the Sudan Defence Force.

The Kaid decided on a plan for the capture of the triangle formed by Kassala, Sabderat and Tessenei, to start on February 9; this was later brought forward to January 19, because of suspicions that the Italians intended to withdraw. And Wavell desired earlier action. Both the efforts of Messervy's Gazelle Force and reports from deserters had shown that the enemy was gradually reducing his forces in the Kassala neighbourhood, prior to an evacuation. Heath's men would drive through Tessenei and along the road to Barentu by way of Aicota. The newly arrived Fourth Indian Division would head along the shorter northern route to Sabderat, Keru and Agordat.

Early in the new year the 2nd Highland Light Infantry (Lieutenant-Colonel B. C. Fletcher, M.C.) were ordered to move by night. This battalion had joined Ten Brigade at Christmas time, after four months in Port Said, to replace the 1st Essex, who were transferred to Palestine after Gallabat. They were to push the enemy from the isolated and volcanic Abu Gamal feature; having two separate peaks, this mountain, whose name means 'father of all camels,' towers with Jebel Kassala some three thousand feet above the surrounding plain. On January 11 the battalion captured the wells from which the Italians drew their water; it covered the track to Tessenei, so preventing the enemy maintenance lorries from bringing in supplies to the garrison; and then dug itself in round Abu Gamal, prepared to besiege the enemy and force his surrender. But the operation was called off. No offensive action was to precede our full-scale invasion of Eritrea. Accordingly, Fletcher withdrew his companies, and left the S.D.F. armoured cars to watch the enemy and to reconnoitre the *jebel* in detail.

Then, on the night of January 15/16, the Italians were reported to have evacuated Abu Gamal. Next morning it was occupied by the H.L.I. without trouble. And on the night of the 17th the enemy slipped out of Kassala, despite a swashbuckling proclamation from General Frusci to the effect that the absurd English would attack Kassala only to be scattered like chaff.

Kassala, a town of some 25,000 inhabitants, consisted largely of mud buildings, with a red-brick market-place in one corner, the old fort, and certain Government buildings and gardens. One of our Intelligence teams entered the place on the heels of the retreating Italian rearguards. Evidence of the enemy's hurried departure was found in two piles of 'In' and 'Out' signals that had not been destroyed. Among the 'Out' messages was one which had given a very black picture of the situation. Its wording ran something like this: "To Brigade. A 17. Am surrounded. Enemy armoured units most active. Will fight to the last for the honour of our Duce and Empire." Looking through the pile of 'In' signals, the Intelligence Officer found the following: "In reply to your A 17. Don't be theatrical. State hour of withdrawal."

The enemy had indeed withdrawn. The Highland Light Infantry, now temporarily under Marriott's command with 29 Brigade, hurried east from Abu Gamal, on the 18th crossed the yielding river bed of Gash on a causeway of palm fronds laid by the Sappers, and headed down the road to Tessenei, knowing that they could no longer cut off the enemy's retreat, but prepared to encounter rearguard ambushes. No Italians were seen. The main body of 29 Brigade, led by the 3/2nd Punjab, occupied Tessenei on the afternoon of January 18.

While this was happening, Slim's Ten Brigade Group, with the 28th Field Regiment, left Khashm-el-Girba and made a complicated night march to Malawiya Pools on January 16-17. In the evening of the 17th news came that the Italians were evacuating Kassala, so off went Ten Brigade on a night march to cross the River Gash at Angaleit. It was hoped that they would be in time to cut off any Italians still holding the Tessenei gap. They reached the river after great difficulties in forcing a route through the undergrowth. The approach to the Gash was marked by dense trees and vegetation; both banks were thick with dom palms, acacias, and long green grass. But there was no water, only five hundred yards of soft sand that could not be crossed by our armoured cars until the Sappers had laid down Army track. There was no resistance from the opposite bank, where the palms and undergrowth were even denser and enlivened by many beautifully coloured birds. Here news was received, late on January 18, that Marriott's 29 Brigade had already entered Tessenei. Ten Brigade was now too late to intercept the retreating enemy, who had withdrawn with the utmost speed to rearguard positions east of Aicota, intending to hold up our advance on Barentu. So it was henceforth a chase to make contact again before the enemy had time to reorganize.

Ten Brigade left the bush and drove along the first main road since leaving Khartoum. The bridges were as impressive as the drainage. But the Italians had sought to delay our advance by strewing the *autostrada* with thousands of four-pronged nails. These caused so many punctures in our vehicles that supplies of repair outfits were soon exhausted and had to be replenished by air from

South Africa. Enemy equipment was found abandoned by the roadside. Eritrean natives gave news of the retreating foe. Slim's two battalions found Aicota empty, and the Italians still out of reach.

The Fourth Indian Division had, meanwhile, advanced swiftly through the tangle of hills by Sabderat, and had, early on January 21, come up against strong opposition in the mile-long and heavily mined Keru Gorge. How best to co-operate with Beresford-Peirse's leading troops had been thought out by General Heath weeks ahead, as the result of a terse comment by General Wavell during a conference.

Wavell listened in silence while the Kaid and his two divisional commanders discussed their plans for the capture of the Kassala–Tessenei–Sabderat triangle. Then he said, "And what if the Italians have managed to creep away?"

The maps had been studied afresh, and General Heath had kept in view the possible advantage of using a diagonal route that was shown on Italian maps as linking Aicota and Biscia. The serious resistance met by the Fourth Indian Division at Keru made it clear that if this route were at all feasible, then a move by one of Heath's brigades towards Biscia might force the Italians to relinquish their grip upon Keru. Accordingly, Slim's Ten Brigade was ordered to advance north-east along this route. And 29 Brigade was directed to fight its way straight ahead to Barentu.

Although the indifferent maps showed the existence of a second-class road between Aicota and Biscia, the route was not defined until the hilly ground was reached. At one time the route had been surveyed for a railway line; a number of embankments had been built, though no bridges, and survey marks in the form of stones could be seen at regular intervals. Fletcher's Highland Light Infantry acted as advance guard to Ten Brigade Group, which they had rejoined. Their progress, slow as it was on account of difficulties in finding the track, was further slowed up by frequent sandy *khors*. These could only be crossed when palm branches had been laid to prevent the vehicles from becoming stuck. Colonel Fletcher went ahead with a small group to reconnoitre a hill some twelve miles out from Aicota. The Brigade Commander and Colonel Welchman decided to do the same thing.

They set off in a truck, Slim driving, Welchman sitting beside him, and the Brigadier's orderly in the back. A small escort of the Highland Light Infantry accompanied them in carriers. Soon they passed the main body of the Scottish battalion and caught up Fletcher and his reconnaissance party. Just then they heard the zip-zip of machine-gun fire. The ground all round was spattered with bullets. Looking up, Slim and Welchman caught sight of two Italian C.R. 42 fighters which had swooped down out of the sun, their engines off. The first attack caused so many casualties among the escort that all our anti-aircraft Bren guns were out of action. And so, when the enemy planes started to circle for a second swoop, there seemed no alternative but to jump out as quickly as possible from the truck and take cover. But there was almost no cover. In trying to leave the driving seat with speed, Slim got caught up in the spare wheel. Welchman found that his right forearm, pierced by a machine-gun bullet, was bleeding. And the Brigadier's orderly had been wounded in the shoulder. Yet somehow the three of them did get out and lay on their faces in a small ditch that ran at right angles to the track.

The two Italian fighters circled round and round, firing their guns. Welchman saw Slim wince as though he had been hit by a bullet. None of the three expected to survive these attacks from above, but the planes soon flew away. The Brigadier now discovered that he had been wounded in the behind while lying on the ground; and one of the escort had been severely hit in the stomach as he tried to fire his Bren gun from one of the carriers. Slim was hurriedly bandaged up, the wounded Scottish private given a shot of morphia, and all the wounded placed in the Brigade Commander's truck. Welchman, his arm wrapped in a field dressing, drove the truck at fifty miles an hour along the track through Aicota to the dressing station at Brigade Headquarters. Slim was able only to recline rather than sit on the car seat.

The doctors dressed the various wounds with all speed, and Slim was told that he would have to be evacuated to the casualty clearing station at Malawiya Pools, and thence almost certainly to Khartoum. The Brigadier cursed and said, "Well, then, that fellow Welcher will have to come along too."

Next morning early, having heard Ten Brigade Group moving off, and bemoaning their ill fortune at thus missing the coming advance, Slim and Welchman set off in a motor ambulance,

Welchman seated in front beside the driver, Slim and his orderly—bitterly apologetic for having failed to protect his Sahib from the *hawai jahaz* (aeroplane)—lying on the stretchers inside and tended by two bearers.

Beyond Tessenei, where General Heath came to commiserate with his two wounded commanders and to wish them luck, the journey was extremely bumpy. Welchman found that he could be of most use by shouting back to Slim, "Another bad bump coming, sir!" whereupon the Brigadier would raise himself by the straps hanging from the ambulance roof. At Malawiya Pools the wounds were dressed afresh, and late that evening the ambulance brought the two senior officers in great pain to Gedaref Hospital, where an Indian doctor operated on Slim without delay. When the Brigadier came round from the anæsthetic, in the small ward in which he and Welchman had been placed, he asked the ward orderly, an Indian Christian named Martin, "Is Colonel Welchman anywhere about?"

"Yes," replied Martin, "he's just over there. Did you want him, sir?"

"Yes, please," said Slim.

So Welchman walked over to the bedside.

"Welcher," said Slim, "the H.L.I. aren't in the right place. They ought to be at so-and-so. Could you possibly see about it?"

Welchman, seeing that Slim, though delirious, was definitely worried about the matter, promptly answered, "Yes of course I can. I'll tell Ripley (Major G. S. R. Webb, M.C., the Brigade Major) at once."

The Brigadier said, "Thanks awfully, that's grand." Then, having given a few clear and matter-of-fact orders about the dispositions of the Brigade Group, he lapsed into unconsciousness.

Next day Welchman managed to send off a telegram to Slim's wife. It said, "Slightly wounded and in hospital. Shall not sit down again for some time." It was later discovered that this telegram had never been dispatched. It had been stopped by the censor because it was not in plain language. Welchman thought that nothing could have been plainer.

One day Welchman, who had been released from hospital and was visiting Slim, found him chuckling over the fact that one of his opposite numbers, an Italian Brigadier, had recently been brought in from the Keru battle, having been hit in the same part of the body as himself. They were able to compare notes, and Slim was very satisfied at the prompt manner in which he had been avenged.

Command of Ten Brigade now devolved upon Colonel B. C. Fletcher; and his second-in-command, Major Charles Harvey, took over the battalion. Welchman returned within a few weeks, but two and a half years will pass before we meet Brigadier Slim again in this narrative, in the role of Lieutenant-General and Corps Commander in India.

* * * * *

We must turn north to watch the Fourth Indian Division at Keru. All through January 22 fighting on the hills took place, with the 4/11th Sikhs bearing the brunt. So stubborn was the Italian resistance at Keru that the Fourth Indian Division might have been held up indefinitely, had the enemy commander, General Fongoli, made adequate provision to protect his left rear. As it was, his troops—the 41st Colonial Brigade—withdrew during the night. They had been disconcerted to find that Ten Brigade, with the H.L.I. in the lead, were threatening their rear. As the Italian commander had never expected our vehicles to negotiate the long disused track between Aicota and Biscia, the defile where the Lowlanders met opposition was held by a mere two hundred Carabinieri—not placed there until Fongoli knew that Ten Brigade was threatening his left rear, and then hastily flung out to stem this threat. To do this would have required two full battalions. The enemy was to pay dearly for underestimating the capabilities of our Sappers and truck drivers.

The H.L.I. cut due north into the hills, and on Jebel Shiba behind Keru came upon the position chosen by General Fongoli for covering the withdrawal of his brigade. As the presence of the Italians here was unexpected, our leading company (Captain P. Hamilton) suffered casualties. But within a short time the Italians surrendered, Fongoli and his staff among them. It was a *débâcle*. Over six hundred prisoners were taken in the engagement, and during the hours that followed groups of thirst-stricken stragglers from the Keru Gorge gave themselves up. A few of the more hardy slipped through our cordon, and some of the native troops reached their homes. This thorough mangling of the 41st

Colonial Brigade exercised a permanently crumbling effect upon Italian morale, both among commanders and lower ranks. And it resulted in panicky reorientation of the enemy's forces.

Ten Brigade now moved into Biscia, through which the Fourth Indian Division had already passed on its way to Agordat, which was not captured until February 1, the day before Barentu fell. After a day of reorganization, the Brigade set off across country once more in the direction of Barentu, this time bent on slipping into the town by the back door. The move was seriously delayed by the many *khors* that crossed the route. And the Sappers were hard pressed to cut approaches for vehicles down the banks of these *khors* and to put down steel-mesh tracks across the sandy bottoms. At this time Marriott's Brigade was still twenty miles from the town. Ten Brigade cut the Agordat–Barentu road on January 26, but a disappointment followed. The Baluch and Garhwal Rifles found the road that winds up one side of the gorge to a crest before dropping down into the cup of Barentu to have been blown. So the infantry battalions climbed up the hills that barred the way into the northern outskirts of the town, now three miles distant. The Italian garrison, some eight thousand men strong, held these heights.

On the 27th the Baluch and Garhwalis drove the Italians from the first line of hills. They now overlooked the Italians, who were installed in heavily fortified rock sangars, with slit trenches behind for protection against shelling and bombs. Fletcher ordered two companies of the Highland Light Infantry to attack on the 28th. 'A' Company under Captain Hare went forward and gained the ridge that faced our positions. But those of his men who reached the enemy's rock sangars were caught in severe enfilade fire and forced back to their starting point. The casualties suffered were numerous, and Hare himself was wounded.

Meanwhile, 'D' Company, led by the dashing Mark Hollis, made across very broken country towards its objective, Conical Hill, the highest feature in that district. The three platoons soon lost touch with one another, and the moment came when Hollis found himself with but a dozen men—P.S.M. Macmillan's platoon. They were still half a mile from the summit, which could only be reached after a stiff climb of some five hundred feet. With great courage Hollis decided to press on with the handful of Scotsmen.

At the foot of the hill Hollis had turned to Macmillan and said, "Well, Sergeant-Major, if it is the last thing I do, I am bloody well going to get to the top of this hill."

And get to the top they did, despite fierce resistance from the Italians, who hurled down grenades. The enemy was driven from the summit, but there was small space, even for the few men that Hollis still had with him. At once the Italians counter-attacked, firing their mortars and crawling up to lob grenades at our men. Hollis was badly wounded in the body and head, and half his little band were killed or wounded. Hollis, realizing that he would not live, ordered Macmillan to withdraw the remnants; but he refused to endanger this move by being carried down the slope himself. Though almost unconscious, he wrote on one of his visiting cards: "I order P.S.M. Macmillan to withdraw—I strongly recommend him." And on the other side of the card he wrote a message to the girl he loved. Then he was left alone to die on his objective.

Three days later, when the hill was recaptured, the battalion found several graves of the men of 'D' Company. One grave had been made with great care. At its head stood a large natural stone. The Italians had honoured the gallantry of this little party, and paid special tribute to its leader.

Ten weeks after this happening, at the capture of Massawa on the Red Sea, the Italian Admiral in command there asked General Heath to speak to the General who had commanded the Italian Division holding Barentu. Their conversation was interpreted by the Admiral. The Italian General wished to offer his congratulations upon the extreme gallantry displayed by the Highland Light Infantry before Barentu.

P.S.M. Macmillan was decorated with the Distinguished Conduct Medal, and Mark Hollis was recommended for a posthumous Victoria Cross. Had there been more witnesses, it is likely that a good case for the award could have been submitted.

On that black day the Highland Light Infantry lost two Company Commanders, ninety-seven men wounded and killed, and three prisoners, the only ones throughout the campaign. All day stragglers and wounded picked their way across the innumerable ravines, among the huge boulders and thorn bushes that studded the hillside, and came back into their own lines. When night fell patrols went out to bring in more of those who had been wounded in the two engagements. It was a night of misery, for the men were without blankets, and the bitter cold of the hills contrasted rudely with the heat of the plains they had left.

During the next two days the 4/10th Baluch, under its commander, Sundius-Smith, were subjected to heavy counter-attacks by two fresh Blackshirt battalions, and although our weak forward posts were overrun and some ground on two features known as Five Tebeldi Hill and White Rocks was yielded for a time, the Italian assaults were beaten back with bayonet charges, fierce yells, and bullets. But our casualties had been serious—over ninety— and only two British officers were not wounded.

* * * * *

Marriott's 29 Brigade, supported throughout by the guns of the 4th Field Regiment, had been fighting along the road towards Barentu. The advance had been arduous and hard fought, with constant delays both from Italian resistance and mines laid on the road. But on the 30th the last ridge west of Barentu was occupied by the 1st Worcestershires, and the one good landmark of the whole district was now clearly visible—a white house by the road junction south of the town.

As soon as Ten Brigade's outflanking move was rendered abortive by the demolition in the gorge north of Barentu, General Heath had moved his Divisional H.Q. from near Biscia down to the Barentu road, and directed operations from near to Marriott's own Headquarters. This transfer presented a problem of intercommunication, for the liaison officers had a drive of more than sixty miles from Ten Brigade Headquarters to that of 29 Brigade. This could only be short-circuited by wireless conversations between General Heath and an officer at Ten Brigade H.Q. in Pushtu, a language considered sufficiently obscure to the enemy.

Next day, January 31, the 6/13th Frontier Force Rifles took a ridge that led up towards Conical Hill, and the Worcestershires, having beaten off an attack by fourteen enemy tanks, advanced a short way. February 1 dawned, but progress was still slow, and resistance stubborn. In his diary Brigadier Marriott observed: "Enemy sticking it well." When the 3/2nd Punjab made an attack, they were in their turn forced back by Italian light tanks.

The garrison of Barentu had been losing ground steadily,

and during the night of February 1/2 the Italians evacuated the town. Barentu was not imposing. It had an airfield, a group of scattered administrative buildings, a few shops. And on the hill, commanding the approaches from both north and east, stood the fort. This merged so well with the landscape that 29 Brigade had been unable to see it until the final day, by which time Marriott's troops were really close.

The Italians had withdrawn most of their troops and had left little equipment. Some prisoners were taken, when our battalions entered, and in the hospitals a number of wounded men had been left to face captivity. Field kitchens in which meals were ready prepared bore witness to the suddenness of the enemy's retreat.

It was the action of the Infantry tanks, giving to the Fourth Indian Division the sweeping victory at Agordat, that was finally responsible for the Italians' helter-skelter withdrawal from Barentu. If the Fifth Indian Division had enabled the Fourth to renew its advance from Keru towards Agordat, so now it was the Fourth's success which allowed General Heath's forward troops to overrun Barentu without opposition on February 2.

Throughout these operations the co-operation between the two divisions was admirable, and owed not a little to the fact that Generals Heath and Beresford-Peirse had been together in the same dormitory at Wellington.

* * * * *

Just where the Agordat road begins to wind down through the Barentu Gorge, the Italians had, as already noted, made an effective block. More than a hundred yards of the hillside had been blown down on to the roadway. Great lumps of rock, some of them as large as a three-ton lorry, were piled one on top of the other. It took the 2nd Field Company five days to clear a way through the block. This demolition had originally been designed to prevent us from continuing our advance through Barentu to Agordat. But the cross-country move of Ten Brigade had so startled the Italian commander that the demolition had been blown there and then, thus stopping all chances of his 2nd Colonial Division joining up with the main Italian forces. Now the only line of retreat open to him lay across country through Arressa.

It took some time before we could establish for certain that the metalled road marked on some Italian maps as having been built from Barentu to link up with the Abyssinian network of metalled *stradas* did not exist east of Barentu. A fair road had been cut for wheeled traffic, though across the plains to the east the road was undemarcated. Did a hewn route exist through the hills beyond the plain? To settle this point finally, after conflicting reports had come from our reconnaissance aircraft, General Heath asked Air Commodore Slatter, the Air Officer Commanding, for a plane to be placed at his disposal.

The two Wellesleys sent to escort Heath's faster Blenheim were both shot down over Adi Ugri, and Heath never saw them at all. But he did find out that a route for wheels did not connect with the main road at Arressa that wound its metalled way to Adi Ugri.

The Sudan Defence mobile columns, now reinforced, and commanded by Lieutenant-Colonel A. D. G. Orr, pursued the exhausted Italians relentlessly. Soon they came upon the vehicles, tanks, ten-ton Diesel lorries, and wheeled guns jettisoned by the 2nd Colonial Division. Hundreds of prisoners fell into our hands. Reports from deserters who came into our lines showed that the Italians had suffered crippling losses in the defence of Barentu. The Italian division had been worsted and put out of action as a fighting formation.

And the capture of Barentu opened up direct communication, along a metalled road, with the Fourth Indian Division, already heading east from Agordat towards Keren. Beresford-Peirse's L. of C. could now be switched from the very cut-up Keru–Biscia track to the excellent *autostrada* that linked our railhead at Kassala with Asmara, the capital of Eritrea.

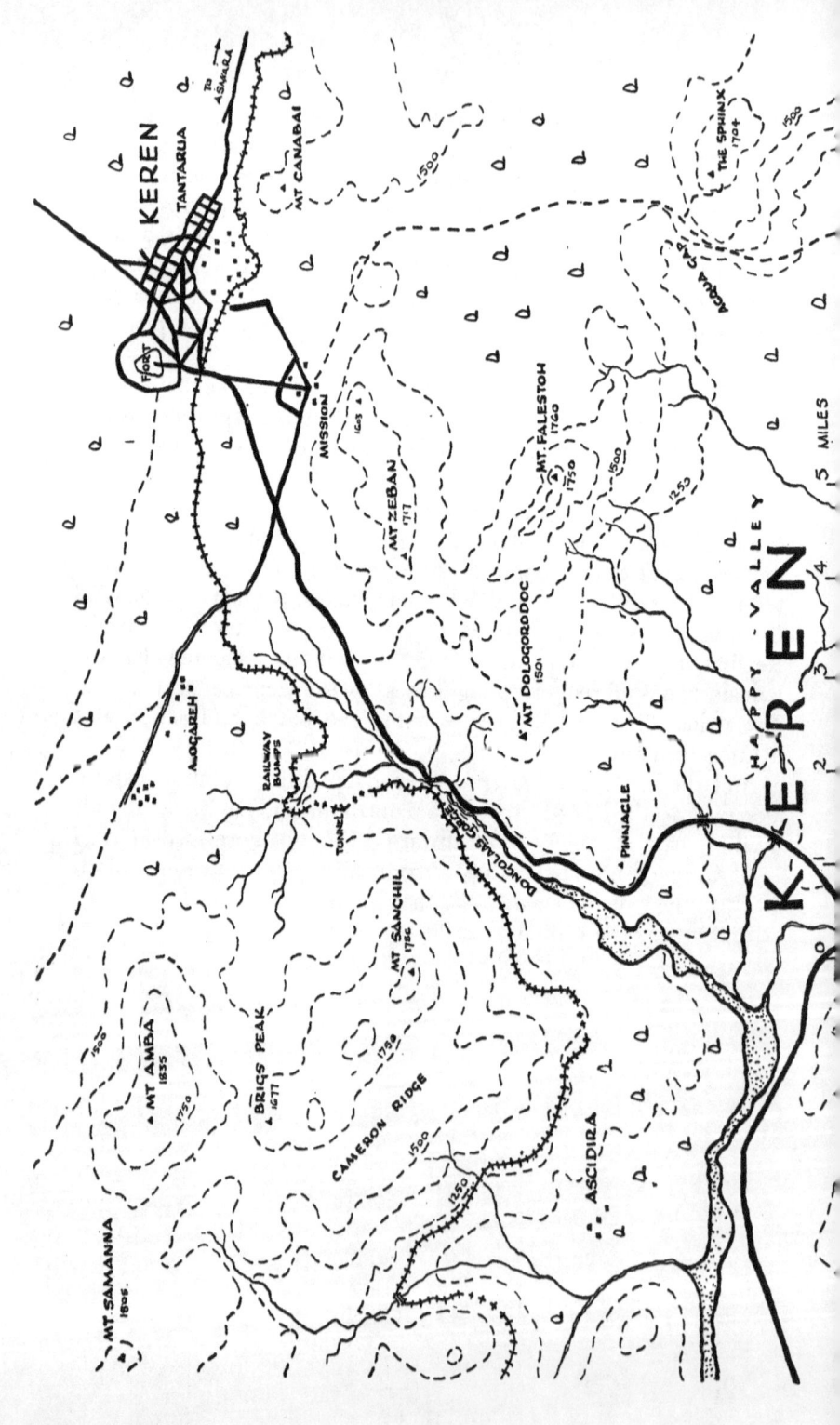

BRITISH TROOPS ATTACKING (Imperial War Museum)

CAMERON RIDGE, BRIGS PEAK, SANCHIL (J. E. B. Barton)

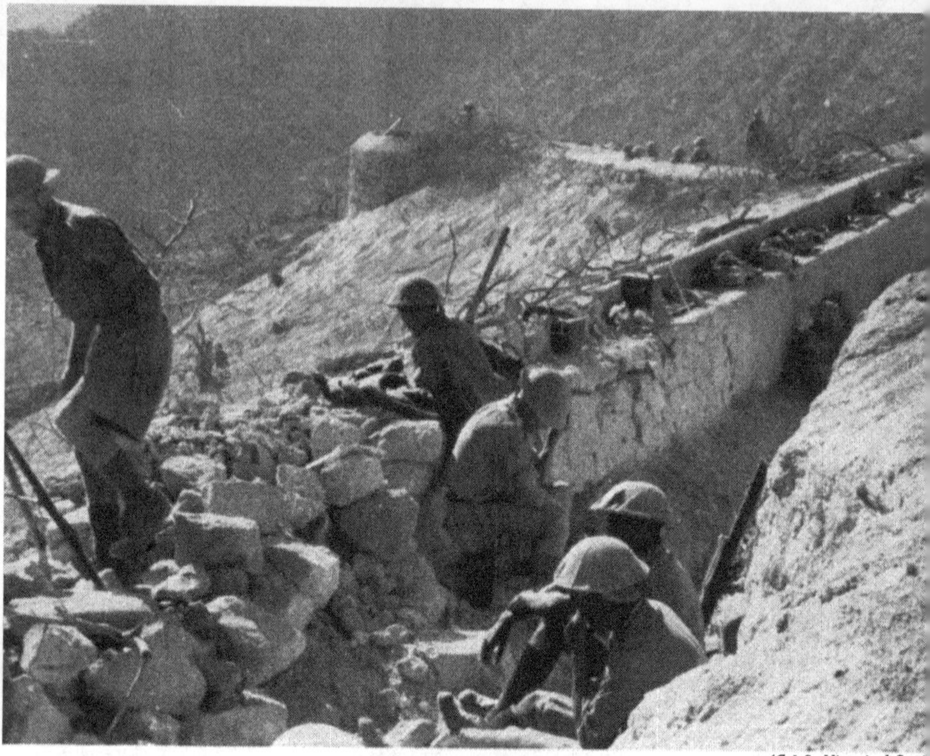

FORT DOLOGORODOC (C.I.S. Historical Secti

MADRASSI LINEMEN WITH MULE (R. C. Watso

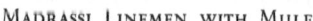

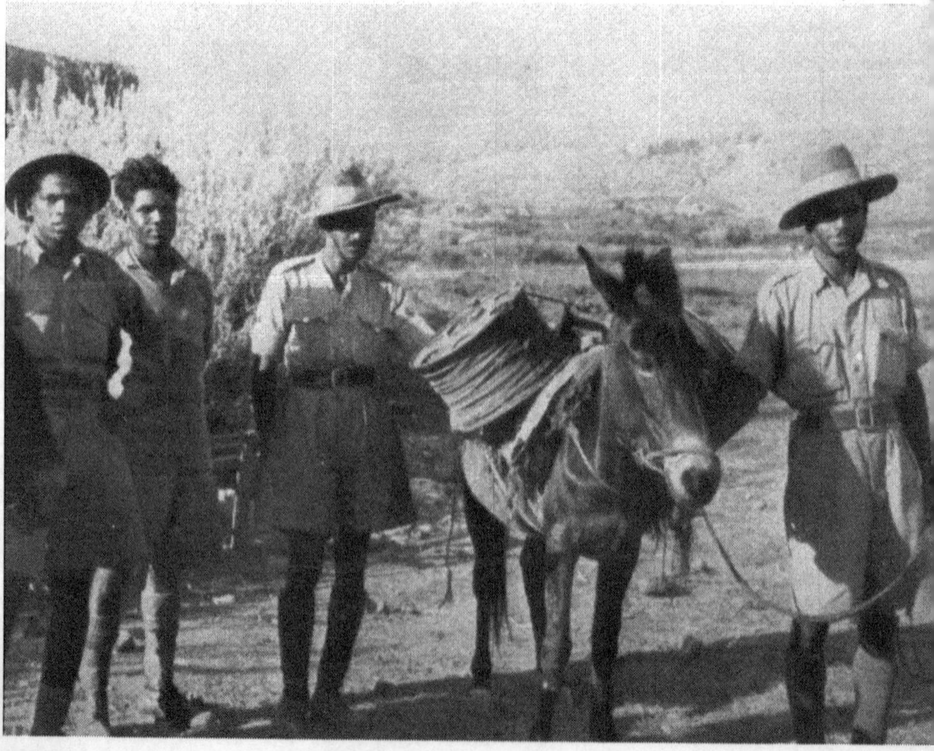

CHAPTER IV

KEREN

FEBRUARY—MARCH 1941

THE battle for Agordat had ended. At once Colonel Messervy, with Skinner's Horse, a squadron of the 4th Royal Tank Regiment, the 390th Field Battery of 144 Field Regiment (under Major E. C. Mansergh, M.C., a future C.R.A. and commander of the Fifth Indian Division), led his Gazelle Force in pursuit of the enemy towards Keren. Some twelve miles out, at the Baraka river, the damaged Ponte Mussolini, whose approaches were heavily mined, held up our advance for a few hours, but by the evening of February 2 Gazelle Force and Savory's Eleven Brigade of the Fourth Indian Division had reached a point only five miles from Keren. It was hoped that by advancing rapidly our troops might reach Keren before Italian reinforcements could arrive. At the beginning of the month it was known that the garrison comprised one Colonial brigade, but within a few days the enemy had reinforced it by another brigade and by part of the Grenadier Division that had been brought up from Addis Ababa.

To approach the town of Keren, which lies 4,300 feet above sea-level, from any direction but the east means an arduous passage through mountainous country. A formidable barrier of hills guards the town as you drive towards it up the road from Agordat. Only one gap exists through this barrier, the narrow and climbing Dongolaas Gorge that takes both road and railway up to the Keren plateau. On the left of this gorge rise the hills of Cameron Ridge, Sanchil, Brigs Peak, Samanna, and Mount Amba; while on the other side are features that became equally famous and bloodstained in the battles that were to follow—Dologorodoc, Falestoh, Zeban. And below Fort Dologorodoc and to the east is the wide Happy Valley, from the north-east corner of which rises the very steep Acqua Col.

The whole mass of mountains, like a bleak and jagged screen, looms up into the sky some 2,500 feet above the green valley of approach. It is steep, high, immense, forbidding. No picture can do justice to the physical effort of climbing past enormous granite domes and through a prickly bush more effective than any barbed wire. The soil crumbles beneath your feet, which can find no foothold; and the rocks, for all the cover they might give to climbing infantry, are easily dislodged if used as a lever to pull yourself up. At every step spear-grass stabs through the toughest clothing, and the skin is torn by the prickly thorn-trees. One of the major problems of the Keren battle was to get our infantry to grips with the enemy in a fit state to fight. The exertion of men laden with equipment, rifles, ammunition, shovels was wearing on even the stoutest, and it is no wonder that those soldiers who did reach the almost unclimbable crests were momentarily too exhausted to make further effort. It was this moment of breathless exhaustion and strain that the Italians were so often to choose for delivering a counter-attack from their points of physical and moral vantage.

The strategic possibilities of this natural position before Keren had been for many years appreciated by the Italians as a defence of Asmara and the highlands of Eritrea. On the Keren escarpment General Luigi Frusci, the sixty-two-year-old commander in the field, who had served in the Spanish Civil War, decided to make his main stand, and to concentrate the bulk of his forces. These included three Italian and ten Colonial battalions that were fresh or had been but slightly involved in the previous fighting, and the remnants of a further four Colonial battalions.

A two hundred yards long block, where the road turns a corner and enters the narrowest part of the Dongolaas Gorge, now held up Gazelle Force. A cliff had been blown down on to the road, and this obstacle was covered by fire. The enemy, moreover, had a very great advantage of remarkable observation posts from which our every movement could be seen, and fire directed accordingly. The tanks of the 4th R.T.R. failed to get past, but on February 3 the 2nd Cameron Highlanders advanced up the hill to the left and secured the ridge that became known by the name of this battalion. A reconnaissance around to the right up Happy Valley failed to find a way of outflanking the enemy, though there was one gap over Acqua Col which seemed a possible line of advance.

So Brigadier Savory decided to push the 3/14th Punjab (Major C. C. Furney) through the Camerons to seize the heights overlooking Keren. During the night of February 4/5 the 3/14th Punjab advanced beyond Cameron Ridge and soon after half-past three occupied Brigs Peak—a series of three little peaks that could be held by no more than four platoons. The battalion was driven off the following day, after suffering more than a hundred casualties. The enemy, daily being reinforced, counter-attacked our troops with great determination.

Brigadier W. L. Lloyd's Five Brigade came up on the 6th, but its night attack two days later against Acqua Col, seeking out a southern approach that would avoid the Gorge, failed because the position was too strongly held. On April 8 Brigs Peak was again captured by Eleven Brigade, but in trying to exploit further on to part of Mount Sanchil we incurred heavy casualties. It was decided, accordingly, to make a second attempt to force a way over Acqua Col. For this purpose Marriott's 29th Brigade was brought from Barentu and placed under command of General Beresford-Peirse; the Brigade was not to be used to force Acqua Col, but only to exploit towards Keren if Five Brigade were successful.

The commanders had decided to press the attack through Acqua Col because, if it did succeed, the enemy's lines of communication would be cut and thereby a large part of his forces in and around Keren encircled and captured. On the other hand, to maintain two brigades in Happy Valley presented formidable administrative difficulties.

On March 11 our troops were again forced off Brigs Peak and retired to Cameron Ridge. Despite great gallantry our second attack next day on the Acqua Gap failed to reach its objective, and Beresford-Peirse decided to end the operation. Accordingly, 29 Brigade was sent back to Barentu and the rest of the Fourth Indian Division was also withdrawn successfully from Happy Valley. Messervy's Gazelle Force was disbanded after four months; there was no room for further manœuvre and no route over which its armoured vehicles could be used. Its harrying role was over. And on the 15th Colonel Messervy left to take command of Nine Brigade.

* * * * *

Good progress had attended the efforts of the Divisional Sappers to open the road to Aressa, but Orr's mobile troops lacked the punch to overcome the commanding positions that covered Aressa. And the track which had been built to within a few miles of the town was inadequate to bear the movement of a large force. It was therefore decided to use Orr's troops as a continuing force, ready to advance through Aressa on Adi Ugri, and to employ the Fifth Indian Division to reinforce the Fourth to smash a way through the Keren defences.

The most attractive plan that then appeared to offer success was a renewed attempt, employing the Fifth Indian Division, to advance and capture Acqua Col. This was considered feasible, provided that the attack had the support of artillery from both divisions, and air bombardment of the reverse slopes astride Acqua Col.

It was important that General Heath should have three infantry brigades for this projected assault. Accordingly, Nine Brigade, less detachments to hold our positions on the Gondar road, was ordered to concentrate at Tessenei. And as transport was quite insufficient to supply both divisions in the Keren area and simultaneously to build up reserves adequate for such a large-scale assault, the Fifth Indian Division also moved to Tessenei, there to undergo a period of hard training in mountain warfare on the stiffest hills within reach.

When, on March 1, General Heath set up his advanced headquarters alongside that of Beresford-Peirse, plans had to be entirely changed. Heath found that much had altered in the interval since he last saw the Keren front. The Italians now dominated Happy Valley. The bulk of the Fourth Indian Division's artillery had been forced to withdraw from forward positions below the Keren heights. These guns would no longer be able to give an adequate measure of support in the direction of Acqua Col.

Fresh reconnaissance from every angle possible led to the belief that the best plan that now offered was to attempt to capture Fort Dologorodoc, and from there to exploit success towards Falestoh and Zeban. The initial attack would start on the lee of Cameron Ridge, for the Italian artillery had the main road accurately covered, and all movement was fired on. By night the road was harassed.

This plan was ambitious and, as will be seen, had to be varied as the action developed. It should be remembered that General

Heath was at this stage working on the assumption of the Fourth Indian Division's Sappers that the demolition blocking the Dongolaas Gorge would require ten days' work to make the road fit to carry wheeled traffic.

The new plan for the two divisions was as follows. The Fourth Indian Division would gain the hills on the left of the road, thus keeping the enemy preoccupied on Sanchil. It fell to General Heath's men to attack along the south of the Dongolaas Gorge, aiming to capture Fort Dologorodoc and to exploit towards Falestoh and Zeban.

This line of attack had certain obvious disadvantages, the most noteworthy of which was that Dologorodoc was exposed to the dominating features of Sanchil, Falestoh and Zeban.

Measures to reduce vulnerability from these hills were to obtain the maximum possible support from the Royal Air Force. Such support was unstintingly arranged throughout the battle by Air Commodore Leonard Slatter. It speaks much for his wholehearted co-operation that every pilot was required to trace his orders on the sand model of the area that had been prepared in order to acquaint the ground troops with their objectives.

As regards Fort Dologorodoc, the factor which made the plan attractive was that the Italians would be robbed of the advantage which had so contributed to their success in all the previous abortive attacks by the Fourth Indian Division against objectives lying along knife-edge ridges. In fact, it was the spinal conformation of the ground with the almost precipitous reverse slopes which rendered the Italian supports and reserves—and even their forward troops thinly scattered among boulders—immune from our heaviest artillery fire.

It was only when our concentrations had to lift, owing to the proximity of our attacking troops, that the Italians' real strength was exposed to view. And then they were able to rain automatic fire and grenades upon our toiling infantry, who were unable to reply effectively. As will be seen, it was this important difference in the configuration of the ground, lying behind Dologorodoc, as compared with the rest of the Keren front, that was to present us not only with the Fort, but was ultimately to give us victory at Keren.

In order that each division should have the largest possible number of guns in support, our two attacks were to be consecutive rather than simultaneous. The day fixed was March 15. Secrecy was to be gained by bringing the Fifth Indian Division into the Keren back area at the last possible moment, and to bring the attacking troops forward and deploy them for the fray under cover of darkness. They would move by an easy approach route which was not the target of enemy predicted fire.

The line of approach brought our troops right up to a starting line under the slopes of Cameron Ridge below the Tunnel. A factor which had not been reckoned with was the volume and intensity of fire which the Italians were able to deliver against our men after they crossed the starting line and as they crossed the Dongolaas Gorge and mounted the slopes beyond.

At a final meeting on the 14th, to 'button up' small details of timing and co-operation, General Platt told the officers gathered round a model of the Keren features:

"Do not let anybody think this is going to be a walk-over. It is not. It is going to be a bloody battle: a bloody battle against both enemy and ground. It will be won by the side which lasts longest. I know you will last longer than they do. And I promise you I will last longer than my opposite number."

Beresford Peirse's plan was as follows: Eleven Brigade, strengthened to five battalions, would assault Sanchil, Brigs Peak, Saddle, Hogs Back, and Flat Top Hill, all on the left side of the gorge. Five Brigade, by capturing Mount Samanna, would secure the left flank and thus protect Eleven Brigade's attack from Italian opposition on Mount Amba.

It fell to Messervy's Nine Brigade, with the 2nd Highland Light Infantry under command, to capture Fort Dologorodoc; 29 Brigade prepared to go through and attack Mount Zeban. The H.L.I. were not to go forward until the Fourth Indian Division had occupied Sanchil and Brigs Peak, because in the event of Sanchil's not being taken, enemy shelling from there would seriously impede Nine Brigade's advance.

The Fourth Indian Division's attack started at seven o'clock on March 15, half an hour after sunrise. And although, three hours later, Sanchil and Brigs Peak had not been captured, some progress had been made, especially on the outer flank. General Heath now recommended—and obtained the permission of General Platt—

the launching of the Fifth Indian Division's attack. It was fully realized that the task would be much more difficult than if, as originally planned, Beresford-Peirse's troops had first obtained a lodgment on or, better still, a grip on Sanchil.

The Fifth Indian Division was all set for its assault. And had this not been now sanctioned, it would have been difficult to visualize how a better alternative could have been created.

*   *   *   *   *

Just after 10.30 the Highland Light Infantry, now under Lieutenant-Colonel E. L. Percival, who had arrived in Tessenei, went forward to attack the first bump up Dologorodoc, named Pinnacle. The leading company, commanded by Major P. H. T. Hoare, crossed the starting line—a large sandy *khor*. At once Hoare's men came under heavy fire from both sides of the road and from well-concealed automatics in culverts along the railway line that ran across the lower slopes of Sanchil. Despite casualties, the company reached the far side of this *khor* and the sandy hillocks just below the main road. Then, while encouraging his men, Percy Hoare was badly hit. But he was safely carried back across the *khor* by one of the stretcher-bearers, Private Sinclair.

Meanwhile the other two attacking companies, led by McKeig Jones and P. St. G. Maxwell, were also held up below the road by accurate sniping and intense fire from Italian mortars and machine-guns. When McKeig Jones was wounded in the leg, Maxwell took command of both companies. By noon the H.L.I. found themselves pinned to the ground at the foot of Pinnacle.

Throughout that day the men lay out in the great heat, taking cover among the bare rocks and hillocks. The day was close and thundery, with not a breath of air. Thirst and heat exhaustion assailed the companies as they waited in the open, exposed almost without shade to the full glare of the sun. They were also exposed to the full attentions of the enemy, who had by now beaten back the attack of the Fourth Indian Division. From their commanding positions the Italians could observe our every movement. The least stir by one of the H.L.I. provoked a hail of machine-gun fire. Particularly troublesome were the enemy mortars; and snipers took their toll.

This reverse might have been averted had the enemy been

alarmed by the seizure of Sanchil. But no provision had been made to engage the scattered and concealed flanking posts from which the Italians brought such devastating fire to bear on the H.L.I.

It became apparent that no further advance during daylight was possible along this route, and equally that the Scottish battalion would be unable to move back until dusk brought some measure of protection. To recross the open ground to the original assembly area behind Cameron Ridge was out of the question. The men had to stay out for a further six hours, without supplies, and suffering casualties throughout the afternoon. At length, towards seven o'clock when the sun went down and darkness fell, the Highland Light Infantry withdrew to safety.

But in the meantime General Heath, accompanied by Messervy, had crept forward to the end of Cameron Spur, overlooking the Dongolaas Gorge, and had made a fresh plan. At three o'clock they decided to surprise the enemy and launch a new attack, this time in darkness and from a fresh direction, the west, up the steepest slopes of Pinnacle. The plan aimed at slipping the attacking battalion, the 3/5th Mahratta Light Infantry, commanded by Lieutenant-Colonel Denys W. Reid, across the valley which had been under such heavy fire as to hold up the H.L.I. The Mahrattas would cross a good deal lower down, and when the light was failing. After a timed artillery concentration upon Pinnacle, that towered a thousand feet above the level of the valley, and upon Dologorodoc, Reid's Mahrattas would capture Pinnacle and Pimple, the next bump up towards the summit. For this attack Reid was given Dean's 3/12th, less two companies, under command. One company from each battalion was being used for porterage up the hills. Finally, Rodwell's West Yorkshires, preceded by further support from our Gunners, would advance to seize Fort Dologorodoc.

The passage through the welter of boulders was much hampered by thorn scrub. And the enemy emerged from these boulders in far greater numbers than had been anticipated. Twice, artillery concentrations had to be repeated in order to help forward our attack on Pimple, and for the final assault up to Fort Dologorodoc.

These Mahrattas always wore green hosetops, and when not in actual battle under the protection of a steel helmet, wore a green and red hackle in their caps. At first sight an unimpressive fellow, quiet in his bearing and demeanour, and not looking his best in uniform, the Mahratta displays a superb physique when stripped. These men from the Deccan are splendid wrestlers, and their suppleness and wiry activity are remarkable. Slow to rouse, they are when roused like terriers with a little red glow in their eyes. When that happens there is trouble. Physically adaptable, they stand up to extremes of cold and heat almost better than any other Indian troops.

At last light the Mahrattas set out with the utmost determination and vigour. Even in daylight, and without the burden of arms and equipment, hands and feet must be used to climb Pinnacle. Yet these sturdy men, fully accoutred for battle as they were, scrambled eagerly up the boulder-strewn slopes towards the summit and the enemy. 'B' Company, under Subadar Shirang Lawand, led the way. Behind toiled 'C' and 'D' Companies, led by J. d'Issa Boomgardt and Seymour. The Italians resisted stoutly, relying on hundreds of their little red bombs that they threw down on the Mahrattas. The combat raged. Amid the crash of bombs and shells and the crackling of machine-guns, the war-cry of the Mahrattas—'Shivaji ki jai!'—came floating across the moonlit valley to where General Heath and Brigadier Messervy waited in the Battle Headquarters that had been established among rocks at the foot of Cameron Ridge.

Major George Munn, of 144 Field Regiment and attached to the Mahrattas, has recorded how he sat with Colonel Reid and watched this attack. They could hear the fighting in the dusk but could see little beyond the flashes on the hillside. Three times the troops were driven back. A fourth attempt was made. Every now and then the Mahrattas would give a cheer, and Reid would mutter, "Good little chaps," "Stout little chaps." When the success signal did go up about eight o'clock, after more than an hour of bitter hand-to-hand fighting, he could hardly contain himself for elation and pride.

Reid, Dean and Munn followed the companies up, and on Pinnacle Reid said, "My chaps seem to have shot their bolt. It's up to you now, Dean." And so, just after midnight, Major A. J. W. McLeod's Pathan company of the Frontier Force Regiment, with Maurice Curtis' Dogra company, were put into the battle because all the Mahratta reserves had been expended; and casualties had been heavy. The Italians fired wildly in the dark, but Dean's men stormed their way up the terrible slope, taking nearly an hour to reach the summit. On the last few yards shouts and screams mingled with the bomb explosions and the shots. The Frontier Force had captured Pimple.

The 2nd West Yorkshires, who had been brought forward ready to take advantage of any success gained by the 3/12th on Pimple, were quickly on the scene. Colonel Rodwell gathered his company and platoon officers and issued final orders. He drew attention to the spirited manner in which the Mahrattas had fought that night, undoubtedly urged on to white-heat passion by the utterance of their strange slogan, and he said, "We must have a war-cry. Can anyone suggest a suitable one?" A pause followed. At last a ranker platoon commander hesitantly murmured, "What about 'Fook, Fook,' sir?"

Supported by the guns of both 28th and 144th Field Regiments, fortified by their newly found battle-cry, and led by Captain Michael Osborn's company, the West Yorkshires climbed along the knife-edge ridge towards Dologorodoc. The slopes were precipitous, the thorn scrub tenacious, the going severe. But the enemy seemed dazed by the bombardments, and surprised by an attack from this side. And after hard fighting across extremely difficult ground, the West Yorkshires captured the Fort and fired their success signal. The time was now half-past six in the morning.

The Italians, on their side, had not been idle. At four o'clock they counter-attacked Pinnacle. Our troops here were still disorganized and busy consolidating on the newly won hill. After stern night-fighting the enemy were driven off, even though at one time they came to within fifty yards of the summit. As dawn lit up the hills, the Mahrattas caught many of these Italians as they toiled back to the Fort. Colonel Reid had to knock one of his men off the machine-gun he was firing, for the eager young Mahratta was loosing off belt after belt of ammunition at corpses thrice over. The scattered remnants of the Italian attack climbed back up the hill, only to discover to their dismay that the West Yorkshires were already in possession. In this way the Italian garrison of Fort Dologorodoc had been depleted by a vain counter-attack, which had, in itself, materially eased the task of Rodwell's battalion.

The Fort was merely a concrete trench running round the hilltop that was perhaps an acre in extent. Dugouts were few in number, and their entrances now faced the wrong way. The summit was of rock and nothing could be buried. For some days Dologorodoc was a perilous place, with a bomb, a shell, a burst of machine-gun bullets arriving every few minutes. Yet our casualties were comparatively few, because within a short time the men built large sandbag traverses and walls over the reverse slope of the hill. And the Fort itself was held with the minimum number of soldiers.

Colonel E. G. Woods, Brigade Major to Messervy at Keren, has furnished us with a picture of the scene. "I myself and 95 per cent. of the Brigade could never have imagined what the noise of that battle was going to be like. For twenty-four hours it was deafening. We were stuck in a horseshoe of rock-covered hills. All the enemy guns were firing at us, all our own guns were firing three hundred yards ahead of us. General Heath was with us at Brigade Headquarters. He slept behind a rock which was also my cover. The Italians brought up some big guns; the first shell landed very close to us. I jumped. General Heath turned and said:

" 'What is the matter, Lakri?'

"I replied: 'Rather a big one and rather close, sir.'

"General Heath turned over and went to sleep, murmuring 'Squibs!' "

Supply and maintenance of the forward troops on the summits and slopes was a military feat. Unrelaxed vigilance by the enemy on Sanchil, coupled with his effective shelling, made regular use of the road to the foot of Pinnacle out of the question, though occasional vehicles were able to run the gauntlet. A limited number of ambulances, and trucks carrying commanders and liaison officers, passed that way. But the main supply line went by Hell Fire Corner—aptly named, for it was under constant fire—and thence to a large supply dump under the lee of Tunnel Spur. Carriers transported ammunition and supplies forward from this point to the base of Pinnacle.

It was the transport onward that presented the real difficulty. The climb to below Pinnacle's summit was stiff enough, but beyond this the narrow col and knife-like ridge were barraged at uncertain intervals by Italian guns. And for those caught in these barrages there was no means of taking cover. When the battle started, either a platoon from each company or a company from each battalion had to act as carriers, and a number of fighting soldiers continued as such throughout the operation. The result was an inevitable reduction in the men available to hold the ground so stubbornly gained. And with more troops back in harbours bringing up ammunition and rations in trucks, a sorting party at railhead, casualties, and escorts to prisoners, it was not long before a battalion commander who had three hundred men in his defensive area was considered well off. The entire Division was combed for porters. Among units there was conflicting opinion as to whether ammunition or water should take priority of place in this porterage.

It was several days before a mule track was built up to the top, and until then everything had to be man-handled to the forward troops. Imagine carrying a two-gallon petrol tin or a box of ammunition up a thousand feet, under fire and in over 100 degrees of heat. There was a continuous stream of men going up and down the path.

A few days later, when the Cypriot Mule Company arrived from the Middle East and took over part of the carrying duties, the man-power situation did ease, but the mules were an ever-present threat to stretchers being carried down from the firing line. More than one wounded man had the misfortune to be knocked off his stretcher by a mule or, worse still, by a string of three which had been startled by a shell and were bolting. Though stretchers of a special pattern were used, the ground was so difficult that six men were often needed to carry one patient. Often in the momentary chaos on this narrow winding track mules laden with panniers or leather *yakdans* would go rolling over and over down the mountain side, carrying to perdition precious water or new batteries for wireless sets. At the best the mule path was four feet wide, and many days passed before an up-and-down track was constructed by the Sappers and Miners of the Division. The labour involved was tremendous, for the hillside was very steep, and covered with huge boulders and stunted scrub. Casualties from enemy artillery amongst muleteers, mules, and carrying parties were numerous, but the trying work was carried on from day to day without a murmur of complaint.

Many problems peculiar to mountain warfare faced our Gunners. The maps available were very inferior. Meteorological information was usually late and inaccurate, and the local winds in the mountains and valleys tricky. Predicted shooting was difficult. So too were concentrations on account of the many different types of guns in use: 5.7 inch, 4.5 inch and 6 inch Howitzers, 18- and 25-pounders. And gunpits down in the valley, being dug in sand, were constantly falling in.

Communications were at this period largely by line, and very long lines they were. Relay stations had to be established, and here two signallers would live by themselves and patrol the lines. The quantities of cable used were prodigious. Laying wire behind infantry battalions and Forward Observation Officers was an immense problem, and the teams carrying the heavy drums of cable were difficult to control and easily became scattered during an attack. For example, during the assault by the Highland Light Infantry and Mahrattas, Major Munn had seventeen men toiling uphill with seventeen miles of cable on drums, a No. 11 wireless set, telephones, and signalling lamps.

All through that Sunday morning, March 16, the enemy sent his troops in determined counter-attacks against Fort Dologorodoc. All these attacks were beaten off by Messervy's Nine Brigade. The capture of the place had put us in a very strong position, for though it lay exposed to Italian observation and fire from both Sanchil and Falestoh, this vital hill of Dologorodoc was a key to the enemy's whole defence. That he was determined to get it back was shown by the very fierceness of his efforts to this end, in which he suffered many casualties from our shell fire, machine-guns and bombs. It was this reiterated failure to recapture the Fort with his crack troops that spread despondency in the enemy's ranks, and this in turn paved the way for our ultimate success.

* * * * *

We must now turn to watch the progress of the Fourth Indian Division.

On the morning of March 16 the Kaid rang up General Heath and informed him that Savory's Eleven Brigade had reported the existence of a gap in the enemy front near Brigs Peak. The Kaid understood that through this gap there was an opportunity of passing a brigade to exploit towards Keren. As all Savory's battalions had been committed, it was suggested that Ten Brigade be used for this passage. Heath had no reason to doubt the truth of this report, and as exploitation through such a gap was likely to crumble the Italian resistance on the Fourth Indian Division's front, he readily assented to the Kaid's placing his Ten Brigade at General Beresford-Peirse's disposal.

But no such gap existed. Information was lacking. For proper reconnaissance there was no opportunity. And this fruitless attempt against the enemy's strongest defensive position on the left of the Dongolaas Gorge was perhaps our one great error of the Keren battle.

At first it was proposed that a thrust be made over the col between Sanchil and Brigs Peak. But at a conference this plan was vetoed as suicidal, for the Italians were in great strength and held all the commanding ground. Instead, the 3/18th Royal Garhwal Rifles were to assault Sanchil, while the 4/10th Baluch would attack up Brigs Peak, at ten o'clock that night.

The Baluch suffered fifty-three casualties when two mortar bombs landed among the waiting Pathan company while Colonel Sundius-Smith was giving out his orders. This company was detailed to carry supplies, and the Dogra company led the attack instead. The battalion moved off up Brigs Peak. A shell landed and Sundius-Smith thought his men had been spotted. But nothing followed. The rock of Sanchil is almost unclimbable, so steep are the slopes on every side. Below the rocky summit was a score of yards of loose shale, guarded by barbed wire that ran round to the saddle between Brigs Peak and Sanchil. It was to the right of the rock that the Dogra company climbed. Suddenly the Italians came to life; mortars were fired rapidly and little red bombs hurled down in profusion. To climb such a hill in shirts and shorts, in peaceful conditions, was a tremendous effort. How much greater was the strain of clambering up the mountain side, heavily laden and under intense fire from above! It was too much.

Sundius-Smith tried his Punjabi Mussulman company farther to the left, and these men reached the barbed wire, only to be forced back down the slope. They were almost on the summit, but to remain there was beyond human possibility. At dawn Colonel Fletcher, temporarily commanding Ten Brigade, arrived up, discussed the situation, and decided that to send the H.L.I. through the alleged gap would be hopeless. Nor could the Baluch stay where they were on the slopes of Sanchil.

And the Garhwalis were no more successful. They were, in fact, severely mauled. Two hundred yards from the top the attacking companies encountered unusually fierce opposition. For more than half an hour the entire face of Sanchil appeared to be one sheet of flame. The commanding officer, Lieutenant-Colonel S. E. Tayler, D.S.O., was killed. Every British officer on the slopes was wounded. At one period the battalion was commanded by a subaltern who had climbed up with a party of porters; then he, too, was wounded, and eventually the second-in-command, Major S. K. Murray, arrived to take over.

It was decided that these two battalions could not be maintained where they were. Their casualties continued to be heavy, and no reserves were available to press the attack. Accordingly the maimed Ten Brigade was withdrawn from both hills to re-form in Happy Valley.

So the day passed. At two-thirty on the following night, March 16-17, 29 Brigade passed through the 2nd West Yorkshires to attack Falestoh and Zeban. The Worcestershires were to take the first hill, the 3/2nd Punjab (Lieutenant-Colonel F. A. M. B. Jenkins) the second. This attack had originally been timed for eleven o'clock, but was then postponed for three hours; Brigadier Marriott had found the climb so ghastly that he realized that his battalions would not arrive in time. No daylight reconnaissance had been possible, though the commanders did study air photographs and a large-scale sand model. The only examination of the actual ground was made just prior to the attack in moonlight. Time was needed for commanding officers to point out the objectives to their company commanders, and for these to make their own limited reconnaissance and issue their orders accordingly. Moreover, owing to the stiffness of the climb, to an inadequate supply of guides, and to the enforced use of a single narrow track, which was infested with hastily-laid telephone cables and men who had fallen asleep, the last of the attacking battalions did not reach the area of Fort Dologorodoc until one o'clock in the morning.

This climb has been described by Captain Brian Gomm, one of Marriott's two Signals officers. "We moved up the narrow track towards the heights, a long line of heavily laden men—a whole brigade. The moonlight was shining on the Fort, which seemed a very long way above us. Soon the ground below was out of sight, and the only sounds were the scraping of boots on the mule track and the mortar shells whizzing over us to crash lower down. We were glad to leave that area, for the slope of the mountain protected us.

"Slowly the line of men snaked upwards towards Dologorodoc, accompanied by mortar fire and desultory shelling from our own field guns. The last hundred yards were quite the worst of all. There was no track—it was just a mass of powdered stone and dust which slipped away as we scrambled up. I remember making a last effort, and by a great heave reached the low wall of the Fort. I looked over this wall and leaned against it. Infantry stood in the small trench behind the wall, but there was no Fort at all, only a rocky plateau about one hundred yards in diameter, with a small building to one side."

The Brigadier had been right to postpone the zero hour until half-past two for the 1st Worcestershires and a quarter of an hour later for the 3/2nd Punjab. The 6/13th would exploit through the Indian battalion to the cross-roads west of Keren.

Bucknall's Worcestershires, after a late start, made good progress, but met heavy enemy resistance soon after four o'clock. Despite this they had, by 7.30, established themselves on a pimple one hundred yards south of Point 1552 on the Falestoh ridge.

Meanwhile, from behind our infantry the enemy had counter-attacked eastwards against Fort Dologorodoc, and had reached to within fifty yards before they were beaten back. For two hours that morning Italian artillery heavily bombarded the Fort—particularly the concrete blockhouse on the north side in which Brigadier Marriott had established his battle headquarters. This was later moved, because of the vicious strafing, into one of the trenches of the Fort, although these were already overcrowded. Marriott noted in his diary that evening: "My battle H.Q. was shelled so heavily that we were literally shut in."

For Marriott, the situation remained obscure for several hours, because the liaison officer of the 3/2nd Punjab had been wounded and the Worcestershires' wireless set damaged beyond local repair. The maintenance of telephone cables to the forward companies was an acute problem. All the lines had been cut by shelling, and heliograph was used. But eventually news did come through that, although progress was slow, the enemy had been severely hit. Two very determined attacks by Bucknall's men had failed to gain Falestoh; one company now held positions on the lower slopes and the rest of the battalion were astride the Fort road some five hundred yards short of Zeban Minor.

It was then learned that on the left Jenkins' 3/2nd Punjab, after a splendid attack during which they captured four enemy guns, were again held up by Italian fire from the direction of Sanchil. The battalion was now within half a mile of Zeban Minor. Then, at 7.30, 'B' Company of the 6/13th Frontier Force Rifles, under Captain Anant Singh Pathania, put in an attack on the left flank of the 3/2nd Punjab to protect it from counter-attacks. With great gallantry this company rushed over ground that was swept by Italian guns from Railway Bumps and Sanchil, and captured forty prisoners. And our forward infantry held on to the very exposed ground they had gained, in the face of heavy artillery shelling and sniping. The remainder of the 6/13th acted as porters, carrying water, rations, grenades, Very lights, small-arms and mortar ammunition up to the other two battalions of 29 Brigade.

At half-past ten Colonel Bucknall walked back to Brigade Headquarters. To Marriott he explained the impossibility of hanging on indefinitely to the positions already gained on the slopes of Falestoh, or of making further progress. His forward companies, now virtually isolated, were suffering casualties from enemy guns on Zeban and Falestoh. On being informed of this situation, General Heath at once telephoned back for supplies to be dropped. Urgency demanded that the stores be packed on the spot; there were no proper containers. No airmen there had been trained in Army co-operation. But this supply-dropping flight was arranged with great speed by Air Commodore Slatter, who was with the Kaid at his forward headquarters near by.

Soon after one o'clock that afternoon a Vincent and a Wellesley aircraft flew as low as they dared in the mountains, and dropped hard-scale rations and small-arms ammunition for both forward battalions. A flight-sergeant lay on the floor of the Vincent and pushed the stores out through a trap-door in the floor. Accuracy of dropping in the difficult conditions was hardly to be expected, particularly in view of the fact that the Worcestershires had been unable to demarcate their dropping zone with the conspicuous white 'X' asked for by the Royal Air Force. Some of the ammunition was bent; many of the supplies fell so far from the battalion areas that they could not be retrieved. The ammunition, jettisoned in bandoliers, fell over an area of the hill three-quarters of a mile long. In addition, enemy shelling caused casualties to the parties of men who were gathering in the supplies. Finally, to add to these difficulties, our aircraft drew a large volume of enemy groundfire from Sanchil and Falestoh.

Later in the afternoon, because of the problematic maintenance with ammunition and water, and having regard for the exhaustion of the Worcestershires, General Heath ordered Marriott to withdraw his forward troops to the tip of the depression half a mile in front of Fort Dologorodoc. At nightfall, and not before, was this move possible. Bucknall brought his men back to the Big Rocks area, on the reverse side of the Fort. A party of the 6/13th Frontier Force Rifles helped them to carry in the wounded and dead, who now numbered fifty-five and twenty-three. At six o'clock Marriott also brought his battle headquarters away from its uncomfortable position—the target of snipers on Sanchil and of airbursts—and established himself between two huge rocks, also on the reverse slope. And the 3/2nd Punjab held on to their positions eight hundred yards in front of Fort Dologorodoc.

*   *   *   *   *

Brigadier John Marriott, then forty-five, had won the D.S.O., M.C., and Croix de Guerre while serving with the Northamptonshire Regiment in the First World War. After a year on the staff of our Military Attaché in Washington, he had transferred to the Scots Guards. By 1938 he was commanding the 2nd Battalion, and sailed with them to Egypt in December of that year.

His spare figure stepping precisely round his brigade parish, wearing Scots Guards hosetops and long puttees immaculately rolled, was familiar and stimulating. At all times he demanded the highest standard, his discipline was rigid, and he kept his troops constantly on their toes. Though he was never over-friendly with anyone, and allowed no liberties to be taken, he was greatly liked and respected, for his sense of humour was dry, his mess comfortable, his hospitality generous. Whether his mess was between two rocks high up on Keren, or in an Italian house, or, again, in a dark cave, Marriott was a gourmet, eager when someone shot a guinea-fowl or a gazelle, and particular about his sherry.

One of the best jokes his staff ever enjoyed was the episode of the Brigadier's cake. This gorgeous iced cake had been sent down from Cairo by his wife, and when 29 Brigade left Port Sudan, the two-thirds that remained were packed in a round cake-tin by the Brigadier's batman, Guardsman Sharpe. Great reference was made by Marriott during the next two months of campaigning, as to how this cake was to be eaten. And after the battle of Ad Teclesan the cake was sent for. The tin was brought in by the Indian cook, Suzi, and opened for Marriott's inspection. There was no cake. In its place, lying snugly in the tin and fitting as if this had been specially made for it, was—Guardsman Sharpe's hat!

Brigadier Marriott astonished many by the way in which he took quickly to Indian Army manners and methods. These must have been strange to him, for he had not been to India, and had always served with British troops. He was asked one day how he managed to get on so well with the Indian soldiers, seeing that he spoke no Urdu. The audience was intrigued by Marriott's reply.

"Oh, I just go round and smile at them and say 'Tigeri, tigeri' and they seem to like it."

On further inquiry it was discovered that John Marriott's 'Tigeri, tigeri' was a phonetical attempt at "Tagra hai?" which means "Are you on top of your form?"

He was invariably turned out impeccably, even in battle; his manner was urbane, polished, unruffled. Very rarely was he anything but his smooth and dapper self, sociable, definite, punctilious—a Guardsman commanding an Indian Infantry Brigade with marked success. Of the sepoys he was extremely fond, and his admiration for them mounted as the weeks passed. He could climb the steep hills with the best of them.

It was a help, perhaps, that General Alexander, himself an Irish Guardsman, was Colonel of the 3/2nd Punjab, and so, as Marriott expressed it: "I suppose they felt that to have a Guardsman as Brigadier was not too unsatisfactory." A characteristically British understatement!

* * * * *

At seven o'clock that night, while the Worcestershires were

being evacuated, 'B' Company of the 6/13th out on the left flank was heavily counter-attacked by a battalion of Savoy Grenadiers. Captain Anant Singh Pathania displayed magnificent courage and leadership in this action. Although wounded in the face and in both legs, he collected his company headquarters and any other men he could muster, and pushed the enemy out with the bayonet. Only then, and under orders, did he hand over the company to his second-in-command, but the latter, too, was wounded by bomb splinters.

Major Munn, who was now Forward Observation Officer with the 3/2nd Punjab and commanded 389 Battery of Sussex Yeomanry, happened to be passing by when this engagement began. He walked up to the company commander and asked if he could help. Munn was himself wounded by bomb splinters, but gallantly rushed back to Fort Dologorodoc, and had two sections of Rodwell's West Yorkshires sent forward with all haste to assist the Frontier Force men, who had by now suffered 35 per cent. casualties. They held their ground notwithstanding, and again drove the enemy back at the point of the bayonet.

So ended the first phase of the offensive as it was originally planned. General Heath decided to hold on firmly to the vital gain of Dologorodoc and the ground beyond, such as it was, while he thought out a plan for the next move. The fact that 29 Brigade had failed to gain the high ground and to exploit further made our hold upon the Fort seem precarious, and for a number of days entailed constant efforts by the Royal Air Force and the Gunner regiments of the Division to subdue the enemy along the ridges.

There followed a week of holding on to what had been gained, while the Italians, day after day, counter-attacked with the utmost determination in their efforts to recapture the vital Fort Dologorodoc. During this week no fewer than eight such onslaughts were launched. The defenders of the Fort drove back every one.

On March 19 Major W. H. Langran, M.C., assumed command of the 2nd West Yorkshires in place of Lieutenant-Colonel R. L. Rodwell, A.F.C., who went to Division to act as Corps Liaison Officer.

29 Brigade, being relieved in their position by Nine Brigade, moved to the reverse side of Pinnacle and were heavily shelled

during the take-over. They were now responsible for Pinnacle and Pimple.

On the 20th the troops were all able to spend a quiet day, and batches of men were sent out to Kilo 116 to wash. During the following three days the West Yorkshires, for example, 'rested' behind Fort Dologorodoc. But the heat was intense, and from the east blew a hot, dust-laden wind that freshened at night. Small parties were sent back for a bath and a rest, but shelling continued day and night, and the battalion had most of its casualties during four days of otherwise comparative inactivity. Three shells burst in the same place in as many minutes and caused casualties among the stretcher bearers. One shell burst beside the signal exchange, wounding the signal sergeant. Another landed in battalion headquarters.

Reports from the Fourth Indian Division, from interrogation of prisoners, and from the active patrolling carried out during this period of preparation indicated an imminent enemy withdrawal towards the Zeban front. The enemy seemed to be drawing in his battalions from the right flank preparatory to a general retirement, using Zeban and Falestoh as a screen. Many deserters, mostly from the Colonial battalions, had been crawling under the wire on Acqua Col—the seats of some trousers verified this—in spite of the risk of being shot by their own officers.

CHAPTER V

THE FALL OF KEREN

MARCH 1941

THE Division, after hard fighting, had not gained Falestoh and Zeban; nor had the Fourth Indian Division yet captured Sanchil and Brigs Peak. General Heath had no reserves. The only brigade he had not used was the Tenth, which had already suffered severely on the slopes of Sanchil. But he determined to maintain pressure against the enemy, and to feel his front for points of weakness. With this in mind he investigated the chances of repairing the breach in the main road up the Dongolaas Gorge, for it had occurred to him that the Italians might be neglecting their defences there. During the original reconnaissance a distant view of the road-block had been obtained from Cameron Ridge, and a preliminary estimate made of the time and labour required to clear it. But it was not until after the capture of Fort Dologorodoc that a close reconnaissance was possible.

On the night of March 16 a Sapper officer from 2 Field Company went out to examine the breach. He did this without interference from the Italians, and came back with the information that the block consisted of two craters about twenty yards long, with a debris of large boulders at each end and between the craters. The total length of the obstacle was over a hundred yards. The officer estimated that the road could be made passable to tracked vehicles with some forty-eight hours' work.

The next night a further reconnaissance enabled the C.R.E., Lieutenant-Colonel Arthur Napier, to look at the road-block himself. A patrol of the 6/13th Frontier Force Rifles—the only troops available to give protection to the Sappers—was sent along the railway line towards Railway Bumps. They met no enemy in advance of their fixed defences overlooking the block, but an Italian sentry at the Keren end of the breach was disturbed.

It had been Napier's intention on this occasion to start clearing the debris of boulders, using gun-cotton charges where necessary. To drown the noise, a programme of artillery and small-arms fire had been arranged. But the enemy, being on the alert, opened fire. After a brief engagement, Napier realized that he could not carry out his task and withdrew the little force. Thus a plan for a stealthy demolition of some of the larger rocks on the block, which was attempted on the night of the 18th, failed.

General Heath decided that a second attempt should be made on the following night, with a covering party strong enough to deal with enemy opposition on both sides of the Dongolaas Gorge. Once again the Frontier Force Rifles—a company of them this time—met two enemy picquets and sustained casualties from bombs showered down on the leading platoon. Twenty of our men were wounded, and the operation had to be abandoned.

But despite failure, the information gained was so valuable that on sifting it General Heath exclaimed, "Keren is ours!" He had had an inspiration after realizing that Sanchil, hitherto regarded as the key to the whole position, could be ignored, and that the real key was Railway Bumps. These closely overlooked the road-block and could be approached with considerably less opposition by the railway line from the tunnel below Cameron Ridge.

For the third attempt Heath had to wait until the heavily mauled Ten Brigade had been reconditioned. Nothing less than a full-dress attack would succeed. A major operation would have to be staged before the Sappers could start their job, and for this operation the Division would need its third brigade. But Ten Brigade would not be ready for a further severe effort until March 23 at the earliest.

The Fourth Indian Division reported on the 20th that they would be able to clear the tunnel on Cameron Ridge spur within two days. It was through this tunnel and along the railway line that Ten Brigade was to advance, under cover of darkness, for its attack. The G.S.O.1 of Beresford-Peirse's Headquarters, Colonel T. W. Rees—a stocky little Welshman known as "Pete," a teetotaller and non-smoker who, four years later, was to capture Mandalay—came across to take command of Ten Brigade. This had been led by Fletcher of the H.L.I. ever since January 21, when Brigadier Slim had been wounded. Now Bernard Fletcher formed a mobile column, known as Fletcher Force, composed of the Central Indian Horse, together with thirty-six brigaded carriers and the remaining fourteen Infantry tanks. The column stood ready to advance through the Gorge to Keren to mop up Italian reserves so soon as the road-block should have been cleared.

While the Fourth Indian Division would hold the enemy on the left flank and divert his attention, Messervy's Nine Brigade on the right had instructions to push forward and capture three small features that lay between Fort Dologorodoc and Mount Zeban—they were known as Hillocks 'A' and 'B,' and Red Hill. After this had been accomplished, Brigadier Marriott was to send his troops through to take Zeban and, further to the east, Mount Canabai, which looks down on Keren and guards the road to Asmara.

It is General Heath's opinion that this exploitation to Zeban and Canabai would not of itself have caused the Italians to give up. They would still have had sufficient troops in hand to defeat the small force that we might have established on these two objectives. Administrative problems would have precluded us from strengthening the force. What the Italians were not prepared to face was a thrust through their central defences by our much-feared Infantry tanks, for which they believed they had no adequate antidote.

The main attack was fixed to start early on March 25. It had been postponed by a day. Just before midnight on the 24th patrols from Captain Timbrell's company of the 2nd West Yorkshires, after hearing enemy talking on the reverse slope of Hillock 'A,' occupied this small feature. And by half-past four two companies had been established there by Colonel Langran. At the same time Reid's Mahrattas took Hillock 'B' against heavy opposition. Their attack was due to start at half-past four. It was later discovered that an Italian counter-attack had been planned for the same time, but was postponed because the supporting tanks did not arrive. So Reid's men found themselves outnumbered and fighting against an enemy well dug in. By seven o'clock on March 25 the Indian troops had surprised the enemy on Red Hill. Our casualties were heavy when the Italians retaliated from Falestoh with mortar fire, but the defences of the road-block to the south had now been cleared.

Meanwhile, Ten Brigade's assault on Railway Bumps had started that morning, the 25th. Brigadier Rees and Sundius-Smith had made several perilous reconnaissances, during which mountain guns had fired at them at point-blank range.

The Highland Light Infantry and Baluch spent the night in the tunnel. The scene was like some Rembrandt painting, as the men waited in the darkness that was pierced by an occasional light and by the glow of cigarette ends. From time to time tea and rum were served out. The Indians remained silent by contrast with the 'Jocks,' who chattered away and suddenly burst into the strains of *Annie Laurie*. Brigadier Rees walked to the end of the tunnel to see whether the sounds could be heard, but all was well.

The troops were ordered to scatter to left and right of the railway track if firing broke out. Who knew but that the Italians had fixed-line machine guns trained on the exit from the tunnel? When our men debouched they might encounter some Italian patrol, and such a meeting would start an inferno of shooting and grenades. At 3 a.m. the troops tiptoed forward. Brigadier Rees waited anxiously, watching the seconds tick by on his watch. As each minute passed he knew that the men had reached a certain distance without being discovered. What troops the enemy held on Railway Bumps was unknown. The moment was tense, and in no man's mind was there any sense of an easy attack, still less of a walk-over.

Each battalion had two companies to fight, and one to carry stores, ammunition, rations, water. The leading Scottish company then left the track and started to scramble up the hillside, only to meet a shower of Italian red bombs. The other two attacking companies, led by Major Maxwell, went farther along the line. Both parties made good progress. The enemy, now thoroughly awake and in some state of panic, hurled down bombs and grenades, but put up little effective resistance. The Italians had been taken by surprise, and our concentrated artillery barrage on the ridge had thrown them into confusion. Several Dogra fighting patrols were sent up the slopes of Sanchil and had hectic little engagements against odds. When a number of Italian soldiers walked down from above with their hands raised, Major Doyle sent out a patrol. The sepoys were greeted with a further storm of red bombs—a favourite Italian trick.

By half past five most of the objectives had been gained. Some five hundred prisoners were taken. Several admitted that they had never seriously considered that anyone would risk an attack along the railway track. The colonel of the Bersaglieri battalion holding Railway Bumps surrendered with his headquarters in their dugout to the H.L.I.'s Intelligence sergeant. He was brought back to Brigadier Rees. He was almost speechless with rage at having been surprised. So long had the tunnel been quiescent, that his eyes had been on Sanchil. A battery of pack guns and another of anti-tank guns that had been defending the road-block were captured.

Our attack had been successful. Now it was a question of holding on until the Sappers had repaired the road through the Gorge. The Italians still held the upper slopes of Sanchil, but here the mountain side rose so abruptly that the enemy could scarcely bring down accurate fire on the positions held by Ten Brigade.

At half past six that morning 2 Field Company started work on clearing the block. The Sappers had asked for two nights and one day in which to clear the road for the passage of tanks; they were given two days and one night. After the first day Napier's three Field Companies, aided by another loaned by the Fourth Indian Division, relieved each other every five hours. The task was accomplished to time, in spite of frequent shelling of the block and its approaches.

Throughout the period of work on repairing the demolition, the Royal Air Force continued to bomb the enemy on Falestoh and Zeban. The Italians made several cut-and-run raids with their speedy Savoia bombers directed on our forward guns in the road bend below Pinnacle. These howitzers of the Kashmir Mountain Battery were positioned there to keep quiet the enemy troops on the lower slopes of Sanchil. Other guns to engage Railway Bumps were placed at the mouth of Happy Valley, the control of which had by this time been regained from the Italians.

During March 26 the Fourth Indian Division reported signs of enemy artillery moving away from their front. Ten Brigade reported movement eastwards across the plain of Keren. Nine Brigade, too, noticed a decrease in shelling and anti-aircraft fire from the Italian side. Indeed, the 2nd West Yorkshires noted that this was the quietest day they had spent since the battle for Keren began.

On the same day the Commander-in-Chief, Middle East, General Sir Archibald Wavell, visited the battle area with the Kaid. After viewing the situation on the Fifth Indian Division's front from Dologorodoc, General Wavell expressed a wish to visit Brigadier

Marriott at 29 Brigade. Heath strongly advised the Commander-in-Chief not to do so, because the enemy artillery seldom failed to engage movement observed on the road forward of Divisional Headquarters, and Savoia bombers came at intervals bent on strafing the mountain battery just short of Marriott's headquarters.

But General Wavell was stubborn, and was already edging down the spur towards the roadway when five Savoias flew overhead and dropped bombs, as anticipated, on the battery position. The bombs straddled the road. Those officers and men in and around Divisional Headquarters who stood within splinter range of this attack threw themselves down in the cover of rocks.

Wavell smiled, and only then was persuaded to give up his intention of going forward to visit Marriott. Instead, he sent a message of good wishes for 29 Brigade's attack next morning.

The work of repairing the demolition of the roadway through the Dongolaas Gorge and making the road fit for the passage of tracked and wheeled vehicles being now within an ace of completion, the time was near for Marriott's Brigade to round off the operation by securing the upper part of the Dongolaas Valley.

Accordingly, that night (March 26-27) 29 Brigade launched its attack at half past four through Nine Brigade's positions. The night was very dark, the troops burdened, and the approach march difficult in consequence. But within an hour the Worcestershires had raced to the top of Zeban Minor. Falestoh Ridge was occupied without opposition. And by half past seven two companies of the 6/13th had seized Zeban Major.

The enemy had had enough. He had worn himself out with reiterated and vain counter-assaults. He had lost heart for the fight. His resistance was now poor. At six o'clock the 3/2nd Punjab spotted white flags flying from the summit of Sanchil, and during that morning similar white flags appeared on Brigs Peak, Mount Amba and Samanna.

The Italians had managed to withdraw over half their guns from Keren and all their troops from the east side of the road into Keren. On the Sanchil side, on and around the commanding heights which the Fourth Indian Division had been so valiantly attacking for more than seven weeks, over 3,000 Italians were left marooned. The battle of Keren was at an end.

We must now return to the road-block in the Dongolaas Gorge.

At the end of the second day, March 26, when the road had been cleared to a width of twelve feet, it was decided to defer the passage of Fletcher's mobile column until the following morning. A further night of intensive work was necessary to prepare for the tracked vehicles, but the shelling had now died down, and by dawn all was ready. The column passed through, not without incident. The 'I' tanks went first, driven by their incomparable crews; then the carriers, and finally the wheeled vehicles. The leading carrier stuck on the incline of the former block, and delayed matters. One officer's staff car became wedged and had to be thrown over the precipice to allow the remainder to pass.

Beneath the rebuilt road lie the bodies of brave men of the Sappers and Miners who gave their lives in clearing the block; and of the 6/13th Frontier Force Rifles who died in winning the information which brought success.

By ten o'clock Fletcher Force had entered Keren. When the Air Force had reported, three hours earlier, that the Italians were evacuating the town the role of this column, which had originally been to destroy all Italian communications, reserves, headquarters and guns in the Keren neighbourhood, was changed to that of pursuing the enemy. The 4/10th Baluch and Highland Light Infantry were placed across the valley to stop fugitives. Marriott established 29 Brigade in the area south of the road by Keren. That afternoon Nine Brigade also moved forward from Fort Dologorodoc and down to the water point below Zeban. The stern battle had been won.

* * * * *

In a letter to his wife, Lieutenant-Colonel W. E. Dean, of the 3/12th, wrote: "We have been very short of sleep—only two nights did we have a blanket, and latterly we've been climbing, and the nights have been cold. Only one change of clothes in the eleven days of the battle, and no water all that time for anything but drinking. I had a long, almost white beard when it was over, and my face and hands were incredibly grimy. The result of that was that every graze went septic at once, and we are all a mass of bandages. No hot meals—all cooking was below, so we had no hot meals except for an occasional cup of tea; and no washing up of plates. We just forked and spooned things out of communal tins, or ate curry puffs, sausage rolls, etc., sent up from behind. One curious thing was that, after ten days, one felt no more dirty than after three, and far less sensitive to the hordes of flies—another inevitable result of the conditions of unburied bodies and no sanitation."

The compiler of the narrative for the Official History of this campaign has summed up the battle in these words: "So Keren fell after fifty-three days of siege. It is estimated that the Italians employed in the battle a peak total of thirty-nine battalions and thirty-six batteries, and that during the total period of operations they disposed in all of something over 30,000 infantry, supported by 144 guns. Many of these were fresh troops, and although the British forces never succeeded in driving their opponents from the main peaks on either side of the Gorge, and suffered over 4,000 casualties in their attempts to do so, it is true to say that the enemy brought defeat on himself and finally wore himself out in his eight fierce but fruitless attempts to retake Dologorodoc Fort. It was here that his best and freshest units were driven back with crippling losses. In General Frusci's own situation reports, which were captured, he reveals that 3,000 dead were left at Keren, including General Lorenzini and five senior officers. . . . Practically all had been staked on holding this great natural fortress, with the result that, at the end, there were but three battalions and a few batteries uncommitted between Keren and Asmara."

And Lieutenant-General Sir Reginald Savory, who commanded Eleven Brigade during this fighting, affirms, as have others, that "no enemy but the Italians would ever have allowed us to take the place. It was practically 'impregnable,' and even with Italian defenders we suffered heavily and at times began to wonder if we ever would succeed."

The Italians, particularly the regular troops such as Savoia Grenadiers, Alpini, and Bersaglieri, were proud of their resistance at Keren. It was one of the few occasions on which they really fought with tenacity and fervour.

It is probable that without the specialized training at Tessenei, and experience gained by nearly all the Indian, and some of the British, battalions in operations and columns on the North-West Frontier of India, our troops would not have proved so sharp a thorn in the Italian side. For the battle had been one of endurance and holding on. The Fourth Indian Division had been sent straight into the fight without the priceless opportunity of training for the battle ahead.

Co-operation between the two Indian divisions was at once intimate and generous, as General Heath has put on record. The Fourth set the Fifth a very high standard in fighting against the enemy and physical difficulties. Beresford-Peirse's men bore the brunt of the battle for six weeks before the advent of the Fifth Indian Division. And it was natural that the Fourth should have wanted to win through. Indeed, it would merely have been justice had they done so. But in the end, when the final and successful solution to the Keren barrier had been found as the result of trial and error, it was the Fifth who were able to exploit the weakness in these defences. The hitherto impregnable Sanchil, scene of many a valiant and vain assault, grave of many scores of gallant fighters, was taken in reverse by men of the Fifth. None were more pleased at this success than their comrades of the Fourth.

CHAPTER VI

THE ROAD TO ASMARA

APRIL 1941

MEANWHILE, Fletcher Force was pursuing the enemy. After searching Keren for an hour, the tanks set off along the Asmara road. They halted at noon to await the arrival of the carriers and armoured cars which were more fitted for pursuit. Soon our column met some two thousand disorganized Italian stragglers. These readily obeyed Fletcher's instructions to stack their arms by the roadside, and then trailed back towards Keren.

The first opposition to our progress was encountered at K.59. From this point forward for several miles the road twists along the side of a valley, while below the road the ground slopes steeply away into a gorge. The Italians had realized the defensive qualities of this stretch and had improved upon the natural strength of the position for delaying action by demolitions covered by cunningly emplaced guns.

At five o'clock that evening, March 27, General Heath arrived forward to find that Fletcher's leading armoured car had been knocked out by an unlocated gun. Reconnaissance made it clear to the Divisional Commander that something stronger than Fletcher Force would be needed to deal with the opposition ahead. Besides, the tanks being restricted to the road, infantry were required to deploy to the flank. Accordingly he summoned Marriott's 29 Brigade, while Fletcher's men picketed the neighbouring heights. A further bad road-block had been discovered three kilometres on towards Asmara.

Brigadier Marriott reached Fletcher Force early next morning, the 28th, and took over the position, Fletcher himself returning to command the Highland Light Infantry back in Keren. That afternoon the 3/2nd Punjab and 6/13th Frontier Force Rifles cleared the first block. The country here was hilly, more thickly vegetated and less rocky than Keren, and the road was carved out of the hillside. This made things very difficult for our Gunners of 28 Field Regiment. The guns supporting the Brigade were in action just off the road, and were a long way back so as to be able to clear the crests. Consequently the range was greater than could be efficient. Moreover, the enemy had succeeded in withdrawing more than half his artillery from the positions defending Keren, and had he not worn himself out in the recent battles, the Division's task of breaking through the block would have been even more difficult and costly.

29 Brigade, with its Headquarters and Signal Office in a large cave, was now faced with an obstacle reinforced with a landslide demolition. This was K.56. Before 20 Field Company could start to clear the block, the Italians had to be driven off the flanking hills. By noon on March 29 the Sappers had worked so well at the obstructions that a column consisting of one light tank, some armoured cars, one squadron of the Central India Horse, and three 'I' tanks was soon through. By four o'clock this force had advanced five kilometres. Then it came under heavy fire and was obliged to withdraw. One of our armoured cars had been set ablaze. Several burning Italian lorries were blocking the road.

At the same time an attempt was made by the Divisional Commander to outflank the enemy by moving Ten Brigade down the railway line with a detachment of Skinner's Horse and one M.M.G. company of the Sudan Defence Force. But this effort was foiled by serious demolitions, although the number of guns and amount of Italian equipment later found there did indicate that this flanking move had served the general operation by causing the enemy to divert troops from the main battle.

Early on March 30 Brigadier Marriott reported that he hoped to push along the road at first light next day with 'I' tanks. Colonel Russell, the G.S.O.1, visited him to say that the enemy seemed to be on his last legs. Everything possible must be done to complete his destruction.

Later that morning General Heath made a reconnaissance and decided that Messervy's Nine Brigade should pass through and continue the advance. After lunch the Italians started to range their guns on the stretch of road between K.55 and K.51, and soon afterwards regular harassing fire was opened upon a certain bend in the road. Here salvoes of four rounds descended with accuracy every sixty seconds. Brigadier Messervy and the West Yorkshire reconnaissance parties ran the gauntlet and came through without harm. But later, when General Heath and Dudley Russell tried to get through to the rear, they found that the road had been completely blocked by trucks and corpses.

General Heath has told the story. "The firing continued well into the afternoon, and the time came for our departure. So we started off and waited down the road, waiting for the regular salvo. It did not arrive on time, so we drove on, round the bend, and found the road blocked by smashed vehicles. A couple of hundred yards away a few trucks untouched by fire had been left. I alighted and said, 'We will take one of those.' I had gone a few yards when 'crump,' 'crump,' and my Bombay bowler (sun helmet) was sent spinning by a shell splinter. I quickened my pace and walked round the next bend. Only then did I look back. There was no sign of Russell. I waited a few minutes and then started to retrace my steps, and there came Russell, coolly driving the staff car. He had, with the aid of a signaller on line-repair duty, pushed a couple of vehicles clear, and had then driven his car through the gap. It was a cool appreciation that the Italian gunners, from their observation post high up in the hills to the north of the road, would not be able to release another salvo from their old-fashioned pieces for fifty seconds or so."

Next morning, March 31, a little before five, the 2nd West Yorkshires attacked. Within an hour their first objective had been taken, and 460 prisoners, including nineteen officers, captured. Heavy shelling prevented a second company from exploiting along the ridge on the other side of the road. But that evening the 3/12th Frontier Force Rifles attacked what was known as White Rock Ridge covering the road-block at K.45, and the feature was gained.

Meanwhile, the 1st Worcestershires, assisted by part of the 6/13th Frontier Force Rifles under Major Vidya Dhar Jayal, had taken two more hills against stern resistance. A hundred more prisoners had fallen into their grip.

Thus ended the enemy's final resistance before Asmara. During the past two days prisoners and deserters had been numerous. The Italians had, in a last effort to hold our advance, moved fresh troops into the line, but when one particular Colonial battalion reached the fighting many of its native soldiers at once deserted.

On that last evening of March, at eight o'clock, the 2nd Field Company set to work on the road-block. Though it was a hundred yards in length, the Sappers had cleared a route through the block by two o'clock in the morning. The day was now April 1. While the 3/12th Frontier Force Regiment took possession of Ad Teclesan village, a mile forward, Rees' Ten Brigade, with a squadron of the Central India Horse and a few 'I' tanks under command, passed through to the front. Their task was to pursue the enemy along the remaining twenty-five miles into Asmara.

An hour later a black car with a white flag flying from the windscreen was seen approaching from the direction of Asmara. The car contained two police officers who bore a request that the capital of Eritrea should be treated as an open town. They were sent back to Brigade Headquarters and met by Brigadier Messervy, who was at that moment riding into Ad Teclesan in a tank. While Ten Brigade continued its advance, the two Italian envoys were sent back to meet General Heath. The Divisional Commander agreed to the enemy's request on condition that dumps, vehicles and military stores were handed over, that civil plants and public services in Asmara were not damaged, and that roads and airfields were cleared of mines and booby traps. With these terms the two police officers returned to Asmara, having been instructed to meet Brigadier Rees outside the town with their accredited leaders.

Three miles short of the capital, Rees was received by the Bishop of Asmara and by the heads of the Government and Police. After a conference held inside an Italian motor-bus, Rees went forward into the town. The time was now half past ten. He was accompanied by the Italian delegates and escorted by the Central India Horse and tanks.

Brigadier Rees arranged that his three battalions and the leading battery of Welchman's 28th Field Regiment should march through the city, the four colonels and himself driving in state to the Governor's palace. The five trucks moved in a stately and dignified procession. Much to the astonishment of the British officers, there were plaudits of welcome from the inhabitants, and Welchman's faithful bearer, Abdullah, sat up very erect in the back of the vehicle and acknowledged the cheers on behalf of his *Sahib*.

The arrival of British forces was welcomed by the inhabitants, because the evening before one of the Colonial battalions had mutinied and rioted, and the Italian civilians were anxious to have law and order restored without delay. But in the meantime most of the people shut themselves up in their houses and stayed there until our troops entered the town.

Asmara was formally surrendered. A slight drizzle rather spoilt the ceremonial in front of General Frusci's palace, where an unusually scruffy guard presented arms execrably. Then, at the General Post Office, loudspeakers announced that Asmara would be treated as an open city. All traffic would drive on the left of the road.

General Heath arrived at eleven o'clock. By midday the Highland Light Infantry had reached the outskirts of Asmara, where a halt was called. They had come up the road past a continuous stream of thousands of prisoners. These all seemed to be cheerful, notwithstanding the surrender. As they trudged back, they mingled with large parties of Eritreans who came in from the hills to meet the British column with shrill songs of greeting. But bands of them also roamed about the bare plateau and edged towards the booty stacked near the road. The Italians had to hurl stones to keep off these would-be looters. The road, too, was strewn with the debris of the retreating Italian army: litter of all sorts, and such trophies as revolvers, binoculars and compasses.

At one o'clock the H.L.I. were ordered to dismount from their lorries. Led by Pipe-Major McLean, the battalion marched into Asmara, the first infantry unit to enter the town. The streets were now lined with large crowds of Italians and Eritreans. Many hung out of the windows to wave and clap. The people's first comment, on seeing the Scottish pipers, was that the British Army must be hard pressed if it could not afford to give its soldiers a proper band !

* * * * *

On the evening of the day our troops entered Asmara, General Heath sent for Colonel Fletcher and ordered him to lead a column south along the Via Imperiale that linked Asmara and Adigrat, a distance of a hundred miles. He was to pursue those Italians who were reported to have retreated in this direction. The column, called "Flitforce" after the nickname of its commander, comprised the Central India Horse and two M.M.G. companies of the Sudan Defence Force.

Bernard Fletcher, commissioned into the Highland Light Infantry in 1916 at the age of eighteen, had won the Military Cross and been gassed with mustard gas in France during the last two years of the Great War. Thereafter he had served for a few months in North Russia, before going with his battalion to Egypt and Palestine. For nearly a year in 1923 the H.L.I. had occupied Turkish territory in Asia Minor, at Chanak, and was then sent to India. Fletcher, now speaking both Arabic and Hindustani, passed into the Staff College in 1929, served in India again during the thirties, and in 1938 was appointed to command the 2nd Highland Light Infantry in Palestine.

It was clear that if any Italian prisoners were to be captured, they must be cut off. Accordingly, Fletcher sent the C.I.H. to make a direct pursuit down the road through Decamere to Adigrat while the two M.M.G. companies took the western road that passed via Adi Ugri to Aduwa. Then they would turn east and cut across to Adigrat.

Adi Ugri was reached without incident. Here a stop was made to release from the Italian camp a number of our prisoners of war, taken when Italy invaded Somaliland. The former prisoners had the pleasant duty of escorting their Italian guards back to Asmara. Then the pursuit was renewed. Some forty miles farther south the S.D.F. came upon a large barrack-like block of buildings, which turned out to be an Italian detention barracks. To have captured the staff would have obliged Fletcher to look after the prisoners, so the Italian staff were left in charge and placed upon their best behaviour not to interfere with any traffic on the road that "Flitforce" was leaving behind it. As Fletcher rightly commented, "Such a course would not have been possible with any enemy other than Italians."

Aduwa was reached at nine o'clock next morning. Here a cousin of Haile Selassie, Emperor of Abyssinia, named Ras Seyoum, presented himself, but could give no information about the retreating Italians, for none had passed that way. Leaving one S.D.F. company in Aduwa, Fletcher turned east with the other and headed for Adigrat. As the road climbed up to cross the Alequa Pass, so the column gradually spun out until the S.D.F. company was stretched over five miles. Hopes that our advance was a secret were dashed when the top of the pass was reached. For there, nearly ten thousand feet above sea-level, among the clouds that drifted over the neighbouring crags, waited an assembly of women and priests—a reception committee. While the women ululated their welcome to Fletcher's men, the priests advanced with crosses and chains of beaten silver, which they held out towards our officers. These latter did not quite know what to do, but they touched the crosses.

Then the column descended into Adigrat. A subaltern of the S.D.F. found a complete Colonial battalion, with lorries drawn up facing south, about to set off down the road to Amba Alagi. With armoured cars he drove up to the officers who were seated beside the road taking their commander's orders, and induced them to surrender. The men were marched past an open space where they laid down their arms prior to filing into an enclosed camp, while the officers were taken to huts in another part of Adigrat. This easy capture was marred by anxiety at the non-arrival of the C.I.H., who were no longer in communication by wireless. Accordingly, Fletcher sent for the second S.D.F. company that had been left in Aduwa; this force arrived next morning. The number of prisoners had meanwhile been swelled by the arrival of further parties from the north, and they now outnumbered Fletcher's columns by more than ten to one. Nor was there sufficient diesel oil to send these prisoners back to Asmara via Aduwa. Only the officers were driven away.

Fletcher sent out a patrol to search for the C.I.H. Within ten miles they were found driving calmly down the road. They had been held up on the way by a fair-sized Italian force. The enemy commander had telephoned to Adigrat. He had been told by the Italian District Commissioner, in whose house Fletcher had slept the night, that it was useless to continue resistance, for the British were already in Adigrat. "Not many of them, but they are here," he added. At once the force opposing the C.I.H. surrendered and were dispatched to Asmara.

The ten-ton lorries belonging to the Colonial battalion were packed to capacity with prisoners and sent off in relays to the Eritrean capital. One S.D.F. company returned to Aduwa, the second remained to send off the rest of the two thousand prisoners, and the C.I.H. moved still farther south towards Amba Alagi. At Quiha, a small Italian cantonment, the enemy could have arrested our advance with a few determined men. He did no such thing. When Fletcher arrived with the commander of the C.I.H., the officer of the advance guard came up excitedly and said, "I've got them to surrender all right, but the Italian colonel wants you to have lunch with him."

"Oh, nonsense !" retorted Fletcher. "There's far too much to do without worrying about lunch parties."

And there was, as Fletcher has described. Quiha was a depot, a hospital and an aerodrome. Everything was in confusion: deserters and natives were looting the hospital, the ground staff of the aerodrome were wandering about carrying luggage, and the ten-ton lorries which had been prepared to take the garrison to Amba Alagi were effectually blocking the main road.

"But you must have lunch with him," insisted the advance guard commander. "It was one of the terms of surrender."

"Oh, all right," Fletcher agreed. "Tell the Italian commander that I will lunch with him on condition that these lorries are turned round facing north, and loaded complete with his garrison by two o'clock." And so it was agreed. Fletcher lunched in the Italian depot mess, and the column of prisoners left on time, the lorries overcrowded with 300 Italians and 700 native troops, not to mention a few women. One hitch occurred before the lorries drove away.

"Who is going to escort us to Asmara ?" queried the Italian commander.

"A troop of the Central India Horse."

"But I am a Colonel, and you have two Lieutenant-Colonels here. One of you at least should escort us."

"The officer commanding your escort belongs to a distinguished English family," said Fletcher, neglecting to add that he was also the junior subaltern !

At the market town of Macalle the local Ras, another cousin of the Emperor Haile Selassie, was commissioned to maintain law and order in the district until such time as the officials of our military government could take over.

This brought the operations of "Flitforce" to an end. The Central India Horse rejoined the Fourth Indian Division bound for the Western Desert, and were replaced by Skinner's Horse (Lieutenant-Colonel I. F. Hossack). They reconnoitred as far as

Amba Alagi. At no cost to ourselves "Flitforce" had, in Fletcher's own words, "collected, rather than captured, 3,500 prisoners."

*   *   *   *   *

Asmara lies on a plateau, 7,000 feet above sea-level, in stony surroundings. The town, whose climate was cool after the heat and dust of Barentu and Agordat, and open by comparison with the sheer cliffs and narrow gorges of Keren, is built on rolling downland, bare of all but a few trees. This capital is a mixture of modern Italian and more primitive Eritrean; the native population dwells in settlements of mud-brick houses, clear of the European quarters. It is a modern city, with a wide main street—the Viale Mussolini, as it then was—and many shopping streets that lead off on either side. The Italian residential area is composed of small, well-built villas in pleasant gardens.

There is an imposing red-brick cathedral, a market-place, modern cinemas, tennis courts and cafés, excellent hotels and garages, an airstrip, and a radio station. On the hill stands Fort Baldissera, strangely out of keeping with the rest of Asmara that it overlooks. Its ramparts and barbed-wire defences harmonize ill with the general view of white houses and tree-lined avenues. It was in this fort that all Italian troops were collected into custody, while native soldiers were kept in another fort. Over the white prisoners guard was kept by the 4/10th Baluch.

The Highland Light Infantry were billeted that first night in the Colonial Police barracks, which were in a state of hideous filth, and which housed, besides the battalion, twice as many Italian soldiers and officers, who wandered aimlessly about while waiting to be evacuated as prisoners of war. Asmara contained a far greater number of armed enemy troops than British and Indian. Not that they made trouble. Indeed, they seemed more afraid of the natives than of anyone else. Platoons of Indian soldiers picketed Asmara to quell the sporadic disturbances that broke out among the local population, trying to loot food and clothing stores. All Italian officers were placed on parole and instructed to return to their homes and to report again within a week.

Hasty plans had to be made for the evacuation of these prisoners to the Sudan. During April some 25,000 were sent back from Asmara alone. It was fortunate, indeed, that the city was well stocked with food, enough to last for nearly two months, for the Italian authorities were able to supply rations to all their own soldiers. The withdrawal of the Fourth Indian Division to Egypt, on Wavell's orders, meant that for nearly two weeks all available transport and railway stock was needed for their move. Three trains a day had been taking prisoners from Keren to Agordat, but these soon had to be stopped, and the number of prisoners in Asmara rose to the alarming total of over twelve thousand. The number mounted as more and more were rounded up in outlying areas, but on the whole they behaved well and gave no trouble to our minute escorts.

The inhabitants of Asmara were most affable to the troops of the Division, and in typical Italian manner appeared to bear not the least malice towards their conquerors. Rather did they treat our troops as peaceful tourists with money to spend. And in the surprisingly well-stocked modern shops, goods were by British standards cheap, owing to the fictitious rate of exchange fixed by the authorities on April 7. The shopkeepers did an excellent trade in cameras, watches, clothing and stationery, even though they could not provide spirits or beer, tinned food or soap.

On the night of our entry into the city, Divisional Headquarters were quartered at the Albergo Ciano, and the Mess President ordered a special dinner to be prepared. Judge the surprise of General Heath and his staff when they sat down to dinner and saw menu cards headed:

"5TH INDIAN DIVISION. CELEBRATION DINNER."

It was indeed a celebration dinner, but the officers had scarcely expected the Italian manager of the hotel to enter so thoroughly into the spirit of the occasion, even though he had spent five years as a waiter at the Savoy Hotel in London, and a further two at the Piccadilly Hotel.

* * * * *

The occupation of the capital of Eritrea, with its large number of Italian civilians, presented many problems to the staff officers of the Division. All restaurants, cafés and food shops were placed out of bounds—except for liquid refreshments—because if our troops fed there, there would be a shortage of food for the local population, and particularly for the children. Already many children of Asmara were suffering from the shortage of milk. Troops of the 3/12th Frontier Force Regiment suggested that they might be allowed to surrender one-fifth of their milk ration on behalf of these youngsters. But fresh milk in churns was flown up each day from Khartoum.

House-to-house searches for arms were made in the native quarters. The Baluch threw a cordon round the area and a number of rifles, pistols and bombs were found. Patrols in trucks were sent out on the roads towards Adi Ugri and Decamere to catch any people trying to escape from Asmara. The Baluch also placed ambushes on the road between Keren and Massawa, to catch odd bands of Eritreans still roaming in the hills.

Enemy ordnance equipment, such as saddles and capes, which were repaired by the local tailors, and tents and hurricane lamps, were issued to the Division. Wooden bungs had to be made for two-gallon petrol tins before these could be dispatched forward. Supplies had to be held for prisoners of war, who could now only be evacuated at the rate of six hundred a day; and medical attention had to be available, if necessary, before this evacuation. The local Italian police and municipal workers continued to function. So did the hospitals. The Italians dealt with their own food supplies. Rates of pay for officers and men billeted in hotels and requisitioned buildings had to be fixed. An organization known as O.E.T.A., and consisting of Brigadier Kennedy-Cooke, Colonel Cumming, and a handful of officers and clerks, was set up to deal with the varied and numerous civil problems.

At one period during the month nearly every available officer and man was on duty at traffic control posts, which were established throughout Asmara, to check the passes of individuals and motor vehicles. No fewer than five hundred motor-cars alone were impounded and placed in a vehicle park because they were without passes. The town major, the billeting officer, the requisitioning officer, salvage officer, officer in charge of the prisoners-of-war cage, and the deputy assistant provost marshal were all overworked.

Salvage, too, presented a major problem. Thousands and thousands of tons of military equipment were located in many places within the Divisional area. Although as many of these dumps as possible were guarded, once they had been located, some looting of supplies, petrol and oil, and vehicles went on. The amount of transport needed to collect and backload the tens of thousands of rifles and the vast quantities of ammunition and other weapons was enormous.

Ten Brigade, after its operation to capture Massawa,[1] remained throughout the latter part of April and May on guard and internal security duties in Asmara. The battalion patrols intervened in fighting between Italians and natives in villages outside the capital. One day they went off in search of five armed Italians and an officer who were reported living in a tent. They found nothing. In response to Italian complaints that Eritreans were coming by night armed with bombs and rifles and taking away building material from shafts in the mines area, intensive searches for arms were made in outlying villages. But most searches had no result. On one occasion several 40-gallon barrels were stolen by natives from our petrol supply depot; the thieves held up the attendants at the point of the pistol. A farm outside Asmara was wrecked by natives with hand-grenades.

Early one morning a report was received that two Italian ladies had gone shopping in the market. The Eritreans had refused to supply them and had eventually kicked one lady in the stomach. The lady called to three Italian policemen, who were standing near by, to arrest the man. But the police were set upon by the crowd, who chased them to the police station. From time to time the Italian police lost control of the Eritreans, various shootings and looting incidents would occur, and every day platoons of the Baluch, West Yorkshires and H.L.I. had to stand by in trucks, in case of trouble.

---

[1]Chapter VII.

CHAPTER VII

MASSAWA BY THE SEA

APRIL 1941

THE Fifth Indian Division had beaten the enemy in the Keren stronghold, broken through his resistance at Ad Teclesan, and entered Asmara. The next task was to capture Massawa, the principal port of Eritrea on the Red Sea. Seven Indian Brigade, led by Brigadier H. R. Briggs, which had blocked the northern flank of Keren and thus assisted directly in the eventual capture of the town, was already concentrated thirty-five miles north of Massawa, and a mobile column had been pushed forward down the coast to reconnoitre the place.

In the original plan Seven Brigade was to have captured Massawa alone. But when the Italians evacuated Asmara, this plan was changed. Briggs was in the process of establishing Monclar's Free French Brigade (*Brigade d'Orient*) from Chad, less one battalion astride the Asmara–Massawa road near the point where it enters the plains. This operation materially assisted in the opening of the mountain portion of the road down from Asmara.

General Heath suggested that the operation for the capture of Massawa would be greatly simplified if he sent his 'I' tanks down the main road with such troops of Rees' Ten Brigade as could be hurried there. This suggestion was approved by the Kaid, who instructed Heath to take command of the whole operation.

During the night of April 1/2 General Heath was directed to convey to the Italian commander there, Admiral Bonetti, the following message:—

"Now that the British forces have entered Asmara and are advancing on Massawa, I am to inform you that if any of the ships in Massawa harbour, of which I believe there are twenty-five, are scuttled, the British forces will consider themselves relieved of all responsibilities either of feeding the Italian population in Eritrea or Abyssinia, or of removing them from those countries. This message is being conveyed separately to the Duke of Aosta, Viceroy of Italian East Africa."

A rare event in war then occurred. The ordinary telephone lines between Asmara and Massawa were, of course, out of action. But a direct private line from the electric light supply in the port that generated electricity and transmitted it up to the capital was discovered by Divisional Signals to be intact.

Brigadier Rees, utilizing Lieutenant Bellwood, Italian interpreter at Divisional Headquarters, was able to speak direct by telephone with the Italian Headquarters. Bellwood talked to Admiral Bonetti's senior staff officer, Capitano di Frigata Berretta. The Kaid's ultimatum was translated, and Rees directed that the Italian commander should give an immediate promise that the terms would be fulfilled. This was at five o'clock on the afternoon of April 2. An hour and a half later Berretta telephoned to say that a reply would be given next morning. But no assurance would be given that the port facilities would not be destroyed in the interim. When morning came it was learned from Berretta that the Duke of Aosta had ordered Admiral Bonetti to refer the matter to Mussolini in Rome, as he was not prepared to handle this personally. From Rome came orders to resist our entry into Massawa and to give no guarantee about shipping and harbour works.

Early on April 4 Ten Brigade moved out from Asmara. Rees' force had already been preceded by one battalion and some Sappers, who had by now cleared the main demolitions in the Nefasit Gorge. Massawa lies sixty miles distant, and seven thousand feet lower than the Eritrean capital. The climate of the uplands had been marked by cool breezes and thunderstorms. In the Massawa coastal belt day-time temperatures rose thirty degrees above those of Asmara; the heat was intense, the humidity weakening, the stickiness odious.

Though the winding road was still blocked in several places, notably at Nefasit, the clearing of these further obstacles presented no great difficulties to the Sappers. In fact, one block was cleared by the Italian demolition party who had just made the block. They were captured by the Free French, and set to work feverishly under the eye of a French soldier armed with a stick, which he brandished vigorously. He described the efforts of the working party as "Merveilleux ! Magnifique !" The road was not mined, though on the outskirts of Massawa a great variety of improvised mines were discovered, made of canisters filled with explosive, shells and even sea mines buried in the earth.

That same day Ten Brigade was joined by the French *Brigade d'Orient*. Colonel Monclar was a fire-eater, who bore the scars of many wounds and who had the habit of placing all his officers under arrest. The leader of what Welchman termed the ' arrest ladder ' had been under arrest for one hundred and ten days. He seemed to thrive on it.

The afternoon of the 4th was devoted to taking up preliminary dispositions. The French Foreign Legion battalion was on the right of the road, and Ten Brigade was on the left. The guns of Welchman's 28th Field Regiment and two 3.7-inch howitzer batteries of the Sudan Defence Force were trained on the town, but with orders not to fire. There was no wish to damage the town. Nor was it then known whether women and children were still present there. Patrols were sent out to make reconnaissance.

At half past one next day, the 5th, an Italian lorry bearing a white flag approached. This was fired upon in error by the Sudan Defence Force. Later a British flag party, consisting of *Bimbashi* Sims of the S.D.F., Bellwood the interpreter, and Young, a subaltern from the 3/18th Royal Garhwal Rifles, went ahead and was met at the wire by the Italians. Admiral Bonetti asked for our terms. These were transmitted to him that evening, after consultations by telephone with General Heath and the Kaid. The Admiral, having read the terms, announced that he must consult Rome. It was agreed that neither side would shoot until a reply had been received. Bonetti was ordered by Rome to defend the port to the last man, so hostilities were resumed at one o'clock on the 6th.

That afternoon a conference was held at Ten Brigade Headquarters with Rees, Briggs and the Divisional Commander. A concentric attack on Massawa by the two Indian brigades and by the French was to be launched on April 8. The plan for the attack was simplified by the discovery, in the map room of the Italian War Office at Asmara, of a drawing of the Massawa defences. This map showed, in particular, the position of enemy guns, and as a result our own artillery and aircraft were enabled to provide most effective counter-battery assistance to the infantry. The map also showed that anti-tank obstacles had been constructed across the wide *khor* traversed by the main road into Massawa. In planning the attack these defences were given a wide berth, and it was as well, for a most formidable cement dragon's teeth, interspersed with sea mines, had been built over a frontage of thousands of yards.

The garrison numbered some ten thousand men, a mixed collection belonging to many different units—remnants of the formations defeated at Keren and Ad Teclesan, a naval battalion, coast defence and customs units. But before the attack our estimate of the enemy strength was half this total.

Ten Brigade's objectives were a series of hillocks—leading to Signal Hill—that ran parallel to the road on the left-hand side. The Garhwalis would capture the first of these features. The Highland Light Infantry were then to pass through and take the remainder. Monclar's *Brigade d'Orient* were to wrest from the enemy a number of fortified hills covering the port—Moncullo, Fort Moncullo and Fort Vittorio Emmanuele. The forts each mounted heavy naval guns sited so as to fire either seawards or landwards. Briggs' Seven Brigade would attack from the north.

On the evening of the assault Brigadier Rees, when reconnoitring forward, could find no sign of the enemy on the first objectives. Accordingly he changed the plans and sent the Garhwal Rifles on at once to establish contact with the Italians, but not to involve themselves if serious opposition were met. Before eleven that night the Garhwalis had occupied two hillocks: they could hear voices on the next ridge ahead, and could see enemy fires from the prominent Signal Hill. So far not a shot had been fired. It was after 3 a.m. on the 8th when the Highland Light Infantry went through the Indian battalion to take Signal Hill, but again only if slight opposition were encountered. Otherwise the original plan of advance beneath an artillery barrage would be adhered to.

Led by Captain R. Wallace's company, the H.L.I. reached a white road cut in the side of the plateau. This was a landmark noticed earlier in the day and chosen as the starting line for the original attack. The leading section then announced the sound of talking and the movement of enemy transport ahead of them. As the remainder of the battalion moved to cover below the road, Very lights and star shells started rising into the darkness. The

Italians switched on a searchlight. Yet they failed to discover our troops who were tucked in below the hill, even though it seemed certain that the men must be visible whenever a parachute flare went up. For half an hour they lay crowded by the road embankment, hearing quite distinctly the voices of the enemy just above on the high ground.

It was now four o'clock in the morning. Word was passed to the two leading companies under Wallace and Maxwell to advance up on to the plateau above the road. They breached the barbed wire, took the Italians completely by surprise and occupied the feature without shooting. Then 'C' Company, commanded by Captain P. T. Telfer-Smollett, rushed up to Signal Hill and took it after a sharp fight. Resistance was soon overcome by the use of grenades and tommy-guns, which the Adjutant had previously 'confiscated' from the Asmara Police Barracks. The company was unable to deal with the crowds of prisoners who were wandering about in confusion. But at this point 'D' Company came up and organized their evacuation. Most of the prisoners were sullen, in particular a Naval Captain, who had only arrived the evening before to command this sector of the defences.

With the dawn came Breda and mortar fire on the hill, but few casualties were suffered, for our men took shelter in the trenches which the Italians themselves had dug on the crest. A short delay then occurred while the Free French, who were delayed on account of losing their way in the dark—they were not alone in this—came up to attack Moncullo. They were due to assault this as soon as Signal Hill was ours, so as to guard the H.L.I.'s right flank. But the French were ready on this flank before eight o'clock, and set out for their attack against the three forts on the ridge that ran southwards from the road south of the Swedish Mission—itself the final objective of Brigadier Rees' troops.

About the same time the squadron of 'I' tanks from the 4th Royal Tank Regiment roared forward, with the 4/10th Baluch in the wake, to drive the enemy from the hillocks on the left flank of the Highland Light Infantry—Black Bumps and Ridge 86. The tanks helped to smother the machine-guns that fired persistently on the Baluchis, and by 9.15 both hills were in our hands, to say nothing of many more Italian prisoners. It was the appearance of the tanks that above all else unnerved the enemy.

The Swedish Mission was taken without incident. Before half-past eleven the French soldiers had entered Fort Vittorio Emmanuele. The battle was all but ended. White flags appeared all along the front of attack of the Free French and Ten Brigade. But in the north Seven Brigade had met stronger resistance, and for two hours, once the day had lightened, Briggs' attacking battalions, the 1st Royal Sussex and 4/16th Punjab, were pinned to the ground by a prolonged and heavy barrage of land and naval guns. Briggs was without his third battalion. There was no alternative but to await the result of the attack from the west by Ten Brigade and the French. No sooner was this finished than tanks were dispatched to help Seven Brigade, and the opposition was speedily dealt with.

The town is built on low coral reefs linked with the mainland by a long causeway, the seaward end of which forms one side of the harbour. Massawa shimmered in the heat of the early afternoon. Clouds of smoke billowed up from the town and harbour, black and smelly from the oil and petrol tanks that had been shelled during the morning by a British destroyer. Dumps of ammunition and war material still smouldered on the north-western outskirts. Obviously, the Italians had been busy destroying prior to surrender.

And at 2.20 p.m. General Heath, accompanied by Brigadier Rees and escorted by a column of 'I' tanks, by armoured cars of the Sudan Defence Force, and forty men each from the 3/18th Garhwal Rifles and 4/10th Baluch, set out from the Swedish Mission. They had been preceded, strictly against orders, by the Free French Commander, unable to restrain his impatience, at the head of a platoon, promptly followed by an ardent posse of war correspondents. Now Heath's party made its formal entry into the town and drove through the streets and along the causeway to Admiral Bonetti's headquarters. Here the Admiral, with four generals and his staff, formally surrendered; their bearing was at once subdued and dignified. It was one of these generals, as we have already noted, who complimented Heath upon "the gallantry of your Highlanders (Highland Light Infantry) at Barentu." Two hours later the Italian commanders were on their way to Asmara with General Heath.

The damage done to Massawa harbour had been great; masts and funnels emerging from the water presented a sorry sight.

THE MULE TRACK AND SANCHIL

The Highland Light Infantry enter Asmara
(Imperial War Museum)

Major Graham, Colonel Russell, Brigadier Rees, Major-General Heath at Asmara
(C.I.S. Historical Section)

A score of ships had been scuttled, some across the dock entrance, some alongside the quays, some in the outer harbour. A floating dock had been sunk. Guns and tanks had been pushed into the sea. The crews of barges had thrown their cargoes over the side. The foreshore was stiff with black oil from sunken ships. Go-downs filled with supplies were captured; more than a hundred Italian guns and much rolling stock fell into our hands. All night the light standards on the quayside were kept burning—there was no fear of aerial bombardment, and the illumination added some attraction to an otherwise desolate harbour.

Brigadier Briggs was left in command of the vanquished port. It being late afternoon, he kept most of his troops outside the town except for certain guards, one of whose tasks was to prevent the enthusiastic Free French from looting. Briggs ordered the Italians, who were still armed, to report to the aerodrome by ten o'clock next morning. It was a memorable and ludicrous sight to watch eleven thousand Italians and another thousand Colonial troops walking to this aerodrome, followed by local porters with barrows laden with one suitcase per head. Briggs placed a guard of only one company of the Chad Regiment over these prisoners. One strand of wire encircled the hangars that became their prison.

Fourteen Italians, whose wives were living in Asmara, decided to make a bid to escape and rejoin them. But they were caught by the Chads and, bareheaded, hung up by their thumbs in the open air. The Chad colonel found the unhappy prisoners in this state, and said that this was all very well, but 'le Général,' meaning Briggs, was British and would be very angry. A compromise was therefore reached. The Chads pitched tents over the fourteen captives. There were no more desertions.

* * * * *

With the taking of Massawa, eleven weeks after the opening of the campaign, more than forty thousand prisoners were in our hands, and 250 guns. Many Colonial troops had dispersed to their homes, and had been encouraged by their officers to do so. Our own casualties at Massawa were small, while the enemy lost twelve thousand men into captivity.

It now appeared as though the Italians who had got away to the south to re-establish the northern front in Abyssinia were defending two main areas: Amba Alagi, that covered the road to Dessie and Addis Ababa, and Gondar, above Lake Tana farther to the west.

Meanwhile, certain important changes took place. Ten Brigade moved back to Asmara to rejoin Nine Brigade. Marriott's troops were still busy out at Ad Teclesan, rounding up deserters. At Wavell's insistence, the Fourth Indian Division set off back to the Western Desert, where the two divisions were to meet once again a year later. The Kaid was making certain that the Asmara district was a sure base for further operations to the south. For our railhead was still back at Tessenei, and Massawa would not be usable for some time to come.

Then, suddenly, General Heath was promoted to command a corps in Malaya. After touring all units of the Division to take his leave, he was seen off by a guard of honour from Asmara on April 12. He was succeeded by the former commander of Nine Brigade, Brigadier A. G. O. M. Mayne. Heath and his wife were taken prisoner in Singapore within a year, and spent the remainder of the war in Japanese hands.

CHAPTER VIII

AMBA ALAGI

MAY 1941

MASSAWA had fallen. The Italians withdrew their remnants from Eritrea along the two main roads that led southwards from Asmara to Amba Alagi and to Gondar, in northern Abyssinia. Although these forces were no longer in a condition to threaten the Sudan, and had little hope of success if they made a counter-offensive to recapture Eritrea, their presence in the south constituted a source of nuisance. It was determined that they should be destroyed or brought to surrender. The task of attacking the immense position of Amba Alagi was entrusted to the Fifth Indian Division.

Amba Alagi lies 235 miles south of Asmara. The strength of the enemy there was estimated at between five and seven thousand troops. These men were reported to be ready to make a last-ditch stand. However, there were some optimists among our commanders, as General Mayne has recorded, who thought that the Italians, after Keren, Ad Teclesan and Massawa, had little fight left in them, and that they would hoist a thousand white flags the moment we made an ugly enough face at them. Others, on the contrary, after hearing from local informers and the first prisoners we took how elaborate were the honeycomb defences which had been carved into the cliffs and crags—already formidable enough in themselves—expected the enemy to fight stubbornly and well under the royal eye of their Viceroy, the Duke of Aosta. When General Cunningham's troops from the south took Addis Ababa on April 5, the Duke moved his headquarters from there and chose Amba Alagi of the three rallying points for the Italian soldiers.

The battle was a hard one, though less costly in lives than Keren had been. The first sight of Amba Alagi gave the beholder a shock. Shaped like a cone, it was the highest mountain encountered during the campaign: close on 11,000 feet. The hills, higher than those at Keren, were just as steep. Moreover, the great problem of maintenance over such a distance from Asmara imposed a heavy burden upon the service units and administrative staff, and compelled General Mayne to reduce his forces to a minimum. In any case, though he would have wished to have his whole Division for the assault, Mayne was required to leave behind four battalions for internal security and to garrison Asmara. As we have seen, Rees' Ten Brigade was selected for this work, with the 2nd West Yorkshires under command in place of the Garhwal Rifles.

By Amba Alagi the road into Abyssinia crosses a spur of this mountain at the Toselli Pass, defended by a fort that bears the same name. These are called after an Italian, Major Toselli, whose force was overwhelmed at Amba Alagi by the Abyssinian Army in December 1895. A little chapel to his memory stands on the summit of the peak. The approach from the north winds steeply for some miles through a narrow valley, overlooked on both sides by commanding heights. North-west of Amba Alagi itself is a long ridge, of which prominent features became household words for the Division: Little Alagi, Middle Hill, Elephant, Pinnacle, and Sandy Ridge. South-west from Amba Alagi runs the narrow Castle Ridge which ends in Castle Hill. Some ten thousand yards to the east of Amba Alagi lies the Falaga Pass, the approach to which is a rough road, the Stretta di Meyda Merra, leading from Mai Mescic, where the Division concentrated, to the Pass where the road finishes abruptly.

Though the dumping of food and ammunition began at once, transport was not plentiful, and not all of it could be allotted for the ferrying of supplies. Certain infantry units had to be sent forward early to make reconnaissance; the artillery needed to range on likely targets; the tasks awaiting the Sappers were innumerable. In this way supply and maintenance once more became major factors in deciding the earliest date on which our offensive could be staged.

It proved impossible to concentrate the force before the last day of April, so May 3 was chosen as the date for attack. But later, owing to difficulties of organizing donkey transport, the offensive was postponed by one day.

At Amba Alagi, though the distance and height from the forward troops to truckhead were considerably greater—six miles and over

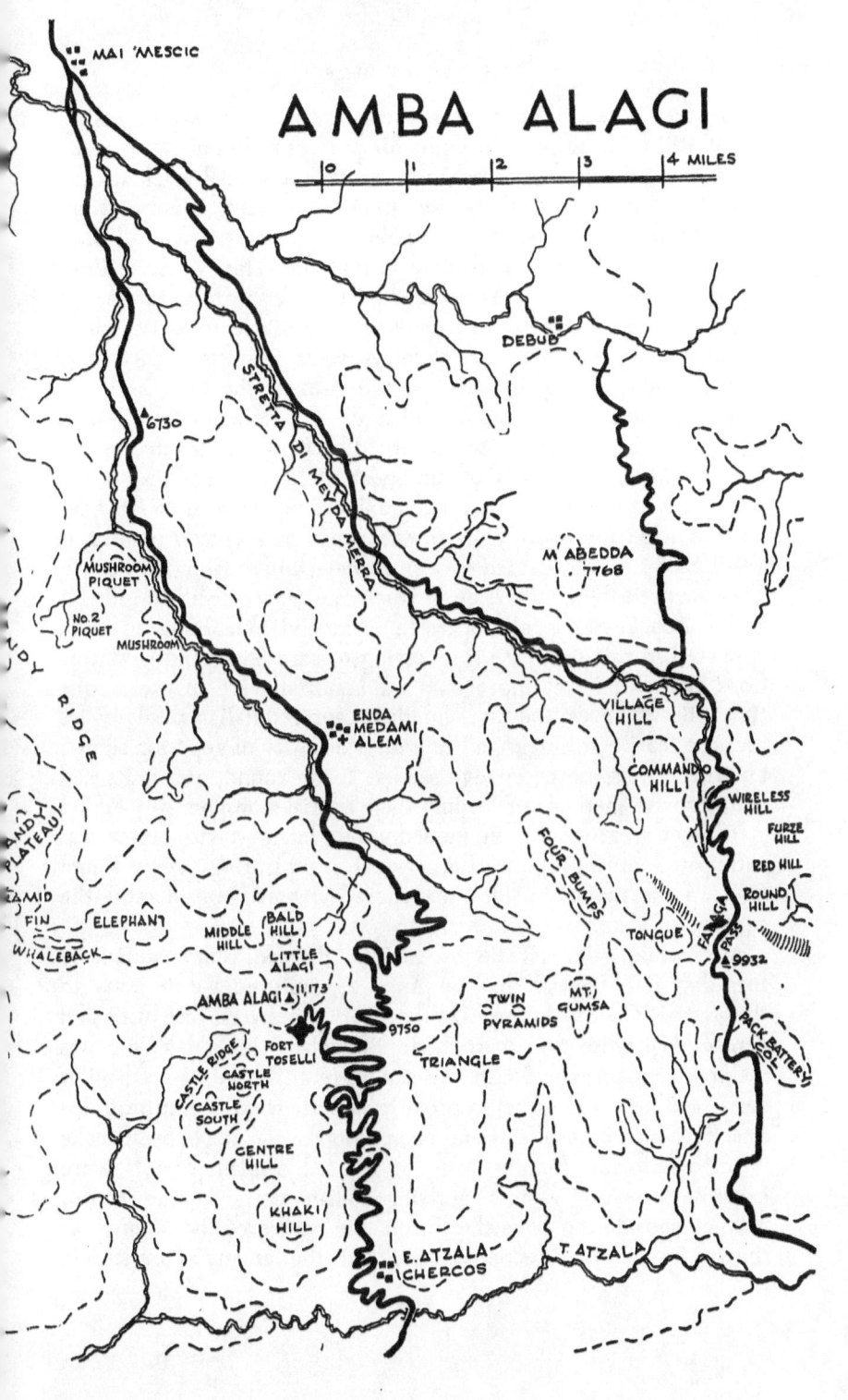

3,000 feet—than at Keren, the routes were on the whole easier. But it still took up to eight hours for porters and donkeys to reach the leading companies. The Sappers made a special track up the mountain, marked with white stones. Initially, dumps were established as far forward as possible by fighting troops, aided by two companies from a reserve battalion. This time, neither Cypriot mules—there was no transport to ferry them forward— nor men from a Labour Company were available to assist, but a number of local Abyssinian donkeys were impressed each day. The Division gave up listening to promises by the local headmen that were never kept and rounded up the donkeys by its own exertions. The animals were collected by *Bimbashi* Martin Harvey, D.S.O., M.C. (an officer of the Sudan Defence Force), who was doing duty as interpreter and topographical expert with 29 Brigade. He had lived for many years in the Sudan as a cotton planter at Wadi Halfa. He was aided by a small detachment from the S.D.F. They scoured the countryside in trucks and roped in all the likely-looking donkeys. In all, between eight and nine hundred were collected in this manner. But, owing to sore backs and to desertions at night, never more than six hundred were in use at one time. Between two and three hundred captured Italian saddles were brought from Asmara, together with a quantity of rope for slings; but there were never enough saddles to go round, and units had to improvise methods of loading their animal transport.

Though great trouble in supplying our infantry with water was anticipated during the battle, several good springs were found high up the mountain sides, and these shortened considerably the carriage of water to the forward troops.

Meanwhile, the 1st South African Brigade, commanded by Brigadier Dan Pienaar, had on April 28 captured Dessie away to the south. The Italian forces still operating between that place and Amba Alagi were thus marooned. But when General Mayne was making his plans, the South Africans were still two hundred miles away, and he could make no provision for their co-operation in his attack; while road-blocks and enemy opposition might well make it impossible for them to assist at all. Abyssinian patriots were exerting pressure against outlying Italian posts in the south. Mayne, considering both the formidable nature of the country as shown by detailed reconnaissance and the enemy's immensely strong positions with posts hewn into the sheer rock, was not fully confident that his plan would succeed with the forces at his disposal. A final appeal for at least one more battalion was turned down by the Kaid. He would not spare it in view of the internal situation at Asmara, Massawa, and elsewhere. But General Platt did take control of operations on the Gondar front, so that Mayne was free to devote his full attention to Amba Alagi.

There were three possible ways of attacking the Italian forces, who had for months been making tremendous fortifications in the Amba Alagi–Toselli position, who had dug large tunnels into the mountainside, and had built up stocks of food and ammunition sufficient to withstand a siege of many months' duration: to the east by way of the Falaga Pass; astride the road straight at the enemy stronghold; or from the right, along the ridge from Sandy Hill to Amba Alagi itself. The enemy, as at Keren, had a double advantage: he held ground which he himself had selected as being naturally almost impregnable; and he had magnificent observation of our movements from the heights he commanded.

But the position had one exploitable weakness: it extended over a distance of more than ten miles, and this made a very wide front for some five thousand men to hold. The enemy could not be strong at all points. From deserters it appeared that Amba Alagi was guarded mostly by Italian troops, in the proportion of four Italian to two Colonial.

General Mayne's plan aimed at threatening the enemy at three points, and consisted of a double feint. Noteworthy is the fact that the Kaid obtained a copy of a book written by Marshal Badoglio about the Italian campaign against Abyssinia in 1935-36. This volume contained a lengthy account of the Amba Alagi district and, more particularly, of Badoglio's own attack against the Falaga Pass. The Marshal contended that this was the best way of attacking Amba Alagi. After careful study, Mayne felt sure that many of the Italian staff officers would have read Badoglio's book, and that they would consequently expect an onslaught against this Pass. Thus the first bluff was to send a force against this flank to demonstrate just where the enemy was especially susceptible to threat. A new Fletcher Force was created for this task.

In the centre Murray's 3/18th Royal Garhwal Rifles, with a detachment of Sappers and Miners, would advance astride the main road and demonstrate boldly throughout the night that preceded our attack. They were to simulate the first steps of a full brigade assault.

And the main attack was to be carried out by Marriott's 29 Brigade at first light on May 4 against the enemy's western flank, advancing along Sandy Ridge. Secrecy for this move was essential. Yet the starting areas were in full view of Amba Alagi. So, too, was the truckhead some miles away. Forward from here no transport was allowed to move. The maps provided for the Division were very bad, and the Italian sheets made from aerial photographs stopped short, tantalizingly, at the Toselli Pass. Detailed knowledge, therefore, of the country south of this line remained meagre until our own photographs could be made available, and it was incomplete until the arrival of the South Africans.

General Mayne relates an incident when, during the preliminaries before the battle proper started, it was brought home to him—not for the first, and certainly not the last, time—how very close, even affectionate, were the ties between the British and Indian troops in the Division.

"I had puffed and panted my way to the top of a sheer peak which afforded the best available observation of the enemy's position at Toselli. The Garhwali tactical headquarters were there, and so was an important O.P. from the 28th Field Regiment. As I arrived exhausted at my destination, a party of British gunners caught me up and were hailed with obvious enthusiasm by some Garhwali signallers, who were brewing tea in a dugout. I stopped for a breather before scaling the last fifty feet to the look-out, and saw out of the tail of my eye much hand-shaking and then the Englishmen squatting down beside the Indians and accepting the tea and cigarettes that they offered.

"Having finished my own business in half an hour or so, I began stumbling down the hill again, only to be stopped by the same Garhwali signallers and led into the dugout. There I, too, was given tea, biscuits, and a cigarette. I took them thankfully, but with mild protest, knowing that every half-pint of water and morsel of everything else had to be carried by hand from a water point over a mile away and nearly a thousand feet lower down, and I asked the Garhwalis whether it was their habit to entertain every

Tom, Dick and Harry who came their way. Their answer was a flat denial. Not a bit of it. It was business enough to keep their own tummies full, and normal hospitality had to go hang. But in my case it was different. I was, after all, the Divisional Commander and a very old man too ! Then what about the British soldiers, I asked. 'Oh, that's quite different,' they replied, 'they belong to the 28th. They belong to us.' "

* * * * *

The new Fletcher Force was formed on April 29. It consisted of Skinner's Horse (Lieutenant-Colonel I. F. Hossack), 51 Middle East Commando, 'B' Company of the 3/12th Frontier Force Regiment, under Major A. J. W. McLeod, D.S.O., and one section of 2 Field Company. This Commando, led by Lieutenant-Colonel Miller, was formed of 60 per cent. Palestine Jews and 40 per cent Palestine Arabs, and included in its ranks Spaniards, Egyptians, Czechs, Armenians, Germans and Circassians. Its officers had been seconded from British regiments. (The artillery allowed to the force was one troop of 6-inch howitzers from 244 Medium Battery, 'B' and another troop of 25-pounders from 28 Field Regiment, and 'A' Troop's 3.7-inch howitzers from the Sudan Regiment.)

Skinner's Horse had already secured Village Hill on April 27 with, fortunately, but few casualties from the Italian pack-artillery fire. This was surprising, as the valley at this point was so narrow that there was no opportunity of escape, and the enemy artillery fire had been at an intense rate.

The one feature which dominated the whole Stretta di Meyda Merra was Commando Hill. This looked straight up the valley with a clear view for mile after mile of the Mai Mescic track. At some points the track was hidden behind a spur, only to emerge clearly a few hundred yards farther on. The enemy appeared to have all the ammunition he needed, and used to amuse himself by sniping at individuals. The individuals concerned promptly left the track and walked along the stream bed, hoping to remain unobserved. Not that the enemy fire stopped. The Italian gunners merely shortened their range every few minutes. For this reason, a visit to Skinner's Horse was likely to be exciting. Possession of Commando Hill and the fact that until April 29 we had no artillery available on the Falaga Pass side made the enemy careless. Men were sometimes to be seen walking on the skyline; thin wisps of grey-blue smoke showed that the Italians were cooking food.

A Commando patrol reported that the north-east slopes of the hill named after them were almost unclimbable. As Colonel Fletcher later wrote in his report: "So they were, but the north-west slopes, which were subsequently climbed, were even steeper."

Fletcher now made his plan for the capture of Commando Hill. The enemy guns were to be driven back by our 25-pounders, which could engage them from well out of range. Then the Italian posts would be shelled by concentrations from our combined artillery, to force their withdrawal from the forward slopes. And in order to make certain that these posts were not reoccupied by night, our Gunners were to put down a further series of concentrations, starting at midnight. McLeod's Frontier Force company had instructions to take up a covering position on the spurs running north from Commando Hill at dusk on April 30. From here they were to support 51 Commando should these men be unable to surmount the feature. Besides, they would be well placed to go on top themselves if 51 Commando needed help in holding the hill. At midnight on the same date 51 Commando were to begin their climb. Dawn on May 1 would see the crest line of Commando Hill assaulted.

The plan worked. On April 30 our 25-pounder guns silenced the enemy artillery and made them change their positions. Miller's Commando had an uneventful approach march to the foot of their hill, which was found to be even steeper than expected. Near the top rose an almost vertical step. Up this step most of the men had to be pulled or pushed. In the darkness few could climb it unaided. But fortunately the time allowed for reaching the crest had been generous. When at length the summit was reached, the enemy infantry posts were found to have been abandoned.

The large flat top of Commando Hill had been ploughed ready for the rains. From the centre of this plateau rose a small mound with a cluster of trees; otherwise the top was without cover. The entire feature, being overlooked by the enemy on a hill called Tongue, was subjected to mortar, machine-gun and artillery fire from pack guns firing over open sights. For this reason 51 Commando held only the bare edge, where they could suffer no counter-attack except on their extreme right. To meet this possible threat, McLeod's company climbed the hill and took up positions. All that night the Italians fired on the track, and in the early morning light flashes of their pack guns could be clearly seen.

The capture of Commando Hill changed the tactical situation. Fletcher Force could now move about in the Stretta with reasonable freedom. Fletcher decided to make a further advance on the following morning, May 2.

Meanwhile, our observation post on Commando Hill noticed a wisp of smoke rising from the foremost fringe of Wireless Hill. Through the glasses were spotted first one, and then another, of the enemy's trenches and breast-works hidden under camouflaged waterproof sheets. They were engaged with 6-inch howitzers to good effect, as a patrol later found. Strips of white cloth had been hung up on rough stakes. The enemy had evacuated his position. And by three o'clock that afternoon Wireless Hill was securely in our possession.

Work was now started on the track leading up to this hill. It had to be made fit for steady traffic by 15-cwt. trucks, because hitherto an excessive strain had been put on all units to maintain themselves. The tufts of grass, which had served as hand and foot holds on the steepest part of Commando Hill, had quickly been pulled out and the only way it was now possible to climb the western face was by means of a rope let down from a tree on the summit. Inevitably, evacuation of casualties had become a matter of extreme difficulty.

Fletcher Force had to maintain pressure on the Falaga Pass until at least midnight on May 3-4. One effect of our artillery fire and of the operations which had already taken place was to cause several hundred Colonial troops to desert to our lines. These men reported that the enemy's defences were very weak. There were, they said, only about thirty Italians on the Falaga front. So Fletcher decided that the moment had come for a bold stroke to capture Falaga Pass. The enemy must be persuaded that our pressure in this direction was no mere feint but a serious threat to his flank and rear.

Accordingly, Skinner's Horse was ordered to secure a ridge that numbered among its peaks Red and Furze Hills. Miller's Commandos were to advance over the top of Commando Hill, move along its two slopes, cross the north-east flank of Tongue, and secure the Falaga Pass. They would also capture small hills named Step and Rump, which controlled this Pass. The attack had to be made at night because the long approach was overlooked from Tongue.

51 Commando's attack did succeed in securing both Step and Rump, but as the approach march took longer than anticipated, these two features were occupied an hour after Skinner's Horse attacked Red Hill. The Commando came under such heavy mortar fire that Colonel Miller judged that, while he could hold his positions by night, he would certainly be unable to stay there in daylight. For this reason he ordered his men to withdraw.

Meanwhile, the enemy moved along the top of Tongue and tried to push down the spur which ran on to Commando Hill. But here they were met by McLeod's Frontier Force company. An engagement was fought until dawn, when the Italians retired. Fletcher noted: "The last which was seen of this battle was a party of some ten Italians running back up the forward slope of the hill while three shells from our 25-pounders burst neatly amongst them."

By this time one squadron of Skinner's Horse on our left flank had reached Furze Hill unopposed. But so stiff was the opposition met by the right-hand squadron in its efforts to capture Round and Red Hills, that one troop leader was wounded very early in the action and the squadron suffered numerous casualties. Eventually the squadron, which had numbered only forty men at the outset, had to be withdrawn by Lieutenant-Colonel Hossack.

Then, late on May 4, Fletcher received orders to continue to exercise pressure on the Falaga Pass. This was no easy order to carry out, for full pressure had already been maintained on the enemy for a day longer than originally intended, and now this pressure had ended with an unsuccessful attack. His men were thoroughly tired.

* * * * *

We must look for a moment at the centre of the Amba Alagi front. On the afternoon of May 3 the 3/18th Garhwal Rifles made their feint. While their carriers entered the Enda Medami Alem valley and occupied it before half-past five, the rifle companies seized, one after the other, the hills west of the village.

And so the last thing the enemy saw before darkness fell was a steady advance towards his positions. After dark our bluff was kept up by active patrolling; one patrol even scaled the precipitous Bald Hill, and this bold enterprise so enhanced the realism of our threat that the Italians thought they had repelled a determined attack. In the background, carefully controlled signs of activity and a display of lights gave the impression that we were arranging preliminaries for a further and more powerful advance later that night.

If the failure on the Falaga front may have seemed a setback to those immediately engaged, it certainly was not so in actual fact, as was realized at the time by Divisional Headquarters and afterwards fully endorsed by the enemy.

The Duke of Aosta later told General Mayne that the Italians had expected our attack to come from the Falaga direction, and had taken it for granted that this was so when we started that way with Fletcher Force. Then, during the night before our main assault, when the Garhwalis made their realistic feint against his centre, the Duke and his generals felt that they must have been wrong in their ideas about our Falaga advance. It must have been a bluff. So they reinforced their centre during the night at the expense of their left. Great was their discomfort when, at dawn, Brigadier Marriott with his brigade attacked the depleted left flank and rolled it back as far as the inner defences of Amba Alagi itself.

General Mayne wrote in his report on the operations: "When looking back from the enemy's point of view on the Alagi feature, it seems incredible that he should not have known of the concentration near Sandy Ridge; yet we have it on good authority that he did not. He failed to carry out any reconnaissance and he had no aircraft."

During the night of May 4 the two attacking battalions of 29 Brigade, the 6/13th Frontier Force Rifles and 3/2nd Punjab, moved to their forming-up positions in the dip north of Sandy Village, while the 1st Worcestershires established themselves in the nullah north of Sandy Ridge. At 4.15 a.m. our artillery concentration opened. The infantry followed close behind. By five o'clock Colonel Malden's Frontier Force Rifles had taken Sandy Ridge and Hill. When the shelling ceased, 'D' Company, who had felt their way to the foot of Pyramid and had found two single tracks on the north and north-east sides of this rocky feature, scrambled to the summit too quickly for the shaken enemy to stop their advance. The officer commanding the left sector of the Italian defences was captured with all his staff officers, 110 other ranks and much war material.

Then the 3/2nd Punjab moved through and by five-thirty had taken Whale Back. An hour later Whale Head was seized and the battalion continued at great speed up the very steep hill named Elephant. This was reached within fifty minutes. Just after half past seven, 'B' Company moved through the bushes on the north face of Elephant and occupied a ridge of the same name.

Later that morning the commander of the 3/2nd Punjab reported that the route to his next objective, Middle Hill, lay along a narrow undulating ridge devoid of cover and dominated by both Bald Hill and Alagi. Brigadier Marriott's reconnaissance showed that an advance straight down to the main road south of Alagi was impossible because of the vastness of the country. As further progress in daylight would be too expensive, he postponed the next attack until the early hours of May 5. The maps issued to the Division had given little idea of the extreme steepness and narrowness of the ridges now facing 29 Brigade.

At 4.15 next morning the attack on Middle Hill went in. 'A' Company of the 3/2nd Punjab captured the hill after a fight with grenade and bayonet. The first line of attacking troops had to bomb the enemy out of his caves and dugouts, which were many and deep. We suffered no casualties, and twelve prisoners were made.

Half an hour later Captain F. E. Baker led the Worcestershires through towards their objective, Little Alagi. They were late. Already the light of day was on the hilltops. They might have got across in darkness, though to have remained in position would have been extremely hard. But now Baker's men were stopped by barbed wire and by heavy machine-gun fire from Little Alagi and Bald Hill. One platoon did penetrate the enemy wire, but the whole company was pinned to the ground, unable to move. Eight men were killed and twenty-eight wounded.

No further daylight progress was possible owing to the narrowness of the front, which lay within five hundred yards of twelve Italian machine-guns. The Worcestershires were ordered to hold the ground they had gained, for the battalion could not be extricated by day. There had been fifty casualties by now, and our wounded were obliged to wait until darkness before they could be carried back. Baker's troops had the misfortune to be bombed and machine-gunned from the air by our own planes during that day; but at six o'clock they were successfully withdrawn to the ground north of Whale Back.

It seemed that 29 Brigade was definitely checked between Middle Hill and Little Alagi. Any further attempt here would have proved too costly.

In the meantime, we may look to the other side of Amba Alagi, to the south and east. Pienaar's South African Brigade had made good progress from Dessie, and was now placed under Mayne's command to complete the encirclement of the Italians and to assist in finishing them off.

It had also become clear that still greater pressure would have to be exerted on our left flank by Falaga Pass, but for this purpose Fletcher Force needed more infantry. General Platt agreed that, as our lines of communication in Eritrea were now more secure, the 3/12th Frontier Force Regiment could be spared from garrison duty. Accordingly, this battalion joined Fletcher Force. So, too, did the 3/18th Royal Garhwal Rifles, who relieved Skinner's Horse.

Marriott's Brigade now prepared to attack on May 8. The plan had been for the Worcestershires to make a second attempt against Little Alagi, but after receiving the patrol reports from the 3/2nd Punjab about the wire and defences there, Marriott was doubtful. He spoke to Mayne, and made it clear that to attack there would be inadvisable. Mayne asked whether the 6/13th could attack Castle Ridge and Hill. The Brigadier agreed that this could be done on the 8th. They were to execute an outflanking movement, while Fletcher Force would attack the Falaga Pass. A further demonstration on the main road would also be made. The 6/13th, with one company of Worcestershires under command, gathered at the Togora Pass on the evening of May 7. They had orders to carry out a silent attack at first light, their objectives being Khaki and Centre Hills, and Castle Ridge.

Throughout that night, in heavy rain and over extremely difficult country, this body moved to within assaulting distance of Castle

Ridge. The men had to descend two thousand feet into a narrow valley. From here they climbed up to their starting line. The approach along this steep and unreconnoitred route had taken eight hours. Their attack was launched silently a few minutes after four o'clock on the morning of May 8. For deception purposes the 28th and 144th Field Regiments put down an artillery concentration so as to give the impression that our troops were about to make a fresh attack on Little Alagi and Bald Hill.

By a quarter past five Khaki Hill and Centre Hill had been captured without opposition by 'B' and 'C' Companies of the 6/13th, led by Lieutenant Sadiq Ullah Khan and Second-Lieutenant G. B. Singh respectively. Then, just before six o'clock, 'A' Company of this battalion, commanded by Major Vidya Dhar Jayal, was seen from the observation post to be fighting its way with bayonet and bomb up the southern escarpment of Castle Hill. The Italians could be seen throwing grenades profusely. These were followed by accurate mortar fire. When our forward platoon forced its way on top of this feature, a strong enemy company was observed to be collecting on the northern end of Castle Hill. At once a thick mist came down for half an hour and observation was difficult. An attempt was made to bring fire on the gathering enemy to break up the coming counter-attack. But owing to the lack of previous registration—this had been deliberate in order to preserve secrecy and surprise—to the extreme range at which our guns were firing, and to the difficult shape of the ground, effective fire could not be brought down in time.

On the left of Castle Ridge some of the enemy put out the white flag as a signal of surrender. When Major Vidya Dhar Jayal sent a platoon to occupy the enemy's defences it was greeted with a shower of bombs, and suffered many casualties. Our attack came temporarily to a halt. General Mayne asked that world-wide publicity be given to this disgraceful episode of treachery, and a protest was dropped on the Duke of Aosta's headquarters. Mayne wrote: "Your Excellency. It has been brought to my notice that, during the engagement on the morning of May 8, certain Italian troops, after putting up the white flag in token of surrender, fired and inflicted casualties on my troops as they advanced to make prisoners of war. I prefer to leave the matter of the punishment of these offenders to your sense of duty, and write rather to warn

Near Ad Teclesan (J. E. B. Barton)

Distant View of Amba Alagi (J. E. B. Barton)

TRIANGLE AND AMBA ALAGI (*J. E. B. Barton*)

COLONEL RUSSELL, MAJOR-GENERAL MAYNE, THE DUKE OF AOSTA
(*Imperial War Museum*)

you of the reprisals that I shall feel compelled to take in the event of any repetition of this treacherous breach of the laws of civilized warfare."

Thanks largely to the gallantry of Sepoy Saudagar Singh, the position was finally taken. He was found lying dead on top of the body of an Italian soldier, whose chest the Sikh had pierced with the bayonet. Four other Italians, who had met a like fate, were stretched out beside them. Earlier in the attack the section commander had been killed. Saudagar Singh took control. When the section was held up he charged forward with his bayonet, even though he had been wounded. Thick scrub tore off his puggree. With his long, uncut black hair flying loose, he must have looked like some demon scaling the hill. Inspired by his example, the rest of the Sikhs followed up the slope and captured Castle Ridge. Sepoy Saudagar Singh was recommended for the Victoria Cross, but was awarded, posthumously, the Indian Order of Merit.

Very soon, when the mist lifted, an Italian counter-attack came in. This first attack was checked with heavy losses. A second advance with stronger forces succeeded after the Sikh company had held on resolutely until they had sustained over seventy per cent. casualties and had run out of ammunition. The wounded alone numbered sixty-two, though most of these were walking cases. Then the remnants of the company were given permission to withdraw. At half past eight our Gunners fired a heavy concentration on Castle Ridge. Half an hour later, owing to maintenance difficulties and to the possibility of it becoming isolated, the Frontier Force company on Khaki Hill was recalled. It would have been possible neither to reinforce it nor to maintain it effectively in the event of yet another enemy counter-attack. 'A' Company had suffered no less than sixty-seven casualties on Castle Hill.

Brigadier Marriott decided to hold all the ground gained, even though Centre Hill was overlooked from the Castle feature. And he sent this message to the 6/13th Frontier Force Rifles: "Will you please convey to all ranks my admiration for the action carried out by the battalion. How they reached their objective is beyond my comprehension. I very much regret the casualties incurred after such a magnificent effort. I am indeed proud to have your battalion under my command."

Meanwhile, the demonstrations by the Garhwalis in the centre had continued to keep the Italians apprehensive of an advance there, and the amount of fire that the enemy put down in this area was indeed impressive.

* * * * *

And what of Fletcher Force? Colonel Fletcher had made a suggestion: now that the Italians were withdrawing troops from his front to resist 29 Brigade's attack on the right, there was a good hope of breaking through. Accordingly, General Mayne decided to replace Fletcher Force by a reconstituted Nine Brigade. Fletcher was promoted to Brigadier—Messervy having been transferred to the command of the Fourth Indian Division—and remained in command of the Force. It had been arranged that the Sikh company of the 3/12th should assault Red Hill at two o'clock on the morning of May 8. They did so with success. The enemy found himself trapped. At a cost of ten men wounded, we captured seven Italian officers and 113 other ranks. Both Red and Round Hills fell into our possession.

Then, as the sun rose, our troops saw for the first time the ridge that ran west from Green Hill to Rump. Beyond this was a deep ravine. On the far side could be seen a higher ridge on which the enemy had established a battery of pack guns. It was obvious that 51 Commando would have great difficulty in raiding these guns. Fletcher planned for them to advance at dusk along the two ring contours towards Rump. Throughout that day our 25-pounders kept up harassing fire on the hill. The Italians were being given no peace, and at three o'clock that afternoon, when an officer of the 3/12th fired a burst from his machine-gun into the opening of an enemy shelter on Rump, they reached the end of their tether. At once small white flags began to appear all over the hillside. Our men were cautious. They beckoned to the Italians to walk over. With some reluctance an enemy officer and forty other ranks did so. It now appeared that the enemy had either been pushed off the Falaga Pass or were finally evicted that night.

Then fresh instructions came from General Mayne. The motorized part of Nine Brigade was to try to penetrate behind the enemy down in the Atzala Valley, while the infantry would fight their way up on to Mount Gumsa, nearly 11,400 feet above the sea. The night of May 8/9 was bitterly cold and wet. 51 Commando tried to advance along the escarpment of Tongue towards the ridge below the enemy pack guns. They lost their direction in the clouds and darkness. By the time they and Dean's 3/12th Frontier Force Regiment had reached Pack Battery Col—the name of the ridge—the Italians had left. Next morning, by nine o'clock, 'B' Company of the 3/12th had occupied Tongue and mopped up all resistance there. It was found that beyond Rump the Falaga Pass road had never been finished. It was thus impossible to send our motorized units through to the Atzala Valley.

On the morning of May 10 another of Colonel Dean's companies moved forward from Tongue and captured a feature known as Four Bumps, from which, on the previous day, the enemy had fired on our troops with machine-guns and mortars. The company then advanced farther towards a hill that rose to the north of Gumsa, and caught sight of some two hundred Italians disappearing on the farther slopes of this hill. Four pack guns were found abandoned and partially dismantled.

The 3/12th had now been fighting for six days with scarcely any sleep and with only three of its companies present. So that afternoon a company of the Garhwal Rifles was sent through to occupy Mount Gumsa. Although on a fine, windless day it might be quite warm at noon, it became bitterly cold on a windy night. Fletcher considered it impossible to ask his troops to operate on these heights without their blankets; in fact, he asked that the men should have extra blankets. As a result, it took three days to get the Garhwalis completely into action on Gumsa. The weather broke and added to the difficulties. So slippery did the road up to the Falaga Pass become that it could no longer be used by trucks or cars. This fact added a further four and a half miles to the mule lift. Some idea of the time and distance is given by the fact that it took six hours to walk from the bottom of Wireless Hill to the crest of Gumsa.

It was from this crest that Nine Brigade had its first sight of Amba Alagi. Fletcher saw that any advance forward from Gumsa would have to be made along a ridge that resembled the edge of a saw. As the Brigadier expressed it: "Each serration of the saw was held by little posts built up with stones and manned by machine-guns, and there seemed no possibility of advancing this way."

Prisoners taken during these days stated that preparations for the defence of Amba Alagi had been started six months earlier, and included many deep shelters and several minefields. These bomb- and shell-proof shelters were to be found mostly in the final peak of Amba Alagi, some way below the church on the summit. The garrison, said these prisoners, had sufficient food and ammunition for several months, but only one source of water, a spring that our Gunners were able to harass by night. It appeared that the presence of the Duke of Aosta with the garrison had had a salutary effect upon the Italian officers. The Duke's headquarters were in a rock gallery between Amba Alagi and Little Alagi. Not that the Duke tied himself to the cover of his gallery. He was frequently out visiting his troops in the forward areas.

*   *   *   *   *

Meanwhile, heartening news had been coming in from the South African Brigade which had advanced quickly northwards from Dessie. So far, concerted planning with Brigadier Pienaar had been impossible, but Mayne now sent an officer across by air to establish liaison. The report showed that our Divisional staff had been a trifle optimistic. The South Africans had not advanced as far as had been thought, and direct assistance from them was not to be expected before May 11. On that same day General Mayne flew over to meet Pienaar and to carry out a close reconnaissance of the Amba Alagi massif from the south.

General Mayne has related his experiences that day. "I was really frightened when I flew high over the battlefield to make first contact with Dan Pienaar's brigade. It wasn't so much the journey over enemy-held territory that frightened me as the foreboding I had that the South Africans would resent being put under an *Indian* Divisional Commander, and might be rather difficult to deal with. They would object, perhaps, to tasks I might give them to do and, may be, appeal against them to their own South African Headquarters at Addis Ababa.

"Never were anyone's forebodings so utterly confounded. From the moment I met Dan Pienaar—he came to the strip where I landed—I knew from his open and cordial welcome that he was glad to see me. And after half an hour's talk in his car on our way forward to his headquarters, there was no doubt in my mind that

I was dealing with a man who was an ardent patriot, an enthusiast, an indefatigable thruster, a highly qualified professional soldier, and one who had a fund of battle experience and was trusted, respected and loved by every single soul under his command.

"When I took him—or, more correctly, when he took me—right forward to view the battlefield from the back, Dan Pienaar asked me innumerable questions, each one constructive and dead to the point. His artillery and infantry commanders were equally inquisitive, and sound in what they wanted to know. Due to their eagerness to see more clearly everything that there was to be seen, we went forward a little bit too far, and just over the crest of the hill which was our selected viewpoint. The Italians from the summit of Amba Alagi, eight to ten thousand yards away across the foothills, valleys and ravines, were quick to react to our mistake. We were well within range of their anti-aircraft guns, traversed down for ground targets, and we had to scatter very hurriedly indeed, luckily without worse damage than a few scratches."

It seemed to Mayne clear that the approach to Amba Alagi was easier from the south than from any other direction. And the capture of the feature named Triangle immediately east of Amba Alagi appeared to be an essential prelude to the final assault on the enemy's inner fortress. Accordingly, the South African Brigade was ordered to seize this hill. Support was promised to them both from our artillery and from Fletcher's Nine Brigade.

Now, quite unsolicited, the Abyssinian Patriots took a hand. Throughout this stage of the battle they proved a mixed blessing. To control them was difficult. Besides the real Patriots, who obeyed the orders of Ras Seyoum, the chief who had been placed in command of all Patriots in that area, there were large numbers of local inhabitants—robbers, looters and even murderers—who joined in for what they could gain. These had no leaders; they ignored requests from British officers, and gave constant trouble to ourselves, the South Africans, and the Italians. The prospect of loot and massacre tended to divide the Patriots' attention, and Mayne issued orders that every endeavour should be made to keep them out of the battle. But before these orders could be enforced, the Patriots had started interfering in the Triangle area.

Entirely without warning to our forces, Ras Seyoum's men stormed two pyramid-shaped hills. Their line of approach was not along the saw edge which would have been Nine Brigade's axis of advance, but rather up the southern and almost precipitous slopes of these two pyramids. The Italians resisted stoutly on Pyramid West, but were overwhelmed. The Patriots then endeavoured to push forward to Triangle, but the ridge up which they had to advance was barred by two double-apron fences of barbed wire, and by many fascines, all of them covered by numerous machine-gun posts. Our Gunners did their utmost to knock out these posts. But they were too well dug in. As a result, the Patriots failed in their gallant effort to cross this heavily defended defile. They fell back to Pyramid West, only to be caught between pack guns and machine-guns from north and south. They were obliged to take refuge on the lower slopes between the two pyramids. On May 12 the 1st Royal Natal Carabineers had established themselves on Khaki Hill and the adjoining crest to the east in order to clear the valley between Khaki and Centre Hills. Contact was made by 29 Brigade with the South Africans here, and a telephone cable laid by Captain Brian Gomm, Marriott's Signals Officer, and his Sikh linemen. Then, on the following day, a patrol found that the enemy had slipped away. This now enabled the Transvaal Scottish to assault their first objective, Triangle, despite heavy and continuous rain throughout the night.

On May 14 they set out deliberately up Triangle. This, like most of the neighbouring hills, began with a fairly easy slope. But then followed a series of cliffs some sixty feet in height, strongly wired on top, and interspersed with comparatively gentle grass slopes that covered a hundred yards or more. The faces of these cliffs were honeycombed with caves, in which the Italians had hidden machine-gun posts and riflemen.

After being checked by machine-gun fire and driven back slightly by one counter-attack when the Italians disgorged from their caves, the South Africans that evening reached a point five hundred yards from the summit. On the grounds of safety, they had refused artillery assistance from the Division. And air targets were now limited to Amba Alagi itself, and to the neighbourhood of Toselli Fort. Brigadier Pienaar came to the conclusion that the objective was too formidable for his brigade to capture on its own. Co-operation was arranged accordingly.

During the night of May 13/14 the 3/18th Garhwal Rifles had

occupied Twin Pyramids. So now, on ground practically level with Triangle, but at right-angles to the line of Pienaar's advance, was a battalion which could provide support. It had been hoped that the Garhwalis would remain unobserved so that they could open surprise fire in the event of an Italian counter-attack developing. But so many Patriots had joined them that all idea of secrecy had to be abandoned. It was now arranged that as the South Africans approached the summit of Triangle, the Garhwalis would make a noisy diversion and help to the best of their ability with cross-fire. Further, between seven and eight o'clock on the morning of May 15 the Divisional artillery would strafe Triangle prior to the final assault.

In support of the South African attack, Sappers of 20 Field Company with Nine Brigade successfully blew lanes in the two rows of barbed wire between Pyramid West and Triangle. This occurred at three in the morning. At dawn the Garhwalis sent forward a patrol which found an Italian straggler. He stated that his company had left the hill during the night, and he proceeded to explain to the patrol the lay-out of the defences. The artillery bombardment was cancelled.

Let General Mayne take up the story.

"The time came when the Italians realized that Triangle was lost. The South Africans were scaling the heights on a fairly broad front, and the troops on the left, directed against the crest of the hills on the Amba Alagi side of Triangle, were making quicker progress than the troops on the centre and right, heading for Triangle itself. So, before South African met Italian man to man, the Italians, thinking discretion the better part of valour, bolted to Amba Alagi, leaving behind their casualties and much booty.

"The moment the Italian fire started to fade away the Garhwalis hurried on, picking their way through the mines and making gaps through the wire with Bangalore torpedoes. The South Africans, too, finding things suddenly very quiet, with less bullets humming about, raced up the last few hundred feet of the precipitous slope as fast as their active legs could carry them. Thus the Scottish from the Transvaal and the highlanders from Garhwal arrived at Triangle at about the same moment.

"Unknown to most if not all of us, the Garhwalis, having seen the Sudanese who were fairly black and the Ethiopians, who were blacker still, expected that the Springboks, whom they had never set eyes on but who sprang, as they knew, from a country very much farther south than the Sudan or Ethiopia, would be quite black!

"On their part, most of the South Africans, never having seen the Indian Army, imagined the Sepoy would look the counterpart of the Indian coolie, with whom they were only too familiar in their own country. Not very much of a man, and certainly not a fighter!

"Astonishment when they met was mutual and profound, but what capped it all was when Lieutenant-Colonel Hartshorne, commanding the Transvaal Scottish, rushed forward and spoke to the Garhwalis in their own, little-known language. The South Africans were fairly surprised, and happily surprised, at what they saw—sturdy brown highlanders, bulging with muscles, who smiled and looked them straight in the face. But the Garhwalis could hardly believe either what they saw or what they heard. Here were people from the far south who were not ebony black at all, but just bronzed, and obviously as white as their own British officers. How could it possibly happen? And, mystery upon mystery, apparently they talked Garhwal, too. But, unhappily, that was not quite true. It was only Hartshorne who talked it. After having lost an arm while fighting with a British battalion in Gallipoli, he took a regular commission, was posted to the Indian Army, and served for some years with the Garhwalis before deciding to retire and seek his fortune in South Africa.

"It must have been a happy little episode up there on the top of Triangle. And the Italian behaved himself. He did not trouble to shell the scene of this first battlefield meeting between Indian and South African. He probably thought that some of his own men were still there. And they were, his dead and wounded. So there was a lull in the battle and a little time for the Springboks and Himalayans to introduce themselves to each other."

CHAPTER IX

SURRENDER WITH HONOUR

MAY 1941

THE seizure of Triangle was a direct threat to the heart of the Italian defences by Toselli Fort. The enemy was now hemmed in on all sides. Nevertheless, General Mayne estimated that our final assault would cost us many hundreds of casualties. He pictured the Italians, firing from the comparative security of their dugouts, taking a heavy toll of our men as they toiled up the cliff face, and then hoisting white flags from each successive cave as it was overrun. It was a very nasty prospect. All that Mayne could hope to do was to draw the enemy's attention towards 29 Brigade and then assault with the South Africans and with Fletcher's battalions, while the Italians were looking, and getting busy, in the wrong direction.

Suddenly, unexpectedly, the Italians capitulated. At half past seven on May 16 Mayne was on the point of setting out with his C.R.A., Brigadier van Straubenzee, on a six-hour climb to the joint headquarters of Fletcher and Pienaar, in order to make final plans for the decisive assault. News arrived that two Italian officers and an interpreter, envoys from the Duke of Aosta, had come into the headquarters of Skinner's Horse under a white flag, and were craving an interview. Mayne postponed his expedition and sent for the envoys. The latter, blindfolded and under escort, arrived in half an hour. The senior officer's name was Colonel Tramontano. His mission was to ask for an armistice in order that the Italians might be able, "in the cause of humanity"—those were his words—to evacuate their many hundreds of casualties into our charge. Would General Mayne also allow the Italians access to water? When Mayne declined to be so magnanimous, he was asked whether he would receive a senior envoy to discuss, on behalf of the Duke of Aosta, terms for capitulation. Mayne agreed.

Why did the Duke of Aosta decide to capitulate at this stage, when he should have been looking forward to the prospect of mauling us without risking many Italian lives? The answer was, as the Duke told General Mayne several days later, that on the night before he sent his envoy, a burst of our 6-inch howitzer fire had struck an Italian P.O.L. dump high upon the slopes of Amba Alagi, and the petrol and oil had flowed downhill into the Duke's last remaining source of fresh drinking water. That finished him. And it was indeed a fortunate burst that saved many British, South African and Indian lives.

And so General Volpini, the Italian plenipotentiary, was sent down to meet Colonel Dudley Russell, Mayne's G.S.O.1, at three o'clock that afternoon, May 16. Russell, nicknamed "Pasha" on account of his bushy black moustache and his manner, was to be seen about the Division wearing a Sam Browne belt over his khaki shirt and shorts, a broad-brimmed hat on his head, with a chin-strap beneath his firm jaw, open-leather *chaplis* on his feet. His legs were distinguished by black stockings and white ankle-socks. Under his arm he carried a walking-stick. During the 1914-18 war he had been wounded in France while serving with the Royal West Kent Regiment, had transferred to the Indian Army, and gained the Military Cross in Allenby's final advance through Palestine. Between the wars his service had varied between four years as Recruiting Officer for Pathans on the North-West Frontier of India, a period at the Staff College at Camberley, and the post of Assistant Director of Intelligence at Peshawar. On the outbreak of war Russell was commanding the 6th Royal Battalion, Frontier Force Rifles.

Russell went to the rendezvous at the appointed time. Volpini never arrived: he had been murdered on the way by free-lance Abyssinians. Indeed, Russell found a battle going on between the Italians in their forward defences and certain undisciplined parties of Abyssinians who were seeking to storm the Italian positions in quest of loot and murder.

The armistice was to be observed from one o'clock that day until seven in the evening. Plans were still carried forward for a Divisional attack by the South African and Nine Brigades in the event of our terms being refused. Some hours later an urgent message arrived from the Italian headquarters: "Rebels surround our positions and are impeding the passage of our envoys as shown by the death of Volpini. We beg you most earnestly to send your envoy with Colonel Tramontano. We ask you to agree to extension of armistice until 1200 hours tomorrow and to stop movement of your troops to south of Amba Alagi. We assure you we will only fire on rebels who are attempting to penetrate our positions. We are constantly expecting to hear from you."

This request was agreed to. Colonel Russell would go next morning from Medami Alem across Bald Hill to Amba Alagi, there to communicate the terms of surrender. During the whole of the next twenty-four hours, and despite the armistice, there was continuous rifle, machine-gun, and mortar fire and bomb-throwing between the Italian forward defence lines and the Abyssinian would-be looters. Nevertheless, on the morning of May 17 at six-thirty Russell, accompanied by Captain C. W. Ridley and Lieutenant C. H. P. Bellwood, the interpreter, with a suitably strong escort of gunners from 144 Field Regiment, made their way unscathed up Bald Hill to Amba Alagi. They arrived soon after midday. The Italians were pleased to see Russell and his companions, and insisted on Russell drinking half a glass of neat brandy after his climb. This he did, after some protest, as he thought it might help to create the right atmosphere. The British officers were then taken to the place where the negotiations were to take place; this had been carefully selected on a narrow path along the face of the precipice. Here Russell met the senior Italian general, General Trezzani, who insisted that Russell should have a glass, this time of neat whisky, before the talks began.

There were two tents a short distance apart, one for the British, one for the Italians. The latter frequently retired to their tent to use a telephone which, as Russell later discovered, was connected direct to the Duke of Aosta.

Two hours later a message was sent to the Italian commander saying that a reply to General Mayne's terms of surrender was expected by three o'clock. Three o'clock came and no reply had been received. Accordingly, at four o'clock a message was sent from Divisional Headquarters to Russell, saying that an immediate report was to be sent by wireless, as the time limit granted to the Duke of Aosta for the acceptance of our terms had already been extended. Half an hour passed, and then Russell was able to announce that, after prolonged negotiating, our terms of surrender, with minor modifications, had been accepted by the Italians. It is not without interest to quote certain passages from Russell's report of his parley with General Claudio Trezzani, which led to the agreement over terms of surrender:

TREZZANI: We have read your proposals. I would now like, with your permission, to make some counter-proposals.

I think that you do not care very much about the honour and glory of the victory of Amba Alagi. What you really want is to open the road between Addis Ababa and Asmara. This you must do, owing to your superior forces. I am going to ask you to save His Royal Highness the Duke of Aosta from humiliation. The terms I will now suggest will in no way affect your object and will in fact differ materially but little from your own.

We propose that we remain in Amba Alagi; we leave you with full use of the road; we will take no action whatsoever against you; you may send an agent here to act as liaison officer; we ask to be allowed to remove our wounded, and such Italians as are unwilling to remain here shall be disarmed and handed over to you; we have sufficient food here and shall not require assistance from you; in fact, our concentration camp will be Amba Alagi: we shall be your prisoners, but we shall avoid the actual act of surrender; we will keep only enough arms to protect His Royal Highness and his garrison against Abyssinians.

RUSSELL: We are prepared to protect you against the Abyssinians.

TREZZANI: But this will relieve you of this responsibility which you will find difficult *vide* the death of General Volpini.

RUSSELL: Yes, until such time as we take over the Amba Alagi position. General Volpini was killed under the very eyes of your defences through your failure to provide the requisite escort.

It is impossible for us to allow a nation, which is unfortunately at war with us, to hold a strong point on an important line of communication for the duration of the war.

TREZZANI: The Duke would guarantee that arms are not used against you.

RUSSELL: I am most desirous, on behalf of His Excellency the Commander-in-Chief, to save the Duke from any form of humiliation; but there seems to be no difference between a disarmed Italian force in this 'Island' and the Duke being kept as a guest of the Commander-in-Chief at Asmara.

TREZZANI: No, here in this 'Island' he would be free.

RUSSELL: He would be free in Asmara.

TREZZANI: If allowed to stay here the Duke will avoid the act of surrender.

RUSSELL: The distinction is so nice as not to be worth considering.

TREZZANI: Then why not accept it?

RUSSELL: He would be living in a prison.

TREZZANI: But he would be in charge of his soldiers.

RUSSELL: Disarmed soldiers.

TREZZANI: No, armed soldiers; that is, sufficient armed soldiers to protect us.

RUSSELL: We will protect you when we take over. The pride of His Royal Highness will have to take second place to our war effort.

TREZZANI: We understand that, but our request does not in any way thwart the British Government, since the road would be open and we guarantee not to use arms against you.

RUSSELL: I must disagree, because the prestige of the British Government depends on reconstruction in Abyssinia; that will suffer if the Italians—unfortunately fighting against us—are allowed to remain in the middle of the country.

TREZZANI: This would only last until the end of the war, and I do not think you will be able to do anything material in the way of reconstruction during the war.

RUSSELL: You can be assured His Royal Highness the Duke will be treated as his rank desires. I am sure the Duke will not want to take such action as will cause more casualties and suffering.

TREZZANI: If left here we will guard ourselves.

RUSSELL: We will ensure his safety, comfort and prestige, if he comes to Asmara. We must have complete control of these Amba Alagi defences.

TREZZANI: You will have practically complete control. Your movement, etc., would not be affected.

RUSSELL: While the war continues we cannot allow such an important personage as His Royal Highness to remain in Abyssinia.

TREZZANI: If you are prepared to be kind to His Royal Highness why not leave him here?

RUSSELL: There are other parts of Abyssinia in which war is still going on. Therefore His Royal Highness must be removed until the situation is cleared up.

TREZZANI: His Royal Highness will give his personal guarantee not to communicate with any other part of the country.

RUSSELL: I must disagree on behalf of the Commander-in-Chief, as the retention of such an important person in Abyssinia is bound to influence the people of the country.

TREZZANI: I do not think the Duke being left here would have much effect.

RUSSELL: I consider such a compromise more humiliating than facing facts. His Royal Highness is a famous soldier and is, I am sure, ready to face facts. In face of our superior material the Italians have put up a fight they need never be ashamed of.

TREZZANI: But the Duke has in effect been a prisoner for some time, so there would be no further humiliation.

RUSSELL: The policy of the British Government is to restore peace and prosperity in Abyssinia. The retention of this small Italian garrison would be a disturbing factor.

TREZZANI: Yes, but the Abyssinians have revolted against Italy, so the presence of the Duke will not affect you in that way.

RUSSELL: There are still a number of Abyssinians sitting on the fence which delays the furtherance of the country's welfare. This would be further delayed by such a compromise.

TREZZANI: The chiefs have never helped the Italians with their administration; the Duke's presence would have no effect.

RUSSELL: We are anxious not to aggravate difficulties of administration, and I have therefore been instructed by the Commander-in-Chief to put the terms before you which you have already seen.

TREZZANI: It does not matter what your policy may be, the Abyssinian has no regard for either Italian or British. The presence of the Duke will make no difference.

RUSSELL: Thank you, but that is not in agreement with those now trying to administer and bring peace to the country.

TREZZANI: I apologize. I was not trying to give you advice, I was only stating facts which we have learnt after some years of experience (*slight laughter*). You may have different ideas, and I hope you will succeed where we have failed. The Abyssinian sides with the strong party.

RUSSELL: And that is why I insist on these terms, we want them to side more with us.

TREZZANI: All they want is to be independent and to steal.

RUSSELL: Right or wrong, our present policy entails the removal of the Italian forces from Amba Alagi. This is a necessary factor to the cessation of hostilities.

TREZZANI: I am sorry you will not understand our point of view. I am a soldier and no diplomat. I cannot agree with your arguments, and I do not see your point of view.

RUSSELL: To be quite straight, we are in a position to dictate terms. Fighting has been the soldier's argument.

TREZZANI: In effect you came here to make proposals, so I have made counter-proposals. If you merely came here to state terms all this discussion might have been saved. We have asked for a discussion, not because we are unable to hold this place, but because, for the sake of humanity, we want to evacuate the wounded.

RUSSELL: In situations like this, as shown in the history of sieges, it is endurance that always brings one side or the other victory.

TREZZANI: If we had sufficient accommodation for our wounded we should be all right. Generally in a siege it is a case of shortage of water. We are not troubled by that, but we have not had sufficient time to make caves for our hospitals.

RUSSELL: In war we always want more time. We have already allowed many wounded, and those whom you did not want to accommodate within your defences, to be evacuated to the south. This will now stop.

General Trezzani then requested to withdraw and discuss the situation with His Royal Highness the Duke. While he was away luncheon was served in a friendly atmosphere.

Meanwhile it was arranged for Major Graham, with a small British escort, to go and look for General Volpini's body. The Italians had already tried to do this, but had failed on account of local marauders. This party went off and recovered the body, and also the bodies of three officers who had been killed with General Volpini.

The discussion was resumed at half past one, when General Trezzani put forward a number of requests, many of which, after a little discussion, were agreed to. The modifications were then written out in both English and Italian and were compared. The

Italian copy, a typed one, was signed by Trezzani and Russell at half-past five on May 17, 1941. One copy was retained by each. Russell signed and pocketed the English copy, handwritten in pencil.

General Mayne has set on record the reasons why, after reference to the Kaid, he allowed the Italians the concession of 'Surrender with Honour':—

" 'Surrender with Honour' was an idea that had never occurred to me and nothing of the kind was included in the terms of surrender which I sent by hand of Colonel Russell to the Duke of Aosta. The suggestion originated with the Duke himself, and as soon as it was communicated to me I felt that I could make capital out of it—that it was I who would benefit much more than the Italians. This is why I thought of it that way.

"Amongst my terms of surrender, which Colonel Russell was to elaborate verbally, was a demand that the battlefield should be handed over 'clean'; all mines, booby traps and such like were to be clearly defined and their location shown to those troops of mine who were to take over the area; there was to be no sabotage or destruction of any kind of guns, equipment and stores; none were to be hidden and all were to be handed over intact to my representatives. All that was very easy to say and equally easy for the Italians to accept. But would they play up honestly? Obviously not, I thought. It would be nothing else than normal, underhand, war-time practice for them to spend the intervening hours between now and the march-out, hiding or sabotaging the breech-blocks of valuable guns and anything else that might be of use to us; and it would be only natural for an enemy conveniently to forget to show us some of the places where mines and booby traps had been laid, and many of our men would be blown up for the price of their 'forgetfulness.'

"But if I put the Duke of Aosta 'on his honour' it might, I thought, put things on an entirely different footing. He was, as I knew, an honourable man and, as a popular Prince, his word ought to be unbreakable law to every single soldier in his army. So, for the price of allowing the Italian troops to march out in military formation—handing over their arms a couple of miles away from the battlefield instead of on the battlefield itself—I should, as I hoped, get a clean and complete hand-over of valuable equipment and stores. And, more important still to my way of thinking, I should save the lives of men who might otherwise stroll over ground that looked harmless, but, in fact, concealed death-dealing contraptions of many kinds.

"As events proved, I was quite right. The Duke of Aosta was delighted with my concession and, as he told me, gave a rigid and unmistakable edict that the hand-over was to be complete and clean, making it quite clear that any breach of his orders would mean that he had broken his own word. So the Italians did play up. We got everything intact and no one, save Abyssinian patriots who broke all bounds in their search for loot and deserved their fate, suffered so much as a scratch from a hidden mine, although there were plenty of them about."

Russell and Ridley had to spend the night at Amba Alagi, owing to the break-down of their truck and to the firing that was going on on all sides. They slept in General Frusci's dugout, where he and his staff were drinking up the wine that remained in their mess. All the Italian officers were gay and pleased about the surrender. Their manner towards the two British representatives was most cordial. Gramophone records were played during the evening, and one record ended up with the Italian National Anthem. Everyone rose to his feet, and Russell and Ridley did the same. The Italians took this gesture kindly, and hunted through their records to find one of *God Save the King*, so that they might return the compliment.

General Mayne sent a message to the Duke of Aosta to say that a parade and an exchange of compliments would be held on May 19 at noon.

Meanwhile, all units of the Division had been informed that the Italians were to start evacuating their positions at six o'clock next morning, May 19, and that they would leave small parties of reliable men to await the arrival of our forces. No British troops would enter Amba Alagi before eight o'clock. The 18th passed as a day of grace for the Italians, granted in order that they might bury their dead. Our troops were busily engaged in preparations for the morrow's move and in drilling the guards of honour.

Next morning Brigadier Marriott led his brigade across into enemy territory at Middle Hill, and took over the Amba Alagi position. Accompanied by his battalion commanders, his Brigade

Major, Charles Nash, and other officers of his headquarters, Marriott crossed in front of the 3/2nd Punjab positions, walked along the narrow track that led to the impregnable Amba Alagi itself. No mines had been laid here, but the approaches were guarded by wire. At the back of the fortress stretched a large open space. The road—an earthy track—fell away in twists and turns to join the main road at the top of the Falaga Pass. Marriott and his party waited for a little while. Then, all of a sudden, a tall figure, obviously the Duke of Aosta, and a smaller staff officer emerged from half-way up the rock and walked towards the Brigadier, who was standing in advance of his companions. They saluted and shook hands.

No incidents occurred. In his diary Marriott noted at the time: "An amazing sight of abandoned material, filth, and the Italian garrison." He also expressed the feeling of all when he wrote: "What a relief that it is all over." The conditions under which the Italians had been living were dirty beyond words. Very little attention had been paid to sanitation, and the place seethed with flies.

The scene high upon Amba Alagi was memorable. The view across hill and valley seemed to be without end. And on every side were precipitous drops into the valley. Everywhere was rock and still more rock; protective parapets had been built of smashed boulders; rocks overhung every narrow track. Bald Hill was honeycombed with caves and tunnels. Of battle debris there was abundance: sheets of corrugated iron, oil drums, splintered wood, smashed basket work, packing-case lids, boxes, splintered flakes of rock, buckled tin boxes, tents, smashed lorries lying in the ditch, planks, metalwork, hundreds more boxes with metal bands, casks. Our men came upon ration and ammunition stores, and even a huge stone bust of Mussolini. Down on the astounding hairpin bends of the Toselli Pass could be seen rows of abandoned vehicles, in their scores. Toselli Fort itself was now but a disordered mass of plaster and bricks, collapsed roofs, corrugated iron that had fallen in, and rubble.

At one place a knotted rope led down the rock face to an Italian cache. Kilometres of telephone wires straggled through the grass and across the rocks. In the caverns used for living quarters were rucksacks and topees, bed sheets and camp beds with gay spreads.

Officers were found sitting on wooden boxes, drinking wine from bottles placed on a packing-case table. One Italian sat on such a case while his hair was being cut.

Besides the Duke of Aosta, the following Italian officers of high rank were captured at Amba Alagi: his Chief of General Staff, General Borgini; General Trezzani; the Chief of the Air Forces, General Pietro Pinna; General Luigi Frusci, former Governor of Eritrea and Commander-in-Chief of the northern front; and General Alberto Cordova di Montezemmo, who until recently had commanded the only Italian field regiment. The balance of the garrison numbered 185 officers, 4,180 Italian troops, and 412 Colonials.

It appeared that General Frusci had fallen from favour, and had been made the scapegoat for the defeat of the Italian Army at Keren. Many of the Italian prisoners remarked on the effectiveness of our shelling. The enemy gunners were emphatic about this, but their connoisseurs were perhaps most concerned about a certain shell which had landed in their cellar and destroyed a vast quantity of Chianti wine. The majority of the captives appeared glad that the fighting was at an end; some of them went so far as openly to express the hope that the British would win the war.

* * * * *

At 11.15 a.m. on May 19 the defeated remnant of the Italian Army marched out of Amba Alagi and filed eight abreast down the hill. As they passed, a guard of honour of one officer and twenty-five men drawn from each battalion of the Fifth Indian Division presented arms. General Mayne stood beside the road, a slim and impeccable figure in service dress, and took the salute. The pipe band of the 1st Transvaal Scottish played *The Flowers of the Forest* and other melodies as the Italians came by. In a group up the hillside, a little way behind the saluting base, were Brigadiers Pienaar, Marriott, van Straubenzee, Fletcher, and senior staff officers of the Division.

In his diary Marriott noted tersely: "A memorable and historic occasion. What a rabble they looked." This comment was indeed the truth. The Italian officers tried hard to maintain some semblance of dressing and soldierly bearing among their troops. But with men stumbling and even falling headlong—just in front of where

General Mayne stood—under the weight of machine-guns, enormous cabin trunks and suitcases that some of them carried on their backs in addition to haversacks, they found it an impossible task. And the lament of *The Flowers of the Forest* ill suited the Italian marching and upset their step. The headgear was motley and contributed by its variety to the air of untidiness that prevailed among the marching Italian garrison; they wore peaked caps, forage caps, topees, broad-brimmed hats, or steel helmets. The officers, some of whom wore polo boots and spurs, and carried ice axes or swords, gave the Royalist or Fascist salute, according to their units. At the back of several companies walked a group of black mammies, and even a few gaily-dressed boys.

After the march-past the Italian Chief of Staff, General Borgini, was presented to Mayne. His companion, Trezzani, wept at the surrender. When the parade was at an end the Italian troops deposited their arms in neat piles in Medami Alem, and took yet another sorrowful look at the bleak background of hills that towered above—Amba, Little Alagi, Triangle, Elephant, Castle Hill, and the other peaks and ridges which they had failed to hold against our determined pressure and assaults. Then the Italians entered the prisoner-of-war cages.

On May 18 special permission had been obtained for Colonel Dods, Colonel Lynn, the A.D.M.S., and an interpreter to enter Toselli Fort in order to discuss with the Italians the best means of evacuating their sick, wounded and prisoners. On the day of the surrender ceremony no fewer than 1,500 prisoners were evacuated by lorry to Quiha. Those remaining in Medami Alem were sent away within two days. And only some 1,200 were retained to help our Sappers to repair road-blocks, to clear the battlefield of salvage, and to put as many as possible of the captured lorries in working order. Between the top of the Alagi Pass and a point three kilometres to the south, three hundred and fifty Italian vehicles were recovered. The abundant salvage to be cleared from the battlefield ranged from naval and heavy anti-aircraft guns to a vast quantity of assorted ammunition and equipment.

This was no easy task that faced the 'Q' staff of the Division, but it was accomplished with exemplary speed and success. In his detailed report composed soon after the battle, Colonel Dods recorded these facts: "The sick and wounded were adequately dealt with, but the lorries with kits intermingled with cars full of generals and their entourage, and marching prisoners, caused a terrific congestion. . . . That a few prisoners got away on arrival at Asmara was due to inadequate escorts and to our lorries being properly spaced out. The majority of these escapees only wanted a few days with their families before resigning themselves to the fate which awaited them. And the civilian population naturally thronged the streets when each convoy arrived, in order to see if their relatives and friends were among the survivors from the battle. Most of these prisoners who did get away gave themselves up voluntarily—the remainder were apprehended in a general round-up before the Division left the country."

*   *   *   *

We must return for a moment to the closing scenes at Amba Alagi on May 19.

The Duke of Aosta was not present at the formal march-past and capitulation. From Mayne he had asked permission to remain for another day up in his cave headquarters with but two members of his personal staff. He had begged General Platt to get him away from his commander-in-chief and other generals, now that the fighting was at an end. The Duke, having lost his official status as Viceroy, was anxious to cut adrift from his military companions.

Amadeo Umberto Isabella Luigi Fillippo Mario Giuseppe Giovanni, Prince of Savoia-Aosta, Duke of Puglie and Aosta, nephew of King Victor Emmanuel of Italy, was at this time in his early forties. He spoke perfect English and had had an English nurse. He fought through the 1914-18 war as a gunner, and a lowly one at that, for he scorned to follow the custom of his fellow Continental princes and take nominal command of an army. When peace came, the Duke began what he described to General Mayne as his 'republican days,' when he surrendered all claims to royal privileges, went into business in England, and travelled in Central and East Africa. Then he was, as he expressed it, enticed back by an offer of command of the Cavalry and Camel Corps in Tripolitania. He became a royal personage once again. Later, he took up what was to be his life's hobby, flying, and after instructing fighter pilots, he returned to Italy as head of the Italian Air

Forces. Lastly, he had, in 1937, been asked by Mussolini to go to Abyssinia to succeed Marshal Graziani as Viceroy.

On May 18, the day before the surrender ceremony, Mayne took lunch with the Duke of Aosta in his headquarters. This was almost disappointing in its simplicity. Hewn out of rock as it was, the room was dark and dank, and devoid of all luxury. "At lunch that day," records Mayne, "he was very discreet in what he said. He talked English perfectly and was at pains to translate into Italian, for the benefit of those of his generals and staff who were invited to meet me, anything of particular interest that passed between us. But after lunch he led me aside by myself and opened out a little. It was then that he asked to be separated from his generals.

"The Duke was keenly interested in the composition of the Division. He seemed to know a great deal about Indian troops, and told me that his men had not been fond of them at all, having expected to find them troops of very inferior quality. He talked much about England, and especially of London. Were the Hammam Baths in Jermyn Street still functioning? Did I think we should ever get back to the days when one lunched at the Cavalry Club and then went down to watch the finals of the Inter-Regimental polo at Hurlingham? Had I met so-and-so lately, and how were they? What fun it was to meet his old friend John Graham again—he was my senior liaison officer—not having seen him since Graham was coaching polo teams in Rome some years before."

Brigadier Marriott, too, recalls the Duke's great charm, his dominant and delightful personality. He had already met the Duke in Cairo, before Italy entered the war. When Marriott toiled up to the Italian headquarters on Amba Alagi after the surrender and march-past, the Duke asked: "Have you had any food? Oh! but you must have lunch." So they sat down in the cavern, and ate tinned *foie gras*, an Italian equivalent of bully beef, hearts of artichokes, and tinned peaches. The British officers were offered Chianti or whisky and soda. Later a bottle of the very best port was brought in. Marriott and his companions were scarcely used to such food and drink at so great an altitude. All the while the Duke's chief of staff sat at the table, looking miserable, and the A.D.C., the son of a postmaster from Southern Italy, did his best to help the general talk along and to see to the needs of his master's guests.

Next morning, the 20th, Marriott again met the Duke by the little cemetery near his headquarters. Here were a score of white crosses, to mark the graves of Italian officers killed during the fighting upon Amba Alagi. The Duke, a very tall and slender figure in his breeches and leggings, knelt down in the cemetery and prayed for a few moments in the morning sunlight. He had been extremely affected by the murder of General Volpini, a close personal friend. Then, his last tribute paid, he rejoined Marriott, and together they walked down towards the main road. On the way the Duke questioned Marriott upon the procedure for inspecting the guard of honour that was waiting for him at the bottom. Three officers and fifty men from the 1st Worcestershires were drawn up in position. With General Mayne beside him he inspected this guard before driving away to Quiha with the Divisional Commander. Here he was met by the Kaid and taken further to Adi Ugri, and later to Khartoum.

Within a year he had died in Kenya from tuberculosis.

CHAPTER X

FROM PILLAR TO POST

JUNE—OCTOBER 1941

As June gave way to July, the Fifth Indian Division set sail from Eritrea. Only Marriott's 29 Brigade stayed a little longer, stretched out as the units were in Asmara, Quiha, Dessie, and Senafe. But all Divisional troops and the three brigades embarked one by one in the humid heat of Massawa. One by one they journeyed to the port on that remarkable railway that spirals down the mountainsides so that you can look out of the carriage window and see other sections of the line hundreds of feet below. On the broiling quayside a number of men collapsed from the intense heat. Up the Red Sea steamed the convoy of ships, and brought the men of the Division without mishap to Port Tewfik.

Three weeks were spent in the dusty base camps of the Suez Canal—Qassassin and Tahag—where the Division re-equipped and trained. Then came orders for a westward move to the Desert for a period of training in mobile desert warfare, combined with the task of preparing defence positions on the Alamein Line. The South African Division was already engaged in digging and wiring near the coast at El Alamein itself. To the Fifth Indian Division were allotted two positions: one "Fortress A," on the edge of the Qattara Depression in the south by Naqb Abu Dweiss; the other half-way to the coast, at what was known as "Fortress B." Up the famous Barrel Track drove the units, heading west from the Alexandria road not far from the Half Way House at Wadi Matruh, and crossing a soft and desolate tract of desert—the area of fossilized forests in which the troops could pick up pieces of fossilized trees.

No formation had made this crossing before. Each brigade moved by battalions, each battalion moved in four parallel columns, driving in desert formation. A brigade column might well stretch to a length of fifteen miles, and by noon on the first day many of

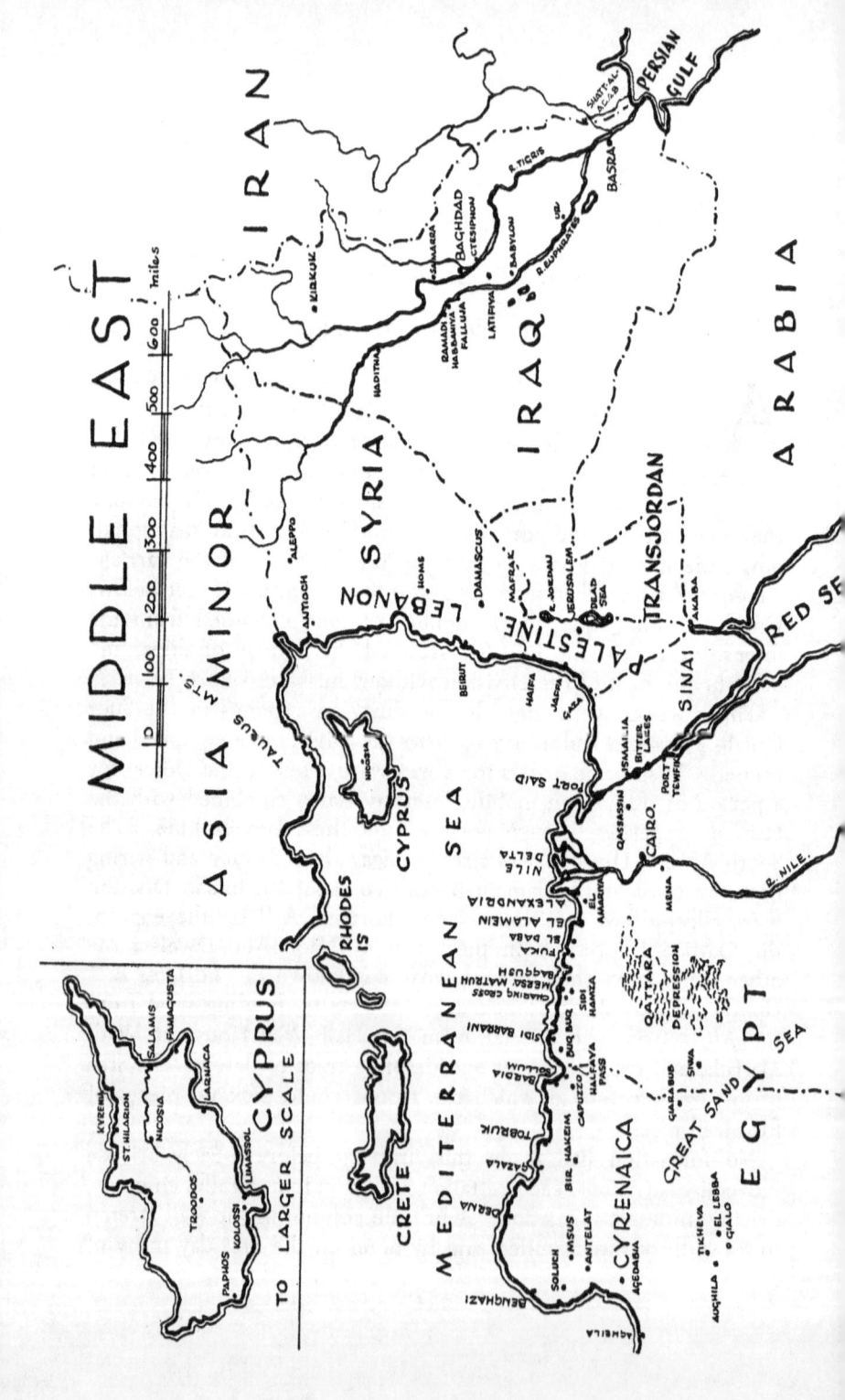

the vehicles had become stuck in soft sand. But next day the drivers had gained experience. By putting all the metal sand tracks and mats of each group into the rear lorry, and ensuring that this particular lorry had a four-wheel drive, progress was less uncertain.

For several days senior officers made one reconnaissance after another, constantly coming to fresh decisions about the precise location and size of these defence positions. The plans were many and varied, but at length agreement was reached. The fortress was designed as a strong harbour in which soft vehicles could take shelter and from which powerful mobile columns that included tanks could sally forth to attack the enemy in the event of an attempted break-through towards the Nile Delta and Cairo. Little did the members of the Division think at this time that they would occupy these same positions and others even closer to Alexandria in the following year.

But on August 22 the digging of fortifications was interrupted quite suddenly. The Division was to move next morning. Rumour spread, as it always spreads, from mouth to mouth. Where? Why? The Division was hurried from the Desert to Iraq to reinforce the Eighth and Tenth Indian Divisions for operations against Persia, and to take its share in maintaining the internal security of Iraq, where the uprising of Rashid Ali and his followers was being quelled in Baghdad.

So once more the Division set off on its travels, this time towards the East and into Asia. A glimpse of Cairo, a night spent beside the Suez Canal at Ismailia, a long drive across the grim and picture-book Sinai Desert to Gaza. Many of the vehicles were new. So were their drivers. The engines needed running in and were prone to frequent overheating. Each day the men woke at half past four and drank their mug of tea by the light of cookers. As they motored across Sinai the sun sometimes shone down through a reddish mist, which suddenly melted away till the road ahead showed clear. And the drivers could not brake their trucks too harshly for fear of piercing the tarmac surface of that road. Palestine was green, hilly and inhabited, which were virtues in the eyes of the Division, and a man must have been pagan indeed who had not heard or read of this Holy Land. Over Jordan and high on the plateau of Transjordan came disillusion, at Mafrak, dreary, desolate, dusty and lashed by swirling, blinding, coating sandstorms. Even the interest of a nearby Roman amphitheatre, villa, and pillared temples could not make weight against the fury of the storm, and two days of Mafrak sufficed. Only the uniforms of the Frontier Force of Transjordan gave colour to the scene of flat desert, black Bedouin tents, a ramshackle village and the local mud-coloured fort.

Then the convoy struck eastwards across mile after mile of seemingly endless, featureless desert, a waste of brown and black boulders, of soft sand in which many a vehicle became bogged, even if it escaped the ravages of engine trouble. The rear trucks of each column were obliged to race and jolt along in order to keep up with those in the lead, and the workshops fitter who brought up the rear was a busy man during that prolonged and arduous crossing into Iraq beside the oil pipeline. Later the Division passed through towns once more, and drove along the black strip of road—Ramadi, Falluja, Habbaniya with its Royal Air Force station and the lake whose shores glitter with flakes of mica.

It was here that the news was brought that the disturbances of the Rashid Ali revolt had already been quelled by the Household Cavalry and other troops who had hurried to Baghdad. General Mayne, having seen his troops start from Egypt, had flown over to Baghdad to get himself in the picture of recent events. He was met by General Quinan, commanding the Tenth Army, with the news that the war with Persia was over suddenly and unexpectedly, and that, although he would put in a plea to retain Mayne's Division, it would probably have to return to the Desert at once.

But having travelled so far, the Division was sent further north to the oilfields of Kirkuk, in case of renewed trouble. No one was allowed to stop in Baghdad, for the Iraqis were still hostile. Our troops had been warned to sit smartly in the backs of their three-ton lorries, with their rifles across their knees, and not to react to acts of open hostility, such as the throwing of bricks or rotten eggs. But there were no acts of any consequence; only an occasional spit, and the throwing of a harmless grape or two by way of a gesture of defiance and disapproval.

The heat of Kirkuk had the touch of hell in its power, and was reflected from the steel structures and the oil drums. It mingled with the all-pervading smell of oil and the melting, sticky roads made of crude oil. Three weeks the Division remained in this place, sweltering in the heat, training, marching as though dazed to the river, and there bathing with a sense of sudden ecstasy in deep pools of gin-clear water that was far cooler than the air above. And a few fished, shot sand-grouse, and enjoyed the club of the local oil people, with its bathing pool that was better far than lying in sweat on your bed and longing for the dusk of evening.

But this vexatious episode ended just as suddenly as it had begun. And at the beginning of October, but a few days after the tail units reached Kirkuk, the Division was heading towards Egypt once again by the same route. It gained valuable experience of travel over immense and wearisome distances, and learned the mysteries of convoy discipline, 'vehicles to the mile,' and 'miles in the hour.' While Ten Brigade and Divisional Headquarters and troops drove to Mena outside Cairo in order to train in Desert warfare with tanks in support, Fletcher's Nine Brigade settled down at Kabrit on the shores of one of the Bitter Lakes, there to train for combined operations. Here for several weeks the men ran up hills, stumbled in the sand, climbed rope ladders, learned to row whalers and cutters, talked the jargon of bollards and bulkheads and other naval matters. For a short time the Divisional staff were engaged in planning a landing in Sicily, to take place in conjunction with the success of Operation 'Crusader' in the Desert, but this project was abandoned at an early stage. It was nearly two years before its time.

And then suddenly again the Division, less 29 Brigade, which had remained behind during the rapid trek to Kirkuk and was now commanded by Brigadier Denys Reid from the 3/5th Mahrattas, was ordered to Cyprus. At first the destination was unknown, and some were disappointed to learn on arrival among the orange groves of Haifa that they were to embark in destroyers for an island. But it was good to discover that the sun which shines on a destroyer cleaving its way through the sea is by no means the same sun that beats down on a three-tonner bumping across the Desert. The crossing to Famagusta, the eastern port of Cyprus, was cold, and the newly issued battledress very welcome.

It was on this journey that 161 Brigade joined the Fifth Indian Division. Brigadier J. A. Salomons, then in command of the 4/7th Rajputs, relates how at Port Said his Officers' Mess had acquired a Nubian named Sambo to serve as dish-washer. He volunteered to accompany the battalion, and was issued with an extremely ill-fitting battledress. The captain of the destroyer had never before had contact with Indian troops, and he said to Salomons that he would like to walk round to see them before darkness fell. On deck there was no room for the men to lie down, so they had to stand or squat. In the dusk it was scarcely possible to distinguish anyone, but suddenly the naval captain came upon Sambo, who was grinning broadly. "I had no idea," he remarked, "that Indians had such negroid features." Salomons was at a momentary loss, for he did not know what would be said were it discovered that the Rajputs were taking an Egyptian subject without a passport. He mumbled something about Indians varying greatly from fair-skinned Pathans to very dark Tamils, and no more notice was taken of Sambo.

CHAPTER XI

FROM GIARABUB TO GIALO

OCTOBER 1941—APRIL 1942

WHEN the remainder of the Division headed east to Baghdad and Kirkuk, Marriott stayed behind with 29 Brigade, and on September 8 moved from Tahag to Burg el Arab. With them as before were the 21st Field Ambulance, the 2nd Field Company, and 23rd Ordnance Workshops. The 144th Field Regiment (Lieutenant-Colonel Clements) was already there, but a week later left Marriott's command.

The Brigade Group, being the general reserve for G.H.Q., was warned that the enemy might attempt seaborne or parachute landings along the coast and the Western Desert pipeline during the last days of September. For a week 29 Brigade kept guard along the coastal stretch east of El Imayid, while the 2nd South African Division watched as far west as Daba. Then the Brigade, being relieved of its responsibilities by the South Africans and a battalion of the Libyan Arab Corps, on September 28 left for Giarabub, many miles distant to the south-west.

Giarabub, a tiny fly-ridden oasis with a Senussi mosque, strange hill formations, and water whose effect is like that of Epsom salts, lies at the extreme southern end of the Italian barbed-wire boundary running down from the coast at Sollum. Between Giarabub and Siwa, seventy miles to the east, a series of salt-water lakes continue from the Qattara Depression.

The plan was to send two parties: to Giarabub the 3/2nd Punjab and 6/13th F.F. Rifles under Lieutenant-Colonel F. A. M. B. Jenkins; and the second party, commanded by Lieutenant-Colonel J. C. O. Knight, with his 1st Worcestershires, the Field Ambulance and the Workshops Company, to Siwa. Both groups were due to reach their destinations on October 4.

By the next evening 29 Brigade had taken over the two oases from Briggs' Seven Brigade, and "Oasis Group" came under the direct command of General Cunningham and the Eighth Army.

It was expected that enemy moves upon the Oasis area would take the form of attacks by airborne or parachute troops against water points, dumps and communications, or of sudden raids by armoured cars, light artillery and lorried infantry, or again, if the enemy made substantial advances in the coastal sector, of a full-scale attack in force. And the order was given: "Oasis Group will, in the event of attack, hold their positions to the last man and the last round."

In Giarabub the outer defence perimeter was held by the 3/2nd Punjab, whose task was to deal with any landings on the town aerodrome; the 6/13th on the inner line would repulse landings in the dump area and on the new airfield. Active patrolling was maintained to give warning of the enemy's approach. More locally, a close watch was kept on Arabs who tried to enter our defence areas. Then at the end of October Marriott's group provided transport, escorts, and an unloading party for two convoys which arrived not far away to establish an R.A.F. landing ground and to make a fresh dump of stores.

On October 15 Brigadier Denys W. Reid, former commander of the 3/5th Mahrattas, was flown down from Mafrak—he was on his way back from Kirkuk—to take command of 29 Brigade; Marriott, a Guardsman himself, had been appointed to the 22nd Guards Motor Brigade near Baggush.

Brigadier Reid's career had taken him into tight corners and the less usual parts of the world where British soldiers served. In the First World War as a subaltern he fought with the Seaforth Highlanders in France and Flanders. He was wounded at Thiepval on the Somme in July of 1916, and again at Passchendaele in October 1917. His first Military Cross was awarded after a raid in January 1916, and the bar for a rearguard action across the Canal du Nord in March 1918. Reid won the D.S.O. for a strenuous attack in May of the same year, on Wytschaete Ridge, south of Ypres.

With the end of the war he discovered that, unknown to himself, an uncle had sent in his name to the India Office in answer to an appeal by the Indian Army for officers. He was accepted, and transferred to the Mahratta Light Infantry. With the first battalion of his regiment he served for seventeen years in various stations, including the North-West Frontier and Burma, spent over a year in the Andaman Islands, and commanded the detachment that acted as escort to the British Trade Agent in Gyangste, Tibet. Throughout the inter-war years he served as a regimental officer, and neither held a staff appointment nor went to the Staff College.

Denys Reid was a man in every sense of the word. Blessed with a tall figure and magnificent physique, he was quite unafraid in any sort of action, under every type of fire, for all his claims to be "a fearful man." Often he was the despair of his staff as he moved calmly among his men in the forward areas. At once commanding in presence and forceful in speech, his was a colourful character, charming and outspoken. His characteristic pose was with his red-banded hat cocked on one side and his steely eyes grilling you. But in those eyes hovered a gay twinkle, as friendly and mischievous as his playful sense of humour. He delighted in pulling other people's legs, and revelled when his own leg was pulled. It is said that he was at his best during a "liar dice" session in the Brigade Mess. He would cover the dice with a huge hand and literally compel you to take a load of rubbish under the cup. If you hesitated, he would roar at you, and lesser spirits would quail and accept what he offered. But those who knew their Brigadier well would refuse time and time again. One officer, an Indian tea planter, would often say to Reid: "I don't care if you do command this Brigade. You don't command these liar dice, and you *are* a liar." Whereupon the Brigadier would roar with delight and slap the officer on the back.

For all his hatred of paper work and his admittedly terrible handwriting, Reid gave out his orders so that no man doubted what was required. And if his decisions were sometimes unorthodox, they were usually sound and even brilliant. In the early days he was frequently unpredictable in his sudden decisions, and could be most obstinate, but when he saw the results of his obstinacy he was quick to apologize and most contrite. He stood up to the worst conditions of weather, battle, physical and mental strain with exemplary fortitude and calm confidence, and was never seen to be flustered.

On the outbreak of war he was second-in-command to his battalion of Mahrattas. That he had been misjudged was shown by his rapid promotion and great success as commander of the 3/5th Mahrattas, of 29 Brigade, and, once he had escaped from an

Italian prison camp, of the Tenth Indian Division. He was a born leader of men in battle, outspoken, dynamic, cheerful, a lovable character at once inspiring and entertaining, who aroused trust and admiration in all those who served alongside or under him.

In the forthcoming operations Oasis Group had as its primary task the protection of such of our air forces as would be operating from the Desert. It was hoped that it would be found possible to establish a series of landing grounds far to the south of the coast and well west of the boundary wire. From these landing grounds our aircraft would endeavour to disrupt and harass enemy columns moving in either direction along the coast south of Benghazi.

It would be the task of Oasis Group to establish, escort and protect such landing grounds and the Air Force staff who manned them.

Alternatively, or even in addition, Brigadier Reid was to plan to advance on Gialo with the maximum force he considered he could adequately maintain. The first object of such an advance was to draw off as much of the enemy's air strength as possible from operating against the Eighth Army's main advance along the coast.

In order to stimulate the deception that Reid's force was far stronger than in actual fact, transport activity was increased between Siwa and Giarabub, dummy camps were erected, and finally it was announced over the wireless that an Indian division was moving westwards from Giarabub towards Agedabia.

An armoured car company of Lieutenant-Colonel P. H. Grobelaar's 7th South African Reconnaissance Battalion, having carried out a disrupting task to the north-west of Giarabub, would operate under Reid's orders; while Colonel Prendergast's Long Range Desert Group was to assist Reid's force by watching enemy movements along the northern approaches to Gialo and keeping in touch with Grobelaar's armoured cars.

For the first fortnight of November, 29 Brigade at the Oases had little of importance to report, but then came plans for the long approach march over the sand to capture Gialo. As Reid himself was not allowed to make a reconnaissance, Colonel Jenkins and Major Kennedy Shaw, navigation officer of the L.R.D.G., were sent as far as Bu Etla, from which it was known that good tracks led the last eighteen miles to Gialo.

It was Reid's intention to attack from the north and west, and

Surrender with Honour (R. C. Watson)

Passing the Guard of Honour (R. C. Watson)

not by the obvious eastern approach from Giarabub. By the 15th he had received no definite orders, so when next day Major Towsey flew down from Eighth Army to act as liaison officer, Reid asked what his Brigade's task was to be. Towsey replied: "Oh! They all reckon you are going for Gialo." And so they went to Gialo.

The column, known as 'E' Force, moved off on the morning of November 18. It experienced no real difficulty either with the going or with the vehicles until the 21st, when two deep wadis with sheer sides had to be crossed. The force was deliberately split into three parts (Reid's idea was that if enemy aircraft appeared, it might seem that our strength was greater than in actual fact): an advance guard with a company of infantry from Jenkins' 3/2nd Punjab, a section of anti-tank guns, and the 6th South African Armoured Car Regiment, all under the command of Lieutenant-Colonel V. C. G. Short. Then followed, in Brigadier Reid's charge, the main body, with the 6th Light A.A. Regiment (Major Sidderfin). And in the wake came the maintenance column consisting of a hundred lorries and trucks, escorted by a squadron of the 7th South African Reconnaissance Battalion, and part of Major Allen's battery of 56 Anti-Tank Regiment. This third portion of the Gialo force was attacked six times that day by enemy planes, which bombed and strafed our vehicles, but to little effect, thanks largely to the gallant action of 6th Light A.A. Regiment.

Next day Colonel Short's column, with Leatherdale's company of the 3/2nd Punjab, drove across the Desert from Bu Etla to the north-west of Aughila, and approached from the south, on Reid's orders, in order to cut off the enemy's line of retreat. This was done successfully. The fort at Aughila was attacked. The Italians waited until Short's armoured cars had driven to within three hundred yards before opening fire. With their large Bredas they knocked out one car, and then hoisted a white flag. Forty-nine of the Bersaglieri, wearing huge cocks' feathers in their head-dresses, were captured.

Following on three hours later, the main column was led farther west than it should have been, owing to an error of seven degrees in the compass bearing that was followed. Appalling soft sand and scrub were encountered instead of good, firm 'going.' As a result, the head of the column did not reach Aughila until two o'clock that afternoon, and then only in a piecemeal condition.

Vehicles were being pushed, winched, or abandoned over a long stretch of the Desert route, so Reid wisely decided that any advance on Gialo was impossible before the 23rd. Moreover, larger stocks of petrol were needed than had been anticipated, because our transport, in particular the armoured cars, had so far used an average of half a gallon for every mile. Major Towsey, the liaison officer, and Captain Trout of the 3/2nd Punjab drove all that night back to Bu Etla, eighteen miles north of Gialo, and next morning fetched enough petrol to enable the force to continue on its way. The maintenance column had once again been bombed without respite from ten o'clock in the morning onwards, and in relays three enemy planes had kept up a constant patrol overhead.

Meanwhile Colonel Grobelaar's force, which included Pearson's company of the 3/2nd Punjab, had also been in trouble, meeting bad 'going,' being heavily bombed, and later engaged by Bredas when approaching the outpost village of Jikhera, three miles north-east of Gialo. But on the evening of November 23, Grobelaar, supported by Jackson's section of A.A. guns, successfully attacked this small oasis.

Reid had been unable to head for Gialo on November 23 as hoped, for the artillery only brought their last gun in after dark, and could not be ready in time. So on the afternoon of the 23rd Reid took his unit and company commanders forward to reconnoitre Gialo, then some thirteen miles away. They approached from the south-west, drove across firm, flat sand, then dismounted and stalked forward until they could look carefully at the oasis from two miles away. Before leaving Giarabub, Reid had been told by our Intelligence that the Italian garrison of Gialo numbered no more than fifty men of low morale. But now local villagers reported that there were more than ten times that number. Gialo, extending perhaps four miles in length and five across, comprised a large group of palm trees with scrub growing beneath. In the centre appeared the top of the fort. To the east and west the sand was undulating, and small clumps of huts, wells and pumpkin patches were visible.

Brigadier Reid decided upon a night approach march and a dawn attack from the south-west: the Italians afterwards confessed that they had considered this quite impossible. 'E' Force had little time to prepare, and none of the troops had ever done night driving on such a scale before. The little column assembled at midnight—three weak companies of Jenkins' 3/2nd Punjab, the company of armoured cars, eight 25-pounder guns, and a battery of anti-aircraft and anti-tank guns.

Very early in the morning of the 24th they set out, moving through the night with fifteen yards between one vehicle and the next. They travelled eleven miles and came to the assembly area three thousand yards from the edge of Gialo oasis. Reid's headquarters remained here, dug themselves in, and camouflaged their vehicles. The infantry climbed out of their lorries and deployed for the attack. To reach their objective—the fort—meant a very exposed approach march through heavily bushed sand mounds and belts of palm trees.

Short and his armoured cars, with Leatherdale's Dogra company, created a diversion over by Gialo aerodrome and towards El Libba. They came under heavy fire from Italian Breda guns, but destroyed an enemy plane on the ground. One squadron of the 7th South African Reconnaissance Battalion, under Captain Flint, demonstrated noisily along the western flank of Gialo, and was fired upon.

The leading companies of the 3/2nd Punjab had in the meantime set off across the soft sand and met no opposition for a mile and a half, when the men made a temporary halt to regain their breath before the final assault. The going had been hard and exhausting. It took an hour to make contact with the enemy. Ahead rose a series of large mounds fifteen feet or so in height, covered with evergreen bushes. Towards the first of these mounds walked the leading platoon on the left. When they came to within 150 yards they were received with intense fire from six Italian machine-guns and Bredas. The Punjabis dropped to the ground as though dead, but not one man had been hit, as was found when the platoon was later extricated. They were for the time being pinned to the ground, and spent two most uncomfortable and indecisive hours. Each pimple seemed to be defended with Bredas and machine-guns, and our artillery could not destroy them, because nothing less than a direct hit would achieve this in the soft sand. And to judge distance and so find the range was in itself a problem.

By midday it was obvious that unless each individual mound could be dealt with by mortars, anti-tank guns or field artillery, any further advance would be most costly. No progress was being made. Force headquarters had been bombed and ground-strafed in unpleasant fashion by four German Messerschmitt fighters. Just in time came a pair of our Hurricanes to drive off the enemy aircraft and shoot down one of them. At length Brigadier Reid decided, after making a further reconnaissance, to send the Punjabis in to attack from the west at half-past seven that evening, after a short artillery concentration.

Accordingly, two companies under Major W. V. S. Leatherdale and Captain F. N. Betts walked forward soon after sunset. The advance was silent and determined. The bushy pimples, so heavily guarded by fire power, were this time captured one by one at the point of the bayonet. Throughout their attack our infantry were supported by a squadron of Short's armoured cars, which shone their lights and demonstrated vigorously from the eastern flanks and approaches to Gialo, and by our medium machine-guns, although these were in turn fired on with tracer and explosive bullets.

In the meantime the company on the left, having made a long detour, charged the fort with great dash and courage, and took it. Only this was not the fort after all, but only part of the Arab village. The real fort must be taken before nightfall. Soon the Punjabis spotted it, attacked with grenades, Tommy guns and the bayonet, and took the mud-walled fort to the shouts of their war-cry, "Ali, Ali." The men found a dozen Italians dead or wounded within the walls, and a further twenty were taken prisoner. The success signal was fired. Silence fell.

At once Brigadier Reid and Jenkins jumped into a truck and were driven by Trout at full speed to the fort. They flashed their headlamps all the way across the mile and more of sand, to give warning of their approach and to prevent the Punjabi company from firing in error at their own commanders. Reid was met by Major Leatherdale and a score of dejected Italian prisoners. He looked round the fort and interviewed these prisoners, one of whom spoke French. This Italian volunteered to lead the Brigadier to a nearby building, the Presidio, where the enemy commandant was thought to be. So Reid, with Jenkins and three other officers, walked down and there found two sentries standing outside the gates of this white-painted Presidio with its crenellated walls. A pistol was held to their heads, the sentries opened the gates with unusual haste, and there inside in the darkness the British party heard a sound like the hum in a theatre during the interval. This noise turned out to be about fifteen Italian officers and seventy soldiers, who meekly handed over their weapons and lined themselves against the wall outside. The officers had been on the point of sitting down to a good dinner. Reid summoned an escort from the fort. Not that the Italians gave any trouble. They seemed to regard our five officers as sufficient guard. When an escort did arrive the Italian officers were locked up in their own mess, while the men were placed in the large court-room, on the walls of which hung two immense portraits, one of King Victor Emmanuel, the other of Benito Mussolini.

That night our patrols combed the oasis, many more prisoners were brought in, and by morning the court-room held more than a hundred captives. King Victor Emmanuel still hung on the wall, but Mussolini lay on the floor with a boot through his face.

When daylight came the whole area of the fort and Presidio was in our hands. At eight o'clock Betts' Sikh company cleared the western oasis, attacked and captured several Breda and machine-gun nests, and rounded up another forty Italians. In the El Libba area to the east Colonel Short's South African armoured cars were engaged on the flank, and when the cars became stuck in the very soft sand there, Short collected a dozen of his men—most of them mechanics—and led a successful bayonet charge. They cleared up the last pocket of resistance.

All day prisoners came in, and by late afternoon, when the enemy resistance finally ceased, the total number of Italians captured was 670. And Reid's armoury was the richer for twenty-five large Bredas and a wide selection of other weapons.

* * * * *

We must rapidly summarize the activities of 'E' Force during the next three months. Its first task was to co-operate with Marriott's 22nd Guards Brigade in getting across the enemy's line of withdrawal near Antelat in the country south of Benghazi. Contact was not made until Christmas Eve, and touch was also gained with the 1st Armoured Division, commanded by Major-General Frank Messervy. Reid had columns out each day harassing the enemy on the coastal road towards El Agheila, and this district was the scene of many little actions in which his columns, made up of armoured cars, platoons of the 3/2nd Punjab and one or two guns, attempted to stem the stronger patrols and larger columns of the enemy. Early in January the 7th Support Group, led by Brigadier Jock Campbell, arrived in the same area and started operating columns alongside Reid. This only lasted a fortnight, after which Campbell's troops went back to Egypt, and Reid was ordered to return to disband his force in the Delta.

But then the Germans struck back, and for the next month Reid's little columns were engaged side by side with the Fourth Indian Division in the withdrawal of our forces step by step, counter-attack by counter-attack. During this period 'E' Force operated under the 1st Armoured Division, and on its southern flank, in the withdrawal by way of Msus to Cherrubba. From there it was suddenly ordered into the Jebel to join the Fourth Indian Division, under whom it fought in the withdrawal to the Gazala line. In February Reid took command of Tobruk, with 29 Brigade reunited after ten weeks. The Worcestershires and 6/13th F.F. Rifles rejoined, and the Brigade stayed in Tobruk until the end of March. Then, having handed over to the 2nd South African Division, 29 Brigade moved back through Capuzzo to what were known as "The Kennels" by El Hamra. Here Reid and his men worked on the defences and trained and improved their standard of navigation and Desert craft till it reached the highest standard. Nothing of great importance occurred until the coming of the Fifth Indian Division to the Western Desert from Cyprus.

But first we may see how the Division spent its time on that beautiful and historic island.

CHAPTER XII

CYPRUS INTERLUDE

NOVEMBER 1941—APRIL 1942

To the men who had come from the Desert and Iraq, Cyprus was an utter contrast. Gone were the sandy miles of no landmark, no green thing, no tree. Now there were flowers and hills, rivers and trees. Those who disembarked in Famagusta and drove along the coast road could wonder what lay round the corner, what the brow ahead concealed. In the Desert there were no such hidden bends. The Division had quitted the Egyptian desert, still scorching in the hot season. Cyprus was now on the brink of winter. The first rains would fall within a month.

After Egypt, Cyprus was to the troops an island that seemed backward, under-developed, and content to remain so. It was a place cut off from the mainland by more than the Mediterranean Sea. Though from the mountains about Troodos could be glimpsed the deep shadow of Syria and the Lebanon sixty miles distant to the south-east, and in the north, still closer, the mountain peaks of Taurus in Asia Minor, nine-tenths of the people of this island had never left its shores.

In Cyprus, too, East meets West, for the Turks and Greeks live together. The Turk still wears his fez and the *vraka*—quaint, voluminous pleated trousers made from cloth that is indigo or black. The Greeks are to be found rather among the merchants, lawyers and money-lenders. At their doors the shopkeepers sit, smoking their hookah pipes. In the coffee-houses of the towns and villages men drink black coffee while they talk and play dominoes. Cyprus is an island of peasant farmers, fishermen and craftsmen; and of the people three-quarters work on the land.

The villages in the hills and valleys are either all Greek or all Turkish. Those in the hills consist of little better than primitive hovels with sun-baked walls of mud and straw, attractive when seen from afar. In narrow lanes the flat-roofed houses stand close one to the next, their wooden balconies gay with a splash of flowers. Often a slim minaret casts its shadow across the village and recalls the Orient to those who see it. On the coast the villages are more advanced, by virtue of a shop or two and some small café. Down the narrow streets of the towns walk black-robed priests of the Greek Orthodox Church. Here and there women pass by, wearing their coloured veils. And in the gutters and squares the naked children play.

Wealth lies in the hands of the few—usually the Greeks—and to gain a living demands a struggle. In Lefkara in the south and centre of the island the women still weave their lace. Many a girl has worked till her eyes have become too weak to do more than the lace edgings. You can watch a mother and her three daughters at work upon the same bedspread.

Cyprus is a blend of wooded mountains and arable plain. Terraced hills with dark forests slope down to a coastline shaped by little bays edged with white sand and half shielded by rows of olive trees. There are cedar trees and cypress, tall pines and massive gum trees. Acacias grow, and oaks, and the grey-green eucalyptus tree. Acres of land are given up to row upon row of orange trees and olives, citrus and grapefruit. From the dark and glossy carob trees comes the bean sent across the sea for cattle food. Of fruit there is abundance and variety: oranges and peaches, figs, apricots and pomegranates, lemons and cherries and olives. Dense vineyards cover large stretches of hillside and plain. Waving fields of barley and wheat catch the eye, as do red poppy splashes and clusters of purple bougainvilia against the white stone houses.

Along the dusty roads, when the rains are still awaited, sway the rough country carts pulled by oxen. These beasts are yoked to the plough in the fields. Strings of camels lurch past, laden with timber and merchandise. From the thousands of goats that wander about the island in their flocks come milk and cheese and sustenance for the poor. Fierce dogs bound and bark by the country farms, and Cyprus possesses countless stray dogs that prowl about the streets and villages. Watchful lizards lie basking on sun-warmed rocks or scuttle from sight at the sound of footsteps.

This is an island upon which the marks of religions and history, traditions and personalities remain vivid and strong. Almost

CYPRUS INTERLUDE

nineteen hundred years before, Paul and Barnabas had landed at Salamis, then the commercial capital, and crossed to Paphos, in the south-west corner. Here they had converted to the Christian faith the Roman pro-consul. More than eleven and a half centuries later Richard the Lionheart had married Berengaria of Navarre in a chapel at Limassol. Cyprus had been owned in turn by the Knights of the Temple, the Lusignan family, and the Venetians. Then had come the Turks to conquer and to hold for three hundred years, a period as long as that during which the Lusignan dynasty held sway.

Othello the Moor was said to have murdered Desdemona in the tower at Famagusta. And the legend tells how Aphrodite, Goddess of Love, was born of the foam, off the coast by Paphos where the Mediterranean waves break on rocks. In the early eighties the future Kitchener of Khartoum, then a captain of Engineers, was Director of Survey.

The civilizations of Greece and Rome, Christendom and Islam, Venice, Genoa and Turkey had left their imprint upon the island. And witness to this is borne by such splendid ruins as the fortified palace of the Lusignan dynasty in Kyrenia, the castle of St. Hilarion on its precipitous mountain top, the beautiful Abbey of Bellapais that lies in the green foothills behind Kyrenia, the Venetian walls and gateways of Famagusta and Nicosia, the square keep of Kolossi Castle, built by the Knights of the Hospital, and the traces of Greece and Rome in the temples, forums and pillars of Salamis, Curium and Paphos.

It was to the defence of this island and its people that Mayne's Division came in the first days of November 1941. It relieved the 50th British Division. To bluff the enemy Intelligence, advanced headquarters in Nicosia was given the designation of 18 Corps, rear headquarters at Larnaca received that of an Indian division, while all those units in the Nicosia area that had been placed under the command of Brigadier van Straubenzee, the C.R.A., were known collectively as the 7th Division.

The task of the Division was to prepare against an enemy airborne attack on Cyprus. General Sir Claude Auchinleck, Commander-in-Chief, Middle East, had told Mayne before he left Egypt that Cyprus must be held at all costs. There would be no question of withdrawing the garrison, even in the event of enemy attack on the heaviest scale. Nor was there to be a repetition of our failure in Crete. To that end the garrison was to be made "to fit the island" instead of pretending, as hitherto, that the island was adequately defended by whatever garrison happened to be there. Mayne was to demand such additional reinforcements of units and equipment as he deemed essential for his plans. This directive smoothed his path, and in due course—in fact, quite soon—he received all that he asked for, including the Household Cavalry and the Yorkshire Dragoons to add punch to the counter-attack troops. Four battalions from the Indian State Force came to relieve the regular battalions from their task of static defence of the main landing grounds that we intended to use.

The principle of defence was contained in the dictum: "Mobile and aggressive defence based on secure harbours." It was considered that invasion might be made by enemy forces from Southern Anatolia as well as from Crete and the Dodecanese Islands. General Mayne laid down his intention in these terse words: "To deny to enemy forces, whether seaborne or airborne, access to the Island; and to preserve the security of aerodromes for the operation of our own aircraft."

To these ends, Rees' Ten Brigade Group, which included the Household Cavalry, was entrusted with defending the eastern part of Cyprus; 161 Brigade Group under Brigadier Stamer, with Skinner's Horse attached to it, was responsible for the north-west area; and to Fletcher's Nine Brigade went the problem of guarding the south-west. Van Straubenzee's 7th Division, comprising the 3rd Hussars in tanks, the motorized Sherwood Foresters, 1st Field Regiment of 25-pounders and a field company of sappers, was quartered around Nicosia and formed the counter-attack reserve under control of the "Corps" Commander.

A system of coast watching and inland observation was set afoot. The sappers of the Division under Colonel Napier made preparations to demolish, in case of dire need, the all-weather runways of aerodromes and harbours, jetties and port facilities, particularly along the south coast of the island, and to block the vital roads across the Kyrenia hills. Minefields were laid. Plans were drawn up for the destruction of dumps, in case some of them fell into the enemy's hands. Prohibited areas were announced. Great attention was paid to camouflage; preparations were made for the disposal of civilian transport in the event of a "stand to"; and the role of the civilian governor in the event of an invasion was settled. So, too, was the control of the local population, to prevent panic and streams of refugees. To all landowners with large expanses of flat land went orders for the erection of mounds five feet in height, spaced at 100-yard intervals and designed to obstruct aircraft landings.

During the first month in particular all the units of the Division were busily engaged in completing their defensive arrangements. They built new battalion command posts and signal offices. Camouflage was improved, dumps were dispersed or resited.

The 4/7th Rajputs, who defended the airport of Nicosia, had taken over from the 8th Durham Light Infantry. These men, who were mostly Durham miners, had dug deep, and the Rajputs continued the work. Digging was nothing new to them, for during the first winter of war the battalion had dug a complete defensive position in the sandhills near Mena, outside Cairo. On this the original Army of the Nile had practised attacks in co-operation with tanks. In the following summer the Rajputs had been called on to dig yet another defence position to the east of Mersa Matruh. The airfield outside Nicosia was their third full-scale effort.

General Mayne had decreed at the very start that each infantry battalion was to make at least two companies mobile. Salomons has recorded the episode that ensued. "At first," he writes, "this was a bit of a shock, as we had just finished positions for the whole of the battalion. And when Brigadier Stamer came round to 'vet' my proposals for the defence of the airport with only two companies, we certainly looked a bit thin on the ground . . .

" 'I hope,' said Stamer, brushing up his moustache with the thumb and forefinger of his left hand, and with the usual twinkle in his eye, 'that posterity will not say: Who were the two fools responsible for the loss of the Nicosia airport? Couple of S's they were—ah, yes—Stamer and Salomons.' "

Later, when reinforcements of static Indian State Force battalions and of equipment had arrived, it was possible to fully motorize practically every regular battalion and to organize really strong mobile columns of all arms from each of the three brigade groups. It was then, at the end of January 1942, that the Division began to feel fully confident in itself and sure that if the invasion came to pass, the enemy would get the knock-out he deserved. And the "Fighting Fifth" would add fresh laurels to the reputation it had already won.

As the main instrument of resistance to invasion was the employment of mobile columns of all arms, one of the urgent tasks was the improvement and widening of certain new roads in Cyprus. Some were narrow and bad. Mobility demanded good arteries for rapid communication. Columns must be able to be rushed from point to point to meet any threat anywhere. Accordingly, the units lent aid to the engineers in the form of men and lorries. Local labour, too, was employed on these roads, and even the women could be seen at work on excavation.

During December and January this labour on roads and defences was hampered by the heavy rains. These fell in periods of two or three days, with a dry day in between. All but the main roads became impassable to transport for three-quarters of the time. Many were the trucks bogged in deep mud, and minor accidents were frequent.

Although these works were to be carried through at speed, units sent men to demonstrations and on courses; TEWTS and mobile exercises were planned and held at every level—battalion, brigade and division—and gas-masks were worn on what were known as "Brigade Gas Days." To add zest or disappointment to the daily routine, there came the usually fruitless or groundless reports of unidentified aircraft, investigations of flashing lights at sea, explosions and Very lights.

These four months provided a happy though strenuous interlude for the members of the Division. Despite the meeting of East and West, Cyprus appeared more like Europe than any place they had been in for many months. True it is that some men found the island cramping and oppressive; once the novelty of Cyprus had worn thin they longed to return to the Desert, where they had left behind their comrades of the 29th Brigade, and a few began to suffer from what they called "islanditis." But for most soldiers Cyprus, with its good food and abundant wines, its syrupy and amber-coloured Commanderia, famous from the days of the Grand Commander of the Knights of St. John of Jerusalem, its white Aphrodite and its sherries, with the green fertility and pleasing climate, induced a sense of well-being and enjoyment. Opportunities for extensive sightseeing were closed to all but a few, though some fortunates recaptured the joys of winter sports in the snows about Troodos, or enjoyed good duck shooting.

British and Indian alike made firm friends among the islanders. Dances were held, and parties in the hotels.

By contrast there were some who recalled vividly the combined Sunday service in the ruins of the church at Famagusta. The church, which was full to the outer walls, had no roof, and tufts of grass were growing inside. On a cold November day the theme of the service was *Then and Now*, and during its course the congregation dedicated themselves to the same cause as that fought for by the Crusaders.

One of the R.E.M.E. workshops had an Indian whose father was a parson. This Madrassi Telugu played the organ in the little church in Larnaca on many Sundays, and when the time came for the Division to leave Cyprus the Christian Indian other ranks presented a lamp to this church. Remarkable, it appears, was the look of wonderment upon the faces of the British troops.

CHAPTER XIII

ENTRY INTO THE DESERT

APRIL—MAY 1942

TEN BRIGADE, now commanded by Brigadier Charles H. Boucher, Rees having left to take the reins of the Tenth Indian Division, were the first to sail away from Cyprus. On March 12 they travelled in the *Antwerp* to Haifa. Trains bore them south across Palestine and Sinai to Qassassin again. Then on April 8 the Brigade set off for the Western Desert, and moved through Amariya and Mersa Matruh to Halfaya. Meanwhile Fletcher's Nine Brigade embarked early in the month at Famagusta and sailed direct to Alexandria. During this crossing to Egypt the ships, escorted by a destroyer, were bombed by a German plane, fortunately without damage or casualties. It was a Sunday, and when the attack started the West Yorkshires and others were at church service, in the act of singing the hymn "For those in peril on the sea."

On April 15 Divisional Headquarters and Nine Brigade moved westwards to the Sollum box, and in company with all other divisions in the Middle East reorganized on a Brigade Group basis. This meant that artillery regiments, field companies of engineers, field ambulances and other service units and detachments were placed under direct command of the brigade in question and helped to form the group.

Here in the Desert Reid's 29 Brigade, already at El Hamra, rejoined the Division after a long period away with the Eighth Army. Nine and Ten Brigades concentrated first on the flat, stony ground near Sollum, and then on the 25th linked up with Reid's force at the Kennels by El Hamra.

The Desert here was stony and almost bare of sand, and when the winds blustered in from the sea they could swirl but little dust. There were no caves or buildings as at Sollum, where the Highland Light Infantry had housed their mess and orderly room in caverns.

But the water of the Kennels was sweeter than before; at Sollum it had tasted brackish and salt, no doubt tolerably palatable with tea or gin and lime, but horrid with whisky. And the water ration increased to one gallon a day for each man, with the same quantity for the vehicles. Throughout this period frequent and heavy dust storms blew up, and the men learned to endure days on end of the *khamseen* with its stinging blast. The heat was often fierce, and many suffered from heatstroke. But while at Sollum parties had driven down the Halfaya Pass to the seashore and bathed. Anti-aircraft sentries were mounted, and the men took grenades in case they met a shark.

This was a time of changes within the Division. In Cyprus the 3/5th Mahratta Light Infantry, the 6/13th Royal Frontier Force Rifles, and the 3/18th Royal Garhwal Rifles were posted away: the Commander-in-Chief decided to strengthen six Indian brigades without battle experience by drafting to each an Indian battalion from the Fourth and Fifth Indian Divisions. To replace the Mahrattas in Nine Brigade came the 3/9th Jats, commanded by Lieutenant-Colonel H. V. Bragg, M.C. At the beginning of May, while 29 Brigade were in the Kennels box, they were joined by the 1/5th Mahratta Light Infantry. And to Brigadier Boucher's command came the first Gurkha battalion to serve with the Division, the 2/4th Gurkha Rifles. This was appropriate, for Boucher himself had been with a Gurkha regiment.

Then on May 8 the Divisional Commander, who had led Nine Brigade in the Sudan and Eritrea, who had won the battle on the heights of Amba Alagi and taken the surrender of the Duke of Aosta just a year before, Major-General A. G. O. M. Mayne, was promoted to command a Corps in Iraq. For a few days the reins of command were in the hands of the C.R.A., Brigadier G. M. Vallentin, and then a week later came Major-General H. R. Briggs, known to the officers, and no doubt to the men, as "Briggo."

He had left Bedford and Sandhurst in time to go to France in 1915 with the King's (Liverpool) Regiment. After a year he transferred to the Indian Army, joined the 31st Punjabis in Mesopotamia, and later served in Palestine. Then in 1924 Briggs joined the 1/10th Baluch, saw action on the North-West Frontier six years later, and after another such period was given command of the 2nd battalion of his regiment. When Seven Indian Brigade left

Poona in 1940 with the Fourth Indian Division, Briggs was its commander, and he led it at Sidi Barrani, behind Keren and at Massawa, as we have already seen. He continued to command the Brigade during operations in the Desert in 1941 and 1942, took part in the capture of the Omars and Derna, and planned and led the celebrated break-out from Benghazi.

Briggs was every inch a soldier, and a fighting one rather than a passive or staff soldier. The battle was for him the one thing that counted at the time, and, though he might lack the urbanity proverbial in an ambassador, he was as fine a commander in battle as could be found. In action he could be fierce and quick-tempered, but he was neither petty nor vindictive. He was at times shy and retiring, and unbent to but a few of his staff officers; maybe it was from this shyness that sprang the impression of fierceness.

He was resourceful and cheerful at heart, a man who did his share and more. As a leader he went out of his way to ensure that good work was appreciated, and as a strong personality he stood no nonsense. He seldom relaxed, but smoked many cigarettes. Severe sinus trouble caused him moments of suffering that were masked in moods of taciturnity or of barking at those who surrounded him during a battle. But he had a sense of humour, and the smile that played on his lips just before he made a "crack" was worth waiting for in the grim warlike days.

He was imperturbable, a good leader for the tight corner, and never allowed himself to become rattled. Having done all that was humanly possible, he did not appear to worry—surely a great trait in any commander. When in July and August he had to put inexperienced troops into battle on Ruweisat Ridge, he gave no undue commiseration, no embarrassing apology, no incorrect picture-painting of the task ahead. He credited his commanders with sufficient imagination and confidence in him to understand that the gravity of the situation justified this action. Briggs therefore issued orders and offered his personal assistance, the help of his staff and of any hands experienced in warfare to help carry them out. To one Brigadier he telephoned and said: "Old —— has got rather a tough one. His brigade is a bit new. I wonder if you would be good enough to drive across and see if you can help him."

He had not been to the Staff College—he had refused—and did

WHEEL-MARKS IN THE SAND (C.I.S. Historical Section)

A DESERT TRACK (C.I.S. Historical Section)

A Tent in the Desert (J. H. Dale)

Mr. Casey with Major-General Briggs on Ruweisat Ridge
(Imperial War Museum)

not interfere with his staff and their working. He trusted them implicitly, and devoted himself to forward planning and deep thought on moves that were open to the enemy, or to visiting his troops. He had a nose for danger, and many a time he was found in his caravan by a staff officer with a map in front of him. He would say both what he planned to do, and what the enemy would do as a result. Seldom was he wrong in his anticipation of the enemy's reactions.

He was not the showman, he did not advertise, but none was more successful, more trusted, more "true blue." He would not allow himself to be bullied or the Division imposed upon by his superiors, and he would fight to get equipment and men and the fair deal that he gave to others. He would never make rash, proud promises to Corps and Army Commanders, and was ready to say firmly that a certain hill could not be taken by next Tuesday. Far from committing himself and his troops to capturing the hill as early as Monday, he would give assurance that success would be ours by the Thursday. He was usually right. And the casualties were much fewer than might otherwise have been.

The Division's equipment was by no means complete; much had to be improvised; spares were hard to obtain; materials for the Signals and Engineers were scarce. Not that such shortages, problems and improvisations were a new feature of war in the Middle East; indeed, units had become well versed in overcoming them. But now the time for gaining experience of the Desert was short, and there was none for exercising as a division, owing to the wide dispersal of brigades and battalions and to lack of transport.

Particular attention was paid to practice in desert navigation, to the use of the sun compass, to the establishment of brigade group boxes, then known colloquially as "cowpats." The battalions practised moving in desert formation and trained in minelaying. Senior officers of the Division liaised closely with their opposite numbers in brigades—particularly Reid's 29 Brigade—already experienced in the ways of the Desert, and picked their brains for help, suggestions and sound advice.

29 Brigade was hampered by the lack of an artillery regiment in the group, for though the 3rd Field Regiment had been allotted, it did not arrive from Iraq until May 21, by which time the Brigade had moved to the area of Sollum, Halfaya and Capuzzo for

the defence of the railhead and dumps. And ill-timed confusion and reorganization followed the transfer, at this very moment, of the 4th and 28th Field Regiments from their Indian establishments of two batteries to the British establishment with three.

All this time Fletcher's West Yorkshires, Jats and 3/12th Frontier Force Rifles formed part of the Tobruk garrison. They had moved there on May 17 after training near Halfaya, and the companies were now well spread out along the perimeter, the reserve companies and headquarters further in towards the centre, and the telephone cables far longer than the resources of a battalion signal platoon were supposed to manage. But manage they did by reeling up many miles of old British and Italian cable and by taking drums of it from the local Ordnance Supply Depot.

Before we trace in detail the fortunes of the Fifth Indian Division in the desperate campaign that was to follow these weeks of preparation and initiation, it is of vital interest to describe this unique battleground, the Western Desert. Those who wish to understand the human side of battles should remember always the conditions in which the men fought and lived. And those conditions, with the peculiar setting and spirit, were uncommon enough and not to be forgotten by soldiers who spent any time there.

The landscape of the Desert was painted in the colours of brown and yellow and grey. And the fighting men learned to hide themselves in this Desert, which at first sight had no natural cover, by skilful use of these same colours in the paints and camouflage nets that adorned their vehicles. It was a land of fawn or black rocks, of beige sand: a scene without interest, being drab in its slight undulations, its occasional low ridges, its steep escarpments. The endless stretches of monotonous Desert were broken by greyish clumps of scrub, by stones and grit, by ridges of stone, by rocky outcrops and by rare hillocks. The Desert provided no obstacle to motor transport, beyond here and there the cliff, the softer patch of sand, and to the south of El Alamein the Qattara Depression. This gave you an unusual sense of freedom. If you wanted to go to a certain point on the map, you could go there on a straight course, provided that your navigation was sound. Sometimes the ground was firm and rocky, defiant of the shovel and pickaxe; sometimes it was powdered dust that swirled up when a vehicle's wheels rolled through it. There were not the usual restrictions of route imposed by river, bridge or mountain. Movement was slower than along a road, the wear and tear on the lorries greater.

There was the coast road and the railway as far as Capuzzo, but otherwise nothing better than tracks. No camel, no wall, no tree, no river, not even a stream, no grass, no civilian. It was the green trees that the men up in the Desert missed most. Those who passed the fig plantations at Burg el Arab on their way up were not impressed. But on the way out some months later these same trees would seem beautiful and were admired, as they grew in their groves against the white sand of the coast.

The Desert has been described, acidly but with no little justice, as "miles and miles and bloody miles of absolutely damn all." There was a seeming eternity of barren, inhospitable nothingness. And this lack of physical features and recognizable landmarks by which to find your way made navigation a problem to all, and was particularly baffling to the newcomer to the Desert. You learned to move by map, compass and speedometer. You were never really certain that you were actually at the point from which you thought you were starting, and you had to take your map reference on trust: there was no guarantee. It was hard to tell how far away the horizon was. Your sense of direction became befuddled, you were haunted by the constant risk of losing the way. After a time you developed a sense of direction in daylight; but at night, though to proceed in a general direction was tolerably simple, it was no light matter to pin-point a unit or a rendezvous. You might search for a group of tanks reported to be leaguered at a certain map reference, and you might spend hours driving round the sand, when all the time the tanks were only a mile distant. Unless it was extremely urgent that they be found, it was wiser to camp down for the night and wait until daybreak. Usually the tanks were then visible towards the horizon.

You had to step out of your truck or jeep, lorry or staff car whenever you needed to take a new compass bearing. You kept a watchful eye on the speedometer. And you found your way back by observation of tiny details: a pile of stones or jerry cans that someone had dropped, or a strip of red flag on a hillside, or a tin of bully beef lying in the sand. All vehicles looked alike, and to search for your unit was sometimes like looking at a sea of transport as though in a nightmare. You gazed upon acres of flat desert studded with scores of trucks, and these were poor landmarks—they might move at any time.

And you had to learn to drive without sticking in soft sand, when there was no other jeep or four-wheel-drive truck to tow you out. Then there was the problem of finding the gap in our minefields, which were often only protected, and marked, by a strand or two of barbed wire. Many were the vehicles travelling at some speed which blew up on the first few mines of the field. After dark a driver might find the gap, and still drive off its narrow path and blow up. Perhaps it was best to be blown up in a jeep, for the resistance was slight, and you might be thrown clear.

All vehicles could be seen moving from afar because of the trail of dust that billowed up behind or to one side. When two trucks did meet, each driver tried desperately to steer to windward and so avoid the dust of the other vehicle. You might wear sand goggles, but your face was coated with sand, that caked itself into a beige mask, clinging to the sweat of your countenance, collecting in the corners of your eyes. Hands and arms, necks and knees, became coated with this same sand, which penetrated under your shirt, and caught in your throat, and made your eyes smart. Your hair became matted and bistre. Along your limbs the trickling sweat would cleave little rivulets through the sandy coating.

All day long thousands of vehicles shod with balloon tyres or with tracks were moving about, each with its plume of sand, that poured up over the mudguards, penetrated into the carburettor, came through chinks in the truck's body, or round the edge of a staff car's windows. The tanks cut deep ruts in the sand. Half the surface of the Desert might appear to be in the air at one time, and drivers would keep their windscreen-wipers going in order to clear the dust and so see a few yards ahead. For in a sandstorm, with its blown and gritty sand that lashed the human body and was blasted everywhere that particles of sand can go, there was an opaque yellowish fog ahead, into which you could peer for but a yard or two. It was as though some shuddering beige curtain had been drawn across the face of the Desert; the light of day became unreal in its strange hues; you stumbled over tent ropes and into slit trenches; minefields became a still greater source of danger; while maps were invisible beneath the layer of dust that stuck to the marks of chinagraph pencils—red, blue, yellow and green — on the talc sheet above. And those who were trying to work out map reference or signal codes found their stencils clogged.

Although you were permanently coated with sand when driving or when the wind blew up, baths were impossible and you grew accustomed to being dirty, to washing seldom. Water was short in the Desert, scarcer by far than petrol. On a gallon a day for all purposes it became an art to wash, shave, clean your teeth, wash your feet, all in a mug of water, with the resultant glutinous fluid being strained and poured into the radiator of your truck. Some men planned to wash a third of their bodies each day, for the sand became matted on the hairy parts of the body, and they felt the imperative need for washing it away, even though a fresh lot of sand was picked up at once.

But few cared deeply about washing so long as there was no shortage of drinking water. And, with rare exceptions, there was always enough to drink. Yet the water was either brackish or salt to the taste, and to make a good mug of tea was hard. A new officer might well drive up to join a unit, and the Colonel would ask him whether he had any water and where he came from. If the new officer said he had filled up at, for example, Mersah Matruh, and the unit was now at Gazala, there would be a shout of joyous triumph: "Boys, we've got some Matruh water!"

Just as the Desert possessed few natural sources of water, so too it provided the opposing armies with no raw food. The rations were good, but men lived from tins. Bully stew, with onions, peas, beans, or whatever was to hand, formed the evening meal, cooked before sunset, and good it all was. You might, in default of a cooker, cut a four-gallon petrol tin in half, fill one part with sand, pour on petrol and set it alight. You then cooked your food in the other part of the tin, using it as some rough pan. Brewing tea became almost a recreation, a form of relaxation, despite the spoiling taste of the water. And for the porridge of the Desert—known as 'burgoo'—you came to know which issue of biscuits made the best dish, oatmeal or wheaten or other types. You cooked the mess in water, added a dollop of condensed milk, and sugar if you had it. Some men added cocoa to make a sort of chocolate pudding, and on occasions marmalade was used in the mixture.

When the evening meal was eaten, officers and men bedded down in the Desert, some in the open alongside their lorry or truck, some in the canvas side-shelters of their vehicles; others erected small bivouac tents in the lee of a dune or a lorry. Each slept the sleep of the weary, rolled in his blanket, for the nights could be cold after the heat and glare of the daytime. Though many worked stripped to the waist by day, they pulled on battledress blouses and even greatcoats at sundown and at first light. Some men lay naked on top of their blankets, and when the night grew colder towards the early hours they pulled up the blanket over their bodies. They cleared the stones and scooped little hollows in which to rest their hips and shoulders. They slept wonderfully, and awoke refreshed for the day ahead. And after spending some period in the Desert, men found it oppressive to sleep in a large square tent or in a building. They had slept beneath the stars, and could not forget. At night they experienced a sense of rest and relaxation in the impressive silence. When the light of evening failed, and the lengthened shadows were fading into night, the air grew cooler to the feel, and there was blessed relief. You could sit down and smoke a cigarette, or sip a whisky and tepid water, and there were no flies till the morrow, and the peace of it all was astounding. After sundown you could strip and stand to enjoy the gentle breeze blowing in from the sea and cooling—slightly, but enough—the hot, sweaty, dusty skin. And in the early morning, too, you drank your mug of tea, and a cigarette was really worth-while smoking. On rare but memorable days you could reach the shore and plunge with a sensation approaching ecstasy from the gleaming white sand into the blue waters of the Mediterranean.

General Briggs has drawn the distinction between the two main phases of Desert life. "You were either 'put' in defences, where you just had your unit vehicles with you, or you became mobile and lived in your lorries (troop-carrying) and were self-supporting in food, water, petrol, blankets, ammunition. When 'put' you were digging all day, wiring or laying mines, with certain days set aside for training. You always patrolled well out in the Desert by day, and occupied defences by night. You slept in and around your positions, which you tried to make flush with the ground.

"Life 'mobile' had its special characteristics. First, every man had to learn to cook and fend for himself. You learned to dig slit trenches when halted, to avoid frequent hostile dive-bombing. When day broke you moved into Desert formation, each vehicle about one hundred yards from the next, while at night you closed up to avoid losing one another and halted in close 'leaguer.' And when things moved, they did so very quickly. Generally speaking, except at Alamein, the infantry were out of contact with the enemy except when asked to attack, or while being attacked, or whilst on patrol. You learned to debus in close contact with the enemy."

But beyond all these physical conditions that characterized life and war in the Desert, a peculiar spirit existed among the men there. They had a sense of brotherhood and hospitality, as though Man made recompense for the barrenness of Nature. The atmosphere was one of intimacy and friendliness. Life had a new simplicity, and was nomadic, primitive. Men found a new sense of values, and those things that had mattered to them in civilized life now hardly seemed to count; the troops were ready to sacrifice that which normally they considered necessary for ordinary living. Life had been reduced to essentials, and, apart from the fighting itself, eating and sleeping were now the important factors in a man's preoccupation. Most vital was the mere process of existence.

A common danger unites men, and here they were away from civilization, stripped of social barriers and artificialities except for that of officers and other ranks, and even rank seemed to count for less than in other places of battle. You saw the other man as he was, for himself and not for any false position he might have occupied in civil life. You accepted him, and it made little difference whether he was a professor or a bricklayer. You shared things, and there was the spirit of "mucking-in" abroad.

Except during the holding of the Alamein Line, men were always on the move, and perhaps it was this that was conducive to the carefree spirit that was remarkable in the Desert, as were the new code of manners, the lack of regimentation in the soldiering, the atmosphere symbolized by the fly whisk and the pair of suede Desert boots. And by the unifying Good Samaritan spirit that forbade you to pass a man whose truck had broken down without calling out to him, "Are you O.K., Charlie?" In mobile warfare neither side *occupied* the Desert; they merely took up positions for a day or a night; and in this respect Desert warfare resembled that at sea. Men attached enormous importance to the bit of ground on which they landed up. There was delight if they found some scrub bushes, as these made excellent fuel. But groans were heard and curses if the ground was stony. For it was of importance whether or not the area of Desert made easy or difficult the digging of slit trenches.

To analyse this spirit of the Desert is hard, for it sprang from a host of varied factors, and there were many differing views on the life in the sand. But it was exhilarating, and such a different existence from the normal that men felt they had been in the Desert for years rather than for weeks or months. They were cheerful and on the whole healthy, and only asked for a week in Cairo before being ready to return. In such surroundings Man seemed tiny, insignificant, and yet human relationships loomed large. The Desert played its part in restoring men to themselves, and revealed to them some of the riches of their own inner beings and of their companions in battle.

CHAPTER XIV

ROMMEL'S OFFENSIVE

MAY 1942

On January 21, three months before the entry of the Fifth Indian Division into the Western Desert, the enemy had reopened the offensive, outpaced our forces, driven them back from Agedabia to Msus. When a stand was ordered at Benghazi, the enemy feinted successfully, and the Fourth Indian Division found itself without armoured support. Briggs and his Seven Brigade became isolated in the town, but fought their way out with great skill and daring. A series of rearguard actions was fought by this division, until by February 4 it had reached our defence line at Gazala, which the remainder of Ritchie's Eighth Army was busy fortifying.

Our immediate aim was to stabilize a front behind which reserves might be accumulated and a striking force built. Accordingly, a minefield was hurriedly laid from the coast by Gazala south to Bir Hakeim, a distance of some forty miles. And within this minefield strong defensive positions were prepared from Gazala to Sidi Muftah, and at Bir Hakeim itself. Organized in depth as it was, over an area thirty-six miles square, the line was strengthened by Tobruk on the coast, and by positions farther east at Acroma, El Adem and Bir El Gubi. These Gazala defences were manned by General Gott's Thirteen Corps; while far back, near the Egyptian frontier, Thirty Corps, under General Willoughby-Norrie, prepared new positions of defence.

Between the end of February and May the Desert front remained quiet, but both sides made intensive preparations in the race to be ready for the next offensive. Our strength in heavy bombers and naval forces in the Mediterranean did not suffice to prevent the steady reinforcement of the German and Italian armies in Libya. And this strengthening of Rommel's forces had so far progressed by the middle of May that it became clear to our commanders that our own attack was likely to be forestalled.

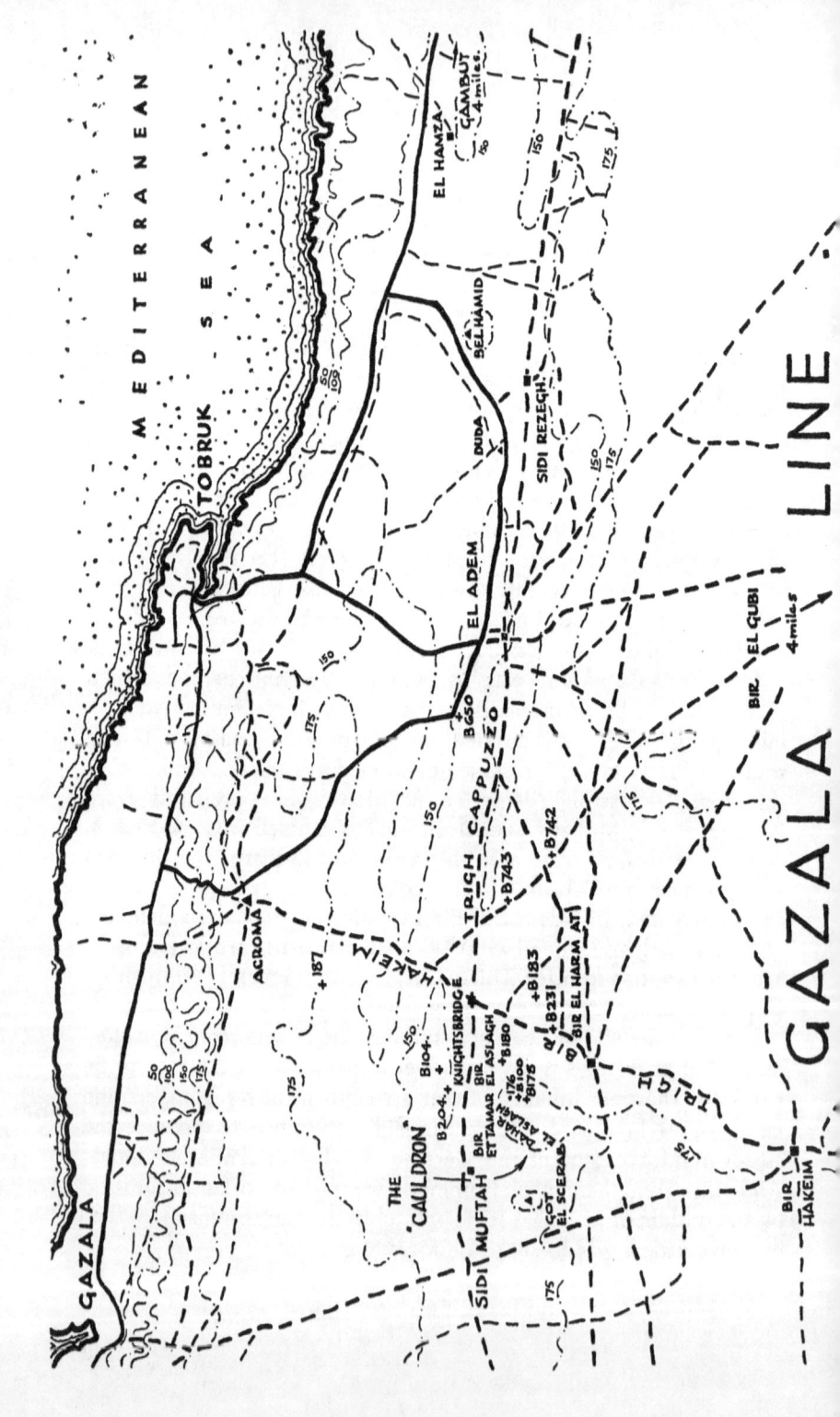

During the first two weeks of May our Intelligence received many indications that the enemy would soon end this period of inactivity. More tanks than usual had been employed in the forward area. There was evidence of a wish on the enemy's part to screen still more effectively his own movements. Our air reconnaissance showed the 15th and 21st Panzer Divisions to be now well forward. The only German prisoner to be taken for some time said that a rumour was about among the troops of an impending attack. Further evidence was gathered when an indiscreet German staff officer from Libya, on leave in the Balkans, stated over his cups that Rommel's offensive was intended to start between May 20 and 27. And whereas during the whole month of March the enemy had unloaded only 1,500 tons of supplies in Benghazi harbour, he was now unloading 2,000 tons a day. Indications suggested that the enemy's most likely course of action would be a feint in the south, combined with a strong attempt to punch a way through our minefields and defences on top of the Gazala escarpment.

We planned to give the impression that our own forces were unprepared, but so to deploy our armoured formations that, having once blunted the enemy's initial thrust, we could contain his tanks in the area between the Gazala line and Knightsbridge. For this plan to succeed it was essential both that the enemy's main attack should come from the south and that the Gazala defences remain firm.

The dispositions of the Eighth Army on May 25 were as follows: the 1st South African Division held the front from the coast west of Gazala to El Hamza. Eastward from this point stretched two brigades of the 50th British Division, while its third, 150 Brigade, had established a detached strong-point at Sidi Muftah. The Tobruk defence perimeter was divided between the 2nd South African Division and Fletcher's Nine Brigade. Of the Thirty Corps formations, the 1st Free French Brigade, led by General Koenig, held another detached position far to the south at Bir Hakeim. Of our tanks, the 1st Armoured Division (Major-General H. Lumsden) was centred round Knightsbridge, while Messervy's 7th Armoured Division was ready a little further south.

It appears that most of our senior commanders thought the enemy thrust would come through the centre, trying to break our minefields. Intelligence reports also gave this impression. But, though it was said to be impossible to go round the south of our line, south, that is, of the French in Bir Hakeim, several senior officers were suspicious, and believed that Rommel planned to try this southern route. Perhaps because of this difference in view, our tanks were dispersed, ready to meet threats from the centre and the south.

Finally, the Fifth Indian Divisional Headquarters and Ten Brigade, in reserve, had the task of guarding the group of airfields north and south of the Trigh Capuzzo by Gambut, and of protecting Advanced Army Headquarters there.

General Auchinleck felt that the Eighth Army had sufficient infantry to cope with any eventuality. But we held no reserve of field artillery. Though we had numerical superiority in tanks, these were inferior in gun power and reliability to those of the enemy. The Commander-in-Chief laid down that, whether the German and Italian forces tried to break our centre by attacking on a narrow front, or whether they tried to pass south of Bir Hakeim— in either case their object would be the capture of Tobruk—our intention must be "to force the enemy to depend on the long and exposed southern route for his supplies, and having thus placed him at a disadvantage, to defeat him in the triangle formed by Gazala, Tobruk and Bir Hakeim." The enemy must be stopped short of Tobruk, then attacked in the flank with armour, in the rear with infantry and guns, and dealt a blow from which he would find it impossible to recover.

What part the Fifth Indian Division would play when battle started was at this time undecided, but was generally thought to be the advance guard for our follow-up. The eventual role was entirely due to an unexpected turn in the tide of operations.

* * * * *

The enemy struck. Once more the sands blew up to the turmoil of mobile warfare. Once more the chinagraph marks on a thousand map cases were altered. Rommel spurred forward his full-scale attack in moonlight on May 27. He did choose to make his main thrust round the southern flank, and the Afrika Korps came against our 3rd Indian Motor Brigade to the south-east of Bir Hakeim. This brigade fought with gallant tenacity but was overwhelmed. By midday on the 28th the enemy was being engaged from Knightsbridge east along the Duda ridge to Bel Hamed, a distance of thirty miles. That evening saw the Germans' main striking force stretched out over a great expanse of Desert. To supply the tanks large numbers of soft-skinned vehicles were driving to and fro amid clouds of dust that could be seen for many miles. The Royal Air Force lost no opportunity of bombarding the enemy columns.

Rommel sent one group against Acroma, but this withdrew. Our tanks began to gain the upper hand, and the enemy forces found themselves not only held along a line between Knightsbridge and El Adem, but pinned against our Gazala line in the area of Desert to be known later as the "Cauldron." All day heavy fighting went on; the contest was maintained from morning till nightfall; the result was not decisive.

Then Rommel drew back his armour into our minefields north of Bir Hakeim. But here it was surrounded and trapped within the triangle bounded on the west by our line of mines linking Gazala and Bir Harmat; to the east by troops from Bir Harmat through Knightsbridge to the coast; to the north by the South Africans near the sea, and by the 50th Northumbrian Division, grouped at intervals down the minefield line. Far too great a reliance was placed upon the effectiveness of these minefields. The enemy was to prove them to be anything but invincible, and he soon turned our defences to his own advantage and protection.

On May 31 he established a corridor through the minefields, under cover of a violent dust-storm. It was a brilliant coup that changed the face of battle. Even while general optimism prevailed among our Army, while its commanders congratulated themselves on having forced the enemy into a dangerous position where he might be destroyed, Rommel's men cut two lines through our minefield in the east, ten miles apart and on either side of 150 Brigade's position at Sidi Muftah.

Thus our opponent formed a bridgehead, and provided a new supply route to his forces within the Cauldron that had hitherto been contained with a diminishing supply of food, water, ammunition and petrol.

150 Brigade, isolated, without armoured support, could not hold out beyond June 1. Despite the efforts of our soldiers and

aircrews, the enemy widened the two gaps, known as Peter and Paul, and reopened the lifeline to his armoured forces. With the arrival of supplies these became once more actively menacing. Our extreme optimism faded. The face of battle had changed again. At all costs these gaps must be closed, or, if this were not possible, the amount of material allowed to pass through them must be severely limited.

Reid's 29 Brigade had meantime moved from El Gubi to El Adem, and was under command of Thirteen Corps. Marriott's Guards' Brigade held Knightsbridge. Nine Brigade under Fletcher had driven down from Tobruk to the same area; while Boucher's Ten Brigade was in the neighbourhood of Bir Harmat. It was planned to form two "boxes" opposite the gaps of Peter and Paul, the northern one at Bir et Tamar to be established and held by Ten Brigade, the southern box two miles west of Bir el Harmat to be Fletcher's responsibility.

But delays occurred. Plans were altered. The days passed. And all this time the enemy was able to reinforce and refuel his units within the Cauldron. Precious time was lost, time that was precious to Rommel and dangerous to ourselves.

Reports varied about the enemy's strength. Some patrols said that all the tanks in the Cauldron were derelict, having run out of petrol. Could we advance far enough to plug the two holes in our minefields? Who was to gain the initiative after the heavy fighting of this first week? Lack of reserves, of fresh troops, and the fog of war caused delay and indecisiveness over our counter-stroke. We delayed four days before attacking in force. We then hurried too late.

Some commanders thought we should pull back to the Tobruk–El Adem line, re-sort properly there, and fight an organized battle. Others considered that an immediate come-back must be staged upon the enemy where he lay. We must fight hurriedly, desperately —in fact, fight with everything in confusion, and hoping that the enemy was in a worse state. The two gaps must be closed, and the enemy forced to withdraw.

But the Germans had meantime brought in many 88 mm. anti-tank guns to stiffen their defences. And to evict them grew more difficult and perilous a task as each day passed. However great the risk taken by the enemy in punching boldly back, so soon as he had realized that he had failed to destroy us, he had now placed himself in the heart of our defences, in positions where we must destroy him or ourselves retire. Rommel had been able to disengage one armoured division, rest and re-equip it, and bring it up ready for his assault upon Tobruk. It emerged just at the same time as our attack on his 'bulge' in the Cauldron.

And our Intelligence erred. For the Italian Ariete Division, facing the eastern side of the Cauldron, had not been correctly located. It had false-fronted us. The German tanks were said to be massed about Sidi Muftah. The 21st Panzer Division was there, it is true, but not the 15th, which lay further south in the Cauldron.

The situation was grave, the time short, the planners not of one mind.

General Briggs wrote that, though the Fifth Indian Division was supposed to be in general reserve at the start of Rommel's offensive, in fact every brigade and some battalions even had been taken out of his control and placed directly under one of the two Corps, or under the Armoured Divisions. In this whirlpool battle, brigades were swapped from one command to another. Contact was sometimes made by wireless alone. Briggs called his own headquarters an "H.Q. on Ice," and was occasionally given formations to look after for a day at a time.

"It was not," he records, "till Rommel had established himself in our minefields, had overrun 150 Brigade, and was threatening Bir Hakeim that I was called in. 'Strafer' Gott, optimistic as usual, sent for me. The Army Commander was coming to a conference in two hours' time. Would I meanwhile consider attacking Tmimi through the South African position along the coast. It was held by a German parachute division and half of 15 Panzer Division, protected by unlocated minefields. I had to collect in the Division, plan, reconnoitre, and attack within thirty-six hours. I never thought harder in my life.

"My answer was in the shape of an alternative. I suggested a Desert move round the south of Bir Hakeim on to Tmimi and Rommel's L. of C., by use of surprise mobility, and in a place where there were no mines. This was agreed to by both Ritchie and Gott, and I thought everything was settled. It looked as if we should have a good, open fight with the whole Division together. Unfortunately the armour intervened. It had been arranged that they should protect my right flank. Now they said they needed a day to refit. In my absence the whole plan was changed to a frontal attack against Rommel in his prepared position. And we were not to be a complete division after all.''

The Army Commander considered that this attack would be the decisive one of the present operations. So it was, but for the enemy. Ritchie ordered Thirty Corps, with the First and Seventh Armoured Divisions and the Fifth Indian Division, to attack from the east, while Thirteen Corps co-operated in an attack from the north with a brigade of 50 Division and the 32nd Tank Brigade. Meanwhile the Free French Brigade would continue its gallant defence of Bir Hakeim. The Thirty Corps attack was allotted to the 7th Armoured Division and the Fifth Indian Division. The 1st Armoured Division would prevent the enemy from breaking out to the north and north-east.

The general plan of Operation 'Aberdeen,' as it was called, divided itself into three parts. General Briggs had charge of the opening phase. Ten Brigade with the 4th Royal Tank Regiment under command would attack first. The H.L.I. (Lieutenant-Colonel Douglas Thorburn, O.B.E., M.C.) was to capture B.180, Bir El Aslagh, Bir Et Tamar and B.204. On the left Sundius-Smith's 4/10th Baluch were responsible for taking B.100 and B.178. The 2/4th Gurkha Rifles (Lieutenant-Colonel Weallans) would remain in reserve. The starting time was three a.m. on June 5. The infantry were to gain their objectives within two hours.

The second phase of the operation, under command of Messervy's Seventh Armoured Division, was the establishment, on a line from Sidi Muftah to B.176, of three boxes defended by infantry battalions to be provided by Fletcher's Nine Brigade, with the 4th R.T.R. under command, and Brigadier Carr's 22nd Armoured Brigade in the lead.

In the third phase of 'Aberdeen,' which never materialized, the Fifth Indian Division would assume command of all infantry in these boxes, and our armoured forces were to rally, in order to exploit any success westwards through our minefields, to complete the enemy's destruction, and to re-establish a line running from Sidi Muftah through Dahar El Aslagh to Got El Scerab.

The enemy force within the Cauldron being largely if not entirely mobile, it was impossible to expect infantry battalions to pin down divisions of German tanks. For this reason our commanders had recourse to this principle of "boxes," the establishment of which was designed to compel the enemy to assault them. At this point our armour would attack the enemy in the back. But to establish such boxes the infantry needed adequate time, to lay anti-tank mines, to site its anti-tank guns with the greatest care and skill. Even had this time been available, the enemy might always be able to concentrate superior force against one isolated "box" and destroy its garrison before our tanks could intervene. In the event, this fate overtook the few infantry "boxes" that were established on June 5.

The whole plan for 'Aberdeen' was ill-conceived, and the preparations rushed. It was carried out by troops who had not trained together, and with a dual control which produced various grave faults. Insufficient attention was paid in the later stages of the battle to the security of the flanks; several units engaged had reached the Western Desert but a few hours before the battle, and had had no time to find their way about or to gain experience in the peculiarities of Desert warfare.

Briggs established his headquarters some three miles south-west from B.743, and at nine o'clock held a conference at Brigadier Boucher's H.Q. to outline the plan of attack. After Ten Brigade's thrust south of Knightsbridge, under Briggs' personal orders, the 22nd Armoured Brigade would enter the Cauldron, advance by way of B.178 to Bir El Scerab and Sidi Muftah, and execute a 'milling attack.' They would enter the Cauldron along its southern side, penetrate deeply, swing right towards the north, and rally at B.104, ready to exploit west of the minefields. Then Nine Brigade, now under Messervy's command, whose Tactical Headquarters Briggs was to share, would follow in lorries, advancing on a general axis of B.742, B.183, B.100 and Bir El Scerab, and would establish the three battalion boxes: the 3/12th R.F.F.R. (Lieutenant-Colonel W. E. Dean) near Dahar El Aslagh, the 3/9th Jats (Lieutenant-Colonel H. V. Bragg, M.C.) just south of Bir El Scerab, and Langran's 2nd West Yorkshires at Sidi Muftah. Each battalion was to be preceded by a squadron of Infantry tanks, which would act as local protection; and under command of each unit would be one battery of 157 Field Regiment.

"Progress of the attack," said Messervy's orders, "will depend on any armoured action in which 22nd Armoured Brigade becomes involved."

At an afternoon conference on June 4 it was decided that Carr's 22nd Armoured Brigade should leave its forming-up area at four o'clock, aiming to reach the Knightsbridge–Bir Hakeim track by 5.15 a.m. Nine Brigade, following behind, would assemble near B.183, cross the Trigh Bir Hakeim, pick up its battery of guns and its armoured squadron. These Fletcher would take forward to the three battalion "boxes." First would go the West Yorkshires. Then, when they had secured their objective, the Jats would follow in, and behind would come Dean's 3/12th Frontier Force Regiment.

CHAPTER XV

THE CAULDRON

JUNE 5, 1942

THE battle to destroy the Germans and Italians in the Knightsbridge Cauldron started in the early hours of June 5, when Boucher's Ten Brigade went in to attack. Sentries walked round to wake the troops at half past two. Just before 3 a.m. our artillery barrage began, and for twenty minutes shells from five regiments thudded and crumped upon the two areas of sand and stone that the battalions were to capture: Bir Et Tamar and Dahar El Aslagh. Then, riding in lorries, the 4/10th Baluch and 2nd Highland Light Infantry crossed their starting line behind a screen of armour. In moonlight the visibility was good.

Soon after three o'clock the H.L.I. were fired upon on the way to B.180. Our tanks and carriers retaliated, and the battalion reached the first objective in good order. The enemy gave no sign of his presence; but fifteen derelict tanks, relics of a previous battle, lay on the sand like black monsters. At B.180 'A' Company dropped off to mop up, and rejoined two hours later. The battalion pressed ahead, and the firing became heavier. At first the direction taken was too far north, and our tanks became split up; the left half of the squadron disappeared into the night. The H.L.I. were unable for the moment to find Bir Et Tamar, so Colonel Thorburn formed a 'cowpat' before daybreak. He sent out Kindersley's 'B' Company, with a troop of Valentine tanks and a section of carriers, to search for B.204, a little distance to the north of the battalion's position.

In this part of the Desert the ground was flat. With the dawn came the enemy shells in great numbers, before the Scottish troops had finished digging their trenches and weapon pits. 'C' and 'D' Companies now went forward in transport, preceded by five Valentines, to the southern edge of Bir Et Tamar, to capture the second objective. They dismounted and advanced on foot towards the northern edge. The men were shelled and machine-gunned all the way. On seeing this, Colonel Thorburn came up and stopped the two companies going any farther; they dug in on the northern edge, while Battalion Headquarters established itself a short way to the west. Meanwhile, Kindersley's 'B' Company had formed its independent 'cowpat,' and had dug in, with the guns taken off their portees. From the frequent Very lights that rose in the west, it was plain that the enemy was not far away.

Soon after this, Thorburn sent his carrier platoon officer, Captain Bromley Gardner, to tell 'B' Company to retire. Kindersley was found to be holding the position with a dozen men. Around him lay the dead and the wounded. Only two vehicles remained undamaged. The others were burning and all the time fresh shells came crashing into the small area. The remains of the company crowded into what transport could still be driven, and withdrew to the rear of the main battalion defences.

The tanks from one regiment of the 22nd Armoured Brigade came into position west of the H.L.I., who kept on hoping that our armour would attack, for the enemy guns could be seen a thousand yards away.

The main attack on Bir Et Tamar was launched at half-past six; the objective was a series of bumps on top of a long ridge. Heavy shelling obliged the companies to dismount from the lorries and cross the last two hundred and fifty yards to the first bump on foot, with bayonets fixed. Casualties mounted. Shells and machine-gun bullets hailed down on the advancing infantry, and there was no cover of any sort. A number of German tanks were now visible on a ridge west of the Bir. At this moment Thorburn arrived on the scene to order his companies to consolidate their gains, with 'D' Company on the forward end of the ridge. 'C' Company settled in just behind, with headquarters in the rear and 'A' Company on its left.

Then, soon after eight o'clock, while the H.L.I. were attempting to dig in, six enemy tanks moved to within 1,500 yards of 'C' Company on the left flank, and it was soon obvious that the Germans had forestalled our own armour in occupying this area. Part of the 22nd Armoured Brigade that had advanced level with this company was unable to go farther forward without coming under fire from the deadly 88 mm. guns.

While this had been taking place, the 4/10th Baluch had captured

Dahar El Aslagh, B.178 and B.180. Their green success signal was fired at a quarter past four. Half an hour before this the adjutant, when asked for a report by Boucher's Headquarters, had said, "I think we have overrun the position, but the situation is not yet clear." Within a very few minutes the battalion commander, Lieutenant-Colonel B. L. Sundius-Smith, announced that he had just heard a loud cheer from one of his forward companies. "They are," he said, "obviously mopping up." But soon afterwards the Baluch were reporting heavy and accurate shelling on their position.

The third battalion of Ten Brigade, the 2/4th Gurkhas, were covering the minefield gaps at Bir El Harmat, to the south-east. They had to await the arrival of the 1st Duke of Cornwall's Light Infantry before rejoining the Brigade.

And so, by half past six, Boucher's forces had taken their objectives. The first phase of 'Aberdeen' was over. Casualties had been comparatively light, success was complete. Four artillery regiments now moved up in readiness to support the 22nd Armoured Brigade and Fletcher's Nine Brigade in the second act of the battle, which was to pass through and secure Sidi Muftah.

* * * * *

At 6.45 a.m. Fletcher's attack began. The Brigadier wrote in his report soon after the battle this instructive paragraph:

"If we examine this plan from the point of view of Nine Indian Infantry Brigade, we find that battalions were expected to advance in the dark, over ground they did not know, to an assembly area, the centre of which was marked by a barrel; to do a further advance to a point 'east of B.100,' where they were to be joined by a battery of a regiment which they did not know (it had arrived from Iraq two days previously), and by a squadron of the 4th R.T.R. which had already been in action in the dark. The axis of advance was marked out by the Brigade Intelligence Officer (Captain Livingstone) with lamps, some of which went out during the night. The leading battalion, however, reached the assembly area by 5.45, and the Brigade's first group, consisting of the 2nd West Yorks and supporting troops, crossed the Trigh Bir Hakeim at 6.35 behind the 22nd Armoured Brigade."

The 4th R.T.R., which had fought in support of the H.L.I.

earlier that night, now covered the advancing West Yorkshires, under whose command was the machine-gun company of Royal Northumberland Fusiliers (Major Martin). Our own minefields were reached without opposition, but the battalion was then heavily engaged by German tanks and 88 mm. guns.

"The first thing," records Captain Wiberg of the West Yorkshires, "that one remembers about the attack on June 5 is that it was mounted in a great hurry. The second thing is that there was an entire absence of detailed information about the enemy, and we were told that we would very likely meet only very slight opposition. The haste was necessary and justifiable; even if the appreciation of the enemy's dispositions and intentions was correct—but, of course, it was not—so that the haste only produced added difficulties. Just before it got dark, the battalion close-leaguered in the formation it was to adopt for the approach march next day; *i.e.* the carrier platoon leading on a broad front followed by the rest of the battalion in five columns. Battalion Headquarters and Headquarters Company, led by Colonel Langran, standing up with his head through the roof of his station wagon, made up the centre column, and the four rifle companies the others. We moved off well before dawn, and slowly bumped our way, nose to tail, radiator to radiator, in an ungainly line across the Desert, through the darkness. That was stage one, and it was depressing.

"The battalion opened out at this point, and we halted in an area inhabited by other units, and here picked up the Valentine tanks which were to precede us on to the objective. Behind me were troops sitting in their 3-ton lorries, more or less impassive, as is their wont on such occasions. Very shortly the scene began to change; the ground became slightly undulating; battered vehicles of other units appeared, and the signs of battle, too, in the shape of unkempt tired men, working on their guns or vehicles.

"I felt the threat of a crisis. The battalion surged forward again, and now shells began to fall among the vehicles. Just a few at first, then more thickly. Colonel Langran, leading his troops into battle, literally even in this modern age, increased speed so that very soon we were all advancing in fine style and no doubt keeping the German gunners very busy shortening range.

"I can remember seeing the rear of a 3-ton lorry full of troops suddenly burst into flames, and the efforts of the men to tell the

THE CAULDRON

driver in his closed cab, quite oblivious to what had happened, to stop.

"As soon as this last forward movement started, we left the undulating ground behind and came on to flat desert, which was No-Man's-Land. The slight hill or ridge ahead was the enemy's forward position, and our objective. Langran stopped a few hundred yards before the hill and stepped out of his car. 'B' and 'C' Companies, commanded by Majors Dawson and Timbrell, continued forward toward the ridge, our tanks and carrier platoon having already arrived there. The Valentine tanks (4th R.T.R.) rallied to the rear sharply, as soon as our infantry arrived, and that was the last we saw of them. They had two-pounder guns: the German tanks had 75 mm. Battalion Headquarters was simply a spot on the open desert, where Colonel Langran had originally stopped. There was no cover, except from vehicles and an odd slit trench or two.

"It must have been about now that the German armour (15th Panzer Division) counter-attacked. They had, of course, been waiting to do this, and completely overran our two forward companies and more or less wiped them out. All nine officers were killed except one, who was taken prisoner. The tanks stopped at what had been for so short a time our forward position. From there they used their guns on us. Had these tanks advanced we should have been destroyed, because all the anti-tank platoon guns had been put out of action almost before they had had a chance to fire. But we learned afterwards that the enemy tanks formed part of a force that was after bigger game, namely, Ten Brigade on our right, which they were virtually to destroy later that day."

At seven o'clock the 22nd Armoured Brigade had informed Brigadier Fletcher's headquarters that they had completed their attack and were rallying north to B.204, to the north-east of Ten Brigade. They had met no enemy tanks, but had incurred a number of casualties from German anti-tank guns near Bir El Scerab, covering the 21st Panzer Division at Sidi Muftah.

German resistance from this quarter was more severe than might have been expected. The 32nd Army Tank Brigade, having run into a minefield, was unable to attack Sidi Muftah from the north. It failed to influence the battle, and to divert the enemy's strength which could concentrate to meet our attack from the east.

The withdrawal of the 22nd Armoured Brigade was to leave Langran's West Yorkshires in the open, to be attacked by German tanks.

Half an hour later, at half past seven, the West Yorkshires reported that they were being engaged by forty tanks and seventeen armoured cars (15th Panzer Division). On being informed of this fact, the Armoured Brigade, in its turn, announced the presence of German armoured units (21st Panzer Division) near B.204. This was true, for as we have seen, six German tanks were giving trouble west of the H.L.I. position. So were several 88 mm. guns.

Then, some time after nine o'clock, Ten Brigade told Divisional Headquarters that the H.L.I. had been subjected to a fierce tank attack and forced off B.204, having suffered many casualties. They were now concentrating at Bir Et Tamar, and enduring heavy shelling from guns and tanks near Barrels 174 and 175. The infantry were complaining that our own tanks were sitting behind them and not attempting to assist in the fight.

It should be here stated that the 22nd Armoured Brigade was not an Infantry Tank Brigade. Nor was it armed with the type of tanks designed for close-support action with infantry. Moreover, having once wheeled to the north-east, it is likely that the Armoured Brigade considered that to re-enter the Cauldron would be to leave open a dangerous gap between the Fifth Indian Division and the First Armoured Division, a gap now covered from the direction of Sidi Muftah by the position they had taken up.

Since May 26 these crews had had little sleep, some hard knocks, and many days of stern fighting. A number of their tanks had become casualties. They had no Grant tanks to stand up to the German tanks. The squadrons rarely started a battle at one hundred per cent. strength, and there were frequent mechanical breakdowns before the fighting area was reached. Moreover, after several days of action, a regiment might well be reduced to one composite squadron without reserves. Only two out of three tanks had a wireless set that worked on this occasion. Two hours before the start of the engagement, several tanks had broken down, and last-minute changes of crew and commander had been made.

But resolution did not mark the handling of our armour at the crisis of the battle. By the very nature of our attack we had challenged the enemy Panzer divisions to a decisive battle, but we had failed to concentrate our tank forces for this challenge.

For two hours, from ten-thirty, the H.L.I., who wore the red and white hackle on their bonnets and the Mackenzie tartan, were shelled and machine-gunned steadily. Their wounded were evacuated in carriers, for this was the sole means of getting them back over shell-torn sand. Brigadier Boucher appealed for assistance to our own tanks, and was backed up by requests from the Divisional Commander. But these waited still, a few hundred yards behind the infantry position; they drew down heavy fire on the troops, and could do nothing themselves to intervene, for fear of undue exposure.

It was at ten-thirty that Thorburn had come forward across the desert to 'D' company's position to tell Major Robertson that some two-pounder guns were being sent up to deal with the German tanks. One hour later these guns had not appeared. Then, about midday, the enemy tank attack developed. Preceded by intense shelling, machine-gun fire and mortaring, small groups of tanks slowly approached from right, centre, and left. It was a dangerous moment. Complete surprise had been achieved by clever use of ground.

No sooner had the 22nd Armoured Brigade moved back from its position near Thorburn's command post than this German tank pincer movement started. And 'C' Company—enfiladed on both sides—had to retire through a murderous hail of fire from every type of weapon. This cost them dear.

One platoon of the H.L.I. and their Gunner O.P. were seen to be trapped in a position from which no withdrawal was possible. Just after one o'clock the men tried to escape away to the right. But at once they met four enemy tanks approaching from that flank. One of the platoon, Private Campbell, was last heard shouting "Withdrawal impossible!" He charged a tank, firing his Bren gun from the hip. Most of these brave men were killed or wounded on the spot.

German tanks continued their methodical advance. They mopped up slit trenches one by one. At 1.15 p.m. Major Robertson decided that to stay longer would be to lose the whole of his 'D' Company to no good purpose. Accordingly, he led back the remnants to the Gurkha box at B.180, three miles away to the east.

When the armoured onslaught first began against his two forward companies, Colonel Douglas Thorburn realized quickly that unless support arrived very soon, the ridge of Bir Et Tamar could not be held except at a price: the destruction of the Highland Light Infantry. The Colonel did his utmost to urge our tanks to go forward. It was while standing on top of one tank, talking in a tone of fierce urgency to the squadron commander and imploring him to do something to stem the German progress, that he was struck on the head by a piece of shrapnel. His wound was bandaged with a field dressing. He carried on. He summoned Captain J. H. Rolls and ordered him to drive with all speed to Ten Brigade Headquarters. There he would inform Boucher that to hold the ground without reinforcements was now impossible. Thorburn needed the Gurkhas, the Brigade M.M.G. Company, and some guns that would take on the German tanks.

Rolls stood up to salute. At once he fell on the sand, shot clean through the forehead. He died instantly. Into his place hurried Captain Bromley Gardner, who commanded the battalion's carriers and had been striving throughout the morning to carry back the wounded to safety. He arrived at Brigade Headquarters. He explained the situation to Boucher. The Brigadier at once ordered the Gurkhas and the M.M.G. company to hasten to the aid of the H.L.I., and he added that the 28th Field Regiment had already been summoned forward. Bromley Gardner was on the point of leaving when there came a message on the wireless from Thorburn to announce that both his forward companies were being overrun and were withdrawing. A stand was to be made at battalion headquarters.

Boucher straightway cancelled the move of the Gurkhas, for to expend more man power would be fruitless. Instead, he did everything he possibly could do to persuade our tanks to counter-attack and save the situation. His attempts were unavailing.

Meanwhile Thorburn at Bir Et Tamar found himself obliged to give up his plan for making a last stand with his headquarters and the few men from the forward companies who still remained there. The position had by half past one become untenable, and he decided to retire. The battalion re-formed at B.180 behind the Gurkhas, having withdrawn on foot across the Desert under constant fire.

THE CAULDRON

Douglas Thorburn was driven back for attention to his wound. It is sad to record that he was killed a year later in the landings in Sicily. Major Kindersley assumed command. As that afternoon was drawing towards evening the battalion was taken out of the line in its own lorries. The casualties of the day now made room in the surviving transport for the whole number. Kindersley took them south to B.231 near Bir El Harmat, on the track that ran from Bir Hakeim to Knightsbridge. The men were meant to rest and sleep, but they had been in the new quarter of Desert but twenty minutes when they were both bombed and shelled. Soon after this, carriers from the D.C.L.I. rattled in with news that enemy tanks (15th Panzer Division) were approaching. Almost at once these came in sight. Kindersley telephoned to Brigade Headquarters for orders. He was told to take his men back until such time as he found opportunity to form up and dig in again. The battalion moved, but became badly split into little groups. An hour past midnight they had reached a point six miles beyond El Adem, having travelled some twenty-five miles to the east.

Meanwhile, General Messervy had ordered Fletcher to inspect the area now held by Langran's West Yorkshires, and to report whether or not it could be held. Messervy thought that the battalion would have to be withdrawn, as it seemed to be much in advance of our rear-guard position. Fletcher visited Sundius-Smith and the Baluch at B.178, and then walked to Langran's position, which he found in a little hollow. To the north, seventeen German tanks could be seen heading very slowly for B.178. The West Yorkshires' transport was burning in amongst them, but these tanks paid no apparent attention to our infantry in the hollow.

Fletcher ordered Langran to withdraw as soon as he was able to, adding that he would probably have to wait for darkness before he got an opportunity. However, at 2.15 p.m. the tanks rumbled towards B.178, soon came under our fire, and themselves began to shoot. Langran now saw a chance of escaping from his present exposed position. With great coolness he brought his battalion out in good order. Let Wiberg describe the withdrawal:

"When the time came for this, we just got up and slowly walked away across the desert. In contrast to most battles that end in defeat, we came out of it a good deal more slowly than we went in, leaving behind something like 180 dead and much wrecked transport and equipment, including our six 2-pounder anti-tank guns." The wounded were carried in Langran's staff car and in the very few trucks that had not been either sent back or set on fire.

A dangerous situation now arose on the left flank. The forward battery of 157 Field Regiment had originally been part of the West Yorkshire group. But when Langran's companies withdrew, this battery did likewise. Fortunately the situation was reported. At once the battery was ordered back into action, with an escort of one company of Jats. The line from B.180 to 100 now looked secure. At least four field regiments were in action. Our two flanks were near to the main minefield on the left and to the Knightsbridge position on the right.

General Briggs, in consequence of arriving at Boucher's Headquarters during a heavy Stuka raid on the terrible conglomeration of vehicles in the area, ordered Fletcher to form a composite brigade and to move with the West Yorkshires, H.L.I. and 3/12th R.F.F.R. to B.742, where the two British battalions could reorganize and the Indians be held in reserve. These moves were completed by half past six, when the enemy began to shell from the south.

"We were all sitting," wrote Wiberg, "round the mess table, having just finished eating, when a 3-tonner drove up at high speed and came to a stop in a cloud of dust and smoke. The driver jumped down and dashed up to Colonel Langran. Before he had a chance to say anything, Langran gave him a severe 'rocket' for making a dust. That over, the man blurted out the information that a German armoured column had broken through and was heading in our direction. He was quite right, as we soon discovered. Very soon there was further evidence. All manner of transport from other units, including, I am sad to say, perfectly good anti-tank guns, appeared, entirely unorganized, moving eastwards as though they were in a gold rush. We watched this in amusement for a moment or two, and then a carrier with a British officer went past near by. Langran stopped him. It was the carrier platoon commander of the 3/12th R.F.F.R. He also talked about German armoured columns breaking through. Having given all the information he could, he went forward, to the great relief of his Sikh driver, who had been saying 'Get going, Sahib,' throughout the thirty seconds' conversation.

"Langran hesitated, as well he might, undecided. We watched him. Then the matter was settled by the unmistakable sounds of small-calibre shells bursting in the area. The Colonel said 'On Truck,' and before you could say 'Knightsbridge' every man-jack had his feet off the ground, in spite of there being only half enough transport left from the day's war.

"Away we went, and not too soon, for German armoured cars were already running neck and neck with us. But we outstripped them, and the whole battalion headed eastwards at no mean pace."

Meanwhile, disaster had occurred on the left flank. That afternoon the 1st Duke of Cornwall's Light Infantry, after a forced march from Baghdad, arrived at Bir El Harmat to relieve the 2/4th Gurkhas. This new battalion, commanded by Lieutenant-Colonel H. W. Dean, had expected a day's rest before going into action, but patrols were sent out and found the enemy a few miles to the south-west of their position. The D.C.L.I. formed the sole barrier between the Eighth Army Headquarters area and lines of communication on the one hand, and any enemy attack from the south-west on the other. The battalion had the task of blocking lanes through our minefields, which came out near Bir El Harmat.

The companies had arrived piecemeal throughout that afternoon, armed with the normal issue anti-tank guns. Their position was critical. Behind them the remnants of the H.L.I. were unfit to assist. Beyond the Scotsmen stretched the echelons of various forward units. And at five o'clock, by which time the guns and tanks supporting the D.C.L.I. had been ordered into the front battle, Rommel chose to send tanks round this vital flank. The D.C.L.I.'s position, after being shelled and mortared, was attacked from the rear by a strong armoured force. The one rifle company charged with the bayonet. But infantry without tanks or guns were of no avail. Soon German tanks moved forward, and the battalion ceased to exist.

Briggs had ordered the 4th Field Regiment (Lieutenant-Colonel Truscott) to support the D.C.L.I. on our left flank, but later these gunners had been summoned by the Seventh Armoured Division to support its tanks. Later again, the 2nd Armoured Brigade, which had also been watching this flank, though from some distance to the rear, had been called into the main battle. This latter move caused Briggs to ask for 157 Field Regiment to be attached to the D.C.L.I. to operate in a column southwards. But the Armoured Division said this was unnecessary, as the flank was watched. In effect, it was precisely the unguarding of this flank which allowed the enemy tanks free access to the rear units of both divisions.

Of significance on this grave issue are Brigadier Fletcher's comments at the time:

"Our left flank had evidently not been guarded. Its protection was such an obvious necessity that it never occurred to me personally to ask what that protection was. I assumed that my Brigade and Ten Brigade would not be asked to advance five to eight miles into the enemy positions without adequate steps having been taken to protect the southern flank.

"There appears to have been a complete misunderstanding between the 22nd Armoured Brigade and Nine Brigade as to the capabilities and tasks of the two brigades. The 22nd Armoured Brigade appears to have thought that a battalion could establish itself in a box in the Desert in a matter of half an hour; while Nine Brigade thought that the 22nd Armoured Brigade, with its one hundred tanks, had been given the task of destroying the enemy tanks in this area in which it was to establish itself. In point of fact, the Armoured Brigade appears to have made no attempt to go to the assistance of the 2nd West Yorkshires when they were attacked by forty tanks and seventeen armoured cars; and when the position held by the 2nd H.L.I. was attacked by forty tanks, the 22nd Armoured Brigade began a slow withdrawal. Later, it reported itself faced by ninety tanks. The opportunity of destroying the two small concentrations of enemy tanks had passed.

"I consider that infantry who have to operate with tanks should be trained with them. There would not then be this wide divergence of opinion as to the tasks and capabilities of the two parts of a force engaged in any one operation. In the Desert infantry require forty-eight hours in which to establish a box which can stand by itself against an enemy tank attack. In addition, they must be allowed to lay mines. Lack of mutual understanding and of common doctrines extended beyond the failure of tanks and infantry to understand each other.

"The two companies of Royal Northumberland Fusiliers arrived in the concentration area at dusk on the evening before the battle. They had been stationed in Cairo without arms and unable to train. Suddenly they were issued with arms and ordered to entrain for the front. This was not fair on the men. 157 Field Regiment had arrived from Iraq two days before the battle, and the 3/9th Jats had come a fortnight before."

*   *   *   *   *

And what, meantime, was happening to the 3/12th Frontier Force Regiment ? By the afternoon Dean had moved his battalion back to a point two miles south of Bir El Harmat. Then he set off in search of Brigadier Fletcher, was directed to Messervy's headquarters, found the General in a trench, still outwardly cheerful, but Fletcher had already left to return to Nine Brigade Headquarters. At length Dean obtained orders to take his men back to their harbour area of the previous night: Fletcher had formed a new brigade of the West Yorkshires, Highland Light Infantry and 3/12th.

They drove towards the harbour, reading the numbers on the barrels as they went towards the east. And all the time scores of vehicles surged past, heading at great speed towards what their drivers deemed to be safety. When Colonel Dean and his battalion, driven by R.I.A.S.C. men in pool lorries, reached their destination, their eyes saw a vast concourse of vehicles that occupied several square miles of Desert. Dean chose the only empty space in this gathering, drew the battalion up in five company lines, ready to move off in any direction at short notice.

Suddenly the silence was shattered. Several shells landed near by. A few more whined overhead and crumped into the sand. The effect was startling. In Dean's striking simile, it was as though a teacher had taken a duster and wiped clean the blackboard of the Desert. The concourse of vehicles vanished into the dusk: And their wake of dust was caught just above the horizon by the setting sun.

Within a few moments only the 3/12th remained in the area. Then one of Dean's officers spotted a number of men three-quarters of a mile away. When these men started to run towards the Indian battalion, it was thought that an attack was coming in. One company was set in defence positions, but it soon became obvious that these were no enemy approaching, but a large party of the West Yorkshires, under Major Osborn. When the first shells landed they had been standing on the sand, having dismounted from their lorries. The R.I.A.S.C. drivers, following the general departure, had driven away hastily, leaving the British infantry alone, with no means of transport.

Soon after this a group of armoured cars came past. Dean stopped the first and asked what was happening behind. He was told that the Boche had broken through and was now driving east along the Trigh Capuzzo towards the El Adem box. Dean had no communication, and could apply to no one for orders. Only from passers-by could he glean news of the battle. A troop of Bofors guns now arrived, and then two of the battalion's anti-tank guns, so with these firing in turn at the German tanks which had meantime appeared on the horizon, they all moved slowly back.

This firing at the tanks, though it could have little effect, did hearten the troops, for it was a gesture of pulling faces at the enemy. Darkness had now fallen, and down on the Trigh Capuzzo fires were springing up, each one nearer to the east than the previous glare. This seemed to prove that the Germans were heading along the route, but it later turned out to be some of our own vehicles blowing themselves up on the minefields. Dean at the time thought that the German tanks were shooting up our retreating lorries. But as he could not get down the escarpment to the Trigh in darkness, he decided to report for orders to Brigadier Reid in El Adem.

After holding a census to see that the lorries had an equal share of petrol, the battalion, with Osborn's West Yorkshires and the Gunners, moved along the top of the escarpment. Air raids could be seen and heard over Tobruk. Noise was coming from the Trigh below. At length they came to the El Adem wire, and turned along the outside edge of the minefield until the sole entrance on the north side was found.

Dean went inside to find Brigadier Reid, and was ordered to take the 3/12th to B.650. This was a position some four miles north-west of El Adem, just where the road crossed the escarpment. This road was of vital importance to the enemy. When we held the port during the first siege, the Italians had built it as a metalled highway to bypass Tobruk. Now, if we held Tobruk again, the Axis troops would need this bypass for their pursuit and exploitation.

THE CAULDRON

At B.650 Dean found Gleeson's 3/2nd Punjab. Within an hour the hand-over was made, Gleeson's battalion on its way, and the 3/12th Frontier Force Regiment established. And here for the moment we must leave them.

* * * * *

Having overcome the D.C.L.I., thrown out to protect our southern flank, the enemy tanks now overran the joint tactical headquarters of Messervy and Briggs, and that of Ten Brigade. This happened at seven o'clock. Lieutenant-Colonel C. L. Morgan, commanding the Divisional Signals, was with General Messervy at the time. A heavy dive-bombing raid coincided with the tank attack. When things were particularly fierce the General said to Morgan in a quiet voice: "Don't you think it is time we left here?" Morgan agreed heartily. Messervy jumped into his armoured car, but Morgan and the others had first to extract the Signal Office lorry which had been dug in. They got away with the loss of only the small cook-house truck.

Morgan tapped in on the cable to Main Divisional Headquarters, and warned the G.S.O.1, Colonel A. R. Barker, known as 'Tochi,' of what had occurred. When Morgan did reach Main Division he found an atmosphere of calm disbelief in the likelihood of unpleasant events. The headquarters staff of the Divisional artillery were about to have their supper, all laid out on a table.

Just then a young officer of the D.C.L.I. came up, and told the C.R.E., Colonel Napier, that he had a small detachment near by. He could see some German tanks in the distance. Napier passed this information to Barker, but before anyone could act, an airburst overhead showed that the headquarters vehicles were now coming under fire. At that moment General Briggs arrived. On his return from seeing Boucher at Ten Brigade, he had approached his tactical headquarters, only to find it in enemy hands. Briggs, ignorant of what had taken place, received a very hostile reception. Chased by German tanks, he headed at full speed for Main Headquarters and ordered a hasty move. A rendezvous was fixed. A few seconds later the command vehicle was seen to be moving off, followed by such other trucks as were ready. Signals had some trouble in getting the heavy Signal Office lorry clear of its many telephone cables and out of its pit. Enemy tracer being now directed upon Signals vehicles, Morgan's car stopped a bullet in one of its rear wheels. The car was driven on a flat tyre, with Morgan's orderly sitting on the Signalmaster's knee, and the back of the car tight with men. Finally the whole wheel collapsed, but those in the car were picked up by an Ordnance lorry and taken to El Adem.

Meanwhile, Napier's vehicles in headquarters, and those of the C.R.A., Brigadier Vallentin, still had their camouflage nets down. By the time the Engineers had packed up ready to move off, they were under close-range machine-gun fire. Napier's small headquarters, the last to leave, moved away in a group of five vehicles, hotly pursued for four miles by streams of tracer bullets. Not one truck was hit, nor was there a single casualty. And at dusk the enemy abandoned the chase. He established picquets, and fired Very lights every few minutes as was his custom. As no one was found at the given rendezvous, Napier considered the wisest course of action. "I was," he wrote, "surprised to find more lights going up in the east, as though there were German advanced posts in that direction also, but my field glasses revealed a number of vehicles apparently blowing themselves up on a minefield. This we found indeed to be the case, a most extraordinary scene of confusion. I believe some Indian drivers thought they were under shell fire and so tried to run the gauntlet at speed, only to be themselves blown up.

"This was the position outside El Adem, held by the 3/12th R.F.F.R., who were desperately trying to guide the vehicles through the unmined gap. We crept through, and on the road beyond found ourselves taking part in a 'gold rush.' By this I mean a disorderly stream of miscellaneous trucks and lorries, going away from the enemy, with a tendency to hurry and apparently motivated by fear. It is only fair to say that on this occasion it was dark, there were many vehicles of different units and formations, the majority not of our division nor indeed of any division. Some of them, one would have thought, should never have been in a forward area at all during a battle. The scene was a road on the escarpment, a defile, whereas we were all accustomed by now to the open Desert spaces. Under these circumstances, great confusion was inevitable, quite apart from the tension caused by the very unfavourable turn of events."

Napier gave up the attempt to reach Rear Division with his small party. Instead, they turned off the road and slept till daybreak.

We must leave this scene of confusion and hurried escape, typical of the experiences of hundreds of men that evening and night, when the enemy seemed everywhere, the tides of battle running against us in every quarter, the lack of information oppressive, and the sudden comings and goings a source of anxiety and despair. Many there were who did not know what they were meant to do. They were just fighting the enemy wherever he was encountered. Few knew what was now our main object, for the original plan of attack had been thwarted and turned against us. The troops who had set out that morning in darkness were now being smashed and decimated and split and driven in flight, overrun and captured, pursued and harried, shelled and dive-bombed, encircled and crushed by armoured forces. Men needed their firmest courage in such an hour as this. Officers and N.C.Os. were forced to take sudden decisions upon which their lives depended, but without news of where the enemy or our own units now were. Messages were flying but communications were breaking down whenever a cable was torn and cut, a wireless set shelled, a headquarters put to retreat or captured.

Well might A. E. Housman have called June 5 "the day when heaven was falling, the hour when earth's foundations fled." During these hours many acts of great gallantry were performed that will for ever go unrecorded. If there were the few who crumpled under the weight of such desperate events, they were far outnumbered by those who showed a resolute example to their companions and to those whom they served or commanded. In the hour of trial, as was frequently observed, some men proved themselves to be better than ever they had been given credit for. Perhaps, even, they stood firmer than they themselves had imagined possible.

The memories of that day and the night that followed are burnt deep into those who came through the testing. But there were hundreds who did not survive; instead, they lay on the sands in attitudes of sudden death, in prolonged agony, or with fatal wounds, with flies to torment, the sun to scorch their suffering bodies, no water, burning tanks and trucks around them, hastening arrivals and departures, and slowly diminishing hope as the fighting ebbed and flowed, and became ever graver towards our own situation. Those who were captured that day numbered as many as the dead and wounded. Suddenly they were swept up in the swirl of mobile warfare. Without warning the enemy was upon them. Their trucks broke down or were hit, and they could not escape the pursuing foe. Or these men fought their guns to the last, until they were taken prisoner. Or in driving to what they believed was safety they blundered into a German column and were taken.

* * * * *

But for a moment we must turn back to watch the misfortunes that beset Boucher's Ten Brigade. At 6.30 p.m. on June 5 the enemy delivered a severe bombing attack north-east of Brigade Headquarters. Then he shelled the area from the south. And, finally, a few of his tanks came into view 1,500 yards away. Forbes, the Brigade Major, ordered the H.L.I. to withdraw in a north-easterly direction. The Headquarters remained. But at seven o'clock it was overrun by tanks and forced to withdraw. Many escaped in trucks before the enemy could mop them up. In the course of this withdrawal, communication with the battalions was lost, never to be regained. Brigade Headquarters became separated and, when darkness fell, split up into groups of vehicles, all moving somewhere in the stretch of Desert between Tobruk and El Adem.

Brigadier Boucher was missing, but this was not yet known to most of his troops. He was returning from visiting forward troops to his Brigade Headquarters, accompanied in a carrier by three Indian ranks. Shot and shell began to fall about them from directions where no enemy should have been. The Signals and escort trucks lost contact. Time and again Boucher was frustrated from following the bearing on his route: heavy shelling and the presence of German and Italian groups and columns prevented this. When night fell the carrier had suffered a direct hit, one man had been killed, and further progress was impossible, so Boucher and the two remaining Baluchis took refuge in a derelict three-ton lorry. During that night long columns of tanks passed to and fro, without giving signs as to whether they were friend or foe. At daybreak the two sepoys crept out to pay their usual early morning visit. They saw tanks to the east of them, and more tanks to the west. Both groups had leaguered close to one another. Both knew that they had no forward outposts where this lorry was standing. On seeing the two figures moving, both sides opened fire on the derelict. A battle ensued, and the British tanks were forced to withdraw from the scene. Boucher sheltered in a handy trench with the Indians until the firing died down, and then set off across the sand on foot towards the Baluch position. Soon a further group of vehicles appeared from the south-west. This time it was part of the German 90th Light Division, who machine-gunned the Brigadier and his companions.

By now the three men were tired. They could see the 4/10th Baluch fighting ahead by the horizon, and the sounds of battle reached them across the Desert. And then a German battery of guns came into action near where Boucher was. He had just time to find a slit trench, bury the two Indians with sand, and cover himself in the same way, with twigs of scrub to allow an air passage, before the German artillery arrived. For some time Boucher lay concealed. All round him the enemy guns were firing. In the lulls he could hear shouts and orders. Men were passing near him. Soon the British artillery ranged on this battery and shelled it heavily. The R.A.F. bombed it. A German gunner saw the slit trench and jumped into it, right on top of the Brigadier. It happened that one of the Brigadier's boots was showing out of the mound of sand. The German soldier saw this boot, was tempted to steal it and its fellow from the supposed corpse, and yanked out Brigadier Charles Boucher with the coveted boot. Thus was he captured. The two Indian ranks, seeing what had happened, stood up and were captured too.

To turn back to the late afternoon of June 5. General Briggs had placed the 3/9th Jats with Ten Brigade to replace the battered H.L.I. Two companies moved forward under Major J. J. Waite to find the Brigade. But when news reached Lieutenant-Colonel H. V. Bragg, the Commanding Officer, that Ten Brigade Headquarters had been forced to disperse, he went to look for Waite and his men. With him were Captain Schubert, Lieutenant Rowling, and an attached R.I.A.S.C. officer. This party caught up the two companies, and began to discuss plans. Rowling was sent off on a mission. Then a shell landed among the group, and all these officers were killed outright by the direct hit. This was one more disaster in a day of disasters.

The rest of Ten Brigade, with the motor battalion of the 22nd Armoured Brigade and Truscott's 4th Field Regiment, stayed in their positions on Dahar El Aslagh, to hold the ridge. Here they awaited the enemy's next move, with orders to hold on to the last. To dig in the guns was impossible. The commanders of the First and Seventh Armoured Divisions realized the gravity of Ten Brigade's position, and formed plans for a counter-attack to rescue the infantry from the encircling enemy. General Messervy found that his 22nd Armoured Brigade was in no fair condition to take part in such an attack; sixty tanks had been lost from shell fire or mechanical failures during the day's fighting.

And the guns of the German tanks could penetrate our tanks while remaining two hundred yards outside the furthest range of our own tank weapons. The enemy tanks were thus enabled to reduce our armoured strength while they themselves escaped almost unscathed.

Our 4th Armoured Brigade, which had been reinforced by a regiment, made slow progress from the north. And, worst of all, owing to a misunderstanding of orders, the 2nd Armoured Brigade attacked too far north and found its advance blocked by an impassable escarpment. The tanks could only intervene in the battle at long range, and this was of little value. And so the armoured counter-attack proved abortive on June 6, and failed to prevent the enemy from overwhelming our infantry and artillery.

That morning, June 6, Ten Brigade, unprotected by armour, was attacked on Dahar El Aslagh. At seven o'clock heavy shelling started, and sixty tanks slowly approached the 4/10th Baluch, making use of the ground, hull down. They halted beyond effective anti-tank range, and all our six-pounders were knocked out of action without being able to retaliate with success. The 4th Field Regiment was slowly destroyed. Our guns were obliged to use their ammunition sparingly. Should they fire shells at too great a range for accuracy, or wait till the German tanks came near enough to hit with effect? If the guns did wait, they were exposed to terrible fire, for their positions were exposed. One by one, slowly, systematically, the field guns were blown up.

By half-past nine only two 25-pounders were still firing. The

Baluch carriers had been overrun. At the same time the leading company commander telephoned to Lieutenant-Colonel B. L. Sundius-Smith and said, "The tanks are coming through now." Ten minutes later the Colonel ordered another company to retire to the box at B.180. His battalion headquarters was taken by the first group of tanks that roared across the position. With no opposition but small-arms fire, they came forward, and sat over our slit trenches, their guns trained at point-blank range, while dismounted lorried infantry gestured "Get out—or else. . ." And so our infantry were mopped up, still fighting, but with their ammunition exhausted or very low. It was this battle that Brigadier Boucher had heard when walking over the Desert that morning towards eventual capture. Only scattered remnants of Ten Brigade escaped to tell the tale and to fight another day.

The Highland Light Infantry, saved from annihilation by Briggs' order to join Nine Brigade, re-formed in the El Adem "box." Stragglers and small detachments came in all that day. When the roll was called, of the twenty-five officers and 678 men who entered the battle, fifteen officers and 467 other ranks remained to answer their names. In the early morning rain fell heavily. And Richard Bromley Gardner noted in his diary: "A good thing; it washed the blood off our vehicles."

And so it ended. Our counter-attack against Rommel's forces in the Cauldron had failed. Far from destroying the enemy, we had ourselves been severely mauled, our tank strength had been gravely reduced, and one brigade of infantry had been wiped out save for isolated parties who made their way back to safety after strange adventures. Four artillery regiments had been lost, their guns spreadeagled or damaged, their crews killed or captured. So great had been our losses, so widespread the disorganization, so bewildering the confusion and lack of control, that a withdrawal of the forces round Knightsbridge became inevitable. Tobruk, El Adem, and Bir Hakeim were the next bastions in our defence, and it will be seen how each in turn was to fare, and in what way the defenders of each were to conduct themselves.

CHAPTER XVI

FIGHTING RETREAT AND REARGUARD ACTIONS

JUNE 1942

ALL this time Denys Reid's 29 Brigade, with the 3rd Field Regiment (Lieutenant-Colonel P. H. Teesdale) under command, had been deployed round El Adem. The Brigade found itself taking orders direct from Thirty Corps Commander, General Willoughby Norrie, who was also in El Adem.

During the first twelve days of June Reid operated two mobile columns whose task was to harry the enemy along his lines of communication between Bir Hakeim and the Cauldron. Our small columns normally comprised two platoons of infantry, a battery of 25-pounders, one troop of two-pounder anti-tank guns. Sometimes a machine-gun section or a troop of Bofors A.A. guns was added. These columns, whose movements were directed by Messervy's Seventh Armoured Division, were led by Majors Leatherdale, Hale, Hind, Dodd, Syme, and Captains Digby Trout and Haslehurst. They remained out for three days at a time, and were relieved in turn.

No column came back without having shelled enemy troops and transport, though the infantry never came to close quarters, and the anti-tank guns had few opportunities for action. On one successful day 'Leathercol,' with its platoons of the 1/5th Mahrattas, destroyed twenty-seven German tanks near Bir Hakeim, having received word that these tanks were immobilized through mechanical defects and lack of petrol.

Lieutenant-Colonel Dean's 3/12th Frontier Force Regiment was placed under Reid's command for the purpose of completing and garrisoning the partially constructed auxiliary box at B.650, some three miles to the north-west where the Acroma road descends the escarpment. This battalion, had not, as we have seen, been engaged in the Cauldron, and was left behind when the rest of Nine Brigade withdrew to Bagush to re-form and refit. On

June 8 the 1st Worcestershires (Lieutenant-Colonel J. C. O. Knight), with a battery from the 3rd Field Regiment and a troop of Bofors guns, occupied a second auxiliary box at Pt. 187, a further ten miles north-west of El Adem, and a little to the south of Acroma itself. Here they came under the 22nd Armoured Brigade. In the light of events, this decision to form two subsidiary defence positions was wrong, Reid being left seriously short of artillery in the main box at El Adem. The results of this dispersal of strength were disastrous.

Rommel had started his attacks against Bir Hakeim on June 6, and they continued with growing intensity despite the valiant resistance of Koenig's First Free French Brigade. So grave did the situation there become that by nightfall on the 8th it was apparent that unless immediate outside support were given to the French garrison, it could not hold out. When a further two days had passed, the Army Commander ordered Koenig to evacuate Bir Hakeim. And the Free French were withdrawn during the night of June 10, escorted by Messervy's Seventh Armoured Division.

Having overcome our opposition at Bir Hakeim, the German 90th Light Division advanced swiftly north-east. On its left flank moved the 15th Panzer Division. As, by nightfall on June 11, the enemy's forward troops with some thirty tanks were but ten miles from El Adem, Messervy ordered Reid to withdraw his mobile columns into the box. The remnants of Nine and Ten Brigades had already, four days earlier, withdrawn east of Sollum, near to Buq-Buq. These remnants were indeed few: of the 4/10th Baluch five officers and 190 men survived; the 3/9th Jats had only seven officers; of the 2/4th Gurkhas one officer and 156 men remained; the Highland Light Infantry, now under Nine Brigade and commanded by Major E. L. Percival, D.S.O., could muster fifteen officers and just over four hundred men. Ten Brigade Headquarters was almost complete, except for Brigadier Boucher, who was now a prisoner of war. 28th Field Regiment H.Q. had vanished in the battle of the Cauldron, and the 4th Field Regiment had been severely mauled. The only battalion of Fletcher's brigade which had not suffered heavily on June 5 was the 3/12th F.F.R., now attached to 29 Brigade.

On June 12 the German 90th Light Division made its first

assault against the El Adem box. Shells fired from the south-west landed inside our defences soon after dawn that day. Our own artillery retaliated. And Brigadier Reid sent out a mobile column with guns, under Major W. G. Hale, to delay the enemy. Hale's column at once sighted a strong German force south of our box. When the 25-pounders engaged this target, they were immediately fired on themselves and one of our guns was knocked out within a few minutes. So Hale brought his small force back into El Adem.

Meanwhile, carriers of the 3/2nd Punjab (Lieutenant-Colonel L. D. Gleeson), also sent out to delay the enemy, had been dispersed and cut off by the Germans, and withdrew to Tobruk.

During the first part of the morning German lorried infantry occupied a ridge and a deserted Arab village—no more than low broken walls and piles of rubble—that lay south-east of the box. Though several tanks were destroyed by our guns, though the 1/5th Mahrattas (Lieutenant-Colonel W. D. Marshall), when approached by thirty German armoured troop carriers, forced the enemy to dismount, and though our machine-gunners fired to good effect, these Germans could not be prevented from digging in.

The main El Adem box was now surrounded. Our gun positions, in particular, were intermittently subjected to heavy shelling. Colonel Teesdale and several Gunner officers were wounded, and three guns hit. At this time Reid only had six 25-pounders in action. Enemy transport frequently presented excellent targets, but so heavy a counter-battery fire did our Gunners draw down upon themselves whenever they did shoot, that they were ordered to hold their fire as much as possible. We could not risk the loss of all our field guns during the early days of the siege.

Meanwhile, Dean's Frontier Force box away across the sand at B.650, though shelled from time to time, was not seriously attacked either on the 12th or 13th, and remained in wireless communication with Brigade Headquarters.

Early on June 13 Royal Air Force Kittyhawks strafed the enemy round the El Adem box. Daylight brought renewed shelling of our gun positions. From the south and west, where a tank battle was being fought, came the sound of heavy gunfire. To the east our troops could see the enemy being shelled from behind by certain British columns that were operating outside.

Then, during the late afternoon, a fierce duststorm so reduced visibility that the defenders of the box lost sight of these engagements. They lacked news of what was happening beyond their own perimeter.

Towards evening another battle raged, and the enemy started withdrawing south from El Adem. The aerodrome was evacuated. And at nightfall a large column of German transport drove away from the ruined village and moved westwards along the crest of a ridge south of the box. Silhouetted against the sky, these vehicles offered a perfect target. For twenty minutes they were bombarded by every gun at Reid's disposal, including sixteen light and heavy anti-aircraft guns. When this three-mile-long column vanished into the dusk, twenty hulks, four of them blazing, were left clearly visible on the skyline.

It was midnight before the sound of gunfire died away. Our patrols came back with reports that no enemy troops were to be found in the neighbourhood, except for one German party attempting to recover vehicles from the ridge. Six prisoners were taken. Next day, June 14, the enemy was still absent.

To General Auchinleck's mind it was essential to hold El Adem in order to prevent the permanent isolation of Tobruk. Accordingly, he ordered Ritchie to reinforce the position at once. But this proved impossible. On the afternoon of June 14 began the evacuation of the Gazala line, held by the First South African Division. The Eighth Army was now, by defending a line through Acroma and El Adem, to save Tobruk from encirclement and siege. To 29 Brigade was assigned a mobile covering role, and all troops in the Brigade Group not required for the immediate formation of three columns were to be sent back next day to El Hamra.

But by midday on the 16th the transport needed for such a move had not reached El Adem. Instead, the Germans had again surrounded our positions. No sooner had an early attack against the 1/5th Mahrattas on the west side of the box and against Gleeson's 3/2nd Punjab on the opposite perimeter been repulsed, than the enemy began to dig in. All day fighting continued. Upon the enemy were inflicted many casualties, and during that afternoon German and Italian ambulances made no less than six trips along our minefield wire to pick up their wounded. When great numbers of enemy vehicles passed north of the box, Reid's staff were able to direct the Royal Air Force on to many suitable targets that our pilots engaged with promptitude and accuracy.

This encirclement of El Adem had also isolated our two auxiliary boxes held by Knight's Worcestershires and the 3/12th. The British battalion was attacked at B.187 during the afternoon of June 15. The defenders made a devoted stand, and endured an artillery bombardment for hours on end. When German tanks formed up and attacked the position, they were met by accurate fire from our 2-pounders. Several tanks were destroyed. The rest withdrew. For twenty-four hours Knight's men held off the enemy, and in that time knocked out seventeen tanks.

At dawn on June 16 the enemy, enraged at his failure to break through on the previous day, launched a second armoured assault. This, too, was vain. All that morning Stuka dive-bombers were sent to raid the Worcestershires' lonely corner of the Desert. All that morning bombs thudded and exploded, and erupted showers of sand and flailing metal splinters. Casualties mounted among the resolute, tenacious defenders. But each time the German tanks probed their way forward through the dust, our anti-tank gunners drove them back.

Ammunition, food, water were by now low. And that afternoon the Worcestershires were ordered by the First Armoured Division to leave the position at B.187. To offer further resistance would mean the total loss of the battalion and supporting gunners. Nor could it now serve any good purpose. The 1st Worcestershires escaped in good order to Tobruk, but only a handful of the gallant fighters survived the subsequent disaster there. An immediate D.S.O. was awarded to Colonel Knight.

And what of our other small box? On the previous evening Colonel Dean had been summoned to a conference in El Adem. He arrived after a nightmare drive, and was greeted by Denys Reid with food and beer. He learned that the South African Division in the Gazala line and the 50th Division were drawing back. Tobruk would be held. Dean was to evacuate B.650 next morning. Lorries would be sent up for his use, and the 3/12th F.F.R. was given a rendezvous behind Halfaya.

Dean returned to B.650 before daybreak, and gave out his orders. Then with daylight came a large German column, driving

FIGHTING RETREAT AND REARGUARD ACTIONS

along the escarpment between our two boxes. The defenders of El Adem fired at the enemy. The guns in B.650 did the same. Though a few vehicles were hit, the others remained dispersed over the sand, and took little notice. But away to the west the German 90th Light Division, from its halting-place of the previous night, could overlook B.650 and see Dean's artillery firing. At once the Germans started to shell our guns. Soon eight enemy batteries were shooting at the Frontier Force box.

Our troop of 2-pounders was ordered not to disclose their positions until a serious attack came in. Otherwise they would be blotted out by the enemy, who was only too eager to discover our anti-tank weapons. Dean realized that none of the promised lorries could reach his box. Brigadier Reid had told Dean in Urdu on the wireless that there would be no move without orders from higher authority. In any case it was now clear that to leave B.650 was impossible. Parties of the enemy were manœuvring on all sides. A first tank attack was launched, but retired after losing seven tanks on or near our minefield.

That afternoon the 3/12th were attacked a second time, after our anti-tank guns had been heavily shelled. German tanks roared in from the west, blasted 'A' Company, under Major G. N. Heath—son of the former Divisional Commander. Enough mines were lifted to allow one tank to pass through. Behind came other tanks and lorried infantry. They routed out and destroyed each section and platoon one by one. Our only vehicles in the box—one truck for each company—were burning amid the haze of dust and smoke. This made it very hard to see what was happening. One 25-pounder was still firing, and each fresh crew lasted just long enough to fire one or two rounds before being killed or wounded and replaced by more gunners, who in their turn fired to the end. Dean was without communication: every cable had been cut, and the wireless aerial taken down, because it was too obvious a landmark for enemy artillery.

Dust spurted up from bullets that found a grave on every side. By now Colonel Dean and his jemadar adjutant were firing rifles themselves. And the German tanks were penetrating the box. Dean saw the crew of the Bofors gun near the entrance walk out with their hands up. Major Stanley Raw was killed leading 'D' Company in a counter-attack. The carriers were told to attack, but their officer, Donald Baird, was struck down by a shell as he climbed into his leading carrier.

Then a line of German infantry advanced into the centre of our position. Dean took aim at the tallest German and killed him. Every spare man was firing at the approaching line of troops, but still they came on. Dean went down into his small command-post that was linked to other dugouts by a crawl-trench, and looked at the enemy through the window. A German soldier flashed past, and hid behind a mound of sand. One tank, summoned by the shouts of this soldier, came right up close. The crew called on Dean and his companions to come out. "Herauskommen!" they shouted through the noise of battle. There was no alternative but to come out. All secret papers had already been buried in the sandy floor of the command-post. The adjutant, Hugh Philips, smashed the telephone.

As soon as they walked outside they were covered by German guns. Dean learned that 'A' Company had been overrun, and Heath captured. Maurice Curtis had been shot as he led 'C' Company in a final charge. The battalion had suffered close on a hundred casualties in the day's fighting. The officers were kept separate from the sepoys, and both groups were ringed with Germans armed with automatic weapons. Dean ordered his men to fall in, called the roll, and took a list of survivors. At this time the Germans made no attempt at interrogation. One German subaltern gave Dean an overcoat and brought a chair from his truck, for Dean had only what he stood up in and a blanket. His attaché case that contained washing and writing kit had been taken from him.

The German manner was correct throughout. But our prisoners were given neither food nor water; their captors explained that no supply columns had yet arrived, and they were still fighting a battle. So desperate with thirst did the Indian soldiers grow that Colonel Dean persuaded the German staff officers to send one of his company commanders and a lorry back to B.650 to collect packals of water and tins of biscuits that the battalion had buried. Dean records that one havildar was so heartbroken at the plight of his battalion, which could fight no more, that he wept, and said: "Pultan tut gaya" (the regiment is broken.)

Eventually Dean and his officers were taken to Derna and flown to Italy. The Indian ranks were escorted in a column too close to our positions at Acroma, were fired on, and managed in the confusion to make contact with the British garrison. They went inside and later made their way to Tobruk, only to be captured a second time when the town capitulated.

* * * * *

We must return to follow the fortunes of the rest of 29 Brigade. Throughout June 16 the El Adem box was shelled from all sides. When the Germans tried to approach our wire they were forced to retreat by our machine-guns. Great numbers of enemy vehicles drove past the box, heading towards the east. That morning Brigadier Reid received orders from the Seventh Armoured Division to extricate his brigade during the coming night. He summoned a conference and explained his plan of withdrawal. The gathering had no sooner broken up than Reid was called to the wireless set. From General Messervy he learned that these orders to withdraw had now been cancelled by Higher Command, and that 29 Brigade would remain where it was and fight to the last. But at four o'clock Messervy again spoke to Reid on the wireless, and the decision to move out or to stay fast was left entirely in the Brigadier's hands.

At length Denys Reid made his decision. The troops would move back that night, given a fair chance of extricating the most important equipment. But to avoid having yet again to reverse his plans, Reid disclosed these to no one until the last possible moment. He merely gave orders for the infantry to maintain their patrols that night. He needed early information about the enemy's strength and whereabouts in the south and south-eastern sectors of El Adem. On this information would depend the Brigade Commander's final decision.

The patrols brought in favourable reports, and at half past nine a fresh conference was held. Reid issued his orders. Two gaps would be made in the minefield. Petrol and stores were to be destroyed. A detachment of Sappers would remain behind and start demolitions at three o'clock in the morning.

The withdrawal started at 2 a.m. on the 17th. The troops moved, independently, due south for a dozen miles in the direction of El Gubi to a point where transport of the Seventh

Armoured Division had been instructed to pick them up. Sending ahead their vehicles, with all guns and valuable equipment, the 3/2nd Punjab and 1/5th Mahrattas walked out of El Adem in small parties. Most succeeded in filtering through without meeting the enemy patrols in the dark, but two Punjabi companies which stumbled into enemy leaguers had to fight their way through with bayonet and tommy-gun. A few men, less fortunate, walked straight into prepared positions and were killed, captured or scattered.

At the rendezvous transport was found, and these trucks continued to pick up stragglers all through the next morning.

Though all our anti-tank guns had been lost in this withdrawal, the six 25-pounders and several Bofors guns were brought out safely, and most of the equipment. Of Marshall's 1/5th Mahrattas 150 men were missing, and of the 3/2nd about ninety.

On June 19 Reid's brigade, such as it now was, moved to El Hamra beside the Fifth Indian Division. To General Briggs' command had been added Five Indian Brigade, summoned in haste from Palestine to join the Eighth Army. This brigade was led by the former G.S.O.1 of the Division, Brigadier Dudley Russell, and normally belonged to the Fourth Indian Division. It had moved into the Kennels area on June 14, and left Briggs' command four days later for Sollum, when the Fifth Indian Division handed over the defence of El Hamra to the South Africans and went back into reserve at Sofafi.

On the 19th General Briggs and his headquarters entered Bagush and reassumed command of what remained of Nine and Ten Brigades, together with the 1st and 2nd Free French Brigades. Reid's 29 Brigade also came into Bagush, on June 22. The 1st Worcestershires were replaced by Percival's 2nd Highland Light Infantry, and the 32nd Field Regiment (Lieutenant-Colonel Biscoe) joined the brigade to replace of the 3rd Field Regiment. The Division was given a role on the Lines of Communication between Mersa Matruh and a point west of El Alamein.

But in the meantime the Eighth Army and the whole world had been shocked by the news that Tobruk had fallen on June 20. The place, so grimly defended in the previous siege, had become encircled three days earlier, when we had been forced from our positions at Sidi Rezegh. The Germans attacked from the east;

FIGHTING RETREAT AND REARGUARD ACTIONS

in the previous siege our artillery had been moved to beat off just such an assault from the same quarter. Its direction had been foreseen. Now our transport was gathered in that part of the perimeter, and our guns were less mobile than before.

The disastrous losses of men and materials in Tobruk angered our troops. Far from causing depression, this blow stirred the Army to more resolute determination, to still greater exertions.

On June 22 orders were received that Ten Corps, the headquarters of which had just arrived from Syria, would hold Mersa Matruh at all costs and prevent the enemy from establishing himself east of a line running south to Sidi Hamza. The forces to hold this line were the Tenth Indian Division in the Matruh defences, the First Armoured Division south and west as far as Bir Qaim, Freyberg's New Zealand Division, which had also just hurried down from Syria, at Minqar Qaim, twenty-five miles from Matruh, and the Fiftieth British and Fifth Indian Divisions in the area of Sidi Hamza and of the minefield by the main Matruh–Siwa road.

Three days later General Auchinleck assumed personal command of the Eighth Army from Ritchie. Meanwhile, far back between El Alamein and the Qattara Depression, Thirty Corps was busy organizing a line of defence with the First South African Division and the 2nd Free French Brigade.

The Germans and Italians had reached Bardia on the 22nd, and pressed on next day south of Sidi Omar. Sidi Barrani had been passed, two columns struck towards Halfaya, a third headed for Maddalena. And so it came about that the enemy drew close to Mersa Matruh.

Our infantry divisions were instructed to organize themselves into battle groups having the largest number of field guns available, and enough infantry and no more to protect these guns. Artillery was now our only striking weapon; we had mines for delaying purposes. Such a mobile defence could be moved from point to point wherever the danger was greatest. Accordingly, Brigadier Reid sent out two columns: 'Gleecol,' led by Lieutenant-Colonel L. D. Gleeson, with a battery of 25-pounders, another of anti-tank guns, and two platoons of the Highland Light Infantry; and 'Leathercol,' under Major Leatherdale, that had two platoons of the 3/2nd Punjab, and a similar force of artillery. Their task was to delay the enemy north-west of the Siwa road.

The Mersa Matruh position, apart from the perimeter round the town itself, comprised a covering line to the west, in front of which ran a deep minefield from the coast to Charing Cross, and two further minefields that had been laid northwards from Sidi Hamza, on high ground fifteen miles south of Matruh. It was the passage between these two groups of minefields that 29 Brigade was ordered to close with all speed. But the Brigade was to prove too weak to halt the enemy tanks, which eventually broke through, as will be seen, and forced our columns back. Our mines caused the enemy but little delay.

While 'Gleecol' and 'Leathercol' searched for the enemy west of our minefields, the Sappers from 20 and 21 Field Companies, aided by those from the New Zealand Division, worked all day and night to close the gap between our two minefields. By eleven o'clock that night they had done the work, and our columns, which had made no contact with the enemy during daylight, withdrew behind the mines. Soon afterwards several German tanks, preceded by a lorry, approached from the west. The lorry blew up on the minefield, which had deliberately not been marked by wire. On seeing this, the tanks withdrew at speed.

That afternoon the last train steamed out of Matruh. The last British armoured forces moved within the perimeter. Then next day, June 26, the enemy arrived at Charing Cross, seven miles south of Matruh. At half past three two German armoured columns scouted along the minefields in search of gaps, and after bombarding 29 Brigade's position, attacked it. At a quarter to seven our transport was withdrawn from the box. At seven o'clock 'Gleecol' reported that one hundred enemy tanks had broken through the minefields in the north-west corner and were advancing towards the column's position. The German engineers rode on the tanks, ready to jump down and deal with mines. From that moment onwards the wireless failed. The two columns and our Gunners were too busy fighting the battle to pass back details of the engagement. 'Gleecol' and 'Leathercol' did their utmost to delay and destroy the enemy, but they had not the strength. The Germans did lose tanks and many vehicles on the mines and from our shelling.

The enemy took but thirty minutes to penetrate our minefield. Their infantry followed the tanks. 'Leathercol' was overrun, but a few men and guns got away, including Major Leatherdale himself. He was to command the 3/2nd Punjab while Gleeson continued to lead his column, which fared a little better in the onslaught. At eight o'clock the 3/2nd were ordered to withdraw with Brigade Headquarters to a rendezvous seven miles north-east from Hamza. Our retreating columns were promptly bombed by Stukas. One Punjabi and one H.L.I. company were left in the Hamza box to cover the withdrawal, and these were overrun next day. All guns had been spiked, and the men left in groups of two and three, hoping to march south and then east towards El Daba. Most of them did reach our lines after hours of anxious walking. The Medical Officer, with three wounded men, escaped in the only truck, bringing the gun-sights.

All that night of June 27/28 General Briggs and his staff worked to gather in our forces withdrawing from Matruh—the town was no longer to be held to the last. They sought to regain contact with units that had become scattered in darkness and confusion, and to form fresh battle groups from an assortment of men and guns. By morning the position had been momentarily reorganized; three mobile columns had been put together and pushed forward to regain touch with the enemy. These three columns were: 'Gleecol,' once again, with a company of the H.L.I. and eight guns from the 32nd Field Regiment; 'Scotcol,' under Lieutenant-Colonel Scott of the 1st Field Regiment, made up of two companies of the 1/5th Mahrattas and twelve guns from Scott's own regiment; and a reserve, consisting of Reid's 29 Brigade Headquarters, two platoons and headquarters of the H.L.I., a company of the Mahrattas, and another of the 3/2nd Punjab.

Brigadier E. C. Mansergh, who had succeeded Vallentin as C.R.A. of the Fifth Indian Division, records how at two o'clock in the morning the G.S.O.2, Major F. B. B. Noble, came to him and reported that the Germans were in a certain position. What should be done? Briggs must be consulted for a decision. Briggs was at that moment asleep. Mansergh and Noble woke him. "What is it?" he asked. They told him about their information, the signals received, the location of the enemy. Briggs thought for a moment. Then he instructed them to do this and that, to send this signal and that order. He lay back on his blanket and fell asleep once more. His decisions were right, and they were acted upon. Next morning, when Noble asked the General why he had given those particular instructions, Briggs was puzzled. He remembered nothing of it. No recollection of the night conference remained in his mind. He had been so weary, yet somehow had risen, more than half asleep still, and made the correct decisions.

During June 28 'Scotcol' had a brush with a German column, and was obliged to retire a short distance. Gleeson was ordered to take his small force back to El Hamza, but this move was intercepted by the Corps Commander in person, and 'Gleecol' redirected westwards to Fuka. It was here that the remains of Briggs' division was to make a rearguard stand, to allow the Eighth Army to withdraw from Matruh to the Alamein Line.

* * * * *

And so the hours went by, one by one. The battle raged. The frontier of Egypt drew ever closer. The delaying actions became more desperate as our casualties in troops and vehicles mounted steadily. One unit, one column, one detachment, one headquarters after another was overrun or forced back. Some escaped to fight again; others were destroyed or captured. But all the time the Eighth Army was extricating itself bit by bit, hammering at the exultant enemy, hanging tenaciously on to Rommel's forces all the way back. It took every opportunity for offensive action, giving as good as it got, and often better. But our men were outnumbered and outgunned at every halting place and in every running engagement.

This was a period of uncertainty and distress, at once mental and physical. Men woke to the sound of exploding bombs. At night scares were frequent: "Ninety enemy tanks have broken through and are heading this way." Enemy flares dropped to illuminate the darkness were particularly unnerving. Small units, headquarters, dressing stations, were being overrun when columns of German tanks roared through, by-passing our positions that were hurriedly evacuated. At any moment the cry might come: "The enemy is upon us." Staff officers began to shout irritably down their telephones. Many were the narrow squeaks and close shaves during this month of retreat. Few were not in a high state of nerves. But they did their best to look unconcerned, and to set a good example to their fellows. Journeys became as terrible as nightmares, and most perilous. Trucks were often without food and water. Even reserve rations had been finished or abandoned. How often did men groan or curse at the slowness of the vehicle in front of them in a convoy driving towards Egypt. How frequent were the outbursts of impatience.

In the diary of Christopher Perowne, the Division's Senior Chaplain, we find written such entries as :

"Wash off dust and bloodstains from my meagre wardrobe."

"Dusty, tired, bearded, but in excellent spirits."

"Everyone tremendously depressed. Almost impossible to get any enthusiasm."

Day and night he drove from point to point, tending our wounded in an advanced dressing station—usually set up in a pair of lorries, with side shelters in which the wounded lay on stretchers on the sand. Never did these stretchers suffice. And men were continually being brought in for urgent attention. At night the doctors and orderlies had to work by hurricane lamps in a complete blackout. Scores of the dead had to be buried, often in stony ground. Picks and shovels and arms to wield them were short. As far as possible the graves were dug in groups, but so often the wind-blown sand blotted out all trace soon afterwards. Through all the days of bewildering strife, celebrations of the Holy Communion were held, a few men here, a group there, by the side of a car, in a truck or tent, or, more often, in the open air.

For all this apparent atmosphere of nervous tension, of confusion, of lack of any clear picture of events, of sudden moves in the nick of time, of scares and alarms, of muddled journeys and frequent moves, almost always towards the east and ahead of or beside the tired but triumphant enemy, most men kept their heads. The troops fought where they were told to fight. They did their utmost to hold back the enemy's onrush, to save their friends from being overrun, and to make the Germans and Italians pay dearly for their successful advance.

And through it all the spirit that prevailed has been exemplified by Brigadier Dudley Russell, as he then was, commanding Five Brigade. The Brigade was ordered to hold Mersa Matruh.

"The New Zealand Brigadier I relieved there said, 'Thank God, I am getting out. You never will.'

"We were, in fact, surrounded there, and completely picketed by German armour. We all thought we were 'for it.' We collected all the papers of value at Brigade H.Q. and made a bonfire and threw all identifications on to the fire. This was a sad moment, but my Brigade Major, a magnificent fellow, produced a bottle of whisky, and we danced round the fire and drank to all the courts martial, courts of enquiry, and other difficult problems which were going up in smoke.

"That is the spirit you want when things are going badly. We made a hazardous bid for a break-out in a completely unexpected direction, and after a hectic night in the Desert, got away with it."

* * * * *

On June 27 Brigadier Reid was ordered to hold a rearguard position on the Fuka escarpment, to cover the withdrawal of Thirteen Corps. He arrived there during the afternoon. The troops available for this task were two platoons of the H.L.I., two companies of the 3/2nd Punjab, headquarters and one company of the 1/5th Mahrattas, a part of 21 Field Company, organized as infantry, three medium machine-guns, and five 25-pounders from Biscoe's 32 Field Regiment. The orders were these: "The position will be held until it is impossible to hold it without being cut off. Withdrawal from this position will be to Naqb Abu Dweiss" (on the edge of the Qattara Depression and south-west of El Alamein). The two main passes six miles north-east and eight miles due south of Fuka were to be held by 'Gleecol' and 'Scotcol.' General Briggs told Reid that he would if possible send four guns from 'Scotcol' to help 29 Brigade. The 3rd Field Regiment was also on its way. But neither of these reinforcements arrived in time.

Fuka was not a good position to hold. The escarpment could be descended in many different places. Ahead of 29 Brigade were our 12th Lancers, watching the German 15th Panzer Division east of Mersa Matruh. When Reid went out to visit the Lancers he was assured that they would report any enemy approach, for they had a screen five miles deep from the coast.

On the morning of the 28th Reid received a staff officer who came from General Auchinleck to be put in the picture about the situation at Fuka. Reid told the officer all he could, and then said to him, "My compliments to Sir Claude, but I reckon I shan't be here tonight."

Nor was he, as will be seen.

At half past seven that evening the 3/2nd Punjab, who had established a position on top of the escarpment, saw large numbers of armoured fighting vehicles approaching. At first they thought this transport was our own, and reported it as such to the Brigadier. But five minutes later they telephoned urgently. "By God," they said, "it's not our own. It's the Hun." And it was a sight at once magnificent and menacing to see the Panzer Division rumbling by, some sixty tanks in all. A wind blew from the west, and the upchurned dust swept over the 3/2nd Punjab to blind their vision.

The Germans split their force. Part moved west along the escarpment, part moved east; some of the tanks deployed along the crest, others started to descend the pass. When shells began to fall among the Brigade 'B' Echelon trucks, Reid instructed his Staff Captain, Alan Passingham, to lead them back twenty-seven miles along the railway. This was done. Then a score of German tanks lumbered down the escarpment towards Brigade Headquarters and the Mahrattas, who were near Fuka railway station. Though several tanks were forced by our 25-pounders to turn aside or halt, the main body came on in line ahead towards the centre of the Brigade position.

Brigadier Reid now told Lance-Corporal Macpherson of the Signals to smash all wireless sets. Reid sat in a slit trench while this blue-eyed, ginger-haired Scot went about his business. A few minutes passed. Then Macpherson ran back and saluted. "All the wireless sets busted, sir." They went to ground, Reid, his new Brigade Major, Richard Pease, and the Signals Officer, Brian Gomm. The tanks were all round the position, firing across the dip in which Brigade Headquarters was spread out. Life in those moments was hideous. In the growing dusk German soldiers rounded up our men, one by one, group by group. At least six tanks headed straight for Reid's Headquarters. When two guns from the 32nd Field Regiment, concealed behind a low ridge, scored four direct hits on the enemy tanks at two hundred yards range, the advance was momentarily arrested. But such resistance could not last. The gun portees were hit by machine-gun fire and set ablaze.

German tanks then roared into the middle and stopped. Our resistance also stopped.

The Brigadier waited till nightfall. He knew the moon would rise later. Gomm advised Reid to wait a little longer, as things were not yet settled enough for an escape. But Reid said no, they must go now. So they crawled out to the Brigadier's truck. Then four Indian soldiers came by, talking at the top of their voices. At once a German patrol captured them. This patrol walked round the truck and saw the Brigade Commander and his companions. These had no alternative but to crawl out ignominiously and be taken prisoner. And Denys Reid remained a prisoner, in company with Brigadier Charles Boucher, until November 9, 1943, when he escaped back into the lines of the American Fifth Army. Soon afterwards he was given command of the Tenth Indian Division, at that time fighting up Italy with the Eighth Army.

Meanwhile the small remnant of the Highland Light Infantry had watched this disaster to 29 Brigade Headquarters. Colonel Percival recalls that he was just eating some tinned peaches when the noise on top of the escarpment began. He dashed away to his command post, and later discovered that he was still clinging to the spoon and a tin of fruit.

At eight o'clock the German tanks had been in 'hull down' position five hundred yards in front of Percival's platoons. The two Mahratta mortar detachments fired on these tanks with good results and caused them to veer off. Instead of coming through the H.L.I. they swung round the flank, through the 3/2nd Punjab on the left, and headed straight for our guns and Brigade Headquarters. All this time there was continual counter-battery and anti-tank shelling, for enemy guns had been sighted on top of the escarpment. It was a little before nine o'clock that the H.L.I. saw the Germans on top of Brigade Headquarters. Our forward 25-pounder guns had been overrun. Lorried infantry could be seen on the escarpment. One tank was blazing, and its flare was rivalled by that of two burning portees.

It was now beginning to get dark. Percival ordered his men to climb into their trucks and lorries. He planned to take up an alternative position farther back, where the battalion's transport might be better protected.

FIGHTING RETREAT AND REARGUARD ACTIONS

The route to choose was a problem for Percival. He could not lead his men south into the Desert, for this was occupied by dark masses of the enemy. To drive eastwards would take them straight among the German tanks. On the north lay the railway embankment that could not be crossed. Percival decided to make northwest towards the enemy.

They could do no good by staying. The only chance was to get to the east of the enemy tanks before these cut the road once and for all. The attempt succeeded, but it was a close shave. They came through with less than two hours to spare.

With the aid of four carriers all the troops were got away safely, but our vehicles were heavily overloaded. The transport was inadequate. A number of Indian soldiers who had come down from the escarpment had to be carried and wanted to be driven to safety. It was fortunate that the battalion was not shelled as the men embussed. Percival's own truck normally carried six men; now it was weighed down with twenty-four. In an attempt to reach the main road, they drove under the railway lines through a small drainage tunnel. The cab roof of the first lorry scraped the tunnel. The second vehicle was still higher, and its roof had first to be taken down. As it was, the lorry touched on both sides. Behind, the night sky was slashed by rising white Very lights, signs that the Germans had overrun 29 Brigade Headquarters.

Would the H.L.I. strike an ambush? Had the road been cut behind them? No one could tell. They tried to drive across the sands towards the sea, but so bad was the going that they were forced back to the road. Now they headed east. Every man kept his finger on the trigger, ready for a sudden brush and a burst of firing. Several abandoned lorries were found, but their engines could not be started; most of them had in some way been damaged, and time was short.

By midnight the H.L.I. had met a picquet of the 12th Lancers a dozen miles west of El Daba, and it was here that Percival and his men spent the remaining hours of the night. Next day they drove back to El Alamein, and from there down the defence line to join Nine Brigade at Naqb Abu Dweiss. As for the 3/2nd Punjab at Fuka, Lieutenant Bhag Singh got away with some men of Headquarters Company, marched all that night along the coast, and early next morning met patrols of the 12th Lancers.

* * * * *

What, meanwhile, had happened to Briggs' Divisional Headquarters? On approaching Fuka, the Headquarters column found German artillery in action, firing at 29 Brigade's positions. Our leading trucks all but ran into the enemy guns. But these took no notice, and Briggs' column was able to swing away and halt below the escarpment to the west of Fuka.

Divisional Signals picked up on the wireless a running commentary describing the assault on 29 Brigade. When, at eight o'clock, the set with the Brigade went dead—smashed on Reid's orders as we have seen—a staff officer, Major J. N. Chaudhuri, was sent over to discover what had happened. He found the Germans holding the exits to the minefields. It was apparent that Reid's formation had ceased to exist. Divisional Headquarters were now alone. On all sides rose enemy flares. General Briggs asked permission from Thirteen Corps to withdraw south and then eastwards. General Gott was not available. His Chief of Staff was not prepared to grant permission, despite Briggs' personal telephone call. For Briggs to speak in person was a rare event and indicated the gravity of the situation. What could be accomplished with a Divisional Headquarters, Signals, and the remains of some columns? Very little that would serve the Army. If this small force was to get away, it must do so at night.

At one o'clock, having heard nothing further from General Gott, Briggs ordered Divisional Signals to close down communication with the Eighth Army and Thirteen Corps. The locations of the German advanced posts had meanwhile been checked by compass—they were obvious from the flares and Very lights—and by halving the widest gap, a safe course was found. The night was clear. The stars shone brightly. The sand glittered under the moon's cold light. In a compact column Briggs brought his force and some remnants thirty miles south and then turned east.

Looking over the side of the trucks, our men could see the freshly made tracks of German tanks set in sharp relief by the moon. At one point the column was unwittingly escorted by German armoured cars. A furnace fire gleamed through the darkness, and the clink of hammers could be heard—German fitters were repairing their tanks. A motorized column approached from the flank. Both halted. Was it friend or foe ? We never found out, for the other group of vehicles passed across the front and vanished. Mersa Matruh and Bagush were being evacuated at the same time, so these unknown rovers may well have been British.

Then, one hour before daybreak, a mist came down upon the Desert. Some tanks were heard approaching from the east. Brigadier Mansergh, the new C.R.A. of the Division, was sitting beside Briggs. He jumped out and ran over the soft sand to the nearest tank, to see to whom they belonged. He leaned against the tank, but could see nothing. The tanks did not move. Then a turret opened. Mansergh heard one member of the crew ask in a foreign tongue who these b———s in front were. Of all the men then serving with the Fifth Indian Division, Mansergh was probably the only one able to recognize this language as Cape Dutch. He had spent the first sixteen years of his life in South Africa. Any other officer sent forward to investigate might in error have thought the tanks to be German. Firing would have broken out and a needless battle ensued. As it was, no harm came. The four tanks from the South African Division went their way. And Briggs' column reached in safety the southern end of the Alamein Line, where Fletcher's Nine Brigade was already established.

Thanks to the gallant rearguard of Reid's 29 Brigade, Ten Corps had been able to break out from Mersa Matruh. But the enemy pressed on along the coast. By the evening of June 29 he was fifteen miles west of El Alamein. Next day our armoured and motor brigades, operating behind the hurrying enemy, were withdrawn into reserve. Gott's Thirteen Corps took over the defence of the southern half of the Alamein Line, with the remnants of the Fifth Indian Division and Freyberg's New Zealanders; while Thirty Corps, having under command the First South African and Fiftieth British Divisions, assumed responsibility for the coastal sector of our defence line.

In a message to his troops the Army Commander stated that the enemy was stretched to his limits and thought us a broken army. "He hopes to take Egypt by bluff. Show him where he gets off."

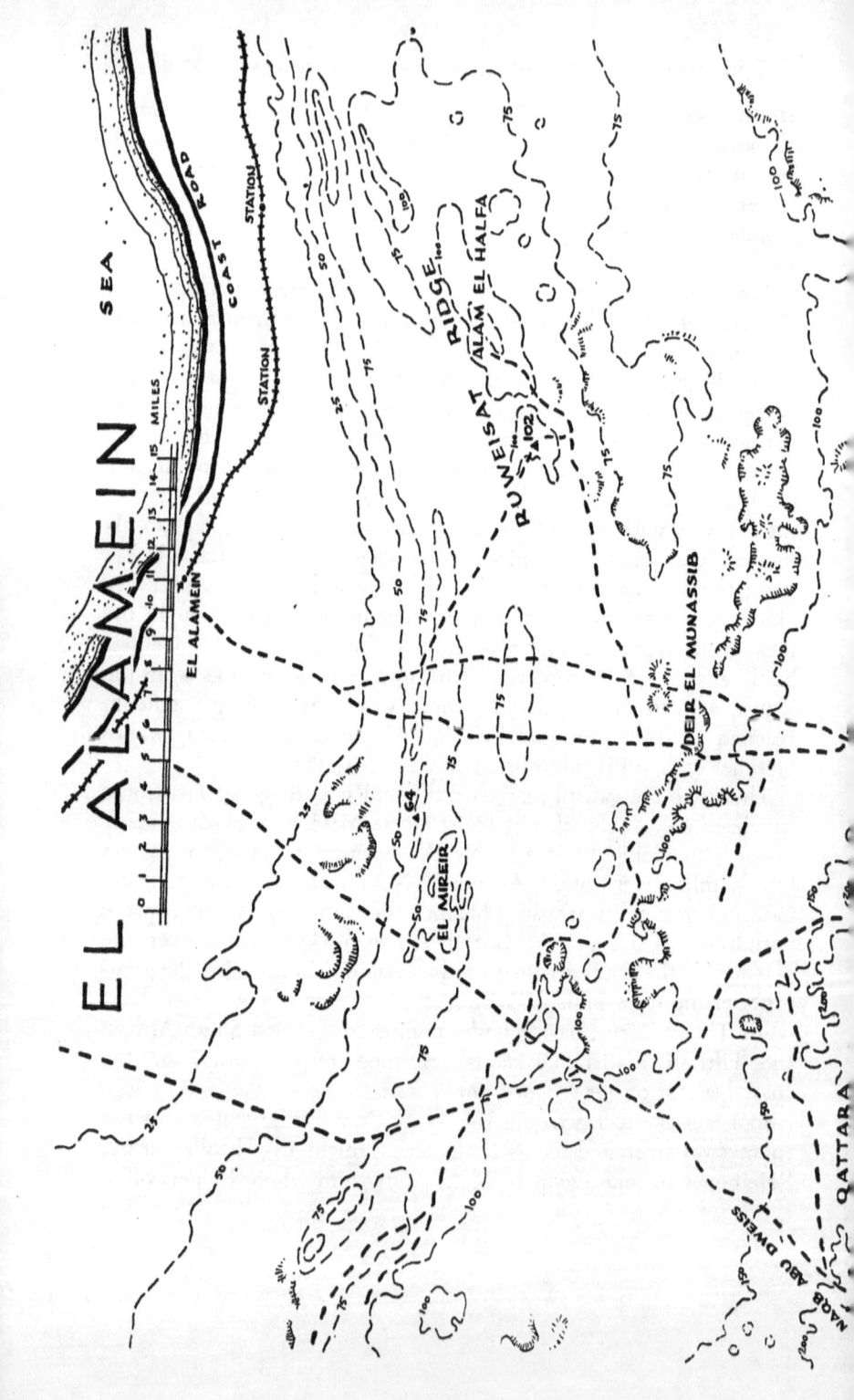

CHAPTER XVII

RUWEISAT RIDGE

JULY—SEPTEMBER 1942

JULY saw the transition from mobile warfare to static, costly, and often abortive aggression in the interests of holding the line of defence. This was a time when the Eighth Army sought desperately to defeat Rommel's forces before they were properly consolidated and in a position to launch a further offensive into the heart of Egypt. Our attacks during this period were hurried and unrehearsed, and became more and more costly in proportion as the enemy dug himself in. Brigades were often set difficult tasks, with little opportunity to ensure that the operation would be successful. Co-ordination between infantry and supporting armour was seriously deficient; officers were frequently working without proper information as to what they were meant to be doing; conferences were too few for those who mattered most in the planning and launching of our attacks; liaison between neighbouring brigades engaged in the same operation was often lacking. And brigades came and went from one division to another. During one period of four weeks the Fifth Indian Division had no less than twenty-three changes in brigades, and these involved eleven different brigades, attached for a few hours, for a night, for a week.

Air photographs were not available when most urgently needed for the preparation of an attack; minefields could not be marked or cleared for want of time. Orders were issued and cancelled, given out again, and cancelled a second time. The resultant uncertainty was inevitable. But despite these difficulties and shortcomings, the Army held the line.

Tank battles went on spasmodically in one direction or another; heavy artillery duels were fought out across the ridges and depressions of the Desert; both the enemy and our own troops endured desultory shelling; the Gunners on both sides of No-Man's-Land shot harassing fire over the stones and sand and scrub. After an attack the ground was strewn with the dead and the dying, with abandoned vehicles, blazing tanks and trucks, and ambulances. The nights would be broken not only by flares and butterfly bombs, by tracer bullets, exploding ammunition lorries, and the rippling flashes of guns firing a concentration, but also by the moans of the wounded, the thudding of artillery, the scream of shells passing overhead, and the crunch of landing shells.

There were moments of terrible anxiety when units in action went out of touch by wireless. Failures and casualties, minor successes and more casualties, confusion and frustration were the order of one day after another. At times the commanders were gripped with the sense of helplessness and uncertainty, the battalion strengths were low, and the general feeling one of alternating depression, elation, cynicism, hope, anger and pride. Whether by day or by night it was often hard to decide what was happening in an engagement; in the haze visibility was bad, and in darkness every sound, flash and flare was confusing.

During July the Eighth Army maintained pressure along the whole front. The object of this policy was at once to improve our position, to meet any enemy offensive that might develop, and to make ready for our own attack when the time came.

General Auchinleck, finding that the enemy was preparing to attack the northern part of the Alamein defences, held by the First South African Division, decided to relieve pressure here and to regain the initiative by counter-attacking from the south against the enemy's flank. For this the New Zealanders and what remained of the Fifth Indian Division were used. Our northward thrust went in on July 3. Part of the El Mreir feature was occupied by the New Zealanders. The Italian Ariete Armoured Division was forced to retire with the loss of over forty guns and many prisoners. Our troops drew near to Deir el Shein, which had been taken by the Germans on the 1st.

Then the enemy, though battered by the Royal Air Force, hurriedly reinforced his southern front with tanks and infantry. At once his opposition stiffened. As we had no reserves with which to further the attack, our advance from the south came to a halt. This operation neither destroyed the enemy, nor outflanked him, much less brought us to the coast. But it did force him to regroup, and so relieved pressure against the South Africans. And it gained time for tank reinforcements and the Ninth Australian Division to arrive in the line.

* * * *

During the first days of July General Briggs formed three new mobile columns, controlled from a small headquarters. The 2nd West Yorkshires, who had been withdrawn to the Nile Delta to refit after the June battles, supplied the nucleus of 'Langcol,' led by Lieutenant-Colonel W. H. Langran, M.C. The other two columns were named 'Gleecol' and 'Scotcol.' These three moved westwards in the formation of two up and one in reserve. To each column came similar experiences, and we take those of 'Langcol' as typical.

Langran had under his command an infantry company of less than fifty men, seven 25-pounder guns in the charge of the distinguished mountaineer, Major H. W. Tilman, and one troop of light anti-aircraft guns. The second and third columns were of similar strength and composition.

'Langcol' moved westwards to Jebel Himeimat; for the troops engaged, this proved a novel experience. They had grown accustomed to retreating in the opposite direction. The column's task was to harass enemy 'soft' transport and gun positions; and the method, to establish guns in a good battery position, with one protecting platoon of infantry on either flank. Two observation posts were then sent forward under escort, until they could see enemy vehicles. Meanwhile, Bofors guns were placed round the perimeter to engage any hostile planes that flew over.

At night Langran's column leaguered in four lines of vehicles, facing in a predetermined direction, and ready to move off should hostilities break out. On the morning of July 9 two Messerschmitts flew over 'Langcol' at a height of three hundred feet. The leading plane was hit, and crash-landed between our two observation posts, a thousand yards in front of the gun positions. The second German plane landed, picked up the crew of the crashed aircraft, and took off again, in full view of Tilman's seven guns and all the Bren gunners, who, as though petrified, just watched the rescue and took no action. Then a South African armoured car did open up with the anti-tank rifle in its turret, but this had no effect.

Later in the day thirty German tanks approached Langran's position. While one tank acted as an observation post, the others stayed out of sight and fired their guns. Again and again our Gunners located these tanks and shelled them. But 'Langcol' was slowly forced back towards the Alamein line. There was no time for digging; the infantry sat around the guns; our sole target was the hull of a lone tank. That evening 'Langcol' reached the area near Fortress 'B,' and when about to leaguer was dive-bombed by Stuka planes. Further casualties were sustained. Under cover of night Langran brought his column east to the Jebel Himeimat area once more, and although on the two following days our guns were in action against enemy transport, on the 13th 'Langcol' drove back to the Barrel Track. Three days later it rejoined the rest of the 2nd West Yorkshires, now returning from the Delta.

Meanwhile, the Ninth Australian Division had concentrated by the coast. On July 10 it launched an attack to capture Tel el Eisa, on the railway west of El Alamein. Supported by the First South African Division, this attack succeeded and the ground gained was held despite heavy enemy counter-attacks. Shortage of reserves again prevented us from exploiting success. The enemy's resistance was strong. But the new salient was important by virtue of its threat to Rommel's positions further south.

Then, four days later, the New Zealand Division, which had already incurred more than a thousand casualties since it first entered the battle, was ordered to advance six miles north-west and to capture part of the Ruweisat Ridge. This vital feature ran west and east into the centre of the Eighth Army's positions. Its possession would be of great tactical importance. The Ridge was narrow, and its average height some two hundred feet: on the map the altitude was marked in metres—an example is Point 64. Russell's Five Brigade, attacking on the right flank of two New Zealand brigades, was to seize the eastern stretch of the ridge. This night assault was also designed to break through the enemy's centre and thereby destroy his forces east of the track running south-west from El Alamein to Naqb Abu Dweiss.

Russell's battalions, the 3/10th Baluch and 4/6th Rajputana Rifles, gained the larger part of their objective, Point 64. The Brigade overran two battalions of the Italian Brescia Division, and took nearly a thousand prisoners. When, next morning, Rommel put in a counter-attack, this was dispersed by our field artillery and by the 6-pounder anti-tank guns that had just arrived. Thereafter, many derelict enemy tanks and lorries lay strewn across this quarter of the Desert.

The New Zealanders became engaged in heavy fighting; support from the tanks had not been co-ordinated; the 4th Brigade was overrun when counter-attacked in daylight by the German 15th Panzer Division; they lost nearly 1,500 men, and took a similar number of prisoners, though this total would have been far greater had not the German tanks rescued large numbers of prisoners from our hands. The New Zealand brigades were forced to withdraw, and took up positions some 1,200 yards south of Ruweisat Ridge. They faced north, with their left flank against El Mreir.

Then, on July 17, Langran's West Yorkshires were ordered to pass through Five Brigade and to attack westwards along Ruweisat Ridge to capture Point 63. This lay 12,000 yards ahead of our forward positions. Already that day the enemy had made two vain and costly counter-attacks. Now he was digging in, having been reinforced by fresh troops that had just arrived from Crete. By contrast, the strength of the West Yorkshires at this time was a mere 250: no reinforcements were available in the Nile Delta, and Langran's strongest rifle company numbered fifty men. But the artillery support for this operation was very powerful, for a medium regiment had been added to the guns of the New Zealand, South African and Fifth Indian Divisions. The resulting barrage provided a memorable spectacle.

Dunlop's 'C' Company led the West Yorkshire attack along the southern slopes of the Ridge, while 'D' Company trudged forward along the northern side; O'Hara and Osborn followed with their two companies. When our men had gone several hundred yards the enemy troops suddenly left their positions and retreated west; some even gave themselves up. Then, because the advance had been too rapid, 'D' Company walked into our own artillery barrage. The objective was not well marked, and our infantry merely pushed ahead until the opposition became too strong. In this way 'A' and 'D' companies went a mile too far and had to be recalled to Point 63 by Langran. Lieutenant J. R. Barton's platoon overshot the battalion's objective by three thousand yards, but retired when counter-attacked by German tanks.

Our troops suffered frequent casualties from enemy shelling and machine-gun fire, and in the platoon led by Sergeant-Major Neville every man was killed or wounded except Neville himself. He went forward alone. By now the strongest company could muster no more than fifteen men. The advanced dressing station had received a direct hit, and Langran's regimental aid post was overcrowded with casualties.

At last light the battalion found it impossible to dig in, because the Ridge here was formed of solid slabs of rock. Instead, the men built up the rocks to complete a number of sangars abandoned by the enemy; only our anti-tank guns could be dug down a little. Later that evening, when German tanks attacked, they did not press, but were pulled out after twenty minutes and leaguered a thousand yards to the north. Then a section of 20 Field Company drove up to lay a minefield around the battalion's position. One three-ton lorry was at once illuminated by enemy flares; a burst of medium machine-gun fire caused this lorry-load of hundreds of mines to blow up with a tremendous explosion.

Next day, July 18, the 2nd West Yorkshires were troubled by accurate enemy sniping and shelling. At ten o'clock Stukas dive-bombed our position, and one bomb wrecked Langran's truck. The battalion held its position for two days until the total strength was under a hundred. Then, on July 20, the weary Yorkshiremen were relieved by the 1/4th Essex.

On the same day 161 Indian Motor Brigade joined the Division. Now commanded by Brigadier F. E. C. Hughes, this brigade had, after leaving Cyprus, been in Qatatba under direct command of G.H.Q. Its battalions were the 1/1st Punjab (Lieutenant-Colonel M. H. W. Wilson, who was killed by a shell within a few days), the 3/7th Rajputs (Lieutenant-Colonel G. F. M. Stray), and the 1/2nd Punjab (Lieutenant-Colonel D. Barker).

161 Brigade was ready to play its part in attacking against the centre of the enemy's line. This fresh attack was designed to sever the enemy's communications, to force him to extend his front and disperse his reserves, and having done this, to roll up the northern part of his force. And so, at last light on July 21, Hughes' brigade advanced along Ruweisat Ridge, while the 6th New Zealand Brigade attacked northwards across the El Mreir depression. They aimed to make a breach through which the 23rd Armoured Brigade

could pass. Despite strong enemy resistance and shelling in darkness, and heavy casualties, the 1/2nd Punjab and 3/7th Rajputs made good initial progress.

The 1/1st Punjab of 161 Brigade attacked along the Ruweisat Ridge and made progress, though failing to reach as far as had been expected. The Sappers and Miners of 2 Field Company assisted by the New Zealanders, began to clear the minefield, but this proved a very difficult task, for the men were under continuous fire. The enemy then counter-attacked, and the 6th New Zealand Brigade was disastrously overrun by German tanks.

General Gott now ordered the newly arrived and inexperienced 23rd Armoured Brigade forward, to carry out the second phase of the operation. The tanks charged through such gaps in the minefield as had been made, pressed on through intense fire, and came on to another minefield. The armoured thrust was defeated with very considerable losses in tanks. And although the attack was renewed later in the day by the 2nd Armoured Brigade, our main assault had failed to split the enemy forces. Valuable ground had been gained, but at great expense.

General Briggs returned to his headquarters late in the afternoon of July 22 to learn that orders had come from Corps for an attack on the Deir el Shein depression, by dawn the next morning. This attack would be in conjunction with advances by the New Zealanders and tanks on the Division's left flank. The depression was at this time held by the 15th Panzer Division.

Briggs telephoned to General Gott at Corps Headquarters, and stated that this attack was too large, the time too short. He added that, if the urgency warranted it, he would limit the assault to an attempt to seize the end of the Ridge, so as to allow 161 Brigade to widen its base and dominate the El Mreir depression with fire. It would thus be made untenable to the enemy. 'Strafer' Gott agreed to this proposal.

Briggs decided that Fletcher's Nine Brigade should make this attack. Nine Brigade had spent July 22 in column in lorries, waiting for news. About four o'clock that afternoon General Briggs sent for Fletcher and showed him on a map the positions thought to be occupied by our troops. Briggs asked Fletcher whether he thought he could mount a night attack to gain certain objectives beyond the point on Ruweisat Ridge gained by 161 Brigade. Three hours remained for reconnaissance. The attack was to be made in the dark, from starting lines that had not yet been reconnoitred. It was therefore decided to make the attack "silent without artillery."

At this time Nine Brigade consisted only of the 2nd West Yorkshires, who had already had a very difficult time, and the 3/14th Punjab (Lieutenant-Colonel W. A. Putnam), who had recently joined from Qatatba. Although this battalion had fought in Eritrea with the Fourth Indian Division it had not yet been in action in the Desert. Fletcher decided to carry out the attack with the 3/14th, and to move up the West Yorkshires when the objectives had been captured. An anti-tank battery was placed under command.

Then Fletcher set out with Colonel Putnam and the reconnaissance groups to make certain where our own front line was. They had to find a start line, point out objectives, and take compass bearings. On the way forward this party was delayed by a Stuka raid, which badly disorganized the anti-tank battery. As Fletcher and his companions approached our front, they abandoned their trucks and walked across the sand of Ruweisat Ridge, passed through 161 Brigade's forward defences on foot, and came under machine-gun fire. A point on the ridge was found from which Fletcher was able to point out to Putnam what his objectives were. Then darkness fell. The company commanders of the 3/14th Punjab had not seen their objectives, and Fletcher wanted to postpone the attack until the following night, thus enabling the battalion to dig in in front of 161 Brigade. But it was essential that the attack be launched without delay. So Colonel Putnam established his headquarters on the southern slope of the Ridge, and the companies were ordered up to the start line before the moon set at 2 a.m.

Unfortunately the whole area through which the men had to advance was studded with vehicles, criss-crossed with telephone cables, and dotted with packets of men belonging to 161 Brigade and supporting units. And the sepoys had to pick their way through a minefield. The moon set at the appointed time, but the 3/14th were not ready. For Fletcher and Putnam it was an anxious time. When a ground mist rose the companies literally vanished into the darkness and the mist. No firing was heard. Touch with the advancing companies was lost. Putnam walked forward to investigate.

About eight o'clock he reported back that he had made touch with his company commanders; the attempt to advance by night had led to confusion, and some reorganization had proved necessary. But he had now ordered a fresh advance to be made at nine o'clock. At this time the 3/14th Punjab attacked in lines with great gallantry and reached Point 63. The sepoys tried to consolidate, but were unable to dig in on the stony surface. Heavy casualties were suffered from enemy fire. German tanks that were dug into the sand engaged the Indian infantry with disastrous results. Colonel Putnam and his leading company commander were killed. And when the Germans counter-attacked, the battalion suddenly broke, and fell back through 161 Brigade's positions.

Nine Brigade was taken into reserve once more, and Lieutenant-Colonel W. H. Langran took over command from Brigadier Fletcher.

*   *   *   *   *

During the rest of the month a lull intervened along the front. The Fifth Indian Division had orders to cause the enemy to expect an attack south of Ruweisat Ridge, and our artillery harassed the German and Italian positions in the Deir el Shein. Throughout this period a grave shortage of transport and controlled stores within the Division led to constant juggling and improvisation. The remnants of 29 Brigade had been almost literally 'milked' of everything to make the 2nd West Yorkshires mobile and capable of functioning, though on a reduced scale. So grievously had 161 Brigade suffered in attacks on Point 63 and the Deir el Shein that two battalions had to be replaced. The 4/7th Rajputs (Lieutenant-Colonel J. A. Salomons), which had left the Brigade in Cyprus, came from the Sudan to relieve the 3/7th Rajputs; while the 1/2nd Punjab gave place to the 1st Argyll and Sutherland Highlanders (Lieutenant-Colonel R. J. F. McAlister).

And this feeling was reflected in an appreciation of the situation, written on July 27 by General Auchinleck, who decided that the Eighth Army required re-equipping and training before it would be fit for further offensive operations. We were strongly placed for a defensive battle, but lacked the strength to deliver an attack sufficient to dislodge the enemy from his strongly-held front.

Auchinleck estimated that unless we made a serious mistake the Germans would, during the first half of August, have no defensive superiority in troops. Though they held a greater strength of armour, their artillery was inferior, our air strength greatly superior. The Eighth Army was obliged to husband its ammunition; its transport deficiencies were mounting rather than decreasing; none of its formations was adequately trained for offensive battles. The great need was to provide an Army reserve. Two courses lay before us: either to persist with attacks in the hope that the enemy would crack before he was reinforced by fresh troops, or to adopt a defensive policy until we were strong enough to attack with every hope of success.

Auchinleck did not believe the Eighth Army could be made ready for a full-scale assault before the middle of September, whereas the Germans and Italians might be ready as early as the last week of August. It was decided that our best course was "the defensive, combined with offensive gestures from time to time, including raiding."

Accordingly, the month of August was spent by the Fifth Indian Division, which had suffered 3,000 casualties during July, in reorganizing its defences on Ruweisat Ridge, in extensive mine-laying, artillery shoots, and active patrolling—including a number of strong raiding parties.

* * * * *

On Ruweisat Ridge were to be found most of the characteristics of static war and life in the Desert. It was an underground existence for the infantry, overlooked as they were by the Germans and Italians. Often the ground was too hard to dig, and so sangars had to be built of stones and rocks. No one in the forward positions could move with safety during daylight, nor could vehicles approach without drawing fire upon themselves. So the men sat in their trenches, or lay down at the bottom on a blanket, cleaning and oiling their weapons. A piece of mosquito netting was stretched across the opening of the trench.

In the beginning many officers tried to construct fly-proof trenches with these nets, but a net made the trench very hot to sit in. And even with its aid, and that of an arsenic trap which deposited a black carpet of dead flies on the sand, it was impossible to deal with the flies. They were vicious throughout each day, and never ceased to torment those who dwelt on the Ridge. If you so much as moistened your lips, twenty flies would be clinging to them. A drop of tea in a mug attracted flies in hundreds. You had to shield the mug all the way to your lips, otherwise the tea was undrinkable. And it was the same with a plate of food. The side of a lorry that formed one wall of a certain officers' mess was permanently black with flies by day, and a similar horde swarmed and buzzed around after food either on the table or on men's faces. One British officer who had been ill was in such a poor state that he remained oblivious of the flies crawling in the corners of his mouth and eyes. It was not a pretty sight.

Then there was the sickening odour wafted across by the breeze from former Italian positions in front of our trenches—a horrible stink of unburied corpses, and of burnt-out tanks that rose like blackened tombs from the dazzling sands.

At times, when little happened, life was boring. But the men in the line lived on anticipation, on the certain knowledge that something was bound to happen sooner or later. German planes flew over most nights to drop flares and bombs. The bombs crumped in the sand, and the dazzling flares gave men a sense of nakedness. In daylight Stukas would come to dive-bomb our positions, or to attack the congested and dust-cloaked 'C' Track. The Royal Air Force and the Luftwaffe fought each other over the heads of the divisions between El Alamein and the Qattara Depression, and to see pilots swinging beneath a white parachute was not uncommon. Our fighters made frequent raids over the enemy's back areas, and would fly home very low and often be caught by Messerschmitts that waited high above. Sometimes our men saw smoking German planes struggling to reach their own lines before making a forced landing.

Once again sundown was the best time of the whole day. Soon after dark the battalion Quartermaster would arrive up the dusty track with his ration convoy. They drove through a minefield gap, maybe, or over an empty stretch of Desert, or up a shallow valley between two ridges, bringing hot meals in dixies for the troops. In this case the lorries were able to go right up to the forward companies. Sundown was also the time for sick parade, when a large proportion of each unit might attend. Under different circumstances many of these men would have been in hospital, but with the great shortage of soldiers in the line, a man had, as Wiberg expressed it, to be on the verge of *rigor mortis* before he was permitted to become a casualty through illness.

Dusk and nightfall were the moments for men to take exercise and to stretch their limbs that had been cramped in the narrow trenches. For those who had dysentery the end of the day was a lull during which they could in safety empty the tins that they needed with such painful frequency. At night, infantry patrols crept forward to report upon the enemy in his dispositions and activities, and to shoot up enemy mine-laying parties. Sometimes they caused German tracer to whip across the dark sky, though a greater danger lay in treading on a mine when walking through minefield gaps.

And the Sappers would be out, improving the minefields, putting down more mines, erecting barbed wire. And across the sands walked Signals linemen, who searched for a break in a frail cable. In dugouts and in vehicles wireless operators kept a listening watch, and sent or received messages. Constantly alert was the operator on the telephone switchboard; hard at work would be found cipher operators who encoded and decoded messages. In every command vehicle a duty staff officer was awake, ready to deal with each urgent piece of news. And so it went on, night after night.

During the day, notable for the searing glare and an atmosphere that was clear save when the wind blew up or a mirage appeared, units remained widely dispersed against air attack. No two vehicles were parked together. Camouflage nets hung everywhere in evidence. Little trenches had been dug beside each vehicle. It was possible to stand in the centre of Divisional Headquarters and not to realize that you were there. No unity seemed to exist between the scattered office lorries, staff cars, caravans, jeeps, trucks with side shelters outspread, between the tiny greenish bivouac tents, khaki figures trudging across the sand, and many little signboards that indicated the occupant of each office.

One track looked like every other track, and the wire netting that the Sappers had staked into the sand hardly aided a driver in distinguishing one from another. Occasionally, if you stood on the upper ridges and looked towards the northern skyline, you could glimpse the slim blue streak of the Mediterranean. All else was Desert and men at war. On every side the sands stretched on and on towards a horizon that was broken by no feature but columns of black smoke rising from smouldering tanks, trucks and aircraft, by funnels of dust, and by the few rocky points. Into the hazy distance rolled the ridges and hollows; over the hot and gritty sand trudged the men about their business; and against particles of sand and the fierce glare of the sun overhead, strained eyes were puckered. Countless wheel and track marks criss-crossed on the ruffled surface of this Desert. Men and lorries and tanks that passed later would blur the outline of these tracks, and so would the wind. And across the Desert's face lay mile upon mile of single and twisted cable, half-buried by the loose sand, ripped by tank tracks, followed and repaired by Indian linemen, followed too, by trucks and soldiers who had lost their way and firmly believed that a telephone cable must lead to some unit or formation headquarters.

And the hollows of all these tyre marks and boot tracks were filled with dark shadows when the sun sank low. The evening turned cool, the dust was stilled, the surface of the sand took on a reddish light that swiftly faded, leaving the sand matt and tinged with grey. Eyes that were bloodshot and weary opened wider. Stars shone and twinkled in the heavens. And no white puffs from anti-aircraft shells could spoil the long-awaited evening peace.

* * * * *

It was in the middle of August that General Auchinleck handed over command of the Eighth Army to 'Strafer' Gott. Gott was to have a few days' leave before taking up his new post; he set off for Cairo, but the plane in which he flew was shot down, and the new Army Commander killed. In this way command of the Eighth Army fell to a successor from England, Lieutenant-General B. L. Montgomery. And, as a result of Mr. Churchill's visit to the Desert, Auchinleck returned to India, and Alexander replaced him as Commander-in-Chief in the Middle East.

The Prime Minister had stated that this was now to be a decisive theatre of war; an open mandate for equipment and reinforcements was given; the Army would make ready to defeat the enemy in Egypt and Libya. An aggressive and offensive spirit was to be instilled into every man. As a token of this resolve, all troop-carrying transport was sent back a long distance. Alternative positions were no longer mentioned. The terms 'box' and 'consolidation' were abolished. The first word was apt to mean that the troops were shut in and unable to operate outside; the second term implied the defensive spirit. Nobody would use the expression 'in the bag' to mean 'captured' or 'a prisoner of war.' All orders referring to withdrawal from, or thinning out of, our present positions were cancelled.

A new spirit went abroad through the Eighth Army. Hope sprang high. Fresh divisions and American tanks began to arrive. Morale rose all round. On his arrival in the Middle East, General Alexander had found the Army, to quote Mr. Churchill's alliterative phrase, "brave but baffled." Now all was changing. But let it be remembered that those who had struggled in the bewilderment and butchery of the Cauldron, who had fought a rearguard action day after day to delay the enemy from El Adem to Fuka, who had seen battalions decimated, brigades overrun, headquarters captured, armoured forces destroyed, transport hurrying towards Egypt—they had played their gallant part in paving the way for the new offensive. Without those early attacks from the Alamein Line, without those day-to-day columns and raids, without the crippling losses, the hundreds of prisoners captured from the enemy, without the untiring handling by commanders and staff, and the valiant fighting of the troops of Great Britain, Australia, New Zealand, South Africa and India—without all this and more, there would have been no line of defence at El Alamein from which the fresh Eighth Army might sally forth to drive the enemy back and back and still further back beyond Benghazi, beyond Agheila, to Tunis.

It was with this eventual onslaught in mind that Alexander directed Montgomery, on August 19, in these words: "Your prime and immediate task is to prepare for an offensive action against the German-Italian forces with a view to destroying it at the earliest possible moment. Whilst preparing this attack you must hold your present positions, and on no account allow the enemy to penetrate east of them."

The newly arrived 44th Division entered the Alamein Line and took up positions on the Alam el Halfa ridge. A further immediate addition to the Army's strength was the Tenth Armoured Division, which established itself on the western edge of the same ridge, between the 44th and the New Zealand Divisions. Thus, on this important ridge we had ranged, in artillery alone, as a threat to the flank of any advance the enemy might make against the southern part of the line, some sixteen medium, 240 field, and 200 anti-tank guns, to say nothing of the guns of nearly four hundred tanks.

From information received of Rommel's plans, it was expected that he would attack about August 25, the night of a full moon. His shortage of fuel, largely due to our successful sinking of tankers in the Mediterranean, delayed the final attack; but his increased concentration of forces towards the south gave us clear indications that one was impending, and of the direction it would eventually take. Rommel's plan—similar to that executed so successfully at Gazala three months before—was to break through on our southern flank, turn north, and advance towards the sea behind Thirty Corps, thus encircling our centre and right. The enemy's main striking force was to consist of the German Afrika Korps, with the 15th and 21st Panzer Divisions.

And what of our own side? This was to be Montgomery's first Desert battle. Our preparations were made, our moves completed, our hopes high. There had been no hurry, no lack of co-ordination, no want of proper co-operation, such as had characterized many of the recent engagements.

*　　*　　*　　*　　*

It was in the early hours of August 31 that the enemy's offensive started. Diversionary attacks were made against the northern part of the line. On Ruweisat Ridge a German parachute battalion overran the forward company of the 2nd West Yorkshires; our wire was crossed, and one company dislodged from its defences. But by the time the 1/4th Essex and some tanks arrived up to counter-attack, the position had been restored.

Then, soon after midnight on the 31st, Rommel's main thrust moved against our southern minefield between Deir el Munassib and Himeimat. In order to make a gap for the armour to go through, our minefields had to be lifted. And this lengthy operation gave the New Zealand and Seventh Armoured Divisions an excellent target for enfilading fire.

Next morning a dust-storm frustrated bombing efforts by the

Royal Air Force, but when the two German armoured divisions moved cautiously north and north-east against our 22nd Armoured Brigade near Point 102 at the western end of the Alam el Halfa ridge, the artillery fire brought upon them was so concentrated that at least a quarter of the enemy's tanks were disabled. His striking force retired. All night our aircraft dropped flares and bombed the German tank leaguers, while the New Zealanders sent out raiding parties to prevent the 90th Light Division from digging itself in.

On the morning of September 1 the enemy again tried to push on to the ridge. Again he suffered heavy losses. And his lack of success during these first two days of Rommel's last fling against the Alamein Line constituted in itself a success for the Eighth Army. Next day Rommel changed his tactics. He did his best to tempt us into counter-attacking him, but our forces did not accept the bait. Moreover, while his troop concentrations were steadily bombed by our aircraft and hammered by our artillery, his fuel situation became critical, and by the evening of September 2 Rommel must have realized that his push was doomed to failure. To remain in his advanced position was out of the question; withdrawal was the sole alternative.

On the following night—the third anniversary of the outbreak of war—the 5th New Zealand Brigade, with 132 Brigade from 44th Division, attacked south to close the minefield gap. During that day the enemy had shown signs of withdrawing slightly to the south-west, though our commanders could not be certain whether this was merely a feint to lure our tanks into a counter-attack, or whether it really was the beginning of a final withdrawal. The attack by the New Zealanders was no more than a partial success; and 132 Brigade incurred very heavy casualties. All the enemy counter-attacks next day were repulsed, and the German columns bombed and harassed by our mobile parties.

The evening of September 5 found the enemy back beside our minefields. Rommel had thus gained a small amount of ground—some five miles of Desert—and he showed his firm intention of holding on to these paltry gains. Accordingly, General Montgomery called off our attack on the 7th, leaving the enemy holding a line on the southern flank from the eastern end of Deir el Munassib to the peak of Himeimat.

The battle of Alam el Halfa not only cost the Germans and Italians severe losses in tanks, men, and motor vehicles; it was their last opportunity of victory before the Eighth Army reached its full strength. On the other hand, by this repulse of a serious offensive, we had regained our morale, and forced the enemy once again on to the defensive.

Three hundred Sherman tanks had arrived in the Middle East on September 3; new divisions were now ready to enter the line; other divisions were drawn out to refit and reorganize. And it was in this process of building up the Army's offensive strength that the hard-fought and weakened Fifth Indian Division was relieved by General Tuker's Fourth. Only Headquarters, Signals, and Langran's Nine Brigade, who had all been fighting continuously since the last week of May, left the Alamein Line. Russell's Five Brigade returned to the Fourth Indian Division to which it really belonged. 161 Brigade, with two fresh battalions, settled into the defences vacated by Nine Brigade, and stayed to fight in Montgomery's October battle of El Alamein.

On September 9 the Fifth Indian Division, which had been but slightly involved in Rommel's last onslaught, handed over to General Tuker's command not only its positions on Ruweisat Ridge, but its battle-worn vehicles and some of its stoutest troops. Then Briggs led out from the Desert those units that were to leave. The column headed for Mena and a sight of the Pyramids.

And so it was that the Fifth Indian Division quitted the continent of Africa. No longer would the Division fight against Italians and Germans. No longer would it serve in Middle East Forces. It was bound for the newly constituted Persia and Iraq Force. Cairo would not be its base and leave centre, nor the Nile its most familiar river. The Division was to cross Nile, Jordan, Euphrates, to settle beside the waters of Tigris.

CHAPTER XVIII

OUTSIDE BAGHDAD

OCTOBER 1942—MAY 1943

A YEAR had passed since the Division drove through Baghdad on its way to Kirkuk and back. Now it returned to Iraq, and settled among the dusty wastes of Quetta Camp, a mile to the west of the capital. At this time the German advance towards the Caucasus was at its height. The Russians might be overwhelmed and brought to collapse. And there waited the Anglo-Iranian and American oilfields as a tempting bait, which would doubtless prove irresistible to the Germans. It was to prepare against an enemy attack southwards through Persia as well as through Turkey that Persia and Iraq Force was formed under General Sir Henry Maitland Wilson in the summer of 1942.

Wilson had at his disposal General Quinan's Tenth Army in Persia, and, in Iraq, the Polish Corps under General Anders. The Fifth Indian Division arrived to constitute a strong G.H.Q. reserve, which General Wilson could move to either country in a mobile role. In order to play this part the Division was reorganized with two infantry brigades, Nine and 161, when the latter came over from the Eighth Army in December, and the veteran Seventh Armoured Brigade, led by Brigadier J. K. Anstice. This brigade comprised the 2nd Royal Tank Regiment, the 6th Royal Tank Regiment, the 7th Hussars, the 14th Royal Horse Artillery, and the 14th Sherwood Foresters. It had fought with the "Desert Rats" in the early battles of North Africa, and its bold actions in Burma had enabled General Alexander to extricate our army from the Rangoon-Pegu area.

Also under command of the Division were the armoured cars of the Guides Cavalry, a fine and picturesque unit from the North-West Frontier of India.

It was not until the end of December that Hughes' 161 Brigade rejoined the Division after its three months with the Fourth Indian

Division. At first it had patrolled south of Ruweisat Ridge and prepared for the great day of October 23, the Battle of Alamein. During this assault, that was to be a turning-point in the war, 161 Brigade made diversionary attacks, raids, and bluffing noises, as did the rest of the Fourth Indian Division, while the main battle raged further north along the front. Then, in November, it had the task of clearing the battlefield and rounding up the hundreds of Italian prisoners.

When, on December 10, the Fourth Indian Division moved up to El Adem, 161 Brigade left its command and returned to Egypt, on its way to Iraq. The British battalion changed, and the 1st Argyll and Sutherland Highlanders were replaced by the 4th Royal West Kent Regiment.

* * * * *

This was a period of flickering local interest, but robbed of any purpose that could finally satisfy the men. There were many who fretted under the lack of action, under the frustration of training and living in so bleak and inhospitable a land. To read of the Eighth Army's all-conquering progress across the north of Africa was but to emphasize the inaction. News from other battlefields only served to magnify the sense of being in a backwater of the war. No doubt the threat of an attack by German armies from the Caucasus through Persia and Iraq was ever present, so long as the Russians were on the defensive or retiring towards the east. But a threat of possible attack could not impress with the same stern reality as could a known and present danger.

And the country itself did nothing to dispel the sense of waiting, of incipient boredom, of futility. The dusty, earthen fields of Quetta Camp, devoid of grass, but prickly with thorns and bumpy from worn banks and ridges, were monotonous and without character. True it is that the rows and rows of square white tents that housed Divisional Headquarters and Nine Brigade were bright with fluttering unit flags and pennants. But the only greenery to relieve the brown tones of the landscape was provided by a roadside hedge and several groups of dusty palms.

And wind swirled up the dust, blew in beneath the tent walls, chilled men's fingers, and added its discomfort to the sting of driving dust particles. If few trains puffed and rattled down the line that skirted one end of the camp, the motor traffic passing along the main road to Baghdad was constant and noisy. But beyond this railway appeared one bright patch: the Palace of the Roses—home of the boy King of Iraq—the white walls and red roof of which could be seen above the trees of the garden. In every other direction the eye met buff and brown, puffs of dust, straggly bushes, tents and lorries.

Nor did Baghdad itself provide much relief. All the troops were disappointed. The city of Haroun al Rashid contained no Eastern glamour, and its only mystery was provided by the acres of narrow, dirty alleys and side streets that were out of bounds. A glimpse of a sunlit courtyard, the blue or golden gleam of some mosque, and the slender grace of a minaret against the sky brought pleasure amid so much squalor and dilapidation, where poverty, dirt and disease lurked round corners. Yet the sight of the outspread city from the Maude Bridge was impressive, though the waterfront itself could not be so described. Many small boats plied on the muddy waters of Tigris, and in the narrow lanes that ran up from the river bank lean, unkempt pi-dogs barked. And the bridge itself seldom stopped from shuddering beneath the rumbling flow of military and civilian traffic.

Many there were who visited Ur of the Chaldees and clambered on the ziggurat and down into deep chambers; who walked beneath the immense unsupported arch of Ctesiphon and photographed the ruins of Babylon. Others went north to the spiral mosque of Samarra, or south to the site of the Tower of Babel, and to other historic cities of the past. The response of the men, both British and Indian, to such expeditions far exceeded the expectations of many of the commanding officers. And Baghdad attracted by its bazaars where collectors of carpets and copperwork, of silver and brassware, of Arab head-dresses and robes, of inlaid boxes and other oriental objects could prowl at will and bargain with the local men who sat behind their goods and gossiped or smoked the hookah.

Though watered by Tigris and Euphrates, though believed to be the site of the Garden of Eden, the country's dominant impression was of dust, or of mud when the rains fell, of uncomfortable winds and lack of green in the bleak landscape. And Quetta Camp at moments recalled some factory town, on account of the smudges of thick

General Alexander Inspects the 3/2nd Punjab

(C.I.S. Historical Section)

Facing p. 242]

Major-General H. R. Briggs

(C.I.S. Historical Section)

The King of Iraq
Visits the Division

(Imperial War Museu

and oily smoke that coiled above the tents and dirtied everything. A severe shortage of wood had made it necessary for the Divisional Sappers to build into all office and mess tents a brick stove which fired on one drip of oil to two drips of water falling into a flashpan. If the heat provided was excellent, the danger to the tent canvas where this touched the chimneys was constant, and hardly a week passed without several tents catching fire.

It was during the spring that most camps in the Division were plagued by 'loosewallahs'—thieves who stole in by night from the villages to steal such kit, arms and equipment as they could make away with. It must be conceded that they were devilish successful and cunning, for they could remove every object inside a tent, except the bedding and camp bed, without waking anyone sleeping in that tent. Belief had it that the loosewallahs could even strike a tent and carry it away, and still the occupants would sleep on undisturbed. So bad did the situation become that units on the edge of every camp were obliged to post guards and man machine-guns. Seldom were the night hours unbroken by the sudden crackling of a gun. Few dawns lit the sky without disclosing a corpse, though the vultures were quick to circle and descend, should the human eye have failed to pick out the dead marauder. To recover stolen property was all but impossible, for women and boys waited among the dunes outside our camps while their men folk crept in and stole. Then the booty was laden on donkeys and taken to a village or to some obscure hiding-place.

For those who had money, the hotels of Baghdad provided meals and drinks at high prices. The shops were unattractive, and poorly stocked. But units organized their own entertainments, concert parties, discussion groups and hockey matches. The chaplains were leading spirits in such work. At Divisional Headquarters in Quetta Camp the Senior Chaplain, the Rev. Christopher Perowne, started a branch of Toc H, and in the Church tent some activity was arranged for almost every night of the week. Lectures were given by Freya Stark, by the head of the Baghdad Police, by a banker, by an expert on irrigation; other lecturers spoke on devil worship or the antiquities of Iraq. Games, debates and community singing took their turn in beguiling the frequent empty evenings. Many of the men borrowed books from the Chaplain's personal library. The Polish Corps in Iraq presented outstanding concerts of music, singing, and folk-dancing in native costumes. The Baghdad cinemas were filled; and in Quetta Camp mobile cinema units provided films for the Indian ranks, who sat on the grass on either side of the open-air screen and enjoyed films in their own language.

Many events at once varied and important to the Division occurred during this winter and spring spent in Iraq. General Briggs lectured on 'The mixed Infantry and Armoured Division' that the Fifth had become. Demonstrations were given by several battalions; battle inoculation was provided for new members of the Division; courses on demolitions were organized by the Sappers. Round sand-table models officers worked out and discussed tactics, and tactical exercises without troops (more familiar under the title of TEWTS) occupied the thoughts and ingenuity both of planners and of those under instruction.

Speed was essential in becoming battleworthy in the new role allotted to the Division. Infantry and artillery units had to learn how to co-operate fully with the Seventh Armoured Brigade, while at the same time they reorganized, re-equipped and trained in their own weapons. Commanders and staff officers at all levels were sent out to reconnoitre the possible theatre of war in the northern parts of Iraq, and both on the ground and on scale models the detailed employment of the Division in each type of fighting was explored and practised.

At a certain bridging demonstration an amusing incident took place that might well have been extremely serious. The Iraq Levies asked to drop parachutists to attack the bridge. To witness this attack, about ninety senior officers from G.H.Q., Paiforce, assembled, and stood round a jeep on a 'bund.' The two transport planes, capable of a speed of little more than fifty m.p.h. and dating from the First World War, dropped their parachutists without mishap. But the pilots then decided to demonstrate a dive-bombing attack on the assembled 'brass-hats.' These were seen to fall in haste from the bund. And this showed their wisdom, for the first aircraft hit the jeep fair and square, and crashed. One rather 'broad' brigadier lay flat on the bund, but as his breadth was out of all proportion to his height, he only escaped by rolling down it. He was seen rushing at speed to report the matter to the Air Officer Commanding.

On the last day of February it was arranged that the young King of Iraq should visit the Seventh Armoured Brigade at Latifiya, thirty miles south of Baghdad. Lieutenant-Colonel F. B. B. Noble, being deputed to fetch the King, reported to the palace, and wore his Highland Light Infantry trousers of the Mackenzie tartan. He had been warned that if the King expressed a liking for anything, he would expect to be given it. On reaching the palace Noble was ushered into a reception room and given a cup of coffee.

Very soon the boy King walked in. Noble was presented. The King sat down beside him, placed his arm round Noble's shoulders, and said, "Will you tell me a story, please ?" Noble, nonplussed by this unexpected request, was unable to improvise. But at once the King expressed great admiration for the tartan trousers, and Noble had several moments of acute embarrassment, wondering whether this was his cue to take off his trousers and present them to the King. His fears were relieved and all went well.

On arrival at Latifiya, the King shook hands sedately with General Briggs and Brigadier Anstice. Then he was taken up into the turret of a tank by Colonel Liardet, commanding the 6th Royal Tank Regiment. He watched one squadron rumble past and fire their guns, but seemed a little uncertain as to whether he liked this display or not. But on noticing a jeep, he at once asked to be driven about in it, and was so delighted with the ride that it was a long time before he could be persuaded to get out of the jeep again. Afterwards the King was presented with a jeep and a model tank for himself.

In the early spring General Briggs held a full-scale exercise called 'Forbid' that was to last ten days at full war pressure. The Division made a night move by road and as dawn broke was seen in full Desert formation ready to advance again. Led by the Armoured Brigade, a manœuvre was carried out with the object of seizing a feature vital to the enemy's communications. These were then raided so as to oblige the enemy to attack the Division on its own ground. Enemy tanks, represented by our own tank transporters, supported by units of the Iraq Army, launched their attack but failed to penetrate the brigade position behind which the Seventh Armoured Brigade was held in support, ready to launch the necessary counter-attack against the enemy's flanks. Then the Division followed up and found the enemy back in a defended position.

Our infantry cleared a minefield and formed a bridgehead, thus enabling the second infantry brigade and the tanks to overwhelm the position.

For such an exercise the troops moved out of their dusty camps, and felt themselves back once more in the Desert. They were on the move, camping out in the open, camouflaging their vehicles, and watching the mirages of glistening water and of sandbanks in the air.

Lighter entertainment was the order of the day when the Division organized a gymkhana on the sands by Latifiya. The sideshows attracted great crowds: cocoanut shies and roulette and a greasy pole, weight-guessing contests, and darts. Close upon the heels of a camel race followed a wild donkey race, which was slow but entertaining, though hard on the donkeys. A jeep race over a most difficult course provided greater excitement, for the hairpin bends, marked out on the sand with strips of camouflage material, and the humpbacked sand ridges tested the competitors to the utmost. Spectators jumped for their lives as drivers, wearing goggles and half blinded by dust, steered their jeeps round corners in a scream of roaring engines and a cloud of sand.

Team races and tugs-of-war were won and lost; competitions were held for dismounting tanks from transporters, and for running out and setting up field guns. Brown-skinned Indian soldiers wearing scarlet shorts wrestled over the sand, heaving and grunting in their efforts to force their opponents flat on their backs. As evening approached, fifty Pathans from the Guides Cavalry, with grey shirts hanging outside their trousers and a red sash round their waists, danced the Khattak dances. By the light of a great wood fire that was constantly replenished with fuel, these tall men danced to the strange music of three pipes and three small drums beaten with the fingers. The dancers shouted and swayed, waving red streamers in their hands. When other dancers came forward, this time with swords, the blades flashed in the firelight. And the dancers' energy never flagged. Indeed, it mounted towards a memorable finale with instruments playing, swords glinting, bodies jumping, bending and twisting. And the huge fire crackled and leaped in the centre.

It was a sight to remember, both for its own sake and because of its rarity in war time. This was one of the very few occasions on which the Division played together, carefree, eager for enjoyment, bounding with health. At other times, when the units were resting and re-equipping, they were split up, or too busy training, or engaged on defence digging, or in some manner occupied. But the end of Exercise 'Forbid' had found the Division united, and ready to relax. And this the men, British and Indian, did with a will. As they walked away in the gathering darkness, the haunting music of the Khattak dances still sounded in their ears.

* * * * *

After six months of constant training in the new role, the Division was never given an opportunity of operating in battle with the Seventh Armoured Brigade. Persistent demands were made by India for the Division to be sent to take part in the war against Japan. India was short of war-experienced formations. The jungle frontiers of Burma did not lend themselves to large armoured formations, but there was a shortage of tanks in the Middle East, and that was where the Seventh Armoured Brigade moved. It was with regret that the Division parted with Brigadier Anstice and his men, for the Brigade was already an integral part of the Fifth Indian Division. Co-operation had been smooth, mutual pride enhanced, and close ties of friendship formed.

And so, during May 1943, the units packed their kits, loaded their equipment and stores, and travelled by road and rail through Ur of the Chaldees to Basra. Here they boarded ships that brought them in a week to Bombay, the Gateway of India. The Indian ranks were overjoyed at the prospect and reality of leave in their homes, from the North-West Frontier to the Malabar coast and Madras. For those who had never before set foot in the vast continent, there was a wealth of unending new scenes and people to watch and absorb. And the veterans who had known India before the war could revive old memories and perhaps discover fresh aspects of a fathomless world.

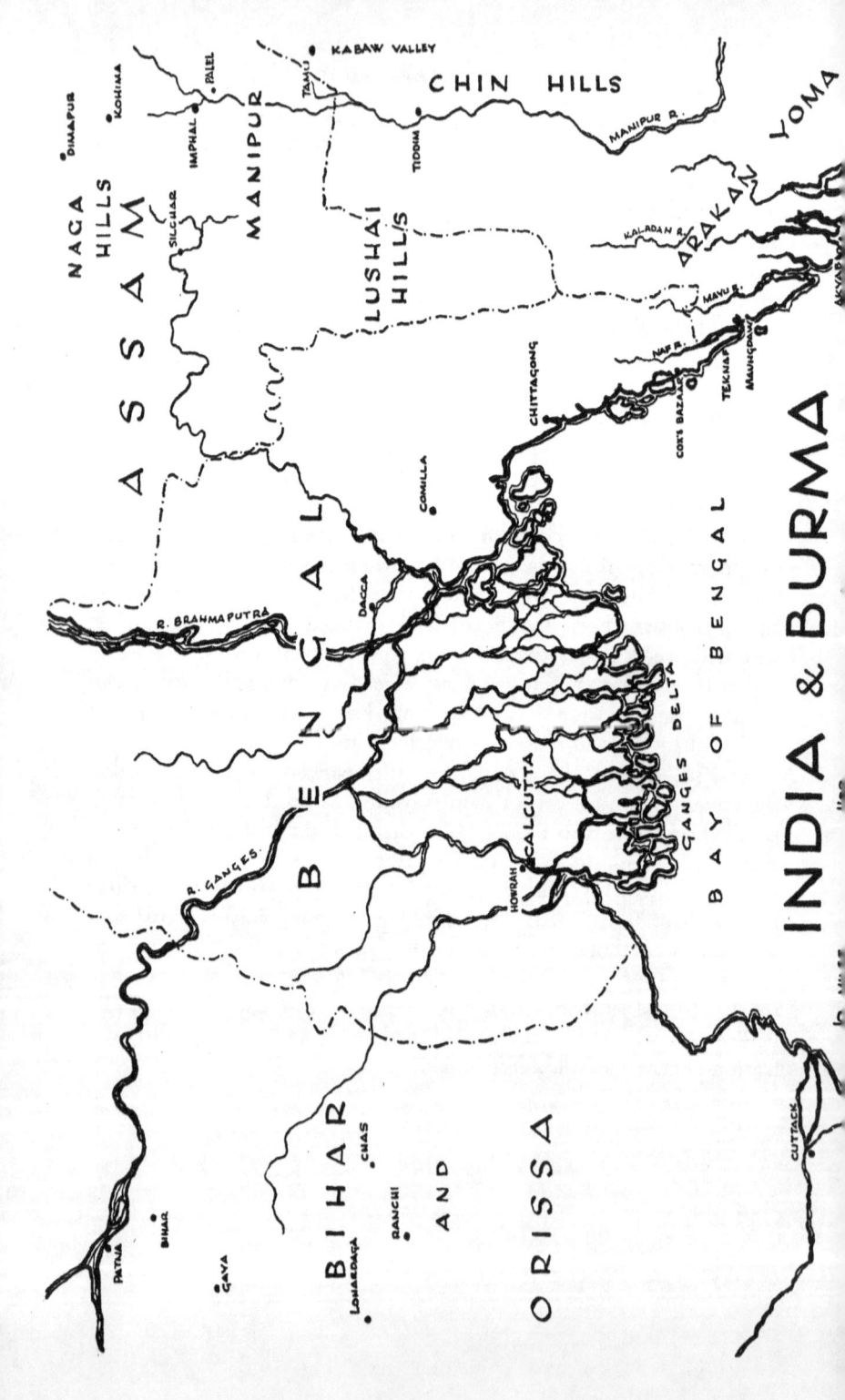

CHAPTER XIX

TRAINING FOR BURMA

JUNE—OCTOBER 1943

IT was in the first weeks of June that Nine and 161 Brigades reached Bombay from Iraq, and moved by road and rail across the centre of India to their concentration area at Chas in Bihar Province.

Chas was an uncomfortable place in which to train. As an introduction to India it was lamentable. The heat was humid and enervating, and mosquitoes abounded in the jungle clearings. In the paddy fields walked the men and women from the nearby villages, and along the dusty roads lurched sleepy bullock carts. There were rivers to cross and distant hills to watch in sunlight or sudden storm. Every unit was at half strength or less because of men away on leave. The Indian units, except for small maintenance and vehicle parties, were sent direct to their regimental depots for well-earned leave. Those who remained were kept fully occupied in training, and in maintaining the daily routine of existence and work. New changes were taking place every week. Fresh units joined the Division, and a rapid transformation occurred between the ways of the Desert and the methods and requirements for the warfare of Burma.

When the Division first reached Bihar, Briggs was called in to Ranchi by Lieutenant-General W. J. Slim, now commanding Fifteen Indian Corps. It will be recalled that General Slim was last mentioned in this narrative in January 1941, when he was wounded and evacuated to hospital soon after the capture of Kassala, Tessenei and Agordat. Since that ill-fated day the former commander of Ten Brigade had led the Tenth Indian Division from Syria to the Caspian Sea, made contact with the Russians in Persia, and led his Corps in the fighting withdrawal from Burma in 1942.

He told General Briggs that the Fifth Indian Division was to go down to the Arakan front in a few months' time, ready for the new campaign that was to open there at the end of the year.

Briggs expostulated, and asked why, considering that there were two fully-trained jungle divisions (the 19th and 25th), and that all jungle text-books stated that troops should not be committed to battle without a year's jungle training. Slim then said that he had particularly asked for the Division, owing to its battle experience, flexibility, and high morale; the morale in Burma was at this time very low. Of course Briggs objected no longer.

At the end of June the Division adopted the organization of combined animal and motor transport. A Divisional Headquarters battalion was added, to relieve the strain on the nine infantry battalions in the brigades. Hitherto they had had to provide detachments for escorts, traffic control duties, and local defence tasks. In addition, the strength of the rifle companies was increased to enable them to turn to a man-handling basis without unduly weakening the rifle sections. Most of the vehicles with less mobility in jungle country than the 15-cwt, four-wheel drive truck were dispensed with. The principle was accepted that all baggage and non-essential stores would be dumped at the start of operations and moved forward by pool transport only when possible during static periods.

The need for close support of the infantry by artillery units, in country in which the normal 25-pounder regiment was thought unable to operate, was met by providing a mixed regiment of 3.7-inch howitzers and 3-inch mortars. The 28th Field Regiment became a Jungle Field Regiment with one battery of sixteen mortars, and two batteries each of eight howitzers. The regiment had no mules, but a larger establishment of jeeps.

The Division was entitled to a regiment of mountain artillery for jungle warfare, and one was tentatively allocated. But the C.R.A., Brigadier Mansergh, was not quite satisfied that this regiment was ready for active service. With other senior officers of the Division he happened at this time, during August, to be making a tour and reconnaissance of the Arakan front, and as a gesture of courtesy he called in to see the positions of the forward-most artillery, the 2nd (Derejat) Mountain Battery, which with the 12th (Poona) formed the 27th Mountain Regiment. Both these batteries had fought with distinction and endurance in the first campaign across Burma. Each had marched some 1,200 miles, and they had lost but two guns between them.

They were on the point of being amalgamated with the 24th Mountain Regiment, which had the 11th (Poona) and 20th Batteries, to form a full regiment, rather than a light mountain regiment which each had been hitherto. Mansergh was shown round the position of 2 Battery (Major P. Hartley) at Bawli Bazaar, and was impressed that the men should be in such excellent shape after five months of continuous action in over 200 inches of rain; most of this period had been spent under canvas, with no cover for the mules. Further investigation showed that the other three batteries were equally sound, and Mansergh decided without hesitation that the 24th Mountain Regiment, commanded by Lieutenant-Colonel Humphrey Hill, was what he was looking for.

The chief event of July was the arrival under General Briggs' command of 123 Brigade, led by Brigadier A. V. Hammond, who was shortly to be superseded by Brigadier T. J. W. Winterton. The battalions of this brigade, which had fought through the first campaign in Arakan, were the 2nd Suffolks (Lieutenant-Colonel Hopking), the 2/1st Punjab (Lieutenant-Colonel W. G. Smith), and the 1/17th Dogras (Lieutenant-Colonel W. A. Crowther).

To command 161 Brigade came Brigadier D. F. W. Warren, who had already served in Burma as G.S.O.1 of the 14th Indian Division. August saw the arrival in the Division of 56 Anti-Tank Regiment and 74 Field Company I.E., the latter being attached to 123 Brigade. The Guides Cavalry left the Division at the end of the month.

While General Briggs and his G.S.O.1 visited the Arakan front for a fortnight, an animal management team toured the Division and gave lectures and instruction in the handling and care of mules. Those officers and men who were not on leave received visits from the Army and Corps Commanders; they went to conferences, attended lectures on Burma, on battle drill, on recent operations in Arakan, on tactics against the Japanese; and they read training instructions. Then, the Fifth Indian Division moved away from the steamy neighbourhood of Chas to the cooler and more hilly landscape of Lohardaga, forty-five miles west of Ranchi.

A foretaste of the campaign ahead could be had from the training extracts issued during this period of reorganization and re-equipment: 'Speed our Training' was the great dictum. The Division, two of whose brigades had been used to fighting the Germans and Italians, had now to learn about the Japanese. Units which had sped about the Desert in lorries had to learn to use animals instead. The enemy was described as "a fanatic" and, therefore, "a menace until he is dead." "His morale at the moment is high from his past successes; his training is good; at present he fears the disgrace of capture more than death. Our morale is good, and our training will shortly be better than his; we shall destroy his morale as we destroyed the Italian and German morale in the Desert. The way we shall do it is thus; it will be our fanatical aim to KILL JAPS; hunt him and kill him like any other wild beast. He is not a superman; he is a good fighter and nothing except death will stop him from obtaining his object. But against experienced troops who know what to expect, he is a nuisance value and plays into our hands. He is anything but a silent and good bushman, and in movement his security is bad. He prefers to keep to trails, and thus is a 'gift' to us when trained in jungle warfare. He is a very bad shot. We could outplay him, too, at his sniping and concealment. Finally, the Jap's stamina is no better than our own, and he simply hates our artillery and mortar fire."

The Japanese tactics were based on deception and rapid manœuvre, and they relied on surprise manœuvre rather than on assault, preferring to force our retirement by infiltrating troops to block our lines of communication and to raid our larger headquarters. The jungle called for better junior leadership than any other theatre of war. Mental and bodily endurance would be essential. Individual fieldcraft, observation and concealment had to be learned and practised. Japanese characteristics and methods were studied with care; the troops were trained in fire discipline and control to avoid shooting at mere noises; they were taught to treat the jungle as a friend, able to supply them with shelter and food. Aggressive patrolling was to be the basis of our tactics.

General Briggs issued his Five Commandments that every member of the Division had to learn:

1. Be determined to kill every Jap you meet, and then some.
2. Be determined not to let the Jap frighten you with ruses and induce you to disclose your positions and waste ammunition. Ambush him and do unto him as he would unto you.
3. Be determined to hold fast when ordered, whatever happens. The Jap will then have to give you the target you want, whilst our reserves are on the way to help you.

4. Be determined to carry out to the letter every task given to you, whether on patrol, in attack or defence. No half measures. Plan for all eventualities, after anticipating enemy reactions. Plans cannot be too thorough. Be observant and suspicious.

5. Be determined—even fanatical.

Among the most unaccustomed and essential aspects of training were the malaria precautions. Units were instructed to become mosquito-minded, because malaria could be as great an enemy as the Japanese. Every man, at seven o'clock in the evening, rolled down his long sleeves and tucked his trousers into socks or gaiters. His face, neck and hands were smothered with anti-mosquito cream, a tin of which he also took to bed with him. Every man not on duty slept beneath a mosquito net which was tucked under the blankets. Sentries and others who were not sleeping wore veils and gloves, and applied mosquito cream every two hours to the exposed parts of the body. Early morning spraying squads visited all tents and huts. The enforcement of these precautions was rigorous, and the penalty for negligence severe.

Each of the three brigades in turn took part in an exercise, attacking a hill with air support and tanks. The country to the west of Lohardaga resembled the hills of Arakan, with thick jungle, streams, muddy roads, and few villages. But heavy rain caused many difficulties in supplying the troops in these outlying parts of Bihar, and imposed delays on a training programme that was already overcrowded and hurried. The actual problems to be faced in the coming campaign in Arakan were faced round a large-scale model of the country. Syndicates from each brigade, and from the Services, worked out their plans of attack, and expounded these to the directing staff and for the benefit of all present.

These exercises and rehearsals much resembled those held near Baghdad, but with one fundamental difference. This time it was quite certain that the experience gained would be used in battle, and against an enemy about whom only 123 Brigade and a few officers knew much at first hand.

By the beginning of October it was decided that the Fifth Indian Division was ready to enter the fighting area. 123 Brigade would go first, and Nine Brigade, which had been the last to reach India from Iraq, and was thus behind the others in training, would move last to Arakan.

CHAPTER XX

ARAKAN

NOVEMBER 1943—JANUARY 1944

A BOAT steaming from Calcutta down the Hoogly River and eastwards across the mouths of the Ganges and Brahmaputra would bring you to the coast near Chittagong. Turn south here and follow that coastline past Cox's Bazaar to the little port of Maungdaw, which lies up the broad Naf River. This is more like an estuary or an arm of the sea, and is protected from the Bay of Bengal by the elongated Teknaf Peninsula. You are in Arakan, a coastal area of Burma that is divided from the central plain and Irrawaddy Valley by the mountains of the Arakan Yoma. The main port of Akyab lies another sixty miles down that coast, and farther still is the island of Ramree.

From a narrow coastal strip some four miles in width, intersected by tidal waterways (known as *chaungs*), planted with paddy, and studded with villages of teak houses and thatched huts and clumps of trees, rises the Mayu Range. These hills, the ridge having a height of between 1,200 and 2,000 feet, are sheer, rocky, and thickly covered with jungle. Beyond this range lies a valley through which flows the Kalapanzin River. The small town of Buthidaung has been built on its banks. Going still farther east over several ranges of mountains, higher than the Mayu, you would reach the valley of the Kaladan.

In the early months of 1943 our forces had been driven back from the Mayu Peninsula to a line that ran across the map from Nhila on the Teknaf Peninsula, over the waters of the Naf River, through Bawli Bazaar, over the Mayu Range to Goppe and Taung Bazaars. The Japanese had advanced no farther than Maungdaw and Buthidaung, and stayed there during the monsoon period that summer. There followed several months of static warfare, active patrols, occasional brushes, constant rain, disease, and a gradual

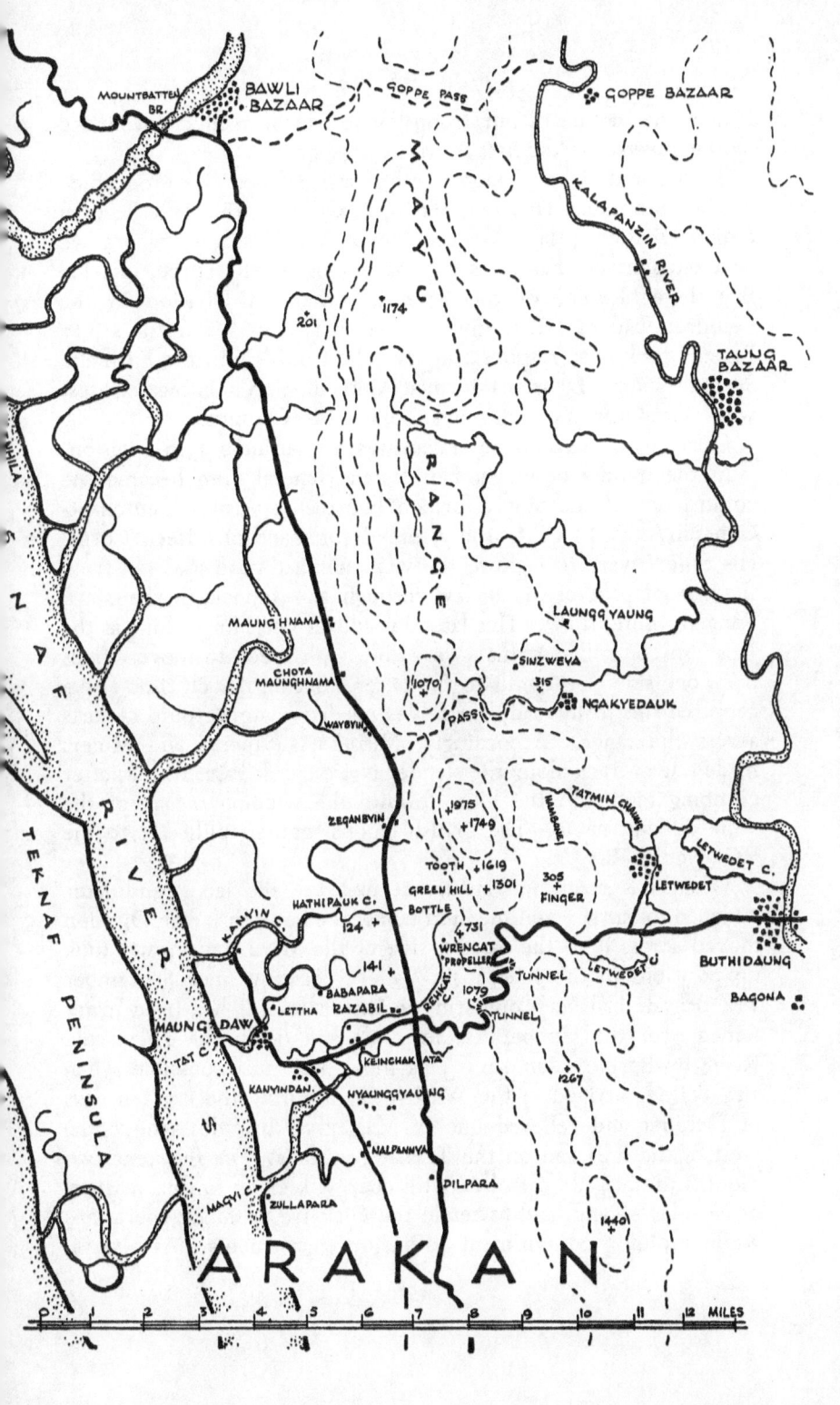

rise in the morale of our troops, who had been much dispirited by our reverses in the first Arakan campaign.

Throughout the monsoon our forward defences were occupied by the 26th Indian Division. Then, in October, came the Seventh Indian Division (Major-General Frank W. Messervy, whom we have encountered before as commander of Gazelle Force, of Nine Brigade at Keren, of the Seventh Armoured Division in the Cauldron battle). This division and Brigadier Winterton's 123 Brigade took over responsibility for the front. Both the Fifth and Seventh Indian Divisions formed General Slim's Fifteen Corps, whose headquarters were moved forward to Chittagong.

Opposing our troops in Arakan was the Japanese 55th Division.

In the middle of November, when General Slim became the commander of the newly formed Fourteenth Army, Lieutenant-General A. P. F. Christison assumed command of Fifteen Corps. His orders were to capture the vital metalled road that ran from the coastal port of Maungdaw through two tunnels in the Mayu Range to Buthidaung. This lateral road was vital, for so long as the Japanese controlled it they were able with speed to move troops from one side of the hills to the other. But until such time as we captured this main road, our forces needed a lateral route of sorts across the range. Accordingly, Messervy's Sappers and Miners made a jeep track along the slender Ngakyedauk Pass, which, after climbing high into the hills, follows the winding *chaung* of the same difficult name. The British troops soon simplified it to the "Okeydoke Pass."

When this track was made, at first to take jeeps, and later widened for lorries and medium tanks, the Seventh Indian Division moved across it to the eastern side of the Mayu Range, and took up positions in the Kalapanzin Valley. Already since September 114 Brigade had been operating in this valley. It had been maintained over the Goppe Pass by mule and down the Kalapanzin River by Burmese sampan. This move was made possible when 123 Brigade arrived in the Waybyin area during the last ten days of October and relieved one of Messervy's brigades (the 89th) west of the hills and on the Teknaf Peninsula. For the next two months the brigade patrolled with energy, seeking to gain mastery of No-Man's-Land, and to retain the initiative in minor operations while avoiding commitment to major engagements. As always, detailed information of the enemy positions and defences was required. New officers and men had the opportunity to gain experience, while those members of 123 Brigade who had already fought in Arakan with the 14th Indian Division renewed their acquaintance with the country and taught the newcomers such wisdom and knowledge of jungle warfare and the Japanese as they had themselves gained earlier that same year.

On November 9 General Briggs assumed operational command of the front west of the ridge of the Mayu hills, with 123 Brigade forward, and Warren's 161 Brigade guarding our lines of communication north of Bawli until the end of the month. Then it moved south to hold the coastal plain by Waybyin and Zeganbyin, and Teknaf across the water.

*　　*　　*　　*　　*

Units erected their tiny bivouac tents among the glens east of the main road, they stretched large tarpaulins on bamboo frameworks and camouflaged their habitations as best they could. Black leeches, an inch long, sucked men's blood and had to be evicted from the flesh with a glowing cigarette end. Tracks had to be made off the road, the gunners dug their gun pits and kept on improving them, and signallers toiled up and down hills laying miles of telephone cable or carrying pack wireless sets on their backs.

The dust of the one and only road reminded veterans of certain tracks in the Desert. Each day parties of Arakanese, dressed in gaily coloured shirts and skirts called *longyis*, threw water on the road surface to subdue the billowing dust. While little boys ran up and down, having great fun with tins of water that they fetched from nearby pools or from a muddy *chaung*, the men and even their women worked on this never-ending job of repair and maintenance. Wide wicker hats shaded them from the sun that beat down on the landscape, shone upon white palm flowers waving on long stalks, and brought out the rich colours of paddy and watercourse, bamboo plant and palm tree.

Up and down the road pass ambulances, jeeps, trucks and lorries. Mules lurch past with their creaking loads, mountain guns can be seen strapped in sections to the mules, wireless vehicles bump along with a slender rod aerial swaying at the back. Little signboards painted with the numbers of each unit show where to turn off the road for a particular brigade or regimental headquarters. On either side the upswished dust coats the trees with a yellowish film. There goes General Briggs in his jeep—the red pennant flies from the bonnet. Behind is an ambulance with red crosses on its body. Farther on the Sappers are repairing a bridge, and every vehicle has to follow a rough diversion that causes the passengers to bump and swear as the driver turns down the bank, steers the jolting truck across a stretch of paddy field, and roars up on to the road once more.

It is up and down this road, with its dust, its bridges, and its hold-ups, that everyone moves. But along the peaceful *chaungs* pass sampans, rowed from the stern by an upright Arakanese. Scores of these little boats ferry stores across the river at Bawli Bazaar, while the new Mountbatten Bridge is being completed. Sampans take stores and dispatch-riders over the Naf to Nhila and the Teknaf Peninsula. Signal cables run beside the road, fastened on poles, tied to trees, hitched to a building, buried under a track crossing. And Madrassi linemen can be seen on top of ladders, armed with pliers and tape, or rolling huge drums of cable, or ringing and buzzing with their telephones when testing the line or looking for a break. A motor-cycle roars by, a man shouts a greeting in Tamil, and the dispatch-rider, wearing his blue and white armband, has vanished round the corner on his way to Divisional Headquarters.

At one place a sign will lead to a water-point made by the Sappers; farther up is the barbed-wire cage for any prisoners-of-war that may be taken. On the right a board with a red cross and the letters M.D.S. reveals the presence of a Dressing Station and one of the three Field Ambulances. Another jeep goes jolting along, a blue flag fluttering in the dust-laden breeze. The pipe and a flash of the sun on spectacles show that Brigadier Warren is visiting one of his battalions.

Perhaps a small convoy of heavy lorries with the sign of the three Roman fives—more like crossed hockey-sticks—approaches from Fifteen Corps Headquarters, laden with stores or ammunition or rations. One or two of the vehicles that use this road bear the golden arrow of Messervy's division over the hills above Buthidaung. Few have time to stand and watch the constant procession of human

Brigadier D. W. Reid

(*Lafayette*)

Brigadier B. C. Fletcher

Brigadier C. H. Boucher

Brigadier W. H. Langran

Arakan Landscape (J. H. Dale)

The Mayu Range (J. H. Dale)

ARAKAN

beings and mechanical transport and animals that go this way. Only the Military Police on duty, perhaps, can stand and watch, because these men must guide and control, halt and send on, divert and direct.

Nor were the Military Police idle at this time. To control the traffic up and down the narrow road was no easy task. And the surface of that road had to be preserved, the clouds of dust diminished, the trucks slowed down. Certain bridges were one-way only, and there were other patches of the road subject to strict police supervision. Near Zeganbyin a warning signboard had been erected. On it were painted these sombre words: "Stop ! If you drive your vehicle past this point you probably won't come back. They didn't." And an arrow pointed down to a picture of the fate that might await any driver who passed our forward defence line through ignorance or lack of caution.

On Christmas Eve the road was brightened north of Maunghnama by a temporary sign erected by the Assistant Provost Marshal of the Division: "A Happy Christmas from the A.P.M . Peace on Earth, Goodwill to All Men, and 15 m.p.h. if you please !"

And a notice at the foot of the Ngakyedauk Pass indicated forcibly, with the pregnant words "A jeep can go anywhere" and a picture of one falling over the precipice, the dangers that awaited every user of that pass.

One day in the middle of December, an open jeep brought a Very Important Personage to visit the Division. This was Lord Louis Mountbatten, fresh to his post as Supreme Allied Commander, South-East Asia, resplendent in Naval uniform, and impressive by his commanding presence. The effect upon the troops was profound, the enthusiasm for Mountbatten's genial informality undisguised, the appreciation of his talks from a jeep bonnet heartening. The Fifth was the first Indian division that Mountbatten visited on the battlefields of Burma. Back in Britain he had been primed about the poor morale he might expect among the troops. Not only did his personal contact with the Division, and, later, with Messervy's Seventh Indian Division across the hills, do much to change Mountbatten's misgivings into confidence, but his presence in the forward areas acted as a vigorous tonic to morale. He spoke to and shook hands with all officers and N.C.Os. at informal parades, he addressed the British ranks as a crowd, and to certain Indians he spoke individually, using but three Urdu expressions. He pretended to understand the excited replies. They referred to him as "Mounting Batten," while to the British he became "Supremo."

While inspecting Winterton's 123 Brigade, Lord Louis watched an artillery shoot laid on a Japanese position especially for his benefit. The shoot did not go according to plan, for the rounds kept falling short. The Forward Observation Officer on the telephone kept firing corrections of "Up 50," but without appreciable result. Eventually Mountbatten impatiently seized the telephone and shouted to the startled gunner at the other end of the line, "Up 1,000." Great was the amusement of all those watching when a cloud of dust and smoke was observed well beyond the target.

* * * * *

The first engagement of 161 Brigade was Operation 'Jericho,' which opened as the old year passed away to make way for 1944. The great obstacle that barred our successful advance down the coast to enable us to gain control of the road linking Maungdaw with the Tunnels and Buthidaung was the Razabil Fortress. Here, on the hillocks that guarded a pair of T-roads, the enemy had entrenched himself with prodigious care and forethought. Before the Division could assault this Fortress, the low hills that led to it had to be secured.

And the first of these was Point 124. This feature lay on the west of the main road. It overlooked on the southern side an important gap at Hathipauk which led through these foothills and gave access to the coastal flats, intersected by numerous winding, tidal *chaungs*. South-west across this stretch of desolate coast, with its few little villages, lay the port of Maungdaw. Although we could approach this place without using the Hathipauk gap, we could not supply troops there by road so long as Razabil remained in enemy hands. So it was that Point 124 presented itself as the first objective of Warren's Brigade, which had under temporary command the 3/9th Jats.

While the 4th Royal West Kents moved round secretly to attack from the south and east, Salomons' 4/7th Rajputs assaulted the hill from two villages on the west. All four of the rifle company commanders had made a night reconnaissance of the position, and these patrols, though they heard the Japanese soldiers in their defences, were not molested. Then, on December 30, the battalion moved up to its assembly area in darkness, and crossed the Hathipauk Chaung before daybreak. The hour had been chosen deliberately, to allow our men to cross after the moon had gone down, and at low tide, for at any other time it would have been impossible to wade across. Supported by the mortars of the 28th Field Regiment, two Rajput companies were to advance on one route, two companies on a second.

The two leading companies crossed the *chaung* without incident. No sooner had the sepoys started to climb the hill towards Point 124 than the Japanese opened fire with mortars and small arms. The resistance was fierce, the enemy well dug in, and our own guns hampered by the proximity of our men to the target, and by the thick undergrowth on the slopes. Though the rest of the 4/7th Rajputs crossed the *chaung*, by midday Salomons' entire force found itself pinned to the ground, unable to advance. More than ninety casualties had been suffered, and these could not be carried back until darkness fell and gave cover. Then Colonel John Young, with the stretcher-bearers of 45 Field Ambulance, came right forward into the battle area and cleared all our casualties before daybreak.

Outstanding during this first attack was the exemplary conduct of Major C. C. Ansell, who commanded 'A' Company and led his devoted men up the hillside with absolute disregard for his personal safety. His gallantry was inspiring, for he went on until gravely wounded, having been shot through the stomach and in the face. For his leadership that day he was awarded an immediate D.S.O., and he survived to command his battalion nearly four years later.

The 4/7th Rajputs attacked Point 124 continuously for the next six days. On several occasions the leading sections reached the triple fence of barbed wire round the top trenches before being driven back down the slope by hand grenades that the Japanese soldiers lobbed at them.

Each little scrub-covered hilltop had rings of trenches dug round the summit, and each was covered by the fire of at least one machine-gun from another hillock. When a particular hill was attacked by our men, the defenders would fire a red Very light and at once take cover. This was the signal for all other Japanese posts giving covering fire to open up with machine-guns on the post being attacked. The enemy soldiers holding the post would lob showers of grenades over the parapet, when the assaulting troops were only five or ten yards from the crest.

A policy of strangulation, starvation, and attrition was adopted, but it was not until January 7 that the enemy positions were found to be abandoned. The Japanese had slipped away by night; the sounds of their retreat were covered by the wind and the teeming rain.

Two days later the Royal West Kents drove the enemy off the next hill beside the road, Point 141, and the British companies moved into positions from which they could watch if not dominate the Razabil Fortress.

* * * * *

Meanwhile what of Langran's Nine Brigade, the last to arrive in Arakan, and now ready to do battle against the Japanese for the first time? Early in the New Year the Brigade gathered its parts near Wabyin. Cree brought his West Yorkshires across from the Teknaf Peninsula, and to this battalion fell the task of leading forward to reach the line of the road between Maungdaw and Keinchakata. This latter place was the nearest point we could approach to Razabil without becoming engaged in a desperate struggle for the fortress itself.

During those first days of January, while the West Yorkshires travelled from Nhila to Bawli Bazaar by river steamer, the rain fell with prolonged force. The dust on the road and tracks vanished within an hour. In its place reigned deep mud, so bad that the Engineers closed our one all-important road to traffic. Only brigadiers and wounded men might use jeeps. The rest walked, and a few went to and fro on horseback. The mules squelched their way through the mud, their drivers urging them along, cheerful despite the rain that lashed at their broad-brimmed hats and monsoon capes. Across the Mayu Ridge blew the dreary, penetrating mist. And then the rain ceased, the sun shone again, and steam rose from the sodden earth towards a cloudless sky.

Once more the scars of bare rock gleamed on the range as the clear sunlight bathed the coast and the hills. The sky was reflected in the sluggish *chaungs*. A soft wind fanned the grasses and swayed the growing crops in the flat paddy fields. Clumps of trees showed where the villages lay. And the sun served not only to disperse the damp gloom that had descended on the neighbourhood when the rain teemed down, but to emphasize the tawny layers of dust that hovered intermittently above each track and stretch of the road. No sooner had the dust died away in one place than it was churned up farther along the same route. No sooner had the first disturbance settled than another jeep, a pair of lorries, or a dozen mules would appear round the corner and send the dust swirling up to blur the blue sky and to coat the leaves of such trees as grew beside the road. The dazzling sun gave a hazy brilliance to the view of a landscape that, for all the forces of destruction and suffering waiting in its shadows and on its crests, was very beautiful.

On January 6 the West Yorkshires set out, prepared to cross the *chaungs* that barred the way to Maungdaw. Abroad among the companies was that spirit of suppressed excitement and expectation for the action for which they had spent many weary hours training. In the words of one company report, written in block capitals in pencil: "The real thing again, everyone determined to show the Jap that here was a force ready and capable of proving false the myth of his supposed superiority and of retaking the ground he has held far too long."

That evening 'A' Company (Major C. O'Hara) led the way to a point on the first *chaung* where a number of folding assault boats had been assembled. The men embarked and propelled themselves to the far bank, using the boats as a ferry service. Six boats were hauled out of the water; the remainder were left behind for Dunlop's 'B' Company, who were following. The six boats, saturated by the first crossing and now doubly heavy, were carried across two miles of paddy fields to a second *chaung*. Again the boats were launched, and the crossing made without mishap or enemy interference. Though exhausted by this strenuous advance, the leading company reached Babapara village during the night and prepared defensive positions for the morning.

When Dunlop's men had moved through into Lettha village, 'C' Company (Major J. P. Roche) advanced south-west, skirted some opposition in Kanyindan, and chased the few remaining Japanese soldiers out of Maungdaw.

On January 9 Kanyindan was cleared of enemy troops. These withdrew south to cross the wide Magyi Chaung, only to find themselves ambushed near the iron bridge by Lieutenant Hazell's guerilla platoon. Ten Japanese were killed at nightfall. At the same time, 'D' Company, under Major Brian Sellars, moved eastwards to capture a village named Zullapara that guarded the approach to Razabil and to Keinchakata. The enemy strongly opposed this attempt, and fighting lasted throughout the night. Then, in daylight, mortars and artillery aiding, the Japanese were driven out and the village occupied completely.

Maungdaw presented the grim spectacle of a derelict town. The Arakanese had fled; grass grew over the warped verandahs; half-ruined shacks with caved-in roofs stood side by side with more solid brick buildings which had been robbed of doors and windows, and chipped by shell and bomb alike. In every corner among the piles of rubble and fallen beams lay perished rubber gas-masks and the oozing contents of food tins that had burst. And these combined to pervade the ruins with a putrid stench that was wellnigh intolerable. All trace of the bazaar had vanished. The streets had become dusty tracks invaded by an army of thriving weeds. And a little way downstream, where the Naf River and the green hills north of Teknaf came into view, stood the mouldering steamer station, with its wooden piers bleached by the sun, its little red tin hut rusted and empty, and the muddy water lapping at the green slime level. The bridge across the Tat Chaung linking Maungdaw and the island to the north had been destroyed.

But the West Yorkshires did not dawdle in the town of the dead —a place of bitterness and weeds, of mould and neglect, of evil smells and dismal memories.

General Briggs had by now issued orders that a bridgehead across the Magyi Chaung was to be formed at Nyaunggyaung. From here the battalion would patrol southwards and seek out the rear defences of Razabil. But this was the beginning of trouble. While Cree's headquarters and one company remained in the village of Nalpannya, the other three companies moved eastwards across the paddy fields to the main road. Sellars' 'D' Company dropped off at Bagona, to maintain a halfway base, and 'A' and 'C' Companies under Majors O'Hara and Roche crossed the main road and started north among the foothills. Their object was to comb these densely covered hillocks and thereby approach to within a few hundred yards of the southern edge of Razabil Fortress. They were out to discover the flanks and rear of the Japanese position.

So far the enemy had not opposed these moves, but on the evening of January 14 Roche's leading sections came upon what appeared to be a main enemy defence position. The company established itself on a hill where the Japanese had dug a considerable system of communication trenches and other defence works. O'Hara's men settled on the rear half of this hill, and only some thirty yards separated the two companies, who were linked by a trench. The enemy had but recently given up this strong redoubt, and the position seemed strong if isolated.

During that night large parties of Japanese moved north over the coastal paddy fields. They attacked Sellars' platoons in Bagona, severed contact between this company and the two companies in the foothills, launched violent but vain and costly attacks upon one company of the 3/9th Jats under Major Petrie-Hay, holding the iron bridge that spanned the Magyi Chaung.

As a result of these night hostilities, Colonel Cree ordered O'Hara to take his company back to the position in the foothills that had been occupied before the northward move began. This was a little way from the main road, and due east from Bagona. It proved to be a disastrous move. Roche's men were meant to do the same, but the message was never received. So long as both companies had been together, they were strong and could resist the enemy. Now Roche's 'C' Company was alone.

The Japanese occupied that part of the hill vacated by 'A' Company, and our men had to block the trench that had linked the two company defences. At half past five next morning, January 16, the enemy attacked from all sides. He strove to drive Roche and his men from their part of the hill. He infiltrated through the dense jungle. He got a machine-gun on to high ground and threatened to enfilade the whole of Roche's headquarters. But a gallant attempt to destroy this fatal gun succeeded and it was driven back, though at some cost to ourselves.

A report was sent back to Colonel Cree by Morse, the sole means of communication that remained intact. Ammunition was needed. Our water point was in enemy hands. We had food for another day, but almost no water. Three stretcher cases needed urgent attention, while three other men had been less severely wounded. Cree said he would do his best to send help, but the company must be prepared to fight its way out.

At first Roche decided to get out by night. But the enemy harassed our positions with artillery during the hours of darkness; any move would be more easily heard by the watchful Japanese; if our withdrawal were discovered, the resultant confusion in the dark would be such as to risk our men shooting one another as well as the enemy.

On the other hand, to retreat in broad daylight entailed crossing open paddy fields, without cover of any kind. The enemy's field of fire would be clear. No sooner had Roche decided on a night withdrawal than it was noticed that the scrub across the road had caught alight, and that a northerly breeze was blowing smoke across our front. This smoke seemed providential, and Roche warned his company to move in half an hour.

The dead were placed in a fire trench and covered over, but no time remained for the burial service. The stretcher cases were wrapped in blankets and carried to one of the exits. Then the scrub fire died down. When the first platoon crossed the road they were caught in heavy fire, the mortar was damaged and could give no support, and the three men on stretchers were hit on the way down.

It was now a matter of every man for himself. Men threw themselves on the ground, crawled behind low paddy bunds, or made a dash for any piece of cover that might protect them from the fierce machine-guns. The more fortunate ones managed to reach a water hole four hundred yards from the enemy. This hole was six feet deep, fifteen feet across, and had two feet of water in the bottom. Here, in the space of the next hour, a score of the company gathered. Outside there were a dozen more men, some of them unscathed, sheltering behind a bund. One badly wounded soldier was calling out for water, of which there was none save the filthy liquid in the hole. Another wounded man shouted for the stretcher-bearers, but of these one was dead and the other a casualty.

At last, about half past four, when the sun was shining into the faces of the enemy, an attempt was made to escape from the water hole, but a few bursts of fire showed just how hazardous this would prove. It was not till dusk that Roche and his men were able to move off in safety, some to the bridge by Kanyindan, others back to Cree's headquarters in Nalpannya. 'C' Company had lost, in this day's fighting, one officer and eleven ranks killed, another eleven men missing, and two officers and nineteen men wounded.

* * * * *

While the West Yorkshires were battling in the foothills and paddy fields south of the Maungdaw-Razabil road, the 3/9th Jats (Lieutenant-Colonel B. C. W. Gerty) were in Kanyindan and Keinchakata, with Petrie-Hay's company still guarding the Magyi Chaung bridge. On January 16 'D' Company, commanded by Major Ritchie, crossed this *chaung* and occupied the straggling and heavily wooded village of Nyaunggyaung without opposition. And 'C' Company (Major Lambert) went east to hold the bridge farther up the same *chaung* by Razabil South. Here they stayed for nine days, overlooked by the Japanese in the foothills south of the fortress, subjected to nightly attacks, sometimes three in one night, and to sniping by day. All supply and evacuation of a score of wounded Jats had to be done during darkness.

The night of the 17th was the battalion's first real tussle with the Japanese. At nine o'clock one of Ritchie's reconnaissance patrols reported that the enemy had occupied the south-eastern corner of Nyaunggyaung wood, three hundred yards from our positions. When the reserve platoon moved out as a fighting patrol, it was attacked on two sides. Meanwhile the main Japanese force had crept south of Ritchie's position and engaged his southerly platoon. The centre of our defences was also attacked, just where the reserve platoon had been before it sallied out to engage the enemy.

Here the Japanese gained a footing, and were followed by Sikh Jifs who set fire to the position with a miniature flame-thrower. Just before dawn the Japanese withdrew, after making repeated attacks against 'D' Company. The dozen Jifs called out in Punjabi to our Jats to come across and join the Japanese. Their temptations were greeted with indignant bursts of firing. Jifs (Japanese Indian Forces) were Indian soldiers, who, being prisoners of the Japanese, had been forced or cajoled into fighting for their enemy.

Two nights later the enemy troops again attacked Ritchie's men, and, although repulsed, they managed to dig themselves in only twenty yards from our forward trenches. Unless the Japanese were ejected, they would be able to cover both the exit from the iron bridge held by Petrie-Hay's 'A' Company, and the track leading from this bridge to Nyaunggyaung. So next morning Colonel Gerty decided to launch a counter-attack from the east, using Petrie-Hay's company and two sections of carriers from the 81st West African Division Reconnaissance Regiment.

No sooner did these carriers stop, after crossing the open paddy and taking up a firing position 300 yards to the flank, than an enemy anti-tank gun opened fire and knocked out three of the carriers. The others were withdrawn. 'A' Company was held up by heavy flanking fire from machine-guns, particularly from one that had been tied high up in a tree. While co-ordinating the Jats' attack, the second-in-command of the Battalion, Major R. H. White, was killed. And Major W. E. Petrie-Hay was badly wounded in the arm. Eventually the Japanese machine-gunner in the tree was brought down by a Jat sniper who crept up close.

It was only on January 24 that the enemy positions were found abandoned, and our troops burnt down all those parts of Nyaung-gyuang that we had not occupied.

* * * * *

123 Brigade spent the first fortnight of January in aggressive patrolling among the foothills of the Mayu Range, east of the main road from Hathipauk, and centring round Point 731 and a feature known as 'Wrencat' after the nearby Rehkat Chaung. The 2/1st Punjab, 1/17th Dogras and 2nd Suffolks all had brushes with the enemy among these scrub-covered hillocks. Patrols had sharp encounters on the banks of the many waterways running down into the coastal plain. Names such as Green Hill, Bottle, Tooth, and Mutton Chop became familiar to the British and Indian soldiers as they explored the Japanese positions and approached closer to Point 731 and to the eastern part of the Razabil Fortress.

On January 28 the Dogras attacked 'Wrencat,' and its little neighbour 'Wrenkitten' without success. Within a hundred yards of the summit the enemy had placed a bamboo fence with only one gap, and grenades and booby traps prevented more than one of our men from going through at a time. The jungle had been dense bamboo, but the ravages of artillery, mortars and dive-bombers had transformed the hill into one great sand dune, bare and precipitous on certain approaches.

The Dogras had virtually to pull themselves up the hill by the remaining bamboo stumps, always in the face of savage fire. Major Ghulam Qadir led four separate attacks, and won the Military Cross. Again and again the little Dogras climbed slowly up 'Wrencat,' through the black smoke of showers of grenades exploding, and the sun glinting on their bayonets. Each time the men no sooner reached the top than the enemy on neighbouring hillocks opened fire with mortar and machine-gun and forced the Dogras off. A severe loss to the battalion was Subadar Narain, who fell leading an attack on the main Japanese bunkers. He was awarded, posthumously, the Indian Order of Merit.

Though these assaults by two companies failed, they did provide accurate information of the Japanese defences and guns, and the best and worst routes to the summit were revealed at a price—five killed and forty-six wounded.

The 2/1st Punjab held the crest of the range, and notably three peaks known by their altitudes as 1975, 1749 and 1619. They patrolled along the ridge to the next peak, Point 1301, in Japanese hands, and also captured the right-hand of three knobs, two of which were already held by our troops. The 2nd Suffolks (Lieutenant-Colonel H. R. Hopking) shared Bamboo Hill with the enemy, and on January 28 made a very determined effort to capture the hill. They reached the top, only to be forced to withdraw.

These attacks were part of Operation 'Jonathan,' at once the most ambitious conception and most complete failure of the month. By night the redoubtable tanks of the 25th Dragoons (Lieutenant-Colonel Frink) rumbled into hiding behind the infantry battalions. They came forward in darkness, hoping to conceal their arrival from the Japanese who watched our activities from the Mayu Range. The tanks were ready for this full-scale offensive against the cross-roads at Razabil and the surrounding hills. Among these were Tortoise and numerous little hillocks that rose from the paddy fields and bore such names as Propeller, Squiggle, Hop, Step and Jump, names often coined in imitation of the shape of the particular feature, and used as an easy and temporarily secure means of reference.

The plan was for our Strategic Air Force to bomb targets in the Razabil area, and for the battalions of 161 Brigade to drive through the foothills to the cross-roads. On January 26 Mitchells, Liberators, and Vengeance dive-bombers roared overhead, and soon a pall of smoke and dust hung above Razabil and Tortoise. Immense explosions reverberated against the Mayu Range. The aircraft returned low down across the *chaungs* and paddy fields. All that day and the next the Royal West Kents, 1/1st Punjab and 4/7th Rajputs attacked the little hillocks east of the road. In their support fought the 25th Dragoons. Fire from Mansergh's Divisional Artillery was at their call.

Success was limited, casualties mounted, and the enemy fought tenaciously. Our bombing had been neither effectual nor accurate. Japanese counter-attacks were beaten off at night and in daylight. Though Squiggle was captured by the 1/1st, attacks by the Sikh company under Captain Roxburgh-Smith failed, proving costly against barbed wire and dense machine-gun fire from the hillocks. The company was reduced to twenty-one men before it could be extricated. And the battalion, which entered the battle 163 men under strength, came out with this figure at 279. The Rajputs had also suffered heavily during the month. Twenty-seven men had been killed and 129 wounded. The Commanding Officer, Lieutenant-Colonel J. A. Salomons, had been promoted to command Nine Brigade instead of Brigadier W. H. Langran, who had returned to India. Major J. Cargill, the second-in-command, took Salomons' place.

Salomons was one of the best-liked battalion and brigade commanders the Division ever had. Few were more highly esteemed than "Sally," by which name he was referred to if not called on every side. He was a bald, lean Scotsman in his forties, a man whose energy astounded officers and men years his junior. He never spared himself, and tramped up one hill after another, or along a series of paths through the jungle, to visit his forward battalions. Accompanied by his liaison or intelligence officer, he became a familiar figure near the battle. If his voice was harsh, this did not reflect his character, for the very opposite was true. He could be quiet and reticent to a degree, and to the casual visitor may have been deceptive. But if he did not appear dynamic and full of fire, in reality he merely weighed the chances a little longer than most, and then, quietly and without fuss, ordered his troops into the attack at the right place and the right time.

His brigade was a happy one, for he welded what he always liked to term "the Brigade Group" into a united team, and his pride and care in its well-being and achievements were shared and reflected. Seldom was he to be seen without a cheery greeting on his lips, and his sense of humour accorded with his youthfulness of spirit.

Although in the Division he commanded an *infantry* battalion and brigade, he had started his service in 1920 with the Royal Sikh Pioneers, where one of his brother officers was Brigadier Freddie Warren. He served with the Pioneers for thirteen years, until they were disbanded. All officers were then posted to infantry regiments—Salomons to the 7th Rajputs. But as a number of the men were transferred to the Sappers and Miners, volunteers were called for to remain behind to see the men settled in to their new units. Salomons stayed for two years, and was the only infantry officer to have his name on the list of adjutants of the Bengal Sappers and Miners at Roorkee.

From 1935 onwards he served with the Rajputs, and, just as Denys Reid had done some years before him, he commanded the company that was escort to the British Trade Agent in Gyangtse. His appointment was known as "O.C. Escorts, Tibet."

Further variety to his peace-time service was provided by a trip to Chitral as Column Staff Officer, and by a period as Personal Assistant to two Residents in Kashmir.

When the war came, he sailed from India to the Middle East with the Fourth Indian Division.

Of Salomons, one of his officers wrote: " 'Sally' is one of the great names in the Division. He had no enemies, countless friends, and was beloved by the *jawans*—one can say no more."

Operation 'Jonathan,' a frontal assault directed upon the Japanese fortress of hillocks round Razabil, had failed. Bunkers, wire, bamboo stakes—sharply pointed and known as *punjis*—and withering fire had brought our ambitious offensive to a halt, with but small gains to record.

The Division learned a lesson. For the future, tactics were based upon those of tanks. Operations in the Desert had proved that to win a tank battle you did not attack enemy tanks on ground of their own choosing, only to find their tanks behind a defensive screen of anti-tank guns and infantry. Rather did you seek to manœuvre with the purpose of seizing ground which was, or could be made, so vital to the enemy that he was forced to attack you instead. Encirclement, hooks from the left or right flank, and guile were to replace the more direct assault.

Meanwhile, Fifteen Corps decided to switch our main offensive to the eastern side of the Mayu Range. While the coastal plain and the range itself were held and made uncomfortable for the enemy, Messervy's Seventh Indian Division prepared to attack south to seize Buthidaung.

CHAPTER XXI

THE NGAKYEDAUK BOX

FEBRUARY 1944

AT the beginning of February 1944 General Christison's Fifteen Corps was making ready to capture Buthidaung and destroy the Japanese in the eastern bastion of the Tunnels fortress. At the same time heavy pressure was maintained on the Fifth Indian Division's front along the crest of the Mayu Range and in the coastal strip that was so intersected by winding *chaungs*.

The operation of Messervy's Seventh Indian Division against Buthidaung was due to start on February 8. To strengthen this attack 89 Brigade (Brigadier Alan Crowther, former commander of the 1/17th Dogras) had been taken into reserve from the eastern Mayu foothills. Its place was taken by Nine Brigade, less Gerty's 3/9th Jats, who remained south of Maungdaw to hold the line of the Magyi Chaung, and to patrol between the west Razabil crossroads and Bagona village. The greater part of Colonel Frink's 25th Dragoons had also been transferred from the west to the east side of the hills, as had the 6th Medium Regiment of artillery under Colonel Fox. And Fifteen Corps established a small headquarters in the administration area of Messervy's division, at Sinzweya, where the Ngakyedauk Pass debouches into the Kalapanzin Valley.

A mile north of the eastern Tunnel and of the road that linked Maungdaw with Buthidaung the 3/14th Punjab (Lieutenant-Colonel C. C. Furney) took over positions from the Gurkha battalion of 89 Brigade. With these Punjabis, to hold such features in the actual foothills and several isolated hillocks that rose like queer-shaped islands from the paddy fields and bamboo thickets, went one company of the 2nd West Yorkshires under Major Brian Sellars. The positions that these troops defended had been given such names as Finger, Octopus, Italy; one of them, perhaps the most important, was called by its title on the map, Point 305.

Less than a mile farther north were Nine Brigade Headquarters and the rest of Cree's West Yorkshires, while in charge of a strangely elongated and sharp hill called Hambone, running north and south beside the Tatmin Chaung, were 20 Field Company, commanded by Major Philip Hatch. And high up on the Mayu Range itself, by Point 1619 and facing the enemy along the narrow ridge, were Gleeson's 3/2nd Punjab, who had been placed under the command of Nine Brigade so that there might be no gap in our front. Along the banks of the Tatmin Chaung camped 24 Mountain Regiment under the white-haired Humphrey Hill.

Such was the state of Nine Brigade among these paddy fields, dense patches of jungle, and thickly growing trees through which narrow, dust-clogged tracks had been cut. The density of the jungle made dispersion off these tracks most difficult. All tents had to be concealed among the trees, for the Brigade was in full view of the Japanese who looked down from their vantage points. Two miles away towards the east, across the flat paddy fields that were marked bright yellow on the maps, straggled the village of Letwedet, through which the wriggling Tatmin Chaung flowed towards the Kalapanzin River, on the banks of which rose the buildings and shacks of Buthidaung.

And to Nine Brigade came a new brigadier—Geoffrey Evans.

When the Fourth Indian Division first left India, Evans was Staff Captain to Five Brigade. He was promoted Brigade Major of Savory's Eleven Brigade before the first battle of Sidi Barrani in December 1940, and in that post he remained until after Keren, by which time his reputation as an efficient staff officer stood high. He went to a planning job at G.H.Q. in Cairo, but had not been there long before he was urgently posted to the Western Desert to command the 1st Royal Sussex in Briggs' Seven Brigade. Into this battalion he instilled a spirit that had previously been lacking—the effect of his arrival has been likened to a cyclone. He subjected the men to intensive training. His energy was as abounding as his drive, and so great was his influence that when, five months later, the Royal Sussex was ordered to attack the strong German position of Sidi Omar the battalion took its objective within four hours, despite over two hundred casualties. And Geoffrey Evans rode into battle on the leading tank.

As a memento of those fighting days in the Desert he carried a steel-shod staff, presented by the officers of the 1st Royal Sussex, and as treasured in its way as had been Colonel Welchman's near Gallabat. To it was fastened a silver plaque which bore the words: "Begush, Sidi Omar, El Gubi, Martuba, Benghazi and the Great Trek back." This staff was a familiar weapon with which the Brigadier, who had in the interim risen to the posts of Commandant of the Staff College at Quetta and B.G.S. of Four Corps, helped himself through sand, up dusty or mud-caked hillsides, and through jungle undergrowth.

Already Evans had earned the Distinguished Service Order and bar. Throughout his career, which had started as a subaltern in the Warwickshires under Montgomery, he had displayed utter fearlessness, and a dynamic, nagging vitality and push. He worked harder than almost any, and on occasions took the power out of himself with over-exertion. During operations he seemed hardly to sleep. Nor did his brain appear to rest. And often his staff or gunner officer would be woken during the night to answer some point of detail on which Evans was concentrating his thoughts.

He brooked neither hesitancy nor delay, neither incompetence nor pretence. His own manner could be curt and brusque when events were urgent, and when he was spurred forward to his most intense efforts. Yet he forgot nobody who had served beside him, and his words of praise were as forthcoming as those of criticism and impatience.

To Evans may be applied Lord Wavell's description of Allenby: "To those who knew him well, and to those who faced him fairly and without fear, his dominant personality was an inspiration and support; to those who met him for the first time or were at all nervous in his presence he was without doubt alarming and disconcerting, especially in his official capacity. His manner was often gruff and abrupt; his questions were straight and sharp; and he demanded an immediate, direct reply. Any attempt at prevarication, any indefiniteness, even hesitation, might provoke a sudden explosion of anger that could shake the hardiest."

*   *   *   *   *

Our preparations for attack were almost complete. The day was fast approaching when Messervy's troops were to fight for

Buthidaung and the Tunnels road. But the enemy attacked first. Our plan was forestalled by his own. Our plan had to be stored at the back of the mind so that our every particle of strength, energy, skill and endurance might be devoted to beating the oncoming and cocksure Japanese.

The 55th Japanese Division had been split into three parts. The main force commanded by a skilful and thrusting leader, Colonel Tanahashi, was composed of four battalions of 112 Regiment, Tanahashi's own. Its task was to push silently northward to the east of the Seventh Indian Division, capture Taung Bazaar on the Kalapanzin River a dozen miles upstream from Buthidaung, swing south-west to encircle Messervy's troops, sever the vital Ngakyedauk Pass, and thus trap the Seventh Division on the eastern side of the hills.

Meanwhile, a separate Japanese battalion would strike still farther north across the narrow Goppe Pass to the western foothills of the Mayu Range, cut the main road in the rear of the Fifth Indian Division, and so separate our forward troops from Fifteen Corps Headquarters and the Lines of Communication. And a third enemy force would hold the original front between Maungdaw and Buthidaung by means of limited attacks. The Japanese then planned to annihilate Messervy's Division, as it tried to withdraw across the steep range, and to crush the now isolated Fifth Indian Division, which, so thought the enemy, would be obliged to attempt an escape in little boats across the Naf River to the Teknaf Peninsula.

On February 4 Tanahashi struck. Reports came in that during the night an enemy force of unknown strength had slipped through Messervy's positions east of the Kalapanzin. The Japanese, moving in a compact body, passed across the rice fields in the area held by our 114 Brigade. They were not spotted in the dark, even though some of our men did run into a mule. The noise of the column was thought to be our own transport.

Early on the morning of the 5th Taung Bazaar fell into enemy hands. Crowther's 89 Brigade was sent to intercept Tanahashi's force, and was engaged in fierce fighting all through that day. The Japanese had now turned south-west to threaten from the rear Messervy's main positions, and our efforts to halt their advance were not successful. That same day enemy artillery was

THE NGAKYEDAUK BOX

unusually active along the whole divisional front, and Japanese aircraft made frequent sweeps over the area, paying particular attention to the eastern end of the Ngakyedauk Pass.

General Messervy wondered to himself: Should his headquarters move or stay put ? As he had been preaching the doctrine of no withdrawals by anyone when the Jap came round the flank—this was a new policy from the earlier campaigns—he decided to keep his headquarters at Launggyaung, two miles north-east of the administration area in Sinzweya. He knew that to stay was a risk, but a good example would be set. Moreover, to move his headquarters at such a critical moment might mean the disruption of communications just when they were most needed.

But it was upon this very headquarters, unprotected as it was by infantry, that the assault fell. The only troops defending Launggyaung were Lieutenant-Colonel P. M. P. Hobson's Divisional Signals, and part of an Engineer Battalion. At six o'clock the air was rent by wild shouts from the Japanese. A few shots were almost smothered by a roar as of some vast football crowd, intermingled with catcalls and yells. All was uncertain in the half-light and morning mist. The members of headquarters took up their prearranged battle stations. The Signal Office was attacked. Parties of the enemy infiltrated into the Signals area, and towards Messervy's headquarters. Machine-guns and mortars began firing into our positions from short range. Several attacks were beaten back, but all telephone lines were cut. Communication between the different parts of the headquarters was broken. Messervy with part of his staff was isolated on a steep hillock and pinned to the ground by fire. He decided that the place must be abandoned, but could get no message to this effect through to the rest of the staff and to Signals. Eventually he and a few companions managed to slip away, waded down a stream, made their way through the jungle and reached the administration area at Sinzweya.

Meanwhile Colonel Hobson, finding his men hard pressed, his casualties mounting, his wireless sets being overrun and destroyed, consulted Brigadier Hely, the C.R.A. It was decided to fight on, but soon the Japanese had established machine-gun posts along a ridge that overlooked our strong-points. Some tanks of the 25th Dragoons, which had just arrived here, were firing at these machine-guns, but groups of our men found themselves caught between the two lines of fire.

The position was perilous. Resistance could not long be maintained. Hely gave the order to evacuate Launggyaung. A rendezvous was made: the eastern end of the Ngakyedauk Pass. But many new casualties were suffered in this withdrawal, and some confusion, for Japanese mortar fire broke up our parties and the main line of retreat was covered by the enemy. In all, Hobson's Signals had seven officers, eight British and ninety Indian ranks killed or missing from that morning's fighting.

* * * * *

What, meanwhile, had happened to the Fifth Indian Division? General Briggs had already pointed out the danger of taking away his only reserve—Nine Brigade—which alone could counter-attack any infiltration on to the Mayu Range or the Ngakyedauk Pass, for Fifteen Corps had no immediate reserves of its own. On February 5 he was showing the Army Group Commander, Sir George Giffard, round the Divisional area. When the news of the Japanese crossing at Taung Bazaar came in, Giffard remarked that Seventh Indian Division's dispersion had rather invited this stroke. Briggs, feeling it best to return at once to his own head-quarters, left General Giffard to cross the Ngakyedauk Pass and visit Nine Brigade in the company of a staff officer.

Briggs' immediate reactions were to send the 4/7th Rajputs (Lieutenant-Colonel J. Cargill) to the top of the Pass at the western end, but this plan was countermanded by Fifteen Corps, who insisted upon half the battalion for the protection of the Goppe Pass farther to the north. Odds and ends had to be collected to hold the crest of the Ngakyedauk Pass, while the remaining Rajput companies were sent back to deal with the strong Japanese force that had crossed the precipitous hills above Chota Maunghnama. The enemy, beaten back at the approaches to Goppe by a mule company, and thinking that pass to be strongly held—which it certainly was not—had decided to cut the coastal road behind the Fifth Indian Division farther south than originally planned. At half past two in the early morning of February 6 our 44 Field Park Company and a Workshops Company were attacked near Briasco Bridge. The enemy burnt a few vehicles, damaged the bridge, and withdrew into the foothills. When daylight came the

Rajputs operated carrier and infantry patrols up and down the road to Bawli, and communications were soon opened. But the enemy still lurked in the neighbourhood to waylay convoys or single trucks, and the road was by no means safe.

The administrative units of the Division had, thanks to wise forethought, been brought into various defended boxes as soon as the reports of danger near the hills arrived. The bulk of the Division's supplies were already coming forward by boat to Maungdaw, and General Briggs arranged for his two brigades to be supplied by water. In this way Briasco Bridge was cut out.

* * * * *

When Briggs heard that Messervy's headquarters had been attacked and that communication with the Seventh Indian Division was impossible, he instructed Brigadier Evans to hold his positions frontally with the 3/14th Punjab, and to take the 2nd West Yorkshires to try to keep open the Ngakyedauk Pass if possible. Nine Brigade was already too late to effect this, but it was in time to save the Admin. Box, as it was henceforth to be called.

It was a stroke of good fortune that the bulldozer with Hatch's 20th Field Company, who were improving a jeep track that ran north and south by the Tatmin Chaung and repairing several culverts, should have broken down on February 5. It refused to start. Next morning, when Brigadier Evans received his orders, heavy rain fell. Had newly-shifted earth lain on the four crossings where the Sappers were to have smoothed out the approaches, Nine Brigade's vehicles could not have withdrawn along the tracks through the jungle. Upon such small factors does war so often depend. As it was, the tracks became slippery and treacherous within an hour.

The Mayu Range misted over, and dark rain-clouds blew across the thick and already gloomy jungle. Into the few clearings the mist drifted, and the hills were veiled from sight. The dusty surface of the winding tracks soon clogged with damp. Rain set in steadily, mud was turned to slush, and the countryside became sodden with rain. Vehicles skidded, jeeps were abandoned, camps hurriedly packed up, mules saddled and loaded, stores collected for transportation on trucks, and other equipment buried beneath the dripping trees.

Evans had ordered all units back to the Admin. Box at the end of the Ngakyedauk Pass, while 20 Field Company stayed on Hambone and Furney's 3/14th Punjab prepared to resist the enemy in positions of isolation but great importance, for they could block the southern approach, in so far as any block could be effected in the Arakan jungle.

The rain poured down upon this jungle and its narrow tracks. The mud deepened, the branches dripped in melancholy rhythm, and progress towards the Admin. Box was slowed down most seriously. Jeeps skidded into streams, heavier trucks became embedded in the mire and blocked the way through the scrub oaks and undergrowth. Nobody knew quite what had happened, and some knew nothing except their orders to move to a given point. But it was clear, even without facts, that events were turning against us. Much had gone astray, and that right quickly.

Anxious and confused, men slithered on the slopes, sweated and swore as they struggled to drag their frightened, obstinate mules uphill. So slippery was the muddy surface of the tracks that even when mule loads had been taken off the saddles and laid in the slush, the mules still stumbled and kicked in their game efforts to mount the slope. Mule drivers fell to their knees and held on to saddle ropes to stop themselves from rolling down to the bottom. For those who had only their own bodies to care for, it was best to cling for support to branches and bamboo shafts. While Bren-carriers flailed their tracks deep into the mud and ruined what remained of the tracks, and to little purpose, drivers of jeeps and ambulances looked aghast at the scene and decided to wait unless they were obliged to move on. And few did this without skidding into a bank.

The tanks were unable to go out from the mud, and had the sun not shone mercifully that afternoon to dry up the tracks, the situation might have deteriorated to a most grievous extent. But until the rain ceased and the skies cleared, it was a grim scene that met the eye at the eastern end of the Pass. Troops hung around waiting for someone to tell them to do something. Others straggled in from Messervy's headquarters that was now in enemy hands. The Police, who had set up rallying posts for the men who wandered in all that day, soaked and weary, many of them wounded and drooping, with a mixture of bewilderment, fear and relief at escaping alive from the early morning ordeal, strove to bring order to the disoriented soldiery.

In the centre of the Box, where the headquarters tent of the administration area had been, stood Brigadier Evans, with Cree of the West Yorkshires, and Colonel Cole, who commanded the 24th Light Anti-Aircraft Regiment already in the Box and had drawn up full plans for defending this Box with such troops as were available. The group was joined, when he eventually arrived after a hazardous journey through the jungle, by General Frank Messervy himself. With the troops available it would not be possible to man the entire perimeter. Accordingly, the Brigadier had decided to hold the eastern and north-eastern sides by fire alone. Evans had made a rapid tour of the position with Cole, who had been in charge of the area until that morning. He had allotted sectors of the defence perimeter to various units which comprised the garrison: mule companies, workshops, clerks from Ordnance sections, medical orderlies, drivers, signalmen, who, with their inexperience of infantry fighting and lack of training in defence and attack, outnumbered the three companies of West Yorkshires, the two squadrons of the 25th Dragoons, and two batteries of 24 Indian Mountain Regiment.

The debt owed to these tanks and their crews cannot be over-emphasized. It was their accurate, high-velocity, close-range blasting which put our infantry back whenever the Japanese penetrated our defences or captured any vital position.

Outside the tent, that was now a command-post with officers listening eagerly to the wireless messages, stood Evans. He leaned on his staff, while the rain dripped from the wide brim of his bush hat. His energy infected those with him, and those who plodded past along the road, or walked in from outside the Box. His decisions in this hour of peril were definite, unhesitating and wise. Using with but slight adjustment Cole's defence plan, he ordered the positioning of mule companies, supply depots, tanks, infantry reserves, mountain and medium and light anti-aircraft guns. All his experience of rapid thought in tight corners of the Desert was called out to organize as strong a defence as might be offered to the Japanese, who were now approaching. Where would they strike ? What was their strength ? These things were not known to our commanders.

* * * * *

Early on the morning of February 7 the Japanese cut the Ngakyedauk Pass, thus separating the two divisions. 89 Brigade, which had been fighting out east of the Box, was ordered to withdraw to hillocks on either side of the Ngakyedauk Chaung and near Point 147. Only two battalions were available, the 2nd King's Own Scottish Borderers and the 7/2nd Punjab. The third, the 4/8th Gurkhas, were holding a ridge at the eastern gate of the Box, and were having trouble round Point 315, the main feature of the whole position.

On the previous day this battalion had suffered heavily and two companies had lost contact when ordered to retire towards the Box. Now, on the 7th, a serious emergency occurred. The Japanese attacked the depleted Gurkhas, whose battalion headquarters were forced back by heavy sniping and grenading. The time was after 'stand down,' while our men were having breakfast. The first counter-attack failed. At this critical juncture Brigadier Evans summoned up Dunlop's 'B' Company of the West Yorkshires, ordered field, anti-aircraft and mountain guns, mortars, and a line of tanks to fire point-blank at the advancing enemy. The hillside crumbled under the tremendous force of the bombardment. Smoke veiled the scene. And at noon Dunlop's troops attacked and reoccupied the ridge, and helped the Gurkhas to re-establish themselves in their defences. An anti-aircraft battery acting in the role of infantry, was sent to reinforce them.

Just south of the nullah that ran through the Box, and on higher ground, were the tents, dug-outs and ambulances of the Main Dressing Station. The trees were coated with dust, the roadside cemetery grim where the dead lay beneath the rough wooden crosses. This was a place of life and of death, of devoted service by doctors and orderlies to save the wounded and to cure the sick. But the Japanese made of it a place of hideous memory, where lust and the savagery of wild beasts were let loose to work themselves upon almost defenceless men. Here was committed an appalling crime.

Two hours before midnight on the 7th a strong party of Japanese, with a group of Jifs—those Indians who, as prisoners, had been coerced or persuaded to fight against the British and Indian forces—entered the hospital. They attacked and overran it. The West Yorkshire protective section was wiped out. Every doctor they could find was murdered. The British patients lying in the darkness in the long tents were butchered. Nor were the Indians unmolested. Japanese and Jif soldiers prodded them with bayonets, robbed them of cigarettes, and stabbed some to death, before turning upon the next tent to continue their looting and killing. The discovery of a rum store only inflamed the attackers the more to foul deeds.

Many of the Indians escaped into the jungle, where they hid for several days until they dared to return. Three doctors did escape: one was stunned by blast when, miraculously, a pistol held to his ear misfired; two owed their survival to the perfect blackout of their tiny operating theatre below ground.

A West Yorkshire patrol was sent to find out what had happened, but was repulsed by grenades. To help while it was still night was out of the question. To have mortared the enemy would have been to kill many of our own men. To have risked our sole reserve company of infantry in a night attack without reconnaissance or artillery support would have been to court disaster.

Next morning, O'Hara's 'A' Company of the West Yorkshires attempted to clear the dressing station, while a platoon of Dunlop's 'B' Company created a diversion in the rear of the Japanese force. Throughout the day O'Hara's men continued to comb the area. Most of the surviving casualties found there were passed back. but the operation was difficult and exacting, for the ground was broken by numerous *chaungs* and the undergrowth was thick. The Japanese, with devilish cunning, had constructed machine-gun positions covered by stretchers in the wards and operating theatre, and these positions were hard to spot. No mortar or artillery support could be called for, on account of our wounded who were still lying out under the trees. Nightfall was approaching, and at five o'clock O'Hara's Company withdrew from the area and took up positions with the tanks. The West Yorkshires reoccupied the M.D.S. next morning. Those of our wounded who still remained alive were brought out. So, too, were the bodies of four doctors and thirty patients.

That afternoon the Admin. Box was shelled from one o'clock

onwards for an hour, heavily and accurately, and an ammunition dump at the western foot of Ammunition Hill was set on fire. Hundreds of cases of ammunition, stacked on terraces cut into the hill, lay in the open, a ready target for the enemy's shelling. Few days passed without some shell setting off one or other corner of this great dump. Indeed, to start the ammunition exploding or to start a store of petrol blazing seemed to content the enemy gunners. But to those within the Box such explosions were a peril and a prolonged strain upon the ears. Hour after hour small-arms ammunition crackled like a burning clump of bamboo. Hour after hour shells of varying calibre whined off across the valley to thud into some distant field or hillside. The sounds were alarming, the clamour strident and exhausting. Squads of fire-fighters worked desperately to localize the danger, but their task was dangerous, with shells exploding at the rate of two a minute, and ammunition whizzing off laterally to cut down anyone caught in its path. Foremost among these fire-fighters was Lieutenant-Colonel R. B. Cole.

* * * * *

For a time the only wireless link working consistently between General Briggs' headquarters and Nine Brigade was the 'Q' link, which, during those anxious hours when the ship of our battle-front was beginning to rock violently in the unexpected and violent storm, carried the great volume of Signals traffic across the Ngakyedauk Pass. The Madrassi operator, Naik Balasundaram, worked throughout forty-eight hours, while Major Roe and his Staff Captain, Peter Gell, sat in the office tent with three telephones and the remote control of this precious wireless set.

The first air drops of supplies upon Seven Division and Nine Brigade had to be arranged. The impossibility of getting all the necessary information through by wireless made the location of our troops and their requirements of food and ammunition largely a matter of guess work to the staff officers west of the Mayu Range. But one thing was indelibly certain; those supplies had to reach the garrison of the Admin. Box. All night the staff worked on the demands, and the last details did not reach Fifteen Corps until three o'clock in the morning. Later their hearts thrilled to watch, with eyes weary from lack of sleep and a night's work by the light of a flickering hurricane lamp, the first supply-dropping planes

THE NGAKYEDAUK BOX

roaring over the hills, led by the American Brigadier-General Old. The Japanese might curse the spectacle, but there was not a Briton or Indian who did not heave a sigh of relief and take new courage and hope at seeing the Dakotas circling above the narrow valley. This was, to both divisions, the first experience of an air supply on which the troops became so dependent during the remaining stretches of 1944.

Day after day those who defended the Box turned their bloodshot eyes northwards when their ears caught the drone of approaching aircraft above the noise of shells and bullets, tank engines and men's shouts and the clattering of mules beneath the trees. Through the hatch doors of these planes were pushed boxes of ammunition of many sizes, shiny tins of petrol for the tanks of the 25th Dragoons, bales of equipment, rations, and countless items that could feed, protect, and hearten the garrison below. Fodder for the mules, bundles of the newspaper *SEAC*, batteries and spare telephones, telephone cable—all these and more came drifting slowly to the open paddy field, swaying from a host of white parachutes. The loads, when they were not dropped 'free,' bumped heavily on the ground, where the dropping zone quickly turned into some vast laundry of drying linen. To brighten this strange scene came parachutes of green and blue, orange, red, yellow, bearing special loads that had to be distinguished from the others by these gay colours of some peace-time regatta.

When the dropping for the day had concluded, Indians of the Service Corps ran out and dragged in these bales and bundles and tins. They cut loose the parachutes and stacked the stores ready for distribution to all units within the Box. Often a fickle breeze or an inaccurate approach by one of the planes would cause a parachute or two to drift away from the dropping zone; and the load might drop into the upper branches of a tree on Ammunition Hill, or drag itself across the turret of a waiting tank. It might even fall outside the defence perimeter, and that was a sad spectacle, for the Japanese were in dire need of supplies to alleviate the starvation that soon threatened their columns.

*   *   *   *   *

The Japanese had chosen as a rendezvous the point where, just south of Nine Brigade's 'B' Echelon, the muddy road crossed a stream. No more fatal gathering place could have been found, for on the high banks of this dried-up stream men of the West Yorkshires, under their Regimental Sergeant-Major, Maloney, and of 23 Animal Transport Company, had established machine-gun posts. This was the southern fringe of the Box defences. Soon after dawn on the 9th, a party of forty-three Japanese soldiers and an officer marched up the stream-bed in close formation. Our men held their fire until the enemy reached the bend by the crossing. Then, at a sign from Maloney, the defenders of 'B' Echelon hurled down their grenades from the high bank. Most of the enemy were killed. Those who turned and ran into the undergrowth found themselves caught at the foot of the opposite bank. They could not escape. They were shot down in the bushes or as they tried to scramble up the road into the jungle. The Japanese officer was killed.

Several days passed before the enemy abandoned this rendezvous, now called "Blood Nullah," and their perseverance cost them dear. But their attacks against the Echelon, commanded by Captain E. D. Chaytor of the West Yorkshires, were many and ferocious. With admirable support from 24 Mountain Regiment, Chaytor's men withstood frequent assaults and gave a memorable account of themselves. In the western part of the Box, this was the most attacked part of our perimeter.

Just before noon on February 11 a strong force of Japanese soldiers occupied the south-east crest of Artillery Hill. This overlooked the nullah and the centre of the Box. If the enemy could haul guns up that hill, our position below might become untenable. Evans ordered a general stand-to. One platoon of O'Hara's 'A' Company was sent to restore the situation. A second platoon was posted in the nullah just west of the foot of the hill, to prevent any attempt at infiltration by the enemy.

The climb was long and steep, and by the time our first platoon reached the top, the enemy had occupied the entire summit. O'Hara withdrew his men. Evans ordered all available guns, mortars, and tank weapons to bear upon Artillery Hill. The bombardment was an awful spectacle. Trees were splintered, bare patches appeared on the hillside, smoke and dust rose from the jungle. The noise was deafening, with mountain and field guns accompanied by the cannons of the tanks and their fierce, snarling machine-guns. To the men who watched, it was a heartening sight.

THE NGAKYEDAUK BOX

To the officers of the Fifth Indian Division who heard the bombardment from the other side of the Mayu Range, it was alarming. Some thought that the Japanese were launching an all-out and final attack to overwhelm the garrison of the Box. But this was not so.

Two of the West Yorkshire platoons had taken up positions within safety distance of this shelling. No sooner did the fire lift than they attacked and captured Artillery Hill. The enemy had retired. By half-past five the vital position was again in our hands, and never again was it allowed to be taken from us. Next day its defence became the responsibility of one company of the 7/2nd Punjab (Lieutenant-Colonel R. Rowse). This battalion of 89 Brigade came into the Box, and was caught in the open by a strong Japanese bombing attack. Its headquarters were destroyed, many sepoys killed and wounded, and the remainder disorganized by this unhappy blow. The least affected company was placed under command of Colonel Cree, and joined the West Yorkshires as a temporary measure.

* * * * *

At the same time as this bombardment on Artillery Hill lifted, General Briggs at his own Headquarters was in conference with his senior commanders. He expected the 26th Indian Division from the North to be in contact next day. The 36th Brigade had taken over responsibility for clearing the rear areas of the Fifth Indian Division, north of Maunghnama and Briasco Bridge. Warren's 161 Brigade, with the Suffolks, Jats and Dogras under command, was to take over the Division's southern front, between the crest of the Mayu Range and the coast. Briggs declared his intention of increasing the momentum of advance towards the relief of the Ngakyedauk Box by reopening the Pass from his side with all possible speed. His plan would be executed by 123 Brigade, composed, for this operation, of the 2/1st Punjab, 4/7th Rajput, 1/18th Garhwal Rifles, 24th Engineer Battalion, 28th Jungle Field Regiment, 74th Field Company, and a detachment of the 25th Dragoons.

The advance started on February 12. The 2/1st Punjab (Lieutenant-Colonel W. G. Smith) and 4/7th Rajputs (Lieutenant-Colonel J. Cargill) pressed on through the Pass, from its summit at 'Cresta

Run.' One company of Garhwalis held the important hill of Point 1070 that commanded the centre of the Pass from the northern side.

The early hours of the 14th were marked by a severe blow, the news of which frustrated the relieving force and cast a gloom upon the garrison of the Ngakyedauk Box. Their hopes of an early relief were dashed. During the night of February 13/14 some two hundred Japanese soldiers continuously attacked the Garhwali positions on Point 1070. Their onslaught from the east and west was made regardless of cost, and just before first light they managed to drive the 1/18th Garhwal Rifles from the hill.

This was a serious setback. Further delay might imperil the besieged garrison. Accordingly, General Briggs ordered 123 Brigade, now temporarily commanded by Lieutenant-Colonel W. G. Smith of the 2/1st Punjab, to take every reasonable risk to open the Pass at the earliest possible moment.

That afternoon two companies of the 4/8th Gurkhas, who had withdrawn across the Mayu Range on the 7th of the month, being the companies which had lost contact with the rest of the battalion, passed through the 2/1st Punjab on the crest of the range and re-entered the Admin. Box near 'B' Echelon. With them came a line party from the Fifth Indian Divisional Signals, and for the first time in a week telephone communication was established between the two divisions. This communication lasted just long enough for the two Generals and other leading staff officers and commanders to talk to each other; but within three hours the slender telephone cable had again been cut by the enemy. And this time no communication except by wireless was possible until the end of the siege.

Meanwhile, General Christison had ordered the 26th Indian Division to hasten its leading battalion, the 1st Lincolnshires, towards Point 315, so as to ease the situation of the Admin. Box. On the same day the Gurkhas, supported by Frink's 25th Dragoons, cleared the enemy off the eastern and lower slopes of this same vital Point 315, and thus opened the road leading in at the eastern end of the Box. As a result, Crowther's 89 Brigade H.Q. and the 2nd King's Own Scottish Borderers were able to move within the Ngakyedauk defences. Their entry was marred only when the mule convoy of Brigade Headquarters was stampeded by mortar fire and many animals were killed or lost in the darkness. The mobile force of West Yorkshires was becoming so exhausted and decimated that it was essential to have 89 Brigade inside to strengthen the garrison and enable it to act more offensively.

Early next day, February 16, three companies of the Lincolnshires attacked Point 315. They failed to take the hill because of very fierce Japanese opposition. Their casualties were heavy. The battalion was withdrawn into the Box with the aid of tanks and carriers, so that their wounded might be transferred to the main dressing station, which had now been established in a new position round the foot of a hill. The Lincolnshires then returned to their own brigade at Prinkhaung, escorted by tanks.

By now the casualties in the main dressing station awaiting evacuation totalled no less than 478. Rows of wounded men lay in the shade of bamboos that grew in a stream bed. Others lay there patiently, weakened as they were by malaria and dysentery. While harassed, overworked medical orderlies hastened to give out food and drink, to dress wounds, pour out medicines and take temperatures, the wounded and the sick used their diminished energy to brush away the flies that attacked, buzzed, and distracted all day long. Many lay there with their clothes still stiff with clotted blood, their blankets stained and alive with greedy flies. Day by day they lay waiting for the promised deliverance. Day by day they endured pain and weakness, watching men beside them die and be taken out, while new casualties were carried into the shade and laid on the empty space of bare earth. They talked and laughed, guessing what was happening outside, or telling of how they had been wounded. Their beards grew darker, their faces became more drawn. And at night they struggled to fall asleep and often failed, so disturbing were the sudden splutters of fire, the glows and flashes that their tired eyes watched on the leafy roof above their strange ward. The unknown danger stirred more deeply than the peril that was known; the menacing sounds and lights of darkness played upon their suffering bodies and their strained nerves. And so the days and nights dragged on.

Outside, by the road that led down the Pass, jostled strings of mules, jeeps that had edged forward, and Military Police who did their best to prevent blocks from forming. Here, in the sunlight, worked the few remaining doctors and medical orderlies, who tended those men who had just been brought in on stretchers. Inside a *basha* operations were performed, blood transfusions given, limbs amputated, bleeding stopped, pain relieved. Across the dusty road gaped a wide pit for the dead, and from the loose soil rose crosses roughly made from boxes and inscribed in pencil with the name, rank and number of the men who had been killed or who had died from their wounds.

A description has come down to us of a visit paid to a sport-loving officer who had been twice wounded and whose leg had been amputated. "I found him lying with his eyes closed, his face grey, and his features distorted with weariness and hopelessness. I spoke to him. He opened his eyes, but there was no light of welcome there, although we had known each other well for a long time. Finding it difficult to know what to say, I asked him how he felt. He twisted his head from side to side on the 'pillow,' and his face screwed up with suffering. He said, 'I'm all f———d up.' The way he said it took away the coarseness of the word he used. He seemed too exhausted to talk, so, after telling him I would bring him some lime-juice which he had asked for, I went out. On the way I saw one of our sergeants who had also been badly wounded. I asked him how he was getting on. He said, 'I shall be all right, sir. I shall be out of it soon.' And he did not mean over the Ngakyedauk Pass. He had been shot in the stomach."

* * * * *

At any moment during the day a shell might land in some part of the Box. So crowded was the area that few shells did not strike some man or mule, some ammunition or petrol store, some tank or jeep, some tent or shelter. The hundreds of mules presented a most vulnerable target, and the mule drivers, assisted by such veterinary officers as were with the garrison, did their best to dress the wounds in leg and flank. But the mules struggled and kicked. They were frightened, and often the task of bandaging some limb was delayed or rendered impossible. And many animals were so gravely hurt that they had to be killed to end their misery. A group of men might be waiting near the cooking fire for their lunch to be served. A shell would crump and explode. A man would lie dead or moaning on the ground. A jeep would catch fire and burn to a twisted, blackened shell.

Meals and cups of tea were awaited with an eagerness born of the cramped trenches, the constant expectation of shelling, and

THE 25TH DRAGOONS NORTH OF RAZABIL (Imperial War Museum)

MEN OF 123 BRIGADE CLAMBER UP A JUNGLE PATH (Imperial War Museum)

(Walter Stoneman, F.R.P.S.)

BRIGADIER G. C. EVANS

(Lafayette)

BRIGADIER J. A. SALOMONS

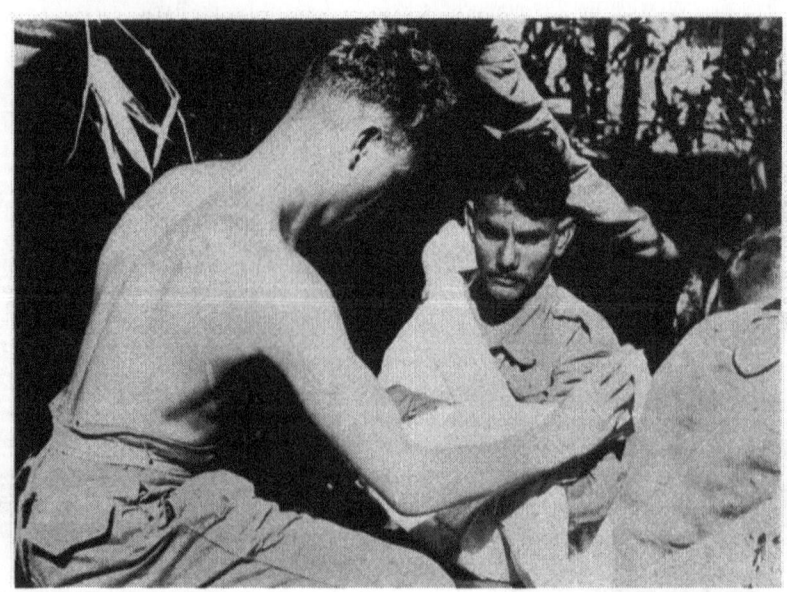

(Imperial War Museum)

CORPORAL ASKE BANDAGES A WOUNDED RAJPUT

the tedium and lack of exercise experienced by all save those who struggled up hills to counter-attack the enemy. Those who had worked throughout the night tried to snatch a few hours of restless sleep. The men deepened and improved their trenches, their dug-outs and underground chambers. They groomed the mules, fed them, worked wireless sets and telephone exchanges, went out to mend a cable or to lay a new one. The tanks were on call to any quarter of the Box to drive off the Japanese with their guns and mobility.

Daily the defenders listened to news, rumours, and forecasts of their relief from outside. Hopes were dashed and then renewed. General Messervy walked twice a day to the armoured scout car and spoke to his three brigades by wireless. And Brigadier Evans held conferences on the telephone, to spare his commanders the time and danger of coming to a central meeting-place.

If the hours of daylight were strained, the night watches wore down the garrison still more sharply. The minutes ticked by, so slowly. Whether a man stood in his trench and peered out into the jungle, alert for the least stirring in the undergrowth; or strained his eyes to peer in search of lurking enemies who might be creeping stealthily towards his outpost; or sat in his stuffy little dug-out, blacked out by a heavy tarpaulin, and listened to the Morse signals on his wireless set, trying through the confusion of atmospherics and intruding signals to pick out and read those transmitted by a battalion or headquarters; or tried to move from one trench to another and was fired at in the darkness—in every case he longed for the first grey light to outline the hills and jungle about him. The defenders could distinguish between the crackling Bren gun and the lower pitched Japanese machine-gun. The explosion of grenades gave place to sudden bursts of automatic fire. And shouts rent the moments of silence as clearly as did a whining shell. Across the Box scurried tracer bullets, and Very lights would swish up into the night sky and illuminate for an instant the crest of Artillery Hill.

Night after night the Japanese flung themselves against some part of our perimeter defences. Always they were beaten back. An hour before first light on February 21 some seventy Japanese soldiers marched down the road through the eastern gate of the Box. They moved in formation, and thought perhaps that they were at Launggyaung. They were savaged by the 4/8th Gurkhas and by the 25th Dragoons. Though some withdrew in disorder, fifty attacked one Gurkha company and were mown down. Forty-two enemy corpses were counted on the ground when daylight came.

And throughout the same night the West Yorkshires and the defenders of Nine Brigade 'B' Echelon fired to repel enemy parties that attacked from the south. One group reached to within twenty yards of Nine Brigade officers' mess and the troop of mountain guns beside the *chaung*. The whole defence sector was in an uproar. Shouts from the Japanese were rivalled by Indian war cries. Then silence fell. And next morning two Japanese lay on the sandy stream bed. Twenty-five other bodies were counted.

* * * * *

On February 21 the 2/1st Punjab, now commanded by Major Sarbjit Singh Kalha, and strengthened by one company of Rajputs and another of Garhwalis, attacked and captured Point 1070 that had been lost a week earlier. The final opening of the Pass was now in sight. Every known Japanese position had been pounded by the Royal Air Force and all available artillery from both east and west of the Mayu Range. Now the only hill to be cleared was the dominating Sugar Loaf that overlooked the Box. This was captured by the 2/1st Punjab on the 22nd. The troops made a wide and precipitous detour in order to approach from the north. Two parties of Japanese were routed on the way, and many enemy dead found in the jungle proved how effectual our bombing and shelling had been. When Sugar Loaf was reached, the Japanese offered no resistance. They had fled after a dive-bombing attack and on hearing the distant war cries of "Allah ki gai !"

The siege of Ngakyedauk was at an end. The Pass had been opened. At two o'clock General Briggs rode up to the command post in a tank, bringing bottles of whisky. And Lomax's 26th Indian Division from the north had gained touch with the defenders of the Box. Upon the Japanese had been inflicted a severe defeat. His dead lay on every approach to our defences, his wounded were being hurriedly borne through the jungle towards a new line of battle. And at last our own wounded and sick were lifted into ambulances and driven across the Ngakyedauk Pass to hospitals and safety, to silent days and nights of sleep without fear. Such was the radiant joy showing in the faces of these men that the sight brought tears into the eyes of the most hardened soldiers. Their uncomplaining fortitude had been an example to all.

*　　*　　*　　*　　*

Messervy prepared his brigades for the assault upon Buthidaung, which was captured on March 11. Nine Brigade returned to the coast and settled into a cleaner, less smelly Maungdaw. Brigadier Geoffrey Evans was transferred to the command of 123 Brigade, and Salomons took his place.

This battle was a turning point in the campaign, not so much for the five thousand Japanese dead that littered the jungle and *chaung* beds, or for the crushing of a serious enemy offensive, but rather for the uplifted morale of our troops who had taken part in the fighting, and for the final breaking of that pernicious legend of Japanese invincibility.

CHAPTER XXII

RAZABIL FORTRESS AND THE FLIGHT TO IMPHAL

MARCH 1944

THE Division's next main task in Arakan was to capture the Razabil Fortress, against which so many vain attacks had already been launched, both on the ground and from the air. Operation 'Jonathan' had been abortive. The Vengeance dive-bombers swooping down upon targets had brought no decisive result. Nor had our artillery concentrations and harassing fire driven out the Japanese, whose defences about Razabil and the hillock known as 'Tortoise' were deep and skilful. No frontal assault could succeed without undue loss of life. Brigadier Warren and his 161 Brigade were charged with bearing the brunt of the new operation, of which the code name was 'Markhur.'

The plan was to substitute guile for direct attack, to close a tight ring around the fortress by surprise, to bring 161 Brigade in from the foothills to the south, and so to sever the enemy's lines of communication. The success of a scheme designed to bypass the fortress and appear on dominating features, so isolating it from the rear, depended on accurate preliminary reconnaissance both of the route and the final positions. Officers of 161 Brigade spent several days behind the Japanese lines, making these reconnaissances. And their daring and careful observation was amply repaid when the operation began.

Evans' 123 Brigade were to simulate a major attack against Razabil from the north, while Nine Brigade would remain in reserve to hold the front, to delay enemy reinforcements from reaching the battleground, to protect our convoys, and thus to relieve the attacking troops of anxiety about their rear and flank. The 3/9th Jats (Lieutenant-Colonel Bernard Gerty) were placed under Warren's command for the attack.

And so 161 Brigade, having gathered together near the village of Kanyindan, moved off in the evening, crossed the Magyi Chaung by the iron bridge, and turned south-east across the paddy fields to the main road that led to Akyab. The Brigade column, headed by the 1/1st Punjab, moved through the night, a night so quiet that the braying of a mule sent cold shivers down the spine, for fear the enemy should become aware of our advance across his line of retreat.

Each battalion of the Brigade was stretched in single file. Walking slowly through the moonlight, the troops felt, as Major T. S. Ware expressed it, as Wolfe's men must have felt filing up the Heights of Abraham. All went well from the start, and notwithstanding inevitable halts and some concertina-like movements of the long, snake-like column, there was neither noise nor major confusion. No command could be exercised, and no order given on such a march. The only orders issued were in anticipation. Weapons were carried unloaded, to eliminate the risk of their accidental, or even intentional, use. For a single shot in the night might have affected the entire operation.

As all patrolling of the route beforehand had been most cursory, in order not to arouse Japanese suspicions, confirmation of the correct route was obtained as well from good memorizing of maps in advance, as from experience in recognizing features on the ground. The hardest task of all was the final move of companies to their positions among the scrub-covered foothills. After leaving the battalion snake, the way of each company was uncharted, and groping is the only word that describes the last stages of this march.

It was not until day-break that company commanders were able to check just where their men were positioned. How strange it was to be facing north on to the rear of the enemy's defences, after two months of frontal assaults! How completely the Japanese were surprised by our arrival was revealed soon after dawn when six enemy soldiers were found washing in a stream. They were shot.

The Royal West Kents advanced north towards Razabil, and suffered heavily when a Japanese gun shelled them over open sights. But skilful shooting by 4th Field Regiment knocked out this gun, and the British battalion pushed on, until soon only Razabil and 'Tortoise' remained in Japanese hands.

The honour of the final assault upon Razabil Fortress was given to Cargill's 4/7th Rajputs, who had fought and lost against these almost impregnable positions during the previous weeks. The attack took place in the morning, after an artillery bombardment unprecedented in that campaign. The area was dense with smoke. The thumping of two hundred guns echoed against the Mayu Range. The whine and crump of shells, the dust, the explosion of bombs dropped by swooping dive-bombers, the crescendo of noise—all heralded a climax. And never were the faces of Indian infantry set with such determination. They were out to capture and to avenge. But the enemy had realized his untenable position. He was surprised by this encirclement, accustomed as he had become to our attacks from the north side alone. And during the night he evacuated the fortress.

When the battle was over, the scene was one of devastation. Some Japanese bunkers had been smashed to rubble and splintered timber by the bombing. But others had not been touched, or else their depth had saved them from wreckage. Inside the hill the enemy had hollowed out an immense cavern, used for a dressing station, and at one place was a corridor with openings at each end, to enable a gun to be fired in two directions. It was then towed back into shelter, thus mystifying our gunners who were trying to destroy the enemy's guns. Strands of barbed wire, sand-bag shreds, bags of rice, and broken ammunition boxes painted with Japanese characters lay about the bare, scarred slopes and crest of Tortoise. The surface had been ploughed up by bomb and shell. Craters and fallen bunkers made the sepoys tread warily as they settled in on top. Corpses still lay out in the sunshine. Boots and muddy uniforms, more and more ammunition and boxes, steel helmets and articles of equipment testified to a recent battleground. Above all, the very bareness of this place by contrast with the surrounding hills, so coated in bushes and bamboo, marked it out as a scene of warfare. Only in the gullies and lower slopes of the fortress was undergrowth still visible.

And there was Colonel Jack Cargill of the Rajputs—"a familiar figure striding along into the attack, cursing hills, jungle and Japs with blasphemous fervour. Who will forget his vast bulk standing out on the skyline above the Razabil Fortress after its capture by his battalion ? Who will forget his kindly welcome in an improvised mess ?" So wrote a Gunner officer of the Rajput's leader, a hard taskmaster who was quick to praise, and whose round, brick-red face shone with soap and smiles.

RAZABIL FORTRESS AND THE FLIGHT TO IMPHAL

No sooner was Razabil in our hands than Brigadier Warren sent patrols forward up the road that led through the two Tunnels to Buthidaung. The enemy must be permitted no respite to recover from his surprise and from our success. No delay in pursuing him must be allowed. The main road ran through a gorge, and the ground on either side was high and rocky. The 1/1st Punjab advanced south of the road, Cargill's 4/7th Rajputs on the north side, with Brigade Headquarters and the Royal West Kents moving along the axis of the road itself. Opposition was met from point to point, but this was either outflanked or destroyed as 161 Brigade neared the first of the Tunnels.

On March 14 the Royal West Kents secured Point 1079, on the left of the road and just short of the western Tunnel. This was at the top end of a stretch where the road runs nearly due north through the heart of the Mayu Range. And although on the next day the 1/1st drove the Japanese from a dominating hill—Point 1267 on the main ridge south of the road—these operations were marred for the battalion, and, indeed, for the entire Division, by the death of the commanding officer, Lieutenant-Colonel D. I. Morrison, known as "Digger." He was wounded in the shoulder. The bullet must have been deflected to the lung by a bone, for although he was cheerfully smoking a cigarette as he lay on a stretcher on his way back to the Advanced Dressing Station, he had an internal hæmorrhage, and died in Maungdaw that night.

* * * * *

Meanwhile 123 Brigade had been active against the enemy. On March 12 Alden's 'B' Company of the 1/17th Dogras attacked a small hill named 'Propeller' that rises steeply from the surrounding paddy fields between the road and the foothills. To approach this lone hill was perilous, for the paddy fields provided no good cover. But the attacking company hoped, in the short period of darkness before the moon rose, to crawl up in the shadows cast by the narrow paddy bunds and so to reach the foot of Propeller unobserved. Alden's men did in fact reach their objective but were checked by heavy fire when they attacked. A second assault was made after midnight, again without success. But at four o'clock on the morning of the 13th it was a case of third time lucky. A ground mist thickened by cordite fumes provided some measure of cover.

And with a dash and determination made almost reckless by the anger at having twice failed, the Dogras rushed in to the attack, shouting their war-cries in the moonlight and appearing out of the mist with such suddenness that the Japanese turned and fled from Propeller. The Dogras suffered not a single casualty in this final assault.

Four days later the battalion was ordered to capture the battered Wrencat hill, further east into the foothills. This, as has been described, was the scene of five vain attacks during January. Now, for three hours before the attack on March 17, the guns of the Division pounded the target. Then, at half past two that afternoon, Captain Pat Meek led his 'C' Company of Dogras against Wrencat. The first platoon to clamber up the slopes was that commanded by Subadar Gian Mohd. So spirited was this attack that within seven minutes the hill was in our hands, and the Dogras enjoyed the spectacle of Japanese soldiers bolting from their positions and hurrying into the jungle-clad foothills.

It was indeed fitting that Wrencat should fall to the 1/17th Dogras, who had attacked with such determination on six occasions and had thereby suffered so heavily.

161 Brigade continued to fight along the Tunnels road against Japanese resistance. The gorge was narrow and the hills steep. Bridges presented numerous delays. It was a formidable task to fight on the peaks and highest ridges of the Mayu Hills, looking to the east across into the Kalapanzin Valley and to Buthidaung, and southwards down the range towards distant Akyab. A more familiar view was that over the foothills to the paddy fields and *chaungs* of the coast, with villages marked by their clumps of trees, the road by its line of dust, Maungdaw by its buildings and jetty, and all the battlefields of the past weeks by the bare patches and upturned earth caused by bombardment and assault.

* * * * *

Then came rumours and uneasy reports that the Japanese were invading in the north, threatening the state of Manipur, with its capital at Imphal. The enemy's thrust in Arakan during February had been crushed. Now he crossed the Chindwin and advanced north and west to destroy our central front, to capture the vital advanced airfields of Imphal, and so to threaten our railhead and enormous supply dumps nearly 130 miles farther north. The enemy now threatened the valleys of Assam, the oilfields by the Brahmaputra, and the supply routes toward Ledo and General Stilwell's forces in Northern Burma. The loss of Imphal would mean the unhinging of our defences in this all-important area. Its gain for the Japanese would mean the first stepping-stone towards the invasion of India. It was unfortunate, but also unavoidable, that our battle front ran from north to south for some three hundred miles, from Dimapur through Kohima and Imphal to Tiddim in the south; it ran parallel to the Chindwin and at right angles to the Japanese line of advance. At almost any point the road could be cut. The 17th Indian Division would be isolated if the road were cut between Imphal and Tiddim. If the enemy cut it north of Imphal, then Four Corps would find its supply routes severed. This was a risk that had to be taken. And the roads were cut just as had been foreseen.

The Japanese began their advance on March 8. When the Japanese 33rd Division made its way from the Chindwin up into the hills near Tiddim, the 17th Indian Division found that its route of withdrawal had already been blocked. It was ordered back to Imphal, and had to fight its way through the hills and valleys for close on 150 miles. A second thrust was made by the 15th Japanese Division up the Kabaw Valley towards Tamu and Palel, that guarded the south-east approaches to Imphal; while the 31st Division headed towards Ukhrul in the east and began to threaten both Kohima and Dimapur.

Such was the menacing situation when the Fifth Indian Division began to arrive in Imphal on March 27, in aircraft that had been diverted by Lord Louis Mountbatten from the Hump route to China, because Troop Carrier Command had no planes available to transport the Division in time to reinforce the defenders of Imphal and the surrounding plain.

In Arakan the front was taken over by the incoming 25th Indian Division, and by the 36th Brigade, who continued the fight to clear the Tunnels road linking Maungdaw and Razabil with Buthidaung.

A warning order came that the Division was to move to Imphal by road and rail, a move that would take at least three weeks to complete. The first road parties from each brigade had already left Arakan when the Division received word that the move was now to be made by a "faster method." Indeed, 123 Brigade, the first to leave, had already reached Chittagong before orders came for the troops to be flown to Imphal instead of travelling the whole way by road. Seldom was transformation so abrupt, improvisation so successful, and disciplined planning so indispensable.

That same day a staff officer flew down to Divisional Headquarters from Fourteenth Army, and announced that the entire Division, including mules, guns and jeeps, would be flown to Imphal and Dimapur, because the situation had become extremely serious. The presence of the Division was needed urgently in the north.

The staff officer issued loading tables for every type of unit and then said, "Any questions ? I have to leave in half an hour." None of the Divisional staff had any experience of moving a formation by air, nor had the troops ever trained for this. All that was known was that such a move was supposed to be highly complex, and to involve months of practice. Colonel Maclaurin, the A/Q, his deputy, Major T. C. W. Roe, and their staff were in no position to ask questions on the spur of the moment. Instead, they hoped for the best, and settled down to follow the loading tables provided. These tables had been prepared by Army some months before, in anticipation of such an emergency, and they worked splendidly.

The loading tables showed exactly which men, by ranks and trades, would travel in each aircraft, and which stores and pieces of equipment would be loaded in each. Should any one plane crash, the unit concerned would not have lost all its trained men, all its mortars, all its wireless sets.

And the men were excited at the prospect of such an unusual and unexpected move. It was the first and only time that a division was transported by air out of action on one battle front to immediate action on another front several hundred miles distant. It showed that, given experienced and disciplined troops, an air move was the simplest form for both troops and staff.

The patience and skill with which drivers steered their jeeps up the ramps into the aircraft, the delicacy and controlled strength used to lift and coax the jeep round into its final position inside the fuselage, the tugging and prodding and tempting of the mules up into the planes—all this was remarkable. The Gunners had to work

RAZABIL FORTRESS AND THE FLIGHT TO IMPHAL

with great rapidity. One evening their guns would be taken out of action and back to a concentration area. Next morning the regiment moved by road to the airfield at Dohazari, near Chittagong. They arrived about tea time, dismantled the guns, loaded the pieces into Dakotas on the following morning, flew that day to Imphal, reassembled the guns, which were then ready to enter the firing line on the fourth day. Only one hitch occurred, when a regiment was landed on four different airstrips on the Imphal plain. A special tool was needed for reassembling the 25-pounders, and only one such tool was allowed to each regiment. No more were available in Imphal, so an urgent signal went to Dohazari. The tools were flown up by a fighter aircraft. Then further delays occurred while the instruments were hurried from one airfield to the next.

It is recorded that, while loading mules into one Dakota, a British sergeant was heard to shout to an Indian sepoy who was struggling with a particularly obstinate mule:

" 'Ere, you puckero his topee and I'll gurum his peachi." This meant, "You hold his head, and I'll warm his backside."

There was, it appears, an American pilot who, during a flight, called out to the Indian jemadar who was in charge of the troops in the plane:

"Say, where do you want to go?" To which the jemadar replied, "Malum nahin (I don't know), sahib."

Colonel Roe tells of a second American pilot who asked his passengers: "Say, what's the name of the place we've just left?"

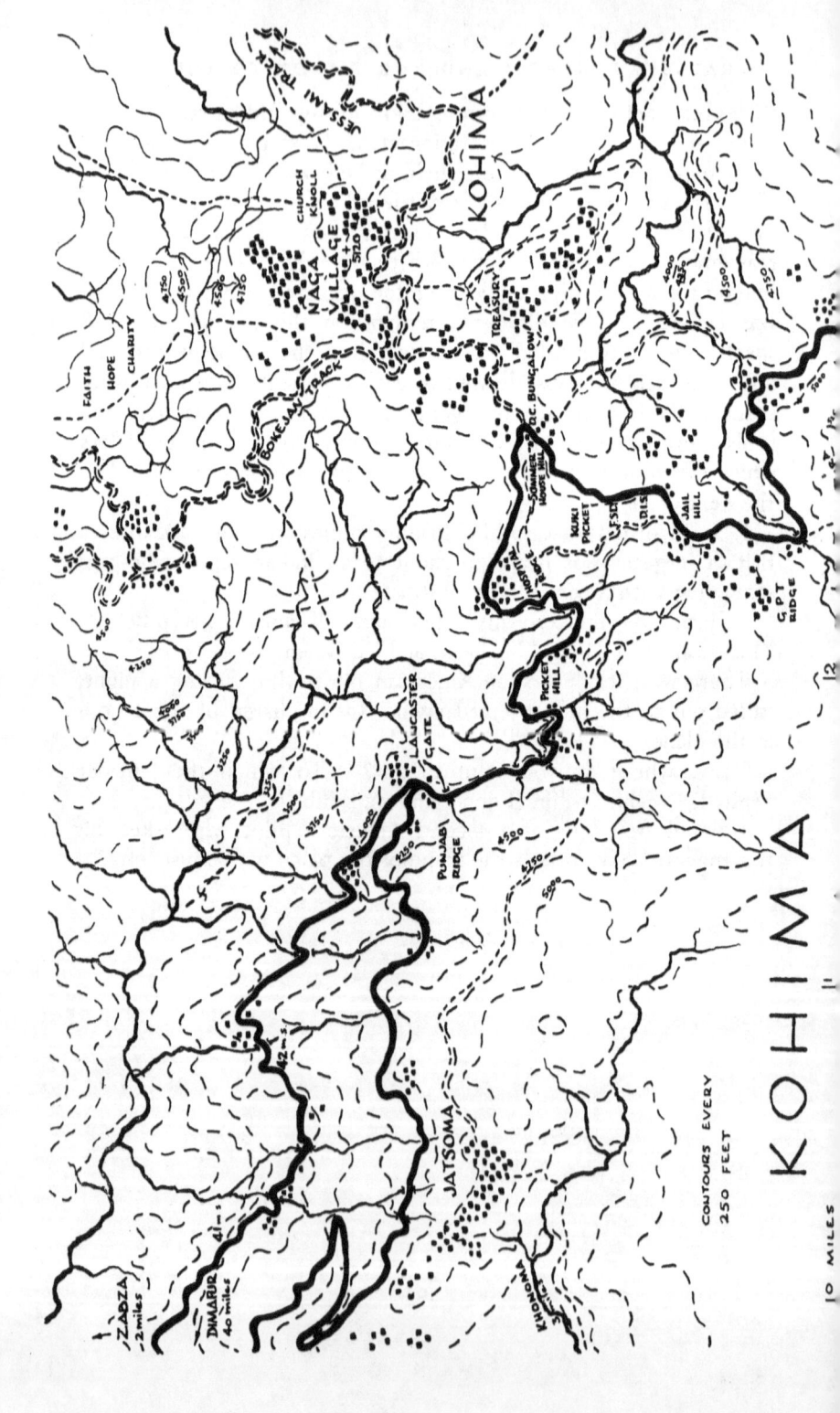

CHAPTER XXIII

KOHIMA

APRIL 1944

A SECOND enemy thrust was directed against our railhead and supply base at Dimapur in Northern Assam. Also threatened was the little town of Kohima, nearly fifty miles to the south and high up among the Naga Hills. On March 29 the Japanese cut the road between Imphal and Kohima, and Warren's 161 Brigade flew from Dohazari to Dimapur, moved by lorry along the main road to Kohima, and settled into evacuated hospital buildings.

Lieutenant John Wright, who commanded the detachment of 2 Field Company with the Royal West Kents, has painted the scene on arrival in Kohima for the first time. The town lay among the hills five thousand feet above the sea, surrounded by precarious cultivation on terraced slopes. The villages had been built on promontories, and there lived the picturesque Naga hill-people, with their gay blankets, their shell necklaces, and their black hair clipped short and straight or else tied on top of the head. To those who had just hurried from the bright heat of Arakan, and before that from the vast emptiness of Iraq and the Western Desert, this beautiful land of wooded hills hardly seemed to be a potential battlefield. The way up from Dimapur reminded some, at least, of the road to Mussoorie, the hill station above Dehra Dun. And it was hard to convince yourself that this arrival in Kohima was not the beginning of a hard-earned leave on the edge of the Himalayas.

You saw a village perched on the very peak of a sharp ridge, and built substantially of timber with red corrugated iron roofs. From afar the Nagas, with prodigious calf muscles, could be seen trotting up the steep paths, with their loads supported by a band across the brow. There, too, a pleasant smell of wood fires lingered on the evening air. Most welcome of all was a nip in the air as the light of day began to fail, with the promise of the luxury of a night slept in blankets, without the oppression of a mosquito net.

Brigadier Warren was occupied with the co-ordination of the Kohima defences, but the difficulties of planning were aggravated by the likelihood of his brigade being ordered back to Dimapur as Army reserve. It was, however, arranged that, on April 1, Brigade Headquarters, Laverty's 4th Royal West Kents, 2 Field Company, I.E., and 24 Mountain Regiment (Lieutenant-Colonel Humphrey Hill) less two batteries, should form a defensive box at the Treasury in Kohima, which had already been occupied by a company of Assam Rifles. This plan proved unsatisfactory: the area was dominated by a hill immediately to the east, which was not held in strength; our water supply in the event of Japanese attacks was most precarious; and the Treasury itself was already adequately garrisoned.

But that afternoon the expected change of plan occurred. The move to the Treasury was cancelled, and 161 Brigade ordered to return next day to Dimapur. Here the 4/7th Rajputs had meantime established themselves, while the 1/1st Punjab (Major Neil M. Brodie) were concentrated along the road between Dimapur and Kohima at Ms.16. While the Royal West Kents moved into Dimapur as Brigade rearguard, the 1/1st Punjab remained under command of the 1st Burma Regiment at Nichuguard. The rest of 161 Brigade settled around Ms.4, being entrusted with the defence of the Dimapur base and with counter-attacking inside this base should the need arise. To this end Brigadier Warren organized two columns, "Thunder," comprising the West Kents, and "Lightning," made up of the 4/7th Rajputs, each supported by a battery of 24 Mountain Regiment.

But the general situation on the front changed next day when the 31st Japanese Division made contact with the garrison at Kohima and drove in our outposts. During the afternoon of April 4 Colonel Laverty received a warning order that his battalion would return to Kohima at dawn on the following day.

The battalion column, with Major Donald Easten's 'D' Company in the lead, set off at half past six on the morning of the 5th. At intervals they met stragglers returning from Kohima, some walking beside the road, others packed in speeding lorries. Several officers whom Colonel Richards, the garrison commander at

Kohima, sent out to meet the West Kents, brought news of the contact battle. They painted so grim a picture of disorganization and lack of spirit within the defence perimeter that Colonel Laverty hoped the situation would not have deteriorated to the extent of a complete collapse before he could reinforce the garrison. Although the Japanese were already in Kohima itself and east of the village, the road to Dimapur had not been cut, and fighting was as yet confined to the first of five hill features on which the defences of the garrison box were based.

Kohima looked much the same as before. But the Nagas no longer trotted through the village. Silent was the usual hum of lorries driving down the Line of Communication main road towards Imphal. Only the roar of the troop-carrying vehicles that bore the Royal West Kents and supporting arms in this last dash into Kohima was heard. The deserted hospital with its unhinged doors and the chaos of abandoned stores could be glimpsed as the column passed towards the cross-roads where the troops were to alight. At that moment our Field Ambulance detachment was fired on, and one of its trucks disintegrated with a flash. Rather than run the gauntlet further, the men behind left the transport and laboriously made their way within the defences of the town.

As Easten's company drove in past the Indian General Hospital, the leading lorries were fired upon by rifles in Kohima Village, away to the east. Easten gave orders to dismount and the men marched the rest of the way to prearranged positions on a hill by the District Commissioner's Bungalow, the home of Mr. Charles Pawsey.

By five o'clock the company groups had unloaded most of their stores, and the fifty lorries had been parked in the shelter of a hill. Much of this transport, which the battalion had been definitely instructed to keep at Kohima in order not to block the rest of 161 Brigade, who moved up to the Jatsoma area on the same day, was to be wrecked in the subsequent battle.

That evening, after a day during which the Japanese had fired spasmodically, the Royal West Kents took up their positions: 'A' Company (Major J. Winstanley) and battalion headquarters on Summerhouse Hill; 'B' Company (Major T. Kenyon) on Kuki Picket; Major P. E. M. Shaw's 'C' Company on D.I.S. Hill; and Major D. F. Easten and his 'D' Company established themselves between battalion headquarters and 53 Indian General Hospital. At six o'clock that afternoon four Japanese guns shelled the whole defensive area for half an hour, concentrating specially on the D.C. Bungalow Spur. But the night was quiet. And save for intermittent shelling and mortar fire, the enemy made no serious attempt to attack.

* * * * *

When the Royal West Kents had returned to Dimapur on April 2, it had been decided that Kohima contained sufficient troops and supplies to withstand heavy attacks. It was known well in advance that the town was an objective of the 31st Japanese Division, but it was thought, wrongly, that the enemy would not launch more than the equivalent of a brigade group against Kohima and Dimapur. In fact, he sent a full division, whose strength far exceeded that of the assorted garrison. Apart from the Royal West Kents, its attached Gunners—20 Battery (Major R. Yeo) of 24 Indian Mountain Regiment—andSappers of 2 FieldCompany, our garrison numbered some 2,900 all ranks. There were the 3rd and 4th Assam Rifles, one company of the Shere Regiment, the 1st Burma Garrison Battalion, part of 313 G.P.T. Company, men from workshop, supply, medical, engineer and 'V' Force units, some signalmen of the Burma Telegraph Company, and soldiers from the 24th Reinforcement Camp who happened to be in Kohima when the road to Imphal was cut. Those units that were organized had already marched many miles across rough country from the Chindwin river, or were generally tired out from hard rearguard fighting among the hills at Jessami and Kharasom, to the east. And that part of the garrison which comprised the non-combatant administrative staffs was later to prove a liability. Not only did the special requirements of protection and disposal impose an extra burden upon the garrison commander, but the morale of these men was low and, therefore, dangerous. In many cases, quite inevitably, the troops had been collected together at very short notice; platoons and sections were composed of men from several units, under officers and N.C.Os. whom they had never seen before; and being men from non-fighting units, their infantry training was naturally inadequate.

If the state of the garrison when the Kohima battle started was

(C.I.S. *Historical Section*)

THE WAR MEMORIAL AT KOHIMA

Across the Imphal Plain (Imperial War Museum)

A Punjabi Defence Post (Imperial War Museum)

not all that might have been desired to withstand a prolonged siege, the defences had also been neglected. Vital wireless sets had not been dug in; few or no communication trenches had been dug before the arrival of the Royal West Kents, although there had been weeks of opportunity. The water points, exposed as they were, lay outside the defence perimeter and, consequently, soon fell under enemy control. Canvas tanks were available, but little effort had been made to construct alternative water points or to form reserves within the perimeter. But to offset these shortcomings, the quantity and the dumping arrangements of ammunition were good, and the presence of the F.S.D. within the defences ensured adequate food supplies at the outset. Yet, here again, the formation of reserves in individual sectors had not been completed. On the medical side, no less than five separate unco-ordinated regimental aid posts were operating when Laverty's battalion reached Kohima. Some were without stores; others had stores in abundance, but were not dug in.

This was the position at nightfall on April 5. 161 Brigade Headquarters and the 4/7th Rajputs had established a temporary defensive box on the hills outside, near Ms. 42, within two miles of the town, and on the morning of the 6th Brodie's 1/1st Punjab, who had been relieved outside Dimapur by a battalion raised from the reinforcement camp there, joined the Brigade and deployed up the spur towards Jatsoma.

Brigadier Warren had decided not to put the whole of his brigade into the Kohima box. He had several reasons for this decision: the area within Kohima was too confined for the guns of Hill's 24th Mountain Regiment to fire effectively, and they could only operate to the best advantage if two mutually supporting boxes were established. Warren's decision did much to save Kohima, for the battery of mountain guns that did go in with the Royal West Kents was unable to fire, and it was the remainder of the regiment which, tirelessly, night after night, gave brilliant covering fire to the British battalion. Most of the fire was called for by O.Ps. in the garrison, with whom wireless communication did not fail. There were nights when the guns were never silent, one or more firing defensive fire targets that ringed Kohima. On one target alone the Regiment fired some 3,500 rounds in five hours. Nor could the infantry have held out without this support.

The Brigade had so great a quantity of transport laden with ammunition and supplies that it would have been impossible to find room for these within the perimeter of Summerhouse Hill. These supplies had either to be protected outside the Kohima perimeter, or sent back to Dimapur. Warren decided to protect them, and accordingly established the Jatsoma box. This box relieved some of the pressure on Kohima by drawing upon itself attacks from which the enemy suffered as many casualties as he did on Summerhouse Hill during the actual siege. It was intended that power of manœuvre should be given to the main part of 161 Brigade. But, owing to the strength of the Japanese, the 1/1st and 4/7th were fully occupied in defending 24 Mountain Regiment so that the Gunners in turn could assist the Royal West Kents by fire.

* * * * *

From 5 a.m. until 11 a.m. on the 6th, Jail Hill and G.P.T. Ridge were heavily shelled and mortared. The jail buildings were rapidly hit, and the crest and forward positions of the 1/3rd Gurkha Rifles under Captain Frew suffered severely. Both British officers with the Burma Rifles were killed, and many casualties had to be sent down to Summerhouse Hill.

At half past ten, by which time the Japanese had infiltrated steadily on the left flank, the ninety Gurkhas remaining on G.P.T. Ridge withdrew to Jail Hill. There were not enough trenches for them, and few of these trenches had overhead cover. Half an hour later the Burma Rifles were forced off Jail Hill, and withdrew towards the F.S.D.

When Jail Hill was captured, Colonel Laverty ordered Easten's 'D' Company up from near the hospital to retake the position. But Easten's men found the Japanese too firmly established to be dislodged by anything less than a full-scale attack. And as the casualties that this might incur could not be afforded, Easten was ordered instead to reinforce F.S.D. Hill. During that morning 'A' Company of the 4/7th Rajputs, commanded by Captain Mitchell, joined the garrison, came under Laverty's command, and took over the positions just vacated by 'D' Company. They had been sent into Kohima by Brigadier Warren to ensure that the road was still clear and to gain touch with the defenders. But this road to Dimapur was cut behind the Rajput column, although small patrols continued for a time to move in and out with messages. When the road was finally blocked, all evacuation of casualties from Kohima became impossible. The telephone cable back to 161 Brigade Headquarters lasted through for six hours more. Then the enemy cut it, and all communication was by wireless.

It was fortunate that the siege began with the dressing stations almost empty; they did not remain so for long. And it was at this stage, when desultory shelling had proved how inadequate and poorly protected were the garrison's medical arrangements, that Lieutenant-Colonel John Young, commanding 75 Indian Field Ambulance, arrived in Kohima by a circuitous route. His arrival was indeed a blessing. At once he organized with devoted energy the centralization of medical stores for the entire garrison. And parties of non-combatant Indians were set digging trenches to protect our wounded from the worst of the shell-fire.

When night fell on April 6 a company of Japanese attacked frontally in an attempt to cross the main road from Jail Hill to D.I.S. Hill, held by Shaw's 'C' Company of the Royal West Kents. While our mortars caused many casualties in the enemy's forming-up areas and on Jail Hill, men of 'C' Company killed scores of Japanese in the open. One strong attack was driven back. But under cover of the dark night an enemy platoon succeeded in infiltrating around the west flank into some *bashas* and pits between 'C' and 'D' Companies of the West Kents. Major Shaw was seriously wounded, and two hours later his second-in-command was hit.

When dawn broke the situation was grave. Something must be done to restore it. Accordingly, Laverty ordered Easten's company to destroy the Japanese who had infiltrated. This counter-attack succeeded. But it was rendered the more hazardous by enemy guns only a thousand yards away on G.P.T. Ridge which fired direct into the flank of our advancing troops. The detachment of Sappers, commanded by Lieutenant J. W. Wright, supported Easten by demolishing the brick walls of several *bashas* in which the Japanese, and some Indians whom they had captured, were hiding. At one moment, some of the enemy soldiers took shelter in brick ovens: they were forced out by grenades. Others sheltered in an ammunition dump and in the D.I.S. Hospital stores. Their choice of refuge was ill-fated, as during the fighting both these caught alight. The confusion of battle was not lessened when a burning *basha* set this ammunition dump exploding. Easten's men did not fail to shoot down the Japanese like rabbits bolting from a haystack. Fierce hand-to-hand fighting also occurred. Many wounded Japanese fled into a nullah on the western side, and after the fighting died down forty-four enemy bodies were counted on the ground. Then Major Easten led his men across to reinforce Shaw's 'C' Company's position, while the Rajput Company took over the defence sector that had been retrieved in this engagement.

The next night a Rajput platoon, using a route across country north of 53 Indian General Hospital, succeeded in escorting out of Kohima, to Ms.41, eighty of our walking wounded and a hundred non-combatant Indian troops. The road from Dimapur to 161 Brigade area was still open. Supplies had been coming in and ammunition reserves were being built up as fast as possible, for it was expected that the road would be cut at any moment. During the night 'C' Company heard the Japanese forming up for an attack. Defensive fire was called for by wireless from the 24th Mountain Regiment, whose guns were outside near Jatsoma, and the attack was dispersed. On the previous night Major Yeo's mountain battery, the only one inside Kohima, had moved two of its 3.7-inch howitzers to the top of Summerhouse Hill, but only on one occasion was it possible to fire the guns from this cramped and wooded space, which was under constant enemy observation. And, later, these two howitzers had to be abandoned.

On April 8 Brigadier Warren moved his headquarters to higher and more defendable ground. The necessity of defending many vehicles, ration dumps, and gun areas had caused 161 Brigade to become extended. One result of this closing-in move was that Warren was enabled to release part of the 1/1st Punjab, in the hope that these troops might be able to open the road into Kohima. A further reason for moving was the reports from escaped prisoners and from one of our patrols, indicating that a serious threat to the Brigade's right flank might develop from the direction of Khonoma.

By eight o'clock that morning, too, the telephone line to Dimapur had been cut, and a carrier patrol of the 1/1st, which drove back ten miles to Zubza, reported that the road had been blocked. Thus, both the garrison of Kohima and Warren's defensive box were surrounded by the enemy. During that day the Japanese installed 75 mm. guns along the ridge south of Kohima village towards Merema, and their artillery on G.P.T. Ridge was reinforced by anti-tank guns. In this way, our garrison was now exposed to direct fire from east, south and west.

And at dusk Kohima was shelled by all these enemy guns together. This concentration coincided with a really ferocious Japanese attack from Jail Hill against the thin line of 'C' and 'D' Companies. The attack was repulsed, as were two others that followed. Major Donald Easten was wounded. And Lance-Corporal J. Harman died performing the acts of high gallantry for which he was posthumously awarded the Victoria Cross. Many a faint heart was inspired by his sacrifice, and urged to fight on with renewed determination. By this time our two companies had inflicted about five times their total strength in casualties on the enemy.

That same night the Japanese attacked from two other directions —from D.C. Bungalow and 53 Indian General Hospital Spurs— and obtained footholds in both these areas. Our mortar fire, which was successful in helping to repulse the attacks on 'C' Company, drew counter-battery fire by the sparks of the charge which were clearly visible to the enemy in the darkness.

This fighting in the hospital area made the garrison's medical and water problems still more acute. No longer could walking wounded be evacuated across country. No place within the perimeter lay out of enemy observation or fire. And the number of stretcher cases had greatly increased. The one small water tap in the District Commissioner's garden was now little more than thirty yards from the enemy positions, and our men had to crawl forward singly at night to fill their bottles. Although four days later another water point was found near the Hospital, this, too, could only be used by night. So desperate had the water situation become that it was rationed to half a mug a day for each man. Subsequently, when the water was supplied by air, the garrison had just enough for drinking and for the more urgent medical purposes.

Unforgettable to those who endured the siege of Kohima was the District Commissioner, Mr. Charles Pawsey, who had spent a score of years among his beloved Naga hill-men. He lived mainly with Colonel Richards, the garrison commander, in a large bunker on Summerhouse Hill, and was to be seen wandering through the thick of the fighting, dressed in grey flannels and an old trilby hat. He encouraged his Assamese and Nagas, and provided a fine example of a British Empire administrator's devotion to duty and to his charges.

Day by day Pawsey watched his bungalow home shelled and ruined, till nothing was standing of what had been a pleasant, rambling, red-tiled house with walls of asbestos sheeting. Its terraced garden had been gay with flowers. Little paths wound up the hill behind to a summerhouse at the end. And his private asphalt tennis court became the No-Man's-Land of a battle. The Royal West Kents held trenches along its upper edge, and before long the Japanese had burrowed their way into foxholes on the lower side. There were nightly, then daily, and in the end almost hourly grenade and rifle duels fought across the width of this court, without a decision for either side.

During the morning of April 9 the Japanese reinforced their hold at D.C. Bungalow Spur. Supported by the usual artillery fire, they made further limited attacks from the Hospital. Although this area was not cleared of enemy troops, heavy mortar fire and onslaughts by the Assam Rifles did relieve pressure.

Meanwhile, outside Kohima, the 1/1st Punjab had moved to the east of Jatsoma and had attacked southwards along a ridge. But lines of enemy bunkers blocked their path, and during the day's fighting the battalion suffered twenty-five casualties Though counter-attacked that same evening, they held the ground they had gained.

As the dusk enveloped Kohima, heavy shelling coincided with a rainstorm and a strong enemy attack from beyond the Bungalow. A fierce charge, accompanied by shouts and yells, was beaten off by Winstanley's 'A' Company, supported by defensive fire from the Mountain Gunners, who took a heavy toll. This first attack, on a pitch-dark night, was repulsed. But the Japanese again probed from the Hospital towards the Assam Rifles, and made a third and most dangerous thrust directed at the West Kents' now seriously depleted 'C' Company. Under cover of showers of grenade-discharger bombs, the enemy gained a definite footing in the trenches in D.I.S. Hill, that could not be manned because of our casualties.

Next day, April 10, Colonel Laverty decided that a counter-attack to regain the lost ground stood little chance of success; the fighting reserve remaining in the garrison was small; severe casualties could not be afforded. Accordingly, plans were made to shorten our perimeter by withdrawing 'C' Company to the F.S.D., by destroying the stores in the huts on D.I.S. Hill, by boobytrapping the approaches to the F.S.D., and by altering the defensive fire tasks of the Mountain Gunners to fit our new defence lines. During the night 'C' Company was successfully withdrawn through the Rajputs. But all this time the Japanese maintained pressure with great strength and tenacity along the two main approaches on which they concentrated throughout the siege: their thrusts from D.I.S. Hill towards the F.S.D. and also from Pawsey's Bungalow. Grenade-discharger fire was used in profusion, and in one mortar concentration the Japanese put down a hundred bombs in ten minutes on the small area between Laverty's command post and Young's dressing station.

April 11 was a quieter day. The Kohima garrison had hopes that Brigadier Warren, operating outside, would be able to relieve enemy pressure. 161 Brigade was now under command of Major-General Grover's 2nd British Division that had been hurried to Dimapur from India. Its 5th Brigade, fighting its way south, was now within ten miles of Kohima. The 1/1st Punjab carrier platoon moving along the road from the west side of the Jatsoma box had been ambushed on the 10th. And next day Major T. S. Ware's 'B' Company, after successfully attacking a party of enemy on the outskirts of Jatsoma village, was twice counter-attacked, but resisted hard pressure throughout the day. The sepoys held their ground.

First light on April 12 brought against Kohima yet another Japanese attack, this time against the Rajput company near the F.S.D. This onslaught was repulsed and twenty-eight enemy bodies later found, but Captain Mitchell, who commanded the company, was killed in the engagement.

* * * * *

Enemy mortaring, in particular from Jail Ridge, had by now made our casualty position critical. Stretchers were scarce, the stretcher-bearers and doctors had suffered casualties, and in the small area of our advanced dressing station barely enough room remained for the lying cases.

The wounded, tended with the utmost devotion and courage by Colonel Young and his team of doctors, by the Indian orderlies of the Field Ambulance detachment and by the men of the West Kents' medical section, were pathetic. Sniped, shelled and mortared as they were in their all too shallow trenches, many were killed, or wounded a second time. Some lay in individual trenches, and some in pits that held half a dozen wounded soldiers. The small operating theatre, which was to receive two disastrous direct hits, lay in an open dugout, covered by a tarpaulin. Here John Young and his surgeons, whose numbers dwindled as the result of shelling, carved, chopped, hacked, stitched, and healed men. And they gave of their best to cheer them and inspire them, even when the days and nights seemed black beyond compare.

The position near the edge of Colonel Laverty's perimeter, on the slopes of Summerhouse Hill, was terribly exposed. The wounded could watch the Japanese loading shells into their mortars, and they could hear the mortar shells landing close beside them. They listened to the shelling and the screaming. They watched bombs dropping from hostile aircraft, and parachutes swaying down with precious supplies. Many died of gangrene, and a few of despair. Burial of the dead was almost impossible, and the smell of rotting corpses became hideous towards the close of the siege.

In the words of Donald Easten, who had commanded 'D' Company: "Many of the wounded I feel sure died in the last few days because they had given up hope. Yet they were incredibly cheerful, outwardly, up till the end. Those who were not wounded were too busy to think much, except perhaps at night, just before the time due for the evening hate, when they wondered whether their turn would come tonight." From the moment when the enemy launched his first attack of each evening against some part of the thinly held perimeter, the night was rendered horrible, laden with noise and fear and blood. And not a man among the defenders but prayed for the break of day and some measure of relief from the dread of this war in darkness.

With nightfall the feeling of isolation increased. There was often neither telephone nor wireless by which to communicate with adjoining positions, and attention became concentrated upon the strip of ground before your own small sector. In nearly every case this took the form of a steep slope that ended in a pool of darkness.

Out of this, records John Wright, seemed to come a commotion of Japanese voices raised in argument. Such sounds of apparent altercation amazed the hearers, and exploded the myth of the Japanese superman noiselessly sneaking up to our positions. You could almost sense a degree of confusion among the enemy as he formed up to attack. And the crump of 3-inch mortars from the Royal West Kent support company and the shells from the mountain guns sailing over to bring defensive fire restored a feeling of security that tided over the anxious defenders.

In the early morning nerves became tensed again. The Japanese trick of lobbing grenades up to our trenches usually brought forth a fusillade of small-arms fire. Whole magazines of Bren ammunition went streaming off into the dark at no particular target. As soon as order had been restored, frenzied shrieks from another quarter told that an attack was coming in elsewhere, and the commotion would again increase.

It was fortunate that our men were not short of ammunition.

Perhaps the most eventful period of an eventful and harassing twenty-four hours was this early morning. After a night of confusion and, possibly, a dawn assault, there were many tired and curious eyes peering out of trenches to observe any changes that had occurred during the night. Great boughs of trees felled by gunfire might alter the scene. Up on the hillock to your left, where earlier a fight had been seen by the light of a burning *basha*, a flow of British profanity now proclaimed to the general relief of all within earshot that they were still among friends. Though secure to your front, an air of uneasiness prevailed, until it became known how much ground, if any, had been yielded in your rear.

But, welcome though the daylight was, it was far more dangerous to move about by day than in darkness. As the trees gradually disintegrated under shell fire, so our troops became more and more exposed. And the consequent development of crawl trenches seemed to leave scarcely one patch of ground that had not been dug up.

Major P. E. M. Shaw, who lay for days among the wounded, recalls with admiration the untiring efforts of Colonel Young and his assistants, whose work was beyond praise. Young was awarded a D.S.O. for his outstanding conduct. Food was brought to the wounded by night, and in daylight Shaw had in his little trench a tin of biscuits and another of tomato soup, which when empty he used for another purpose. The wounded were kept going by the heartening tales brought round by the padre and others who could spare time to visit them. The officers, from whom pistols had been removed when they were first carried in on stretchers, insisted on having their weapons back; some, at least, had decided in the long hours and days of anxiety and fear that, if badly wounded again, they would shoot and be finished with it all. All day and all night they lay and watched and waited. They could talk to those in neighbouring trenches, they could watch the guns firing from outside Kohima, and the tanks of 2 Division some distance down the road. It often happened that those who carried food and drink round from trench to trench were sniped and killed.

Shaw has told how he tried to read a volume of Shakespeare, but could not concentrate on the reading of it. When Randolph, padre of the Royal West Kents, came to see him one day he lent him a Bible, and this Shaw found much simpler to read, against and within the turmoil and restless fury of a battle that raged ever closer from day to day. As the perimeter shrank, so the position of the wounded became more precarious. On the last day of the siege a British private fell into Shaw's trench. He apologised, when Shaw asked with magnificent patience and restraint what was the reason of this abrupt arrival. The man had come to take up a firing position, so restricted had the outer line of our defence now become.

Water and medical stores were scanty. Indeed, it was only when Colonel Young led an unarmed carrying party through the enemy lines one night to reach some trucks abandoned in the open that sufficient blankets were obtained for the wounded. Laverty was obliged to ask Brigadier Warren, with whom wireless communication remained good throughout the siege, to arrange air supply of medical stores, water, and certain types of ammunition, in particular grenades.

* * * * *

The superstition of date was justified, for April 13 became known to the garrison as "the black 13th." This title was due to three main misfortunes that befell the defenders of Kohima. They suffered more than usually heavy mortaring and sniping during daylight, and Young's medical dressing pit received two direct hits. The first supply dropping, apart from one sorely needed pannier of medical stores, was a failure. Despite frantic Very light signals from the West Kents, three entire plane-loads, including 3-inch mortar ammunition, were dropped on the enemy. The full consequences of this dismal sight—urgently needed supplies falling into enemy hands—were realized when our own troops were later bombarded with their own mortar ammunition.

And what of the third misfortune that day? After 'A' Company of the Rajputs had been reinforced at the F.S.D., an attack was put in by one platoon of the Assam Rifles. But when our men came under machine-gun fire from G.P.T. Ridge, they were forced to return before their objective was reached. As a result, the enemy was left with positions thirty-five yards from the crest of the hill, while his guns could still fire directly into our own trenches on the forward slopes. The night that followed, far from being quiet, was rent with bitter fighting. When, at the F.S.D., the Rajputs were forced from their trenches by direct hits from 75 mm. guns opposite, Major Winstanley had to send forward one platoon from his 'A' Company at Kuki Picket to save the front positions. Their place at Kuki was taken by the platoon of Assam Rifles whose attack had been broken up during the day. On 'B' Company of the West Kents the Japanese made a heavy rush attack from the D.C. Bungalow. When one of our Bren guns jammed, enemy soldiers succeeded in penetrating into the shade of a small and important hillock. Lieutenant King, the forward platoon commander, restored the situation by driving them out with grenades, but not before the Bren gunner himself had picked up a shovel and with it attacked his Japanese assailants.

Throughout April 14 the enemy continued to fire his mortars and from time to time smoke bombs landed in our positions. 'B' Company, who near Pawsey's Bungalow had repulsed yet another attack early that morning, were replaced by a company of the Assam Rifles, and took over a less active position north-west of the Hospital.

The war diary of the Royal West Kents comments here: "This was the fourth occasion on which, after statements by the relieving forces that they hoped to make contact on the morrow, hopes of relief, reinforcement, or evacuation of casualties were dashed."

As the days wore on, each one with its rumour of relief, it

became a sort of grim joke that tomorrow they really would be relieved. But tomorrow never seemed to come. 161 Brigade had so far cleared the spur running forward from Jatsoma to Ms.41. Five Brigade, led by the Cameron Highlanders, had driven back Japanese opposition at Ms.38. Next day, the 15th, when both brigades made contact, the Jatsoma neighbourhood was found to be clear of enemy troops.

Meanwhile, in Kohima itself, the defenders had spent their first night without a large-scale attack. The enemy had spent the day shelling 'A' and 'C' Companies by the F.S.D., and the fresh casualties only served to increase the terrible congestion in the dressing station. That afternoon a patrol from the 4/7th Rajputs managed to sneak into Kohima and gain touch with Laverty's headquarters. No Japanese had been seen on the way, and although the main road was still blocked, this patrol was able to return before dark.

A quiet night followed, apart from several local probing attacks and intermittent harassing fire. April 16 saw the occupation by the 1/1st Punjab (now commanded by Warren's former Brigade Major, Lieutenant-Colonel E. H. W. Grimshaw, who had taken over from Major N. M. Brodie) of unoccupied Japanese positions on what were known as Punjab Ridge and Picket Hill. At the same time, Five Brigade relieved the 1/1st Punjab in the Jatsoma box. And by the following day Cargill's 4/7th Rajputs had also been relieved by the incoming British division. Now Brigadier Warren had both his Indian battalions free to open the two miles of road between Jatsoma and Kohima.

But, meanwhile, the weary defenders had been making over-optimistic preparations for evacuating the wounded. This was due both to messages received and to observation that our troops were fighting on the main road north-west of the town. The supply drop of water, rum, grenades, and ammunition was successful, though a very difficult operation, for our pilots had now to drop the stores into an area that was only some eight hundred yards long and three hundred yards wide.

It was estimated that the Royal West Kents had so far suffered two hundred casualties, of which number forty-five had been killed. Many who were not listed as casualties had in fact received slight wounds and heavy shocks from the shelling. And a number of the less seriously wounded had returned to their companies, because the A.D.S. was already overflowing with stretcher cases.

That night, April 16/17, was particularly dark, foggy, and wet. The Japanese took advantage of the weather and attacked from Pawsey's Bungalow. At first their efforts were in vain, but towards morning heavy pressure brought the enemy troops towards the top of F.S.D. Hill, thus gaining some ground that the defenders could ill spare. Having had no water with which to wash or shave since April 5, and an almost negligible amount of sleep or rest, they were extremely weary. But 'A' and 'C' Companies at the F.S.D. were, on the 17th, relieved by the Assam Rifles, who were able to retake a few trenches both in this area and near the Bungalow. 'A' Company returned to its original positions just south of Summerhouse Hill, which by now could scarcely be called a rest area. Although not subject to direct enemy pressure, it had for some days past been under as heavy fire as anywhere else in Kohima.

The thirteenth night of the siege brought further disasters upon the garrison. The enemy put down a concentrated barrage on F.S.D. Hill. Our exhausted troops holding this feature drew back. The Japanese were not slow to exploit this withdrawal, though only in small numbers. Our troops could not be rallied to make a counter-attack, and 'D' Company of the West Kents, at Kuki Picket near by, peering into the darkness, began to be affected by the confusion of their neighbours. The Company Commander was wounded, and C.S.M. Staines, M.M., who had already been blinded in the fighting but had refused to go back for treatment, was killed. As a result, 'D' Company was forced under pressure to draw back. And many good men were lost in this onslaught. One could hear the yelling Japanese, the screams of the wounded and dying. And our wounded men lying in darkness on Summerhouse Hill must have wondered whether the enemy, successful at last, would try to carry the main hill that night. It was fortunate that this time the enemy, though less than one hundred yards from Summerhouse Hill and Laverty's command post, failed to exploit his success. Doubtless the stout resistance by the remnants of 'C' and 'D' Companies and the defensive fire brought down on our abandoned positions by 24 Mountain Regiment had inflicted severe casualties.

April 18 was the last day of the siege of Kohima. Grimshaw's

1/1st Punjab, supported by tanks, cleared the road up to 53 Indian General Hospital, and joined the garrison.

It was about ten o'clock in the morning that Major Ware's company filed up from the road, picking its way through the dead of three nations. "We must," records Easten, "have presented a strange spectacle. Bearded, filthy men with glazed eyes, who had not slept for fourteen days—we all slept a little, I suppose, but mainly standing up. Wounded, with filthy bandages and pale, grey faces, and weak but cheerful grins. The entire hillside was pockmarked with trenches, the trees shattered by shell fire and festooned with parachutes."

But however strange, the siege was over, the isolation relieved, new strength added to the dwindling, weary garrison. And the old comradeship between British and Indian soldier was heartening; the battered hillside rang with shouts of "Shahbash, Royal West Kents!" from the Punjabis, and "Good old Johnnie, everything teak hi now, eh!" from the British.

Over three hundred wounded and some two thousand non-combatant troops were evacuated. Enemy snipers were active throughout the day; and during the evacuation of our wounded still further casualties were caused by enemy mortar and shell fire directed at the ambulances. Colonels Laverty and Grimshaw made readjustments in the shrunken, overcrowded perimeter, and the 1/1st took up positions on Hospital Ridge.

More non-combatants, and the Shere Regiment, were evacuated next day. The supply dropping on a now tiny plot of scarred ground continued to be accurate, though several men were struck when certain packages dropped either without a parachute or with an unopened one.

During the night of April 19 two enemy attacks from near the Bungalow, supported by grenade-discharger fire, had to be repulsed, and in these engagements two company commanders (Captains Smith and Koath) were wounded. Then, on April 20, the 4th Royal West Kents and attached troops, still in good heart though utterly battle-weary, were relieved by the 1st Royal Berkshire Regiment and driven back to Dimapur. Since April 5 they had successfully resisted no less than twenty-five major Japanese attacks, during which more than 250 enemy soldiers were seen to be killed. Sixty-one members of the battalion had been killed in action, thirteen were missing, and 125 had been wounded.

Well might Donald Easten write this passage years afterwards, when the memories had begun to fade and the scene to grow blurred: "But the greatest honours are due to Tommy Atkins. He had fought for six months in Arakan, they had flown him to Dimapur, marched him up to Kohima, marched him back again. Then back once more to Kohima, where he was shot at as he got out of his trucks. He fought hand-to-hand battles practically every night, and his pals were shot down all round him. If he was wounded, he had no hope of evacuation. Day after day he was promised relief which never came; and his platoon, or section, or just 'gang' got smaller and smaller. My own company finished up twenty-five strong; one platoon consisted of a single grinning private, who asked if he could put a pip up. And Tommy Atkins did all that on half a mug of liquid every twenty-four hours."

CHAPTER XXIV

IMPHAL

MARCH—JULY 1944

FLYING into Imphal from any direction you pass over mile after mile of rolling green hills, along whose crests and wooded flanks brown pathways wind like serpents. Hardly a village is seen. Then, suddenly, these hills fall away steeply, "running down into the flat brown and yellow plain of paddy fields and swampy lakes like cliffs into the sea."

At the end of March the encircling hills, having a colour of green and terracotta, clashed sharply with the greys and buffs of the parched plain, where the earth crumbled for want of rain. To dig gun-pits and trenches into the paddy fields was like cutting into iron. But the monsoon was not far distant, and then the dust of the tracks would be changed into mud, and the dry waterways into coursing torrents.

Imphal looked a small town to the troops who, in lorries or on foot, hurried through its blossomed avenues. The town, in reality a series of adjoining villages, has its houses of stone and white plaster, and its wooden thatched huts, surrounded or sub-divided by bamboo clumps. Further out, the small, rectangular villages are enclosed in bamboo hedges, with dusty tracks running through the middle.

The inhabitants of this capital of Manipur State, with its own maharajah, presented a contrast to the people of Arakan, for they wore clean white shirts instead of the coloured *longyi*, and could afford bicycles and wrist watches. As the Japanese invaders drew nearer, the bullock carts that hitherto had creaked slowly along the roads carrying loads of grain or wool were now turned to a different work. Refugees from the outer villages came into the centre of the plain. And their carts were piled high with household goods, with mattresses and wooden bedsteads, with furniture and cooking pots.

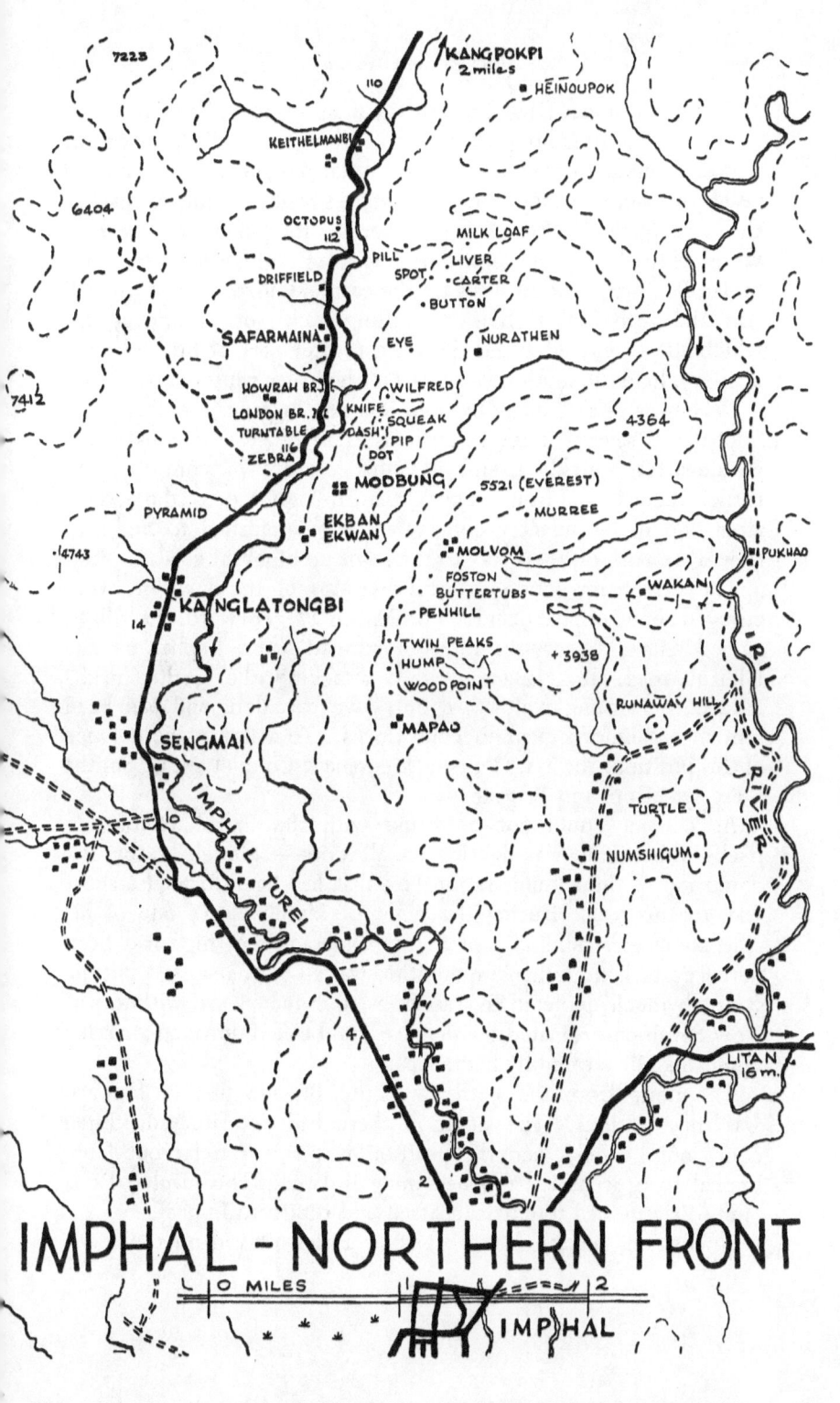

The 17th Indian Division was still fighting its way north up the road from Tiddim, along which it had with great skill staved off the constant threat of encirclement and total destruction. To help it reach our outer defence line a few miles south of Imphal, part of the 23rd Indian Division was sent across, the oncoming Japanese were stopped, and our positions stabilized. This done, the 23rd Indian Division took up posts on the east and north-east of Imphal. And the 20th Indian Division, pulling back from Tamu, against which the enemy advanced with the greater part of his tanks and artillery, held the south-eastern part of the front, centred upon Palel.

When the Fifth Indian Division, less 161 Brigade, first arrived in Imphal, on several different airfields, staff officers of Four Corps Headquarters quickly assembled units company by company, and rushed them to the front. One Commanding Officer, who arrived after two of his infantry companies, was astonished to find that they were both on their way to the front up different roads.

The first main action in which troops of the Division were engaged about Imphal occurred on March 22. Forward of a village named Litan, twenty-six miles north-east from Imphal on the Ukhrul road, the Japanese were attacking the 50th Gurkha Parachute Brigade, which had only two battalions and had been sent in as reinforcement to Four Corps. To assist in the defence of this position, the 2/1st Punjab (Lieutenant-Colonel W. G. Smith) were sent from 123 Brigade.

As contact could not be made with the Parachute Brigade itself—the enemy was fighting on all sides—Colonel Smith took command of the administration box that had been formed a short way to the rear. During the night of March 24-25 one of his rifle companies holding a peak four thousand feet high had been fiercely attacked. When ammunition was all but exhausted and the strength much depleted by casualties, our men were withdrawn. Now Smith co-ordinated the defences, and called down an airstrike upon this hill vacated by his troops.

The news from the 50th Parachute Brigade further forward was most serious. The situation there had deteriorated. Litan could not be held, and the position was now too far out from Imphal to prevent it from becoming isolated. The mauled Parachute Brigade had to extricate itself and return to Imphal.

And when, on the 26th, Brigadier Evans arrived on the scene

with his two other battalion commanders, it was decided that all the troops of 123 Brigade should be withdrawn by the next morning. The 2/1st Punjab covered the retiring administration troops, from the slopes of a peak half a mile west of Litan. Here only two of Colonel Smith's companies were properly dug in; the other companies had been obliged to move after setting fire to such stores as could not be evacuated. And at eight o'clock the enemy attacked.

Now began one of the most nerve-racking nights in the battalion's history. 'C' Company, on a small hill five hundred yards from Smith's headquarters, was attacked by a battalion of Japanese troops. Without a break the battle raged through the night. Part of the company was overrun. Hand-to-hand fighting was of the most ferocious. But the enemy was repulsed. The Company Commander, Major J. Walker, was killed at midnight while directing a precarious defence, and Subadar Walayat Khan took charge. Above the noise of battle his voice could be heard encouraging the men as they drove off one assault after another. He urged them on to kill the enemy troops, who rushed forward without regard for casualties. And with their war cry he led them, until after three hours' stern fighting this brave man, covered with wounds, was obliged to hand over command to another V.C.O. Walayat Khan's gallantry during this critical night was recognized by the award of the Indian Order of Merit.

Though our men held out until daybreak, only six of the fifty who had started the fight remained unwounded. Why the Japanese did not advance down the hill to one side of 'C' Company is not known. Had they done so, Smith's battalion headquarters could scarcely have avoided annihilation. For the men were not dug in; they were dispersed on the slopes. It says much for the fire control of the sepoys that not one shot was fired by headquarters company that night, for all the intense provocation and imminent danger.

It was a tired and shaken battalion that withdrew in the morning through the positions of the 2nd Suffolks and settled into a village eight miles out of Imphal.

* * * * *

During the next two weeks the three battalions of 123 Brigade patrolled the villages east and north-east of Imphal. Their efforts were directed towards cutting the Japanese supply routes up and down the valleys that skirted the Imphal plain, and daily our patrols fought engagements with groups of enemy soldiers. When local villagers reported the presence of Japanese looting parties, the Royal Air Force and Gunners bombarded the place. It was a battle for the lines of communication, upon which the enemy depended so much for his ability to hold out upon the hills which he captured and to maintain the impetus of his invasion, the opening phases of which had been so abundantly successful. Long reconnaissance patrols were sent out for several days at a time to search for the enemy. Raiding parties attacked villages from which the enemy was known to take food by night. Ammunition dumps were bombed and mule convoys strafed.

But although our men gained the upper hand in these small brushes with the Japanese, and inflicted considerable losses upon them both in human lives and in war material, the enemy continued to make progress towards Imphal. And to arrest his advance meant full-scale battles that involved a battalion or more in action. The first of these battles occurred on the Imphal–Kohima road, fifteen miles north of the Manipur capital at a village named Kanglatongbi. By cutting this road, the Japanese had encircled Imphal. The town set in its plain was now besieged. All supplies had to be flown in to the airstrip, near which Four Corps Headquarters had formed the 'Keep,' a defensive box based upon a group of hillocks in the centre that stretched southwards into the plain to within a mile of Imphal. In order to cut down the strength of the garrison and, thereby, the rations needed each day, 50,000 non-combatant troops had either been evacuated before the road was cut, or were now sent out in returning aircraft.

At Kanglatongbi, spread over a considerable area, Four Corps had an Ordnance Dump and Reinforcement Camp. On the night of April 4/5 the Japanese penetrated the area. All the troops from our administration units had been withdrawn into what was known as 'Lion' Box, a mile farther south. The occupants of this box numbered some 12,000 men, of whom the only real fighting units were two Sapper Field Companies and a company of the Assam Rifles.

When the Japanese first attacked astride this main road from the north, Salomons' Nine Brigade was still in reserve. Its task had been to destroy any Japanese who succeeded in penetrating through or round 123 Brigade. The 3/9th Jats and 3/14th Punjab had patrolled with vigour to find out the routes of any enemy enveloping moves, and to anticipate the enemy on any vital hill that covered these routes. But to counter this new threat the 2nd West Yorkshires, supported by one squadron of the 3rd Dragoon Guards with Lee tanks, were at once ordered out to the village of Sengmai, a mile south of Lion Box. The battalion formed a firm base here, and had orders to ensure that the box was not overrun during daylight and that no enemy parties advanced any farther south. On April 5 and 6 West Yorkshire platoons, accompanied by tanks, patrolled forward to Lion Box, dealt with any groups of Japanese troops who had penetrated our defences during the previous night, and mopped up all resistance that remained, before returning to Sengmai at dusk.

Then, on the morning of April 7, strong enemy parties were reported to have entered the box. So Colonel Cree sent one platoon and tanks to evict the Japanese. But, at nine o'clock, the evacuation of Lion Box was ordered. And the task of Cree's West Yorkshires became that of covering this evacuation. Accordingly, the battalion moved forward to positions inside the box. At noon the withdrawal started. The troops marched back along the road into the centre of Imphal, while convoys of lorries were sent up to Kanglatongbi to bring back some of the more important stores from our dumps there. During this evacuation, the enemy shelled the place with a 75 mm. gun. And it was during this bombardment that the A/Q of the Division, Lieutenant-Colonel Norman Maclaurin, was killed while trying to disentangle a traffic block near Kanglatongbi. He had been with the Division for eighteen months, since the days of Quetta Camp outside Baghdad. He was a delightful personality, of varied talents, for besides being a good caricaturist, he was an expert at Scottish dances, and a piper of merit. In rest areas he could be seen walking up and down outside his tent, playing his pipes. And, fittingly, a piper from the nearby Seaforth Highlanders came over to pipe a lament at his funeral.

After much insistence on the part of General Briggs, the vacant post was filled by Maclaurin's deputy, Major T. C. W. Roe, one of the most prominent and veteran members of Divisional Headquarters.

*   *   *   *   *

The second main battle in which the Division was involved

during April was on the slopes and summit of Numshigum. This, one of the most vital hills north of Imphal, was a sprawling feature that butted far into the plain. Its green ridge extended over some seven thousand yards, its highest part rose to 3,800 feet high, and the hill overtopped the surrounding paddy fields by more than a thousand feet.

So committed were Colonel Gerty's 3/9th Jats already across part of our northern front that the only troops available for holding Numshigum were a platoon from his 'B' Company and the Jat guerilla platoon. Of these men a number were newly joined recruits, and of automatic weapons the force had but three. To reach the summit meant a climb of an hour and a half up steep grassy slopes, and when Lieutenant Sain and his men did arrive on top they had little enough time to dig and wire a defence position before darkness fell upon the plain and its encircling hills.

At three o'clock in the morning of April 7 the Japanese sent two companies to attack Numshigum from the north. They chose a time when strong wind and a rainstorm had reduced visibility to a few yards and when the sounds of approaching troops would be covered by the weather's violence. The brunt of this strong attack was borne by the platoon of 'B' Company. The havildar was killed early in the engagement. By half past six the Jats had suffered twenty-four casualties. The position on Numshigum was menaced from all sides by the enemy's superior strength and fire power, and permission was given by Colonel Gerty for the survivors of his two platoons to withdraw from the hilltop. Particular gallantry in this night action was displayed by Havildar Munshi Ram, who, when his platoon commander was killed, went forward to encourage his men. A grenade shattered his hand. He was badly wounded in the foot. And in darkness he was left for dead on the summit. Later that day Munshi Ram survived an airstrike when Hurribombers bombed and strafed the Japanese on Numshigum, but even then his misfortunes were not ended. The Japanese threw him down the hillside. Nevertheless, though weak from loss of blood and shock, this havildar struggled into Gerty's headquarters down beside the road. There he died from his wounds soon afterwards. He was posthumously awarded the Indian Order of Merit.

That Numshigum be recaptured, and with all speed, was

imperative, for there was not one good defensive position between this hill and Imphal itself. Colonel Gerty sent 'A' Company (Major Risal Singh) and the hill was taken, with surprisingly light opposition. The enemy had found the cost of his night attacks so high that he withdrew without offering his usual tenacious resistance. And his counter-attacks that night were easily repulsed.

During April 8 and 9 the enemy made several half-hearted assaults against the Jats, and on the night of the 9th his efforts, though most determined and supported by five machine-guns, served him nothing. An entire battalion was used in these attempts to oust the Jats. It later transpired from a captured diary that the death of four Japanese officers in the early attacks had so incensed the remaining officers that they had determined to avenge their deaths whatever the cost.

The following night 'A' Company were harassed by machine-guns that worked steadily nearer to our positions. When at first light a Japanese 75 mm. gun fired a heavy concentration upon the Jat company, three of our Bren guns were struck. This was a serious loss. And its gravity was felt when, taking advantage of artillery fire, the enemy soldiers moved round the flanks with machine-guns and launched a fierce attack that was pressed forward regardless of casualties. By seven o'clock our forward platoons had been overrun. Ammunition was down to the last few rounds. The company had thirty casualties. And 'D' Company, then on its way up the hillside to reinforce the position, was still some way from the summit. Our men had neither strength nor weapons to keep back the pressure long enough to give time for this hurrying relief to arrive. And so permission had to be given for the mauled 'A' Company to retire from Numshigum, leaving this vital hill a second time in enemy hands.

But the enemy could not be allowed to remain on this dominant ridge. No effort to drive him back must be spared. The threat to our northern front of his presence on this buttress was too grave to be tolerated. Accordingly, Colonel Gerty sent in his 'B' and 'C' Companies, after an inaccurate airstrike and an effective artillery concentration. The plan was for two platoons of 'B' Company under Major G. R. Sell to form base some three hundred feet from the top, while the third platoon secured a knob a short way farther south, in order to prevent enemy flanking fire from that direction.

Then, as soon as 'B' Company was firmly established, Sell's men would pass through to capture Numshigum itself.

There was no cover save a few foxholes. 'B' Company was soon pinned down by heavy fire. The one platoon failed to capture the knob, its commander was wounded, and our artillery could not reach the enemy machine-guns, so well sited were they. Major Graham Sell was killed early on. So was his subadar. When, at 1.30 p.m., it became evident that both companies were losing men to no advantage, and that our attack could not make progress, Gerty brought his men back, after a morning of stern fighting and severe loss. During the withdrawal a party of stretcher-bearers was left behind, trying to evacuate a wounded Jat. For a time this was rendered impossible by Japanese machine-guns, but when, later that afternoon, our aircraft bombed and strafed Numshigum—it was believed that the hill was clear of our men—the naik in charge, Yakub, took advantage of the noise and confusion. Seeing that the enemy had gone to ground, he lifted the wounded soldier on to a stretcher, and had him carried down. He buried two other Jats, and was not molested by the cowering Japanese. Naik Yakub was decorated with the Military Medal for this coolness and presence of mind.

Another day had passed. The Japanese still held the commanding heights. Many good men had been lost in a strong attempt to recapture the summit. The Jats could do no more. The battalion had suffered heavily, and something more powerful than an infantry battalion was evidently required to defeat the Japanese. Accordingly, General Briggs ordered Evans' 123 Brigade to assault Numshigum on April 13. Selected for this assault were the 1/17th Dogras, commanded by Lieutenant-Colonel E. G. Woods, who had served as Brigade Major to Messervy with Nine Brigade in Eritrea, three years before.

In the middle of the 13th morning three squadrons of Hurricanes swooped down upon Numshigum. One by one each aircraft dropped its two bombs, rose again, circled, and entered the smoking lists a second time to spray the Japanese positions on the summit with fire. From the centre of Imphal plain came the thudding of many guns, as the Divisional artillery, aided by a medium regiment, pounded Numshigum with shells that landed amid the pall of buff smoke that swathed the crest. Meanwhile, in the hot sunshine two Dogra companies, one up each of the two main spurs that led to the summit from the east side, had set off, supported by two squadrons of 30-ton Lee tanks from the 3rd Carabiniers. No one knew whether the tanks would be able to climb the very steep gradients. This had never been tried before.

Colonel Woods directed that whichever company with its tanks reached the junction of the two spurs first would be given further orders on arrival. All communication was by wireless. Both companies, commanded by Majors Hugh Alden and L. H. Jones, reached the junction at almost the same time and unmolested by the Japanese, who were momentarily stunned by the shattering weight of shell and bomb brought down by our Gunners and the Royal Air Force. But from this moment the attack became stiff. While the tanks, which had climbed up like big, slow, black beetles, balanced themselves on knife-edge ridges and pumped bullets and shells into every Japanese man and bunker that could be seen, the agile Dogras protected the tanks from interference. And under the armoured cover they assaulted the Japanese trenches and bunkers. The struggle flickered from bunker to bunker. If the successful co-operation between tanks and infantry imbued the Dogras with a sense of invincibility, yet their substantial gains were not won except at a price. Every single officer in that attack was killed or wounded. Jones was wounded, and then a second time in the chest. He was carried away all but unconscious. Alden was also wounded in the chest while directing operations beside a tank. And all Carabinier officers were killed by snipers, as they looked from their turrets to direct the battle. They were unable to close down because the ground was so incredibly difficult, and the position of the tanks so perilous and unusual.

The last half-hour of the fight was ordered by C.S.M. Craddock of the Carabiniers and Subadars Ranbir Singh and Tiru. Between these gallant men language was allowed to present no problem. They continued the fight until no enemy troops remained upon the main Numshigum feature. Craddock won the Distinguished Conduct Medal, Subadar Tiru the I.O.M. Both company commanders were awarded the Military Cross, and to Colonel Woods went a D.S.O.

By nightfall the two companies were dug and wired in. The tanks of the Carabiniers rumbled down the hill again, taking the Dogra wounded. When that night the Japanese counter-attacked in force, from Turtle farther north along the ridge (so called because of its contour shape), our artillery brought down such effective defensive fire upon our barbed wire that the disillusioned enemy was mauled and repulsed. His attack was decisively trounced.

These Dogras come from the foothills of the Himalayas, from Kangra and Jammu. Here, poor but industrious yeoman farmers that they are, they scrape a livelihood from their terraced hillsides. Geographical remoteness has made their education problematic and therefore backward, and they are conservative in their nature. But across the centuries their position among the foothills kept them isolated from the invasions and wars of the Punjab plains. It also kept them from adopting the Moslem religion common to the inhabitants of the Punjab, and in their beliefs they are Hindus. Of their Rajput origin they are intensely proud, and in their own country, if asked, they say that they are Rajput, not Dogra. To them this means membership of an untarnished military chivalry.

In their loyalty and reliability they have few equals. Though small of stature, they are wiry and their stamina and powers of physical endurance remarkable. Shy, in a childlike fashion, they respond at once to courteous treatment, but are quick to resent any attempt at bullying. They are charming little men, staunch, quiet, gallant fighters. And their natural good manners and bearing led their British officers, in more emotional moments, to refer to the "Gentlemen of the Dogra Regiment."

In their hills of the Kangra Valley, Dogras are accustomed to wear little caps, woven by their women in complex patterns of coloured dicings on a white background. When the 1st Battalion was sent to Arakan for the first campaign, their ordinary forage caps could not be supplied. Having no *pagris*, and in need of an alternative to the steel helmet, the Dogras had their Regimental Depot at Jullundur produce these *chesi topis* in khaki. The men, and the officers too, began to wear them and, when official disapproval was expressed, became proud of their unauthorized headgear.

The 3/14th Punjab took over from the Dogras on Numshigum, and Nine Brigade prepared a further assault to drive the enemy from Turtle and the rest of the feature. But the Japanese withdrew. Had they not done so, another attack was to have been made, this time by the 2nd West Yorkshires, from the west up two long spurs that led up to Numshigum and Turtle. This operation was planned but never executed. Instead, the battalion continued its patrolling across country, the very openness of which made this a difficult task. But when our patrols found that two important hills were unoccupied by the Japanese—Point 3938, and Runaway Hill, a very steep little feature guarding the road that ran up the left-hand side of the Numshigum massif—both were occupied by the 3/9th Jats.

It was by Runaway Hill that the Division's third Victoria Cross was won. Before dawn on April 6, during this original encircling movement, at a time when we could not be sure when they would appear next, the Japanese attacked one of Colonel Gerty's standing patrols. By driving the Jats off, they secured a hillock that overlooked the main company position. Jemadar Abdul Hafiz was ordered to recapture the hill with two sections of his platoon. After an artillery bombardment by Bastin's 4th Field Regiment, Abdul Hafiz led his Jats in to the attack. They charged up the hillside that was bare of cover, shouting their war-cry as they neared the top. Then the waiting Japanese opened fire with machine-guns. On the approaching Jats they threw down grenades. Jemadar Abdul Hafiz was wounded at the outset. A bullet struck him in the leg. Yet he dashed forward and seized the enemy machine-gun by the barrel, while another Jat killed the Japanese gunner.

The jemadar then took up a Bren gun dropped by one of his men who had fallen wounded, and notwithstanding the heavy fire from the enemy positions on this hill and on a feature to the flank, he shot a number of the Japanese soldiers. And so fiercely did he lead his men that the enemy ran away: hence the name Runaway Hill. But Jemadar Abdul Hafiz was mortally wounded in the chest, still grasping his Bren gun. To his men he shouted in his own language, "Reorganize! I will give you covering fire." But he died, without having been able to pull the trigger. He was awarded the Victoria Cross, posthumously, and was the first Muslim soldier to win this decoration in the Second World War.

* * * * *

Already before his assault upon Numshigum, the enemy had been active in the Iril Valley, that ran from north to south down the right-hand side of Imphal town itself. He had occupied the principal massif north of the plain, a range that was higher than Numshigum, though less dangerously close to Imphal. This expansive range stretched, as far as the enemy's hold upon its peaks was concerned, from the village of Mapao in the south, with its white-painted American Baptist Mission church standing out as a distinctive landmark, northwards to Molvom, by way of a series of humps and crests nicknamed Hump, Twin Peaks, Foston, Penhill, and Buttertubs. Parts of this ridge soared to a height of five thousand feet above the sea and half that altitude above the plain itself.

It was at first thought that the Japanese had also seized a feature called Wakan, lying between Molvom and Numshigum, but when a platoon of the West Yorkshires, followed by two companies, moved up the long climb to the top, they reported Wakan unoccupied. Cree's battalion established itself there.

On April 21 an operation order was issued from Divisional Headquarters, instructing Nine Brigade to secure positions on the Mapao–Molvom ridge two days later. On the left, the 3/9th Jats were to capture a saddle and a small hump called Wood Point, both a short distance north of Mapao. On the right the West Yorkshires were to take Foston and Penhill. Brigadier Salomons launched the attack on April 23. After Hurricanes had bombed and strafed Mapao, and the guns of the 4th Field Regiment had added to the pall of smoke and dust, the 3/14th Punjab fought their way into Mapao, and the Jats wound their way up the steep hillside to the saddle, and attacked south along the ridge towards Mapao Village. The operation succeeded on that side, but the West Yorkshires were unable to gain a footing on their higher and more precipitous range of hills.

The beginning of May found Nine Brigade doing its utmost to clear the tenacious Japanese from the ridge between Mapao and Point 4364, a distance of six miles by the flight of an aircraft, but infinitely farther when each hump and crest is followed from one peak to the next. While the 2nd West Yorkshires were to hold a firm base on Wakan hill and send out fighting patrols to assail the precipitous heights of Penhill and Foston, Furney's 3/14th Punjab were, with a company of the 15/11th Sikhs under command, to attack the enemy troops holding Hump and Twin Peaks.

During this period 89 Brigade, which had recently arrived in Imphal and was now under General Briggs' command, would hold Sengmai, and clear the area of Kanglatongbi and Ekban Ekwan. And Evans' 123 Brigade would operate from a firm base held by the Dogras far up the Iril Valley. The 3/2nd Punjab would patrol north and west, and the 2nd Suffolks would send patrols to Nurathen and to Modbung, always on the alert for any change in the enemy's dispositions, constantly seeking to disrupt his lines of supply by ambushing a mule convoy or destroying a stores dump or attacking a group of enemy soldiers. Villages where the Japanese habitually obtained food were raided. A *basha* in which some enemy soldiers were sleeping was shot up, and heavy casualties inflicted. In the course of these small raids and pinprick tactics, our troops inflicted upon the enemy more loss than we ourselves incurred.

But the main battles during the first part of May were carried out by the battalions of Nine Brigade. And no obstacle was more difficult to overcome, no hill was more fiercely defended by the Japanese, than Hump, which faced the 3/14th Punjab as it looked north from Mapao and Wood Point. Before the month was out, this battalion had attacked Hump no less than seven times, and had sent patrols to test the defences on many other occasions. It was a corner slope, and refused to yield, for all the effort, bravery, and loss of life. Soon Hump stood out as a landmark on account of its bare face. Every wisp of greenery was churned and burnt away by the shells and bombs that landed on that small piece of hillside day after day, and often at night, when our Gunners were shooting harassing fire at the stubborn enemy.

On May 2 Hump was attacked by two platoons, but the enemy threw grenades and opened fire as our sepoys approached the top. Colonel Furney withdrew the platoons. Two days later repeated attacks were launched, but all in vain. One platoon was counterattacked by the Japanese when only ten yards from the summit. It was estimated that the enemy was holding this feature with at least three platoons, armed with a high proportion of automatic weapons. And by the 5th, when the 3/14th attacked yet again, the defenders of Hump had been reinforced, for the opposition was stiffer than ever.

The situation was serious. Nine Brigade was making no progress, and whatever the total of casualties inflicted upon the Japanese, our own casualties were mounting. It was decided that on May 20 Furney's battalion should attack in strength, and to assist the building up of supplies for this operation, Salomons had a jeep track built by 20 Field Company up the face of the hill to just below Mapao.

But the attack on the 20th was no more successful than its predecessors. Though one platoon did reach the top, it was forced to withdraw by grenade-charger fire from the reverse slopes. On May 22 four platoons reached the crest of Hump, after killing the occupants of at least six pillboxes, and our men remained on the top for twenty-five minutes, lobbing grenades into Japanese trenches and bunker positions. But eventually we were forced off owing to a strong fusillade and showers of grenades from entrenched positions, as before on the reverse slopes. These were the slopes that our Gunners found all but impossible to hit, and the bombing and strafing by Hurricanes was disappointing in its results. On the 24th the ridge between Everest and Hump was strafed five times by our aircraft, but when patrols toiled up next morning, the enemy proved himself to be still in very resolute possession of his points of vantage. Attempts to gain a footing on the ridge between Hump and Twin Peaks and then to attack Hump downhill from the opposite direction, the east, also failed.

At the end of May the Japanese defenders were still on top, having endured a tremendous weight of shell and bomb and mortar fire. A prisoner reported that the company holding the ridge was reduced to seventy men, and that food and ammunition were running low. Given almost no respite by our Gunners, constantly harassed, almost isolated from their fellows, often swathed in damp clouds, sometimes wet from the early rains, these fanatics hung on to their solidly constructed bunkers, and kept at bay our every jab, pinprick, and full-scale onslaught. The monsoon broke in earnest on the 27th, and rain fell almost without a break for forty-eight hours, turning every track into a morass, making slippery every hillside path, and flooding many of the paddy fields.

The 2nd West Yorkshires had, during the first week of May, made attempts to gain a footing on the ridge between Twin Peaks and Molvom. Patrolling had disclosed that the enemy held all spurs running down from the ridge. Two efforts were made to secure a feature christened with the Yorkshire name of Buttertubs.

On the first occasion the British troops were forced off the summit by machine-guns cleverly sited on reverse slopes and in the long grass. The second attempt was made by two companies, the one attacking Buttertubs direct, the other marching farther up the valley and climbing to attack from the north near Molvom. The latter company was delayed by the extremely difficult nature of the ground, and had to advance in daylight, instead of under the cloak of the hour before daybreak. When nearing Molvom the men were engaged by machine-guns and grenade dischargers both from Buttertubs and another Japanese position to the north. All officers and the company sergeant-major were killed or wounded. And Colonel Cree had to withdraw the company. Major C. O'Hara, soon to be awarded the D.S.O. for his fine leadership throughout the campaigns in Arakan and Imphal, was wounded in the jaw and evacuated to hospital.

On May 5 a third attempt was made, but although one platoon of 'D' Company did reach its objective on top of Buttertubs, and beat off a small counter-attack, its strength was by this time so reduced by casualties that it was unable to consolidate the ground won.

Meanwhile, the 3/9th Jats had been sent up the Iril Valley with the purpose of attacking the enemy's line of communication in the Nurathen area. But the plan was changed, and the battalion ordered to capture Point 4364. As, on the morning of April 30, this hill was captured without opposition, Colonel Gerty was now instructed to capture the Molvom ridge from the north, and so to help the 3/14th Punjab in their battle for Hump, and the West Yorkshires' efforts to gain a foothold on Twin Peaks and the main ridge.

The Jats had two main objectives: first Murree, a hill named after the famous leave station above Rawalpindi, and then Everest, 5,521 feet, the highest peak attacked by troops of the Division since leaving Amba Alagi three years before. In moonlight two companies of Jats moved into thick cover on the eastern slopes of Murree. At 7 a.m. on May 4, after an artillery concentration, 'A' and 'D' Companies attacked. The lower slopes were quickly taken. While 'A' Company consolidated, 'D' Company climbed farther up towards the main crest. Japanese snipers and medium machine-guns were outflanked, and the position taken. Then Colonel Gerty sent forward Major S. Lambert's 'C' Company to take Everest, four hundred feet higher than Murree, and lying nine hundred yards to the south-west. After nightfall Lambert's men crept to within half that distance, ready for the morning's attack.

Early on May 5 the Company attacked by two routes. The leading section on the left hand was held up very soon after starting. Machine-guns and grenades made it seemingly impossible for any man to go forward alive. But the right-hand platoon did climb to within twenty yards of the summit. The main opposition came from grenades thrown from trenches ten yards away. Every time the Jats charged up the slope they were driven back by these hand grenades and by flanking machine-guns. Meanwhile, grenade-discharger shells had burst in Lambert's headquarters, and the wireless set belonging to the Gunner F.O.O. had been blown down the hill. The aerial was blown off the small company wireless set, but this was repaired. Major Lambert now committed his reserve platoon on the right side, where the Jats had made least progress. Here the jungle was extremely thick.

Lambert walked forward to examine the situation. As he neared one of his forward platoons, a hand grenade burst directly on him. He was instantly killed.

And at this point, when Lambert's company had already had forty-seven casualties, Brigadier Salomons stopped all further attacks, and 'C' Company was withdrawn from the slopes of Everest.

Nor was this line of attack pursued. Instead, two of Gerty's companies remained to hold Murree and Point 4364, while the rest of the battalion moved across to Nine Brigade's firm base on Wakan, and here relieved the West Yorkshires, who moved into reserve by Runaway Hill. The Jats remained here three weeks, operating against the enemy in the Everest–Penhill area, and patrolling Japanese cookhouses, water points, rest areas, and all approaches to the Molvom ridge. One notable exploit was the destruction by a platoon of sixty maunds of rice, a serious loss to the rice-eating Japanese troops, who were already hard put to it to slip food and ammunition through our screen and carry it up to the hilltops. As 123 Brigade was now switched across to the main road by Sengmai and Kanglatongbi, to join 89 Brigade, General Briggs entrusted to Nine Brigade the task of denying to the enemy

Dogra Stretcher-Bearers below Numshigum (C.I.S. Historical Section)

Milestone 109 on the Kohima–Imphal Road: Major-General Grover, Brigadier Salomons, Lieut.-General Stopford, Brigadier Smith (C.I.S. Historical Section)

CROSSING THE FRONTIER (C.I.S. Historical Section)

MUD ON THE TIDDIM ROAD (Imperial War Museum)

all use of the Iril River as an L. of C., and of holding the ground vacated by 123 Brigade.

*   *   *   *   *

This Imphal battle was a prolonged fight against an enemy who approached from every side. The green plain must be held. The Japanese must be driven from the hills that had been lost or never defended during the initial onslaught. No hill that dominated the plain, no ridge or crest from which the enemy could threaten still further our very existence in Imphal, could be left in his hands. One hill after another was attacked by our aircraft, guns, and infantry. Time and again our leading platoons were forced back from the summit by withering machine-gun fire from well-concealed bunkers. The Japanese troops endured the bombardments and constant harassing fire with a fortitude born of fanaticism. When our men lost a hilltop, this had to be recaptured without delay. And patrols and columns were sent up and down the valleys that ran round the foot of these hills, in order to cut the Japanese supply routes and so to starve out the defenders on high.

These were weeks of failure and success, of slogging effort, often severe casualties, and infectious disappointment. But slowly the tide turned against the enemy. Gradually his grip upon the framework to the plain was broken, for all his tenacity and aggression. All this time the 17th, 20th, and 23rd Indian Divisions were fighting south and east of Imphal. Their battles were of the fiercest and most bloody nature. Brigades and battalions were switched from one part of the front to another, depending on any new Japanese threat that had to be smothered, or on a counter-offensive planned by our own commanders.

Every section, company, and battery within the Division was working at full stretch. The Gunners, under the C.R.A., Brigadier Mansergh, dug their gunpits out in the open paddy fields, or in small re-entrants among the hills. And they fired day and night on targets that varied frequently, but were most often on summits. At night the flash of the guns slashed the darkness that lay across the Imphal plain. The thumping and the more distant explosions echoed round the hillsides.

The Divisional Sappers, now commanded by Lieutenant-Colonel E. C. R. Stileman, were hard pressed with the varied tasks laid upon them. Greatest of these was the construction of jeep tracks up the sides of certain hills. These tracks were needed to take supplies and ammunition to the fighting troops—on a scale impracticable with mulesal one—and to bring back on stretchers men who had been wounded in battle. The building of such tracks was a formidable task, involving rock blasting and the most skilful use of bulldozers. Culverts and drainage systems were required, and places where two jeeps could pass. Water storage cisterns, tarpaulin water tanks, water points and pumping equipment, bridges, tank routes—all these had to be built, strengthened, improved. There were mines and booby traps to render harmless and remove. Many of the tracks used by the mules were inadequate and needed constant repair. The resources of the three Field Companies and 44 Field Park Company (Major M. Keating) were taxed to their limit even in dry weather. But when the monsoon came the work was delayed and became far more difficult to achieve.

For Divisional Signals it was much the same. Problems faced their commander, Lieutenant-Colonel E. J. C. Harrison, and had always to be overcome. The fact that so many battles were fought on the hilltops meant telephone lines of unusual length, and supplies of cable almost unprecedented in the Division's past campaigns. Mile upon mile of cable that in dry weather crossed the paddy fields on the ground had to be raised on poles when the rains flooded the fields. To lay cables up hillsides while keeping clear of mule and jeep tracks taxed the ingenuity of the Indian linemen—Madrassis, Punjabi Mussulmen, and Sikhs. The dispatch-riders taking messages and official letters between brigade and battalion headquarters had long distances to cover, and often when they reached the foot of a hill no track existed for a motor-cycle. The hill had to be climbed on foot, and this lengthened the twice-daily delivery round by several hours.

For mule-drivers the Imphal siege was a nightmare, so great were the distances they had to trudge, tugging their strings of mules from the valley up to the summit, from the crest of one hill along a wooded ridge to the top of another, and then down again to the valley and across the paddy fields on a rough track that was deep in dust when not surfaced with soft mud. To keep the far-scattered units of the Division supplied each day was a problem admirably tackled by Lieutenant-Colonel R. A. Willis and the companies of the Royal Indian Army Service Corps, which had to collect stores, rations, ammunition, clothing and boots, saddles and straps for mules, and a thousand other items of infinite variety and necessity.

*   *   *   *   *

It is necessary at this point to interrupt the narrative and to turn aside from Imphal in order to return to Kohima and follow the final battles among the Naga Hills, and the sequence of events that resulted.

By May 23 Brigadier Warren had collected his three battalions together once more, and 161 Brigade was resting for a short period in Dimapur. On the 11th, after already severe fighting and several vain assaults, the 6th Brigade of the 2nd British Division and the 33rd Brigade of Messervy's Seventh Indian Division, which was arriving at Dimapur from Arakan, had started a full-scale attack against the main positions in Kohima still held by the Japanese: Kuki Picket, F.S.D., D.I.S., and Jail Hills. More than half of these objectives were taken, though at severe cost in killed and wounded. The 2nd Queens captured Jail Hill, and the 4/15th Punjab took F.S.D. So confused did the fighting become that the artillery were ordered to smoke the entire battleground, to allow our troops to dig in. Such a rare smoke screen was a nightmare experience for the infantry. Two days later, and after a day when fighting was prevented by the weather, the ruins of the District Commissioner's Bungalow were recaptured. By the end of the day, the whole of Kohima had been wrested from the enemy. So ended one of the bloodiest periods of fighting known on any front. In this bitter struggle, companies of the 1/1st Punjab and 4/7th Rajputs took over ground that had been regained from the enemy. And the batteries of the 24th Mountain Regiment fired thousands of rounds in support of those attacks.

A description has been preserved of Kohima at the end of the battle. "There was not a tree standing that was not blasted and littered; the more primitive houses were knocked flat, and others were holed and battered beyond recognition. The place stank. The earth everywhere was ploughed up with shell fire, and human remains lay rotting as the battle raged over them. Flies swarmed everywhere, and multiplied with incredible speed. Men retched as they dug in, and a priority task was to clear up as far as possible. But even then the stink hung in the air and permeated one's clothes and hair. It made one realize once again how sub-human the Japs were. A bunker was found in which about twenty men had fought and lived for several days—a bunker littered with their dead companions and their own excreta. These are memories one would like to forget, but they are inevitably linked with the name 'Kohima' "[1].

Now 161 Brigade was placed under the command of the Seventh Indian Division, which had completed its move from Arakan. Warren's troops took the place of 89 Brigade, which was now fighting under General Briggs in Imphal. The Division's final objective was to capture Tuphema, some twenty-two miles south of Kohima, thus guarding the 2nd Division's left flank. But its first task was to open the track eastwards from Kohima to Jessami and, by operating in the hills north of Kohima, to clear such villages as Cheswema and Nerhema, thereby protecting the traffic using the main road between Dimapur and Kohima.

It was stressed by Fourteenth Army Headquarters that no effort must be spared either by the 2nd or 7th Division to open the road to Imphal, for with the monsoon rains falling it was becoming increasingly difficult to supply the garrison by air. It was precisely with the object of delaying the opening of this road to Imphal that the Japanese 31st Division was deployed north-east and south of Kohima. The enemy planned to deny us the Jessami track as a base for any outflanking move round his positions. For the first time on the Kohima front the enemy was, on his own admission, on the defensive, and he was preparing for stubborn if not desperate resistance. The hill country was formidable in its nature, for the height ranged from 3,000 feet in the valleys to 8,000 feet on the ridges, and any operations that aimed at speed were bound to be restricted to the few roads and tracks. And the track to Tuphema would not be passable even to jeeps, once the monsoon rains fell in their full deluge.

But problems of supply and movement also faced the Japanese troops, whose lines of communication were long and tedious. Rice and meat they might find where they did battle, but not ammunition, which had to be carried through the wild hills from

---

[1] Major J. Nettlefield.

the distant Chindwin River. The lengths of the enemy's two main supply routes both exceeded a hundred miles.

On the southern front of Kohima, Grover's 2nd British Division was to attack along the Aradura Spur towards Phesema. Having captured these, the advance would be pressed south along the road to Imphal. On May 27-28 Grover's battalions attacked the Aradura Spur and, although not all objectives were attained, considerable ground was gained in the face of the most tenacious resistance. The Japanese found themselves obliged to counter-attack, but to no abiding effect.

During the first fortnight of June the 2nd Division made strenuous efforts to dislodge the Japanese from the line they were defending between Viswema, Kidima, and Kekrima. Here was encountered fierce opposition. Here were fought most bloody engagements, and the British battalions made several vain and costly assaults against the enemy's positions before they achieved success. But once the Japanese main defence line had been broken, the Division's advance became more rapid, for the enemy offered but intermittent and temporary resistance from hastily prepared positions at various points along the Imphal road.

Meantime, 114 Brigade advanced along the Jessami track, and 161 Brigade under General Messervy's direction had begun to pursue the enemy northwards along the Bokajan track, and to drive him from the villages north and north-east of Kohima, centred upon Merema and Chedema. On June 6 the news of the invasion of France coincided happily with the successful opening of the Brigade's drive along the jeep track. But the monsoon weather appalled all who fought beneath its teeming fury. It barely ceased to rain, and the mules of the battalions and of the 24th Mountain Regiment in support were generally walking hock deep in mud. The mule drivers performed an outstanding service in ferrying stores and ammunition to the forward troops, an achievement only equalled by the young Indian jeep drivers who drove their loaded jeeps and trailers along the treacherous tracks, bringing ammunition to the guns without fail, but living through nightmare journeys to do so.

At this period a special jeep supply column was formed from a London Territorial Regiment. In its ranks were numbered many London taxi-drivers. General Messervy tells a story of one of these jeep crews. "All races produce tough, brave soldiers, but only the British soldier really has that sense of decency and kindly humanity which nothing can upset.

"A Jap was seen skulking in a bush near Jessami, by the side of the track. Out leapt the Gunners and seized him.

" 'Shall we kill the little bastard ? It's what he and his like deserve.'

" 'Oh, no, we can't. We'll take him back with us.'

"After a few hundred yards—"Ere, Tojo, you look pretty miserable. 'Ave a fag.'

"A mile farther on they had a puncture, and it was 'Come on, Tojo, give us a hand.'

"By the time Kohima was reached, 'Tojo' was a mascot, if not a friend."

By June 10 the Brigade were nineteen miles along the Jessami track, with the 4/7th Rajputs in Kekrima, and the Royal West Kents at Chakabama. For two days the Rajputs were blocked by the Japanese on a hill named Charlie, but when the 1/1st Punjab made an outflanking march to skirt Kekrima to the north-east and occupied three hills aptly named Faith, Hope, and Charity, the enemy withdrew. The 15th saw 161 Brigade in Pfutse-Ro, but faced with ever increasing problems of supply and maintenance, problems raised by the monsoon and by the extended line of communication.

On June 17 the two Indian battalions cut the Tuphema–Kharasom track, along which the Japanese had left ample evidence of their recent flight: dead mules, discarded boots, clothing, recently opened fish and meat tins, ashes of camp fires—some still smoking —and fresh footprints. The 1/1st Punjab reached Milestone 78 on this track next day, but beyond this point 161 Brigade's advance farther west was blocked by heavy landslides. Accordingly, the Brigade was brought back to the Imphal road, while the 1/1st Punjab remained to guard the Kharasom track until relieved by the Bombay Grenadiers of 268 Brigade, which arrived to take over the positions of Brigadier Warren's three battalions.

So soon as the road to Imphal was opened, 161 Brigade moved into Imphal, and 33 Brigade of Messervy's Seventh Division was sent across country to eject the enemy from Ukhrul, operating with columns from the 20th and 23rd Indian Divisions.

But the sequence of events has been forestalled, and we must return to the battlefront of Imphal, to follow the hard-fought advance of the Fifth Indian Division northwards up the road to Kohima, to meet the 2nd Division and to crush the fast losing Japanese like nuts in a nutcracker.

*   *   *   *   *

During the second half of May Evans' 123 Brigade battled north from Sengmai to gain ground along the Kohima road. The ground was difficult, the jungle thick, and the site of our dumps in Kanglatongbi wired and mined. Astride the road the three battalions took their turn in hammering at the Japanese. The guns of the 28th Field Regiment supported our attacks, and Hurricanes of the Royal Air Force bombed and strafed enemy-held positions when called upon to do so. Road-blocks had to be cleared, enemy troops driven from bends in the road, from hillocks that overlooked this road, from stream beds and patches of jungle on the right of the road.

89 Brigade was also fighting up the road. But for a week almost no progress was made. Then the Japanese did quit a low hill named Pyramid, on the left of the road, that had delayed our advance, and 123 Brigade moved forward to the northern outskirts of Kanglatongbi, sixteen miles north of Imphal itself. Then General Briggs changed his plans, for it was now of the first importance that the road towards Kohima be opened. The Japanese on Hump and Twin Peaks and Molvom must stay where they were, prevented from taking the offensive against our flank, and perhaps a successful drive up the road below them would force them to leave their sternly defended hilltops.

Accordingly, at the beginning of June Nine Brigade was brought across to the road, to reinforce Brigadier Evans' three battalions, the 2nd Suffolks, 3/2nd Punjab, and 1/17th Dogras.

While 89 Brigade took over our positions on Wakan, Mapao, and Runaway Hill, and Nine Brigade settled into Sengmai and Kanglatongbi, Evans' 123 Brigade, which had been fighting up this road for some weeks, continued to battle its way forward along the line of foothills that ran parallel with the road on the eastern side below Molvom.

Such a move was no easy one. Space had to be found to house

each battalion, Brigade Headquarters, and the Gunner Regiment attached (in this case 4th Field Regiment commanded by Lieutenant-Colonel George Bastin). There was no direct route across, and vehicles, men, and mules had either to go right back into Imphal and out again along the main road to Kohima, or find their way by a series of rough tracks made by cutting down the earth bunds that cut the paddy fields into rectangles. And when the rains came many of these tracks became at once unusable.

On the 6th it was Nine Brigade's turn to take the lead. While Furney's 3/14th Punjab set out on a left hook to cut the road behind the enemy at a culvert nicknamed London Bridge, the West Yorkshires prepared to assault a low hill on the left-hand side of the road called Zebra. After an airstrike on the 6th and an artillery concentration upon Zebra early on the morning of the 7th, 'C' Company under Major J. B. Miller, supported by tanks of the 7th Cavalry, moved forward to attack. 'B' Company guarded the L. of C. of the 3/14th Punjab, while 'D' Company and another troop of Stuart tanks took up positions to guard the flat, open ground on the right of the road, by the Imphal Turel. Before the attack began, 'A' Company had moved round behind Zebra.

It should be noted here that the Divisional artillery, under Brigadier Mansergh, was restricted to six rounds per day per gun. This had to include defensive and harassing fire, and was only relaxed when a regiment was shooting in support of a set-piece attack.

The attack succeeded, and Miller's men took Zebra, though the ground had to be fought for yard by yard. The Japanese from their bunkers defended stubbornly, and had to be driven out from one position after the other. The objective was not finally taken until six o'clock that evening, and the West Yorkshire company was heavily mortared during the night. And next day a Japanese light machine-gun suddenly started firing in the middle of our positions. It was quickly silenced. The tanks were held up on the road by mines, and Lieutenant Yearsley in charge of the Sapper mine-detecting party that went forward with the leading infantry platoon was wounded.

Our own casualties were twenty, mostly wounded, and twenty-six Japanese bodies were recovered after the battle. Further advance up the main road was for the time being prevented by a road-block three hundred yards north of Zebra. This block was covered by a 75 mm. gun and a platoon of Japanese. When 'D' Company and a troop of the 3rd Dragoon Guards tried to clear the obstacle, they were forced to withdraw.

Meanwhile, the 3/14th had been engaged in heavy fighting in the enemy's rear. They had come on to the road a little farther south than intended, and were attacked throughout the night of June 8/9. 'C' Company under Major Anthony crossed the road and secured one of the line of hills east of the road. It was named Squeak, the centre of three, the others being Pip and Wilfred. The latter was held by the enemy, who attacked Anthony's men three times during the night of their arrival. When the Punjabis tried to evict the Japanese from Wilfred they were unable to do so. Colonel Furney had brought the rest of his battalion up to London Bridge, distinctive by its white railings on either side of the road, and on the night of the 9th/10th a large force of fifty Japanese soldiers bumped into the Punjabi positions and were scattered and mauled by firing. Fourteen bodies were counted next morning, and much wireless and other equipment was collected. But time was pressing. The road could not be opened until the road-block was cleared. The 3/14th Punjab had taken three days' rations on their march, and had now to be supplied by parachute drop, but this was difficult in the area involved, and certain important items could not be dropped without considerable warning being given. Anthony's company on Squeak was alone and surrounded, with the enemy sending jitter parties, even though they did not launch a serious attack.

But in the meantime 123 Brigade had made good progress along the ridge of foothills east of the road. Led by the 2nd Suffolks (now commanded by Lieutenant-Colonel K. C. Menneer), they had attacked two features named Isaac and James, by Modbung village, throughout the first nine days of June. The fighting had been severe, and when the Sappers built a track up to the summit and the tanks climbed up to assist the infantry, they got into difficulty. One tank slid over the edge of a spur and had to be abandoned. The monsoon rains had made the slopes slippery, and the tanks needed winches to enable them to reach the crest of the hill. The country was thickly wooded; the hills were surrounded by waterways that made any advance still more difficult than it would otherwise have been against a determined enemy.

All day long on June 7 the Suffolks attacked Isaac, but were held up by enemy troops on the reverse slopes. In the day's fighting we lost nine killed and twenty-eight wounded. On the 8th a strike by Hurricanes produced little result, and one of the tanks was hit and blew up; the crew escaped.

Next day Isaac was cleared, and the 3/9th Jats climbed up to Modbung to resume the advance. This was on the 11th, and the attack was successful. Three tanks had roared up to the top, and waited in the cover of thick trees to help the Jat companies forward along the line of hills. But there was no need, for when the infantry went forward that afternoon they found that the enemy had vanished into the valleys. We secured all the hills, and the Jats linked up with the 3/14th Punjab company on Squeak.

That same morning tanks and the West Yorkshires cleared the road-block, after an intense concentration by mortars. The enemy left sixteen dead. Meanwhile the 3/14th had pushed up the road as far as the ruined village of Safarmaina, and the road was clear to that point by the evening of June 12.

On June 13 the Jats advanced northwards from Squeak to Wilfred. They had orders to brush aside slight enemy opposition and, when the main Japanese defences were encountered, to consolidate their ground. Three days' rain had made the very steep slopes of this ridge slippery. It was impossible to supply the leading companies by mule. Trees grew thickly on the hills, and even where the jungle had clearings, these were covered in high elephant grass that impeded our progress. The leading Jat company under Major Sanson drove some enemy outposts off a knob called Eye. And when 'C' Company passed through to occupy Button, another thousand yards farther north along the ridge, the enemy offered no resistance.

Jat patrols now crept through the jungle to probe the defences of the main hill along this ridge, Liver. There seemed to be little opposition. But this supposition proved to be false, when an attack was made at half-past two by Captain Muskett's guerilla platoon and a platoon of Rowling's 'B' Company, led by a newly joined officer named Armstrong. The Japanese on Liver threw down scores of grenades. Their four machine-guns took a saddening toll. Armstrong and his jemadar were killed, Muskett was wounded by a grenade, and the 'B' Company platoon suffered in all twenty-four wounded and two killed out of a strength of twenty-seven.

The Jat, probably the best farmer in Northern India, comes from the Eastern Punjab, Delhi Province, the Rajputana States and the United Provinces. In the Hindu hierarchy he occupies a position below that of the Rajput, who is of the warrior class that for so long strongly opposed the Muslim invasion of India. But the Jat has also a long and memorable history as a fighting man. He is a great lover of animals and all living creatures, and venerates the cow as a sacred animal almost more than does even the Brahmin. Possibly this explains his inordinate love of milk and of foods made from milk. Some Jats, especially those from the Eastern Punjab, never touch meat in any form, and dislike any dish prepared from animals, birds or fish.

The Jat is of independent character, somewhat intolerant of those he does not know, but his sense of humour is marked. And he loves a party round a communal *huqqa*, which he produces and lights on every possible, and sometimes impossible, occasion.

On the cross-roads below Eye, in the ruins of what had been Safarmaina village, the West Yorkshires had established their headquarters, and on the road thronged men and mules, jeeps and the tanks of Major Dimsdale's squadron of the 3rd Carabiniers, now supporting Nine Brigade. All day and all night the rain poured down. The Jats on the ridge, having neither bedding nor waterproof sheets, remained soaking wet for hours on end. Even those more fortunate soldiers who had tents or tarpaulins, or members of Brigade Headquarters who lived in derelict lorries that had been towed from a nearby dump, found it hard to keep dry. Puddles grew wider and deeper. Water rushed down the hillsides, flooded the streams that already were foaming brown torrents, and tore down plank bridges. The river, which had been fordable at knee-depth, was now swirling branches along at great speed. And men who undressed and tried to ford the torrent were soon out of their depth. Soldiers squelched through inches of water in the fields, and hoisted themselves up slippery paths by means of branches and telephone cables. The mules laden with supplies for the Jats struggled and kicked and floundered up the muddy hillside. Over the dark green peaks to the west of the road hung a white mist, and the whole valley became more depressing and sombre as the hours passed. Even the sun when it broke through the low clouds did little to relieve the gloom that prevailed.

The date was now June 15. After an early strafe by Hurricanes, Liver was attacked by Major Risal Singh's 'A' Company of Jats. When two platoons reached within a hundred yards of the top, fierce fire from bunkers on neighbouring hills held up the climbing infantry, whose sole line of approach was a bare spur. As had occurred before, our shells and bombs, far from ousting the enemy, had effectually diminished what cover grew on the upper slopes. Risal Singh withdrew his men to allow the tanks and guns to fire a concentration, but this failed to silence the Japanese machine-guns, which, as usual, were placed where artillery fire could not reach them. Then a platoon from 'C' Company pushed up from Button by way of Carter to within twenty yards of the crest of Liver, only to be driven back by showers of grenades.

Later, as a result of a two minutes' concentration on Liver and its neighbouring hilltops, and of a prolonged burst of firing from two troops of tanks at all the re-entrants separating these features, 'C' Company (Major J. Campbell) was able to secure Carter. Here the Jats spent a terrible night in pouring rain, overlooked by the Japanese on Liver at a range of one hundred yards. Next day Colonel Gerty had to withdraw the company.

In the meantime Cree's West Yorkshires had been ordered to capture an enemy road-block that was level with Liver but divided from the hills by the flooded, swirling Imphal Turel. The three buildings shown on the map had been nicknamed Driffield, and the nullahs through the jungle there were known as Swale, Ouse, and Avon. One company was to infiltrate round the flank and cut the road behind Driffield at a low ridge called Octopus. When this had been reached, a second company supported by tanks would advance along the road, with a 'scissors' bridge to enable the broken bridge to be crossed.

While moving across a nullah, the leading 'D' Company, commanded by Major Brian Sellars, were suddenly fired at from two directions out of the close jungle. Sellars and his second-in-command, Mallinson, being mortally wounded, refused to be carried back, for this would have endangered other men's lives. But Sellars ordered his company, who had in these brief and alarming moments suffered many casualties, to make their way back. They should try to cross the road and rejoin the battalion by way of the more open strip of country near the Imphal Turel. This was done, and small parties of West Yorkshires did succeed in getting back in the course of that disastrous day. But of a total of three officers and seventy-four other ranks who set out, only the Company Sergeant-Major and forty-seven men returned. And of these, twenty had been wounded. The remainder of the operation was cancelled.

The Division was not making progress. Something new must be tried, for neither the West Yorkshires nor the Jats could make headway against resolute and well-prepared enemy resistance. General Slim had ordered that the limit of our northward advance from Imphal should be Kangpokpi, a village another seven miles ahead. But it seemed that even this would be reached first by the hurrying 2nd British Division, which had by now reached Milestone 78, thirty miles south of Kohima.

General Briggs conferred with Salomons at Nine Brigade Headquarters. It was decided that the 3/14th Punjab, now commanded by Lieutenant-Colonel H. C. A. Baker, who had been second-in-command for a long period, were to make a left hook through the jungle. The road was to be cut behind the Japanese, and the low feature called Octopus seized. Possession of this would give our troops a dominating position by the road. The object would be to force the enemy holding Liver and Driffield to retire, for fear of being cut off and destroyed.

The battalion set off on June 19, and by eight o'clock next morning had reached their assembly point on the left flank. When the guerilla platoon reported that the bend in the road by Octopus was clear of enemy troops, Baker sent his companies forward to occupy the hill. This was achieved without mishap, but during the afternoon the two leading companies were attacked three times by the Japanese, who realized the danger of Indian troops in their rear, and made fierce efforts to oust them before they could establish firm positions. But every attack was repulsed.

Meanwhile, a still wider left hook had been ordered, this time for 123 Brigade. The 3/2nd Punjab and 1/17th Dogras had been sent through the jungle on the left flank with the object of cutting the road in two places near to Keithelnambi, three miles south of Kangpokpi. It had been intended that the Dogras should cross the road at Milestone 109 (from Dimapur) and establish two companies on hills near Heinoupok on the east of the road, behind Liver; but progress through the jungle was seriously delayed by heavy rain, which impeded both porters and mules, who were hard pressed enough making their way without tracks to follow.

On the morning of June 21, a day on which the 2nd Division advanced sixteen miles as far as Milestone 103, three squadrons of Hurribombers bombed and strafed Liver for half an hour. Then 'A' and 'C' Companies of Gerty's Jats, who had lain in cover on the bank of the Imphal Turel, advanced up to capture a lower knob called Pill, just above the road and to the west below Liver. Its possession would give our troops a much needed alternative axis of advance on the summit. Twenty minutes later the artillery fired a concentration so close to Risal Singh's men that three sepoys were wounded by our own shells, but this was worth it, for Pill was taken. The enemy had left their trenches when the shelling began, and had not time to reoccupy their defences before the Jats rushed in and drove the Japanese off the hillock.

At one o'clock a second airstrike was delivered, this time not on Liver itself but on Milk Loaf, a feature that overlooked it from the north, five hundred yards away. During this bombardment Risal Singh and two platoons had climbed up from Pill, Major J. Campbell had brought his 'C' Company up towards Liver from the south-west, and was lying up in thick cover two hundred yards from the top, and Sanson's 'D' Company had worked forward from Button towards Carter. Another platoon was to get astride the spur joining Liver and Milk Loaf, and so take the enemy in the rear. The Jats would in this way approach from four different directions.

Then, at half past one, the 4th and 28th Field Regiments, aided by a troop of 8th Medium Regiment, fired a concentration that lasted three minutes and provided spectators with an awe-inspiring spectacle as the shells tore into the hillsides, ripped off branches, splintered trees, flung up earth, and covered Liver in smoke and dust. The three Jat companies climbed up as far as was safe, and Risal Singh took one bump below Liver and above Pill. But while reconnoitring for a further advance, this fine officer, who had won a Military Cross on Numshigum, was killed by a burst of machine-gun fire from a Japanese bunker. This was a severe loss to the battalion. Major Campbell left Risal Singh's company where it was, and went on with two platoons to attack Liver. He, in his turn, was held up by savage fire that crackled down the bare slope. Meanwhile, the platoon trying to force itself on to the spur behind Liver had lost many men in the attempt, and Sanson's men had only been able to gain a footing on the slopes of Liver. Though a few Jats did get on the summit, they were beaten off by grenades and fire from Milk Loaf.

In view of the many casualties suffered, Colonel Gerty ordered his companies to consolidate where they were for the night. At dawn next day Jat patrols found Liver and Milk Loaf abandoned. The Japanese, having had enough, had slipped away by night. The 3/9th Jats had lost thirty-three officers and men killed, and 111 wounded in the fighting that week.

On June 22 men of the 1/17th Dogras met troops of the 2nd British Division at Milestone 109 on the Kohima–Imphal road. At two o'clock that afternoon a formal meeting by the roadside took place between Lieutenant-General Stopford, commanding Thirty-Three Corps, and Major-General Grover, commander of the 2nd Division, on the one hand, and, on the other, Brigadier Salomons of Nine Brigade. The road had been opened after prolonged efforts and severe loss of life. And that night the first convoy drove into Imphal from the north, the headlights shining into the darkness like a beacon of victory.

Nine Brigade was now withdrawn into reserve in hospital buildings north-west of Imphal, while 123 Brigade stayed for a few days in the area of Keithelmanbi, before moving to the south of Imphal, towards Bishenpur and Buri Bazaar.

The decisive battle had ended. Imphal had been relieved. The Japanese forces had received a severe mauling on the plain and surrounding hills. Indeed, the flower of their army had been destroyed. They had attacked long after such attacks could achieve any result. And the enemy was now faced with no alternative but to retreat south and west through the hills towards the Chindwin, at the height of the monsoon.

General Briggs asked for a rest. He had been told by General Scoones that operations would stop for the monsoon, and that we should not advance beyond the 34th milestone south of

Imphal. The plan for this had already been made, and now Briggs told Scoones that he felt stale, having had no break since the beginning of the war. General Auchinleck had asked for either Messervy or Briggs to command Ranchi area, the training ground for Burma. The two events coincided. Briggs accepted the new post, and General Slim agreed. If ever a man deserved a rest it was Briggs, but for the Division he had led for two years in Desert and Jungle his departure was a tragedy.

To fill his place Brigadier Geoffrey Evans was promoted.

BRITISH GUNNERS (C.I.S. Historical Section)

SAPPERS CROSS THE RIVER (C.I.S. Historical Section)

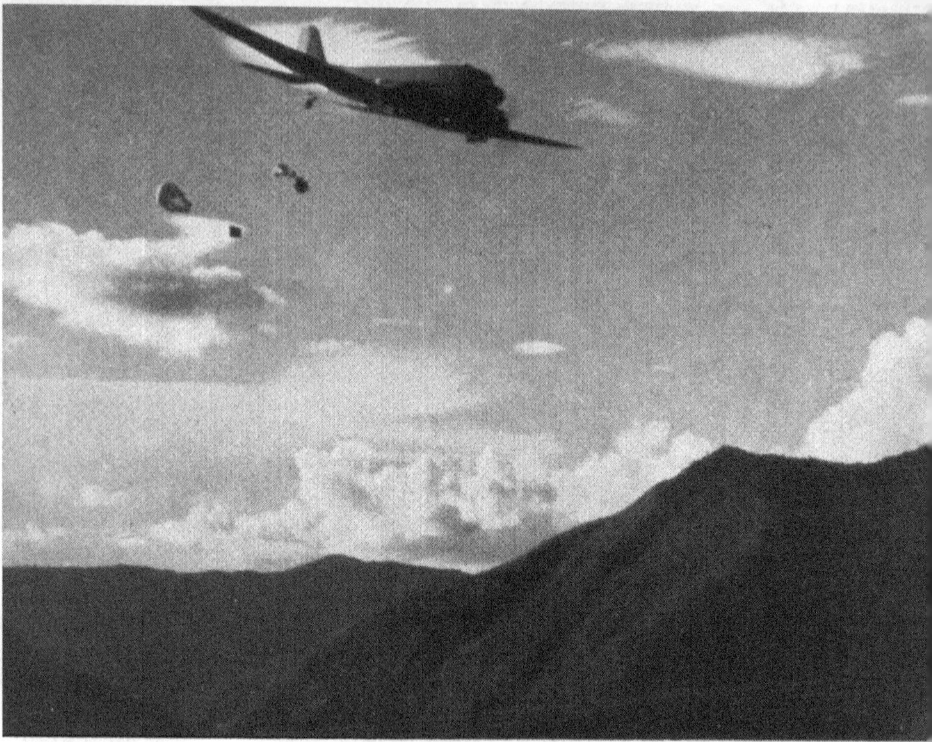

Supply Dropping (C.I.S. Historical S

Fallen Parachutes on the 'Chocolate Staircase' (J. H.

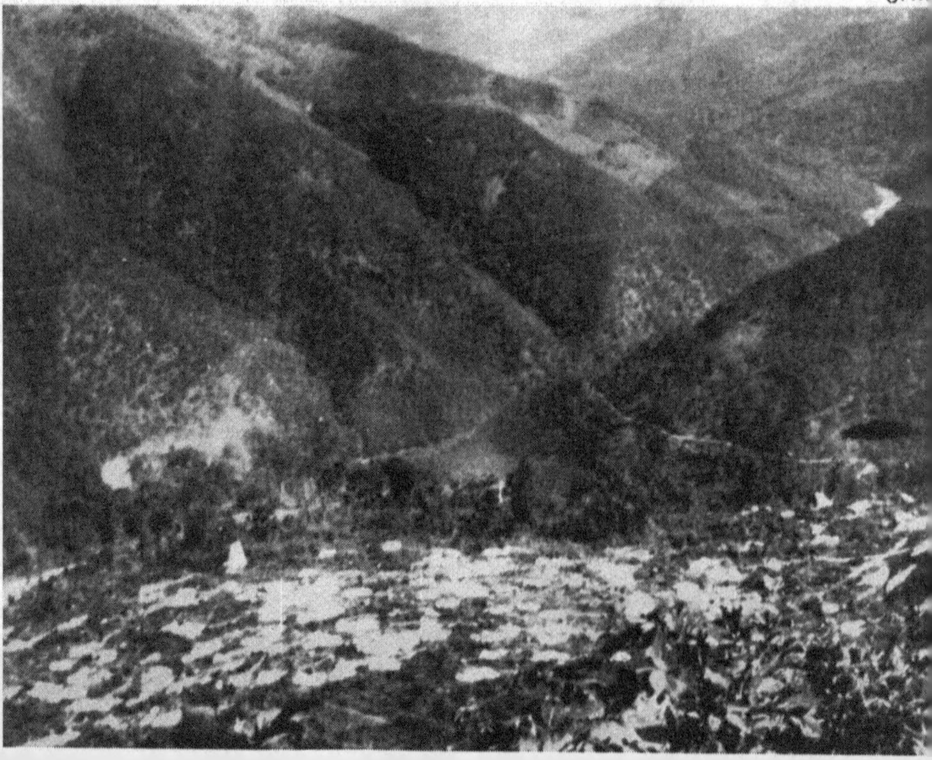

CHAPTER XXV

THE ROAD TO TIDDIM

JULY—OCTOBER 1944

IMPHAL had been saved. The enemy had been driven from the plain in the north and east. A first plan was ordered for the next stage of the campaign. The Fifth Indian Division would pass through the 17th Indian Division south of Imphal, near Buri Bazaar, and establish a strong base by Milestone 36. At this point the high ground would be held on either side of the muddy road that wound away to Tiddim. The Japanese were now retreating rapidly south from Bishenpur and the Silchar track. But it was at first not our intention to pursue them, for the monsoon was in full flood. And for troops to fight and be supplied during the season of pouring rains was considered impossible. So rapidly had the health of the troops deteriorated after nine months of continuous operations that the average monthly evacuation of sick from the Division had now risen to 2,000. The mule companies were tired, and 23 Animal Transport Company was isolated with surra.

But in the third week of July new orders were received: Nine Brigade would advance south as far as Milestone 64—less than halfway to Tiddim—and then withdraw to the edge of the Imphal Plain. The road would be destroyed in the Brigade's wake, and the enemy prevented from ever again using this route.

Finally, when the Division came under the command of Stopford's Thirty-Three Corps, orders were issued that the Japanese be relentlessly pursued despite the monsoon. The Division would drive the enemy back across the frontier into Burma, and force its way through the hills to Tiddim. Then General Evans' troops were to assault the mighty Kennedy Peak, capture Fort White, and march down into the valley by Kalemyo. Here the 11th East African Division, which was at the same time fighting down the Kabaw Valley, would also arrive. This was to be a two-pronged drive against the Japanese. How long would this operation last ?

This could not be prophesied. It depended upon the enemy's resistance, the state of the road, the force of the rains, the incidence of disease, our ability to supply two divisions, the skill, endurance, and resolution of the British, Indian, and East African soldiers.

Salomons' Nine Brigade would lead the way as far as Milestone 82. And the name of the operation was, ironically enough, 'Gallop.' Progress was inevitably slow, for until the third and final plan had been adopted, the Brigade travelled down the first twenty miles with mules and without vehicles. Field and medium guns gave support from the Division's firm base until the leading battalions went out of range. Tanks were unable to accompany the Brigade, for at first the bridges, every one of which had been destroyed by the enemy, were not repaired behind the advance. With Nine Brigade marched 12 Battery (Major Anson B. Howard) of the 24th Mountain Regiment, part of the 10th Field Ambulance, Hatch's 20th Field Company, Bombay Sappers and Miners, the 47th Animal Transport Company, loaned from the 17th Indian Division, and 200 Dhotiyal porters.

While the 2nd West Yorkshires fought down the road along a ridge of low hills to the left, Baker's 3/14th Punjab thrust down the right flank through tall elephant grass and sodden country. They rejoined the road near Milestone 33, where two bushy islands, unsuitably named Duke and Duchess, divided the mud track. Colonel Cree's three companies had by now overcome strong opposition on Julius Cæsar, the first hill that rises from the southern edge of the Imphal plain, but not before the Royal Air Force had bombed and strafed the Japanese bunkers.

Now Salomons' three battalions, West Yorkshires, Jats, Punjabis, leapfrogged down the road, the lead taken by each in turn. To describe in detail the day-to-day engagements would be tedious. Progress was reckoned by milestones. The enemy fought a delaying action all the way, mile by mile. His rearguard waited in concealed defence positions that commanded the winding road, opened fire on our leading infantry section, and killed or wounded several men. If the rifle company failed to oust the enemy, then Howard's mountain guns battered the position with whatever ammunition the limited airdrops had provided.

At first the Japanese were content to arrest our advance for a day or a night. But so prolonged was their resistance near the fiftieth milestone, where the road wound up the side of a hill named "Drake," that Salomons sent for Hurribombers to evict them. For three days the Japanese clung tenaciously to this hill. By firing its steep slopes they denied all cover to the 3/14th Punjab, who were now leading the Brigade. Twice the infantry climbed to attack. Twice they came within four hundred yards of the summit. But each time grenades and machine-guns forced them back. When one fierce assault brought Baker's platoons almost to the top, they could not stay there. The sepoys held positions on the hillside through the next night. In the tense hour before sunrise they endured a fusillade of rare intensity. An attack was expected from above. No attack came. Instead, the Japanese soldiers hurled grenades down into our trenches. Abruptly silence fell. When, at dawn on August 7, the Punjabis crept up the bare and blackened slope, they found Drake's crest deserted. The fierce outburst had been a final defiant gesture. Already the enemy was preparing to delay us a little farther down the road.

And this road—for the soldiers a long, long trail to Tiddim—bore the tracks of a retreating foe. Mud-clogged rifles and splintered packing-cases kept company with dirty webbing equipment, hand grenades and blood-stained, muddy, rain-soaked corpses. From beneath mounds of loose earth appeared legs and arms, even a solitary hand. Over all, and on almost every stretch of the road, hung the sickly smell that betrayed the presence of some dead enemy in a patch of jungle, beneath a dripping tangle of bamboo. At one road fork lay the scorched and buckled shell of a jeep that had blown up. In the bed of one stream was found a small Japanese tank, painted a pale shade of green and adorned in scarlet with the sun of Japan.

Near Drake our patrols found the site of a large Japanese hospital, and close on a hundred graves in the surrounding jungle. Among the trees within a few yards of the road lay two very long brown Japanese lorries. These contained the smashed equipment of a sterilizing unit and X-ray plant, surrounded by wickerwork hampers, chemicals and clothing, and a weighty generator. Inside, too, buzzed a host of savage hornets; one naked corpse lay there, and, pervading all, the smell of death. Back near Milestone 40 were discovered many traces of the one-time headquarters of the 33rd Japanese Division. Here stood brown staff-cars under the scrub-oaks, shelters built of branches and roofed with bits of tarpaulin, cookhouses, mouldy uniforms, blackened pots, and the rain-sodden ashes of a score of fires. Men who searched in Japanese lorries found maps and papers, private kits and coloured postcards, notebooks and personal seals. They found tools and flags, damp newspapers, office equipment muddled up with wireless valves. And from trenches they unearthed heavier, more valuable items of military equipment. At this stage of the campaign it was comparatively rare to find so much belonging to the enemy, and some men, among the West Yorkshires at least, must have cast their minds back to booty captured from the Italians in Eritrea and Abyssinia more than three years before.

No sooner was it decided to go all the way to Tiddim and Kalemyo than Nine Brigade was joined by a squadron of the 3rd Carabiniers, commanded by Major Dimsdale, and the 28th Field Regiment (Lieutenant-Colonel R. A. Collins). The Divisional Sappers repaired the road behind the Brigade. Jeeps and four-wheel-drive trucks were allowed forward, and motor-cycles, though these last were ill-fitted to cope with a road that, already damaged by mules and men, now became churned into deep ruts by tanks, guns and heavy ammunition quads.

Where the Japanese had blocked the road with fallen tree trunks, these had to be cleared, usually under fire; Cree's West Yorkshires had to deal with no less than six blocks of this sort within three days of the second week of August. And on several occasions, where a wider bridge than usual had been blown up, the tanks had to put down a "scissors" bridge, so that the squadron should not be held up too long.

Day by day Nine Brigade moved a little nearer to Tiddim. And the rain poured down. Yet between hard showers the sun's warmth dried out shirts and trousers as the men marched beside the road or went about their work. Seldom did it rain while our columns were actually on the move. But soon after their arrival in a new bivouac, dark clouds would blow across the green hills, which here rose to no great height, and soon the rain would come teeming down for hours on end. The earth grew slippery, yellow rivulets streamed down the slopes, and even when the rain stopped for a while you could still hear the pattering of raindrops off the trees overhead. Dust on the road turned to thick mud. Bivouac tents and large heavy tarpaulins were barely enough to keep off the rain, and the troops went about wearing waterproof capes and wide-brimmed felt hats. Sometimes men woke to a sunlit sky, and their spirits rose in the same proportion as they fell when the sky was weighted with rain and the jungle gloomy and dripping wet.

The passage of mules up and down the road turned its soft surface into mire and holes. Hard-worked mule-drivers toiled with their animals to the forward battalions, linemen unreeled their slender cables, wireless operators set up their little No. 48 sets, and erected rod or wire aerials. Bearded Sikhs passed by with pieces of their mountain guns strapped on their sturdy artillery mules. And always the infantry dug trenches, or patrolled through the jungle, their eyes and ears alert for the enemy's presence, their nerves tense with the expectancy of a burst of bullets from some hidden Japanese in front. Dakotas roared over the Brigade and down floated the white parachutes, bringing precious bales and tins, boxes of rations and ammunition. These supplies had to be collected without delay, and issued by Captain Towning and his men of the R.I.A.S.C., once the reserve battalion had carried in the loads and piled the voluminous parachutes neatly by the roadside.

Communications in the very dense jungle were not always reliable. Patrols seeking a route off the road were often forced to make detours, to slither down hillsides, to wade streams, to clamber and force their way up bamboo slopes; and all this while laden with weapons and equipment, ammunition and packs—and as silently as possible.

Enemy flanking attacks against the road constantly threatened our leading troops. Sometimes Japanese snipers were left behind to shoot at drivers who moved down the road alone and without due precaution. Impatience might lead to disaster, unwariness to serious casualties. Our mountain and field guns harassed the enemy by day and by night. And when the Japanese artillery did retaliate, the often erratic shelling splintered trees hundreds of yards from the road, and sent up puffs of smoke from some ridge or jungle thicket. But on occasions this enemy fire was more accurate, and its consequences unpleasant for the nerves if not harmful to the flesh.

As the days slipped by, so our casualties mounted. More serious than those wounded by shell or shot were the many who lay dangerously ill with scrub typhus. This dreaded and deadly illness brought a high percentage of the battalions, in particular the 3/14th Punjab, to bed with a high fever, intense headache, pains in the chest and back, vomiting and a cough. Colonel Hugh Baker himself was stricken with the fell disease, and yet stayed on his feet until Drake had been captured. Several of his officers were also taken ill. It has been recorded by one doctor that in many cases the British troops were more frightened of typhus than of the Japanese. "Cases used to come in prepared to die of a mild attack of malaria. The Indian was not affected in this way; he was too unimaginative and fatalistic, and one wonders whether this was not a major cause of the much smaller Indian mortality. In the minds of many the word Typhus was synonymous with Death."

And all the time malaria and dysentery robbed the units of their men, until one man was doing the work of two, one officer bearing the responsibilities of another who had been evacuated to hospital. No man knew but that the evening would find him shivering. No commander who did not count his numbers with anxiety to see which men had been taken away. And this toll of sickness mounted in spite of every precaution carried out with strict discipline: mosquito cream was smeared on hands and face, on wrists and neck. When nightfall drew near, shirtsleeves were rolled down and buttoned, mosquito nets lowered and tucked under the blankets, and trousers dabbed or sprayed with an oily liquid named "Skat." Every evening yellow mepacrine tablets were swallowed. But although these precautions did serve to diminish the number of those who went to hospital, they could do little against mite-borne typhus. Evacuation by air was impossible, and the appalling journey back up the road, thirty or forty miles in jeeps specially fitted with stretchers, caused a number of men with typhus to die of heart failure. By the end of August Cree's 2nd West Yorkshires had suffered forty-two casualties from typhus, of whom fifteen died, while the 3/14th Punjab had ninety-seven cases, eight of them fatal.

* * * * *

Just beyond Milestone 62 the West Yorkshires met serious opposition. At a point where the road ran steeply down to a demolished bridge, then swung back and zigzagged up a long hill on the other side, the leading company, commanded by Major A. C. Dunlop, was fired on. Dimsdale's Carabineers were unable to help. Their advance was barred by a wide crater on a bend in the road, and every time the "scissors" bridge showed its nose round the corner it was greeted with fire from grenade dischargers and machine-guns. The driver of the bridge transporter was twice wounded.

Then Colonel Cree sent up 'A' Company (Major S. V. Bishop) in a night attack. The river was crossed by rope. The men clambered up the hill. They dug positions on top, close to the main Japanese defences. At the same time a platoon of Dunlop's company laid an ambush in the enemy's rear. This plan succeeded. The Japanese withdrew. The "scissors" bridge was laid without hindrance and our tanks rumbled slowly ahead.

Prisoners taken were few indeed, and these were usually men who were too weak from disease to retreat with their comrades. One was found bathing in a stream; he was naked and without weapons. Another who had lost his unit in the jungle was emaciated and dismal, his expression woebegone and his features hollow beneath the crumpled peak of his cap. To see a village, or local inhabitants, or cattle near the Tiddim Road was rare. For the road, built by Engineers the previous year, seldom followed the tracks linking the few villages that did exist.

At Milestone 70 the road crossed a river some forty feet in width. Here, as always, the enemy had destroyed the bridge; and the Sappers of 20 Field Company erected a Bailey bridge. But this work took two days. Without waiting, the leading infantry waded through the fast-flowing water. They carried their rifles and Bren guns above their heads, and tugged the mules behind them in a flurry of mud and spray, as the animals heaved out of the stream and plunged recklessly up the far bank.

It was here that contact was made with the Lushai Brigade (Brigadier P. C. Marindin) that had been operating against the Tiddim Road from the Lushai Hills to the west. Its task was to dislocate Japanese traffic, and render the road useless to the enemy as an L. of C. The Brigade, with its four battalions, had blocked the road at several points, prevented the enemy from bringing up reinforcements, and harassed his retreat unmercifully. Marindin's men had marched more than eighty miles across difficult hill country to reach the road behind the Japanese, and had been supplied entirely by air. Their contribution towards the successful advance of the Fifth Indian Division was outstanding. The Lushai Brigade was placed under General Evans' command on August 15.

Three hundred yards beyond the 75th milestone the frontier between India and Burma was crossed, and the last enemy troops driven from Indian territory. The ground now opened out and became less hilly. Resistance weakened. The Japanese rearguards were hastening to the sheer mountainside that rose between Milestones 86 and 100, where this extraordinary road spiralled upwards in dangerous bends. Here was a formidable natural obstacle to our advance. Here the enemy was expected to offer stout opposition.

By reaching Milestone 83 on August 22, the 3/9th Jats completed the task given to Nine Brigade. And Colonel Bernard Gerty, who had commanded the Jats throughout the previous twelve months, was promoted to command a brigade of another division, and received a D.S.O. Nine Brigade had advanced at a speed of just over two miles a day. Thirteen Japanese soldiers had been captured, and eighty-three killed, at a cost of nine killed and eighty-five wounded. But although our men found no less than three hundred enemy corpses beside the road, to say nothing of a still larger number of graves, Salomons' Brigade Group lost over five hundred men through sickness during that period of a month.

* * * * *

Now 161 Brigade passed through and took the lead in driving back the Japanese. For this operation Brigadier Warren had under command 20 Battery (Major J. Nettlefield) of the 24th Mountain Regiment, Dimsdale's 'C' Squadron of the 3rd Carabiniers again; the 2nd Field Company, 82nd Animal Transport Company, and 75th Field Ambulance.

The obstacle that faced Brigadier Warren and his men would have been formidable even in dry weather. But now, with the monsoon rains teeming down, it was doubly so. Only four-wheel-drive trucks were allowed forward, and even these had often to winch themselves out of ruts or up the steepest stretches. Well might the troops call this treacherous route the "Ladder." The road suddenly left the valley, and in one bend after another mounted some two thousand feet in twelve miles. Those parts of the mountain face that were bare of trees soon became broken up by the rains, and down upon the road fell cascades of shale and earth, of trees and rock. After each hairpin bend lorries found themselves a hundred feet or more above the spot where they had been a minute earlier. And the intervening wall of oozing mud had to be held from collapse by immense tarpaulins stretched out and linked together. It was hoped that these would at least shield the bare mud from the rain. But to shield the surface of the road itself from these torrents was quite impossible. Soon the mud was calf-deep, and so wide apart were the ruts made by trucks and lorries that jeeps had always to advance at a sharp tilt, one pair of wheels down in the ruts, the other pair slithering on the surface. The edge of the precipice was very close, and so perilous did the road appear to passengers, if not to drivers, that many hung ready to leap off if the vehicle showed signs of skidding.

At one point lorries weighed down with bridging equipment for the Sappers were stuck for four days, patiently waiting for a day of hot sunshine to dry out the mud sufficiently for them to proceed. One dispatch-rider took sixteen hours to complete a return journey of eighteen miles between Milestones 100 and 109. Though a spell of fine weather during the second week of September enabled stocks of rations to be built up for British and Indian troops and for mules, very heavy rain over the next two days so damaged the road once more that no supply convoys could move. And the road was closed by the Provost unit to prevent its complete ruin.

This state of affairs was to continue all through September and the first part of October, as long as the road was in use. Men had to jump out into the squelching mud and dig the mud from round the sunken wheels. Bamboos, branches, and sacks were laid on the mud, and pieces of rock were pressed in to support the flailing rear wheels. In parts one-way traffic had to be enforced by the military police. Lorries that had become embedded in the mire had to be hauled to one side before other vehicles could be steered past. Mule-drivers tugged sweated, shouted and swore in several languages at their muddy animals, which struggled gamely up and down the hills with their balanced loads creaking from the saddle. Those men who tried to keep their green trousers clean soon gave up the effort, for boots and clothes were rapidly soaked and stained with brown.

Convoys took rations for several days when they set off up the road, for the troops often had to spend two days and more in the open making slow and exhausting progress from one camp, traffic control post, or supply point to the next. On bad corners the Sappers laid rows of logs that helped a little; but these became embedded, uneven, splintered, or they vanished altogether; and lorries found temporary pits in which to sink for hours at a time. Guns had to be winched and man-handled up the slopes.

Throughout this campaign outstanding work was performed by the units of the I.E.M.E., which had in 1943 been renamed from the I.A.O.C. under the direction of the Division's first C.I.E.M.E., Lieutenant-Colonel K. Fryer; 112 and 113 Workshop Companies and 5 Recovery Company (Major J. H. Dale) maintained the vehicles on the road and the technical equipment in action. With each Brigade moved a Light Aid Detachment which performed 'first-line' repairs that could be completed in a few hours. The L.A.D. had, in mobile warfare particularly, to keep pace with its Brigade, and could not be burdened on a move by disabled lorries and other 'crocks.' These were towed back by the Recovery Company to the workshops, where Indian fitters, blacksmiths, welders, carpenters, sheet metal workers and other craftsmen changed engines and effected other major assembly changes. Vehicles, guns, wireless sets and other equipment that needed still more fundamental or lengthy 'third-line' repairs were evacuated behind the Division.

Down the Tiddim Road the Recovery Company was split into sections and attached to each Brigade. Placed at intervals along the road these sections were combined with military police posts. All unit transport officers knew this, and drivers soon learned where to find the nearest breakdown lorry.

On long moves, whatever the campaign, the L.A.D. was always the last in at night, having travelled at the rear of the convoy to repair vehicles stopped by the roadside. The fitters and mechanics worked all night until the column set out again next morning. Any vehicle that was still not going was handed to the Recovery Section to tow.

The tanks had their own workshops, but sometimes needed help from the Division's resources.

Most of the day the rain poured down, until the road's outer edge was swept away; and moving streams of shale and mud, trees and boulders, flowed across the road like lava from some volcano. Certain drivers found their way barred by a landslide that was still in motion. To clear such landslides took Sappers of the 2nd Field Company many hours. Trees were cut with explosives, and rocks broken down to a size that could be dealt with by the bulldozers.

But when the rain did cease, when the clouds were blown away from the hilltops, the view was awe-inspiring. As one Gunner officer, Major C. Morshead, M.C., wrote in a letter at the time: "When you get on the top the ridge is open with pine trees and grass; on the lower slopes it is mostly thick scrub oak reaching to more tropical jungle below. And from the tops the view is of the kind you pay many pounds to travel to see. Rank upon rank for maybe fifty miles run long and featureless ridges of forest, steep-sided in all shades of green, shadow and sunlight. Here and there are long views down deep glens that seem to lead nowhere at all." And he contrasted these hills with the majesty of the bare rock mountains of Persia which he had seen when the Division had driven to Kirkuk, three years before.

His description was a true one. On every side the bluish-green hills stretched their flanks and backs towards a distant horizon. And from point to point the red-brown streak of this infernal road appeared against the lush green of the hillside.

* * * * *

It was during September that the 1/1st Punjab captured an elephant. A patrol discovered it standing sadly on top of a hill near Milestone 116, swathed in cloud and with a little bell fastened round its neck. The elephant was escorted back to Brigade Headquarters, and Brigadier Warren's orderly, who had had experience as a mahout, was charged with its care. The elephant's appetite was huge: a banana tree for breakfast, and a daily consumption of *atta* of one hundredweight, fed in the form of *chapathis*. A large figure 68 was painted on its back for recognition purposes, just as every vehicle had the unit number painted on bumper and tailboard. Being docile, the elephant was used for taking 161

Brigade's laundry down to the river. The *dhobi* used the elephant's hide as a scrubbing-board and even beat out shirts and trousers on its back. When the guns opened fire, this sagacious elephant would move briskly round to its slit trench—a bomb shelter that had previously been dug out of a bank for a 3-ton lorry. For all its docility and wisdom, the elephant possessed a terrible voice, that was likened to the sound of someone tearing up strips of corrugated iron. When the 1/1st Punjab advanced again, the elephant was sent back to Imphal, with three Indian soldiers riding on its back. On the way it met a score of mules and drivers of the West Yorkshires, and caused a stampede among the frightened mules. These could only be persuaded to advance when the elephant had retired up a nullah.

The elephant was last heard of in the stables of the Maharajah of Cooch Behar.

* * * * *

By the end of August it appeared likely that the rearguard of the Japanese 33rd Division opposing 161 Brigade would withdraw rapidly across the Manipur River at Milestone 126. Then another enemy force, composed of two very depleted battalions hard by Tongzang village in the hills some five miles south of the river, would oppose our crossing. At an average rate of progress of two miles a day, it was reckoned that 161 Brigade would reach the banks of the Manipur River by September 15.

123 Brigade, now commanded by Brigadier E. J. Denholm-Young, was to help this crossing by advancing down the eastern flank, across very severe country, over rivers, up and down hillsides, through dense jungle thickets. The object of this march was to establish a firm base on the high ground south-east of Tongzang, from where the Brigade would seek to destroy the Japanese force east of the Manipur River. Having achieved this, Brigadier Denholm-Young was to exploit as far south as Tiddim, along the main road.

Communication would be by wireless only. Support would be given from west of the Manipur River by Collins' 28th Field Regiment: a battery commander and F.O.Os. accompanied the column. So, too, did 74 Field Company, Bengal Sappers and Miners, 45 Field Ambulance, a mobile surgical team, 250 Dhotiyal porters, four troops from three different mule companies, an air support control tentacle, one company of the 2/1st Punjab, and 11 Battery of 24 Mountain Regiment.

By advancing east of the river, the Brigade would avoid having to make the crossing. All villages would be out of bounds except for operational purposes; villages would be ringed before our troops entered, to prevent any southward movement of the local inhabitants. All ranks were to be told the destination of the force, divided into four columns. With each marched detachments of Brigade Signals, 'V' Force, porters, the Field Ambulance, and the Supply Section that was responsible for picking up and issuing all supplies dropped each day by parachute.

Brigadier "Tim" Denholm-Young came to the Division from commanding with distinction a battalion of his regiment, the 13th Frontier Force Rifles. During operations he never spared himself, for nothing mattered except the task in hand. Spurred on by enthusiasm, he would throw himself whole-heartedly into whatever work came to his hand. But when the Division was out of the line, then his parties and hospitality were famous. Sufficient unto himself, momentarily intolerant, and, sometimes having a deceptively fierce exterior, he would go to endless trouble to help those who needed help, and his understanding and sense of humour smoothed many a difficult passage.

Widely read and always mentally alert, his conversation in the mess ranged far and wide. He had rowed with success for the Army Signal School in India and the Royal Connaught Boat Club, Bombay, and he had both stroked and coached the eights.

His lean figure, his long staff, and his small brown eyes smiling from beneath the brim of his bush hat soon became familiar to 123 Brigade and to the Division.

123 Brigade started its approach march south from Shuganu on the fifth anniversary of the outbreak of war. The four columns moved at one day's interval. The track proved good throughout, except for several small bridges that the Sappers had to repair. The weather was fine, although it was the period of the monsoon. But for the unusual dryness, the steep ascents and descents would have been slippery, the many unbridged streams unfordable, and progress slow and even more arduous than in fact it was. Ahead of the leading column moved a patrol screen of 'V' Force and

Chin Scouts, but the first twelve days passed without Japanese opposition. One of the few incidents of this period was the galling sight of the Royal Air Force carrying out an excellent airdrop on a place that the Brigade had left the previous day. No mules could be spared to go back and bring these supplies forward, so the local villagers doubtless fed well for many months to come, and clothed themselves in parachutes.

Then, on September 13, a tiny village named Anlung was reached. Already more than sixty miles had been covered down the track shown as a dotted black and red line on the maps. By sunset two days later a vital hill, Point 5801 just north of Lungtak, was securely in our hands. The Brigade was now level with Milestone 126 and the river crossing on the main Tiddim Road.

One company of the 1/17th Dogras entered Phaitu, three miles south of Lungtak, without trouble. The rest of Middleton's battalion went into harbour along the track between the two villages.

The following day Gleeson's 3/2nd Punjab placed a strong road-block near Tuitum. In vain the Japanese attacked our blocking force all night. They had no course but to withdraw. No longer could they dominate the vital Manipur River crossing. While the 2/1st Punjab in reserve controlled the track south of Phaitu, and the Dogras secured a dominant hill more than 6,500 feet high and established a road-block at Milestone 139, just south of Tongzang, Gleeson's companies set off down the main road from Tuitum.

We must now turn back and see how Warren's 161 Brigade had kept to the estimated rate of progress along the winding, precipitous road. Notwithstanding a delay at the beginning of September a short way beyond Milestone 97, they had driven the enemy fourteen miles that first week. They came in behind from the flank. To do this the troops climbed down and up rain-sodden slopes, crossed swollen streams, and struggled to carry supplies to forward companies, or to evacuate wounded men on stretchers. And all the time the rain poured down, with little respite. Landslides prevented more than one field gun from being brought forward to snipe at the Manipur River.

161 Brigade Headquarters had difficulty in keeping up with the battalions. But Brigadier Warren was there, delighted at playing truant from his H.Q., chuckling, encouraging his troops, and all the time formulating plans for the next move.

"Where," demanded his harassed and incensed Brigade Major, "is the Brigade Commander?" Warren at the time was eating a hastily prepared supper with Nettlefield's 2 Battery of 24 Mountain Regiment. He had given orders that he was not to be disturbed.

"He's up forward," the Brigade Major was told. "But we can relay any message."

"Tell him, for God's sake, to get back to his H.Q. Division have been yelling for him for hours," was the reply.

Warren heard this. "Too bad! Too bad!" was his only comment, as he filled his pipe.

The 4/7th Rajputs had a sharp engagement at Milestone 114, but were then able to press on six miles until a second block arrested their advance. This time it was the turn of the Royal West Kents to lead the Brigade. By hooking behind, as was now the practice, the battalion cleared another four miles of the road. And on September 14 British patrols reached the Manipur River. The enemy was not in sight.

To cross without the assistance of the Sappers was out of the question, so rapid and swollen was the torrent that swirled along between the banks. Waves and small whirlpools broke up the surface, and even to those standing on the bank the river presented a frightening spectacle. Its roar was likened to that of a football crowd.

The river was 110 yards wide at the crossing, and had a fall of fifteen feet per mile as it approached this point. The speed of the current varied with the level of the water, but it averaged twelve feet a second. During one spate the level rose three feet in two hours, and the speed of the current increased to twenty feet a second.

At first it seemed that no boat could cross without being smashed on the boulders round which the yellow-grey waters swirled angrily. But the initial crossing, a terrifying experience, was made on September 16 by Lieutenant D. I. Cordon and eleven men in a folding boat. The Japanese offered no resistance. Then a single cable was thrown across the river by means of an attachment to a 3-inch mortar shell, and this line was caught by the men who had crossed by boat. A double cable was fastened to the end of the single one and hauled across. In the same way lengths of cordage and a 3-inch wire hawser were pulled over the whirling torrent.

The hawser, tightened by a two-ton winch, was secured to the ten-ton-capacity log anchorages that had been built by our troops in April of the previous year, and which, fortunately, had been left both by them and the Japanese. The folding boat was used as a ferry, until a raft was built. On its last trip this boat capsized in the fierce stream and five men were drowned. Two folding-boat ferries were constructed and used after September 19, until the speed of the current proved so great that the bollards, to which the leads of the 'traveller' were secured, pulled out under the strain, and left gaping holes in the boats. It took fifteen men to operate this ferry, and in one hour a dozen return crossings could be made.

A second hawser was stretched across the river thirty yards downstream, and on September 21 a two-pier raft made to bear nine tons, but with deck space limited to twenty feet by ten, was ready for use. When more equipment arrived a week later, two such rafts were coupled together, the deck space was doubled, and mules, ammunition quads, guns, and vehicles with trailers could be taken from one bank to the other. For the mules screens had to be erected on both landing stages and rafts, but later, when the screens were removed, it was found that the mules were willing to go quietly on board. This double raft needed twenty men to operate it, could make six return trips each hour, and carry twelve loaded artillery mules.

Later still, six pontoon piers were lashed together, and the resultant raft bore four tanks across in an hour. These rafts were operated day and night, even in heavy rain. To light up the landing stages and the surface of the river, headlamps were used with effect. The Sappers—Jat Sikhs, Pathans, Punjabi Mussulmen, Rajputs, Garhwalis—who operated the rafts had, as a safety precaution, to be lightly clad, in bare feet or gym shoes, notwithstanding the added risk of malaria. In all, ten men were drowned in the efforts to bridge this turbulent watercourse. Without the rapid work, ingenuity and untiring energies of the Field Companies engaged, the Division could not have crossed. Had 161 Brigade not crossed to time, Denholm-Young's men on the other side might have been placed in a grave position.

It was on September 17 that two companies of the Royal West Kents crossed the Manipur and gained touch with men of the 3/2nd Punjab. Next day the remainder of the British battalion crossed, as did Grimshaw's 1/1st Punjab. They turned their backs to the river and their faces to the enemy. Their arrival on the southern bank freed the battalions of 123 Brigade for a further advance beyond Tongzang.

On the 17th, accordingly, 123 Brigade Headquarters set out from Lungtak to the main road at Milestone 133, seven miles beyond the river and hundreds of feet above it. Things went wrong. No patrols had been along this route before. Brigade Headquarters—staff officers, clerks, mess waiters and cooks, orderlies, sweepers, together with the Signals section and Advanced Dressing Station—walked along the track between Phaitu and Tongzang. At four o'clock that afternoon they were ambushed by snipers. The night was spent beside the track, and next morning a patrol was sent out under the Brigade Orderly Officer, Lieutenant Dutt, M.C. He was to find a route round the Japanese ambush. As the patrol took longer than was expected, Headquarters set off again without waiting for a report. The column plunged down a very steep jungle slope. The going was terrible, and progress slowed up by the carriage of stretcher cases by the A.D.S.

By nightfall the column was lost. Brigadier Denholm-Young had walked on ahead, and was out of touch. Brigade Headquarters bivouacked for the night, and, pocketing their pride, asked one of the battalions to send out a patrol to find them. This they did next day. When the main road was at last reached, it was found that the Brigadier had stumbled in a nullah and strained a ligament in his leg.

Having failed, on the night of September 19/20, to break through the Dogras' road-block at Milestone 139, the Japanese commander decided to jettison his few remaining guns, and to extricate the rest of his troops along tracks to the east and south. Enemy resistance in the Tongzang neighbourhood ceased. 123 Brigade prepared to advance towards Tiddim itself, and, while waiting for the field artillery, jeeps, and replacement mules, the arrival of which had been delayed by bad weather and a rise in the Manipur River, spent the last week of September in searching the land between Tuitum and Tongzang for abandoned enemy equipment, guns, and vehicles, and for graves, of which there were many.

* * * * *

September was a month of changes within the Division. General

Evans was stricken with typhus and taken to hospital. When he did recover, the Seventh Indian Division was entrusted to his charge—General Messervy had been meanwhile promoted to command Four Corps. Brigadier Mansergh was also ill. He left to fill the post of second-in-command to a brigade. And so, on September 23, command of the Fifth Indian Division devolved upon Brigadier D. F. W. Warren, who had long since proved his worth with 161 Brigade. Warren's place was taken by Brigadier R. G. C. Poole.

The next change affected Nine Brigade, resting near Milestone 83. The West Yorkshires had become reduced to two weak rifle companies, and it was necessary to form one strong company from this veteran battalion, place it under the command of Majors J. F. Newman and J. B. Miller, and attach it to the Royal West Kents of 161 Brigade. They, too, were decimated by disease, casualties, and the departure of men on repatriation to Britain. It was essential that at least one British infantry battalion should continue in action, notwithstanding the shortage of reinforcements.

A second change occurred within Salomons' Brigade, when the 3/14th Punjab returned to the North-West Frontier of India, after a long period of service, first with the Fourth Indian Division in Eritrea, and then with the Fifth in the Desert, Arakan, and Imphal. It had been the ravages of typhus that had finally brought this sturdy battalion to a state of weakness. And as the class composition of the 14th Punjab Regiment was being reorganized in India, the battalion was required back at its depot. A replacement was needed to continue the struggle, and this was provided by the 4th Jammu and Kashmir Infantry, commanded by Lieutenant-Colonel Narayan Singh. This battalion of State Forces, untried in battle, led entirely by Indian officers, joined Nine Brigade high up near Tongzang, on October 10.

As the advance to the Manipur River, 126 miles south of Imphal, continued, the L. of C. became more and more stretched, the road ever deeper in mud. It had become increasingly clear that before long the Division would have to be pared down to a bare minimum of men and vehicles. While a large rear party was left at Imphal, the forward troops would have to rely entirely on airdrop supply. And the tortuous road, which required very large numbers of men to maintain it, would be kept open only in the immediate operational area of the Division.

Accordingly, Brigadier Wilson-Haffenden, in charge of Administration at Thirty-three Corps, was asked to come down and discuss the matter. Without hesitation he said, "Of course, the only answer is to abandon the road and put the Division on air supply. I can arrange for seventy tons a day for you."

The advance went on with Division reduced to ten thousand men, stripped of heavy vehicles, but supported by six tanks. Two hospital units were provided to enable up to six hundred casualties to be held forward until Tiddim was captured. Then an airstrip would be built for the evacuation of wounded and sick. Once the road was closed, no reinforcements would be received. Bridging equipment for the Sappers was brought forward. The following units were sent back to Imphal and did not accompany the Division: the 4th Field Regiment, 56 Anti-tank Regiment, 44 Field Park Company (less detachments), 60 I.C.I.S. (less detachments), 113 Mobile Workshop Company, two of the Brigade Light Aid Detachments, the Divisional Recovery Company, the Brigade 'B' Echelons, 238 G.P.T. Company, and most of Rear Division Headquarters.

Formidable, indeed, was the task of supplying the troops down this long and appalling road, with its rutted and muddy surface, its swirling rivers, its landslides, its precipitous hillsides, its dangerous bends. Apart from 160 General Purposes Transport Company (Major R. Runciman), whose Mahsud drivers performed wonders of driving as their trucks brought men and stores to and fro, there was a jeep company, a malaria unit, a mobile laundry and bath unit, a mobile veterinary section, a pioneer company of Dhotiyal porters, and four animal transport companies, all under command to help the Division on its way.

The air supply worked splendidly. Whereas in Europe the Royal Air Force asked for dropping zones six hundred yards in length, in the Tiddim Hills they had twenty-five yards if they were lucky, on the side of a hill. It would take one aircraft half an hour to drop its load. Seventy tons was a small daily tonnage for a division —in Europe an airborne division received two hundred tons—and it could not be exceeded. This meant that every time extra gun ammunition was needed for a battle, the troops had to go on half rations. Strict economy had to be exercised, and stocks for a pitched battle could not be built up other than slowly. And if rations were not received on any one day owing to bad weather, all troops and animals had to go on half rations immediately, until the next successful supply drop was received.

The work entailed for Lieutenant-Colonel T. C. W. Roe and his 'Q' staff was continuous for nearly three months, and fraught with problems that had somehow to be solved. Every day they had to keep within the allotted tonnage, and the priorities were conflicting. Requirements had to be sent by wireless to Corps Headquarters two days in advance. The items were packed on the rear airfields the day before and arranged in plane-loads. On the day itself they were dropped, weather permitting. There were days when flying into the hills was impossible or when the pilots could not see the dropping zones for cloud. To listen for aircraft and to wait for reports of drops imposed a constant strain. And the strain was greater when the drop on an isolated battalion failed, and the men came down to their final reserves.

In addition to normal supplies, two complete sets of tank tracks were dropped, also jeep engines, charging engines for the Signals' wireless batteries, champagne for typhus patients in the hospital, frozen Australian mutton, and many other items: unleaded petrol, kerosene oil, aviation spirit, diesel oil, grease, boxes of grenades, thousands of multi-vitamin tablets, rum three times a week, tubes of toothpaste and packets of razor blades, bars of toilet and washing soap, tobacco, ten thousand cigarettes a day, the newspaper *SEAC*, and many pounds of salt, which had to be taken to counter the loss of body salts through perspiration.

Reserves of ammunition and food had to be built up, parachutes collected and sent back when transport was ready or else dumped in piles by the roadside—a source of joy to the local hill people, who made clothes from the white parachutes. The few coloured ones—red, green, orange—on which were dropped special items of equipment, were eagerly sought after by members of the Division for pyjamas and underclothes.

Within a few weeks American planes joined in the dropping. At first the pilots were very inexperienced. But so keen were they to learn that Major Moriarty, commanding the 3rd Combat Cargo Squadron, drove down to stay with the Division in order to see for himself, from the ground, just what his pilots were doing wrong, and how it could be put right. He quickly sized up the situation, and rapidly the standard of dropping improved. Privately, a special wireless link was arranged whereby at six o'clock every evening Colonel Roe gave Moriarty the results of each day's airdrops and put the American major in the tactical picture.

It is certain that these daily conversations, this close personal liaison, helped considerably to make the pilots feel that they were taking part in the battle and not just dropping supplies impersonally "into the blue." Ground-to-air communication by wireless was also established at the dropping zones, so that direct instructions or advice could be given to the pilots. One day an American was dropping very well indeed, and after every drop a blasé officer on the ground remarked, "Your last drop was perfect." The American pilot got bored with this, and exclaimed, "Say, is there no improvement on perfection?"

* * * * *

During the last days of September the 1/17th Dogras progressed slowly along the difficult gorge where the road runs close beside the Manipur River, between Milestones 140 and 150. Delay was caused by Japanese parties who resisted stubbornly until encircled. Heavy rain and several demolitions also hindered our advance. At the end of this gorge, where the river flows away a little towards the west, the road was crossed by the swift Beltang Lui, a tributary of the main stream. At first fordable, it later rose in spate, and the passage of men and supplies was, until the Sappers built a bridge, only possible by means of a temporary rope and sling.

Leading companies of Gleeson's 3/2nd Punjab crossed on September 28, and secured the high ground near Haupi, a village 1,400 feet below Tiddim, and some five miles distant as the crow flies. The Japanese were holding a position here. But on the first day of October an airstrike and continuous harassing fire by our artillery caused them to abandon their defences and go.

Meanwhile, Appleby's 2/1st Punjab had been marching down the eastern flank, through torrential rain, up and down steep and slippery hillsides, and across flooded streams. The men had ploughed their way along tracks that were deep in mud. Several mules lost their footing in the mire and slid over the *khud* side with all their loads.

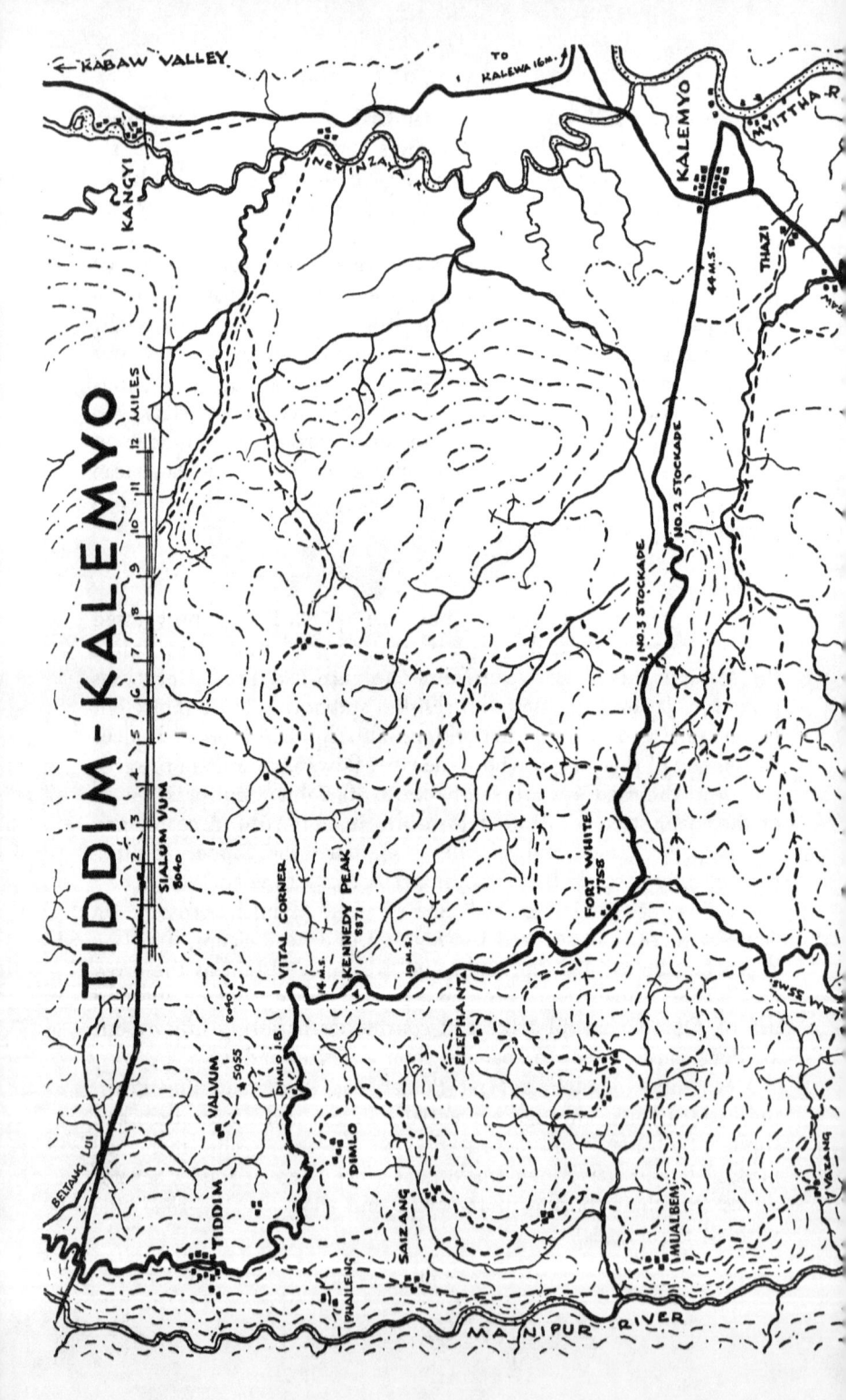

THE ROAD TO TIDDIM

The object of this march was to capture Kennedy Peak, which rises to a height of 8,871 feet, and thereby to cut off the remainder of the enemy division fighting near Tiddim. But the Japanese realized only too vividly the absolute need of defending the long ridge that led up to the Peak from the north. Either they must prevent our advance from this quarter, or see their communications and way of retreat cut.

The sharp bend in the road between Tiddim and Kennedy Peak, where the road turns south towards Fort White and Falam, was christened "Vital Corner," and vital it was. When the leading company of the 2/1st Punjab clambered through dense mist up the slopes of Sialum Vum—the hill that barred the way to the Corner and the Peak—the enemy was found to be entrenched with mortars and medium machine-guns four hundred yards beyond the crest. 'A' Company (Major A. Slater, M.C.) attacked, killed twelve Japanese soldiers, but failed to penetrate the defences. To left and right of the track the ridge drops precipitously from a height of over eight thousand feet to half that altitude in the valleys below. Thus, unless this position was cleared, it would be impossible for Appleby's battalion to move farther south.

Thick mist swirled about the hilltops, and visibility was barely twenty yards even in daylight. One month was to pass before the Japanese soldiers were driven from this magnificent bastion of defence. And the final success was not without cost in human lives.

The battalion dug in on Sialum Vum, and felt itself too close for comfort. Rain, mist and cloud were grave handicaps. Moss-covered creepers growing from the trees dripped ceaselessly. Movement on the abrupt slopes was generally impossible, and reconnaissance patrols were seriously hampered by the wet, slippery ground. For the first five days of October the men lived on half rations, so bad was the weather at the dropping zone. For two days, even, they had no rations. Colonel Appleby tells how a sepoy came to him on the second day and said, "Sahib, I have got a biscuit left and I want you to have it." Eventually the Colonel and the sepoy shared the biscuit. The men slept with one soaking wet blanket between three of them. Having only light tropical uniform of jungle green, they were never dry or warm. Only later, when flying conditions improved, were warm battle-dresses and extra blankets dropped for the battalion. The mules became in bad condition for lack of grain. Six died of exposure and cold. Visibility was normally some twenty yards, but whenever the mist lifted, watchers with field glasses could see plainly Vital Corner ahead, and often enemy troops and lorries on the road were visible.

On October 5 two companies attempted to get round the enemy position on the ridge, but though this move was partially successful at the beginning, the Japanese counter-attacked before our men had time to dig themselves in, and forced our withdrawal.

Then Captain Mohd Jamshed, with the guerilla platoon and three picked men from each company, was ordered to seek a way to the road near Kennedy Peak by going round the enemy defence positions. When evening came the party had reached a hill no more than five hundred yards as the crow flies from their starting-point. The Indians had been obliged to cut a track through the dense jungle undergrowth, and had climbed down some two thousand feet before toiling up the other side to the same level. As Jamshed could go no further, he was ordered to stay on his hilltop.

On several days the battalion positions were shelled by a Japanese 105 mm. gun, and a score of sepoys were killed or wounded. Those who were not hit found the constant threat of shells falling through the mist nerve-racking and unpleasant; it was obviously impossible for everyone to remain all day long in his bunker or trench. And one of the tragedies of Sialum Vum was that any serious casualty had to be evacuated all the way back to the Mobile Surgical Team at Kahgen. A mere six miles on the map, the journey along a bad and mud-clogged track that wound down four thousand feet was terrible. Small chance, then, for any severely wounded sepoy to survive the jolting, prolonged agony on a stretcher. Many good men died of their wounds along that grim track to Kahgen.

The Medical Services of the Division, under the A.D.M.S., Colonel D. Panton, had great problems to face and overcome. Along the Tiddim Road the Field Ambulances took up a new function. Because the road had been closed behind, and no casualties could be evacuated, the Main Dressing Stations became Field Hospitals with a hundred or more beds. Feeding utensils were held only for the authorized twenty-four patients. Though expanded in this way, the hospitals had still to remain mobile and follow the Division at each stage of its advance. And this could only be achieved by opening as far forward as possible, closing as the rearguard overtook them, and then leap-frogging one another.

Jeep ambulances, some of them driven with great skill and daring by volunteers of the American Field Service, proved a success, for they could go in places barred to the ordinary ambulance. Yet, for all their mobility, these jeeps gave an exceedingly rough ride across the ground where they alone could be used, and such journeys exhausted the sick and were hell to the wounded. The sole alternative—hand carriage on stretchers—was too slow and wasteful of man power.

The presence of a surgical team with the Division saved many lives by the emergency operations that were performed. More than any other single factor in saving life were intravenous blood and plasma transfusions. Colonel Steen, who commanded the 10th Field Ambulance, recalls one soldier whom he picked up on the roadside, in a state of complete collapse. He had a tiny hole in his skull behind the ear, and had bled extensively from this single wound. He was lifted into the jeep and driven back to the Main Dressing Station. Within half an hour, after two bottles of plasma had been given intravenously, the man was sitting up and smoking.

*   *   *   *   *

For a time we must leave Colonel Appleby's companies struggling eight thousand feet up in the mist and rain, and go back both in time and along the road to watch the progress of the other two battalions of Denholm-Young's 123 Brigade.

It had originally been planned to postpone an attack against the very difficult features of the stretch of road leading up the mountain face from the Beltang Lui to the summit just short of Tiddim itself. Up these seven miles the muddy road spiralled in a series of some forty hairpin bends. From the colour of the road surface and the appearance of these bends twisting against the green of the hillside, this formidable obstacle was known as "The Chocolate Staircase."

A further obstacle as the Division approached Tiddim was mines—British mines that had been recovered from Tiddim by the enemy after the departure of the 17th Indian Division in March.

The road surface, being too scarred for the Sappers to detect the presence of mines by eye, had to be swept at every point. The fact that, of the six tanks that had crossed the Manipur Road, one had burnt out during an engagement, and a second had been lost when the road beneath it collapsed, made this careful sweeping still more imperative.

No longer was it advisable to wait until the thrusts by the 2/1st Punjab and 3/2nd Punjab against the enemy's L. of C. to Tiddim began to exert an effect on the battle. Bad weather, administrative problems, and opposition were holding up their advance. 123 Brigade must increase pressure along the main road and so prevent the Japanese from concentrating their strength on any one front.

Fortunately the enemy failed to make full use of the natural obstacle that the Beltang Lui was in monsoon flood. On October 3 two companies of Dogras under Major Delme-Murray, who won the D.S.O., made an arduous approach climb on the left flank and blocked the road effectively at Milestone 158, near the top of the Chocolate Staircase. Here they ambushed twenty-five fully equipped Japanese. Seven were killed. The remainder fled, harassed by our guns.

This road-block dislodged the enemy from his positions on the mountainside, and the rest of Colonel Middleton's Dogras were able to push forward to the top of the Staircase. Here they were faced by some two hundred Japanese troops, who occupied old defences near Milestone 160. But a short hook by one Dogra company from the east, supported by two air strikes, drove the enemy from this position on October 16. On the two previous days, which were fine, the Royal Air Force had made eighty-two sorties with four squadrons of Hurribombers against the enemy bunkers in this place. And so enthusiastic was the co-operation of the pilots that in the end they were selecting targets and asking permission to bomb them. Tiddim was found deserted by Dogra patrols on the 17th.

* * * * *

At long last, after three months, after a gruelling advance along 150 miles of mud-surfaced road that had been the constant nightmare of every driver and passenger; past a host of milestones where the enemy had held up our leading platoons for a day and a night, and sometimes for longer; beneath dark skies from which the rain had poured with hampering flood and dismal discomfort—after all these weeks of steady plodding and endurance, of struggle against an enemy rearguard and the ravages of malaria, dysentery, and the dangerous scrub typhus, Tiddim was ours.

It was a small place, that stretched itself below the main road at a point where the saddle of the hill range forms a brief plateau edged with pine woods. Some fifty houses stood on the green slopes, square-roofed buildings of wood and of corrugated-iron sheets that had been painted red. Some were more solid structures of brick, and the windows on the ground floor were covered with metal grilles. Before the Japanese came and forced the 17th Indian Division to withdraw to the plain of Imphal in the spring, officials of the Chin Hills Administration had lived and worked here. Now the place was empty. No men and women and children came from their homes to welcome the incoming soldiers with garlands, though flowers still bloomed in the front gardens—honeysuckle, roses, and a type of bright marigold. Though certain houses had been damaged by the bombing, though pariah dogs prowled and sniffed their four-footed way among the ruins, Tiddim lay outstretched on its eminence, five thousand feet up in the beautiful hills. These were beautiful, when the troops had time to look out across the rolling wooded slopes towards the far horizon. And now, dominated as the little town was by the range of Sialum Vum, Vital Corner and Kennedy Peak a dozen miles forward, there was a special beauty of arrival and achievement to those who set eyes on the place bathed in sunlight. White clouds billowed towards the mountain ridge ahead.

But the Division knew that Tiddim, to which this long road had led for so many weeks, was not the end. Kennedy Peak reared its crest as a challenge for the fast approaching winter months. Beyond lay Fort White, and then suddenly down far below was the warm valley by Kalemyo. Perhaps then the Division would be allowed to rest from its exertions.

CHAPTER XXVI

VITAL CORNER AND KENNEDY PEAK

OCTOBER—NOVEMBER 1944

AFTER the collapse of Japanese resistance at the approaches to Tiddim, Wallace's Dogras encountered but little opposition, and soon reached the fifth milestone beyond the town. Here the road swung sharply left and ran along a ridge for eight miles to Vital Corner. Already the 3/2nd Punjab, operating on the flank, had secured positions on this very narrow ridge that was our sole route to Kennedy Peak, now that Colonel Appleby's battalion was blocked on Sialum Vum.

The 3/2nd had on October 4 occupied the ridge of Valvum, due east from Tiddim, and two days later seized Point 5955. That the enemy considered this hill important was shown by the tenacity with which he attacked our positions there on three separate occasions, each time with greater numbers. The third assault, staged on the 12th by some eighty Japanese soldiers, supported by artillery, medium machine-guns and grenades, failed after an hour's conflict, during which the Japanese evacuated half their number wounded, and left a score of dead on the slopes.

In the next few days patrols of the battalion raided the ridge at various points, and shot up enemy lorries moving along the road. On October 20 a road-block was established near Milestone 8. Next day the 3/2nd Punjab captured the Dimlo Inspection Bungalow a mile farther on. And by the time the Dogras were ready for further operations, the road had been cleared to within a mile of Vital Corner, where enemy positions had been brushed and located. Meantime, the 2/1st Punjab, facing Vital Corner from the misty heights of Sialum Vum, had not been lacking in offensive vigour.

If no attempt had so far been made to go round the Japanese block to the east, towards the cliffs by Vital Corner, it was because this approach looked more difficult from the map than any of the other routes. But the Battalion Intelligence Officer, Captain J.

Arthur, reconnoitred on four separate occasions with his section, seeking a possible line of advance. On the last day he found a route that appeared feasible. Colonel Appleby sent out Major S. Edwards' company to cut a track that ran down to below Kennedy Peak. The chosen route was all but impossible for troops laden with equipment, arms and ammunition, yet somehow they managed to reach their position after a struggle that lasted five hours. It is some indication of the precipitous nature of these hills that a line party that went with the company laid out only two miles of cable during that time.

On October 25 Appleby decided to assault the main Japanese defences on Sialum Vum. From Jamshed Hill 'D' Company (Major Gian Chand) were to launch a diversionary attack, while the principal assault was left to 'A' and 'C' Companies from the north-east. This attack was soon held up by intense enemy fire. But one platoon of 'D' Company, led by Subadar Ram Sarup Singh, did succeed in capturing part of the enemy position. As the forward section climbed the steep hillside it walked into savage fire from machine-guns sited in bunkers. Ram Sarup Singh at once led another section to charge the Japanese defences. This sudden action bewildered the enemy soldiers, who fled from their bunkers, and were severely mauled in the course of their retreat. The Subadar had been wounded in both legs, but took no care for his hurt. Instead, he consolidated the position gained, only to see the Japanese attacking from the flank in three waves of twenty men. Heavy fire from enemy grenade dischargers had just knocked out one of his Bren guns, and the man on the gun was dead.

It seemed that nothing could now prevent the overrunning of the Punjabi platoon, and the Japanese shouted in Urdu, "Don't fire." But Ram Sarup Singh took no notice. He set up another machine-gun and led a charge against the advancing enemy. He was gravely wounded in the thigh. He fell down on the grass. He stood up, ignoring his wounds, and sprang again at the enemy. To his platoon he shouted words of encouragement and courage. At the enemy he flung words of abuse and hatred. No sooner had the Subadar bayoneted one Japanese soldier and shot another than he was himself mortally wounded in the chest and neck by a burst of fire from a medium machine-gun. With his last breath Ram

Sarup Singh shouted out to his havildar, "I am dying, but you carry on and finish the devils."

By drawing upon himself much of the enemy's fire, the gallant Subadar had enabled the supporting platoon of 'D' Company to concentrate its fire on the counter-attacking enemy, and the remnants of our forward sections were extricated. But the attack had to be abandoned, and all three companies were withdrawn.

Before the action Subadar Ram Sarup Singh had shaken hands with his Company Commander and said: "Sahib, either the Japs or myself today." At first sight Ram Sarup Singh's appearance was not remarkable. He looked frail, and in his shoulders there was a suggestion of deformity. But those who were tempted to recall that he had but recently been a Pay Naik were reassured when they talked to the Subadar. To them he would reveal his true self, and his eyes became alight with enthusiasm, while his voice vibrated with eagerness. So profound had been the effect of his example upon the men that when volunteers were called for to bring in his body under the heaviest possible fire, the entire company volunteered. The Victoria Cross was posthumously awarded to Subadar Ram Sarup Singh for his skilful leadership and inspiring bravery in this desperate engagement against heavy odds.

161 Brigade, less the 1/1st Punjab who were engaged near Dolluang, was charged with the task of moving across country in a wide right hook, south through Mualbem and then across eastwards to cut the track between Falam and Kalemyo near Milestone 33. Here they would establish a base and prepare to operate north towards Fort White and the ridge between there and Kennedy Peak. While Nine Brigade drove south from Kennedy Peak, the 1/1st Punjab were to try and come in from the east to the road near Milestone 22.

By the last day of October 161 Brigade was ready in Mualbem. Only five miles of the track south from the main road had proved jeepable. The shortage of mules was serious, the ground very steep. At a bridge over one stream, where only a single mule could pass at a time, the unhitching and subsequent rehitching of groups of mules wasted hours. And as the first week of November came and went, the men of the Royal West Kents and 4/7th Rajputs struggled over hills, along tracks, beside torrents, through jungle, always heading for the road. They strove to discover where the enemy was, to conceal their presence in force, to arrive with the suddenness and success of surprise. The route was precarious, the men grew exhausted, and the mules were overworked, if not overburdened.

Events now moved rapidly. Kennedy Peak and Vital Corner were bombed with great weight. The range vanished in a pall of smoke and dust, from whose midst resounded the explosion of bombs. High into the cloudless sky rose the smoke, far across the hills echoed the sound of the bombardment. Escape routes to the north and east had been blocked by the 2/1st Punjab. Binnie's 3/9th Jats had moved across country from Dimlo, down into the valley, up on to the next ridge, and so had climbed to cut the road behind Kennedy Peak at Milestone 19. Then a brilliant piece of reconnaissance by a subadar and one sepoy from the 3/2nd Punjab led to the discovery of a way up the almost vertical position to Milestone 14, just at the back of the enemy holding Vital Corner.

Up this difficult route clambered one company under Major R. Groome. The enemy was surprised. Fighting continued during that night, when the Japanese counter-attacked ferociously. Groome's Punjabis held fast, and heard enemy vehicles driving past towards the south. The retreat was on, the enemy was pulling out, and when daybreak tipped the hills with light, on November 3, Kennedy Peak and Vital Corner were ours for the taking.

Nine Brigade now took the lead and pursued the Japanese. The Jats were already in position. The 4th Jammu and Kashmir Infantry went forward to what was their first major engagement with the enemy. The infantry went on alone, with supporting guns and tanks. Behind, the road was congested. Mines were being lifted, and the police had made a single way for traffic. Nine Brigade was moving up, mules and linemen, dispatch riders and ambulances, brigadiers and staff officers, ammunition trucks and a score of jeeps—all these bid for priority in the wake of the advance. It was ever the same. After a hook or two hooks behind the enemy, and a subsequent withdrawal of the Japanese, there was haste to catch up with the forward troops. Urgency was in the air. Success lightened men's faces. A new stage had been reached. There were smashed bunkers to be seen, as well as piles of Japanese shells, rice, picks and shovels, graves, and unburied corpses. There among the immense bomb craters and disintegrated bunkers stretched the dead, proclaimed by the bitter smell that was so familiar to a soldier's nostrils. And even that smell was a sign of success. The sunshine of the first days of November made the monsoon seem like a far-away memory of mud and rain. The road had dried up, the ruts were hard, the grass slopes glossy. On the ridge grew many great trees. And from their branches hung festoons of creepers thickly covered with dark green moss. The effect in darkness was at once grotesque and frightening. From the great height of Kennedy Peak men could look back and see the road as it followed the ridge past Dimlo. Tiddim was visible in the middle distance, its red houses framed in white parachutes. And steep down at their feet the soldiers saw hamlets of which the only sign was a bare patch of soil, the curling blue smoke from a chimney or a woodman's fire, and a dozen thatched huts.

These splendid views of hills and valleys as far as the eye could see were a joy each day as the Division advanced along the ridge from Kennedy Peak. On November 6 Salomons sent the Jammu and Kashmir Infantry to attack a hill known as Elephant. But before the companies moved up the grass slopes, Hurricanes droned over, dived sharply, and bombed the enemy positions. Earth and stones and limbs erupted through the smoke. The chatter of bullets and the greater crump of landing bombs reached the ears of the waiting troops, of the Gunners, of all who were engaged in this assault. It was a terrifying spectacle, this hail of fire and metal upon a hilltop. It seemed that no man could withstand the onslaught, however deep his trenches, however strong and cunning his bunkers. Nor did the Japanese remain to fight it out. When the sepoys stalked forward, they found the enemy gone, and ruin smoked on Elephant.

On the next afternoon the Jammu and Kashmir Infantry fought their way, this time against opposition, through the mist of clouds on to Point 8225, a mile farther south. This hilltop, too, had been bombarded, and so devastating had been the attack that no inch of the once grassy summit was not transformed into craters of upturned soil, or loose mounds, or caved-in bunkers. As the men hurriedly dug their trenches, in case of counter-attack, they

Moving up the Tiddim Road (C.I.S. Historical Section)

Tiddim (Imperial War Museum)

THE 3RD CARABINEERS ON KENNEDY PEAK (C.I.S. Historical Sec

MADRASSI WIRELESS OPERATORS (C.I.S. Historical Sec

stumbled over a veritable series of pits and giant mole hills. Clouds concealed the view on every side. Indeed, it was impossible even to see the hill that had just been captured, so dense was the swirling mist. And the muffled sounds of voices, of digging, the clink of shovels, the clatter of ammunition boxes being stacked on the ground, made this an eerie sight. The men felt the chill at 8,000 feet, now that the sun did not shine through. They wore sweaters against the cold, and still were not warm. At night, however warm the day might be, the cold was intense. The mosquitoes no longer buzzed, but blankets were few enough.

Immediately ahead nestled what remained of Fort White—named after Sir George White, V.C., defender of Ladysmith—lower down in a wide crescent of the hill range. The cold mist hid the ruined huts, and on the hillside lay beams, and strips of corrugated iron, and broken brickwork.

The enemy had gone right back now, and it was near Fort White that patrols of the 4th Jammu and Kashmir Infantry met patrols from the 4/7th Rajputs. This occurred on November 8.

Now Tiddim was out of sight, though Denholm-Young's 123 Brigade still guarded the hospital and supply dumps there. And casualties were being flown out each day to Tamu from the little airstrip at Saizang, 3,000 feet above sea level, six miles south of Tiddim, and the only possible site on the hilltops. It had taken the Sappers, with three bulldozers, nearly a week to construct a landing strip 750 yards in length. Three more nursing sisters were flown in, and a hundred casualties evacuated in Auster aircraft.

But what was behind was also the past, and a new view spread itself before the eager eyes of the troops. Beyond the jungle-clad mountainsides that dropped abruptly thousands of feet to the valley of the Myittha River which flowed into the Chindwin at Kalewa; beyond the paddy fields that surrounded Kalemyo; beyond the patches of forest in the lush valley—far, far beyond, lay the Chindwin and the Irrawaddy, and the plain of Central Burma. Behind rose the green, tree-studded hills that had just been captured. Ahead, fading into the distant haze, lay the real Burma that had still to be reconquered from the Japanese. If the distance to Mandalay seemed appalling, how much longer was the route to Rangoon.

And if these cities were to be reached, no delay could be tolerated, no effort spared. Nor was there delay, or any slackening of the Division's impetus. 161 Brigade, having completed its long cross-country march from Mualbem, went forward where the road turns eastwards towards Kalemyo. Ahead lay Falam and Haka, the centres of the Chin Hills. Both these small towns had been found clear of Japanese by Brigadier Marindin's Lushai Brigade. It was to the two Stockades that the Rajputs and Royal West Kents, with their company of West Yorkshires, pushed on. Those who expected a wooden palisade and rifle slits were disappointed. At Number 2 Stockade—a clearing in the jungle where the road reached a stream—Grimshaw's 1/1st Punjab rejoined from its successful harassing of the retreating Japanese among the foothills between Kennedy Peak and the valley down which the 11th East African Division had been fighting its way all these months. A company of Cargill's Rajputs made touch with the East African askaris on November 12. Thus was achieved the object of this two-pronged drive through the monsoon, down the Tiddim Road and the Kabaw Valley.

Then progress was swift. Into the valley, down the almost countless bends of the road, down seven thousand feet, went the Rajputs, the Jats, Nine and 161 Brigades. Now at last men could drive at forty miles an hour in top gear, rather than lurch forward at little more than walking pace. The enemy had gone, but must be pursued relentlessly, both to the east down the Myittha Gorge towards Kalewa and the Chindwin, and southwards in the direction of Gangaw. Both Divisions sent out units to attack, to explore, to reconnoitre. The Air Force continued to attack every target notified by our troops below. The East Africans drove the Japanese down the Myittha Gorge, and fought stern engagements on the way. The 3/9th Jats went south. The 1/1st Punjab prepared to help the East Africans with diversionary attacks. But the rest of the two brigades, and Divisional Headquarters, settled near Kalemyo and Thazi.

At the entrance to Kalemyo stood a signpost at the cross-roads. Pointing back up the road a white arm showed Tiddim, 48 miles. To the right was Falam, 66 miles away. Straight ahead indicated a little place named Pyinthaseik on the banks of the Myittha; while north went the dusty road towards Kalewa, 24 miles distant.

Kalemyo was a ruined township. The Burmese had fled from its crumbling walls to villages that were safe within the jungle, and the few Indian shopkeepers and moneylenders had gone the same way. Now the town lay deserted by its former inhabitants, and only nature grew apace among the ruins. The roads were overgrown with weeds. Trees and creepers stretched up to the broken windows, and the splintered balconies were vanishing beneath tall undergrowth. And this same undergrowth concealed the roofs that had fallen down, and the rubble caused by bomb and shell. A moat, now derelict and thick with weeds, surrounded this town, which had become like this during the two years since the Japanese first came inside its walls.

But with the arrival of the Division a new life hummed within Kalemyo. Jats, Rajputs and Punjabis pitched their little tents between one tumbled house and another, and the smoke of cooking-fires curled over the ruins and vanished among the trees of the nearby jungle. Shouts echoed in the town, and sepoys picked their way through long grass and fallen bricks. And here at last the scene more closely resembled the Burma that had been imagined, for great effigies of the squatting Buddha stared impassively across to the slender white pagodas that were to become so familiar a part of the Burmese landscape. A few had escaped without a scar, but more often their white surface had been chipped.

The Division did not linger in this green and beautiful valley, or in the comfort of wooden houses in the villages close to Kalemyo. The existence of peaceful rest—bathing and fishing in streams, eating and drinking, washing clothes, and lying out in the sunshine that bathed this small corner of Burma—was soon ended. For the Sappers constructed an airstrip, and in the last week of November and in early December the Division was flown back to Imphal. The transport and mules went up the Kabaw Valley, by way of Tamu and Palel.

The monsoon had ended. The Fourteenth Army was moving in all its strength for the recapture of Central Burma and the crossing of the Chindwin and Irrawaddy. Mandalay was the immediate goal, though the road to Mandalay was not that of Kipling. Other divisions were on the move. A brigade of the 20th Indian Division relieved the Fifth, which settled in tents high in the Naga Hills round Maram, south of Kohima.

The Division had earned its rest. It had been fighting without a break for fourteen months. In the course of its advance down the Tiddim Road it had killed 1,316 Japanese—fresh corpses counted on the ground. It had wounded 533, who were actually seen being helped away from the battlefield, and had taken fifty-three prisoners. Our own losses during that period had been eighty-eight officers and men killed, 293 wounded, and twenty-two missing. This had been an outstanding advance in the face not only of an enemy fighting a stiff rearguard action over nearly two hundred miles, but of very serious diseases, the worst furies of the monsoon, mud and steep places on a tortuous road, and a host of administrative difficulties.

The Division had earned its rest. But the men guessed that the rest would be short-lived. They were right.

CHAPTER XXVII

TRAGEDY AT JORHAT

DECEMBER 1944—MARCH 1945

During December the Division lived five thousand feet up among the Naga Hills, resting, training, and re-equipping. At night the cold was intense, but the views by day were remarkable and never palled. To the west rose great hills behind which the afternoon sun sank early. But to the east the eye could see far across terraced hillsides, villages built on promontories, and valleys often filled with mist. You gazed across these to hills and other valleys that rose and fell on and on to the distant horizon, and far beyond.

The black tar ribbon of the Dimapur–Imphal road wound among these hills, and the Division's camps were on the roadside, in tents or under huge tarpaulins stretched on a wooden framework. The Nagas, picturesque and colourful in their scarlet or black and green blankets, were to be seen chipping stones beside the road, or walking with the gait of hill people up and down the slopes.

Christmas 1944 was spent in this beautiful setting. But then, because of supply problems, the Division moved again, this time farther north to Jorhat beside the Brahmaputra River. In winter this flowed by many branches round islands and between long stretches of white sand flats tufted with long grass. Inland, beyond the paddy fields, the patches of jungle, and the untidy villages, lie the tea gardens, acres of little close-trimmed, flat-topped bushes laid out beneath slender-branched 'shade trees.'

Outside Jorhat the Division set up a new camp in open green fields. Tents were pitched, flagposts erected, signboards and fences painted and installed. Smartness prevailed, and for the first time since Quetta Camp outside Baghdad two years before, the Division gathered together in a great cantonment of tents. Once again flags and pennants fluttered above the white tents. Once again inspections, conferences, office work, the dispatch of leave parties, the listing of stores deficiencies, and the training of reinforcements were the order of the day. But no smoke from drip-flash stoves blackened the camp. No loose-wallahs prowled through the camps under the shield of darkness. The dust was scanty until the main tracks became stripped of grass and churned up by the to-and-fro of trucks and jeeps, lorries and marching feet.

The Division was no longer to operate with mules. Two of its brigades were to be fully motorized. Nine Brigade was designated for an air-landing role. The animal transport companies and the unit mules went away, and jeeps and trailers and four-wheel-drive 15-cwt. trucks took their place. The Divisional strength in transport rose overnight by nearly 2,000 vehicles. All these had to be collected, and issued to units. To find drivers for this influx of vehicles taxed the skill and ingenuity of every unit, the training of these drivers, and the painting of numbers and Divisional flashes on the front and back of every vehicle, occupied many hours each day.

Concert parties came to entertain the troops, mobile cinemas gave shows, football matches were organized. A race meeting on the Jorhat track was an outstanding success, and so were parties given by the Division to the Assam tea planters and their wives, who had made members of the Division so very welcome with generous hospitality in their homes and clubs.

* * * * *

While the Division was resting in reserve, in the Naga Hills and near Jorhat, the advance into Burma across the Chindwin by Messervy's Four and Stopford's Thirty-Three Corps was at once rapid and spectacular. Shwebo had been entered on January 7, and the first crossing of the Irrawaddy made two days later. By the third week of February four divisions and a tank brigade had crossed this great river and established bridgeheads on the east bank at widely different points. These bridgeheads had been fiercely attacked by the Japanese, but had been held against every assault. North of Mandalay the 19th Indian Division, led by Major-General Rees, whom we have met as commander of Ten Brigade in Eritrea, had crossed the Irrawaddy. West of Mandalay crossings had been made by the 2nd British and 20th Indian Divisions. And to the south-west, between Pakokku and Pagan, the Seventh Indian Division, commanded by Major-General Geoffrey Evans, had struck across to hold the eastern bank. And, behind, the 17th Indian Division waited in reserve.

The Japanese fought hard to contain us in our bridgeheads, and rushed troops from other fronts to attempt to destroy our forces. The fighting was bitter and prolonged, the casualties serious, the odds at first heavy. Both sides suffered many casualties, but gradually the bridgeheads were extended, and supplies and reserves built up for a break-through. Across the river were ferried men, weapons and transport, in readiness for a drive on Mandalay and Meiktila. And it was to balance the strength of the opposing forces and to ensure every chance of routing and destroying the enemy that the Fifth Indian Division was hurriedly re-equipped, despite the greatest administrative problems to be overcome in the process. General Slim needed a sixth division without delay, to help oppose the seven enemy divisions that were being reinforced hurriedly from other parts of Burma.

Early in February orders had been received from Fourteenth Army that the Division must be ready to enter the battle of Central Burma on March 15. General Warren, with his new G.S.O.1, Lieutenant-Colonel P. S. Pryke, flew south to Kalemyo to confer at Army Headquarters. They were to be briefed as to the future employment of the Division. On February 11 they set off on their return flight. The small aircraft vanished among the hills. Its occupants were reported missing and were never found.

This was a grievous blow to the Division, a piece of news that shocked everyone who heard it. Gloom and a sense of personal loss prevailed, for Warren—first of the Divisional Commanders to be killed—had been held in warm affection.

The troops knew him as "Daddy" Warren, or as "Freddie" Warren. His hair had greyed, deep lines ran across his face, he wore spectacles. If at first sight he did not seem to be awe-inspiring, or typical of the senior Army officer, but more like a farmer, your first impression was certainly one of a real human being. Characteristic were his slow, deliberate way of speaking, his dry Irish sense of humour, the merry twinkle in his eyes, and his companionable pipe.

If the British troops of the Division liked and respected him, the Indians adored him. He never passed anyone without talking to him. Though in the company of his colonels and staff, Warren would break off the conversation to speak to a Punjabi muledriver, to a West Kent stretcher-bearer, to a group of Sikh Sappers. For the humblest *jawan* Warren had a friendly smile, an encouraging word of cheer. He greeted a private soldier, not as a toy of war, but as another human being. His memory for names was astonishing; and his unusual fluency in Urdu and Punjabi gained him a closer touch with the Indian troops than would otherwise have been possible. Moreover, he could make jokes that were understood and appreciated by the *jawan*.

To work for him was a pleasure, because he knew exactly what he wanted and always gave a decisive answer to his commanders and staff. They found him approachable, for he made time to see them. His brain was as shrewd in administration as it was in operations. He was sure of himself, and prepared to back himself and his men to the hilt. He had faith in those under him, and the gift of making them feel this confidence. He gave an impression of slowness that deceived some men, but once he had made his decisions he would act swiftly, and was prepared to take a risk that had been calculated and deemed justified. But he would not be hurried by the highest in the land. He believed in the motto of "More haste, less speed," and would often say, before coming to a decision, "Let's think the problem out first."

And he had a habit of suggesting a plan of action to his junior commanders, rather than giving them an inflexible order that might seem meaningless. In this way he took them into his confidence and inspired deep loyalty. His troops felt that whatever orders he gave would ensure success with the minimum casualties, and that he would never push them into a disaster.

He knew no fear, and in a tight spot he was an inspiration to all those around him. His bravery and enthusiasm infected his Brigade and his Division; he was never seen to be ruffled or excited. Even when the tide of battle was at its roughest, he remained cool on the surface. Indeed, he was at his best when faced with the utmost difficulties, and did not let the burden of adversity bear him down. His strong temper he kept perfectly under control, and many have commented how he never spoke out of turn to his subordinates, however exasperating, though he could be outspoken and challenging to his seniors when he disagreed with their policy or when the situation warranted it. He was always prepared to hold out against what he considered ill-advised decisions.

During a battle Warren was invariably well forward, dropping in on a battalion, company or even platoon headquarters with his friendly manners and dry humour. Commanders loved to have him in the forward areas, for he did not interfere, though a word of advice was ready if needed. He would arrive on a captured position before it had been consolidated, and start to plan the next move ahead.

Despite his age and corpulence, he was a tremendous walker, and he clambered up and down hills in Arakan, by Kohima, and down the road through Tiddim to Kennedy Peak and Fort White with amazing speed and energy. One officer of the Royal West Kents recalls how, in a very exposed position in Arakan, Warren arrived on the very first day after we had occupied the feature. He said, with his gay twinkle, that he was walking round the walls of Jericho. Then, in full view of the enemy, down a gully between the two leading companies, where no man had ventured except running and crouching, Brigadier Warren walked without haste. And the sight of him there braced the infantry and gave them good heart. Always he carried a long staff to help him up the slopes, he wore a wide-brimmed bush hat, and his hands, when they were not holding or filling his pipe, were stuck in a very loose web belt and holster.

It was ironic, perhaps, that Warren, who had been born in Japan where his father was a missionary, should be fighting the Japanese. But he knew his enemy thoroughly, and his decisions about them were right. Sometimes his predictions, to the exact time and place, long before they occurred and before others were prepared, seemed uncanny. It was in 1917 that he transferred to the Indian Army, after two years' service with the Royal Munster Fusiliers. He and Brigadier Salomons had been together in the 34th Royal Sikh Pioneers, building roads in Waziristan. When the Pioneers were disbanded he transferred to the 8th Punjab Regiment, worked in the translation section at Army Headquarters in India for four years, and attended the Staff College at Camberley under protest, being afraid that he might end his days as a 'chairborne' soldier. In 1940 he raised the 6th Battalion of his regiment, Warren's Foot.

He was a versatile man, shrewd, widely read, gifted with an outstanding memory. Conscientious and methodical by nature, he worked at his languages, won prizes for short stories and military essays, and intended one day to take up writing seriously. If he was not athletic like so many soldiers, he was fond of riding, despite several nasty falls; he loved a game of golf as this did not interfere with his pipe, and he looked forward to the day when he would go sailing. The social life peculiar to the Army in India did not attract him, for all his friendly disposition. His ambition was to do a good job of work in India and then retire to the peace of a country home where he might read and write and make things in wood. But that was not to be. Instead he died at the height of his career, planning the new role for his Division whose confidence and affection he had so richly won during the eighteen months he had served with it.

* * * * *

Brigadier Salomons took over the Division for a few days, and then, at a moment when the troops were preparing to re-enter the battle and when a leader who knew and was known by the Division would be invaluable, General Mansergh was posted to command. He had only recently taken over the 11th East African Division, and their loss became our gain. Mansergh was a veteran of the Fifth Indian Division, he had commanded it temporarily on many occasions when Briggs or Evans had been away or ill, and now he returned where he belonged.

"Bob" Mansergh had served with 144 Field Regiment (Surrey and Sussex Yeomanry) during the campaign in Eritrea and Abyssinia four years back. When he went to command the Royal Artillery Depot at Almaza near Cairo, he widened still further a knowledge of Gunner officers which he had built up while adjutant of the Royal Military Academy at Woolwich before the war. He had been born in South Africa, and spent the first years of his life there. Training in diplomacy had come his way when he served on the Military Mission to Iraq as a captain. It is told how he wanted to go north to the border to paint and sketch. No leave was obtainable to do this, as the area was politically *verboten*. But Mansergh went without leave, only to be caught by the Kurds and cast into a prison cell. He denied that he was an army officer, and claimed to be a school teacher on holiday. He gave a fictitious name. This was cabled to London, where all knowledge of him was naturally denied. After several days of discomfort, when convinced that it was his only course, Mansergh confessed.

As a Gunner he was among the most capable, as a C.R.A. he was unsurpassed, both in the skill with which he managed his regiments, the unbounded confidence that he aroused in successive Divisional Commanders, and the admirable relationship he established between his officers and the infantry battalions they supported. He had been C.R.A. for more than two years, and then, being told that this would be his only avenue to higher promotion, he had gone as second in command of a brigade with the Seventh Indian Division. At the end of the Tiddim Road campaign, General Slim had sent for Mansergh, told him that he had no brigade that he could give him to command. Then, as though by an afterthought, to assuage very evident disappointment, Slim added that he was entrusting the command of the 11th East African Division to him.

Mansergh was a man of commanding presence, great height, and massive build. His manners were polished, his bearing at once urbane and impressive. His innate, sincere charm was famous, for he went out of his way to make others feel at ease, because, perhaps, he liked to be at ease himself. Characteristic was his treatment of regimental officers who visited 'A' Mess at Divisional Headquarters. They were likely to feel overawed at entering this group of senior officers, but from the moment of Mansergh's entry all shyness was forgotten. He would insist upon your sitting near him, and he was one of those few people who make you want to talk of your own interests. As one Gunner officer commented long afterwards, "What boring hours he must have endured listening to us all."

This same officer recalled that once, happily, the General spent a night with his regiment. "I remember asking him which, of all the men he had met, he would most prefer to dine with. His answer was unhesitating: 'The Duke of Aosta and Lord Louis Mountbatten.' "

To the Gunners of the Division Mansergh seemed almost their personal property, for he knew all the officers by their Christian names; he had been the welcome guest of almost every troop, battery and regimental mess at one time or another; and his unfailing tact, patience, and outstanding competence were widely known and respected.

His judgment of men was as admirable as were his confidential reports on them. Two particular gems have been recorded: "Geared low but pedals hard," and "I should hesitate to breed from this officer." One regimental commander, describing General Mansergh's amazing capacity for being able to call a man by his name—one of the secrets of his success—added that Mansergh knew more of the men of this particular regiment by name than ever did its commander, even at the end of his period of command.

He was artistic, loved music, and painted or sketched; *Alice in Wonderland* travelled in his kit through the campaigning years; he watched natural life with keen interest; he collected Persian carpets and rugs, and when in Baghdad would spend hours in the bazaars bargaining like an expert.

He could enter into everything easily without ever losing his dignity, whether it was visiting a troops' mess on Christmas Day or sitting unobtrusively on a bench at the back of the tent during a Toc H meeting in Baghdad or at some lecture. Or, by contrast, he was an ideal introducer to such a lecturer as Freya Stark, and a chairman of ease and tact. Though he was good at smoothing down the indignant and irate, he was also able, without becoming angry, to make those who had displeased him feel unutterable worms and vow that they would never again incur such an interview. Where any problem arose over a man's pay or his reputation, Mansergh took time and the greatest pains with detail to examine the question. Humane and attentive to paperwork, friendly to every rank, he was in battle a bold and imperturbable commander. And when a soldier needed to be a diplomat, as will be seen later in this history, he had the gifts required.

CHAPTER XXVIII

MEIKTILA

MARCH 1945

MEIKTILA, eighty miles south of Mandalay on the main road and railway to Rangoon, was a vital centre of communications for Central Burma. It was, too, an area devoted to Japanese supply depots, base hospitals and maintenance units. The town was of the utmost importance to the Japanese in their battles to prevent Slim's Fourteenth Army from crossing the Irrawaddy, and in the defence of the Mandalay front. To capture Meiktila would for us be a fruitful blow in the enemy's rear. We should sit astride his lines of communication, his lines of supply, and, perhaps, too, his eventual lines of retreat from the north.

And so, having once crossed the Irrawaddy, by the bridgehead secured and held by Evans' Seventh Indian Division, the 17th Indian Division (Major-General D. T. Cowan), supported by 255 Tank Brigade, moved east from Pakokku, captured Taungtha on February 24 in the face of determined resistance, brushed aside opposition down the road leading through Mahlaing, seized an important airfield, to which the Division's airborne brigade was flown, and assaulted Meiktila itself.

The Japanese, surprised by this invasion of what they thought to be a back area, hurriedly mustered their forces, which were larger than we had anticipated. To defend the town they fought with tenacity and fanatical recklessness. Hand-to-hand fighting lasted for a week. Enemy posts had to be evicted from one house after another. Many quarters of Meiktila were reduced to ruin. It was a battle in which the Japanese held out in small groups in their cellars and dugouts. The defence was unco-ordinated if savage, and by March 4 the men of Cowan's Division had captured the larger part of the town.

If our thrust had been rapid and decisive, the reactions of a startled enemy were no less swift and vigorous. This enemy had to regain the town at all costs. And he spared no effort to do so. The roads were cut, Taungtha was recaptured, the 5,000 soft vehicles of the Division and Tank Brigade blocked from reaching Meiktila. Above all, the Japanese sought to gain the airstrip on which all our supplies were landed, two miles north-east of the town. The pressure increased for the enemy outnumbered our troops in Meiktila. General Slim's nearest reserves were the Fifth Indian Division, still at Jorhat; but Jorhat was seven hundred miles away. And so it was that Salomons' Nine Brigade, which had trained for an airborne role, was ordered to be flown in to reinforce the defenders of Meiktila. This was no passive defence. Its very nature was offensive, for, daily, strong columns of tanks and infantry sallied out to break up enemy troop concentrations before these could attack the town.

Dakotas began to fly in the Brigade on March 15. Brigadier Salomons has recorded how he attended the briefing of the American pilots who were to fly in part of the Brigade next day. "Half an hour after the briefing conference was due to start some of the pilots had still not returned from that day's sorties. But the briefing officer said he could not wait for them and indicated that those present would just have to pass on the orders later to the others. Occasionally the briefing officer said casually that it might help to take a note of this (this being a bearing to fly on after crossing a certain line, or the altitude to be adhered to on certain stretches of the run). As the pilots jotted these figures down on the backs of envelopes and other scraps of paper, those of us listening all hoped that our own pilot would be one of those receiving this information at first hand and not from a pal some hours later."

On the first day fifty-four sorties were made from Palel airstrip. Salomon's Tactical Headquarters and the 3/2nd Punjab (Lieutenant-Colonel Lakhinder Singh) were the first to arrive. The flight was uneventful across the Irrawaddy and the dusty, hot-looking plain of Central Burma. How sharp a contrast this buff landscape presented with the green, jungle-clad Mayu Range and Chin Hills! Gone were the cool and clouded summits, the awe-inspiring panoramas. From now on the men would see a country of slender white pagodas.

The planes started banking and, there below, the passengers saw Meiktila and its lakes. From the air these lakes appeared vividly

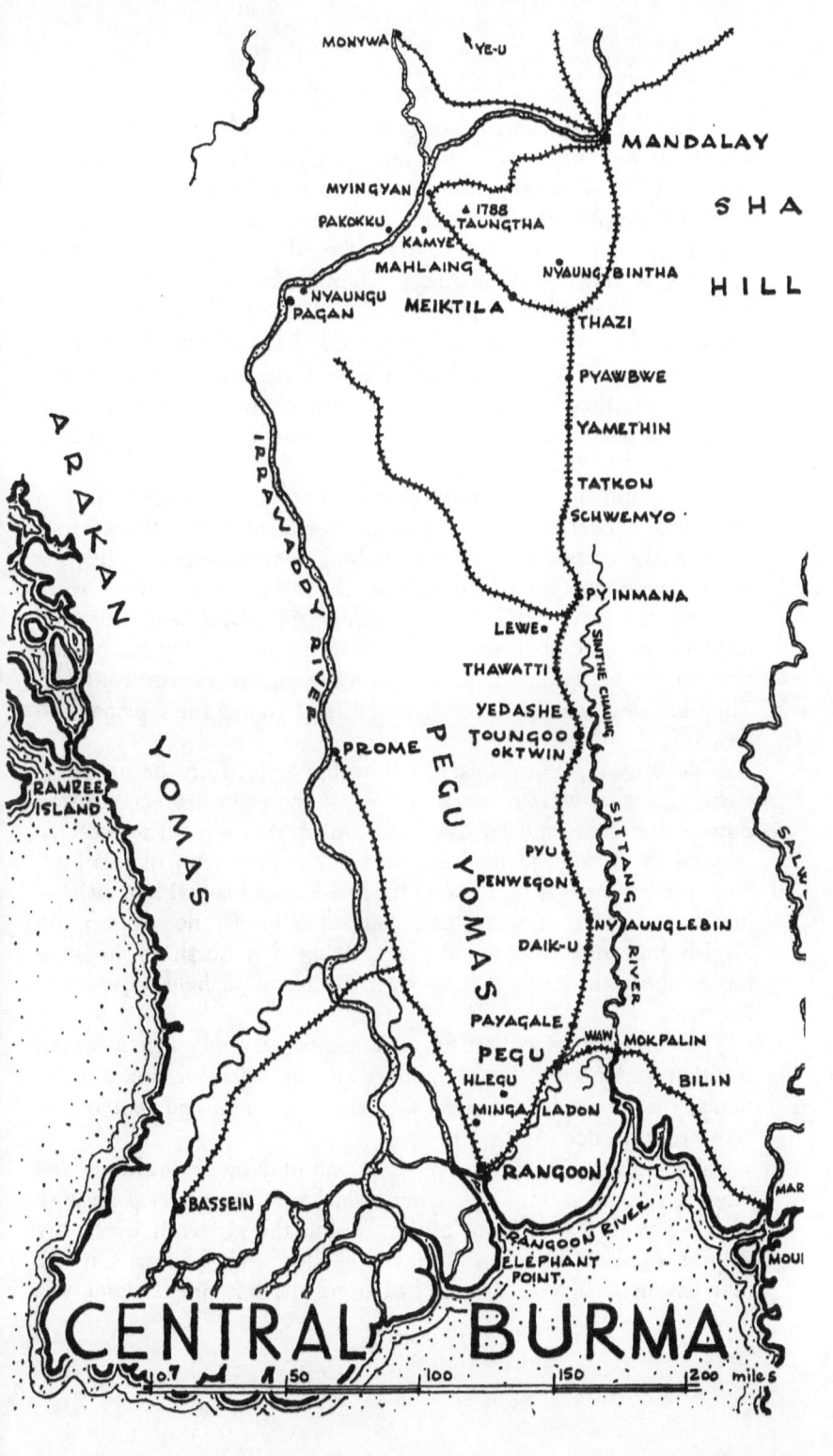

blue, fringed with a luxurious green that quickly gave way to the vast outer belt of brown—the hot, scrubby plain. As the planes came in to land on the airfield some two miles out of the centre of the town towards the north-east, Japanese anti-aircraft guns fired. The troops could hear the sounds of battle on the ground above the roar of the planes' engines. They looked down at bursts of smoke on or around the airfield. And these sights and sounds surprised the men, who had expected that at least the landing would be easy. As the Dakotas touched down and roared across the airfield, their wheels put up clouds of dust. The American pilots shouted to our men to "get out quick, for God's sake!" They leaped to the ground.

The equipment was thrown out hurriedly. A fortunate lull in the firing occurred while the doors were open and the aircraft were being emptied. But the shelling was renewed while our troops were waiting to be told where to go. The pilots were splendid the way they helped to unload the planes and yet found time to photograph some of the dead Japanese lying round the airstrip, or to inquire if there were any enemy swords available. They did not waste a second, but turned round their planes and flew off.

Nine Brigade, or that part of it which arrived on the first day, went into what was known as 'D' Box—the main defence position outside the area held by the 17th Indian Division. The western edge of the airfield formed one side of the perimeter of this box. Here the ground was bare, flat as the Desert, studded with occasional bushes and trees. Leaving two companies in 'D' Box, the 3/2nd Punjab moved across to 'B' Box, lying due north of Meiktila beside the main road. On its own the battalion held an exposed ridge.

The entire Divisional artillery, concentrated as it was in a central position in Meiktila, could support all our defensive boxes. The tanks, too, were held centrally in the town area and sent out as they were needed.

During the next three days the rest of Nine Brigade arrived safely on the airstrip. The flying in had been speeded up because of the Japanese who were milling round the airstrip. Every day snipers were active and the enemy shelled both boxes. On the first day none of our aircraft had been hit, but one Dakota was

(C.I.S. Historical Section)

Major-General D. F. W. Warren

Major-General E. C. Mansergh

(Elliott & Fry)

LORD LOUIS MOUNTBATTEN INSPECTS 3/2ND PUNJAB GUARD OF HONOUR AT JORHAT

MAJOR-GENERAL MANSERGH IN CONFERENCE NEAR MEIKTILA

(C.I.S. Historical Sec

destroyed by fire on March 16 and six men were wounded while escaping from the plane.

In 'D' Box, apart from Nine Brigade Headquarters, Bailey's 2nd West Yorkshires and two companies of the 3/2nd Punjab, there were certain miscellaneous units of the 17th Indian Division, some R.A.F. ground staff, a large hospital, various stores dumps, and many vehicles.

The whole Box was crowded. Each of the many little bivouac tents, which were far too close together for safety, had a slit trench beside it into which the occupant could roll or jump when the shelling started. In between the mass of tents stood the vehicles: these had been dug down forward so that their engines were to some extent protected by the ground from intermittent shelling.

On the second night after the arrival of Nine Brigade a party of Japanese came on to the airfield. Lack of troops prevented us from holding a perimeter round the landing ground, although the enemy thought at first that we were doing so. Next morning the Japanese patrol was driven off so that our aircraft could continue to land, but during the next night a platoon arrived, and it took a West Yorkshire company more than an hour and a half to drive off the enemy. The Dakotas were held up. During daylight standing patrols guarded the airstrip. Then, on the fourth night, a whole Japanese company, supported by one gun, established itself on the airfield, having good cover in the low scrub between the runways. Two British companies, aided by tanks, fought until midday to remove the enemy. And so it went on, each day the situation growing worse, until it would take half a battalion, with tanks, to evict the Japanese, before our Dakotas could land with further units of Nine Brigade.

The Japanese guns approached nearer, and their gunners shot at the aircraft. They hit none, but the planes had to unload at very great speed, the American pilots helping to lift out the stores on to the dusty ground. When the Dakotas took off again straight away, using the very runway they had landed on, the Japanese fired from the north end of the airfield.

On March 23, the last day on which our planes were able to land, they had to be turned back in mid-air because the airfield was not cleared until two o'clock. This left only three hours for the planes to come in. As many as possible landed, for it was now realized that next day it would be impossible to clear off the Japanese. Most of our wounded were evacuated on these last few planes.

Brigade Headquarters was situated right on the edge of the Box. The command post was dug down in the shelter of earth walls that had been built previously to protect aircraft. A bamboo matting roof shielded the men from the sun. The signal office, the officers' mess, and the command post of the West Yorkshires, had also been dug underground. Inside it was pitch dark and stuffy, and lights from wireless batteries had to be kept on all day.

On March 22, to everyone's regret, Brigadier Salomons had left Meiktila, after a disagreement with General Cowan over the employment of Nine Brigade. He was succeeded by Lieutenant-Colonel K. Bailey, commanding the 2nd West Yorkshires. On the following day Bailey was standing in the approach trench to the Brigade command post with his Brigade Major, W. S. Armour. The Intelligence Officer, Captain Leslie-Smith, was standing between them. All three were studying a map. Suddenly a shell landed outside the command post: the Brigadier's batman was killed, and Armour was wounded in the arm and back. Bailey, a heavy man, being wounded in the back, aggravated his condition by falling backwards down the twelve steps that led into the command post. Leslie-Smith, too surprised to duck, was unscathed. Shell fragments that wounded his two companions passed on either side of him.

Armour was taken to the dressing station, and when this was shelled soon afterwards, he received a further slight wound. Then he was sent to the airstrip to be evacuated with the other wounded. As the last Dakota with wounded on board was warming up ready to take off, a Japanese anti-tank gun fired straight down the runway and set the plane alight. Some R.A.M.C. orderlies unloaded the burning aircraft. Armour had again been hit, badly this time, in the head. When all the wounded except him had been unloaded and the plane was blazing fiercely, the orderlies said "He's had it!" and discussed the need for removing the dead body from inside the Dakota. One of them said " Anyhow, you can't let the so-and-so burn. Let's take the body out."

Billy Armour heard this, but could not speak. On being taken outside, however, he indicated that he was still alive. That night he slept in a dressing station near the light aircraft strip, and was to be evacuated the following day in a light plane. As this strip had also been shelled, Armour was, not unnaturally, chary of lying about waiting his turn to be loaded. So he insisted on being placed in a small hole, and only when the other men were on board and the engine was running did he get off his stretcher and totter to the aircraft.

* * * * *

At six-thirty on the evening of March 24 the occupants of 'A' Box heard enemy tracked vehicles moving from west to east across their front. The same noise was then heard by 'B' Box away to the north-east of their position. When, at eight o 'clock, a Japanese tank rumbled down the western runway, toured the airstrip twice and halted, our troops thought that it was a British tank and did not fire until too late. The tank made off towards the north-west. Soon after this several more tanks, supported by Japanese infantry and heralded by a heavy bombardment from six guns, pressed close towards the east side of 'B' Box. By clanking squeakily up and down the airfield for half an hour only fifty yards outside our wire, the first tank made some of the defenders uneasy. Later, it appeared near one of the Box's back exits which had been wired up for the night, and stopped within fifteen yards of the only two Bofors guns held in 'B' Box. An officer opened the turret and said something in very plain Japanese. Still no one fired. In the silence he realized that he had come to the wrong place and he and the tank dashed away untouched. No one fired even a parting shot at him. It was now clear that the tank's movements up and down the airfield, far from being aggressive, had merely indicated that the Japanese officer had lost his way.

Though enemy tanks knocked down a portion of the perimeter wire to prepare for an advance, the infantry supporting the tanks were held off by accurate artillery shelling and by machine-gun and rifle fire from the 3/2nd Punjab. The attack was continued in vain until dawn by the Japanese, and next day over twenty bodies were recovered. During the same night 'D' Box was attacked by jitter parties, who maintained their harassing activities until dawn, accompanied by shelling. Our men repulsed all these attacks without loss. Daylight revealed blood and equipment all over the place. But it also revealed the unpleasant fact that some thirty Japanese had dug themselves and an anti-tank gun into the aircraft bays. And this gun soon opened fire on 'D' Box, wounding a number of Indians as the day wore on. Our own mortars and field artillery were unable to damage the gun owing to its deep pit.

During the same day Brigadier H. G. L. Brain arrived to take over command of Nine Brigade from Colonel Younger, who had stepped into the breach when Brigadier Bailey was wounded. To replace Armour as Brigade Major came Major P. P. Steele, who had been Adjutant to the 2nd West Yorkshires for a considerable period. A further change occurred when Major J. A. E. Newell was promoted to command the 3/2nd Punjab in place of Lieutenant-Colonel Lakhinder Singh. Command of the West Yorkshires devolved upon Major P. W. P. Green.

The next two days were fairly quiet except for intermittent shelling of 'B' and 'D' Boxes and occasional jitter parties and patrolling during the night. But after dark on March 27 the Japanese were extremely active along the whole Brigade front. They started at ten-thirty by attacking Newell's 3/2nd Punjab in 'B' Box with a platoon of infantry. They charged up to the wire, firing their every weapon. The attack was beaten off. A West Yorkshire patrol moving towards Milestone 340 on the Mandalay Road was fired on by rifles and drew back, but was then mortared in the light of flares and had to scatter. Some returned to 'D' Box, others to 'B' Box; there were six casualties in all.

At midnight, sixty Japanese attacked 'B' Company of the Jammu and Kashmir Infantry, holding a position out at Milestone 342. For some days past our tanks and supply columns had been trying in vain to fight their way through to relieve this company, commanded by Major Harnam Singh. Now the men, already reduced to half-scale rations, were bombarded by three tanks which stood off a thousand yards away, firing into our positions with machine-guns and grenade dischargers. Then at two o'clock in the morning the Japanese tanks and infantry both closed in towards the company area, but did not press their attacks. Next day a sweep by our own tanks and a company of the West Yorkshires and another from the 3/2nd Punjab was made towards Milestone 342. But again this column failed to reach the Jammu and Kashmir company, being held up by extremely heavy fire from the village of Wathit, in which there were at least two hundred Japanese troops.

* * * * *

Each day the 17th Indian Division sent out a Gurkha battalion with guns and tanks to clear the villages outside Meiktila. These villages were often a mile in length, stretched out in a belt of trees. And it would take the greater part of a day to comb such villages. But these tactics brought good results, and the average number of Japanese killed during these sweeps approached two hundred. As there were comparatively few Japanese to the north and north-west of the town, most of these daily sweeps, which involved considerable fighting on a fierce scale, took place to the south and east of Meiktila. Nine Brigade itself had not enough troops to do more than hold on to its positions.

On the whole the Japanese were heavily damaged by the offensive sweeps and were kept away from Meiktila as a result. But on one night the Japanese did put in a heavy attack against a brigade of the 17th Division astride the road south of the town. It was a very strong wired position. About three hundred yards in front, on a lone mound the top of which was a cemetery, a platoon of the Jammu and Kashmir infantry was holding an isolated position. The hillock overlooked the approaches from the south. Its defenders, who had dug their trenches among the gravestones, would be able to warn the main brigade position if any enemy troops bumped against them during the night.

On this particular night they heard the sound of approaching troops. Though they did not know it at the time, this was a Japanese battalion moving to attack and occupy the airfield. The battalion, having lost its way, now arrived on the southern front. Part of the leading sections ran straight into the Indian platoon position. The attack was a mistake, and surprised the Japanese. While their left-hand party attacked the Jammu and Kashmir sepoys on their hillock, the remainder of the battalion charged forward in a mass and ran into the main 17th Division position. In pitch darkness the Japanese troops charged with screams and yells. Defensive fire by the divisional artillery and by local mortars was put down in front of the perimeter wire. The Japanese battalion was stopped. It suffered huge losses. Caught in the fire of artillery, mortars and criss-crossing medium machine-guns, the enemy soldiers were cut to pieces.

Until morning nobody knew quite what had happened, but with daylight the ground was seen to be littered with dead. Some two hundred and thirty bodies were counted; others had no doubt been carried away by the Japanese under the cloak of darkness. The bodies lay in swathes; you could see where five sections of eight or nine men marching in file had been caught by a machine-gun and had fallen in line. The wounded and the dead had been rewounded and terribly mutilated by the heavy fire which continued for more than forty minutes. Never had our troops seen dead who were so very dead. The bravest of all the enemy, perhaps, were a small party who heaved forward the battalion gun. When the firing first broke out they did not, as might have been expected, put the gun into position and fire hopefully ahead. Instead, the Japanese gunners started to run forward, carrying the ammunition and tugging their gun alongside the infantry. Into the terrifying inferno they went; they reached a point ten yards from the wire, stopped there, and attempted to fire their gun. How many of the crew were still living at that moment will never be known, but during the next few seconds the Japanese gunners, without protection, were wiped out to a man. The gun was never fired. And at daybreak there lay the muzzle towards the British position, with its crew heaped about it.

Those who had attacked the cemetery mound had been repulsed and decimated with their companions. Several Japanese soldiers were found sprawling across the wire; while some had actually penetrated the Jammu and Kashmir defences and lay slumped across the tombstones. The few who still lived—and most of them had been wounded—stayed where they were, and sniped at our positions, until they were killed, one by one.

* * * * *

On March 30 an operation order was issued by the 17th Indian Division. 48 Brigade, having cleared a number of villages, was to operate eastwards along the road to Thazi as far as the seventh milestone, 99 Brigade would occupy the area of Nyaungbintha and Tamongan, while 63 Brigade with tanks operated north and east of the town to contact the advancing troops of the 20th Indian

Division. Nine Brigade, meanwhile, became responsible for the defence of Meiktila town north of the railway.

That night the airstrip was found to be clear. Next day, the last of the month, patrols all round the Nine Brigade area had nothing to report. For the first time in a week planes were able to land on the airstrip where previously the supply dropping zone had been. It appeared that the Japanese, realizing they had no chance of recapturing Meiktila, had decided to withdraw eastwards towards Thazi and southwards towards Pyawbwe.

CHAPTER XXIX

THE RACE FOR RANGOON

APRIL—MAY 1945

FROM Jorhat to the Irrawaddy was a long and arduous journey, day after day of driving in convoy for hours on end. The roads were unspeakable over the second part of the route beyond the Chindwin. And if the distance was less than that covered by the Division on its way to Kirkuk at the end of 1941, or from Cairo to Baghdad a year later, neither journey had been so exhausting or so difficult.

The two brigades, which left Jorhat at intervals from March 5 onwards, drove through Kohima, past the greened-over scars of 'Liver,' the plain of Imphal surrounded by its ring of all too familiar green hills, and the breath-taking, precipitous stretches of road between Palel and Tamu. East of Kalemyo the country was fresh to the troops, but otherwise dry, scorched and devoid of freshness. Indeed, that drive through the teak forests, with the roadside shells of abandoned cars a grim reminder of the retreat from Burma when the country was first occupied by the Japanese in 1942, was as dusty and jolting as any track in Arakan, as any in the Desert. Each vehicle moved in the backlash of dust from its predecessor in the column. Every driver and passenger grew coated with yellow dust, mouths became dry, and thirsts compelling. This land seemed unnatural in its loneliness, for villages were rare, and no well or river was passed that had any water.

All day long the sun beat down upon this torrid waste. With infrequent halts the vehicles of 161 and 123 Brigades bumped their way forward towards the halting-place for the night. The teak trees gave but little shade, and the oppressive heat was an ordeal. But at last the landscape changed to softer lines, to green paddy fields and villages built among bamboo clumps. And by the roadside stood Burmese villagers, shyly watching, and offering eggs and vegetables for sale. White pagodas were passed in their hundreds, and outside the temples stood guard the strange, symbolic Chinthes, beasts carved in stone and not unlike a lion having a dragon as a forebear.

Through the ruins of Ye-Yu drove the brigades, farther and farther into Central Burma. Near Monywa—Headquarters of General Slim's Fourteenth Army—the Chindwin was crossed a second time, on ferry boats that chugged to and fro between the river banks. On and on moved the convoys, across the parched plains, past pagodas that gleamed white in the strong sunlight, through undamaged villages, past lurching bullock carts and static water tanks. The villagers, dressed in white shirts and gaily coloured *longyi* skirts, hopped off the road when the jeeps and lorries roared by, just as nimbly as did the yellow-robed monks.

No more signs of war were met until Pakokku came in sight, but here the telegraph wires hung in festoons, wooden crosses beside the road marked the graves of British and Indian soldiers who had fallen during the fight by the Seventh Indian Division to secure a bridgehead across the Irrawaddy. 161 Brigade crossed the river in ferry boats, on March 16, at the same time as the main part of Nine Brigade was landing on Meiktila airstrip. A little to the south, on the far bank, our troops could see the gilded temples and pagodas of ancient Pagan shimmering through the morning mist. The waters of Irrawaddy flowed with relentless speed—one more river to cross. From the past rang out the names of other rivers that the Division had crossed: Atbara and Gash, Nile, Euphrates and Tigris, Ganges and Brahmaputra. Veterans added one more to the list of rivers in which they had bathed.

The road from Nyaungu on the east bank seemed more uneven and dust-clogged than ever before. The sun's heat was no less fierce. And the glare stabbed into men's eyes and made them crease up their faces. Burma at this time of year seemed to be a land without green. Only an occasional group of palm trees provided scant shade beneath which the leading vehicle of a convoy might halt. Then the jeeps and trailers behind would close up and stop also. The canvas *chaguls* of water hanging on the side of every jeep were tipped up; the dust was washed from the lips, and dry throats were eased by the cool water. But there was no ease for smarting eyes.

Ninety miles beyond the Irrawaddy the Division, led by 161

Brigade, established itself in Kamye, facing the green massif of Taungtha, held by the Japanese. The Division's task was to clear the dominating Taungtha hills, that rise to a height of 1,700 feet, and the road between Myingan and Taungtha. The country round Kamye is flat and arid. Thick hedges of thorn and cactus, and trees by the roadside and among the village buildings, are the only landmarks, save for the countless white pagodas that are met with on every hand and round each bend in the dusty road. Taungtha is an important road junction, linking Myingan to the north, Mandalay to the east, and Pagan to the west.

In order that our L. of C. to Meiktila should be secured, and the road through to the besieged forces there be opened, the Japanese holding these hills had to be destroyed or driven away. So long as the enemy remained to threaten the area, the Division could not move down into Meiktila. While 33 Brigade of Evans' Seventh Indian Division advanced south from Myingan—it was temporarily under General Mansergh's command for this operation—Grimshaw's 161 Brigade would encircle the southern ridge by Taungtha and assault the main hill, Point 1788.

The battle started on March 25, and was a success. 33 Brigade soon reached a line five miles north of Taungtha. Little enemy opposition was encountered, and our artillery silenced the Japanese guns. The enemy was found to be holding two hill features with strong forces. When the 1/1st Punjab tried to capture Point 1788, they failed. Though our troops penetrated among the foothills, they had to withdraw in the face of frontal resistance and heavy mortar fire. It was not until the night of March 29/30 that the Taungtha hills were finally occupied by 161 Brigade. The Japanese restricted their activities to sniping and the laying of booby traps. Their retreat was hastened when the Divisional Reconnaissance Battalion, the 3/9th Jats (Lieutenant-Colonel R. A. M. Binnie), went round behind Point 1788, cut the Mandalay road, and linked up with the leading battalion and tanks of 33 Brigade.

As speed was essential, planning for the move to Meiktila—seventy miles distant to the south-east—continued throughout these operations near Taungtha. On the last day of March the Division moved to Meiktila along the good metalled road. With it travelled a great column of soft vehicles belonging to units in the Meiktila garrison, in particular to Nine Brigade.

THE RACE FOR RANGOON

On the same day Appleby's 2/1st Punjab, reinforced with a squadron of armoured cars, a battery of field guns, a detachment of 74 Field Company (Major D. Brunt), and some anti-tank mortars, were left to establish a firm base at Mahlaing, a small town half-way between Taungtha and Meiktila. Appleby's force was to keep open the road. Within two hours of arriving in the town, it received news that a party of Japanese were in a village three miles away. Major Jamshed's company and the armoured cars went out and killed sixty-one enemy soldiers without casualty to themselves. The Japanese, caught unawares, lost more than half their number.

At the end of March the troops of the Division entered Meiktila, passed the blue-grey lakes, drove through streets of ruined red brick and plaster houses. On every side were buildings without roofs, windows, doors, heaped about with blackened timber and broken brickwork. Bridges had been destroyed. But in the sunshine the scarred town had beauty, for trees still lined the streets, palm groves cast their shadows into the lakes, and the white façades of those houses that still stood unscathed gleamed among the deep red of walls and roofs.

The Divisional troops and 123 and 161 Brigades settled in quickly in the southern part of Meiktila. The enemy had withdrawn from the town, south to Pyawbwe, east by Thazi.

* * * * *

Preparations for the pursuit of the Japanese to Rangoon were pressed forward. As soon as the 19th Indian Division arrived at Meiktila from Mandalay, it would be possible for the Fifth Indian Division to take part and help Cowan's 17th Indian Division, which was fighting for Pyawbwe, some twenty miles south of Meiktila. Planning had to be intensive and careful, for under General Mansergh's command were 34,000 troops with over 4,500 vehicles and tanks. And it was proposed to operate two divisions down the one main road between Mandalay and Rangoon.

The first phase of the operation was the capture of Pyawbwe by General Cowan's troops. When the Fifth Indian Division had secured Pyinmana and Toungoo, and the vital airfields there, the 17th Indian Division would pass through and continue the southward advance.

The distance between Meiktila and Rangoon is 384 miles.

The monsoon was expected to break at the end of April. Speed of advance, therefore, was the first essential.

With the capture on April 8 of Pyawbwe, Cowan's Division completed its first task. The Fifth Indian Division started to pass through the forward troops on the 11th. In the lead was Denholm-Young's 123 Brigade with, under command, tanks of the 7th Cavalry (Lieutenant-Colonel Barlow) and 116 (Gordons) R.A.C. (Lieutenant-Colonel Blackater), and the 18th Field Regiment. The Brigade was divided into nine separate columns and numbered over 1,200 lorries and tanks, trucks and jeeps, armoured cars and bridging vehicles.

At half past four that afternoon the two leading columns, composed of tanks, guns, and two companies of Dogras, reached Yamethin and passed through the town without trouble. But as the next group, two batteries of guns and a company of Jats, was entering the place it was engaged by Japanese east of the main road. A unit of over 300 enemy soldiers had slipped into the town and dug itself in among the houses. The remaining companies of the 3/9th Jats commanded by Major Campbell were soon on the spot, but nothing could be done that evening. The night was spent, with the armour on its own south of Yamethin, the rest of Denholm-Young's force to the north. And all round our hastily prepared defences the enemy was most active.

Early next morning our rear column was attacked by four Japanese aircraft. These, roaring low over the road, bombed and strafed the vehicles, which could not escape. Twelve ammunition lorries still in harbour were destroyed, and Major Meraj-ud-Din, second-in-command of the 2/1st Punjab, and former Brigade Major to Nine Brigade, was killed—a severe loss to the Division and to the Indian Army.

Two companies of the 7th York and Lancaster probed forward into Yamethin, but were held up by fire and compelled to withdraw. That afternoon, as soon as our artillery had shelled Yamethin, the British battalion with two squadrons of 116 R.A.C. in support advanced again. Meanwhile, Campbell's Jats were clearing the town west of the road and making good progress, but later, when a company of the York and Lancaster ran into trouble and suffered heavy casualties, all troops were withdrawn.

After a night during which the Jats were twice attacked, the

York and Lancaster again probed forward, only to meet strong opposition among a group of pagodas. The Jats secured the road and rail crossing in the centre of Yamethin, and at half past eleven Brigadier Denholm-Young sent out the 2/1st Punjab with a squadron of tanks to advance down either side of the road. Though the two leading companies had cleared the southern outskirts of Yamethin within two hours, considerable firing was still coming from the Japanese soldiers who had dug themselves in on the eastern edge of the town. Accordingly, two companies were diverted towards this quarter, but came under intense fire. The leading platoon ran on to a minefield and suffered a dozen casualties within a minute. Then our companies were ordered back, to allow a Divisional artillery concentration to be brought down on the area. Part of its object was to destroy this unexpected minefield.

When the British infantry went forward with three companies, they were again held up, and forced to retire under cover of a screen of mortar fire and snipers. While the Jats held the north-west part of Yamethin, the 2/1st Punjab consolidated along the line of the main road. All through the night our Gunners harassed the enemy in the eastern streets and buildings, and the morning brought an attack by four Mitchell bombers and a second Divisional concentration. Then the 2/1st, with a company of Dogras protecting either flank, moved eastwards from the road, and by half past one Yamethin was in our hands. Contact was made with the two columns that had become isolated south of the town. Our advance had been held up for two days, the enemy had been difficult to dislodge, and the fighting to secure Yamethin had been severe and costly.

Now the 4/7th Rajputs of 161 Brigade took over Yamethin, the 7th York and Lancaster assumed responsibility for protecting the Divisional administration box just south of Pyawbwe, and 123 Brigade resumed their southward drive on April 16. Tatkon, twenty-two miles from Yamethin, was reached before nightfall.

Between Yamethin and Pyinmana the main road runs alongside hilly country and thick jungle, and at the Schwemyo Bluff, eight miles south of Tatkon, it was known that the Japanese would attempt to make a strong stand. While the Division had been hurrying south to capture this most formidable of all obstacles along this stretch of road, the enemy had been rushing reinforcements up from the south to meet the threat. Our leading troops were held strongly on the line of the Sinthe Chaung and on Schwemyo Bluff itself. But 161 Brigade succeeded in securing a bridgehead across this *chaung*, while Denholm-Young's men made a wide left hook on to the Bluff from the east. The 2/1st Punjab and 1/17th Dogras took the hills. And so a strong position, which the enemy would in earlier days have held with great tenacity, was wrested from his grasp. Pyinmana, another twenty miles nearer to Rangoon, became our next objective.

Nine Brigade was brought forward from Meiktila to Tatkon, where a Dakota strip was rapidly constructed. 161 Brigade pushed ahead down the road with the tanks, which had difficulty in recrossing the Sinthe Chaung, owing to enemy sniping and to the presence of mines and serious demolitions. Nine Brigade was directed to advance against Pyinmana via the railway line, which runs west of both the *chaung* and the road. Most of the equipment had to be conveyed on local bullock carts, for the Brigade was not a motorized but an airborne formation, and had to adapt itself with rapidity and skill.

By April 19 123 Brigade had been relieved on Schwemyo Bluff, and was moving down the foothills east of the Sinthe Chaung. 161 Brigade and the armour, making all speed along the main road, reached Pyinmana early next day, and, thanks to the dash of the Gordon Highlanders and 7th Cavalry, the bridge over the *chaung* was secured intact, although it had been prepared for blowing. The Japanese soldier responsible, being asleep, was killed before he was aware of our sudden arrival. The tanks rumbled amongst the Headquarters of the Japanese 33rd Army, killed hundreds of enemy troops and, as it later transpired, missed capturing the Army Commander by a matter of minutes. While Nine Brigade was left to mop up enemy resistance in Pyinmana, 161 Brigade and the tanks by-passed the town by a diversion, and continued south. The first rains fell that evening, a warning that speed must be quickened if Rangoon were to be reached in time. Part of the town was still strongly held, but as the 17th Indian Division was following close behind, our leading troops could pursue their advance without anxiety about the road behind them. 161 Brigade captured the airfield at Lewe—more vital to our advance than any single town—and 123 Brigade, using the same diversion that bulldozers had made to the east of Pyinmana, reached Thawatti that evening, April 20. Great difficulty in crossing a wide *chaung* just south of Lewe meant that the tail of Denholm-Young's column did not arrive in until three o'clock the next morning, in darkness.

By the evening of the 21st our tanks had brushed aside light opposition along the road, and had reached Yedashe. This town lies some sixty miles beyond Pyinmana, and only 184 miles from Rangoon. The rapid advance continued, the enemy being bewildered by its speed and unable to hold up our tanks except by destroying bridges. Small pockets of Japanese resistance had to be left for the following troops to destroy. Groups of enemy and Jif soldiers surrendered. Many nights the Japanese attacked our positions, which were never anything but temporary halts, so constant was the progress towards Rangoon. The enemy laid ambushes, posted snipers, and sent out 'jitter parties' to harass our men by night. In daylight both sides used their aircraft to strafe and shoot up convoys, points of opposition, and road-blocks. The last had to be cleared by the Sappers.

On April 22, after covering fifty miles, the tanks and 123 Brigade captured the Toungoo airstrips. No opposition was met there, and the 7th York and Lancaster, who had now rejoined the Brigade, hurried into Toungoo behind the armoured column. Two companies of this battalion went on to Oktwin, while the 2/1st Punjab and 1/17th Dogras guarded the airfields, and the rest of the British troops held the town itself. The first tanks of the 7th Cavalry that entered Toungoo overran the Japanese traffic police at the northern outskirts of the town.

No sooner had fifty Japanese been killed than the remainder took fright and fled. More than 3,000 members of a Jif division surrendered, just in time to start work on repairing the airstrips which made Toungoo of such importance. Rangoon now lay 166 miles away, and our fighter aircraft would be able to cover that distance if based on Toungoo.

This was the last place until Pegu was reached where the Japanese could make an effectual stand. The enemy's position was now critical.

After a day for maintenance, during which the Royal Air Force, by some fortunate error, dropped thousands of eggs on to the troops, so that men could go about ordering omelettes made from ten eggs, 161 Brigade headed south again on the 24th, and the Royal West Kents and tanks reached the next town down the road and railway—Pyu. The remainder of the Division was delayed till the following day by the rains, which flooded the river south of Toungoo, made the fords unusable, and necessitated the building by the Sappers of a floating pontoon. No sooner was the pontoon completed than the Division, making use of a full moon, moved south during the night, and caught up the leading troops at Pyu that evening. Only Nine Brigade, still under command of the 17th Indian Division, remained behind at Pyinmana.

The river bridge at Pyu had been destroyed by the retreating enemy, but fortunately the tanks and Dogras managed to cross by a ford, and by April 26 had secured Penwegon, seventy miles south of Toungoo.

In fourteen days the Division had advanced 211 miles, killed more than two thousand Japanese, and captured much equipment, many guns and prisoners. Cowan's 17th Indian Division now passed through and took the lead in the drive on Rangoon, little more than one hundred miles distant.

The advance had become a race, for it was now known that on May 1 Fifteen Corps would assault Rangoon from the sea.

The armoured column that led the 17th Indian Division did not catch up with the fast retreating enemy until within two miles of Nyaunglebin. These Japanese, mostly horsed cavalry, were scattered or destroyed, and our leading troops reached Daik-U, only eighty-five miles from Rangoon. More determined opposition was met at Payagale, where the enemy had placed many mines and where he launched expensive attacks against our tanks. But an airstrike and a brigade attack demolished all resistance, and by the evening of April 29 the tanks with the 17th Indian Division were just east of Pegu, and the rest of the troops just to the north.

Stiff opposition was met in the town. The Japanese commander had hurriedly gathered every available man to defend Pegu. But to do this he had almost denuded the garrison of Rangoon itself. The monsoon broke in earnest; the tanks were blocked by a canal; the river was in spate and could no longer be forded; the two northern bridges were down. Although the railway bridge and the southern road bridge had remained intact, the latter was unfortunately destroyed by the enemy during the last night of April. Airstrips became waterlogged and unusable. Neither tanks nor vehicles could operate away from the road. The rain poured down. But though soaked to the skin, on half rations, and weary, the troops fought with the greatest enthusiasm, established a bridgehead across the river, and had cleared Pegu of all but a few Japanese snipers by the evening of May 1. Until the bridges were repaired, no vehicles could move south of the town, but the infantry of Cowan's Division hurried on.

On May 1, as planned, a Gurkha paratroop battalion had landed at Elephant Point, at the mouth of Rangoon river. Next day the 26th Indian Division landed from the sea unopposed. Rangoon was entered on May 3. Abandoned by the enemy, the city bustled with welcoming Burmese crowds, and elated, thankful Allied prisoners of war who were delivered from their prolonged and arduous captivity. The meeting between the 17th and 26th Indian Divisions took place on May 6 at Hlegu, twenty-eight miles north of Rangoon. The infantry coming from the north had been seriously delayed by mines, by destroyed bridges, by swollen waterways. And they had been obliged to swim several *chaungs* in order to make any progress at all.

Now Burma was ours. All that remained was to mop up the retreating enemy forces, disordered, leaderless, out of touch, dejected, liable to be trapped, and faced with a country flooded by the violent monsoon rains, with rushing streams and rivers, paddy fields deep in mud, and British and Indian troops ready to destroy or capture the straggling Japanese as opportunity offered.

CHAPTER XXX

MOPPING UP IN BURMA

MAY—AUGUST 1945

THE situation on May 5 was as follows: Messervy's Four Corps, comprising the Fifth, 17th and 19th Indian Divisions, held the corridor of the main road and railway between Mandalay and Rangoon. To the west Stopford's Thirty-Three Corps, formed of the Seventh and 20th Indian Divisions, was advancing astride the Irrawaddy towards the Burmese capital by way of Prome.

The Japanese Army was now doing its best to escape from Burma in two main parties. The first—some 10,000 men—was still in the Irrawaddy Valley and could only get away over the Pegu Yomas and across the Sittang River. Most of the second and larger party was making its way slowly southwards through the Shan Hills, hoping to reach the Bilin road via the Salween River.

To withdraw eastwards across the Sittang River was difficult, for the enemy troops had to cross the axis of first one corps and then the other before reaching the river. They had to traverse country that is thick jungle, sparsely populated, without roads and with few good tracks. Then they were faced, between the Mandalay–Rangoon road and the Sittang, with flat, open paddy fields, devoid of cover save in the elongated villages with their clumps of trees. Here, too, the roads were few and bad.

The Division was ordered to pursue the enemy in the direction of Waw, a station on the railway between Pegu and Moulmein, and also to the east bank of the Sittang, towards Bilin, a place farther down the line to Moulmein. Moulmein seemed an obvious rallying point for the disorganized bands of Japanese making their way through the gaps between our two corps. Our object was to intercept as many of these Japanese as could be, and to prevent their reaching Moulmein or crossing the Sittang River.

Nine Brigade (Brigadier H. G. L. Brain) was flown south from

Lewe to Pegu and at once started operations towards Waw and the Sittang. At the same time, 123 and 161 Brigades began to engage the enemy forces who were seeking to escape across the main road south of Pegu. Every report of Japanese troops had to be investigated. Many small parties were encountered, casualties inflicted, prisoners taken, and all at very light cost to ourselves. Nine Brigade met heavy opposition east of Waw, and in several battles caused severe loss to the Japanese. It was planned for the Brigade to cross the Sittang to Mokpalin, but when patrols of the 3/9th Jats reconnoitred on the east bank, they reported communications to be so bad that the plan had for the time being to be abandoned.

Once the monsoon had broken in earnest, the whole district east of the main road became flooded to a depth of two feet or so, and patrolling was well-nigh impossible except along the paddy bunds between the villages. The Divisional Engineers organized a jeep railway which pulled some of the old metre-gauge coaches, and this was the sole means of supplying our battalions forward of Waw.

On May 10 the 2nd West Yorkshires (Lieutenant-Colonel P. W. P. Green), supported by tanks, attacked the enemy at Nyaungkashe, killed some two hundred Japanese soldiers, and captured the village, which had for some days been a collecting point for parties of Japanese moving towards the river. It was when the enemy, driven from strongly defended positions, broke cover that they were mortared, shelled and machine-gunned by the infantry and 7th Cavalry, who had two troops of tanks in support of the battalion. Our total casualties for this successful operation were twenty-four. On the previous day the stores had been brought up on seventy bullock-carts, collected locally, and on an assortment of railway trucks, including seven captured Japanese bogies, that were pushed by fifty villagers. This strange party was met by a solitary Japanese sniper on the railway line. He was soon disposed of.

If the West Yorkshires met with success on this occasion, they ran into trouble five days later, in a village named Letpanthonbin, where a local villager had reported the presence of a score of Japanese. Two platoons under Captain H. Evans approached across the flooded paddy fields, and when fifty yards from the edge of this village were received with heavy fire. Evans was killed early in the engagement, and a serious number of other casualties were incurred. There was no cover and the range was short. Another platoon sent out to reinforce the forward troops was unable to approach nearer than six hundred yards, because of accurate fire that pinned them to the ground. Six hours passed. Then 'B' Company managed to join this second platoon, with a F.O.O. from the 4th Field Regiment. All day the rain poured down, all day the men wounded in the first brush near the village lay in the water or across the muddy bunds, waiting for darkness and the cover of night. Artillery fire was brought down on Letpanthonbin, in order to assist these wounded men. It was early next day that survivors trickled back to battalion headquarters in ones and twos. Corporal Venables, who had been wounded, reported that all bodies lying round him had been bayoneted by the Japanese during the night. He himself had feigned death, but was taken prisoner. A Japanese officer addressed him in English, and told him to wait until he had finished his meal. But a fierce downpour of rain provided Venables with a chance of escape. He took it and reached safety.

This fight cost us twenty-six men killed and six wounded. It was but characteristic of similar engagements fought out among the villages and across the swamped fields by the other battalions of Brain's brigade—the 3/2nd Punjab, 3/9th Jats and 1st Burma Regiment. Operations were extremely difficult, the weather grew worse, the floods expanded and deepened, and Japanese bands kept on coming from the west. They seemed to occupy villages at intervals and for short periods, trying thereby to protect their scattered remnants. Jitter parties, long and short range brushes, intermittent firing, patrolling as a result of some local report, men squelching their way yard by yard, the rain soaking their already damp uniforms, feet that were wet all day long, mud and slime, and chill discomfort—these were but some of the features of this mopping-up end to a campaign. Only in Waw, with its few wooden buildings raised on stilts, was there any good cover.

* * * * *

During May Appleby's 2/1st Punjab spent a fortnight in the neighbourhood of Mokshitwa in the Pegu Yomas. Here the battalion fought against the remnants of the Japanese Army retreating in disorganization from Prome. It was an area of small hillocks covered with thick clumps of bamboo, and some five thousand enemy troops were said to be trying to escape across the road. Each day patrols of a company strength hounded the Japanese. Airstrikes and artillery concentrations were called down upon places where the Japanese were known to be. Ambushes were laid on likely escape routes. Most nights the battalion perimeter was jittered by enemy parties, and on one occasion a heavy attack was made by 150 Japanese. This was repulsed with severe loss to the assailants. Indeed, the enemy suffered heavily during this period of hunting and skirmishing in the jungle.

The enemy soldiers were running extremely short of ammunition and food, though in many of the villages they were able to find stocks of rice, their staple diet. It was, of course, impossible to deny the enemy access to every village. Not only were they too numerous to guard, but also the problems of maintaining soldiers in inaccessible places would have been insurmountable in monsoon conditions, when all vehicles were bound to the road. Our troops would secure a firm base, and then send out very strong fighting patrols with a Gunner observation officer. They would tour all the villages in a certain area, seeking out the Japanese, who were seldom to be found in villages during daylight. They came in by night, and in the daytime might occupy a small hillock in the jungle, covering the approaches to a village. If the enemy was present in strength, he would be shelled by our Gunners, who harassed at night on targets that they registered whenever possible in daylight. Sometimes the enemy would make a stand, but this only brought him heavier casualties.

During the night of May 29/30 the 1/17th Dogras, now commanded once again by Lieutenant-Colonel F. I. Wallace, who had just returned from leave in Britain, started a full-scale operation up the road to Paunggyi, away to the west of the Pegu–Rangoon road. In support was a troop of the 7th Cavalry. A village named Uwinwa was occupied, and when an armoured car patrol reported that Paunggyi was deserted two companies entered the place next day. Local inhabitants said that the Japanese had left just before the arrival of our armoured cars. They had first set fire to the village.

The Dogras found here forty derelict enemy vehicles, and many tons of burning grain.

At the end of May and early in June it became increasingly obvious that the Japanese were planning a mass break-out from the jungle west of the main road, with the object of crossing the Sittang. To prevent this, our patrolling grew more vigorous still, and the activities of the Japanese were closely watched. Then, in the middle of June the Japanese east of the Sittang, by applying strong pressure against Nine Brigade on the Waw front and occupying several villages on the west bank of the river, proved that they were working to a plan, in order to help their comrades still in the jungle west of the road. It was, however, considered unlikely that this enemy break-out would come within the Divisional area. The pressure against Nine Brigade was thought to be a cover plan aimed at relieving pressure on the Japanese elsewhere. This supposition proved to be correct.

* * * * *

It was at Pegu that the 56th A.A./A.Tk. Regiment said farewell to the Division. An officer has recorded an impression of that occasion. "The General, who must have been as dearly loved by every individual man as any Divisional Commander could ever be, told us that he wished to see as many men as possible. We all stood there in the rain, the water ankle-deep in the field where we had been living for three days. He was at his most charming, and if, instead of telling us that our time was now due for home, he had asked us to follow him for another year, I am pretty certain that we would have gone. I know that I would."

Owing to releases, repatriation, and the shortage of British troops in Burma, the Division lost all but one of its British units: the 4th and 28th Field Regiments, whose guns had supported the infantry during every campaign in which the Division had fought; the 4th Royal West Kents, who had defended Kohima; the 7th York and Lancaster; and 56th Anti-tank Regiment. Their places were taken by the 4th and 5th Indian Field Regiments, the 5th Anti-Tank Regiment, the 3/4th and 3/9th Gurkha Regiments. Of the British battalions, only the veteran 2nd West Yorkshires remained.

The Division was eventually released from active operations against the Japanese at the end of June, and its positions near Pegu and Waw were taken over by the Seventh Indian Division, still commanded by Major-General Geoffrey Evans. Some fifteen miles north of Rangoon among the rubber plantations of Mingaladon was the new area in which the various units pitched their tents and settled down, not to rest from their battles, but to train in a, for them, new type of warfare: combined operations. The Division was to form part of the force preparing to invade Malaya (Operation 'Zipper').

The programme of training to be got through was extremely heavy. Every officer and man in the Division was put through a normal six weeks' dryshod course in half that length of time by a most efficient combined operations training team. The local cinema was kept working for six weeks day after day from seven o'clock in the morning till eleven at night showing instructional films. In three days the Sappers bulldozed a magnificent cutting lined with bit-hess, floored with pierced steel planking, and filled with water by pumps from a leak in the Rangoon water pipe-line which ran near by. Drivers of proofed vehicles were given practice in underwater driving through this trough.

The troops practised swimming in full equipment, and the Royal Lake in Rangoon was used for pontoon bridging and outboard motor-boat training. Units and brigade groups rehearsed beach landings, while the staff made final adjustments to convoy-loading and assault-landing tables. Scrambling nets and sliding ropes were used, scaling towers built by the Sappers and put to good purposes, and the troops rehearsed with landing craft.

The A/Q, Lieutenant-Colonel Tom Roe, who was very soon to say good-bye to the Division after serving on its headquarters for three years, made some interesting comments on the preparations for Operation 'Zipper.'

"I always feel to give people in Europe an idea of the difficulty of mounting the Malayan invasion it is necessary to give them this parallel. A number of troops for the invasion of France were two months before D-Day in action in Italy. Their commanders and staff were summoned to Moscow (fitting in on such air services as existed with no special aircraft available) for planning their part in the invasion. The troops to receive new equipment from America and reinforcements from Egypt. The invasion to be embarked at ports ranging from Marseilles and Gibraltar to Glasgow.

The whole force to rendezvous off a spot on the Malayan coast some days later."

On August 8 news was received of a possibility of Japan surrendering. If this occurred, the Division would sail at once for Singapore. Then on the 15th Japan did surrender, and the troops displayed their joy and relief with firing, dancing, Very lights, concert parties, free drinks, and a round of celebrations of all kinds.

But meanwhile the staff officers were working in shifts throughout the twenty-four hours to keep abreast with the latest whim and alteration of the authorities in the allocation of shipping for 'Zipper.' Changes were frequent; some ships already loading had to be unloaded; but in good time all the many problems were resolved in one way or another, and the Division was ready to embark for Malaya and Singapore. Until the last moment the staff had to plan both for the invasion of Malaya and for the reoccupation of Singapore. Which plan would be implemented depended upon the Japanese.

CHAPTER XXXI

SINGAPORE REOCCUPIED

SEPTEMBER—OCTOBER 1945

THE Division embarked at Rangoon Harbour in the middle of August, but the convoy did not sail for another eight days. The reasons for this delay were that the Japanese surrender party was awaited in Rangoon, and that Lord Louis Mountbatten had to be sure that the Emperor's orders to all Japanese forces had been sent out and received. Eventually the envoys arrived in their two white planes with green crosses, escorted by Spitfires, and the surrender of the remainder of Japanese territory was co-ordinated.

The troops knew that they were bound for Singapore, but no one could tell whether or not our landings would be opposed. Even though the Japanese High Command had decreed surrender, it was not certain that the enemy troops on Singapore Island, many of them fresh and untried in war, would accept such a decision. They might resist it. In an appreciation written on August 29, General Mansergh stated that the possibility of opposition could not be disregarded. There might be isolated resistance by local commanders, or deliberate acts of treachery. And uppermost in the General's mind at this time was the security of his force. For whereas the Japanese numbered about ninety-six thousand on Singapore Island, he would have available on the first three days after landing only ten thousand men.

The convoy of sixteen large and crowded troopships and an equal number of cargo vessels eventually set out from Rangoon on the morning of August 27. The sea was calm, the voyage uneventful. For a week the ships steamed on, until soon after dawn on September 3 our troops saw in the distance the hills of Penang. This was the sixth anniversary of the outbreak of a long war. Veterans of the Division recalled other anniversaries: the Sudan; Ruweisat Ridge and the battle of Alam el Halfa; the moist heat of Bihar Province;

and the mud of the road to Tiddim. This day of eager anticipation was to be the final anniversary, but not the final sea voyage. Some looked back to the weeks when the Division first left India, bound for Port Sudan, or to the humidity of Massawa and the Red Sea. Many remembered the crossing to Cyprus, and the return to India from Basra. Some, even, had gone to Arakan, not by rail and by river ferry across the Brahmaputra, but in ships from Vizagapatam over the Bay of Bengal. And now the Division was approaching Singapore.

In case it should be needed, Brain's Nine Brigade on board the *Corfu* was detached from the main convoy and sent into Penang. In the event it was not required, and thus reached Singapore thirty-six hours after the rest of the Division. It was here, off Penang, that General Mansergh and his A.D.C. were taken in a small boat to H.M.S. *Sussex*, which had come from Ceylon.

Then, next morning, September 4, a surrender meeting was held in the *Sussex*, by now a score of miles from Singapore. The morning was still, and the atmosphere close and muggy. At hand waited Japanese tugs, flying black and white surrender flags. After breakfast one of these tugs was summoned across to H.M.S. *Sussex*. The Japanese representatives were piped aboard, met by naval officers, escorted to a small cabin, and disarmed of their swords.

The conference was held in the Admiral's dining room. On either side of a long table, covered with green cloth, stood a row of chairs; those for the Japanese were some distance from the table, to prevent the vanquished envoys from leaning on the table or using it for writing or keeping their papers. Meanwhile the British senior officers had assembled on their side of the conference table: present at the talks, besides Major-General Mansergh, were Rear-Admiral Cedric Holland and Lieutenant-General Sir Philip Christison—Mountbatten's Navy and Army representatives—, Major-General Ralph Hone, the Civil Administration Officer, a Group Captain of the Royal Air Force, the several chiefs of staff, interpreters and recording secretaries.

Then the Japanese officers were summoned. They marched in, saluted, bowed to each service representative, and, when told to, sat down. It was a tense moment. Representing Field-Marshal Count Terauchi, Supreme Japanese Commander of the Southern Region, were General Itagaki, Commander of the Seventh Area

Army—this included Malaya, Java and Sumatra—and Vice-Admiral Fukodome, who commanded the Tenth Area Fleet. Itagaki looked particularly upset.

In the doorway stood a marine sentry. For a moment dead silence filled the Admiral's dining room. Then General Christison opened the proceedings, speaking through his interpreter.

CHRISTISON: What is your name, rank and appointment?

ITAGAKI: General Itagaki, Commander-in-Chief of the Seventh Area Army.

CHRISTISON: Are you entitled to speak for the Field-Marshal Count Terauchi, Supreme Japanese Commander, Southern Region, on Army matters?

ITAGAKI: Not entirely for the whole area, but only for the landings in the Singapore area.

CHRISTISON: Do you know the Terms of Agreement signed in Rangoon?

ITAGAKI: I know of the Agreement signed in Rangoon and, furthermore, I have complied with what I ought to have done in Singapore with regard to this Agreement.

CHRISTISON: Do you abide by the Imperial decision to cease hostilities and are you prepared to carry out the orders of the Supreme Allied Commander, South East Asia?

ITAGAKI: Yes, I am quite prepared. . . .

CHRISTISON: Is there any sabotage, looting or local civil disturbance taking place in the Singapore area?

ITAGAKI: With regard to the maintenance of law and order there are no riots of a serious nature, but there is every sign of possible looting and some sort of violence of a small nature which is under the guard of our Forces now. And we have also suspicions certain Societies are being formed, but we are taking every possible step to suppress them. We are also collecting information about them.

CHRISTISON: I rely on General Itagaki to keep law and order until my Forces take over.

ITAGAKI: Yes, I will.

CHRISTISON: My Forces will act strictly in accordance with the Laws and Usages of War and International Law.

ITAGAKI: Yes.

The Japanese forces were to be reduced immediately and marched to the mainland. Itagaki objected that no quarters existed there, north of Johore Baru. This objection was brushed aside. Huts must be built in the jungle. Movement would start that night, immediately after the return of the surrender party. This was, in fact, carried out to such good effect that by dawn on September 5 over 35,000 Japanese troops were already across the causeway and building their concentration areas as ordered. The only enemy troops allowed to stay in Singapore were those needed for guard and labour purposes.

Among the terms of surrender were the following instructions and stipulations:

The Japanese forces on Singapore Island and in Malaya were to be treated as 'surrendered personnel' rather than as prisoners-of-war. They would be disarmed, but would continue to wear uniform and badges of rank. Japanese commanders would remain responsible for the maintenance and discipline of their own troops, for public order, the protection of banks, and the feeding of civilians in territories that had hitherto been under their control. Essential services such as light and water were to be maintained and guarded until Allied forces had assumed control; aircraft would be grounded and remain so. No demolitions would be permitted; and damage to bridges, waterways, railroads, telegraphs and telephones, stores of food, and cattle belonging to civilians must be prevented. To implement these instructions, the Japanese would be allowed guards of one hundred men for military stores, dumps and vehicle parks, for dock installations, for bulk holdings of cash, and for Japanese hospital patients who could not be moved.

The location was to be given of fortifications, of camps of Allied prisoners-of-war or internees, of aircraft and airfields, of weapons, tanks, and ammunition. The whereabouts of broadcasting stations, radar and signal equipment, rolling stock, workshops, harbour facilities, war materials and food stocks were to be given. Charts of minefields and booby traps were required from the Japanese; all documents, records, ciphers and codes would be handed over together with nominal rolls, orders of battle, lists of medical supplies, shops used by the Japanese forces, and stocks of petrol and oil; all requisitioned or stolen goods and property must be restored. A record was required of all the graves of Allied troops and civilian internees. All Japanese flags, emblems and memorials other than graves were to be removed before we landed.

To the Japanese Commander of Singapore Island orders were issued that every member of the Japanese forces and puppet forces remaining on the Island was to wear a white armband. Japanese wives, families and members of the Japanese comfort corps were to accompany their respective formations on the withdrawal from the Island. Hospital staffs were to remain on duty. A guard or caretaker would be left in every building that was vacated by the Japanese Army, so as to ensure its safe-keeping and to prevent looting.

On the second day of occupation one hundred large staff cars in high-class condition would be made available for the use of the occupying forces. A further five hundred lorries, with drivers, were to assemble in the dock area, and another hundred at Kallang airfield on the day of occupation.

A curfew from sunset to sunrise was imposed until further notice. All stocks of spirits and liquor shops were sealed and guarded; a report was required of all epidemics or infectious diseases, the location of hospitals and laboratories, together with that of all Allied sick and wounded men. Singapore Military Hospital would be emptied of all Japanese patients except those who were too ill to be moved. It would then be cleaned and made ready for use by the Allied medical services. In addition, interpreters and guides were to be available to help our landing forces.

A Japanese general was selected to report twice daily to General Mansergh for orders. Mansergh had dealings with no other representatives; the other enemy generals—twenty-eight of them— were housed in Raffles College.

The two Japanese representatives took four hours to consider the terms. They raised many points and dragged red herrings. But at length the document of surrender was signed and sealed. Itagaki wept, but Fukodome continued his efforts to ingratiate himself with the British commanders, grinning and winking as he had done at intervals during the proceedings.

* * * * *

Early in September Mountbatten laid down for his Allied commanders rules of conduct for relations with surrendered Japanese forces. We may quote the following:

"There will be no fraternizing whatever between Japanese and

Allied forces. In dealing with Japanese your behaviour will be guarded and coldly polite. You will, in the case of senior Japanese officers, use their correct titles. You will not shake hands with them. . . . . In no case will British and Japanese officers feed in the same room, nor will tea be offered at any meeting. Any Japanese who come to receive orders or report should be kept at arm's length, e.g., with a table between you and them, and they should not be allowed to sit at the same table. . . . . Under no circumstances will either Japanese prisoners of war or surrendered personnel be abused or maltreated, nor will violence be used against them except when necessitated by their own behaviour."

* * * * *

That same morning of September 4 the Divisional convoy entered a swept channel in the Malacca Straits, and during the rest of the day our ships steamed along, some ten miles out from the coast of Malaya. In the afternoon could be seen the actual beaches on which our forces were to have landed, had Operation 'Zipper' been carried through. The men saw gleaming sand with palm trees close to the water's edge, an occasional white house with its red roof and, further back, a mass of green jungle. They saw, too, mangrove swamps, with signs of heavy Japanese defences and mines on the beaches. As the surrender talks on board H.M.S. *Sussex* were completed before nightfall, the blackout was lifted, and the convoy sailed on with its lights blazing. During the night the Division prepared for the landing next morning.

Full war precautions were taken. At seven o'clock on the 5th, the landing craft, many of which had taken part in combined operations in North Africa and Europe, came alongside, and boatload by boatload the troops scrambled down the nets into them. By half past eight the craft were ready in battle formation. On board, everyone felt a thrill of expectancy. How would the Japanese take the surrender? Would there be treachery?

The first flight which steamed in from a distance of some twenty-five miles was composed of, on the left, the 3/9th Gurkha Rifles, and on the right the 2/1st Punjab. 123 Brigade Headquarters travelled with the latter. And the 1/17th Dogras moved off to secure possession of certain islands—Pulau Brani, Blakang Mati, and Pulau Hantu, two miles south of Singapore harbour. These were occupied without incident at 10.30 a.m. The rest of the convoy passed a series of these small islands, striking by their greenness, many of them only two hundred yards or so in length, with sandy beaches and palm trees, and a few white houses.

Then Singapore itself appeared, no longer hidden from view by these islands that cover the approaches. Suddenly the scene opened up, and the water line became visible in its wide semi-circle, a mass of buildings along the front showing clearly against a dull and thundery sky. Soon after eleven a.m. the landing craft, in single file and with pennants gaily fluttering, passed H.M.S. *Sussex*, lying with her guns trained upon the city, and entered the harbour to berth alongside the main wharfs.

In the dock area there were only a few civilians. But a small number of dockers and coolies gave a cheer and a wave of greeting, and several Chinese shouted from the roof of the customs sheds.

The first troops of the Division ashore were 'D' Company of the 2/1st Punjab, under Major Niaz Mohammed Arbad. The battalion was met by two senior Japanese officers, who wore ceremonial swords and highly polished jackboots. All were standing rigidly to attention, at the salute. Behind them again was parked a line of glittering civilian cars, each with a booted chauffeur. On the main wharf Brigadier Denholm-Young was met by the Japanese General who was staff officer to General Itagaki. And soon after midday Denholm-Young held a conference with a number of senior Japanese officers, who showed themselves most helpful. All went as had been planned during the voyage, and no opposition was met with.

The battalions moved out fanwise from the docks, and according to prearranged instructions occupied such key positions as arsenals, installations, airfields, the railway station, and camps. The Japanese officers, assisted by interpreters and by maps, showed our officers the dispositions of all enemy guards in Singapore itself.

Meanwhile, 161 Brigade had landed at the West Wharf, near the Power Station, and were greeted by a lone Chinese boy, full of smiles. Led by the 4/7th Rajputs, they moved straight through northwards across Singapore Island to the naval base and causeway at Johore Bahru.

The main shopping areas were Chinese, and in the shops excited crowds of waving, cheering Chinese, particularly children, watched our troops arrive. Union Jacks were flying from buildings or being waved. The streets were empty of buses, trams and tongas, and the sole means of transport seemed to be a few rickshaws. So few were the Malays and Indians by comparison with the Chinese inhabitants that you might have thought yourself in China.

During the first week very few shops were opened. Nobody knew what would happen. People were scared of looting. But if the shops remained closed, trade continued notwithstanding, and the centre of business was on the quayside. All the Chinese with anything to sell gathered here, sidling up with bulging pockets to transact business with those who had time to drive down to the waterfront. And before the re-establishment of British currency, watches, fountain pens, rings, cameras, and many other articles were offered in exchange for cigarettes, ten the first day, twice that number on the next day, and so on by rapid leaps.

But the troops of the Division had very little free time. They were hard pressed by guard duties during the first weeks of our occupation. They guarded dumps of stores, some that had belonged to the Japanese, others our own that dated from before the war and had remained untouched. In the city itself many buildings had been stocked up with supplies and equipment. An example was the base stationery office. Here our men came upon shelves loaded with bottles of ink, pencils by the thousand, rubbers, and paper stacked up on every side. Crates of paper were taken away to the various headquarters. Bags were stuffed with pencils and rubbers that we badly needed.

But the greater part of the dumps that were guarded had been widely dispersed through the rubber plantations by the Japanese. The dispersion, though a tribute to the activities of the Royal Air Force, meant that our troops had to look after wide areas. Most of these supplies were stored in large bamboo *bashas*, roughly made. These were scattered under the rubber trees over a plantation of maybe a hundred acres.

* * * * *

The Japanese stayed in their concentration areas, ruled and guarded themselves, sent out ration parties, and fed themselves. Our troops were warned not to enter the Japanese camps. The

Japanese discipline was remarkably good. All were smart despite their bandy legs and ill-fitting uniform, that resembled bloomers. They provided a marked contrast to the troops encountered in Burma, where in the fighting line they had been at their scruffiest and most desolate. These enemy troops looked fit and tough. Most of them had been in Singapore ever since they first broke victoriously on to the Island, and they had missed the fighting. They had led a comfortable existence, and at times hardly seemed to realize that they were a beaten army. They had seen nothing of Burma and of their defeated regiments foot-slogging dejectedly south, quickened by fanatical spasms, starving, disease-ridden, often desperate, and truly vanquished in battle.

Efficient they were, if sometimes truculent. Their staff work was excellent, and they did what they were ordered to do. Their bowing politeness was absurdly exaggerated, and their saluting punctilious and rigid. Sometimes they carried this to comic lengths. As one of our officers in a jeep met a lorry carrying a Japanese ration party, he heard an order shouted. All the Japanese soldiers stood up to attention inside the lorry as this bounced along the road, and saluted smartly.

In the diary of the Machine-gun Battalion of the 17th Dogra Regiment (Lieutenant-Colonel R. C. B. Bristow) appears the following outspoken description of the Japanese:

"The Jap is a complete locust. His method of life in an occupied country consists of occupying the best house not required by his seniors; living upstairs with his girl friends or captives; downstairs accumulating and dumping loot of three kinds—food, war material, and private loot which he sells to supplement his poor rate of pay; paying no attention to maintenance or sanitation. Eventually, the country is bare and the dirt indescribable. It does us good now to see him cleaning the drains. His recreations are bayonet fighting, flogging civilians and prisoners, and brothels. Most of them look the part and have criminal faces with beady little slit eyes."

Every day Japanese prisoners were ordered down in working parties for each battalion and headquarters. They worked in long shifts, and were kept very hard at it. Some squads swept the roads, filled in trenches round the Cathedral, unloaded ships and coal. Others, armed with buckets and brushes, whitewashed buildings, walls and gates. Parties cut grass and tended the gardens. Some

Japanese, pulling dilapidated carts through the streets, helped to collect our rations under the orders of a sepoy, or cleaned the drains, just as our own men when prisoners had been made to do.

As Singapore had been a large base area, the surrendered Japanese garrison numbered many tailors, shoemakers and other craftsmen in their midst. So Nine Brigade, for example, could order thirty carpenters and a score of tailors to be included in the next day's working party. The tailoring squad was led off and sat down in the shade of the trees. From outlying dumps a pile of green material was collected, and our trucks brought loads of leather and rubber soles, and wood. Officers and men arrived to be fitted for suits. And all day beneath the trees the squads of tailors kept on stitching away. Thus, shirts and trousers and shoes were made for all, from the Brigadier downwards. Japanese carpenters were kept busy making wooden boxes in which baggage could be kept, while others transformed Japanese tool boxes into smaller cases.

As soon as possible the Japanese remaining on Singapore Island were cleared to the mainland. On September 8 General Mansergh had issued a guide of the kit and equipment which Japanese surrendered personnel would be permitted to retain in their concentration areas. During the initial exodus they had taken an excessive collection of baggage; this was now to be retrieved. They were not allowed luxury articles such as radios, gramophones, mattresses and curtains. Chairs, tables and mess furniture were forbidden; so, too, were expensive clothes, crockery, thermos flasks, refrigerators and cameras. No article that might have been stolen from Singapore could be taken with them. Rugs, cushions, upholstery, electric fans, comfortable office furniture were also banned.

At the end of his memorandum Mansergh stated: "The Commanders are reminded that on the Japanese occupation of Singapore our troops—men, women and children—were only permitted such articles as they could carry on their bodies or in the minimum pack. Every luxury, all spare clothing, and all the normal necessities for the reasonable comfort or decency of our men, women and children were removed. There are instances in which elderly civilian ladies were deprived of every form of clothing except two or three garments. During the three years of occupation these women received one issue of army pants. It is my intention that no Japanese officer or man will be permitted to retain any article other than those strictly necessary for his adequate covering in his correct uniform and underclothes."

The total number of Allied prisoners-of-war in Singapore at the beginning of September was over 32,000. Of these the Indians numbered sixteen thousand, the British over six thousand, Australians five thousand, Dutch four thousand. In addition, there were some four thousand five hundred civilian internees.

Lieutenant-Colonel J. F. Carroll, G.S.O.1 of the Division, wrote at the time: "The bearing and morale of our prisoners-of-war was a sight I shall never forget; it has made one proud of one's fellow men. They were magnificent, despite the appalling times they had been through and endured."

The troops of the Division saw them first in the docks. Groups of British prisoners-of-war had wandered about the quayside looking pitifully thin. Some were dressed in ill-fitting uniforms with shorts too long and jackets too big; some of them, dressed only in an old pair of gym shorts, walked either barefooted or in sandals of their own making. One man wore nothing but a Japanese loin cloth and he carried half a loaf of bread between his thin arm and his chest. Many were in a bad way and had been working on the notorious railway inland. The worst ones were evacuated within the first few days of our landing in Singapore.

Most of them, to judge by the impressions gained from our officers and men, were almost child-like. They seemed quite astonished that here, once again, were their own kind and that they were free to come and go. Many of them were entertained to meals in the various messes of the units and headquarters, and they seemed overwhelmed. Naturally, they could not eat too much, but they were so vividly grateful for all that was done for them. And as they passed by in lorries and ambulances that were taking them to the hospital ships for evacuation, they waved and shouted wildly like schoolboys.

At meals they did little talking and were content to listen to the others. Their silence was most noticeable. All had similar stories to tell: of the weight they had lost, of Japanese brutality, of the magnificent Chinese help, of secret home-made wireless sets, of disease, of improvised clothing and footwear, and of the terrible railway.

But though sometimes pathetic, their spirit was extraordinary.

They had shown the highest endurance, and were in good heart. General Mansergh recalls how our Indian prisoners-of-war mounted small guards armed with sticks on their camps, and how they would smartly present arms with these sticks. One day he walked with General Slim into a camp where many of the Indians were dying of tuberculosis. Slim and Mansergh went from hut to hut, and were deeply moved by the wonderful gratitude and loyalty of these Indians, who were happy now that they had seen their General.

All the civilian internees were housed in the Symes Road camp in the most distressing conditions, though in the same wonderful state of morale as the soldier prisoners. The R.A.P.W.I. (Repatriation of Allied Prisoners-of-war and Internees) control was quickly established in the Goodwood Hotel, under Lieutenant-Colonel Crook, who, with the smallest of staffs, did wonders. And by the end of September most of the prisoners and internees had been evacuated from Singapore in hospital ships.

* * * * *

The supply sections of the Division were the only R.I.A.S.C. units on Singapore Island for a month, and under the command of Lieutenant-Colonel E. A. S. Collison they worked night and day to unload stores in the docks and to issue the supplies, not only to the brigades and Divisional troops, but also to the Army, the Air Force, and the prisoners-of-war and internees in Singapore. To exemplify the enormous strain placed upon the Divisional supply organization, 60 Indian Composite Platoon, which in its normal function would be expected to feed some 4,500 troops from a score of units, fed during September an average of over fifty thousand people a day, from more than 110 different units.

The Sappers and Miners, too, under Lieutenant-Colonel R. Orgill, had many problems to face. The water supply was improved, public utilities repaired, and reconnaissance made of store dumps. In South Malaya communications were restored and airfields repaired. Drains were cleared, anti-tank ditches and potholes filled in, bridges strengthened or replaced, and road-blocks removed. Classification signs were erected on bridges. Stock lists of Engineer dumps were prepared, and sawmills and quarries in southern Johore reconnoitred. All the bridges for the first hundred and fifty miles up from Singapore to Malacca had to be replaced.

At night, while the military police closed the road, a platoon or two of Sappers were hastily stripping an old timber bridge and putting up a Bailey bridge by the glare of headlights.

* * * * *

For those who watched or took part, September 12 was perhaps the most memorable day of all in Singapore. It was on this day that the official surrender of all the Japanese in South-East Asia was signed by Admiral Mountbatten and General Itagaki. This ceremony in the council chamber of the municipal buildings was attended by nearly every senior commander in South-East Asia. In the harbour lay the battleships *Nelson* and *Richelieu*, accompanied by cruisers, escort carriers and destroyers.

At 10.15 a.m. General Slim, Admiral Power and Air Marshal Park arrived. Ten minutes later Admiral Lord Louis Mountbatten drove up with his American deputy, General Wheeler, and was welcomed by the three commanders-in-chief. A combined guard of honour from all three services presented arms and was inspected. The Army guard of honour was provided by the 1/17th Dogras. Then, amid catcalls and jeers from the local population, arrived the Japanese representatives. The enemy generals and admirals were escorted by senior Allied officers, of whom two were Lieutenant-Colonel P. W. P. Green, commanding the 2nd West Yorkshires, and Lieutenant-Colonel Sarbjit Singh Kalha of the 2/1st Punjab.

The enemy delegates with their ceremonial escort marched up the steps and into the council chamber, where soon after eleven o'clock the surrender terms were signed and sealed. Half an hour later the Japanese reappeared and were marched away amidst devastating jeers from the watching crowds.

Mountbatten read the text of his Order-of-the-Day from the steps of the municipal buildings. The Union Jack was formally hoisted and the Royal Marine Band played the National Anthems of all the Allies participating. On behalf of the Division, a seventeen-gun salute was fired for the Supreme Allied Commander by the 11th Battery of the 5th Indian Field Regiment.

In his Order-of-the-Day Admiral Mountbatten said: "The defeat of Japan in the last month is the first in history. For hundreds of years the Japanese had been ruled by a small set of Emperors, and they had been told to look upon themselves as a superior race of divine origin. They had been taught to be arrogant to foreigners and to believe that the treachery they practised on Pearl Harbour is a virtue so long as it ends in Japanese victory. They are finding it very hard to accept defeat, and try to wriggle out of the terms of surrender... I wish to warn, too, of the situation you find when you proceed to liberate other territories in this command. In the new territories you will be occupying, the Japanese have not been beaten in battle. You may well find, therefore, that these Japanese who have not been beaten may still fanatically believe in the supreme superiority of their race. They may try to behave arrogantly. You will have my support in taking the firmest measures against any Japanese obstinacy, impudence, or non-cooperation."

* * * * *

Meanwhile, social life was revived and the troops had plenty to occupy their spare evenings. Local liquor that had been doped with the design of killing our troops caused a poisoning epidemic, and twenty-one men died in one week from the effects. Other victims were claimed by numerous road accidents. But the men were entertained by Chinese families who served them with *frangipani* tea and various sweetmeats; they sang long out-dated songs around the piano and learned to play mahjong. And from these Chinese people the troops heard something about the humiliations of life under Japanese occupation.

A crowd of mixed nationality thronged both sides of the main streets in the evening, stepping off narrow pavements and back again as bicycles and tongas slid past on the fringe of the hectic motor traffic.

Singapore at night became the brightest and noisiest place most of the troops, accustomed as they were to the Burmese jungle, had seen for years. "The Great World," and later "The New World" and "Happy World" amusement parks were reopened. Although at "The New World" there were such items familiar on a British fair ground as 'dodgems' and a ghost train, the place of roundabouts and swings was taken by cinemas, theatres and open-air cafés, each with its own orchestra. If on the one hand Chinese patrons of these cafés insisted on paying for the iced drinks that our troops enjoyed, the Chinese proprietors of such establishments insisted on extortionate prices. In the stuffy, overcrowded dance hall the perspiring troops paid a dollar for four dances with the local dance hostesses or "taxi girls," as they were more usually called. In the ring servicemen boxed or wrestled with local champions. And others reckoned with the intricacies of Malayan dancing. You paid fifteen cents to walk in at the gaudy entrance, with its electric lights hanging on chains. You could sit on a bench in the Chinese theatre and watch the acting and listen to the wailing songs; you could pay to see the fat woman, or throw darts.

To be billeted in a modern and civilized town was particularly thrilling to the Indian troops. The British, though they had been deprived of comfort and luxury during long periods of the war, were accustomed to such things; but never in their lives had the Indians lived in such houses. For them it was memorable to stay in a house as palatial as that into which Nine Brigade Headquarters later moved. The hall and large drawing room had marble floors and pillars. And the garden overlooking the sea front had balconies and balustrades.

* * * * *

Grimshaw's 161 Brigade had in the meantime occupied the area of the naval dockyard and the causeway at Johore Bahru. Torpedo, fuel oil and armament depots were taken over by the 1/1st Punjab and 3/4th Gurkhas. It was noticeable that, although the houses had been left by the Japanese in extremely good condition—it appeared that great care had been taken to give a good impression by leaving the buildings clean and tidy—during the period between the evacuation of the Japanese and the arrival of our troops the local population had indulged heavily in looting, mainly directed at obtaining cloth. To this end they had even ripped covers from chairs and baize from tabletops. The exploring battalions found many tunnels that had been dug into the hills inland, and in these tunnels machinery that had been evacuated from the naval base by the Japanese had been hidden to avoid damage from Allied air attack.

Each day Brigadier Grimshaw issued orders through a Japanese lieutenant-colonel to the enemy senior commander. On September 12, in view of the fact that only a fraction of the one hundred lorries and twenty staff cars which the enemy had been ordered to produce arrived at Brigade Headquarters, a conference was held at which the Japanese Chief-of-Staff was informed that unless the Brigadier's orders were obeyed implicitly in future, he would be arrested.

Chinese resistance forces staged processions and meetings in the Johore area. These meetings, though orderly, appeared to be in protest against the cancellation of Japanese currency. As the civilian population had as yet no British currency, they were unable to buy anything. Consequently, the looting of food dumps tended to increase despite our guards. Further, unrest was caused inland by reports spread by the Japanese to the Malays that when the British arrived, the people would be punished and at least part of Malaya handed over to the Chinese. This led certain sections of the Malays to attack the Chinese resistance forces. And platoons of the 1/1st Punjab had to be sent down to the troubled villages to show the flag. They had to go out again when a Japanese ration lorry carrying food to Japanese forces was attacked by Chinese.

The guarding of dumps stretched the brigade group to the extent of leaving no reserves. In the 161 Brigade area there were no less than sixty stores dumps, ranging from small and valuable collections of food and machinery to large ordnance dumps that contained, in some cases, more than five thousand tons and covered as much as eight square miles.

Early in October 161 Brigade was made responsible for building and organizing a camp beside Kluang airfield from which all the Japanese forces in South Malaya were to be evacuated to the islands of the Riouw Archipelago, south of Singapore. The work was carried out by 2 Field Company, assisted by the 3/4th Gurkhas and a Japanese labour party.

Reception and assembly camps were built, a search point and interrogation centre set up, and white, grey, and black camps constructed to house the Japanese according to their past character and record. The camp was to be ready to deal with up to two thousand Japanese a day. Timber for the camp was obtained by our starting a local steam-driven sawmill. As all the owners and the managers lived in fear of the terrorists, a Sapper officer ran the mill directly through an English-speaking Chinese clerk. The twenty-five sawyers cut six tons of planking a day, and the logs were hauled by lorries from the nearby forest. In this, parties of Japanese under British or Indian N.C.Os. were made to help.

A York and Lancaster Patrol at Yamethin (*Imperial War Museum*)

Sappers Repair the Road to Pegu (*Imperial War Museum*)

APPROACHING SINGAPORE (Imperial War Museum)

LANDING AT SINGAPORE (Imperial War Museum)

Then bricks were needed for the camp, and the adjoining brick kilns and clay pits were reopened. Local labour was extremely difficult. The inflationary price of rice and the general fear of working for less money than the high wages dictated by terrorists caused strikes. One afternoon the whole village population of Kluang marched in procession with banners flying. No Chinese owner dared to show his face, and several were abducted and killed.

On October 8 the first Japanese party arrived in the camp. The Japanese officers, who had been allowed a certain amount of kit over that permitted to other ranks, had grossly exceeded their allowance. This extra baggage, which largely comprised silks and clothing, was removed and placed under guard. And the Japanese liaison colonel was told that, as a result, officers' kit would in future be the same as that of other ranks.

By the end of the month nearly 100,000 Japanese troops had passed through the Kluang reception and evacuation camps.

CHAPTER XXXII

SOERABAJA

NOVEMBER 1945—MAY 1946

THE capitulation of Japan had come with great suddenness. In Britain and America mighty forces were being set in motion to accomplish the invasion of Japan and the final destruction of her forces in Malaya, the Netherlands East Indies and the South-West Pacific. Overnight the responsibility for dealing with the Japanese forces in the Netherlands East Indies, the rehabilitation of internees and for the maintenance of law and order was transferred from the South-West Pacific to South-East Asia Command. Great Britain, already fully involved, had thus to shoulder an additional burden. But neither troops nor ships to implement this new responsibility could at once be subtracted from those already locked up in Operation 'Zipper.' The complicated arrangement had to go on.

Two days before the capitulation of Japan on August 15, Doctor Soerkarno, the collaborationist leader of the Indonesian Nationalist movement, had been summoned to Saigon. He was instructed to form a government and to proclaim the birth of the Indonesian Republic. Before the Japanese invasion of the Netherlands East Indies the Indonesian Nationalist Movement had received little support. During the occupation nationalism had been fostered and the attractive but impracticable idea of the Pan-Asiatic Co-Prosperity Sphere had been imparted. The Japanese had made all preparations to install a form of Nationalist puppet Government which, although under their control, would absolve them from the burden of administering the country whilst allowing them to exploit to the full its riches.

On August 18 Soerkarno broadcast the formation of the Indonesian Republic "with the help of Dai Nippon." He claimed the right of the Republic to recognition by the Allied Nations.

The Indonesian Republic now found itself in sole control of

SOERABAJA

the country. During the ensuing weeks it proceeded to consolidate its position against the delayed arrival of the Allied Forces. It took steps to prejudice the return of the Netherlands colonial administration by virulent propaganda directed against the Dutch. A deliberate campaign of ill-use, brutality, and oppression was started against the unfortunate women and children in the internment camps. All men and boys were seized and imprisoned, leaving the women and children to the mercies of the rough, lawless kampong elements and the brutal fanatical youths of the Nationalist extremist parties.

It was only towards the end of September that the movement of British and Indian troops of the 23rd Indian Division (Major-General D. Hawthorn) from Malaya began. Two brigades were landed piecemeal in Batavia, at the western end of Java. This arrival was greeted with suspicion on the grounds that they were assuming control in order, later, to restore the Netherlands Indies Colonial Administration in Java. Nevertheless, the Indonesian Republican Government accepted the assurances that the tasks of the British force were to succour the internees, remove the Japanese, and help maintain law and order; in fact, no other course existed if they were to obtain the respect of the Allied nations and thus qualify for national independence.

The surrender of the Japanese in East Java had been accepted by a captain of the Royal Netherlands Navy. During the ceremony, the Indonesians had forcibly seized the Japanese arms already handed over and had imprisoned the naval captain. To avoid further participation in a quarrel no longer theirs, the Japanese had handed over the vast residue of arms in Java and had withdrawn into concentration areas in which to await the orders of the Allies.

In Soerabaja Doctor Moestopo, a former dentist, had set himself up as head of the Indonesian Republic in East Java. An excitable, honest figure, whose fanaticism led to lack of balance when confronted with the serious problems soon to arise in Soerabaja, he proved no match for the belligerent military clique headed by Soederman and Atmadji. And he played into their hands, ignoring the moderate advice of experienced ex-colonial administrators such as Doctor Soerio, Governor of East Java.

The institution of the Republican Government was fraught

with difficulties. To prevent the Dutch from interfering, the Indonesians took steps to stifle likely opposition by imprisoning all male internees still at large in the internment camps. They then armed the mob in the kampongs with Japanese swords, rifles and machine-guns. The red and white flags of the new Republic were flown from public buildings and vehicles. In September R.A.P.W.I., the organizers in Java of repatriation of prisoners-of-war and internees, were arrested on fictitious charges of espionage. Some were imprisoned, others were murdered. To avoid any publicity being given to their actions, the Indonesians arrested all newspaper correspondents in East Java and confined them in the Oranje Hotel in Soerabaja, which with unconscious irony was renamed Liberty Hotel. The city remained tense and apprehensive, its conscience uneasy over the reaction of the Allied nations to what had been done.

On October 25, 49 Indian Infantry Brigade, under Brigadier A. W. Mallaby, C.I.E., O.B.E., landed in Soerabaja, charged with the tasks of succouring the internees, disarming and evacuating the Japanese, and assisting the local authorities in the maintenance of law and order. The reception accorded by the Indonesians to 49 Brigade was extremely cool. All over Soerabaja large posters proclaimed Indonesian independence. The Brigade was left in no doubt that its presence was resented and although no hostile acts were actually committed against our troops in the early days, the situation was delicate. As day succeeded day it grew ever more tense.

When rumours that the Indonesians intended to commit violence against the internees greeted 49 Brigade on landing, Brigadier Mallaby decided that a conference must be held with Dr. Moestopo at once, to inform him that any such action carried out would be visited by severe consequences. Moestopo must also be informed of the tasks of the Brigade and his co-operation, if possible, enlisted. The handling of this conference was entrusted to Colonel L. H. O. Pugh, D.S.O., second-in-command of 49 Brigade. That it should succeed was most important. For on the results of this first approach would depend the events of the next few days, the completion of the tasks allotted, and the lives and safety of the large number of women, children, men and boys held in the internment camps and jails.

SOERABAJA

The place was in a ferment. Road-blocks covered by muzzles of machine-guns protruding from nearby houses obstructed the streets. At every halt a horde of excitable youths, armed to the teeth, pressed round the car in which Colonel Pugh was being escorted to the conference. Rifles were thrust through the windows; bayonets all but impaled the occupants of the car; and it was obvious that many fingers trembled on the triggers and that the use of the safety-catch was unknown.

But the conference was a success. The reasons for the presence of British troops in Soerabaja were explained and accepted. And thanks to the reasonable attitude adopted by the representatives of the Indonesian Republican Government, a basis for future co-operation was established and a full-dress meeting between Brigadier Mallaby and Dr. Moestopo arranged for the following morning in the former British Consulate.

The situation in the city was different from that anticipated. A form of Government existed and was prepared to co-operate in accomplishing 49 Brigade's immediate tasks. But it was abundantly clear that any attempt to depose the Indonesian Republican Government in East Java would cause a conflagration. A signal was sent by Brigadier Mallaby to Batavia stating that on no account should leaflets be dropped on Soerabaja, as had been done in West Java, announcing the supersession of local government by a British military administration and ordering the disarming of the people. It was asked that such leaflets be flown to Soerabaja and handed over for distribution at Brigadier Mallaby's discretion.

Meanwhile, 49 Brigade proceeded to occupy the key points of the city in accordance with the brief that Brigadier Mallaby had received. Small detachments were placed in the radio station and the public service installations to protect them against possible sabotage. All questions involving relations with the Indonesians were resolved with the help of a Joint British-Indonesian Committee, known as the Contact Committee, under the joint chairmanship of Colonel Pugh and Dr. Doelwarnwo. Innumerable petty restrictions were met, but relations, though scarcely cordial, remained unbroken and, if anything, tending to improve. One major trouble was the lack of departmental machinery to carry out the orders of the Republican Government. And however willing they might be, results were hard to achieve.

On October 27, a Field Regiment, a Field Ambulance and a squadron of Field Engineers started to move into Dharmo, a residential suburb in the south of the city. Here, in the largest internment camp in East Java, were concentrated many thousands of women and children. The urgent medical needs of these internees could best be met by the Field Ambulance. Steps were taken to bring in by military convoy all small parties of internees scattered in camps throughout Soerabaja. And throughout that day convoys with military escorts ran backwards and forwards collecting many hundreds of these women and children.

During the morning a British aircraft flew over Soerabaja and leaflets were dropped on the city. These leaflets stated the British intention of political interference and of disarming all but a police force of very limited strength. These terms nullified those agreed between Brigadier Mallaby and Moestopo. The prestige of the latter was consequently threatened, and he was placed in the unfortunate position of having apparently been double-crossed by Brigadier Mallaby. At once the situation began to deteriorate. All that night Radio Soerabaja broadcast abuse and vituperation. It called upon the population to drive out the British who, it was alleged, planned to render the Indonesians helpless, preparatory to handing them over to the Dutch. Machine-gun barricades appeared in the streets. Dr. Soerio and his Government of East Java seemed to be losing control of the situation. Indonesian regular forces were secretly regrouped, so that each detachment of Indian troops was covered by superior forces.

The strength of the Indonesian army in Soerabaja was twelve thousand. It consisted of ex-colonial soldiers of the former Dutch forces in the Netherlands East Indies, and had been fully armed and retrained by the Japanese. In addition, the armed mob in the kampongs numbered some seventy-five thousand.

On the afternoon of October 28 the clash occurred. The mob, incited to violence and frenzy by frequent vituperative broadcasts from Radio Soerabaja and by the active propaganda of the Black Buffalo Secret Society, poured out from their kampongs. British lorries which were going about their work in the city were trapped without warning. Eleven officers and fifty other ranks were captured and shot out of hand. A convoy of women and children being driven into Dharmo from the

SOERABAJA

other residential quarter, Goebeng, was attacked. The lorries were set on fire. Despite a prolonged and gallant defence by the small escort of Mahrattas and by the R.I.A.S.C. Indian drivers, only three of the twenty lorries escaped. Many of the women and children were massacred with the utmost brutality. Few escaped with their lives.

After desperate efforts, Mallaby arranged a truce with Soerkarno until the arrival on the following day of Major-General D. Hawthorn, Commander of the Allied Land Forces in Java and of the 23rd Indian Division. The Indonesians ignored the truce and continued to attack our men. The situation of 49 Brigade was now extremely grave. The troops had no ammunition but that actually carried on the men, and all reserves were still in the docks.

When the radio station was set on fire, ammunition ran out, and as the surviving Mahratta defenders fought their way out of the flames, they were killed by overwhelming numbers of Indonesian swordsmen. One company of the Rajputana Rifles were overpowered, and the survivors butchered in the jail they were guarding. The Brigade Headquarters officers' mess was overrun and the mess servants and orderlies put to the sword. And all this time Radio Soerabaja was demanding a national rising. Threats were issued to poison the water, to burn down the city, and to torture prisoners and internees.

On the morning of October 30, Colonel Pugh rejoined Brigade Headquarters by passing successfully through the extent of the Indonesian positions from rear to front. He alone of the officers moving in the town at the time of the outbreak had escaped with his life. He had established himself in Dharmo, where he had been conducting the battle in the southern part of the town. The situation was very serious. The conference between Major-General Hawthorn, Brigadier Mallaby, and Dr. Soerkarno was too late, for the moderate leaders of the Indonesian Republican Government had lost all control. Their authority had been usurped by the extremists who had the bit between their teeth. It was clear that military force alone would bring them to their senses.

Another truce was ordered, but as before, the Indonesians ignored it. Mallaby, seeking a new approach to the desperate situation, proposed sending out British officers with Indonesian officers to tour the city and to try by their personal efforts to bring about a cease-fire. He himself was untiring in this cause, exposing himself ceaselessly to the mercies of the mob, by whom he was murdered on October 30. Two platoons of the Rajputana Rifles, south of Dharmo, were overwhelmed and killed to a man. Units of the Brigade cut off in Soerabaja were now reduced to less than ten rounds of ammunition per man. Brigade Headquarters had sustained twenty-five per cent casualties. The Indonesians, on the other hand, had by this time admitted to no less than 6,000 casualties among their troops and the armed mobs.

Colonel Pugh now assumed command of 49 Brigade. He issued immediate instructions that on no account would any withdrawal take place without his orders. He ordered his troops by the harbour to hold the airfield and docks at all costs. Administrative units, such as the Dock Operating Company of Hull stevedores, Indian Pioneer Company, Field Bakery, Supply and Issue Sections, Workshops, were at once to obtain arms from the Navy or anywhere else and to help defend the port. Demands to surrender were at once rejected. Plans were set afoot to regroup the Brigade into the two main areas of Dharmo and Tandjoengperak—the dock area. And negotiations were opened with Dr. Soerio to abate the fighting and to enable the British and Indian forces to withdraw from the centre of the city.

After protracted negotiations, in which an invaluable part was played by Wing Commander Allan Groom, D.S.O., an ex-prisoner-of-war, Colonel Pugh's proposals were accepted. At four o'clock in the afternoon of October 31, 49 Brigade moved into tactically sound positions. By dusk the regrouping was complete. Supplies and ammunition were assured. The immediate danger was past. But during the fighting eighteen officers and 374 men had been killed, wounded, or were missing. Much equipment had been lost. All the documents and files of Brigade Headquarters had been destroyed, preparatory to the Headquarters fighting its way out from the centre of Soerabaja had negotiations failed. Though 49 Brigade possessed little more than what it stood up in, arrangements were at once started to supply the internees and the garrison in Dharmo by air, to bring

BRIGADIER DENHOLM-YOUNG AND A JAPANESE INTERPRETER
(Imperial War Museum)

LORD LOUIS MOUNTBATTEN INSPECTS 1/17TH DOGRA GUARD OF HONOUR
(Imperial War Museum)

British Troops at Soerabaja *(Imperial War Museum)*

The 4/7th Rajputs beside a Railway Track outside Soerabaja *(Imperial War Museum)*

out the internees, and then to assemble in the area of the port.

* * * * *

On November 2 Major-General Mansergh and a staff officer arrived by air from Batavia, and were met by Colonel Pugh, who emerged from a hole in the ground. The grave circumstances of 49 Brigade necessitated reinforcement in Soerabaja by the Fifth Indian Division. On the previous day 2 Mountain Battery (Major J. Nettlefield) had landed, temporarily without its guns. The situation in Soerabaja was different from that envisaged in Batavia. 49 Brigade, although shaken and depleted, was firmly established. The Contact Committee had been revived, negotiations had started, and some results had already been achieved in operations to bring out the internees, to recover Indian troops held prisoners by the Indonesians, to effect the return of Brigadier Mallaby's body and captured vehicles. Delicate though the situation was, it was completely under control. But as General Mansergh's arrival, if known, would give rise to further suspicion which might upset the delicate balance now held, he agreed to remain in the background; all personal negotiations with the Indonesians would continue to be carried out by Colonel Pugh under his direction. It was thus hoped to protect the arrival of the Fifth Indian Division, and to avoid plunging the city into another 'blood bath.' General Mansergh's brief was to secure Soerabaja and to carry out the tasks originally allotted to 49 Brigade—succouring Allied internees, disarming the Japanese, and assisting in the maintenance of law and order.

Nine Brigade were the first troops to arrive. The port and airfield were firmly held by the 4th and 6th Mahratta Light Infantry of 49 Brigade, whilst the 6th Rajputana Rifles and the Field Regiment garrisoned a strongly defended area in Dharmo.

The convoy of L.S.Ts. carrying the troops of the Division passed through the Madoera Straits as they approached Soerabaja. Off Madoera Island to the east our troops could see many ships that had been sunk by the Netherlands Navy when Java was first overrun by the Japanese. These Dutch vessels, whose masts and funnels were sticking up out of the water at frequent intervals, almost blocked the narrow channel marked by buoys. A moving incident occurred when two L.S.Ts., that had already landed troops in

Soerabaja and were on their way back, came out of the sunny haze ahead and passed the convoy. The boats, laden with Dutch women and children who were being evacuated from Java, were so packed with people that their superstructures were hardly visible for dresses. The women and children waved, smiled and shouted. There was a hooting of funnels. A visible reason for our men going to Soerabaja had been vouchsafed. They began to understand.

The men of the Division knew little of the situation except that 49 Brigade had run into trouble and had been attacked. Little of Soerabaja itself could be seen as they came in from the sea: the city stretches seven miles inland, is long and narrow in shape, and the ground quite flat.

The docks presented a dilapidated and derelict appearance: broken glass, rusty roofs, empty warehouses with here and there green-clad figures loading ammunition and stores into waiting vehicles. In the naval base, some few naval ratings moved amongst the overgrown hedgerows and gardens of houses and sheds. In the distance, half-hidden by trees, showed the spires and buildings of Soerabaja. On walls and roofs could be read slogans such as "Indonesia for the Indonesians," "Remember the Atlantic Charter," "We will pledge our freedom with our blood," and many others. From the docks long avenues, lined with gold mohur trees now in flower—a vivid splash of scarlet blossom—led southwards towards the town. The disreputable appearance of Soerabaja, with its dirty unswept streets and blistered paintwork, was set off by the blue flowers of the jacaranda and the red-roofed houses and avenues of shady trees that lined the Kali Mas canal.

The concentration of the Fifth Indian Division was kept very secret and was covered by 49 Brigade, who continued to hold a perimeter outside the harbour area. On the night of November 6 the battalion and field regiment in Dharmo were safely withdrawn to the docks. Nine Brigade concentrated in rear of 49 Brigade and in due time took over the defence of the airfield on the right. The 3/2nd Punjab and 2nd West Yorkshires held the forward line defences, with the 3/9th Jats in reserve. Forward positions were sited in houses, and holes had to be knocked in walls to give fields of fire.

An uneasy peace reigned. Thousands of Indonesians were massed in front of the defence line held by 49 Brigade. Any small incident might have set the fighting off again. Had this happened during the first few days before the Division arrived in strength, the situation might well have deteriorated and our positions become untenable.

Nevertheless, 6,100 helpless women and children had been brought out of Dharmo by 49 Brigade. This had not been accomplished without considerable effort. Evasions, threats, cajolement and lies continued hour after hour. Convoys had driven through the town escorted only by Indonesian troops in whose reliability 49 Brigade had little confidence. A squadron of light tanks of the 11th P.A.V.O. Cavalry had stood by continuously in case any convoy were attacked. This mass evacuation could never have been carried out but for the calm courage and trust of the Dutch women and children, who allowed themselves to be carried through the sullen, turbulent town, the inhabitants of which had but recently been screaming for their blood and threatening them with every barbarity.

In the streets there was no movement—neither cars, trams, nor buses. There were no Indonesian civilians in the area. If the workshops in the docks were empty, warehouses in the port area by contrast were full of stores. Crates of wines—sherries and hocks, and bales of cloth and rotted nylon stockings abounded. In the port offices, typewriters and papers lay on the desks just as they had been abandoned.

* * * * *

The general attitude of the fanatical Indonesians showed that they would stop at nothing. They had committed unbelievable atrocities on Dutch women and children, on British and Indian personnel, and had gone to lengths that no people worthy of the name would have thought possible. Their activities varied from mutilating the wounded to rape, denying prisoners-of-war food and drink and, eventually, when killing those in their power, dismembering them in public. The whole attitude of irresponsible youths and men in Soerabaja was one which was likely to lead to serious fighting and even greater loss of life. In the meanwhile units and formations of the Division were landing in the Dock area. In the city, there were large concentrations of ex-internees and prisoners-of-war, mostly Dutch women and children, who were hourly exposed to the violence and dangers of a brutal mob. This was the situation on November 7 when General Mansergh attended a meeting with the Indonesian leaders.

This meeting was held in a little house on the edge of the airfield. The so-called Governor of East Java and three or four other reputable Indonesians attended the conference and endeavoured to persuade their youthful and quite irresponsible compatriots that the British were in fact there to relieve distress, rescue prisoners-of-war and disarm Japanese. It was quite obvious, in part from the ill-behaviour of the so-called military and naval representatives of the Indonesian Republic, that any attempt at co-operation was useless, but it also appeared that the Indonesian Army were determined to take complete control from the more stable civilian element.

General Mansergh very carefully explained what had already been put to the Indonesians, that all the British forces wished to do was disarm the Japanese, rescue and help the needy, and ensure safety and order in Soerabaja. He further invited the civil police and the Indonesian Youth Army to help him to achieve this end. He suggested that the lawless mob should be disarmed by being ordered to return quietly to their homes and place their weapons at indicated points. These weapons would then be taken over and placed in safety. At the same time he asked again for the women and children to be permitted to come into the safe area of the Docks. It was quite apparent that the young hotheads had no intention of permitting this. Their behaviour, expressions and general attitude were such that further negotiation was obviously useless. General Mansergh then said that, as his orders were to disarm the Japanese and liberate those held against their wills in captivity, he had no alternative but to enter the town and, if necessary, use force. He added that he would not do this until November 10, so as to enable the Indonesians to reconsider his suggestion. He further hoped there would be no opposition; but if there was, he would be forced to protect his men and rescue the Dutch women and children from their brutal captors.

Pamphlets were dropped in Soerabaja and the surrounding area asking for peaceful citizens either to help with the maintenance of law and order or to keep to their houses. The pamphlet further said that the troops in the Dock area would advance at six o'clock in the morning of the 10th and that it was hoped assistance would be forthcoming from the Indonesian authorities. The pamphlet also stated that should there be opposition, and should it become necessary to use force, such force as was at the disposal of General Mansergh would be used. Details were given of a route out of Soerabaja along which peaceable citizens could leave the area; those who remained behind did so at their own risk.

Between the 7th and 10th the situation became more tense and the Indonesians more aggressive. So that casualties might be avoided, information was received and obtained on the position of internees' compounds, hospitals, orphanages, and other places where there were general concentrations of inhabitants. By the time six a.m. on November 10 arrived, the Division had very good information about the Indonesian dispositions within the city. The battalions of Denholm-Young's 123 Brigade—2/1st Punjab, 1/17th Dogra, 3/9th Gurkha Rifles—advanced on a somewhat misty morning and were almost immediately fired upon. Their orders were, however, only to use their personal weapons unless receiving definite orders to the contrary. Within half an hour it was obvious that the Indonesians were deployed in strength and had numerous weapons including tanks, guns, and mortars. They were inflicting considerable casualties on the slowly advancing Indian and British troops; permission was therefore given to our troops to use mortars. In support of the Brigade was the 5th Indian Field Regiment (Lieutenant-Colonel R. F. D. Legh).

As the morning drew on, considerable opposition and artillery fire were encountered, for the Indonesians were using every form of weapon they possessed. And these included not only rifles and machine-guns, but also spears, knives, swords, krisses, sharpened bamboos, blowpipes, and poisoned arrows or darts. By eleven o'clock the main advance line and headquarters occupied by the Indonesian forces had been located, and it was clear that any further advance without receiving heavy casualties would not be possible. Accordingly, General Mansergh gave orders for the prepared support fire, from the artillery and the lighter units of the Royal Navy, to be put down on the carefully located enemy positions. Certain selected headquarters and artillery and infantry positions were bombed by the Royal Air Force. The whole of this concentration lasted for five minutes, after which there was a pause to give the Indonesians time to reconsider their attitude. Then the troops continued their advance where possible and only used such support fire as was necessary to reach their objectives. At no time during the battle, which lasted for nineteen days, were bombs used except where special targets and strong-points made this necessary. By evening the jail had been reached and a breach was made in the wall by an anti-tank gun. Inside the prison were found some 3,000 Dutch and Allied internees, crammed into a space normally occupied by 1,200 prisoners. The troops arrived at this area just in time and were able to prevent the Indonesians from setting light to many of the cell blocks; in some instances petrol had been poured over the roofs and the unexpected arrival of the troops interfered with what would have been an indescribable massacre of defenceless people.

A very serious event that day was the death of Brigadier Robert Loder-Symons, who was C.R.A. of the Division. Before resorting to bombing that morning, he had asked General Mansergh for permission to fly over the city to see what was happening. When taking off his aircraft failed to rise, and both he and the pilot were killed.

This officer, a most distinguished Horse Artilleryman, who had served outstandingly in the Western Desert and Europe, and was one of the great characters of that period of the war, had come out to join the Division from Norway, where he had been C.R.A. to the 1st Armoured Division. In a very short while in Burma and Malaya he had endeared himself to all ranks of the Division and had managed with quite distinctive success to get to know the Indian soldier who was till then quite unknown to him. The loss of this gallant officer in an air-crash was serious not only to the Division but to the British Army, for he was undoubtedly one of the outstanding junior officers of the war.

* * * * *

During the days that followed our battalions were engaged in close-quarter street fighting, a form of warfare new to the Division. Mansergh's plan was to take over Soerabaja, a Dutch city, with the minimum damage and casualties. In any case, artillery was limited; we were forbidden to use aircraft; no more bombs were available; the Chinese areas were not to be damaged or fired into; and the Dutch camp areas and certain special buildings had to be preserved. The supporting squadron of Sherman tanks from the 13th Lancers were only allowed to fire their 75 mm. guns on direct orders from a Brigadier.

The Indonesians knew the area and outnumbered our troops. They had Japanese light and medium tanks and artillery, and abundant ammunition, but they seldom supported their fanatical attacks by fire. Nor could they pin-point our positions, but they loosed off ammunition in their general direction whenever they felt inclined. And their firing grew wilder as the days passed. No one knew when a shell might not whine over, and soldiers in the most innocent places might have to flatten themselves on the ground.

No civilians were seen as the troops moved forward. Many streets were deserted. At this stage little damage had been done and the looting had been negligible. Most of the smaller Chinese shops were found barricaded. But as the battle crept forward, large shops were passed, full of goods that lay on the counters or glass shelves. Some cupboards had been smashed open, but little had been taken.

To clear the city was a slow business. 123 Brigade had to repel the most bitter onslaughts, in which thousands of young Indonesians fell before the medium machine-guns of Colonel Bristow's Dogras. Continuous sniping made the task of digging in at once difficult and perilous. The Indonesian mortaring was accurate and plentiful, and at this stage their troops were commanded by Japanese.

When our troops reached the Chinese area in the centre of Soerabaja, the Chinese, unlike the Indonesians, refused to leave their homes. Here they had gathered from all parts of the city with their belongings, and houses were crammed with families huddled into one room. The Chinese feared that if once they went, their houses would be open to loot and destruction. And they suffered many casualties when their quarter became No-Man's-Land for thirty-six hours. Later they were right in the heart of the battle, and sections of the 3/2nd Punjab (Lieutenant-Colonel J. M. Worsley) had to dig their positions in Chinese gardens. Often holes had to be knocked from one house to another so that the infantry could get through. Often some of our Indians would be manning machine-guns in the front part of a room in the rear half of which crouched a Chinese family.

By November 17 Nine Brigade had occupied the entire Chinese quarter. The Indonesian resistance had begun to stiffen as they brought up more guns and tanks. Like the Japanese who had trained them, they were often ready to fight to the last in their strong points. By the time our infantry battalions reached the European residential areas of Dharmo and Goebeng, the Indonesians had begun to melt away, to slip out of the city. And an enthusiastic welcome awaited the troops as they entered the Dutch districts. Companies of the 3/2nd Punjab were greeted with kisses and flowers by the released Dutch, Armenian, Arab, and Chinese womenfolk.

The occupation of Soerabaja was completed on November 28, after nineteen days' fighting. Now the city had to be thoroughly searched to ensure that no Indonesian insurgents, disguised in mufti and with their weapons hidden, still remained inside. For several days areas were cordoned off and combed in a house-to-house search. The determination of the Indonesians to continue the struggle had been in no way impaired, and it was certain that they would offer the maximum resistance.

The Division, still without Grimshaw's 161 Brigade which after sailing to Soerabaja had been recalled to Batavia, had taken up positions on the edge of the city. The infantry patrolled out from their forward lines to keep contact with the Indonesians, to prevent them as far as possible from infiltrating back into Soerabaja, and above all to keep their heavy guns or mortars out of range of the city itself. To achieve this columns were sent out to break up any build-up by the Indonesians. An area ten miles wide round Soerabaja was to be kept free from major enemy forces.

From Soerabaja the countryside stretched inland, almost flat, with bright green paddy fields, studded here and there by the darker clumps of villages. In the distance rose blue, hazy, volcanic mountains, always so desirable to look at because they conjured up visions of coolness from the day-long monsoon sweat on sea level. There was little cover for our infantry or for the Indonesians in the paddy fields on either side of the road, and many abandoned guns were shot up and captured. Occasionally, a column of both infantry and tanks would set out on a still wider *chukka* for two or three days, sweeping some ten miles along roads and cart tracks.

SOERABAJA

The column rumbled through the streets, past civilians digging in their gardens or eating breakfast under the trees, and so out into the country. And from then on the crack of a machine-gun, a sniper, or a mine, could be expected at any moment. Nine Brigade carried out two such columns, westwards to Sidoardjo, and to Krijan. And 123 Brigade raided and occupied Grissee on the coast north-west of Soerabaja.

Many of the Dutch women and children had been marched out along the hot, dusty road that led inland, and had been imprisoned in the villages. And our patrols and columns, seeking to release these hostages, missed them time and again by a matter of hours. The villages in which the Dutch were kept lay out of range in many cases, and on the approach of one of our columns these civilians would be sent still further into the interior.

As a result of our columns, the Indonesians began a systematic destruction of bridges on all roads leading out of the city in order to prevent further columns from operating. And this fighting further afield took on the aspect of guerilla warfare. Casualties were suffered by both sides, but the Indonesians paid very heavily in their night raids against our company positions and in their attacks on our patrols. The Indonesian army, trained by the Japanese, had been defeated. Now small organizations had come forward to give battle. But Soerabaja was not seriously threatened. By mid-December the Indonesians had abandoned plans to recapture the city. Their policy seemed to be one of prolonged delaying tactics.

*   *   *   *   *

Although in this third phase of the fighting in and around Soerabaja most of the units had very comfortable billets in luxurious houses and hotels and only the forward companies suffered any discomfort, and although the men had clubs and cinemas on a peacetime scale, yet for many the war became a little unreal and every day patrol clashes took place all along the front. The casualties of the Division mounted. Unfortunately, as was so often the case, the men who were killed in Java invariably seemed to be those with the longest service and the greatest honours. This happened particularly in Worsley's 3/2nd Punjab, where men with four or five years of almost continuous service and many decorations, men who had fought in Eritrea, in the Desert, and through Burma, were killed by a sniper, a mine, or a stray shell.

* * * * *

When the fighting in Soerabaja ended, the city had been largely cleared of Indonesians. But these soon began to drift back into the villages and kampongs on the outskirts and then seeped into Soerabaja itself. To stop them was impossible. The Chinese and Indonesians opened up their shops and set to work in the dockyards. But the civilians were, in many cases, scared of the armed Indonesians, among whom there were alleged to be many murderers and looters. Frequently stories, usually unfounded, of Indonesian ringleaders were reported to Brigade Headquarters. Many were the spy scares and reports of strange lights at night. The Indonesians were said to be coming back into Soerabaja in small parties at dawn, taking advantage of the cover provided by villagers bringing fruit and vegetables to the markets, to smuggle arms and ammunition into the city. Rumour had it that the civilians would later be wiped out.

The Dutch and Chinese, who lived in the better houses of Soerabaja, feared that the Indonesians were grouping in the kampongs. These were large slum areas of mud huts and *bashas*, built in row after row with narrow passageways in between the trees. There would be thousands of Indonesians living in one area. In response to these allegations, the kampongs would from time to time be surrounded by two companies of infantry and a systematic search carried out. The odd grenade was thrown from day to day, and sometimes a sniper would be active, particularly against ration lorries being driven out to the forward infantry battalions.

The battalion in reserve in the town, although on guard duties, lived in excellent quarters—in comfortable modern bungalows with pretty gardens, or in hotels. And in the evenings the officers and men enjoyed themselves. It was quite normal for an officer to fight a fierce battle during the daytime and that same evening to take his Dutch girl friend to dine and dance at the Simpang Club. The Dutch sports and tennis clubs were opened to Allied officers and their friends. Tennis rackets and balls could be bought cheaply in the town and many hours were spent on the tennis courts, in the swimming pools and cinemas. Small shops opened up, and these were full of junk and loot. But a weekly issue of Japanese guilders increased the troops' purchasing power in the local markets. The men found it a new experience in war to have civilians, both European and Oriental, around them.

The month of December was spent in consolidation, evacuation, and rehabilitation. In the city the search for arms continued, and although the situation remained generally quiet, isolated sniping incidents occurred at night.

On December 8 a notice was distributed to the local population calling for the surrender of arms and ammunition within two days. Collecting points were announced, and this was to be a final chance for Indonesians to give up their arms. Henceforth, all people found with arms were to be treated as enemies of law and order. The response to this proclamation was very poor. The inhabitants in many cases seemed either afraid of the consequences of producing concealed weapons or unwilling to part with them because of the uncertain conditions in Soerabaja.

But the cases of looting diminished; the search of the city and its satellite kampongs was completed; the curfew was well observed; the extremist influence seemed to have been destroyed; an ever-increasing number of civilians returned to the kampongs— during one week eight thousand came back; and the prevailing spirit seemed to be one of relief that hostilities within the city were over.

The various communities in Soerabaja were too busy restoring normal conditions for inter-communal friction to be apparent. The Chinese, Arabs, and Indonesians all established food control centres, hospitals, and relief posts. A local police force was raised and labour bureaux began to function. Merchants were encouraged to resume business, and people brought in food to the bazaars. A civil court was opened to deal with cases of looting. The anarchic atmosphere in the kampongs noticeably died down, and at least a surface calm prevailed in Soerabaja.

But although public confidence was thus being restored, there was general uncertainty of the future, and a strong public desire for a clarification of immediate Allied policy in eastern Java. While some of the hysterical fanaticism was melting away in the light of more practical administration, and increasing local help was forthcoming, dangerous elements and extremist leaders were still lying low in Soerabaja. The city's population at this time was about 750,000. The Dutch element comprised chiefly some twenty thousand interned women and children, while the Chinese numbered about seventy thousand, the Arabs ten thousand, and the Indians half that number. The rest were Indonesians.

General Mansergh and the staff of Divisional Headquarters at once set about forming a military government, with departments for police, law, supplies, shipping, education, broadcasting, medicine, and power and light. As, at this time, Soerabaja was virtually besieged on every side except the sea, no supplies came from the mainland outside the Division's defence perimeter. By the beginning of January when a certain number of Dutch civilian officials arrived to help, a police force of some seven hundred men and an ambulance system had been organized. Four schools were running, attended by six thousand children, and four civilian hospitals had been reopened. Lighting was working in all offices, in hospitals, and in the docks. Some forty per cent of the water system was in operation, but there was still a lack of water because the Indonesians were holding the springs. Aided by specialists, the Divisional Sappers established water points, filled from ships, and they restored to working order the sewage system, the gas works, the cold storage plant in the docks, and the bulk oil installations. They also stood by to deal with fires and arson in the crowded kampong areas, where the shacks were built of wood and thatch. The Royal Navy, under Captain Garwood, had the dockyard in action, and the docks were discharging some two thousand tons a day at full pressure. Four daily news sheets in Dutch, Malay, Chinese, and Indonesian were issued, and Divisional Signals had constructed a transmitter which broadcast a midday programme with news and a full evening programme.

In the middle of January 451 Sub-area from Akyab arrived to run the base, and to relieve the Divisional staff of many burdens and responsibilities. It was during January, too, that the Division's veteran British unit, the 2nd Battalion, the West Yorkshire Regiment, who had fought at Dologorodoc and in the Cauldron, at Ngakyedauk and Meiktila, went away, after a fighting record unsurpassed in the Division.

On January 11 the Division and the Indian Army suffered a

very severe loss. The 2/1st Punjab had pushed forward from their positions some miles outside Soerabaja and when this battalion's tactical headquarters was about to enter a place called Domas, the small convoy was ambushed. The battalion commander, Lieutenant-Colonel Sarbjit Singh Kalha, in the foremost jeep was killed outright. The battery commander of 144 Field Regiment (Berkshire Yeomanry), Major Whitcombe, who was following in the second jeep, was also killed. The wireless sets were put out of action by small-arms fire, and the isolated column lost touch with the other companies. One platoon under Subadar Karim Khan took up defence positions and beat back four attacks by the Indonesians—attacks that went on for an hour and a half. The situation was later restored when Major Duncan's company, who were quite ignorant of what had happened on the outskirts of Domas owing to the breakdown of communications, came up to the same place despite machine-gun fire. The bodies of those who had been killed were eventually recovered and buried with full military honours. Subadar Karim Khan, I.D.S.M., was awarded the Military Cross for his gallantry in the command of his platoon.

It was tragic that the last action of any importance in which the 2/1st Punjab were engaged should have been the most disastrous, in that Colonel Kalha lost his life. He had been at the Staff College and had served with the battalion off and on from the first day it went into action. Calm and unruffled in battle, fearless, and with delightful manners, he had won the D.S.O. and bar. His remarkable ability included that of commanding both British and Indian officers, and there was no one in his battalion or in the Division who did not hold him in the highest regard. He was one of those senior Indian Army officers whom India could least afford to lose.

Towards the end of January 1946 the Division was instructed to plan the landing on and the occupation of the nearby islands of Bali and Lombok. The operation was to have been carried out by the Dutch Army Brigade from Bangkok. After many changes and a good deal of worry, the occupation was successfully accomplished with the help of a British mission, led by Colonel Kemp. The Senior Commander of the Japanese Forces on Bali surrendered his sword to General Mansergh at a formal parade on February 18.

It was on February 4 that the first Dutch troops actually landed at Soerabaja, led by a reconnaissance party of the 1st Netherlands

Marine Brigade from America. Early in March this Dutch brigade arrived in strength and at once took over the defences on the west of Soerabaja from 123 Brigade, who were to prepare to leave for India.

By the middle of the month it was finally confirmed that the Division was to return to Ranchi, and operation 'Epilogue'—a fitting title—began. The Division was to be relieved in Soerabaja by a Dutch Army Brigade from Great Britain, and, of course, by the 1st Netherlands Marine Brigade. The necessary divisional staff and troops were to be sent from Holland.

During March there seemed to be a general lull in extremist activities. Whenever they tried to make a stand they were dispersed or put to flight, and there appeared to be no basic plan or co-ordination among the Indonesian forces, no liaison between their various sectors. Despite the continued terrorizing of the villagers, the extremists were regarded with increased contempt by the more moderate population. But the news of the approaching withdrawal of British and Indian troops from Java and their replacement by Dutch caused despondency among the Eurasian and Chinese communities.

Although relations between the British and Dutch troops were in the main friendly and co-operative, it was inevitable that there should be difficulties from time to time. Naturally the Dutch felt sore about their inability to take over and control their own colonies. The orders which were being carried out by the British and Indian forces restricted very considerably the Dutch authority, which was made even more insecure by the extreme scarcity of Dutch troops. At moments feeling ran high, but in spite of the inherent difficulties of the situation, the Dutch forces and the men of the Fifth Indian Division, the Royal Navy, and the Royal Air Force worked in very satisfactory harmony.

During April the various units of the Division sailed back to India, and the relief in Soerabaja was completed by May 8. The hand-over went smoothly, but it was not without a twinge of regret that the Division had to leave behind its transport and twenty 25-pounder guns which had served it so well in the past years. These had been sold to the Dutch.

On April 23 General Mansergh had left the Division and had flown to Batavia to assume the appointment of G.O.C.-in-C.

of all Allied Forces in the Netherlands East Indies. The square in front of Divisional Headquarters, the former Town Hall, was renamed 'General Mansergh Plein.' The new C.R.A., Brigadier G. R. Bourne, took over acting command of the Fifth Indian Division.

Other Indian and British troops remained to complete the difficult task with which they had been entrusted. To the individual Indian soldier this task must have presented serious problems. Their propagandists at home missed no opportunity of comparing the duties that had to be carried out in Indonesia with what they, in India, were fighting against in their efforts to rid India of British occupation. Many of the Indians and Indonesians professed the same religion. The soldiers had been away for years and were longing to return home. Yet, despite these important facts, they carried out their duty to their regiments, their officers and their Commander in the loyal, patient and self-sacrificing way so characteristic of the Indian soldier. Many must have been the temptations, but the vast majority of the troops serving with the Fifth Indian Division remained true to themselves and to their leaders, and completed their task in such a manner that both Dutch and Indonesians expressed gratitude, for "your politeness, your kindness, and your dignified self-restraint."

The Fifth Indian Division returned to India, to Ranchi in Bihar Province where it had trained for the war against Japan three years before. The men were in the highest spirits and morale, having completed their foreign service, a service which no other formation can equal.

EPILOGUE

"The road across these five years was long, hard and perilous. Those who perished upon it did not give their lives in vain. Those who marched forward to the end will always be proud to have trodden it with honour."

WINSTON S. CHURCHILL:
Their Finest Hour.

THE Division returned to India for the last time. Muslim units went north to the new state of Pakistan. Many of the soldiers left the service and returned to their homes. The comradeship of British and Indian troops became a feature to look back on with pleasure. For six years the Division had travelled and fought. Units had come, units had gone, the men had changed. But those who were new became absorbed into the team, and imbued with the Divisional Spirit. Now that team disintegrated, and dispersed across the world. And the years of abundant memory began to fade into the past. But, bringing death or mutilation to many, they contained also the most varied and adventurous memories of many more, who had travelled a very great distance, whose horizons had been widened, whose experience had deepened, and whose characters had become strengthened by responsibility, command, and loyal obedience in dangerous times.

Each man has his own particular memories: passing the regimental mule lines, and seeing all the swishing tails; the record of a nostalgic tune of Tchaikovsky played constantly in Lohardaga; the endless lines of bullock carts on the dusty roads of Burma; the varied bird life for those who had a trained eye to watch; the grazing herd of camels that chewed off long stretches of insulation from a telephone line in the Sudan; a night drive across the Desert, standing with your head out of the trap door in the roof, looking down on the road, and calling to your driver to go left, or right, or straight ahead, or to stop; bathing before breakfast in the turquoise-blue waters of the Mediterranean, and walking happily along the gleaming white sands that stretch for miles beside Burg el Arab. One will remember the fields of Cyprus in spring-

EPILOGUE

time, when scarlet poppies and yellow patches of daisies mingled with the green of the swaying barley. Another will be reminded of shooting duck or sand-grouse. There will be a momentary glimpse of the first Italian prisoners brought in—a bedraggled crowd of native troops wearing coloured scarves round their waists to distinguish their regiment. Or a mental picture of Sikh signalmen in Eritrea, hating the cold, muffled up in greatcoats, and bright with coloured cloths tied round their beards and over the top of their intricate *pagris*. Fishing in a stream near Gallabat; the sound of children on the Teknaf Peninsula chanting their morning prayers in the Buddhist school. Lying on one's stomach in a paddy field on the edge of an Arakanese village, and deciphering code messages by the light of the moon. The Punjabi lance-naik who, when he was going away, seized his officer's hand, and said, "Agar maine koi galati kia hai, to ap muaf kijiye" (Please pardon any mistakes I may have made). The ecstasy with which a battalion Signals Officer could greet the discovery of two miles of telephone cable or a roll of insulating tape. The contentment of listening on a long line to clear, loud speech.

The souvenirs that a man brought back with him would vary with his taste, and above all with the force of his collecting instinct and the circumstances in which he found himself. Few were able to bring heavy items, for baggage was restricted, and very little might be carried out from the battle front. Nor had anyone the space, apart from the corner of some leather *yakdan* box, or a haversack, or a niche in a truck. Yet each man took back some little group of mementos: a Japanese sword to hang above his mantelpiece, an album with photographs and news cuttings, lace table mats from Cyprus, brocade from Damascus, an inlaid mother-of-pearl box bought in Beirut, or an Arab headrope picked up in the bazaars of Baghdad. There might be a Persian rug stretched on the parquet floor, a copy or two of an Indian or Egyptian newspaper, a handful of foreign coins, a photograph of the man himself perched on a camel beside the Sphinx, or postcards of the Pyramids and the Gateway to India at Bombay. You might find in one of his drawers a note-book with Japanese characters scrawled on the white pages; or a musty smelling book with his own name, a date, and Cairo or Haifa or Singapore or Nicosia written on the flyleaf—and this book would, on account of its travels, hold for its owner more intimate associations than its fellows on the shelf.

Up in the attic might be found an old canvas valise, that had been rolled round his bedding and had been spread out night after night for him to sleep in, and rolled and fastened again with straps morning after morning through the campaigns. On the outside would be the traces of his name painted in white, and various sets of code numbers and letters that had signified one ship or unit in a convoy. In some old envelope in the drawer lies a sheaf of creased and folded maps of old campaigning areas, torn at the folds, disfigured by pencil crosses and rings that have lost their meaning, and by faintly pencilled code names for hill features and crossroads. Hanging in the cupboard is a suit of green jungle battledress that is used for gardening, and somewhere or other could be found a small cardboard box filled with dusty officer's pips, or a crown, a Divisional flash or two, bits of faded, crumpled medal ribbons, and disused medal bars of various lengths.

In what different places and conditions these men had slept: in moving trains along the Egyptian coast, across the great continent of India, or through Palestine; on the chilly mountain tops of Keren, Amba Alagi, and Kennedy Peak; beside such rivers as Gash and Atbara, Tigris, Nile, and Brahmaputra, Chindwin and Irrawaddy, and on the banks of slender waterways like the Tatmin Chaung. They had slept in the bustling, over-populated cities of Cairo and Calcutta, and in places emerging from the grip of war and enemy occupation, as were Rangoon and Singapore. Nights had been spent in transit and reinforcement camps, on board destroyers and troopships, in bamboo *bashas*, and in tents that ranged in size from the tiny bivouac to the large, square E.P.I.P. As soldiers they had fallen asleep beneath the clear stars of a Desert sky and the monsoon clouds above the jungle-clad hillsides, on soft or rocky sand, on grass and bare earth, on camp beds and in the depths of a slit trench, on wooden planks, beneath a stuffy mosquito net, under the interlaced branches of teak forests or bamboo clumps, in jolting lorries, on a stretcher, in a slow-moving ambulance.

Nor would the sleepless nights of vigil be forgotten, the battles in darkness, the approach marches for the dawn attack, and the night patrols.

Hands that in peacetime had clipped hedges and weeded flower-

EPILOGUE

beds, cast flies for fishing, pushed a pram, held the plough or driven cattle out to graze, hewn coal, thrown a cricket ball, planted bulbs, sown seed, picked coffee berries and drawn water from the village well—these hands, dark brown or ruddy in colour, had during the years of warfare loaded Bren-gun magazines, pressed forward safety-catches on a rifle, squeezed the trigger, thrown grenades, dug trenches and gun-pits, pitched tents and laid mines, put up barbed wire, spread camouflage nets, tugged mules up muddy hillsides, tapped out Morse signals, dug graves, set fuses, built bridges, searched enemy prisoners, bandaged wounded limbs, joined broken telephone cables, and performed a thousand other daily tasks.

* * * * *

And now it was all over. They had shared in the making of History. They had their wound scars, their medals, their pictures of the mind.

For those who came back from the wars, how varied were the homes and jobs to which they returned: the villages of India and Pakistan, the flats and suburban houses, the country farms, the barracks. The members of the Division are to be found working as *zemindars* and shopkeepers, chartered accountants and doctors, farmers in Devonshire and Guernsey. They have retired to Kenya or a Sussex village, or taken civil posts in Rhodesia, Venezuela, Hong Kong; or they are teachers, advertisers, librarians, insurance agents. And some still serve under the colours.

Some have sent their roots deeper into the soil they had left. Others have started afresh. Others again cannot settle with a quiet mind. Many have taken to themselves a wife, and have created a family, or have seen for the first time a child born in their absence.

They meet in twos and threes, or at reunion dinners. They talk of the past, and recall people and places, and much of human experience that can seldom be set down on paper.

But many there were who did not return to their homes. Their villages and their towns have not again seen their faces. For their hands are at rest. The dead lie on the hills of Keren and Kohima; among the paddy fields of Arakan; in the warm sands of the Desert; beside a coursing river. And they are remembered by those who knew them in peace and in war.

APPENDIX I

Those who helped with the writing of this book and who are not mentioned by name in the Acknowledgments.

Major J. O. Arthur, M.C.; Lt.-Col. Hon. D. A. Balfour, T.D.; Major J. M. Birnie; Major-Gen. Sir Charles Boucher; Brigadier R. C. B. Bristow; Captain R. Bromley-Gardner, M.C.; Major D. Brunt; Major P. Connery, M.B.E.; Lt.-Col. J. F. Carroll, O.B.E.; Major H. F. Davis; Brigadier E. J. Denholm-Young, D.S.O., O.B.E.; Brigadier E. R. S. Dods, M.C.; Major D. Easten, M.C.; Major-Gen. G. C. Evans; Lt.-Col. K. G. H. Fryer, O.B.E.; Brigadier B. C. H. Gerty, C.B.E., D.S.O.; B. Giddings; Major A. N. Gillman, M.C.; Colonel J. M. Graham, D.S.O., M.C.; Lt.-Col. E. H. W. Grimshaw, D.S.O.; Captain S. Hamilton;' Lt.-Col. E. J. C. Harrison, O.B.E.; Lt.-Col. C. Harvey; Brigadier M. L. Hayne, C.B.E.; Captain J. A. Hepburn; Brigadier I. F. Hossack, D.S.O.; Major M. Jacobs; Major-Gen. F. A. M. B. Jenkins; Lt.-Col. T. H. Jessop, M.B.E.; Major L. H. Jones, D.S.O., M.C.; Major A. L. King-Harman; Lt.-Col. M. Lamacraft, M.B.E.; Colonel W. H. Langran, M.C.; Lt.-Col. R. Leckie-Ewing; Major M. Lingane, M.B.E.; Brigadier T. Mainprise-King; Major A. S. Massey; Major P. St. G. Maxwell, M.C.; Major D. B. McTurk; Brigadier C. L. Morgan, O.B.E.; Major C. W. T. Morshead, M.C.; Lt.-Col. G. Munn, M.C.; Colonel A. H. G. Napier, O.B.E.; Major J. Nettlefield, M.C.; Major-Gen. F. L. Nicholson; Lt.-Col. E. L. Percival, D.S.O.; Major-Gen. H. E. Pyman; Major-Gen. T. W. Rees; Major J. Rietchel; Major D. Roxburgh-Smith, M.C.; Major R. Runciman; Lt.-Gen. Sir Reginald Savory; Major A. E. Scott; Major P. E. M. Shaw; Brigadier B. S. Sowton; Lt.-Col. J. Steen; Lt.-Col. O. Walker; Lt.-Col. F. I. Wallace, D.S.O.; Major T. S. Ware, M.C.; Lt.-Col. R. C. Watson; Major G. S. R. Webb, M.C.; Captain J. W. Webber; Major R. L. Wetherall, M.B.E.; Captain C. Wontner-Smith; Lt.-Col. E. G. Woods, D.S.O., M.B.E.; Captain J. W. Wright, M.C.; Captain D. W. Young, M.C.; Brigadier F. E. C. Hughes.

APPENDIX II

Had it not been for the generosity of the following, who subscribed towards the expenses of compiling this book, the History of the Fifth Indian Division could not have been undertaken and completed :

Lt.-Col. C. B. Appleby, D.S.O.; Lt.-Col.G. A. Armstrong, D.S.O., M.C., T.D.; Major J. O. Arthur, M.C.; B. T. Bailward; Major N. P. D. C. Baird; K. T. Baker; Lt.-Col. D. A. Balfour, T.D.; Brigadier A. R. Barker; T. Beamish; Captain A. I. F. Bennett; Major H. A. Bennett; Major-Gen. G. K. Bourne, O.B.E.; Captain H. J. D. Boyton, M.B.E.; Brigadier H. G. L. Brain, D.S.O., O.B.E.; Captain E. A. Brett-James; Lt.-Gen. Sir Harold Briggs, K.C.I.E., C.B., C.B.E., D.S.O.; Major D. Brunt; Captain J. Coates; Lt.-Col. R. A. Collins, D.S.O.; Major P. Connery, M.B.E.; Captain C. N. Cooke; Colonel G. H. Cree, C.B.E., D.S.O.; S. H. Davies; Major H. F. Davis; Major R. E. T. Deakin; C. B. Drayson; Lt.-Col. H. Dumville; Captain C. D. Easthaugh; Lt.-Col. R. Elliott, D.S.O.; Major A. M. S. Fergie; Brigadier B. C. Fletcher, D.S.O., M.C.; T. D. Forster; H. Fraser; Lt.-Col. K. G. H. Fryer, O.B.E.; Major T. R. Gemmell, M.C.; Major C. C. B. Gordon; Major G. Gourlay; Captain S. J. Gregory; Lt.-Col. E. H. W. Grimshaw, D.S.O.; Major J. Gutteridge; Lt.-Col. A. P. Harrington, M.B.E.; Lieut. C. T. Hawker, M.B.E.; Lt.-Gen. Sir Lewis Heath, K.B.E., C.B., C.I.E., D.S.O., M.C.; Brigadier K. W. Harvey, D.S.O., T.D.; Major J. W. B. Hext; Colonel R. H. M. Hill; Major J. D. Holland; Major J. W. L. Howard; Major M. D. Jacobs; Major D. A. James; Major A. E. Jefferies; Captain G. P. Kendall; Major J. Kendall; Captain M. A. Kerr, M.B.E.; Major A. L. King-Harman; Lt.-Col. M. Lamacraft, M.B.E.; Major C. C. Lane, M.B.E.; Colonel W. H. Langran, M.C.; R. F. Legard; G. W. V. Liddal; Major M. K. Lingane, M.B.E.; Major F. Lucas; Major H. R. Maconochie; R. W. Malet, M.C.; C. H. Manning; Lt.-Gen. Sir Robert Mansergh, K.B.E., C.B., M.C.; D. F. Mant; Major-Gen. Sir John Marriott, K.C.V.O., C.B., D.S.O., M.C.; Major P. St. G. Maxwell, M.C.; Major R. G. Maxwell; Major Maxwell; General Sir Mosley Mayne, G.C.B., C.B.E., D.S.O.; Lt.-Col. J. M. D. McIntosh, O.B.E.; Lt.-Col. W. P. Milne, M.C.; Captain H. A. Morrison; Major C. W. T. Morshead, M.C.; Colonel T. Murray-Christie; Major D. W. Naylor; Major J. F. Newman, M.B.E.; Major R. J. Niven; Major F. B. B. Noble, O.B.E.; Lt.-Col. R. Orgill, O.B.E.; J. W. V. Palmer; Brigadier D. F. Panton; Major P. Parsons; Major J. H. Partridge; Major C. D. Pattinson; Rev. C. Perowne; Major W. E. Petrie Hay; W. D. Phillips; Brigadier R. G. C. Poole; Lt.-Col. D. Price; Major C. C. L. Pusinelli; Captain C. T. Ramsey; Major-Gen. D. W. Reid, C.B., C.B.E., D.S.O., M.C.; Major C. G. Rickett; Brigadier D. de Robeck; Major A. H. Robertson; Lt.-Col. T. C. W. Roe, O.B.E.; Lt.-Gen. D. Russell, C.B., C.B.E., D.S.O., M.C.; Brigadier J. A. Salomons, D.S.O., O.B.E.; Lt.-Col. W. A. Schooley; Major A. E. Scott; Major D. C. Sebag-Montefiore; A. Selkirk; Major P. E. M. Shaw; Major

APPENDIX

J. D. Short; Major P. P. Steel, M.C.; Brigadier A. B. van Straubenzee; C. D. Thom; Captain J. H. Tucker; Major T. C. Vesey; Captain G. S. Warren; Lt.-Col. R. C. Watson; Brigadier G. de V. Welchman, C.B.E., D.S.O.; Major R. L. Wetherall, M.B.E.; Major J. Wiberg; Captain A. J. Wiles; F. H. J. Wilkinson; Major C. B. E. Williams; Lt.-Col. H. P. Williams; Major J. Winstanley, M.C.; Lt.-Col. E. G. Woods, D.S.O., M.B.E.; Lt.-Col. T. Woods; Captain A. J. Woolford, M.C.; Captain J. W. Wright, M.C.; 344 (SY) L.A.A./S.L. Regiment R.A. (T.A.).

PERSONAL INDEX

ABDUL HAFIZ, JEMADAR, V.C., 333
Alden, Major H., 297, 331
Alexander, General Sir Harold, 69, 236, 240
Allen, Major, 147
Anant Singh Pathania, Capt., 67, 70
Anders, General, 240
Ansell, Major C. C., 261
Anstice, Brigadier J. K., 240, 245
Anthony, Major R. A., 347
Aosta, Duke of, 94, 101, 111, 114, 118, 123-132, 134-136, 161, 397
Appleby, Lieut.-Colonel C. B., 375, 377, 379, 382-3, 413, 422
Armour, Major W. S., 404-406
Armstrong, Lieut., 348-9
Arthur, Major J., 383
Ash, Capt. M., 26
Auchinleck, General Sir Claude, 155, 174, 205, 211, 216, 224, 231-2, 235, 354

BADOGLIO, MARSHAL, 105
Bailey, Brigadier K., 403-4
Baird, D., 208
Baker, Capt. F. E., 112-3
Baker, Lieut.-Colonel H. C. A., 351, 356-7, 361
Barker, Lieut.-Colonel A. R., 195
Barker, Lieut.-Colonel D., 228
Barlow, Lieut.-Colonel, 414
Barton, Lieut. J. R., 227
Bastin, Lieut.-Colonel G., 346
Bellwood, Lieut. C. H. P., 94-5, 125
Beresford-Peirse, Major-General Sir Noel, 38, 41, 48-9, 53-4, 56-7, 64, 73, 80
Berretta, Capitano, 94
Betts, Capt. F. N., 150-1

Bhagat, Lieut. Premindra Singh, V.C., 35
Bhag Singh, Major, 219
Binnie, Lieut.-Colonel R. A. M., 385, 412
Biscoe, Lieut.-Colonel, 210, 216
Bishop, Major S. V., 361
Blackater, Lieut.-Colonel J. H. F., 414
Blood, Lieut.-Colonel J. A., 32
Bonetti, Admiral, 93-5, 98
Boomgardt, Major J. d'Issa, 59
Borgini, General, 132-3
Boss, Lieut.-Colonel T. H., 18
Boucher, Brigadier C. H., 160-1, 176, 179, 181, 183, 187-8, 190, 195, 198-9, 201, 203, 218
Bourne, Brigadier G. R., 465
Bragg, Lieut.-Colonel H. V., 161, 179, 199
Brain, Brigadier H. G. L., 406, 420, 422, 428
Briggs, Major-General H. R., 5, 15, 38, 93, 95-6, 98-9, 143, 161-2, 168-9, 177-179, 190-1, 195, 199, 201, 210, 213-4, 216, 220-1, 225, 229-30, 239, 244-5, 249-252, 257-8, 264, 278-9, 284, 287-8, 292, 327, 330, 335, 338, 342, 345, 351, 353-4, 396
Bristow, Lieut.-Colonel R. C. B., 435, 457
Brodie, Major N. M., 304, 307, 318
Bromley Gardiner, Capt. R., 182, 188, 201
Brunt, Major D., 413
Bucknall, Lieut.-Colonel, 66-8

CAMPBELL, MAJOR J., 351-353, 414
Campbell, Major-General J. C., V.C., 152

475

Campbell, Private, 187
Cargill, Lieut.-Colonel J., 270, 278, 287, 295-297, 388
Carr, Brigadier, 178, 180
Carroll, Lieut.-Colonel J. F., 437
Chaytor, Major E. D., 286
Chaudhuri, Major J. N., 220
Christison, Lieut.-General Sir Philip, 256, 273, 288, 428-9
Churchill, Winston S., 1, 235-6, 466
Clements, Lieut.-Colonel, 143
Cole, Lieut.-Colonel R. B., 281, 284
Collins, Lieut.-Colonel R. A., 358, 366
Collison, Lieut.-Colonel E. A. S., 438
Cordon, Lieut. D. I., 369
Cowan, Major-General D. T., 399, 404, 413-4, 418-9
Craddock, C.S.M., 331
Cree, Lieut.-Colonel G. H., 262, 264-267, 274, 281, 287, 327, 337, 350, 356, 358, 360-1
Crook, Lieut.-Colonel, 438
Crowther, Brigadier W. A., 251, 273, 276, 288
Cunningham, General Sir Alan, 101, 143
Cumming, Colonel, 91
Curtis, Major M. S., 59, 208

Dale, Major J. H., 364
Dawson, Major R., 185
Dean, Lieut.-Colonel H. W., 191
Dean, Lieut.-Colonel W. E., 58-60, 78, 117, 179-180, 193-195, 202, 204, 206-208
Delme-Murray, Major, 380
Denholm-Young, Brigadier E. J., 366-7, 370-1, 379, 387, 414-5, 417, 433, 455
Dimsdale, Major, 349, 358, 361-2
Dodd, Major, 202
Dods, Colonel E. R. S., 133
Doelwarno, Dr., 447
Doyle, Major P. M. W., 75
Duncan, Major, 463

Dunlop, Major A. C., 227, 263, 282-3, 361
Dutt, Lieut., 371

Easten, Major D. F., 304-5, 308-311, 314, 320-1
Edwards, Major S., 383
Evans, Major-General G. C., 274-5, 279-282, 286, 291, 293-4, 324, 330, 335, 345, 354-5, 362, 372, 393, 396, 399, 412, 425
Evans, Capt. H., 421-2

Fletcher, Brigadier B. C., 5, 8, 39, 41-2, 44-5, 64, 73, 78, 81, 85-9, 105, 107-111, 113, 116-7, 119, 123, 132, 141, 156, 160, 164, 173, 176, 178, 180, 183, 185, 189-90, 192-3, 203, 221, 229-231
Flint, Capt., 149
Fongoli, General, 44
Forbes, Major, 198
Fox, Lieut.-Colonel, 273
Frew, Capt., 308
Freyberg, Lieut.-General Sir Bernard, V.C., 211, 221
Frink, Lieut.-Colonel, 269, 273, 288
Frusci, General L., 13, 39, 52, 79, 85, 130, 132
Fryer, Lieut.-Colonel K., 364
Fukodome, Vice-Admiral, 429, 431
Furney, Lieut.-Colonel C. C., 53, 273, 334-346, 346-7

Garwood, Capt., (R.N.), 462
Gell, Major P., 284
Gerty, Lieut.-Colonel B. C. W., 267-8, 273, 294, 328-330, 333, 337-8, 350, 352-3, 362
Ghulam Qadir, Major, 269
Gian Chand, Major, 383
Gian Mohd, Subadar, 298
Giffard, General Sir George, 278

PERSONAL INDEX

Gleeson, Lieut.-Colonel L. D., 195, 204-5, 211-214, 216, 225, 274, 368, 375
Gomm, Capt. B., 65, 120, 217-8
Gott, Lieut.-General W. H. E., 171, 177, 220-1, 229, 235
Graham, Major J. M., 128, 135
Graziani, Marshal, 135
Green, Lieut.-Colonel P. W. P., 406, 421, 439
Grimshaw, Brigadier E. H. W., 318-20, 371, 388, 412, 441-2, 458
Grobelaar, Lieut.-Colonel P. H., 146, 148
Groom, Wing-Commander A., 450
Groome, Major R., 385
Grover, Major-General J., 313, 343, 353

HAILE SELASSIE, EMPEROR, 86, 88
Hale, Major W. G., 202, 204
Hamilton, Capt. P., 44
Hammond, Brigadier A. V., 251
Hare, Capt. T. R. M., 45
Harman, L/Cpl. J., V.C., 311
Harnam Singh, Major, 406
Harrison, Lieut.-Colonel E. J. C., 340
Hartley, Major P., 251
Hartshorne, Lieut.-Colonel, 122
Harvey, Major C., 44
Harvey, Bimbashi M., 104
Haslehurst, Capt., 202
Hatch, Major P., 274, 279, 356
Hawthorn, Major-General D. C., 445, 449
Hazell, Lieut. R., 264
Heath, Major G. N., 207-8
Heath, Lieut.-General Sir Lewis, 15-19, 22, 28, 34, 38-9, 41, 43, 46-9, 54-56, 58-9, 61, 63, 67-8, 70, 72-74, 77, 80-85, 90, 93, 95, 98, 100
Hely, Brigadier A. F., 277-8
Hill, Lieut.-Colonel H., 251, 274, 304
Hind, Major, 202

Hobson, Lieut.-Colonel P. M. P., 277-8
Hollis, Capt. M., 45-6
Hoare, Major P. H. T., 57
Hone, Major-General R., 428
Hopking, Lieut.-Colonel H. R., 251, 269
Hossack, Lieut.-Colonel I. F., 88, 107, 110
Housman, A. E., 197
Howard, Major A. B., 356
Hughes, Brigadier F. E. C., 228, 240

IRAQ, KING OF, 245
Itagaki, General, 428-9, 433, 439

JACKSON, LIEUT., 148
Jenkins, Lieut.-Colonel F. A. M. B., 65, 67, 243, 146-7, 149-150
Jessop, Major T. H., 36-7
Jones, Major L. H., 331

KALHA, LIEUT.-COLONEL SARBJIT SINGH, 292, 439, 463
Karim Khan, Subadar, 463
Keating, Major M., 340
Kemp, Colonel, 463
Kennedy-Cooke, Brigadier B., 91
Kennedy Shaw, Major W. B., 146
Kenyon, Major T., 305
Kindersley, Major, 181-2, 189
King, Lieut., 317
Kitchener, Field-Marshal Lord, 155
Knight, Lieut.-Colonel J. C. O., 143, 203, 206
Koath, Capt., 320
Koenig, General, 173, 203

LAKHINDER SINGH, LIEUT.-COLONEL, 400, 406
Lambert, Major S., 267, 337-8
Langran, Brigadier W. H., 70, 74, 179, 184-186, 189-191, 225-228, 231, 239, 262, 270

Laverty, Lieut.-Colonel H., 304-5, 307-9, 312-4, 316, 318-320
Leatherdale, Major W. V. S., 147, 149-150, 202, 211-213
Legh, Lieut.-Colonel R. F. D., 455
Leslie-Smith, Capt. P. M., 404
Liardet, Lieut.-Colonel, 245
Livingstone, Capt., 183
Lloyd, Brigadier W. L., 53
Loder-Symons, Brigadier R., 456
Lomax, Major-General C. E. N., 292
Lorenzini, General, 79
Lumsden, Major-General H., 173
Lynn, Colonel G. R., 133

MACLAURIN, LIEUT.-COLONEL N., 300, 327
MacMillan, P.S.M. W., 45-6
MacPherson, L/Cpl., 217
Malden, Lieut.-Colonel C. M., 111
Mallaby, Brigadier A. W., 446-9, 451
Mallinson, Capt. P., 350
Maloney, R.S.M., 286
Mansergh, Lieut.-General E. C. R., 51, 213, 221, 250-1, 270, 339, 346, 372, 396-398, 414-423, 424, 427-8, 431, 436, 438, 451, 454-456, 462-465
Marindin, Brigadier P. C., 361, 388
Marriott, Brigadier J. C. O., 18, 40, 45, 47-8, 53, 65-69, 74, 77-8, 81-2, 100, 106, 111-113, 115, 120, 130-132, 135-137, 143-4, 151, 176
Marshall, Lieut.-Colonel W. D., 204, 210
Martin, Major, 184
Martin, 43
Martini, General, 36
Maxwell, Major P. St. G., 57, 75, 97
Mayne, Lieut.-General A. G. O. M., 15, 18, 32-34, 36-7, 100-102, 104-106, 111, 113-4, 116, 118-9, 121, 123-125, 129-130, 132-136, 140, 155-7, 161
McAlister, Lieut.-Colonel R. J. F., 231
McKeig Jones, Capt., 57

Mclean, Pipe-Major, 85
McLeod, Major A. J. W., 59, 107-110
Meek, Major P., 298
Menneer, Lieut.-Colonel K. C., 347
Meraj ud Din, Major, 414
Messervy, Lieut.-General Sir Frank, 15, 17-19, 37-8, 51, 53, 56, 58-9, 61, 63, 74, 82-84, 116, 151, 173, 178-9, 189, 193, 195, 200, 202-3, 209, 256, 258-9, 272-3, 275-7, 279-280, 291, 293, 330, 341, 343-4, 354, 372, 392, 420
Middleton, Lieut.-Colonel, 368, 380
Miller, Lieut.-Colonel, 107-110
Miller, Major J. B., 346, 372
Mitchell, Capt., 308, 313
Moestopo, Dr., 445-448
Mohd Jamshed, Capt., 378, 413
Montclar, Colonel, 93, 95-6
Montezemmo, General, 132
Montgomery, Lieut.-General B. L., 235-6, 239, 275
Moriarty, Major, 374-5
Morgan, Lieut.-Colonel C. L., 195-6
Morrison, Lieut.-Colonel D. I., 297
Morshead, Major C., 365
Mountbatten, Lord Louis, 258-260, 299, 397, 427-8, 431, 439
Munn, Major A. G., 34-5, 59, 63, 70
Munshi Ram, Havildar, 328
Murray, Lieut.-Colonel, 105
Murray, Major S. K., 65
Muskett, Capt. W., 348-9
Mussolini, 94, 131, 151

NAPIER, LIEUT.-COLONEL A. H., 72-3, 76, 156, 195-197
Narain, Subadar, 269
Narayan Singh, Lieut.-Colonel, 372
Nash, Major C., 131
Nettlefield, Major J., 342, 362, 369, 451
Neville, C.S.M., 228
Newell, Lieut.-Colonel J. A. E., 406
Newman, Major J. F., 372
Niaz Mohammed Arbad, Major, 433

PERSONAL INDEX

Noble, Lieut.-Colonel F. B. B., 213-4, 245
Norrie, Lieut.-General C. Willoughby, 171, 202

O'HARA, MAJOR C., 227, 263, 265, 283, 286, 337
Old, Brigadier-General W., 285
Orgill, Lieut.-Colonel R., 438
Orr, Lieut.-Colonel A. D. G., 49, 54
Osborn, Major M. A. C., 60, 193-4, 227

PANTON, COLONEL D., 378
Park, Air Marshal K., 439
Passingham, Major A., 217
Pawsey, Sir Charles, 305, 311-313, 317, 319
Pearson, Capt. B. R., 148
Pease, Major R., 217
Percival, Lieut.-Colonel E. L., 57, 203, 210, 218-9
Perowne, Major the Rev. C., 215, 243
Petrie-Hay, Major W. E., 265, 267-8
Philbrick, Major G. E. H., 35
Philips, Capt. H., 208
Pienaar, Major-General D., 104, 113, 118-121, 123, 132
Pinna, General P., 132
Platt, Lieut.-General W., (The Kaid), 13-4, 18, 37-8, 41, 56, 63-4, 67, 76, 93-95, 100, 105, 113, 129, 134, 136
Poole, Brigadier R. G. C., 372
Power, Admiral Sir Arthur, 439
Prendergast, Lieut.-Colonel W. H., 146
Pryke, Lieut.-Colonel P. S., 393
Pugh, Colonel L. H. O., 446-7, 449-51
Putnam, Lieut.-Colonel W. A., 230-1

QUINAN, GENERAL SIR EDWARD, 240

RAM SARUP SINGH, SUBADAR, V.C., 383-4
Ranbir Singh, Subadar, 331

Randolph, Capt. the Rev., 316
Rashid Ali, 139-140
Ras Seyoum, 86, 119
Raw, Major S. H., 207
Rees, Major-General T. W., 73-6, 64, 93-8, 102, 156, 160, 392
Reid, Major-General D. W., 5, 8, 32, 58-60, 74, 141, 144-152, 160, 163, 176, 194, 202-207, 209-211, 213, 216-18, 220-221, 271
Richards, Colonel H. V., 304, 311
Ridley, Major C. W., 125, 130
Risal Singh, Major, 329, 350, 352-3
Ritchie, Lieut.-General N. M., 171, 177-8, 205, 211
Ritchie, Major W., 267-8
Robertson, Major, 187
Roche, Major J. P., 263, 265-7
Rodwell, Lieut.-Colonel R. M., 32, 58, 60, 70
Roe, Lieut.-Colonel T. C. W., 284, 300-1, 327, 374-5, 425
Rolls, Capt. J. H., 188
Rommel, Field-Marshal, 171, 173-175, 177-8, 191, 201, 203, 223, 226, 229, 237-239
Rowling, Major W., 199, 348
Rowse, Lieut.-Colonel R., 287
Roxburgh-Smith, Major D., 270
Runciman, Major R., 373
Russell, Brigadier D., 5-7, 18, 28, 82-3, 124-130, 210, 215, 226, 239

SADIQ ULLAH KHAN, 114
Sain, Lieut., 328
Salomons, Brigadier J. A., 141-144, 157, 231, 261, 270-1, 293, 326, 334, 336, 338, 351, 353, 356-7, 362, 372, 386, 395-5, 400, 404
Sanson, Major, 348, 352-3
Saudagar Singh, Sepoy, 115
Savory, Brigadier R. A., 38, 51, 53, 63, 79, 274
Schubert, Capt., 199
Scoones, Lieut.-General Sir Geoffry, 353-4

Scott, Lieut.-Colonel, 213-4, 216, 225
Sell, Major G. R., 329-330
Sellars, Major B., 264-5, 273, 350
Seymour, Capt., 59
Sharpe, Guardsman, 69
Shaw, Major P. E. M., 305, 309-310, 315-6
Sherwood, Major L. V. S., 26
Shirang Lawand, Subadar, 59
Short, Lieut.-Colonel V. C. G., 147, 149-151
Sidderfin, Major, 147
Sims, Bimbashi, 95
Sinclair, Private, 57
Singh, 2/Lieut. G. B., 114
Slater, Major A., 377
Slatter, Air Commodore L. H., 49, 55, 67
Slim, General Sir William, 15, 18, 22-24, 26-30, 40-44, 73, 249-250, 256, 351, 354, 393, 397, 399, 400, 411, 438-9
Smith, Capt., 320
Smith, Brigadier W. G., 251, 287-8, 324-5
Soerkarno, Dr., 444, 449
Soerio, Dr., 445, 448, 450
Staines, C.S.M., 319
Stamer, Brigadier W. D., 156-7
Stark, Freya, 243, 398
Steele, Major P. P., 406
Steen, Lieut.-Colonel J., 379
Stewart, Major H., 35
Stileman, Lieut.-Colonel E. C. R., 339
Stilwell, General, 299
Stopford, Lieut.-General Sir Montagu, 353, 355, 392, 420
Straubenzee, Brigadier A. B. van, 123, 132, 155-6
Stray, Lieut.-Colonel G. F. M., 228
Sundius-Smith, Lieut.-Colonel B. L., 24, 32, 47, 64, 74, 178, 183, 189, 201
Syme, Major, 202

TANAHASHI, COLONEL, 276
Tayler, Lieut.-Colonel S. E., 24-6, 65

Teesdale, Lieut.-Colonel P. H., 202, 204
Telfer-Smollett, Capt. P. T., 97
Terauchi, Field-Marshal Count, 428-9
Tessitore, General, 13
Thorburn, Lieut.-Colonel D., 178, 181-2, 188-9
Tilman, Major H. W., 225
Timbrell, Major A., 74, 185
Tiru, Subadar, 331
Toselli, Major, 102
Towning, Capt., 359
Towsey, Major, 147-8
Tramontano, Colonel, 123, 125
Trezzani, General, 125-129, 132-3
Trout, Capt. D. A., 148, 150, 202
Truscott, Lieut.-Colonel, 191, 200
Tuker, Major-General F. I. S., 239

VALLENTIN, BRIGADIER G. M., 161, 196, 213
Venables, Corporal, 422
Victor Emmanuel, King, 134, 151
Vidya Dhar Jayal, Major, 83, 114
Volpini, General, 124, 126, 128, 136

WAITE, MAJOR J. J., 199
Walayat Khan, Subadar, 325
Walker, Major J., 325
Wallace, Lieut.-Colonel F. I., 382, 423
Wallace, Capt. R., 96-7
Ware, Major T. S., 295, 313, 320
Warren, Major-General D. F. W., 251, 258, 260, 271, 287, 294, 304, 307, 310, 313, 316, 318, 341-2, 344, 362, 365, 368-369, 372, 393-395
Wavell, General Sir Archibald, 38, 41, 76-7, 90, 100, 275
Weallans, Lieut.-Colonel, 178
Webb, Major G. S. R., 43
Welchman, Lieut.-Colonel G. de V., 22, 24, 26-7, 31-33, 41-43, 84, 95, 275
Wheeler, Lieut.-General R. C., 439

Whitcombe, Major, 463
White, Field-Marshal Sir George, V.C., 387
White, Major R. H., 268
Wiberg, Capt. J., 184, 189-190
Willis, Lieut.-Colonel R. A., 340
Wilson, General Sir Henry Maitland, 240
Wilson, Lieut.-Colonel M. H. W., 228
Wilson-Haffenden, Brigadier, 373
Winstanley, Major J., 305, 312, 317
Winterton, Brigadier T. J. W., 251, 256, 260

Woods, Lieut.-Colonel E. G., 61, 330-331
Worsley, Lieut.-Colonel J. M., 457, 459
Wright, Lieut. J. W., 303, 309, 315

Yakub, Naik, 330
Yearsley, Lieut., 346
Yeo, Major R., 306, 310
Young, Lieut.-Colonel J., 261, 309, 313-316
Young, 95
Younger, Colonel, 406

www.ingramcontent.com/pod-product-compliance
Lightning Source LLC
Chambersburg PA
CBHW031842220426
43663CB00006B/474